NURSE'S LEGAL HANDBOOK

SIXTH EDITION

NURSE'S LEGAL HANDBOOK

SIXTH EDITION

CLINICAL EDITOR

Kathy G. Ferrell, BS, RN, LNCC

Board Certified
Medical–Legal Consulting
Thompson's Station, Tennessee

Wolters Kluwer

Philadelphia • Baltimore • New York • London
Buenos Aires • Hong Kong • Sydney • Tokyo

KH

Executive Acquisitions Editor: Shannon W. Magee
Product Development Editor: Maria M. McAvey
Senior Marketing Manager: Mark Wiragh
Editorial Assistant: Kathryn Leyendecker
Production Project Manager: Priscilla Crater
Design Coordinator: Elaine Kasmer
Manufacturing Coordinator: Kathleen Brown
Prepress Vendor: S4Carlisle Publishing Services

9 8 7 6 5 4 3 2 1

Printed in China

Library of Congress Cataloging-in-Publication Data
Nurse's legal handbook / [edited by] Kathy G. Ferrell. — Sixth edition.
   p. ; cm.
 Includes bibliographical references and index.
 ISBN 978-1-4963-0260-1
 I. Ferrell, Kathy G., editor.
 [DNLM: 1. Legislation, Nursing—United States.   2. Ethics, Nursing—United States.   3. Malpractice—United States—Nurses' Instruction.   4. Patient Rights—United States—Nurses' Instruction.   WY 33 AA1]
 RT86.73
 344.7304'14—dc23
                                                                                          2015021076

LWW.com

RRS1507

9/23/16

DEDICATION

This book is dedicated to my husband, Jimmy, who has always supported me no matter how many hours I stay locked away in my office.

I also dedicate this book to the community of caring nurses who work tirelessly to bring health, comfort, and hope to each patient.

Kathy

CONTRIBUTORS

Lanette L. Anderson, MSN, JD, RN
Executive Director
WV LPN Board
Charleston, West Virginia

Edith Brous, RN, BSN, MS, MPH, JD
Nurse Attorney
New York, New York

Rebecca F. Cady, Esq., BSN, CPHRM, DFASHRM
Executive Director of Risk Management,
 Deputy Risk Counsel
Children's National Medical Center
Washington, DC

Leslie M. Durr, PhD, RN, PMHCNS-BC
Certified Clinical Nurse Specialist
Blue Ridge Legal Nurse Consultants,
 Inc.
Charlottesville, Virginia

Kelli M. Hansen, BSN, RN, CMCN, LNC, CSA
Chief Nursing Officer/Founder,
 Certified Senior Advisor
Advocate Nurses, LLC
Plattsmouth, Nebraska

Patricia Iyer, MSN, RN, LNCC
Founder and Senior Consultant
Med League Support Services, Inc.
Flemington, New Jersey

Taralynn R. Mackay, RN, JD
Founding Partner
McDonald, Mackay & Weitz, LLP
Austin, Texas

Frances W. Sills, MSN, APN, CLNC, RN
Assistant Professor
ETSU College of Nursing
Johnson City, Tennessee

Kristopher T. Starr, RN, MSN, JD, CEN, CPEN
Esquire/Associate
Ferry Joseph Attorneys at Law
Wilmington, Delaware

Samantha M. Steiner, JD, RN
Clinical Risk Manager
Office of General Counsel Children's
 Healthcare of Atlanta
Atlanta, Georgia

Mariea Urubek, RN, MSN, JD
Assistant Vice President
Healthcare Risk Management at Allied
 World
Chicago, Illinois

PREVIOUS EDITION CONTRIBUTORS

Sally Austin, ADN, BGS, JD

Penny Simpson Brooke, APRN, MS, JD

Linda MacDonald Glenn, JD, LLM

Ginny Wacker Guido, RN, MSN, JD, FAAN

David M. Keepnews, RN, PHD, JD, FAAN

Janet E. Michael, RN, MS, JD

Susan Salladay, RN, PHD

Beverly A. Snyder, RN, MHA

Jacqueline Walus-Wigle, RN, JD, CPAQ

LaTonia Denise Wright, RN, BSN, JD

FOREWORD

Like all nurses, I started at the bedside where I learned to assess, diagnose, plan, implement, and reassess. However, without conscious effort, I realized that I had developed additional skills such as communication, organization, critical thinking, and prioritization. I grew as a nurse, and these skills provided me with many additional opportunities throughout my career in nursing. One of those opportunities included working with a very talented team of nurses who have shared their knowledge with you in the preparation of the *Nurse's Legal Handbook*, Sixth Edition.

As you read this book, you will note that the contributor to each chapter is a nurse. The role of each nurse expanded from the bedside to include careers in law, risk management, education, leadership, and patient advocacy. Consider how far nursing has evolved in the past several decades. We are so fortunate that each of these contributors agreed to share their time and knowledge with you, the reader.

As nursing opportunities and responsibilities have increased, so have the liabilities. The autonomy gained by nurses has resulted in recognition that the nurse is responsible for her independent decisions and actions. No longer are physicians or facilities held solely accountable for the actions of nurses working under their supervision and employment. Nurses are now routinely named individually in litigation involving patient care.

This book is a resource that offers the nurse guidance in the legal and ethical issues that are encountered daily in practice. Each chapter is designed to provide nurses with current information on the rights, responsibilities, and regulations governing the practice of nursing. The focus of this book is to impress upon each nurse the importance of knowing and adhering to the standards of nursing practice, legal risks inherent in the nursing profession, and steps to prevent being named in a lawsuit or other disciplinary actions.

Chapter 1 includes information regarding each state's Nurse Practice Act and the ANA (American Nurse Association) Scope and Standards of Nursing Practice newly released in 2010, and how these regulations protect society by regulating quality in nursing practice.

Chapter 2 discusses current trends in nursing and health care, and trends in litigation including the supervision of unlicensed assistive personnel, such as nursing assistants.

Chapter 3 provides insight into the controversies over the definition of death and the nurse's response to the patient's request to stop treatment.

The contributor of Chapter 4 wanted nurses to understand the importance of purchasing professional liability insurance and when nurses are at risk for civil and criminal prosecution for nursing errors.

Chapter 5 includes a discussion of the four elements that must be proven in a medical negligence case against a nurse. Specific instructions are provided to the nurse who learns that he/she has been named as a defendant in a lawsuit. Information is also provided on ways some nurses use their education, skills, and experiences in assisting attorney in the preparation of a lawsuit and as testifying nurse experts during litigation.

Chapter 6 continues with a discussion of the litigation process and how nursing standards of care and hospital policies affect court decisions. Special attention is paid to the issue of adequate staffing and the legal risk nurses face due to understaffing.

One of the purposes of the medical record is to serve as a legal document. Nurses often fail to recognize that good nursing documentation is the best evidence of nursing care when presented in the courtroom. Chapter 7 provides the rationale for good nursing documentation and how medical records are used by testifying experts in medical malpractice litigation.

Chapter 8 explores how nurses can protect themselves from possible litigation when providing disaster relief or other emergencies. This chapter answers the question "Do Good Samaritan Laws protect nurses?"

Nurses should know their rights as employees. Chapter 9 describes the types of contracts nurses may be asked to sign at the time of employment and what happens if the contract is breached by either party. Nurses also need to know how laws protect them from prosecution in the event they report wrongdoing by their employer (whistle-blowing).

With today's scientific and technological advances and economic realities, nurses face ethical issues daily. Also, nurses are routinely asked to serve as a resource for families, patients, and staff in making ethical decisions. Chapter 10 discusses how law and ethics overlap in many situations and what framework and principles nurses can use in making ethical decisions.

Chapter 11 continues the study of ethical issues by presenting landmark cases involving the issues of end of life, quality of life, and appropriate use of scarce and expensive resources and the laws, such as the Patient Self-Determination Act, that were enacted subsequent to these cases. The chapter discusses the nurse's ethical relationships not only with their patients but also with their peers. Special attention is given to lateral or horizontal violence nurses face in the workplace, and the ANA's response to this trend.

How can one book address so many pertinent issues? The answer is simple. It was teamwork.

My sincere thanks to an excellent team of professional nurses.

KATHY G. FERRELL, BS, RN, LNCC
Legal Nurse Consultant—Board Certified

CONTENTS

CHAPTER 1

Nursing practice and the law

Mariea Urubek, RN, MSN, JD

A s with other professionals, nurses want opportunities for personal advancement, increased economic benefits, and a sense that their profession will keep pace with the latest technological advances. To help realize these goals, each nurse must keep pace with current nursing trends, provide proper patient care, and understand, accept, and follow the legal and ethical responsibilities of her practice. By performing these actions, the nurse not only puts himself or herself in a good position for advancement but also sidesteps many legal and professional pitfalls that may otherwise present themselves.

This chapter provides fundamental information on the laws that directly govern nursing. It includes detailed discussions of the *nurse practice act*—the state law that regulates nursing. You'll also find out about the role of your state's board of nursing, and you'll examine how nursing law is applied in court. You'll learn about standards of care, including how these standards are applied and how they may be used as evidence during malpractice litigation.

This chapter also explains the legal significance of your nursing license and what to expect if you're disciplined for violating any of its provisions. Throughout the chapter, you'll find practical advice that reflects legal precedents or expected standards of care.

Levels of nursing practice

Four levels of nursing practice exist— the advanced practice nurse (APN), the registered nurse (RN), the licensed practical or licensed vocational nurse (LPN or LVN), and the unlicensed Nursing Assistant. All levels are designed with special, unique functions in mind. APNs, such as nurse practitioners (NPs), clinical nurse specialists, nurse midwives, and nurse anesthetists, are RNs who have national certification or a master's degree in a clinical specialty. The APN performs acts of diagnosis and treatment of alterations in health status. APNs, in collaboration with a licensed physician, may prescribe, dispense, and administer medications.

The RN must successfully pass the national licensure examination for registered nurses after completing a board of nursing–approved program leading to an associate, baccalaureate, or master's degree in nursing or a 3-year diploma hospital-based program. When licensed, the RN is the primary professional who will coordinate patient care. She must make professional nursing judgments and take appropriate actions based on the nursing process: assess patient, assign nursing diagnosis, develop plan of care, implement plan of care, and evaluate response to plan of care. In state law, definitions of the RN's role vary, but basic responsibilities include observing patients' signs and symptoms, recording these observations, notifying the physician of any changes in a patient's health status, carrying out physicians' orders for treatments, and appropriately delegating responsibilities for patient care.

The practice of nursing by a LPN is often defined as the performance of selected tasks and sharing of responsibility under the direction of a RN or an APN and within the framework of supportive and restorative care, health counseling and teaching, and executing the medical regime under the direction of a licensed physician or dentist. The educational background of an LPN is generally 1 year of training in a hospital-based program or technology center program. In some states, the duties of LPNs are more clearly defined in terms of *scope of practice*; for example, states may prohibit LPNs from administering IV chemotherapy, blood products of thrombolytics.

Because of changes in the workplace, including an emphasis on cutting labor costs, the role of the LPN has expanded over the years. For example, in some states LPNs are allowed to administer intravenous push medications into a peripheral line of adults if they have completed a formal intravenous therapy training and competency program and perform this task under the supervision of a MD, RN, or dentist. LPNs are responsible for personal acts of negligence under the law. LPNs are liable if they perform delegated function they are not prepared to handle by education and experience and from which supervision is not provided. In any patient care situation, the LPN should perform only those acts for which each has been prepared and has demonstrated ability to perform, bearing in mind the individual's personal responsibility under the law.

The final member of the nursing team is the unlicensed nursing assistant (NA) or unlicensed assistive personnel (UAP). Regulations regarding the scope of practice for the NA are developed by State Boards of Nursing. Delegation of a nursing task to nursing assistive personnel is a skill requiring clinical judgment and final accountability for patient care and can be performed in most states by the RN of LPN. There is both individual accountability and organizational liability for delegation. Organizational liability relates to providing sufficient resources, staffing, appropriate staff mix, implementation of policies and role descriptions, opportunities for continuing staff development, and creating an environment which ensures teamwork, collaboration, and patient-centered care. Consistent education and training requirements that prepare nursing assistive personnel to perform a range of functions such as patient transfers, feeding, bathing, and taking vital signs will allow delegating nurses to know the preparation and skill level of assistive personnel. Individuals who successfully complete comprehensive educational and training requirements, including passing a competency examination, will be certified as certified nursing aide or certified nursing assistant (CNA). Some CNAs can undergo additional training and become certified to administer oral or topical medications under the supervision of a licensed nurse in assistive care living facilities or skilled nursing facility.

Nursing practice in Canada

All Canadian jurisdictions support licensure (commonly known as *registration*) of RNs and nursing auxiliaries (commonly known as LPNs). However, in some jurisdictions, registration isn't mandatory. Some Canadian nursing associations recognize clinical nurse specialists (who usually have master's degrees or doctoral degrees in a specific specialty) and NPs—nurses in expanded roles oriented to primary health care.

In most of Canada's 10 jurisdictions, professional nurses' associations set requirements for graduation from an approved school of nursing, licensing, nurses' professional behavior, and registration fees.

The Canadian RN may receive her education in a diploma school (such as a hospital school of nursing), in a community college, or in a BSN program. One jurisdiction requires a BSN for entry into private practice, and several others may soon have the same requirement. All nurses wishing to practice in Canada must pass the Canadian Nurses Association Test. A nurse also needs to be licensed in the province where she would like to work. Individual provinces issue their own license to practice. A nurse should contact her province board of nursing to confirm the requirement.

Laws, rules, and regulations

Because nursing care poses a risk of harm to the public if practices by professionals who are unprepared or incompetent, the state, through its police powers, is required to protect its citizens from harm. That protection is in the form of reasonable laws to regulate nursing. More than 100 years ago, state governments began enacting laws that protect the public's health and welfare including those ensuring the safe practice of nursing. Each state has a nurse practice act. Each state's nurse practice act is enacted by the state's legislature. Each nurse practice act establishes a board of nursing that has the authority to develop administrative rules or regulations to clarify and make the law more specific. Rules and regulations must be consistent with the nurse practice act and cannot go beyond it. These rules and regulations undergo a process of public review before enactment. Once enacted, rules and regulations have the full force and effect of law. All nurse practice act include standards and scope of nursing practice, educational program standard, types of title and licenses, requirements for licensure, and ground for disciplinary action, other violations, and possible remedies.

Every nurse is expected to care for patients within these defined practice limits—the most important ones affecting nursing care; if she gives care beyond these limits, she becomes vulnerable to charges of violating the law and losing her licensure. These laws, rules, and regulations also serve to exclude untrained or unlicensed people from practicing nursing. The laws of the nursing practice can only function properly if nurses know the current laws governing practice in their state. Ignorance of the law is never an excuse.

Nursing practice acts

Nurse practice acts in each state are laws that define responsibilities of the nurse and "scope of practice"—the range of activities and services as well as the qualifications for practice. The acts are intended to protect patients from harm as a result of unsafe or incompetent practice, or unqualified nurses. The nurse practice act describes what constitutes unprofessional conduct or misconduct, and investigation and the disciplinary procedures for complaints filed against a nurse.

Scope of practice

Early nurse practice acts contained statements prohibiting nurses from performing tasks considered to be within the scope of medical practice. Nurses could not diagnose any patient problem or treat a patient without instructions from a physician. Later, interdisciplinary committees (consisting of nurses, physicians, pharmacists, dentists, and hospital representatives) have helped to ease this restriction on nursing practice. After reviewing some medical procedures that nurses commonly perform, these committees issued joint statements recommending that nurses be legally permitted to perform these procedures in specified circumstances. Some joint statements specifically recommend allowing nurses to perform venipunctures, cardiopulmonary resuscitation, and cardiac defibrillation. Still other joint statements (as well as interpretive statements issued by state boards of nursing and nursing organizations) specifically recommend permitting nurses to perform such functions as nursing assessment and nursing diagnosis. Such joint statements don't have the force of the law—unless state legislatures amend their nurse practice acts to include them. Many state legislatures have incorporated such statements into nurse practice acts. (*See US and Canadian nurses' associations*).

Conditions for licensure

Your state's nurse practice act sets down the requirements for obtaining a license to practice nursing. To become licensed as an RN or LPN, you must pass the NCLEX and meet certain other qualifications. All states require completion of the basic professional nursing education program. Your state may have additional requirements; examples include good moral character, good physical and mental health, a minimum age, fluency in English, and no drug or alcohol addiction.

In addition to specifying the conditions for RN and LPN licensure, your state's nurse practice act may specify the rules and regulations for licensure in special areas of nursing practice (usually termed "certification").

State boards of nursing

In every state and Canadian jurisdiction, a nurse practice act creates a state or provincial board of nursing, sometimes called the state board of nurse examiners. Board responsibilities center around three broad functions—licensure, education, and practice. The board also interprets state statutes and administrative rules to determine the appropriate standards of practice in an effort to ensure the highest professional conduct. The board initiates the investigation of nurses alleged to have violated the law and rules and is responsible to discipline the license of and/or imposes civil penalties on those found guilty.

The board of nursing is bound by the provisions of the nurse practice act that created it. The nurse practice act is the law; the board of nursing cannot grant exemptions to it or waive any of its provisions. Only the state or provincial legislature can change the law. For example, if the nurse practice act specifies that, to be licensed, a nurse must have graduated

(Text continues on page 10.)

US and Canadian nurses' associations

This chart lists the name, address, and telephone number, plus the Web site addresses (when available) of nurses' associations in the United States, its territories, and Canada. The American Nurses Association has a Web site (*www.nursingworld.org*) with links to each state's nurses' association Web site.

National associations
American Nurses Association
8515 Georgia Avenue, Suite 400
Silver Spring, MD 20910-3492
1-800-274-4ANA (4262)
Web site: *www.nursingworld.org*

Federal Nurses Association
8515 Georgia Avenue, Suite 400
Silver Spring, MD 20910
(301) 628-5049
Web site: *www.nursingworld.org/fedna*

State associations
Alabama Nurses' Association
360 N. Hull
St. Montgomery,
AL 36104-3658
(334) 262-8321
Web site: *www.alabamanurses.org*

Alaska Nurses Association
3701 East Tudor Road,
Suite 208
Anchorage, AK 99507
(907) 274-0827
Web site: *www.aknurse.org*

Arizona Nurses Association
1850 E. Southern Avenue,
Suite 1
Tempe, AZ 85282
(480) 831-0404
Web site: *www.aznurse.org*

Arkansas Nurses Association
1123 South University
Avenue, #1015
Little Rock, AR 72204
(501) 244-2363
Web site: *www.arna.org*

American Nurses Association/ California
1121 L Street, Suite 508
Sacramento, CA 95814
(916) 447-0225
Web site: *www.anacalifornia.org*

Colorado Nurses Association
2170 South Parker Road, Suite 145
Denver, CO 80231
(303) 241-8646
Web site: *www.nurses-co.org*

Connecticut Nurses Association
377 Research Parkway, Suite 2D
Meriden, CT 06450
(203) 238-1207
Web site: *www.ctnurses.org*

Delaware Nurses Association
4765 Ogletown-Stanton Road, Suite L10
Newark, DE 19713
(302) 733-5880
Web site: *www.denurses.org*

District of Columbia Nurses Association
5100 Wisconsin Avenue, NW Suite 306
Washington, DC 20016
(202) 244-2705
Web site: *www.dcna.org*

Florida Nurses Association
P.O. Box 536985
Orlando, FL 32853-6985
(407) 896-3261
Web site: *www.floridanurse.org*

Georgia Nurses Association
3032 Briarcliff Road
NE Atlanta, GA 30329-2655
(404) 325-5536
Web site: *www.georgianurses.org*

(continued)

US and Canadian nurses' associations *(continued)*

Guam Nurses Association
P.O. Box CG
Hagatna, Guam 96933 1
(671) 477-6877
Web site: *http://www.nursingworld.org/*

Hawaii Nurses Association
949 Kapiolani Boulevard, Suite 107
Honolulu, HI 96814
(808) 531-1628
Web site: *www.hawaiinurses.org*

Idaho Nurses Association
3525 Piedmont Road, Building Five,
Suite 300
Atlanta, GA 30305
(888) 721-8904
Web site: *www.idahonurses.org*

Illinois Nurses Association
P.O. Box 636
Manteno, IL 60950
(312) 331-0663
Web site: *www.ana-illinois.org*

Indiana State Nurses Association
2915 North High School Road
Indianapolis, IN 46224
(317) 299-4575
Web site: *www.indiananurses.org*

Iowa Nurses Association
2400 86th Street, #32
Urbandale, IA 50322
(515) 225-0495
Web site: *www.iowanurses.org*

Kansas State Nurses Association
1109 SW Topeka Blvd.
Topeka, KS 66612
(785) 233-8638
Web site: *www.ksnurses.com*

Kentucky Nurses Association
200 Whittington Parkway, Suite 101
Louisville, KY 40222
(502) 637-2546
Web site: *www.kentucky-nurses.org*

Louisiana State Nurses Association
5713 Superior Drive, Suite A-6
Baton Rouge, LA 70816
(225) 201-0993
Web site: *www.lsna.org*

American Nurses Association of Maine
P.O. Box 1205
Windham, ME 04062
(207) 281-2091
Web site: *www.anamaine.org*

Maryland Nurses Association
21 Governor's Court, Suite 195
Baltimore, MD 21244
(410) 944-5800
Web site: *www.marylandrn.org*

ANA Massachusetts
P.O. Box 285
Milton, MA 02186
(617) 990-2856
Web site: *www.anamass.org*

ANA Michigan
P.O. Box 11180
Lansing, MI 48901
1-855-823-2652
Web site: *www.ana-michigan.org*

Minnesota Organization of Registered Nurses
P.O. Box 48269
Minneapolis, MN 55448-0269
Web site: *www.mnorn.org*

Mississippi Nurses Association
31 Woodgreen Place
Madison, MS 39110
(601) 898-0670
Web site: *www.msnurses.org*

US and Canadian nurses' associations *(continued)*

Missouri Nurses Association
1904 Bubba Lane
P.O. Box 105228
Jefferson City, MO 65110-5228
(573) 636-4623
Web site: *www.missourinurses.org*

Montana Nurses Association
20 Old Montana State Highway
Clancy, MT 59634
(406) 442-6710
Web site: *www.mtnurses.org*

Nebraska Nurses Association
P.O. Box 3107
Kearne, NE 68848-3107
1-888-885-7025
Web site: *www.nebraskanurses.org*

Nevada Nurses Association
P.O. Box 34660
Reno, NV 89533
(775) 747-2333
Web site: *www.nvnurses.org*

New Hampshire Nurses Association
25 Hall Street, Unit 1E
Concord, NH 03301
(603) 225-3783
Web site: *www.nhnurses.org*

New Jersey State Nurses Association
1479 Pennington Road
Trenton, NJ 08618-2661
(609) 883-5335
1-888-876-5762
Web site: *www.njsna.org*

New Mexico Nurses Association
P.O. Box 29658
Santa Fe, NM 87592-9658
(505) 471-3324
Web site: *www.nmna.org*

ANA New York
2113 Western Avenue, Suite 3
Guilderland, NY 12084
(877) 810-5972
Web site: *www.ana-newyork.org*

North Carolina Nurses Association
103 Enterprise Street
P.O. Box 12025
Raleigh, NC 27605-2025
(919) 821-4250 1-800-626-2153
Web site: *www.ncnurses.org*

North Dakota Nurses Association
6030 173rd Avenue
SW-Walcott, ND 58077
(701) 223-1385
Web site: *www.ndna.org*

Ohio Nurses Association
4000 E. Main Street
Columbus, OH 43213-2983
(614) 237-5414
Web site: *www.ohnurses.org*

Oklahoma Nurses Association
6414 N Santa Fe Suite A
Oklahoma City, OK 73116
(405) 840-3476
Web site: *www.oklahomanurses.org*

Oregon Nurses Association
18765 SW Boones Ferry Road, Suite 200
Tualatin, OR 97062
(503) 293-0011
Web site: *www.oregonrn.org*

Pennsylvania Nurses Association
3605 Varatb Way, Suite 204
Harrisburg, PA 17110-9601
(717) 657-1222
1-888-707-7762
Web site: *www.psna.org*

(continued)

US and Canadian nurses' associations (continued)

Rhode Island State Nurses Association
1800D Mineral Spring Avenue
P.O. Box 299
North Providence, RI 02904
(401) 331-5644
Web site: www.risna.org

South Carolina Nurses Association
1821 Gadsden Street
Columbia, SC 29201
(803) 252-4781
Web site: www.scnurses.org

South Dakota Nurses Association
P.O. Box 1015
Pierre, SD 57501-1015
(605) 945-4265
Web site: www.sdnurses.org

Tennessee Nurses Association
545 Mainstream Drive, Suite 405
Nashville, TN 37228-1201
(615) 254-0350
Web site: www.tnaonline.org

Texas Nurses Association
8501 North Mopac Expressway, Suite 400
Austin, TX 78759-8396
(512) 452-0645
Web site: www.texasnurses.org

Utah Nurses Association
4505 South Wasatch Boulevard,
Suite 330B
Salt Lake City, UT 84124
(801) 272-4510
Web site: www.utahnursesassociation.com

Vermont State Nurses Association
100 Dorset Street, Suite 13
South Burlington, VT 05403-6241
(802) 651-8886
Web site: www.vsna-inc.org

Virgin Islands Nurses Association
P.O. Box 3617
Christiansted, US Virgin Islands 00822
(340) 244-6874

Virginia Nurses Association
7113 Three Chopt Road, Suite H, final
member of the nursing team
Richmond, VA 23226
(804) 282-1808
Web site: www.virginianurses.com

Washington State Nurses Association
575 Andover Park West, Suite 101
Seattle, WA
98188-3321
(206) 575-7979
Web site: www.wsna.org

West Virginia Nurses Association
P.O. Box 1946
Charleston, WV 25327
(304) 342-1169
Web site: www.wvnurses.org

Wisconsin Nurses Association
6117 Monona Drive
Madison, WI 53716
(608) 221-0383
Web site: www.wisconsinnurses.org

Wyoming Nurses Association
301 Thelma Drive, #200
Casper, WY 82609
1-800-795-6381
Web site: www.wyonurse.org

Canadian associations
Canadian Nurses Association
50 Driveway
Ottawa, ON K2P 1E2
(613) 237-2133
1-800-361-8404
Web site: www.can-aiic.ca

US and Canadian nurses' associations *(continued)*

College & Association of Registered Nurses of Alberta
11620-168
St. Edmonton, AB T5M 4A6
(780) 451-0043
Web site: *www.nurses.ab.ca*

Association of Registered Nurses of British Columbia
100-1450 Creekside Drive
Vancouver, BC V6J 5B3
(604) 737-1304
Web site: *www.arnbc.ca*

College of Registered Nurses of Manitoba
890 Pembina Highway
Winnipeg, MB R3M 2M8
(204) 774-3477
1-800-665-2027
Web site: *www.crnm.mb.ca*

Nurses Association of New Brunswick
165 Regent Street
Fredericton, NB E3B 7B4
(506) 458-8731
1-800-442-4417
Web site: *www.nanb.nb.ca*

Association of Registered Nurses of Newfoundland and Labrador
55 Military Road
St. Johns, NL A1C 2C5
(709) 753-6040
1-800-563-3200
Web site: *www.arnnl.ca*

Registered Nurses Association of the Northwest Territories and Nunavut
Box 2757
Yellowknife, NT X1A 2R1
(867) 873-2745
Web site: *www.rnantnu.ca*

College of Registered Nurses of Nova Scotia
Suite 4005-7071 Bayers Road
Halifax, NS B3L 2C2
(902) 491-9744
Web site: *www.crnns.ca*

Registered Nurses' Association of Ontario
158 Pearl Street
Toronto, ON M5H 1L3
(416) 599-1925
1-800-268-7199
Web site: *www.rnao.org*

Association of Registered Nurses of Prince Edward Island
53 Grafton Street
Charlottetown, PEI C1A 1K8
(902) 368-3764
Web site: *www.arnpei.ca*

Ordre des Infirmières et Infirmiers du Québec
4200 rue Molson Montreal
Quebec H1Y 4V4
(514) 935-2501
1-800-363-6048
Web site: *www.oiiq.org*

Saskatchewan Registered Nurses' Association
2066 Retallack
St. Regina, SK S4T 7X5
(306) 359-4200
1-800-667-9945
Web site: *www.srna.org*

Yukon Registered Nurses Association
204-4133 4th Avenue
Whitehorse, YT Y1A 1H8
(867) 667-4062
Web site: *www.yrna.ca*

from an approved school of nursing, the board of nursing must deny a license to anyone who has not done so. This provision applies even to applicants who can provide evidence of equivalency and competency. *Richardson v. Brunelle* (1979).

In many states and jurisdictions, the board of nursing may grant exemptions and waivers to its own rules and regulations. For example, if a regulation states that all nursing faculty must have master's degrees, the board might be able to waive this requirement temporarily for a faculty member who's in the process of obtaining one.

In most states, the board of nursing consists of practicing RNs. Many boards also include LPNs, health care facility administrators, and *consumers*— members of the community at large. The state legislature decides on the board's mix; in almost every state, the governor appoints members from a list of nominees submitted by the state nursing association.

Violations

The nurse practice act also lists violations that can result in disciplinary action against a nurse. Depending on the nature of the violation, a nurse may face not only state board disciplinary action but also civil liability for her actions. Civil penalties for violations of the nurse practice act vary in most states according to the severity of the violation and the risk of harm to the public. Penalties can be assessed by the board of nursing from $100 to $1,000. The best defense against a disciplinary action is staying current in your nursing practice. Every nurse should know their state-specific nurse practice act and be aware of other laws and rules that govern nursing practice. Ignorance of these laws is not adequate defense in a disciplinary action.

Interpreting your nurse practice act

Nurse practice acts are broadly worded, and the wording varies from state to state. Understanding your nurse practice act's general provisions will help you stay within the legal limits of nursing practice. Interpreting the nurse practice act isn't always easy. One problem stems from the fact that nurse practice acts are statutory laws. Any amendment to a nurse practice act, then, must be accomplished by means of the inevitably slow legislative process. Because of the time involved in drafting, and enacting laws, amendments to nurse practice acts lag well behind the progress of changes in nursing. Your state board of nursing can provide you with interpretation of the nurse practice act.

NURSING DIAGNOSIS DILEMMA

You may be expected to perform tasks that seem to be within the accepted scope of nursing but in fact violate your state's nurse practice act. Consider this common example: Most nurses regularly make nursing diagnoses, although in many cases, their state nurse practice acts don't spell out whether they legally may do so.

Many nurse practice acts do not permit nurses to make diagnosis; others simply state that the nurse is permitted to implement the nursing process. Even some nurse practice acts that do permit nursing diagnosis fail to define what the term means. For instance, the Pennsylvania Nurse Practice Act defines the practice of professional nursing as "*diagnosing and treating* human responses to actual or potential health problems through such services as case finding, health

teaching, health counseling, and provision care supportive to or restorative
of life and well-being, and executing
medical regimens as prescribed by
a licensed physician or dentist. The
foregoing shall not be deemed to
include acts of medical diagnosis or
prescription of medical therapeutic or
corrective measures." This definition
and others like it don't distinguish
clearly between medical and nursing
diagnoses.

Your state's nurse practice act is not
a word-for-word checklist on how you
should do your work. You must rely on
your own education and knowledge
of your facilities' policies and procedures. For example, you know that a
nursing diagnosis is part of your nursing assessment. It is your professional
evaluation of the patient's progress,
his responses to treatment, and his
nursing care needs. You perform this
evaluation so that you can develop and
carry out your nursing care plan. So,
if your state's nurse practice act permits you to make nursing diagnoses,
your sound judgment in applying its
provisions should help you avoid legal
consequences. If your employer's practice and procedures conflict with the
nurse practice act, you may be assisted
in working out this conflict by going
to your state nursing organization to
lobby the nursing board for resolution
of the conflict.

LIMITS OF PRACTICE

Make sure you're familiar with the
legally permissible scope of your nursing practice, as defined in your state's
nurse practice act and board of nursing
rules and regulations, and never exceed
those limits. Otherwise, you're inviting
legal problems.

Here's an example. The Pennsylvania Nurse Practice Act forbids a

nurse to give an anesthetic unless the
patient's physician is present. The case
of *McCarl v. State Board of Nurse Examiners* (1979) involved a hospital nurse
who violated this provision. The Pennsylvania Board of Nursing received a
complaint from the operating surgeon
about the incident and conducted a
hearing. The nurse admitted to knowing about the law's requirement but
argued the requirement was satisfied
by the presence of another physician,
although this physician didn't supervise
his actions. The board ruled that the
nurse had willfully violated a section
of the Pennsylvania Nurse Practice
Act and issued a reprimand. The nurse
appealed, but the court upheld the
reprimand.

WHEN TO ACT INDEPENDENTLY

Most nurse practice acts pose another
problem: They state that you have a
legal duty to carry out a physician's or
a dentist's orders. Yet, as a licensed professional, you also have an ethical and
legal duty to use your own judgment
when providing patient care.

In an effort to deal with this issue,
some nurse practice acts give guidance
on how to obey orders and still act
independently. For example, the Delaware Nurse Practice Act states that the
RN practices the profession of nursing by performing certain activities;
among these are "executing regimens,
as prescribed by a licensed physician,
dentist, podiatrist, or advanced practice nurse, including the dispensing
and/or administration of medications
and treatments." Having said this, the
Delaware statute defines the practice
of professional nursing as "the performance of professional services by a
person who holds a valid license" and
"who bears primary responsibility and
accountability for nursing practices

based on specialized knowledge, judgment, and skill derived from the principles of biological, physical, and behavioral sciences." This wording may be interpreted to mean that a nurse practicing in Delaware is required to follow a physician's or a dentist's orders, unless those orders are clearly wrong or the physician or dentist is unqualified to give them.

If you are confused about an order or question the safety of a physician order, ask the physician to clarify it. If he fails to correct the error or answer your questions, inform your head nurse or supervisor of your doubts. The nurse is responsible and accountable for the quality of nursing care given to patient. This responsibility cannot be avoided by accepting the orders or directions of another person.

A similar problem may arise when you deal with physician assistants (PAs) or APNs. Nurse practice acts in some states specify that you may only follow orders given by physicians or dentists—but medical practice acts in those states may allow PAs or APNs to give orders to nurses. Washington, Texas, and Florida, for example, have decided that PAs and NPs are physicians' agents and may legally transmit the supervising physician's orders to nurses (*Washington State Nurses Ass'n. v. Board of Medical Examiners,* [1980]; Fla. Op. Atty. Gen. [077-96, September 1977]). The state of Delaware permits nurses with advanced credentials to prescribe regimens executed by RNs. Find out if your health care facility's policy allows PAs or APNs to give you orders. If it does not, don't follow such orders. If facility policy does permit PAs or APNs to give you orders, check if such orders must have verification or countersignature of the physician. For further clarification, check with your state board of nursing.

CONFLICTS WITH HOSPITAL POLICY

Nurse practice acts and hospital policies don't always agree. Hospital licensing laws require each hospital to establish policies and procedures for its operation. The nursing service department develops detailed policies and procedures for staff nurses. These policies and procedures usually specify the allowable scope of nursing practice within the hospital. The scope may be narrower than the scope described in your nurse practice act, but it shouldn't be broader.

Keep in mind that your employer can't legally expand the scope of your nursing practice to include tasks prohibited by your state's nurse practice act. For example, nurses who measured, weighed, compounded, and mixed ingredients in preparation of parenteral hyperalimentation solutions and IV solutions (a longtime hospital practice and procedure) were censured and reprimanded by the New York State Board of Nursing, even though their hospital allowed them to do so. They were placed on an 18-month probation and charged with the unlicensed practice of pharmacy in violation of the state of New York's Nurse Practice Act.

You have a legal obligation to practice within your nurse practice act's limits. Except in a life-threatening emergency, you cannot exceed those limits without risking disciplinary action. To protect yourself, compare your facility's policies with your nurse practice act and board of nursing rules and regulations.

READING BETWEEN THE LINES

Most nurse practice acts do not specify a nurse's day-to-day legal responsibilities with respect to specific procedures and functions. For instance, along with omitting any reference to nursing diagnosis, many nurse practice acts do not address a nurse's responsibility for patient teaching or the legal limitations on nurse-patient discussions about treatment. However, board of nursing rules and regulations—depending on the state—may provide more guidance.

In an Idaho case, *Tuma v. Board of Nursing* (1979), a state board of nursing took disciplinary action against a nurse who discussed, at a patient's request, the possibility of using laetrile as alternative therapy. The board suspended her license on the grounds of unprofessional conduct. The Idaho Supreme Court revoked the suspension and ordered the board to reinstate the nurse's license. Why? Because the Idaho Nurse Practice Act contained no provision stating that such a nurse-patient discussion constitutes a violation of the nurse practice act.

Keeping nurse practice acts up to date

To align nurse practice acts with current nursing practice, professional nursing organizations and state boards of nursing generally propose revisions to regulations. Also, the nurse practice act can be changed by amendments or redefinition.

An *amendment* adds or repeals portions of a nurse practice act or its regulations, thereby giving nurses legal permission to perform certain procedures or functions that have become part of accepted nursing practice. Amendments have the same legal force as the original act. They do, however, have a disadvantage: They represent a piecemeal approach that may allow an outdated nurse practice act to remain in effect.

Redefinition is a rewriting of the fundamental provision of a nurse practice act—the definition of nursing practice. This approach changes the basic premise of the entire act without amending or repealing it. Redefinition might be used, for example, to reverse a definition of nursing practice that prohibits diagnosis. How? By clarifying the term diagnosis to allow nurses to make nursing diagnoses. This type of change helps nurses understand exactly what is and isn't prohibited.

When a state legislature changes or expands the state's nurse practice act, it must also repeal sections that conflict with its changes. For example, if a state legislature decides to adopt the nursing board's recommendation for a newly broadened definition of nursing, it must repeal the old definition in the state nurse practice act before it can enact the new definition into law.

Be aware that nurse practice acts are constantly being changed. To help protect yourself legally, you need to thoroughly understand your state's nurse practice act and board of nursing rules and regulations and keep up with any changes. You can do this easily by periodically checking your board of nursing's Web site. (*See State boards of nursing*)

Standards of nursing care

Standards of care set minimum criteria for your proficiency on the job, enabling you and others to judge the quality of care you and your nursing colleagues provide. States may refer to standards in their nurse practice acts. Unless included in a nurse practice act, professional standards aren't laws— they're guidelines for sound nursing

(*Text continues on page 18.*)

State boards of nursing

Alabama Board of Nursing
P.O. Box 303900
Montgomery, AL 36130-3900
Phone: (334) 293-5200
Web site: *www.abn.alabama.gov*

Alaska Board of Nursing
550 West 7th Avenue, Suite 1500
Anchorage, AK 99501-3567
Phone: (907)269-8161
Web site: *http://commerce.alaska.gov/ dnn/cbpl/ProfessionalLicensing/ BoardofNursing.aspx*

American Samoa Health Services Regulatory Board
LBJ Tropical Medical Center
Pago Pago, AS 96799
Phone: (684) 633-1222

Arizona State Board of Nursing
4747 North 7th Street, Suite 700
Phoenix, AZ 85014-3655
Phone: (602) 771-7800
Web site: *www.azbn.gov*

Arkansas State Board of Nursing
University Tower Building, 1123 South University Suite 800
Little Rock, AR 72204
Phone: (501) 686-2700
Web site: *www.arsbn.arkansas.gov*

California Board of Registered Nursing
1747 North Market Boulevard, Suite 150
Sacramento, CA 95834
Phone: (916) 322-3350
Web site: *www.rn.ca.gov*

California Board of Vocational Nursing and Psychiatric Technicians
2535 Capitol Oaks Drive, Suite 205
Sacramento, CA 95833
Phone: (916) 263-7800
Web site: *www.bvnpt.ca.gov*

Colorado Board of Nursing
1560 Broadway, Suite 1350
Denver, CO 80202
Phone: (303) 894-2430
Web site: *www.dora.state.co.us/nursing/*

Connecticut Board of Examiners for Nursing
410 Capitol Avenue,
MS #13PHO
P.O. Box 340308
Hartford, CT 06134-0328
Phone: (860) 509-7624
Web site: *https://www.ncsbn.org/ Connecticut.htm*

District of Columbia Board of Nursing
Department of Health,
899 North Capitol Street
NE Washington, DC 20002
Phone: 877-672-2174
Web site: *doh.dc.gov/*

Florida Board of Nursing
4052 Bald Cypress Way,
BIN C02
Tallahassee, FL 32399-3252
Phone (850) 245-4125
Web site: *http://floridasnursing.gov/*

Georgia Board of Nursing
237 Coliseum Drive
Macon, GA 31217-3858
Phone: (478) 207-2440
Web site: *http://sos.ga.gov/index.php/ licensing/plb/45*

Guam Board of Nurse Examiners
#123 Chalan Kareta
Mangilao, Guam 96913-6304
Phone: (671) 735-7407
Web site: *http://www.dphss.guam.gov/ content/guam-board-nurse-examiners*

State boards of nursing *(continued)*

Hawaii Board of Nursing
Professional and Vocational
Licensing Division
P.O. Box 3469
Honolulu, HI 96801
Phone: (808) 586-3000
Web site: *http://hawaii.gov/dcca/pvl/ boards/nursing*

Idaho Board of Nursing
280 N. 8th Street, Suite 210
Boise, ID 83720
Phone: (208) 334-3110
Web site: *www.ibn.idaho.gov*

Illinois Board of Nursing
James R. Thompson Center 100 W.
Randolph, Suite 9-300
Chicago, IL 60601
Phone: (312) 814-2715
Web site: *www.idfpr.com/PROFS/Info/ nursing.asp*

Indiana State Board of Nursing
402 West Washington Street,
Room W072
Indianapolis, IN 46204
Phone: (317) 234-2043
Web site: *www.in.gov/pla/nursing.htm*

Iowa Board of Nursing
River Point Business Park 400 SW
8th Street, Suite B
Des Moines, IA 50309-4685
Phone: (515) 281-3255
Web site: *www.nursing.iowa.gov*

Kansas State Board of Nursing
Landon State Office Building, 900 SW
Jackson, Suite 1051
Topeka, KS 66612-1230
Phone: (785) 296-4929
Web site: *www.ksbn.org*

Kentucky Board of Nursing
312 Whittington Parkway, Suite 300
Louisville, KY 40222
Phone: (502) 329-7000
Web site: *www.kbn.ky.org*

Louisiana State Board of Nursing
17373 Perkins Road
Baton Rouge, LA 70810
Phone: (225) 755-7500
Web site: *www.lsbn.state.la.us*

Maine State Board of Nursing
158 State House Station
Augusta, ME 04333
Phone: (207) 287-1133
Web site: *www.maine.gov/boardofnursing/*

Maryland Board of Nursing
4140 Patterson Avenue
Baltimore, MD 21215
Phone: (410) 585-1900
Web site: *www.mbon.org*

Massachusetts Board of Registration in Nursing
Commonwealth of Massachusetts, 239
Causeway Street, Suite 500
Boston, MA 02114
Phone: (617) 973-0900
1-800-414-0168
Web site: *www.mass.gov/eohhs*

Michigan Board of Nursing
611 West Ottawa Street,
Lansing, MI 48909
Phone: (517) 335-0918
Web site: *www.michigan.gov/lara*

Minnesota Board of Nursing
2829 University Avenue SE, Suite 500
Minneapolis, MN 55414
Phone: (612) 317-3000
Web site: *www.nursingboard.state.mn.us*

(continued)

State boards of nursing *(continued)*

Mississippi Board of Nursing
713 Pear Orchard Road,
3rd Floor
Ridgeland, MS 39157
Phone: (601) 957-6300
Web site: *www.msbn.ms.gov*

Missouri State Board of Nursing
3605 Missouri Boulevard
P.O. Box 656
Jefferson City, MO 65102-0656
Phone: (573) 751-0681
Web site: *www.pr.mo.gov/nursing*

Montana State Board of Nursing
301 South Park, Suite 401
Helena, MT 59620-0513
Phone: (406)841-2340
Web site: *www.bsd.dli.mt.gov/license/bsd_boards/nur_board/board_page.asp*

Nebraska Board of Nursing
301 Centennial Mall South
Lincoln, NE 68509-4986
Phone: (402) 471-4376
Web site: *www.dhhs.ne.gov/publichealth/Pages/crl_nursing_nursingindex.aspx*

Nevada State Board of Nursing
5011 Meadowood Mall Way, Suite 300
Reno, NV 89502
Phone: (775) 687-7700
Web site: *www.nevadanursingboard.org*

New Hampshire Board of Nursing
121 South Fruit Street
Concord, NH 03301
Phone: (603) 271-2323
Web site: *www.state.nh.us/nursing*

New Jersey Board of Nursing
124 Halsey Street, 6th Floor
P.O. Box 45010
Newark, NJ 07101
Phone: (973)504-6430
Website: *www.njconsumeraffairs.gov/nursing/*

New Mexico Board of Nursing
6301 Indian School Road, NE Suite 701
Albuquerque, NM 87110
Phone: (505) 841-8340
Web site: *www.bon.state.nm.us*

New York State Board of Nursing
Education Building, 89 Washington Avenue,
2nd Floor West Wing
Albany, NY 12234
Phone: (518) 474-3817, ext. 120
Web site: *www.op.nysed.gov/prof/nurs*

North Carolina Board of Nursing
4516 Lake Boone Trail
Raleigh, NC 27607
Phone: (919) 782-3211
Web site: *www.ncbon.com*

North Dakota Board of Nursing
919 S. 7th Street, Suite 504
Bismarck, ND 58504
Phone: (701) 328-9777
Web site: *www.ndbon.org*

Northern Mariana Islands Commonwealth Board of Nurse Examiners
P.O. Box 501458
Saipan, MP 96950
Phone: (670) 233-2263
Web site: *www.nmicbne.com*

Ohio Board of Nursing
17 South High Street, Suite 400
Columbus, OH 43215-3413
Phone: (614) 466-6940
Web site: *www.nursing.ohio.gov*

State boards of nursing *(continued)*

Oklahoma Board of Nursing
2915 N. Classen Boulevard, Suite 524
Oklahoma City, OK 73106
Phone: (405) 962-1800
Web site: *www.ok.gov/nursing*

Oregon State Board of Nursing
17938 SW Upper Boones Ferry Road
Portland, OR 97224
Phone: (971) 673-0685
Web site: *www.osbn.state.or.us*

Pennsylvania State Board of Nursing
P.O. Box 2649
Harrisburg, PA 17105-2649
Phone: (717) 783-7142
Web site: *www.portal.state.pa.us/portal/server.pt/community/state_board_of_nursing*

Commonwealth of Puerto Rico
Board of Nurse Examiners, 800 Roberto H. Todd Avenue, Room 202, Stop 18
Santurce, PR 00908
Phone: (787) 725-8161

Rhode Island Board of Nurse Registration and Nursing Education
105 Cannon Building, Three Capitol Hill
Providence, RI 02908
Phone: (401) 222-5700
Web site: *www.health.ri.gov/for/nurse*

South Carolina State Board of Nursing
110 Centerview Drive, Suite 202
Columbia, SC 29210
Phone: (803) 896-4550
Web site: *www.llr.state.sc.us/pol/nursing*

South Dakota Board of Nursing
4300 S. Louise Avenue, Suite 201
Sioux Falls, SD 57106-3115
Phone: (605) 362-2760
Web site: *doh.sd.gov/boards/nursing/*

Tennessee State Board of Nursing
665 Mainstream Drive
Nashville, TN 37243
Phone: (615) 532-5166
Web site: *health.state.tn.us/Boards/Nursing*

Texas Board of Nursing
333 Guadalupe Street, Suite 3-460
Austin, TX 78701
Phone: (512) 305-7400
Web site: *www.bon.state.tx.us*

Utah State Board of Nursing
Heber M. Wells Building, 4th Floor,
160 East 300 South
Salt Lake City, UT 84111
Phone: (801) 530-6628
Web site: *www.dopl.utah.gov/licensing/nursing.html*

Vermont State Board of Nursing
89 Main Street, Floor 3
Montpelier, VT 05620-3402
Phone: (802) 828-2396
Web site: *www.vtprofessionals.org/opr1/nurses*

Virgin Islands Board of Nurse Licensure
P.O. Box 304247 Veterans Drive Station
St. Thomas, VI 00803
Phone: (340) 776-7397
Web site: *www.thevibnl.org*

Virginia Board of Nursing
9960 Mayland Drive, Suite 300
Henrico, VA 23233
Phone: (804) 367-4515
Web site: *www.dhp.virginia.gov/nursing/*

(continued)

State boards of nursing *(continued)*

Washington State Nursing Care Quality Assurance Commission
Department of Health
P.O. Box 47864
Olympia, WA 98504-7864
Phone: (360) 236-4700
Web site: *www.doh.wa.gov*

West Virginia State Board of Examiners for Licensed Practical Nurses
101 Dee Drive
Charleston, WV 25311
Phone: (304) 558-3572
Web site: *www.lpnboard.state.wv.us*

West Virginia Board of Examiners for Registered Professional Nurses
101 Dee Drive
Charleston, WV 25311
Phone: (304) 558-3596
Web site: *www.wvrnboard.com*

Wisconsin Department of Safety and Professional Services
1400 E. Washington Avenue
P.O. Box 8935
Madison,
WI 53708
Phone: (608) 266-2112
Web site: *www.dsps.wi.gov*

Wyoming State Board of Nursing
130 Hobbs Avenue,
Suite B
Cheyenne, WY 82002
Phone: (307) 777-7601
Web site: *http://nursing.state.wy.us*

practice. Some nurses regard standards of nursing care as pie-in-the-sky ideals that have little bearing on the reality of working life. This is a dangerous misconception. You're expected to meet standards of nursing care for every nursing task you perform.

For example, if you're a medical-surgical nurse, minimal standards require that you develop a nursing care plan for your patient based on the nursing process, including nursing assessment, diagnosis, plan of care, and interventions for implementing the care plan. Standards also call for documentation, in the patient's record, of your completion and evaluation of the plan. When you document patient care, you're really writing a record of

how well you've met these standards. A court may interpret an absence of documentation as an absence of patient care. *Pommier v. ABC Insurance Company et al.*, 715 So.2d 1270 (La. App.3d Cir. 1998).

EVOLUTION OF NURSING STANDARDS

Before 1950, nurses had only Florence Nightingale's early treatments, plus reports of court cases, to use as standards. As nursing gradually became recognized as an independent profession, nursing organizations stressed the importance of having recognized standards for all nurses. Then, in 1950, the ANA (the American Nurses

Association) published the "Code of Ethics for Nursing," a general mandate stating that nurses should offer nursing care without prejudice and in a confidential and safe manner. Although not specific, this code marked the beginning of written nursing standards.

In 1973, the ANA Congress for Nursing Practice established the first generic standards for the profession— standards that could be applied to all nurses in all settings (See *ANA standards of nursing practice*). The Canadian Nurses Association (CNA) has established similar nursing standards. Some states and jurisdictions have incorporated ANA and CNA standards into their nurse practice acts.

As the ANA's organizational structure evolved and specialty practice interests expanded, increasing numbers of specialty nursing organizations emerged to provide pertinent specialty-focused continuing education and professional resources. Many nursing specialty organizations have elected to further describe the "who", "what", "where", "when" and "how" of their specialty by publishing the scope of practice and standards of practice pertinent to members of their nursing specialty. In the late 1990s, the ANA created the Congress on Nursing Practice and Economics (CNPE), which became the reviewing body for all specialty nursing standards of practice. (See *ANA standards for nursing administration* as an example of specialty nursing standards of practice.)

Other organizations have contributed to the development of nursing standards. The Joint Commission, a private, nongovernmental agency that is responsible for evaluating and accrediting more than 20,500 health care organizations in the United States, such as hospitals, nursing homes, health care networks, health care providers, and long-term care facilities, has also developed nursing standards to be used in hospital audit systems. In some states, Joint Commission standards have been incorporated into law, resulting in broadly applicable standards of patient care. In addition, state nursing associations and the specialty nursing organizations actively work with hospital nursing administrators for adoption of standards.

Local or national standards

Standard of care can be local, state, or national. Compared to most local or state standards, the national standards of nursing practice as established by the ANA are broad in scope. The standards are often more narrowly defined at a local level based on policies and procedures established by local health care facilities.

Some state courts use local standards—reflecting a community's accepted, common nursing practices— to judge the quality of nursing care. Local standards are established in two ways: by individual health care facilities, through their policies and procedures, and by expert witnesses who testify in court cases that involve nurses. Every facility establishes standards to fit its own community's needs. An expert witness interprets local standards by testifying about how nursing is commonly practiced in the community.

Legal significance

Even though they are not law, nursing standards have important legal significance. The allegation that a nurse failed to meet appropriate standards of care, and that breach of these standards caused the harm (proximate cause) to the patient, is the basic premise of every nursing malpractice lawsuit.

(*Text continues on page 26.*)

ANA standards of nursing practice

The standards of professional nursing practice are authoritative statements of the duties that all registered nurses, regardless of role, population, or specialty, are expected to perform competently. The standards may be utilized as evidence of the standard of care, with the understanding that application of the standards is context dependent.

The standards below are adapted from standards of nursing practice published by the American Nurses Association (ANA). They developed the standards (last revised in 2010) to provide registered nurses with guidelines for determining quality nursing care. The courts, hospitals, nurses, and patients may refer to these standards. The standards of nursing practice are divided into the "standards of practice," which identify the care that is provided to recipients of nursing services, and the "standards of professional performance," which explain the level of behavior expected in professional role activities.

The competencies that accompany each standard may be evidence of compliance with the corresponding standard. The list of competencies is not exhaustive. Whether a particular standard or competency applies depends upon the circumstances.

This adaptation of the standards doesn't present the additional competencies that are specific to advanced practice nurses.

Standards of practice
Standard 1: Assessment
The registered nurse collects comprehensive data pertinent to the health care consumer's health and/or the situation.

Competencies
■ Collects comprehensive data including but not limited to physical, functional, psychosocial, emotional, cognitive, sexual, cultural, age-related, environmental, spiritual/transpersonal, and economic assessments in a systematic and ongoing process while honoring the uniqueness of the person

■ Elicits the health care consumer's values, preferences, expressed needs, and knowledge of the health care situation
■ Involves the health care consumer, family, and other health care providers as appropriate, in holistic data collection
■ Identifies barriers (e.g., psychosocial, literacy, financial, cultural) to effective communication and makes appropriate adaptations
■ Recognizes the impact of personal attitudes, values, and beliefs
■ Assesses family dynamics and impact on health care consumer health and wellness
■ Prioritizes data collection based on the health care consumer's immediate condition, or the anticipated needs of the health care consumer or situation
■ Uses appropriate evidence-based assessment techniques, instruments, and tools
■ Synthesizes available data, information, and knowledge relevant to the situation to identify patterns and variances
■ Applies ethical, legal, and privacy guidelines and policies to the collection, maintenance, use, and dissemination of data and information
■ Recognizes the health care consumer as the authority on her or his own health by honoring their care preferences
■ Documents relevant data in a retrievable format

Standard 2: Diagnosis
The registered nurse analyzes the assessment data to determine the diagnoses or the issue.

Competencies
■ Derives the diagnoses or issues from assessment data
■ Validates the diagnoses or issues with the health care consumer, family, and other health care providers when possible and appropriate
■ Identifies actual or potential risks to the health care consumer's health and safety or

ANA standards of nursing practice *(continued)*

barriers to health, which may include but are not limited to interpersonal, systematic, or environmental circumstances
■ Uses standardized classification systems and clinical decision support tools, when available, in identifying diagnoses
■ Documents diagnoses or issues in a manner that facilitates the determination of the expected outcomes and plan

Standard 3: Outcomes Identification
The registered nurse identifies expected outcomes individualized to the health care consumer or the situation.

Competencies
■ Involves the health care consumer, family, health care providers, and others in formulating expected outcomes when possible and appropriate
■ Derives culturally appropriate expected outcomes from the diagnoses
■ Considers associated risks, benefits, costs, current scientific evidence, expected trajectory of the condition, and clinical expertise when formulating expected outcomes
■ Defines expected outcomes in terms of the health care consumer, health care consumer culture, values, and ethical considerations
■ Includes a time estimate for the attainment of expected outcomes
■ Develops expected outcomes that facilitate continuity of care
■ Modifies expected outcomes according to changes in the status of the health care consumer or evaluation of the situation
■ Documents expected outcomes as measurable goals

Standard 4: Planning
The registered nurse develops a plan that prescribes strategies and alternatives to attain expected outcomes.

Competencies
The registered nurse
■ develops an individualized plan in partnership with the person, family, and others considering the person's characteristics or situation, including, but not limited to, values, beliefs, spiritual and health practices, preferences, choices, developmental level, coping style, culture and environment, and available technology.
■ establishes the plan priorities with the health care consumer, family, and others as appropriate.
■ includes strategies in the plan that address each of the identified diagnoses or issues. These may include, but are not limited to, strategies for
  ❏ promotion and restoration of health;
  ❏ prevention of illness, injury, and disease;
  ❏ the alleviation of suffering; and
  ❏ supportive care for those who are dying.
■ includes strategies for health and wholeness across the lifespan.
■ provides for continuity in the plan.
■ incorporates an implementation pathway or timeline in the plan.
■ considers the economic impact of the plan on the health care consumer, family, caregivers, or other affected parties.
■ integrates current scientific evidence, trends, and research.
■ utilizes the plan to provide direction to other members of the health care team.
■ explores practice settings and safe space and time for the nurse and the health care consumer to explore suggested, potential, and alternative options.
■ defines the plan to reflect current statutes, rules and regulations, and standards.
■ modifies the plan according to the ongoing assessment of the health care consumer's response and other outcome indicators.
■ documents the plan in a manner that uses standardized language or recognized terminology.

(continued)

ANA standards of nursing practice *(continued)*

Standard 5: Implementation
The registered nurse implements the identified plan.

Competencies
The registered nurse
■ partners with the person, family, significant others, and caregivers as appropriate to implement the plan in a safe, realistic, and timely manner.
■ demonstrates caring behaviors toward health care consumers, significant others, and groups of people receiving care.
■ utilizes technology to measure, record, and retrieve health care consumer data, implement the nursing process, and enhance nursing practice.
■ utilizes evidence-based interventions and treatments specific to the diagnosis or problem.
■ provides holistic care that addresses the needs of diverse populations across the lifespan.
■ advocates for health care that is sensitive to the needs of health care consumers, with particular emphasis on the needs of diverse populations.
■ applies appropriate knowledge of major health problems and cultural diversity in implementing the plan of care.
■ applies available health care technologies to maximize access and optimize outcomes for health care consumers.
■ utilizes community resources and systems to implement the plan.
■ collaborates with health care providers from diverse backgrounds to implement and integrate the plan.
■ accommodates for different styles of communication used by health care professionals.
■ integrates traditional and complementary health care practices as appropriate.
■ implements the plan in a timely manner in accordance with patient safety goals.
■ promotes the health care consumer's capacity for the optimal level of participation and problem-solving.

■ documents implementation and any modifications, including changes or omissions, of the identified plan consumers, families, and health care providers.

Standard 5A: Coordination of Care
The registered nurse coordinates care delivery.

Competencies
The registered nurse
■ organizes the components of the plan.
■ manages a health care consumer's care in order to maximize independence and quality of life.
■ assists the health care consumer in identifying options for alternative care.
■ communicates with the health care consumer, family, and system during transitions in care.
■ advocates for the delivery of dignified and humane care by the interprofessional team.
■ documents the coordination of care.

Standard 5B: Health Teaching and Health Promotion
The registered nurse employs strategies to promote health and a safe environment.

Competencies
The registered nurse
■ provides health teaching that addresses such topics as healthy lifestyles, risk-reducing behaviors, developmental needs, activities of daily living, and preventive self-care.
■ uses health promotion and health teaching methods appropriate to the situation and the health care consumer's values, beliefs, health practices, developmental level, learning needs, readiness and ability to learn, language preference, spirituality, culture, and socioeconomic status.
■ seeks opportunities for feedback and evaluation of the effectiveness of the strategies used.
■ uses information technologies to communicate health promotion and disease prevention

ANA standards of nursing practice *(continued)*

information to the health care consumer in a variety of settings.

■ provides health care consumers with information about intended effects and potential adverse effects of proposed therapies.

Standard 6: Evaluation

The registered nurse evaluates progress toward attainment of outcomes.

Competencies

The registered nurse

■ conducts a systematic, ongoing, and criterion-based evaluation of the outcomes in relation to the structures and processes prescribed by the plan of care and the indicated timeline.

■ collaborates with the health care consumer and others involved in the care or situation in the evaluation process.

■ evaluates, in partnership with the health care consumer, the effectiveness of the planned strategies in relation to the health care consumer's responses and the attainment of the expected outcomes.

■ uses ongoing assessment data to revise the diagnoses, outcomes, the plan, and the implementation as needed.

■ disseminates the results to the health care consumer, family, and others involved, in accordance with federal and state regulations.

■ participates in assessing and assuring the responsible and appropriate use of interventions in order to minimize unwarranted or unwanted treatment and health care consumer suffering.

■ documents the results of the evaluation.

Standards of Professional Performance

Standard 7: Ethics

The registered nurse practices ethically.

Standard 8: Education

The registered nurse attains knowledge and competence that reflects current nursing practice.

Competencies

The registered nurse

■ participates in ongoing educational activities related to appropriate knowledge bases and professional issues.

■ demonstrates a commitment to lifelong learning through self-reflection and inquiry to address learning and personal growth needs.

■ seeks experiences that reflect current practice to maintain knowledge, skills, abilities, and judgment in clinical practice or role performance.

■ acquires knowledge and skills appropriate to the role, population, specialty, setting, role, or situation.

■ seeks formal and independent learning experiences to develop and maintain clinical and professional skills and knowledge.

■ identifies learning needs based on nursing knowledge, the various roles the nurse may assume, and the changing needs of the population.

■ participates in formal or informal consultations to address issues in nursing practice as an application of education and a knowledge base.

■ shares educational findings, experiences, and ideas with peers.

■ contributes to a work environment conducive to the education of health care professionals.

■ maintains professional records that provide evidence of competence and lifelong learning.

Standard 9: Evidence-Based Practice and Research

The registered nurse integrates evidence and research findings into practice.

Competencies

The registered nurse

■ utilizes current evidence-based nursing knowledge, including research findings, to guide practice.

■ incorporates evidence when initiating changes in nursing practice.

(continued)

ANA standards of nursing practice *(continued)*

■ participates, as appropriate to education level and position, in the formulation of evidence-based practice through research.
■ shares personal or third-party research findings with colleagues and peers.

Standard 10: Quality of Practice
The registered nurse contributes to quality nursing practice.

Standard 11: Communication
The registered nurse communicates effectively in a variety of formats in all areas of practice.

Competencies
The registered nurse
■ assesses communication format preferences of health care consumers, families, and colleagues.
■ assesses her or his own communication skills in encounters with health care consumers, families, and colleagues.
■ seeks continuous improvement of communication and conflict resolution skills.
■ conveys information to health care consumers, families, the interprofessional team, and others in communication formats that promote accuracy.
■ questions the rationale supporting care processes and decisions when they do not appear to be in the best interest of the patient.
■ discloses observations or concerns related to hazards and errors in care or the practice environment to the appropriate level.
■ maintains communication with other providers to minimize risks associated with transfers and transition in care delivery.
■ contributes her or his own professional perspective in discussions with the interprofessional team.

Standard 12: Leadership
The registered nurse demonstrates leadership in the professional practice setting and the profession.

Competencies
The registered nurse
■ oversees the nursing care given by others while retaining accountability for the quality of care given to the health care consumer.
■ abides by the vision, the associated goals, and the plan to implement and measure progress of an individual health care consumer or progress within the context of the health care organization.
■ demonstrates a commitment to continuous, lifelong learning and education for self and others.
■ mentors colleagues for the advancement of nursing practice, the profession, and quality health care.
■ treats colleagues with respect, trust, and dignity.
■ develops communication and conflict resolution skills.
■ participates in professional organizations.
■ communicates effectively with the health care consumer and colleagues.
■ seeks ways to advance nursing autonomy and accountability.
■ participates in efforts to influence health care policy involving health care consumers and the profession.

Standard 13: Collaboration
The registered nurse collaborates with health care consumer, family, and others in the conduct of nursing practice.

Competencies
The registered nurse
■ partners with others to effect change and produce positive outcomes through the sharing of knowledge of the health care consumer and/ or situation.
■ communicates with the health care consumer, the family, and health care providers regarding health care consumer care and the nurse's role in the provision of that care.

ANA standards of nursing practice *(continued)*

- promotes conflict management and engagement.
- participates in building consensus or resolving conflict in the context of patient care.
- applies group process and negotiation techniques with health care consumers and colleagues.
- adheres to standards and applicable codes of conduct that govern behavior among peers and colleagues to create a work environment that promotes cooperation, respect, and trust.
- cooperates in creating a documented plan focused on outcomes and decisions related to care and delivery of services that indicates communication with health care consumers, families, and others.
- engages in teamwork and team-building process.

Standard 14: Professional Practice Evaluation

The registered nurse evaluates her or his own nursing practice in relation to professional practice standards and guidelines, relevant statutes, rules, and regulations.

Competencies

The registered nurse
- provides age-appropriate and developmentally appropriate care in a culturally and ethnically sensitive manner.
- engages in self-evaluation of practice on a regular basis, identifying areas of strength as well as areas in which professional growth would be beneficial.
- obtains informal feedback regarding her or his own practice from health care consumers, peers, professional colleagues, and others.
- participates in peer review as appropriate.
- takes action to achieve goals identified during the evaluation process.
- provides the evidence for practice decisions and actions as part of the informal and formal evaluation processes.

- interacts with peers and colleagues to enhance her or his own professional nursing practice or role performance.
- provides peers with formal or informal constructive feedback regarding their practice or role performance.

Standard 15: Resource Utilization

The registered nurse utilizes appropriate resources to plan and provide nursing services that are safe, effective, and financially responsible.

Competencies

The registered nurse
- assesses individual health care consumer care needs and resources available to achieve desired outcomes.
- identifies health care consumer care needs, potential for harm, complexity of the task, and desired outcome when considering resource allocation.
- delegates elements of care to appropriate health care workers in accordance with any applicable legal or policy parameters or principles.
- identifies the evidence when evaluating resources.
- advocates for resources, including technology, that enhance nursing practice.
- modifies practice when necessary to promote positive interaction between health care consumers, care providers, and technology.
- assists the health care consumer and family in identifying and securing appropriate services to address needs across the health care continuum.
- assists the health care consumer and family in factoring costs, risks, and benefits in decisions about treatment and care.

Standard 16: Environmental Health

The registered nurse practices in an environmentally safe and healthy manner.

(continued)

ANA standards of nursing practice *(continued)*

Competencies

The registered nurse

- attains knowledge of environmental health concepts, such as implementation of environmental health strategies.
- promotes a practice environment that reduces environmental health risks for workers and health care consumers.
- assesses the practice environment for factors such as sound, odor, noise, and light that threaten health.

- advocates for the judicious and appropriate use of products in health care.
- communicates environmental health risks and exposure reduction strategies to health care consumers, families, colleagues, and communities.
- utilizes scientific evidence to determine if a product or treatment is an environmental threat.
- participates in strategies to promote healthy communities.

During a malpractice trial, the court will measure the defendant-nurse's action against the answer it obtains to the following question: *What would a reasonably prudent nurse, with like training and experience, do under these or similar circumstances?*

To answer this question, the plaintiff-patient, through his attorney, has the burden to prove that certain standards of care exist and that the defendant-nurse failed to meet those standards in her treatment of him. He must also prove the appropriateness of those standards, show how the nurse failed to meet them, and show how that failure caused him injury.

When the standard of care is at issue, the plaintiff-patient must present expert witness testimony to support his claims. The defendant-nurse and her attorney will also produce expert witness testimony to support her claim that her actions didn't fall below accepted standards of care and that she acted in a reasonable and prudent manner.

The court may consider written standards when considering the standards of care involved in a nursing malpractice lawsuit. The court seeks information about all the national and state standards applicable to the defendant-nurse's actions. The court may also seek applicable information about the policies of the defendant-nurse's employer.

Because of two trends—uniform nursing educational requirements and standardized medical treatment regimens—national standards are gaining increasing favor with the courts. These trends have made the ANA's standards more influential than local standards or the standards of other organizations. For example, in the case of *Planned Parenthood of Northwest Indiana v. Vines* (1980), an NP who inserted an intrauterine device was held to the minimum standard of care that was uniform throughout the country.

As the role of nurses is expanding across the country, so is the standard of care. Nurses who perform the same medical services are subject to the same standard of care and liability as physicians. *Pommier v. ABC Insurance Company,* 715 So.2d 1270, 1297-1342 (La. App. 3d Cir. 1998).

(Text continues on page 33.)

ANA standards for nursing administration

The standards below are adapted from standards for nursing administration published by the American Nurses Association (ANA). They were last revised in 2009. In the original document, the ANA referred to nursing administration as "organized nursing services."

Standards of Practice
Standard 1: Assessment
The nurse administrator collects comprehensive data pertinent to the issue, situation, or trends.

Measurement Criteria
The nurse administrator
■ collects data in a systematic and ongoing process.
■ involves health care providers and other stakeholders, as appropriate, in holistic data collection related to context and environment.
■ prioritizes data collection activities based on immediate or anticipated needs.
■ uses appropriate evidence-based assessment techniques and instruments in collecting pertinent data.
■ uses analytical models and problem-solving tools.
■ identifies gaps and necessary mechanisms to address and resolve missing or insufficient data, information, and knowledge resources.
■ synthesizes available data, information, and knowledge relevant to the situation to identify patterns and variances.
■ documents relevant data in a retrievable format.

Standard 2: Identifies Issues, Problems, or Trends
The nurse administrator analyzes the assessment data to determine the issues, problems, or trends.

Measurement Criteria
The nurse administrator
■ demonstrates the ability to examine and synthesize complex data, information, and knowledge representations.

■ promotes the integration of clinical, human resource, and financial data to support and enhance decision-making.
■ derives the issues, problems, or trends from assessment data.
■ validates the issues, problems, or trends with the health care providers and other stakeholders when possible and appropriate.
■ documents issues, problems, or trends in a manner that facilitates the determination of the plan and expected outcomes.

Standard 3: Outcomes Identification
The nurse administrator identifies expected outcomes for a plan individualized to the situation.

Measurement Criteria
The nurse administrator
■ involves health care providers and other stakeholders in formulating expected outcomes when possible and appropriate.
■ derives culturally appropriate expected outcomes from identification of the issues, problems, or trends.
■ defines expected outcomes in terms of values, ethical considerations, environment, or situation, considering associated risks, benefits and costs, and current scientific evidence.
■ includes a time estimate for attainment of expected outcomes.
■ develops expected outcomes that provide direction for continuity of care.
■ modifies expected outcomes based on changes in the status of the issue, problem, or trend, or evaluation of the situation.
■ documents expected outcomes as measurable goals.

Standard 4: Planning
The nurse administrator develops a plan that prescribes strategies and alternatives to attain expected outcomes.

(continued)

ANA standards for nursing administration *(continued)*

Measurement Criteria
The nurse administrator
- develops an individualized plan considering characteristics of the situation.
- develops the plan and establishes the plan priorities in partnership with the appropriate stakeholders.
- includes strategies within the plan that address each of the identified issues, problems, or trends.
- incorporates an implementation pathway or timeline within the plan.
- utilizes the plan to provide direction to members of the health care team and other stakeholders.
- defines the plan to reflect current statutes, rules and regulations, and standards.
- integrates current trends and research affecting care in the planning process.
- considers the economic impact of the plan.
- uses standardized language or recognized terminology to document the plan.
- participates in the design and development of multidisciplinary and interdisciplinary processes to address the situation or issue.
- contributes to the development and continuous improvement of organizational systems that support the planning process.
- supports the integration of clinical, human, and financial resources to enhance and complete the decision-making processes.

Standard 5: Implementation
The nurse administrator implements the identified plan.

Measurement Criteria
The nurse administrator
- implements the plan in a safe and timely manner.
- documents implementation and any modifications, including changes or omissions, of the identified plan.
- utilizes evidence-based interventions and treatments specific to the problem, issue, or diagnosis.

- facilitates utilization of systems and community resources to implement the plan.
- collaborates with nursing colleagues and others to implement the plan.
- incorporates new knowledge and strategies to initiate change and achieve desired outcomes.
- implements the plan using principles and concepts of project or systems management.
- fosters organizational systems that support implementation of the plan.

Standard 5A: Coordination
The nurse administrator coordinates the implementation and other associated processes.

Measurement Criteria
The nurse administrator
- coordinates implementation of the plan and the associated activities and efforts.
- coordinates human, capital, system, and community resources and measures, including environmental modifications, necessary to implement the plan.
- provides leadership in the coordination of multidisciplinary health care resources for integrated delivery of care and services.
- promotes communication systems for an open and transparent organization.

Standard 5B: Health Promotion, Health Teaching, and Education
The nurse administrator employs strategies to foster health promotion, health teaching, and the provision of other educational services and resources.

Measurement Criteria
The nurse administrator
- contributes to the design, development, implementation, and evaluation of educational programs, including continuing education and other professional development programs, needed to implement the plan.

ANA standards for nursing administration *(continued)*

■ promotes the incorporation of materials, teaching methods, and other educational tools and services appropriate to the situation and the learner's developmental level, learning needs, readiness and ability to learn, language preference, health literacy, and cultural values and beliefs.

■ identifies the need to integrate learning resources into health care systems that address health content topics such as healthy lifestyles, risk-reducing behaviors, developmental needs, activities of daily living, and preventive self-care.

■ promotes awareness and education of the health care consumer with regard to appropriate data collection, information sharing, information access, and associated issues.

■ evaluates health information resources, such as the Internet, within the area of practice for accuracy, readability, and comprehensibility to help individuals, families, health care providers, and others access quality health information.

■ creates opportunities for feedback and evaluation of the effectiveness of the educational content and teaching strategies used for the continuing education and professional development programs necessary to implement the plan.

Standard 5C: Consultation
The nurse administrator provides consultation to influence the identified plan, enhance the abilities of others, and effect change.

Measurement Criteria
The nurse administrator
■ synthesizes data, information, theoretical frameworks, and evidence when providing consultation.

■ facilitates the effectiveness of a consultation by involving the stakeholders in decision-making and negotiating role responsibilities.

■ communicates consultation recommendations that influence the identified plan, facilitate

understanding by involved stakeholders, enhance the work of others, and effect change.

Standard 6: Evaluation
The nurse administrator evaluates progress toward attainment of outcomes.

Measurement Criteria
The nurse administrator
■ conducts a systematic, ongoing, and criterion-based evaluation of the outcomes in relation to the structures and processes prescribed by the plan and the indicated timeline.

■ provides evaluation processes built on appropriate research methods, evaluation tools, and metrics.

■ includes the stakeholders involved in the care or situation in the evaluative process.

■ evaluates the effectiveness of the planned strategies in relation to nurse-sensitive indicators, stakeholder responses, and the attainment of the expected outcomes.

■ documents the results of the evaluation.

■ uses the results of the evaluation analyses to make or recommend process or structural changes, including policy, procedure, or protocol documentation, as appropriate.

■ synthesizes the results of the evaluation analyses to determine the impact of the plan on the affected patients, families, groups, communities, populations, and institutions, networks, and organizations.

■ disseminates the results to the stakeholders involved in the care or situation, as appropriate, in accordance with state and federal laws and regulations.

Standards of Professional Performance
Standard 7: Quality of Practice
The nurse administrator systematically enhances the quality and effectiveness of nursing practice, nursing services administration, and the delivery of services.

(continued)

ANA standards for nursing administration *(continued)*

Measurement Criteria

The nurse administrator
- uses creativity and innovation in nursing practice to improve care delivery and population outcomes.
- implements initiatives to evaluate the need for change.
- drives quality improvement programs and activities.
- uses the results of quality improvement activities to initiate changes in nursing practice and in the health care delivery system.
- incorporates new knowledge to initiate changes in nursing practice to achieve desired outcomes.
- assures the presence of effective mechanisms for the development, implementation, and evaluation of policies, procedures, standards, and guidelines.
- assures the development and implementation of an effective, ongoing program to measure, assess, and improve the quality of care, treatment, and services delivered.
- evaluates the practice environment and quality of nursing care rendered in relation to existing evidence, identifying opportunities for the generation and use of research.
- participates in the evaluation and regulation of individuals as appropriate through privileging, credentialing, or certification processes.
- demonstrates quality by documenting the application of the nursing process in a responsible, accountable, and ethical manner.
- adheres to applicable professional standards and regulations.
- obtains and maintains professional certification if eligible.

Standard 8: Education

The nurse administrator attains knowledge and competency that reflects current practice.

Measurement Criteria

The nurse administrator

- participates in ongoing educational activities related to appropriate knowledge bases and professional issues.
- demonstrates a commitment to lifelong learning through self-reflection and inquiry to identify learning needs.
- seeks experiences and independent learning activities that reflect current practice in order to develop, maintain, and improve skills and competence in the nurse administrator role.
- acquires knowledge and skills appropriate to the specialty area, practice setting, role, or situation.
- maintains professional records that provide evidence of competency and lifelong learning.
- uses current research findings and other evidence to enhance role performance and increase knowledge of professional issues.

Standard 9: Professional Practice Evaluation

The nurse administrator evaluates own nursing practice in relation to professional practice standards and guidelines, relevant statutes, rules, and regulations.

Measurement Criteria

The nurse administrator
- applies knowledge of current practice standards, guidelines, statutes, rules, and regulations in practice.
- demonstrates respect for diversity in all interactions as reflected in such behaviors as cultural, ethnic, and generational sensitivity.
- engages in self-evaluation of practice on a regular basis, identifying areas of strength as well as areas in which professional development would be beneficial.
- obtains informal and formal feedback regarding role performance from professional colleagues, representatives and administrators of corporate entities, and others.
- participates in systematic peer review of others as appropriate.

ANA standards for nursing administration *(continued)*

■ interacts with peers and colleagues to enhance own professional nursing practice and role performance.

■ takes action to achieve goals identified during the evaluation process.

■ provides rationales for practice beliefs, decisions, and actions as part of the informal and formal evaluation processes.

Standard 10: Collegiality

The nurse administrator interacts with and contributes to the professional development of peers and colleagues.

Measurement Criteria

The nurse administrator

■ shares knowledge and skills with peers and colleagues as evidenced by such activities as care conferences or presentations at formal or informal meetings.

■ provides peers with feedback regarding their practice and role performance.

■ maintains empathetic and caring relationships with peers and colleagues.

■ establishes an environment that is conducive to the education of health care professionals.

■ assures the presence of a supportive and healthy work environment.

■ models expert practice to interdisciplinary team members and health care consumers.

■ assists staff in developing and maintaining competency in the analytic process.

■ mentors other registered nurses, nurse administrators, and colleagues as appropriate.

■ participates on multiprofessional teams that contribute to role development and, directly or indirectly, advance nursing practice and health services.

Standard 11: Collaboration

The nurse administrator collaborates with all levels of nursing staff, interdisciplinary teams, executive leaders, and other stakeholders.

Measurement Criteria

The nurse administrator

■ communicates with health care providers and other stakeholders regarding care and services and the nurse's role in the provision of care.

■ collaborates in creating a documented plan focused on outcomes and decisions related to care and delivery of services.

■ partners with others to enhance health care and employee satisfaction through interdisciplinary activities such as education, consultation, management, technological development, or research opportunities.

■ models an interdisciplinary process with other members of the health care team.

■ documents plans, communications, rationales for plan changes, and collaborative discussions.

Standard 12: Ethics

The nurse administrator integrates ethical provisions in all areas of practice.

Measurement Criteria

The nurse administrator

■ incorporates Code of Ethics for Nurses with Interpretive Statements (ANA, 2001) to guide practice.

■ assures the preservation and protection of the autonomy, dignity, and rights of individuals.

■ maintains confidentiality within legal and regulatory parameters.

■ assures a process to identify and address ethical issues within nursing and the organization.

■ participates on multidisciplinary and interdisciplinary teams that address ethical risks, benefits, and outcomes.

■ informs administrators or others of the risks, benefits, and outcomes of programs and decisions that affect health care delivery.

■ demonstrates a commitment to practicing self-care, managing stress, and connecting with self and others.

(continued)

ANA standards for nursing administration *(continued)*

Standard 13: Research
The nurse administrator integrates research findings into practice.

Measurement Criteria
The nurse administrator
- utilizes the best available evidence, including research findings, to guide practice decisions.
- creates a supportive environment with sufficient resources for nursing research, scholarly inquiry, and the generation of knowledge.
- assures research priorities align with the organization's strategic plans and objectives and include an appropriate nursing focus.
- formally disseminates research findings through activities such as presentations, publications, and consultation.

Standard 14: Resource Utilization
The nurse administrator considers factors related to safety, effectiveness, cost, and impact on practice in the planning and delivery of nursing and other services.

Measurement Criteria
The nurse administrator
- evaluates factors such as safety, effectiveness, availability, cost and benefits, efficiencies, and impact on practice when choosing practice options that would result in the same expected outcome.
- develops innovative solutions that address effective resource utilization and maintenance of quality.
- assures that resource allocations are based on identified needs and valid nursing workload measures.
- secures organizational resources to create a work environment conducive to completing the identified plan and conducting the critical assessment and evaluation of desired outcomes.
- develops evaluation strategies to demonstrate cost effectiveness, cost benefit, environmental impact, and efficiency factors associated with nursing practice.

- develops evaluation methods to measure safety and effectiveness for interventions and outcomes.
- promotes the value of the intellectual capital of the organization and appropriate measures to develop and expand this resource.
- establishes strategies and mechanisms to promote organizational acceptance of appropriate roles for the utilization of all staff.
- optimizes fiscal resource allocation to support current and potential objectives and initiatives.
- leads in promoting the appropriate use of innovative applications and new technologies, including consideration of the impact on global environmental health and sustainability.
- promotes activities that assist others, as appropriate, in becoming informed about costs, risks, and benefits of plans and solutions.

Standard 15: Leadership
The nurse administrator provides leadership in the professional practice setting and the profession.

Measurement Criteria
The nurse administrator
- engages in teamwork as a team player and a team builder.
- works to create and maintain healthy work environments in local, regional, national, or international communities.
- displays the ability to define a clear vision, the associated goals, and a plan to implement and measure progress.
- exhibits creativity and flexibility through times of change.
- demonstrates energy, excitement, and a passion for quality work.
- willingly accepts mistakes by self and others, thereby creating a culture in which risk-taking is not only safe, but expected.
- inspires loyalty through valuing of people as the most precious asset in an organization.

ANA standards for nursing administration *(continued)*

■ serves in key roles in the work setting by participating on committees, councils, and administrative teams.
■ promotes advancement of the profession through participation in professional organizations.
■ influences decision-making bodies to improve patient care, health services, and policies.
■ provides direction to enhance the effectiveness of the multidisciplinary or interdisciplinary team.
■ assures that protocols or guidelines reflect evidence-based practice, including accepted changes in care management, and address emerging problems.
■ promotes communication of information and advancement of the profession through writing, publishing, and presentations for professional or lay audiences.
■ designs innovations to effect change in practice and outcomes.

Standard 16: Advocacy
The nurse administrator advocates for the protections and rights of individuals, families, communities, populations, health care providers, nursing and other professions, and institutions and organizations, especially related to health and safety.

Measurement Criteria
The nurse administrator
■ supports the involvement of individuals in their own care.
■ supports access by individuals to their own personal health information and development of awareness of how that information may be used and accessed by others.
■ supports the individual's right and ability to supplement, request correction of, and share their personal health data and information.
■ evaluates factors related to privacy, security, and confidentiality in the use and handling of health information.
■ integrates advocacy into the design, implementation, and evaluation of policies, programs and services, and systems.
■ demonstrates skill in advocating before providers, public representatives and decision-makers, and other stakeholders.
■ exhibits fiscal responsibility and integrity in policy development and advocacy activities and processes.
■ strives to resolve conflicting expectations from populations, providers, and other stakeholders to promote safety, guard their best interests, and to preserve the professional integrity of the nurse.
■ serves as an expert for peers, populations, providers, and other stakeholders in promoting and implementing health policies.

HOW NURSING STANDARDS ARE APPLIED IN COURT

In *Story v. St. Mary Parish Service District* (1987), a 66-year-old man was admitted to the hospital complaining of abdominal distention, pain, nausea, and vomiting. During the next 2 days, he complained several times to the nurses and attendants about shortness of breath and severe pain in his elbows and chest.

One evening, the staff nurse (a new graduate who had only recently taken her nursing boards) wrote in her nurses' notes, "Complains of both elbows hurting severely, denied pain anywhere else. Slightly irritable and confused. Assisted back to bed.

Admits to arthritis. Slight shortness of breath noted. Abdominal distention in moderation noted; soft to touch. Blood pressure 150/98; pulse 88. Will have medicated." She didn't indicate any consultation with the charge nurse. The patient died; autopsy revealed a myocardial infarction.

Pretrial testimony revealed that the patient had stated that the nurses didn't listen to his reports of pain. In the pretrial memorandum, the plaintiff's attorney cited a variety of nursing practice standards, including the following:

- The Louisiana Nurse Practice Act, which describes the nurse's responsibility for performing patient assessment and intervening as appropriate
- A board of nursing rule stating that graduate nurses must have RN supervision when they provide care
- Nursing care standards established by The Joint Commission

Although this case was settled out of court, it provides a good example of the extensive use of nursing practice standards as evidence in a lawsuit.

In *Hodges v. Effingham County Hospital* (1987), a woman entered the emergency department and complained to the nurses that she was having chest pains. No physician was present. After conferring with the nurses by telephone, the physician on call decided to discharge the patient. The nurses didn't tell the physician that the patient had a history of heart disease and had recently taken a nitroglycerin tablet. The patient later died.

The plaintiff alleged that the nurses in the ED demonstrated negligence because they failed to obtain an accurate medical history and to "fully report known and observable symptoms to the physician on call." The physician wasn't sued: The plaintiff thought that the physician had treated the patient appropriately based on the information given to him.

Although the nurses won the trial court decision, on appeal, the higher court found the nurses liable. The higher court stated that because the nursing action in question involved nursing judgment rather than the adequacy of services or facility, the question was whether the nurses followed general standards of nursing care.

Who can testify as an expert—state and local community standards of care

With changes in health care tort reform, many states now define who can be an expert. Beginning in 2004, Arizona statutory law required a plaintiff who asserts a medical negligence claim against a health care professional to support her claim with expert opinion testimony regarding the health care professional's standard of care. (A.R.S. § 12-2603(A), (D); *Hardy v. Catholic Healthcare West*, 2010 Ariz. App. Unpub. LEXIS 1468, 2010 WL 5059602, ★ 2 (Az.Ct.App. December 7, 2010)).

"The expert must be licensed as a health care professional in Arizona or another state, and in the year immediately preceding the occurrence giving rise to the lawsuit, must have devoted a majority of his or her 'professional time' to either: (1) active clinical practice of the same health care profession as the defendant; or (2) the instruction of students in an accredited health care professional school or accredited residency or clinical research program in the same health care profession as the defendant." *Hardy*, 2010 Ariz. App. Unpub. LEXIS 1468, 2010

WL 5059602 at ★ 2 (citing A.R.S. §
12-2604(A)(2) (2005)).

Tennessee has similar rules, under
Tennessee Code Annotated section
29-26-115(a)(1). This statute embraces
the so-called locality rule, which
requires that the standard of professional care in a medical malpractice
action be based upon "the community
in which the defendant practices or
in a similar community." A medical
expert relied upon by a plaintiff must
have knowledge of the standard of
professional care in the defendant's
applicable community or knowledge
of the standard of professional care in a
community *that is shown to be similar* to
the defendant's community.

ALL PHYSICIANS AREN'T CREATED EQUAL

Consider the case of a nurse found
negligent for not recognizing and
reporting inconsistent intentions of the
attending physician and the first-year
resident.

In *St. Germain v. Pfeifer*, 637 N.E.2d
848 (Mass. 1994), a first-year orthopedic resident ordered the plaintiff-
patient, who underwent a midlumbar
osteotomy, out of bed on the second
postoperative day, whereas the attending orthopedic surgeon's postoperative
plan was for the patient to be confined
to bed for 4 or 5 days after surgery.
The charge nurse noted the resident's
order without question and without
considering the patient's care plan, of
which she should have been aware.
Therefore, she should have known and
reported the inconsistent intentions of
both physicians regarding the movement of the patient. The nurse got the
patient out of bed and, as he moved,
he heard a loud snapping sound in
the back of his neck and fell back-
ward, screaming in pain. The hooks

and rods in his back snapped out of
position, and he was severely injured.
The nurse's motion to dismiss the case
against her was granted, but later the
grant was overturned because there
was expert opinion that her acts fell
below the standard of care.

NONNURSING PROFESSIONALS

In the Illinois case *Sullivan v. Edward
Hospital* (2004), a physician was
allowed to testify as to the standards
of nursing care regarding patient care
and treatment. The trial court ruled
that the physician was incompetent
to testify as to the standard of care for
the nursing profession and the deviations thereof. This decision was based
partly on the premise that there is no
universal standard of treatment among
physicians and nurses. This trial court's
decision was appealed and later upheld
by the appellate court.

Many scholars have agreed that
physicians often have no first-hand
knowledge of nursing practice except
for observations made in patient care
settings. The physician rarely, if ever,
teaches in a nursing program nor is a
physician responsible for content in
nursing texts. In many situations, a
physician would not be familiar with
the standard of care or with nursing
policies and procedures which govern the standard of care. Therefore,
a physician's opinions would not be
admissible in many jurisdictions which
hold that expert must be familiar with
the standard of care in order to testify
as an expert.

In cases in which the act of negligence is within the common knowledge and experience of a lay person,
it may not be necessary to produce
expert testimony. In *Jones v. Hawkes
Hospital* (1964), the court instructed
jurors to rely on their own common

sense to judge whether a nurse met standards of practice instead of relying on expert testimony. In this case, a nurse left a sedated patient in labor to assist a physician with another patient in labor. She did this because the hospital had a rule that no physician could attend a woman in labor unless a nurse was present. Left alone with the side rails up, the plaintiff-patient got out of bed, fell, and suffered serious injuries. The nurse wanted the court to allow expert testimony to establish what standard of care should have been applied. However, the court ruled that any reasonably prudent person could determine this case on the basis of ordinary experience and knowledge and that the jurors could decide on their own whether the defendant-nurse's nontechnical nursing tasks met reasonable standards of care. The jury found the nurse negligent.

In a similar case, *Larrimore v. Homeopathic Hospital Association*, a nurse was found liable for failing to read a new order or for reading it negligently. The court stated that the jury could apply ordinary common sense, without an expert witness, to establish the applicable standard of care because the standard of care applied depends upon the given circumstances. (176 A.2d 362, 367-68 [Del. Supr. 1961], *off'd* 181 A.2d 573, 576-77 [Del. Supr. 1962]).

Nursing licensure

Your nursing license entitles you to practice as a professionally qualified nurse. However, like most privileges, your nursing license imposes certain responsibilities. As a licensed RN or LPN, you're responsible for providing quality care to your patients. To meet this responsibility and to protect your right to practice, you need to understand the professional and legal significance of your nursing license.

LICENSING LAWS

Each nurse practice act contains licensing laws. They establish qualifications for obtaining and maintaining a nursing license. They also broadly define the legally permissible scope of nursing practice.

Although they vary from state to state, most licensing laws specify the following:
- The qualifications a nurse needs to be granted a license
- License application procedures for new licenses and reciprocal (state-to-state) licensing arrangements
- Application fees
- Authorization to grant use of the title RN or LPN or LVN to applicants who receive their licenses
- Grounds for license denial, revocation, or suspension
- License renewal procedures.

Most state licensing laws don't prohibit nursing students, a patient's friends, or members of his family from caring for him on a routine basis, provided that no fee is involved. They also permit a newly graduated nurse to practice for a specified period while her license application is being processed, and they allow unlicensed individuals to give care (such as administering cardiopulmonary resuscitation) in an emergency. According to state and federal constitutional requirements, state laws must exempt the following types of nurses from state licensure requirements:
- Nurses practicing in accordance with their religious beliefs
- Nurses traveling with patients from one state to another
- Nurses practicing in federal facilities

LEGAL SIGNIFICANCE OF THE LICENSE

Licensing laws help you to avoid civil and criminal liabilities by defining the scope of your professional nursing practice. If you're named in a malpractice lawsuit, your state licensing laws will be used as partial evidence to determine whether you acted within the legal limits of your profession.

In *Barber v. Reinking* (1966), the court used the licensing laws in the Washington State Nurse Practice Act to rule against the defendant-nurse. In this case, a 2-year-old boy was taken to a physician's office for a polio booster shot. The physician (also named in the suit) delegated this task to the LPN who worked in his office. While the nurse was administering the shot, the child moved suddenly and the needle broke off in his buttock. Despite attempts to remove it surgically and with a magnet, the needle remained lodged in the child's buttock for 9 months.

During the trial, the licensing law for practical nurses became the crucial factor in the court's decision. The court declared that the nurse had violated the nurse practice act by performing services beyond the legal limit of her practice. (Until the 1970s, the Washington State Nurse Practice Act didn't allow a practical nurse to legally give an injection.) The nurse's attorney attempted to introduce as evidence the fact that LPNs in the local community commonly gave injections. This evidence wasn't allowed. Instead, the judge instructed the jury to consider the violation of the nurse practice act along with other evidence in the case, including the physician's liability under the *respondeat superior* doctrine, to determine if the nurse was negligent.

Canadian licensing laws

Because each jurisdiction in Canada has its own nurse practice act, the laws vary somewhat from one to the next. Licensing laws in all jurisdictions except Ontario require nurses to join jurisdictional nursing associations to obtain their licenses.

Canadian jurisdictions require licensure to practice nursing. Licensing laws establish the following:
■ Qualifications for membership in the provincial nurses' association
■ Examination requirements
■ Applicable fees
■ Conditions for reciprocal licensure
■ Penalties for practicing without a license
■ Grounds for denial, suspension, or revocation of a nurse's license
Within those jurisdictions that license practical nurses, licensing laws for LPNs are similar to those for RNs.

KEEPING THE LICENSE CURRENT

When you begin a new job, your employer is responsible for checking your credentials and confirming that you're properly licensed. Make sure your nursing license is current, and be prepared to furnish proof that you've renewed your license, if necessary.

If you fail to renew your license, you can no longer legally practice nursing. In the United States, you can be prosecuted and fined for practicing without a license. Fines vary from state to state. For example, Section 223 of the Professional Nursing Law of Pennsylvania states that practicing nursing without a license is a *misdemeanor*, a crime punishable by a jail sentence of 12 months or less. For a first violation, the nurse must pay a fine of up to $1,000 or face a 6-month prison term. For a second violation, the penalty may be a fine of up to $2,000 or 6 months to 1 year in prison, or both. In addition to the criminal penalty, the nurse may be required to pay a civil penalty of up to $1,000.

States can mandate active practice in nursing to maintain a license. Maryland requires 1,000 hours of active nursing practice within a 5-year period immediately preceding the date of anticipated renewal. (*Title 8 Annotated Code of Maryland, Section 309.*)

License renewal and the law

The courts have addressed questions concerning license renewal, usually during an appeal of disciplinary action taken by a state board of nursing. The courts don't always agree with the boards' decisions. In *Kansas State Board of Nursing v. Burkman* (1975), an RN failed to renew her license and continued to practice nursing. No evidence existed to suggest that she had intentionally not renewed her license or knowingly practiced without it. The state board of nursing ruled that her action constituted a violation of state licensing laws and suspended her license for 6 months. After several appeals, a high court ruled that the board had erred, and instructed the board to renew the license.

In *Oliff v. Florida State Board of Nursing* (1979), the court also ruled in a nurse's favor. In this case, the board of nursing refused to renew an LPN's certificate because her application hadn't arrived on time. Evidence indicated that the nurse had mailed her application before the board's specified date. The court ruled that the board's date was a deadline for applications to be mailed, not received.

Failure to renew

If you find that you've forgotten to renew your license, simple measures can help you avoid legal repercussions:
- Notify your employer.
- Find your original license application and immediately notify the state board of nursing of your oversight. Ask them for a temporary license or for authorization to continue nursing until you receive your license.
- If you can't find your license application, call or write to the state board of nursing for a renewal application and instructions on how to proceed. Then follow the board's instructions exactly. Many states now have renewal applications and instructions on their state Web site.

WORKING IN A DIFFERENT STATE

Until the National League for Nursing established the first standardized examination for nursing licensure, each state had its own qualifications for entry into nursing practice. As a result, arranging to obtain a license in a different state than your own was usually difficult.

All candidates for licensure currently are required to pass the NCLEX-RN or NCLEX-PN, administered under the auspices of the National Council of State Boards of Nursing (NCBSN). Due to national standards, nurses are now able to move more freely to new jobs in different states. In 2000, the NCBSN launched an initiative to expand the mobility of nurses as part of our nation's health care delivery system. The Nurse Licensure Compact (NLC) allows nurses to have one multistate license, with the ability to practice in both their home state and other compact states. The number of states which have enacted the NLC is now at 24.

When you move to another state to practice nursing, you must obtain a license or temporary practice permit from that state before you may legally practice unless both states are members of the NLC. Most state boards of nursing will license you if you're currently licensed to practice nursing in another state or territory. If you're licensed to practice in Canada, most boards will license you if your education fulfills the issuing state's requirements; however, some may require you to take the written licensing examination. The policy of accepting out-of-state licensure is called *endorsement*. Many state boards waive reexamination if you're licensed in Canada and want to practice in the United States. The same usually applies if you hold a US license and want to practice in Canada.

Failure to qualify

If the state board finds that you don't have the necessary qualifications to practice nursing in that state, it may reject your application or require that you complete a written examination—regardless of your education or the laws of the state in which you live.

In *Richardson v. Brunelle* (1979), an LPN who had practiced in Massachusetts for 15 years brought suit after being refused a license to practice in New Hampshire. In her New Hampshire application, she requested a decree of educational equivalency. Although she had originally taken and passed a Massachusetts State licensing examination, she had never graduated from an approved school of practical nursing. At that time, only nursing school graduates were permitted to practice in New Hampshire, so her request was denied. Her lawsuit was unsuccessful in reversing the New

Hampshire decision, and subsequent appeals upheld the original ruling.

A similar case, *Snelson v. Culton* (1949), involved Maine's licensing requirements, which also require a graduation for licensing.

Federal law and licensure

Even though no federal law has jurisdiction over state boards of nursing, federal laws may affect nursing licensure. For example, if you're a nurse in the armed forces who is often subject to transfer, you're required by federal law to hold a current state license but not necessarily in the state to which you're assigned.

A federal public health code requires all state boards that license health care professionals to develop systems for verifying those professionals' continued competence. (42 U.S.C. § 13965-2) (2000).

FOREIGN LICENSURE

If you move to a foreign country, your US nursing license will be reviewed by the appropriate authority, which will either reject or accept it (possibly with conditions). If you're a nurse in the American armed forces working in an American installation, you're exempt from this review.

In a non–English speaking country, the licensing authority may require you to complete a language-proficiency examination.

If you're an RN or LPN licensed in a foreign country, you can't practice nursing in any state, territory, or province until the appropriate licensing authority has approved your application and issued your nursing license. When you're granted licensure in the

United States or Canada, you function at the same legal status as a US- or Canadian-educated RN or LPN. You're also equally accountable for your professional actions.

All states and the federal government require that foreign nurses pass the examination prepared by the Commission on Graduates of Foreign Nursing Schools (the CGFNS examination). If a foreign nurse successfully completes this examination—which includes an English-proficiency segment—she may then take the NCLEX. If she passes, she qualifies for licensure and a work visa.

DISCIPLINARY ACTION

The state board of nursing can take disciplinary action against a nurse for any violation of the state's nurse practice act. In all states and in Canadian jurisdictions, a nurse faces discipline if she endangers a patient's health, safety, or welfare. Depending on the severity of the violation, a state board may formally reprimand the nurse, place her on probation, suspend or refuse to renew her license, or even revoke her license. Other types of disciplinary action include imposing a probationary period, imposing a fine, and restricting the nurse's scope of practice. Some boards may require a nurse to take courses in the legal aspects of nursing.

The list of punishable violations varies from state to state. The most common are given below:

- Conviction of a crime involving moral turpitude, if the offense bears directly on whether the person is fit to be licensed
- Use of fraud or deceit in obtaining or attempting to obtain a nursing license
- Incompetence because of negligence or because of physical or psychological impairments

- Habitual use of or addiction to drugs or alcohol
- Unprofessional conduct, including (but not limited to) falsifying, inaccurately recording, or improperly altering patient records; negligently administering medications or treatments; performing tasks beyond the limits of the state's nurse practice act; failing to take appropriate action to safeguard the patient from incompetent health care; violating the patient's confidentiality; taking on nursing duties that require skills and education beyond one's competence; violating the patient's dignity and human rights by basing nursing care on prejudice; abandoning a patient; and abusing a patient verbally or physically. Several boards of nursing also have sexual misconduct regulations.

Administrative review process

When a nurse is accused of professional misconduct, the state board of nursing usually conducts an investigation, followed by an administrative review if the investigation warrants it.

Usually, the board's actions are "complaint driven," meaning that the board investigates complaints about licensees rather than actively looking for infractions of the nurse practice act to prosecute.

As an administrative body, the state board of nursing wields broad discretionary powers and can issue a decision or ruling. As a result, court proceedings, and possibly legal penalties, may result from the board's administrative review findings. You have the right to appeal through the court system for reversal of the nursing board's decision (*See Disciplinary proceedings for nurse misconduct*). It's important to remember that administrative proceedings are civil proceedings that are intended to be remedial in nature; they have no criminal bearing.

Disciplinary proceedings for nurse misconduct

The flow chart below shows what happens when the state board of nursing takes disciplinary action against a nurse for violation of the state's nurse practice act.

Sworn complaint filed

A sworn complaint is brought before a state board by:

- a health care agency,
- a professional organization, or
- an individual.

If the board finds sufficient evidence, it will conduct a formal review.

▼

State board of nursing review

The board:

- reviews the evidence,
- calls witnesses, and
- determines if the nurse is guilty of misconduct.

If the board finds the nurse guilty of misconduct, it can take disciplinary action.

▼

Disciplinary action

The board can:

- issue a reprimand,
- place the nurse on probation,
- refuse to renew her license,
- suspend her license, or
- revoke her license.

If the nurse wants to challenge the board's decision or disciplinary action, she can file an appeal in court.

▼

Court review

The court will do one of two things, depending on the jurisdiction:

- Reexamine the board's decision and decide if the board conducted the hearing properly.
- Conduct a trial.

If the nurse wants to challenge the court's ruling, she can appeal to a higher court.
If the board wants to appeal the court's ruling, it, too, can appeal to a higher court.

▼

Appellate review

The nurse or the board can appeal for a reversal of the lower court's ruling.

Steps in administrative review

In most states and jurisdictions, the nurse practice act and board of nursing rules and regulations specify the steps that the board of nursing must follow during an administrative review. In some states, a general administrative procedure act (separate from the nurse practice act) specifies the steps; in still other states, the board of nursing determines protocol.

An administrative review begins when a person, a health care facility (the nurse's employer), or a professional organization files a signed complaint against a nurse with the state board of nursing, or when the board itself initiates such action.

The board then reviews the complaint to decide if the nurse's action appears to violate the state's nurse practice act. It may begin the process by requesting a meeting with the nurse to discuss the allegations or ask the nurse to submit a statement about the specific incident that led to the complaint. (The nurse should consult with an attorney, who has experience in disciplinary matters, before submitting any information to the board of nursing.) If the board decides that the nurse's actions were in violation of the state's nurse practice act, it prepares for a formal hearing, including subpoenaing witnesses. When these preparations begin, the accused nurse's due process rights include the right to receive timely notice of both the charge against her and the hearing date.

At the hearing, the nurse has the following due process rights:
- To have an attorney represent her
- To present evidence and cross-examine witnesses
- To appeal the board's decision to a court

At the formal hearing, an impartial attorney may act as a hearing officer (in lieu of a judge), or the board itself may hear the case. A court reporter documents the entire proceeding, or it may be taped. Members of the board act as the plaintiffs bringing the claim against the defendant-nurse. Witnesses—including coworkers—testify for the board and the nurse.

It's possible to buy a medical insurance liability policy to cover legal expenses to defend against a complaint filed against you. Although nurses are usually protected by their health care employer's insurance liability policy, these employer policies only protect the nurse in the event of a civil nursing negligence or medical malpractice action. They don't protect the nurse in the event of an administrative board of nursing disciplinary investigation or hearing. Buying your own professional liability insurance policy provides you with protection against civil and administrative actions. Check with your malpractice carrier and expand your insurance coverage, if necessary.

Canadian administrative review

In Canada, the process for administrative review of complaints against nurses is similar to that in the United States. In some jurisdictions, a complaints committee of the jurisdictional nursing board hears the complaint first and either dismisses or endorses it. If the complaints committee endorses it, the complaint is sent along to a discipline committee for a full hearing. In other jurisdictions, only a discipline committee hears the complaint.

Note that, in many jurisdictions, an employer who terminates a nurse's employment for incompetence, misconduct, or incapacity must report the termination to the board of nursing in writing (this rule doesn't apply if the nurse's employer is a patient). If the employer fails to do this, the board may impose a fine.

Judicial review process

In every state, nurses have the right to challenge the board's disciplinary decisions by the process of appeal through the courts. This basic right can't be revoked by any means; in many states, this right is spelled out in the nurse practice act.

Each state and court jurisdiction sets its own rules on how to file this type of appeal. In some jurisdictions, the nurse, through her attorney, must appeal to a special court that handles only cases from state agencies. In other states, she must appeal to the lowest-level court.

In an appeal, the court reviews the legality of the state board's original decision against the nurse—not the nurse's allegedly improper conduct. The court attempts only to determine whether the board of nursing exceeded its legal powers or conducted the hearing improperly. It decides if the state board's decision is unlawful, arbitrary, or unreasonable according to law, or whether it constitutes "abuse of discretion" (meaning the board didn't have enough evidence to determine unprofessional conduct, and so made a decision without proper foundation). The court may also review the original evidence before deciding whether to sustain or reverse the board's decision.

The court also may allow a trial de novo, in which the court hears the board's complete case against the nurse as though the administrative review had never happened. New evidence, if it exists, may be introduced by the plaintiff (the board) or by the defendant-nurse, through her attorney. The court hears the case and then either sustains or reverses the board's original decision.

If the defendant-nurse loses this appeal, she may—depending on the jurisdiction—appeal to a higher court. (If the nurse wins, the board of nursing can appeal to a higher court.) To begin the new appeal, the nurse's attorney must file it with the lower court that ruled against the nurse; this court will send the trial transcript and the appeal to the higher court. All states have rules and regulations governing appeals, and abiding by them is an attorney's legal responsibility.

The higher court decides whether to hear the appeal, based on its merits. The appeal usually must establish that the lower court made an error of law. The higher court won't hear the case a second time or reconsider facts, but the defendant-nurse and her attorney may continue to appeal through all higher courts up to the state's highest court. Exceptional cases may reach the US Supreme Court.

Canadian nurses may also challenge disciplinary action through the court system. An appeal involves a written application to a superior court. The application states that the disciplinary tribunal made an error and requests that the superior court correct or modify the decision of the tribunal.

Court cases

Consider the following two cases, which describe the experience of two nurses during the administrative and judicial review.

In a Connecticut case, *Leib v. Board of Examiners for Nursing* (1979), a nurse was accused of improper conduct: charting the administration of meperidine to her patient but using the drug herself. After voluntarily admitting to this action, she testified on her own behalf at the board hearing. The board issued an order revoking her nursing license. The nurse appealed the revocation order to the court of common pleas. When this court dismissed her appeal, she appealed to the Supreme Court of Connecticut. This higher court also ruled that the evidence supported the board's findings of unprofessional conduct. The nurse's license was revoked. Other cases in which courts have upheld boards' decisions include *McCarl v. State Board of Nurse Examiners* (1979), where the court upheld the Board's formal reprimand of a nurse who administered an anesthetic in the absence of a directing physician, and *Rafferty v. State Board of Nurse Examiners* (1986), where the court upheld revocation of a nurse license where a nurse removed a comatose patient from a ventilator.

In *Colorado State Board of Nurse Examiners v. Hohu* (1954), a physician filed a complaint of incompetence against a nurse, claiming that her failure to admit an obstetrical patient quickly and to contact the physician caused the patient's injury. The board of nursing ordered the nurse's license revoked. However, when the nurse appealed, the court reversed the board's revocation order. This court ruled that the board of nursing had abused its discretionary powers because the evidence didn't support the physician's charges.

License reinstatement

License revocation, if sustained despite all appeal efforts, is usually permanent. Check to see whether your state's nurse practice act provides for revoked-license reinstatement.

If your license is suspended, you may petition for reinstatement. Every nurse practice act contains a provision allowing reinstatement of a suspended license, and some license-suspension orders specify a date when the nurse may apply. In most states, after a suspension has been in effect for more than a year, the board of nursing will consider reinstatement.

Your first step would probably be to petition the board for reinstatement. Then the board would have to decide whether you're qualified to practice nursing again. In some states, you have the right to another hearing before the board makes this decision.

The board usually bases its decision on current evidence of the nurse's fitness to practice. For example, in a drug violation case, the board may consider whether a nurse has successfully completed a drug rehabilitation program.

SELECTED REFERENCES

American Nurses Association. *Standards of Clinical Nursing Practice*, 3rd ed. Washington, DC: American Nurses Publishing, 2004.

American Nurses Association. *Nursing Administration: Scope and Standards of Practice*. Silver Spring, MD: American Nurses Association, 2009.

American Nurses Association. *Nursing: Scope and Standards of Practice*, 2nd ed. Washington, DC: American Nurses Publishing, 2010.

Arizona Revised Statutes. A.R.S. § 12-2603(A), (D).

Carson, W.Y. "Nursing Malpractice: Protect Yourself," *The American Journal of Nursing* 101(12):81, December 2001.

Clarke, S.P., and Patrician, P.A. "Entry into Practice in Ontario: A New Initiative May Have Implications for American Nursing," *The American Journal of Nursing* 101(2):73–76, February 2001.

Hardy v. Catholic Healthcare West, 2010 WL 5059602, ★ 2 (Az.Ct.App. December 7, 2010). Unpub. LEXIS 1468.

Joint Commission of Accreditation of Healthcare Organizations. 2014 National Patient Safety Goals. Retrieved from: www.jcaho.org.

Joint Commission of Accreditation of Healthcare Organizations. Facts About the Universal Protocol January, 2014. Retrieved from: www.jcaho.org.

McCarl v. State Board of Nurse Examiners (1979). 1979 Pa. Commw. LEXIS 1191.

Michel, L.G. "Leveling the Playing Field: Nurses' Rights in State Board Disciplinary Actions," *Kansas Nurse* 78(1):1–2, January 2003.

National Council of State Boards of Nursing. Retrieved from: www.ncsbn.org

Pohlman, K.J. "Nursing Discipline: Demystifying the Process," *Journal of School Nurses* 12(1):52-57, February 2003. Retrieved from www.ncsbn.org.

Rafferty v. State Board of Nurse Examiners (1986). 1986 Pa. Commw. LEXIS 1927.

Rodgers, S.J. "The Role of Nursing Theory in Standards of Practice: A Canadian Perspective," *Nursing Sciences Quarterly* 13(3):260–262, July 2000.

Tennessee Code Annotated section 29-26-115(a)(1).

Thomas, S.A., et al. "State and Territorial Boards of Nursing Approaches to the Use of Unlicensed Assistive Personnel," *JONA'S Healthcare Law, Ethics, and Regulation* 2(1):13–21, March 2000.

Wacker Guido, G. *Legal and Ethical Issues in Nursing*, 3rd ed. Upper Saddle River, NJ: Prentice Hall, 2001.

CHAPTER 2

Working in diverse clinical settings

Leslie M. Durr, PhD, RN, PMHCNS-BC

Professions such as medicine and nursing are regulated for the purpose of protecting society. Medicine was the first professional group in the United States to develop and seek regulation, not just for the protection of society but also to lend itself credibility, and by so doing also claimed the right to define what that practice is and exclude other professions.

Although each state's and each province's nurse practice act and medical practice act are intended to distinguish between the two professions, the needs of society change and so, too, do the tasks of each discipline, blurring the line between the disciplines. In an era of an increasingly aging population and sicker patients, nurses are now expected and legally able to perform many of the tasks formerly reserved for physicians. Therefore, nurses are required to take on more responsibility, and as the roles of nursing and medicine continue to evolve, the interface between the two professions is not clear cut.

Nursing practice vs. medical practice

Knowing precisely where nurse and medical practice acts differ and where they overlap can be difficult; relevant statutes may lack specific detail. Be aware that not knowing exactly where nursing practice begins and ends can create some legal risks.

When state legislatures began writing medical and nurse practice acts, a physician could legally perform any task a nurse performed. That remains true, although many physicians today are unfamiliar with certain nursing practices. Legislatures also reserved certain tasks exclusively for physicians, and a nurse who performs such tasks does so at her own legal peril. To help limit liability, learn as much as you can about your state's nurse practice act. However, you will find that most nurse practice acts will not answer questions about specific tasks. They are not usually written as a "laundry list" of tasks in recognition that the boundaries of nursing and other disciplines change over time. Practice acts usually involve the elements of the nursing process (assessment, planning implementation, and evaluation) and address the areas of the scope of nursing practice such as this Model Act put out by the National Council of State Boards of Nursing (NCSBN):

Section 2. Registered Nurse (RN)
a. Registered Nurse is the title given to an individual licensed to practice registered nursing.

b. The practice of registered nurses shall include:

1. Providing comprehensive nursing assessment of the health status of patients.

2. Collaborating with health care team to develop and coordinate an integrated patient centered health care plan.

3. Developing the comprehensive patient centered health care plan, including:

a. Establishing nursing diagnoses;

b. Setting goals to meet identified health care needs; and

c. Prescribing nursing interventions.

4. Implementing nursing care through the execution of independent nursing strategies, and regimens requested, ordered or prescribed by authorized health care providers.

5. Evaluating responses to interventions and the effectiveness of the plan of care.

6. Designing and implementing teaching plans based on patient needs.

7. Delegating and assigning nursing interventions to implement the plan of care.

8. Providing for the maintenance of safe and effective nursing care rendered directly or indirectly.

9. Advocating the best interest of patients.

10. Communicating and collaborating with other health care providers in the management of health care and the implementation of the total health care regimen within and across care settings.

11. Managing, supervising and evaluating the practice of nursing.

12. Teaching the theory and practice of nursing.

13. Participating in development of health care policies, procedures and systems.

14. Wearing identification that clearly identifies the nurse as an RN when providing direct patient care, unless wearing identification creates a safety or health risk for either the nurse or the patient.

15. Other acts that require education and training consistent with professional standards as prescribed by the BON and commensurate with the RN's education, demonstrated competencies and experience.

(Portions copyrighted by the NCSBN, Inc. All rights reserved.)

Forces causing change

In part, the law is responding to changes in society: nurses' increasing educational background; patients' increasing expectations of nurses; and the needs of meeting the health care needs of our population. Although patients are filing more lawsuits, nurses have a relatively low probability of being party to a lawsuit. In part, this reflects that nurses are usually employees of hospitals and also that, since 2005, nurses have been named as the most trusted profession in Gallup polls. In addition, hospitals and physicians have delegated more authority to nurses. For example, nursing responsibilities in intensive care units (ICUs) and coronary care units (CCUs) include diagnosis (reading electrocardiograms) and treatment (giving medications according to parameters in medical protocols, performing cardiopulmonary resuscitation). Reductions in health care funding have also led to increased responsibilities for nurses and increased workloads.

Portability and mobility are the cornerstones of technotherapeutic interventions which allow health care delivery to move from institutions to outpatient facilities. Nurses who once practiced at the patient's bedside now find themselves employed in free-standing clinics, in ambulatory care centers, and in home care. This change is not always easy for nurses who were trained for traditional institutional positions. Nurses often mourn the loss of all they used to do for patients within the hospital. However, studies show a direct line from the length of hospital stay to increased morbidity and mortality. Nurses are advised to focus on helping patients make the transition to where they will be healing—at home.

Another recent change in nursing is the focus on evidence-based practice (EBP). EBP has shown to improve patient care and nurse satisfaction, as well as, serves as the foundation for the disease management work done by many nurses.

Other changes in nursing may not be contributing to improved patient care and nurse satisfaction. As the population ages and the number of individuals entering the nursing profession declines, staffing ratios are gaining the attention of management and policymakers. Legislation will not likely play a significant role in addressing this concern. Most of the hospitals in the United States are in the private sector; fewer are government owned. Attempts to legislate staffing ratios are being made in some areas of the country by those facilities that are government funded or owned. Studies are underway to prove that health care quality and satisfaction are directly related to nurse staffing ratios.

A shortage of physicians in family practice and other specialities will increase the demand for nurse practitioners.

Changes in "smart" technology will hopefully provide a positive impact on higher nurse-to-patient ratios and other changes that are perceived as negative by nurses. Tools such as built-in safety checks used on "smart" infusion pumps, "smart" beds that detect blood flow in the patient's legs to alert the nurse of possible deep vein thrombosis, digital communication devices worn by nurses, and other biotechnological advances are being tested to improve health care. Current studies show that nurses spend less than 40% of their time on direct patient care. Technology may help turn this process around.

As is often said, the only thing constant is change. Change will result in new roles for nurses.

Defining medical practice

Medical practice acts may be divided into two types: those that define medical practice and those that don't. Both types forbid nonphysicians from practicing medicine. (No Canadian law related to medical practice defines it.)

When a state's medical practice act includes a definition, it usually defines *medicine* as any act of diagnosis, prescription, surgery, or treatment. However, not every definition includes all four elements, and some states' definitions include additional elements while excluding others.

LEGISLATIVE RESPONSE

Some states have solved the problem of overlap between the nursing and medical professions by passing laws making some functions common to both. New York's law, for example, allows both RNs and physicians to diagnose and treat patients, with the proviso that a nursing diagnosis shouldn't alter a patient's medical regimen. Almost all states permit a nurse to perform patient care that a physician requests, as long as a written or an oral order exists and the requested action is reasonable and safe.

Some state medical practice acts limit physicians' rights to delegate tasks. For example, the Texas Medical Practice Act permits physicians to delegate tasks only to "any qualified and properly trained person or persons," and that too only if doing so is "reasonable and prudent," and if the delegating does not violate any other state laws. Most state courts would probably interpret their state medical practice acts similarly, even if this restriction is not written explicitly in their acts.

In some jurisdictions, the boards of nursing and medicine jointly determine which medical tasks may be delegated to nurses and specify the requirements for appropriate delegation.

COURT RULINGS

The courts are called on regularly to decide whether a specific action constitutes medical practice. One area of considerable overlap between nursing and medicine is midwifery. In the past, the courts often decided that delivering babies was a medical rather than a nursing function. In the early case of *Commonwealth v. Porn* (1907), a Massachusetts court upheld the conviction of a nurse-midwife for practicing medicine without a license. More recently, however, in *Leigh v. Board of Registration in Nursing* (1985), the same court said that the basis for conviction in the *Porn* case wasn't the practice of midwifery per se, but the nurse's use of obstetric instruments and prescription formulas. The court went so far as to hold that the practice of midwifery, in ordinary circumstances, isn't to be considered the practice of medicine since

some states such as Virginia recognize lay midwives who are not RNs.

Some court decisions have concluded that a physician need not be present during patient care once a task has been delegated to a nurse. These decisions have been interpreted to mean that a nurse may perform some medical tasks on the basis of standing orders and nursing protocols as well as on the basis of a physician's written and oral orders. Consequently, a nurse's scope of actions, when working under nursing protocols, can be broad in certain practice settings, no matter how restrictive the state nurse practice act is.

Nursing protocols allow the nurse to perform tasks that involve overlap of nursing and medical practices— such as ICU, CCU, and IV team practice—in states where the nurse practice acts don't typically grant nurses clear-cut independent authority to treat patients.

AVOIDING MEDICAL DECISIONS MAY HAVE LEGAL CONSEQUENCES

In some situations, you have no alternative to starting treatment without medical direction and the courts expect you to do so when a patient requires treatment. In *Cooper v. National Motor Bearing Co.* (1955), a California nurse was accused of failing to make a medical diagnosis of cancer in one of her patients. The nurse defended herself by arguing that state law at that time prohibited her from making diagnoses of any sort. The court ruled against her, finding that nurses were supposed to have sufficient education to tell whether a patient had signs or symptoms of a disease that would require a physician's attention. In *Stahlin v. Hilton Hotels Corp.* (1973), a federal court in Illinois reached a similar conclusion when a nurse failed to recognize that her patient's complaint resulted from a subdural hematoma rather than from drunkenness.

Do not assume, however, that courts always ignore the difference between medical practice and expanded nursing roles. A case in point is *Hernicz v. Florida Department of Professional Regulation* (1980). It involved a nurse practitioner who examined and treated two patients without a physician's orders. The state board of nursing suspended the license of the nurse practitioner, and the court's decision upheld the suspension.

In general, the courts interpret the law in ways most likely to protect patients. If protecting patients means not strictly interpreting nursing and medical practice acts, the courts usually follow that course.

Of course, in all situations in which you have called a physician about the care and treatment of a patient, document that communication and what was communicated in the medical record. Such documentation will support an argument that it was not acceptable for a nurse to make the final decision.

Defining nursing practice

Although nurse practice acts vary from state to state, they set the minimum standards for safe and competent nursing practice. These acts define the legal boundaries of the scope of nursing. However, the scope of nursing is more than about legal boundaries and minimum standards.

According to the Social Policy Statement of the American Nurses Association (ANA), *nursing* is the protection, promotion, and optimization of health and abilities; preventions of

illness and injury; alleviation of suffering through the diagnosis and treatment of human response; and advocacy in the care of individuals, families, communities, and populations. This definition encompasses four essential characteristics of nursing: human responses to phenomena, theory application, nursing actions or interventions, and outcomes. Nursing is both a science and an art. Nurses are concerned with human experiences and responses across the life span. They use theoretical and evidence-based knowledge of human experiences and responses to collaborate with health care consumers and others to assess, diagnose, identify outcomes, plan, implement, and evaluate care.

Regulating nursing practice is a state issue, which often makes it difficult for a nurse to move to another state. During the mid-1990s, the nursing profession experienced severe staffing shortages, forcing hospitals nationwide to scramble to meet sufficient personnel levels.

Nursing leaders then joined forces to remove obstacles that blocked clinicians from getting to where they were most needed in a timely manner. One solution the leaders devised was an agreement among state boards of nursing to accept each other's licenses for RNs and licensed practical and/or vocational nurses as an equivalent of their own. They saw it as a means to eliminate duplication of efforts on the part of both clinicians and governing bodies. The NCSBN spearheaded the project, formalizing the language and details. In 2000, the Nurse Licensure Compact (NLC) was enacted.

In 1997, a compact was adopted by the NCSBN that allows states to recognize the licenses of other states, which made interstate movement easier. In 1999, the council adopted uniform core requirements for RNs and licensed practical nurses (LPNs)/licensed vocational nurses (LVNs).

On paper, each state in the compact—as of 2014, 24 total—agrees to honor the others' credentials to practice. In other words, if you reside in an NLC state, then all other member states will accept your home state license without additional licensure, much like how federally funded facilities—such as Veterans Affairs—accept any state's nursing license as long as it is valid.

State	Date Signed
Arizona	January 7, 2002
Arkansas	January 7, 2000
Colorado	January 10, 2007
Delaware	January 7, 2000
Idaho	January 7, 2001
Iowa	January 7, 2000
Kentucky	January 6, 2007
Maine	January 7, 2001
Maryland	January 7, 1999
Mississippi	January 7, 2001
Missouri	January 6, 2010
Nebraska	January 1, 2001
New Hampshire	January 1, 2006
New Mexico	January 1, 2004
North Carolina	January 7, 2000
North Dakota	January 1, 2004
Rhode Island	January 7, 2008
South Carolina	January 2, 2006
South Dakota	January 1, 2001
Tennessee	January 7, 2003

Texas	January 1, 2000
Utah	January 1, 2000
Virginia	January 1, 2005
Wisconsin	January 1, 2000

Advanced Practice Nursing

In 2002, the NCSBN approved uniform core licensure requirements for advanced practice registered nursing (APRN) practice, that is, nurses with a master's degree or doctorate in nursing; and they approved the NLC for APRNs. However, advanced practice is an area that most closely intersects with the practice of medicine, and states have a variety of restrictions on APRN practice. In some states, APRNs can function independently from medical oversight; in some, there must be a collaborative practice agreement on file; and in some, the term *supervision* is used for the relationship between doctors and APRNs. If practicing as an APRN, it is important to know how the regulations affect you if you move to another state.

Trends in Health Care

In 2008, as a response not only to the aging of the US population and the concomitant increase in the need for health care, but also to changes in the numbers of Americans gaining access to health insurance, the Institute of Medicine, along with the Robert Wood Johnson Foundation, launched a 2-year initiative to make recommendations for a plan for the future of nursing. In 2010, the report was published with four key recommendations:

1. Nurses should practice to the full extent of their education and training.
2. Nurses should achieve higher levels of education and training through an improved education system that promotes seamless academic progression.
3. Nurses should be full partners, with physicians and other health professionals, in redesigning health care in the United States.
4. Effective workforce planning and policy-making require better data collection and an improved information infrastructure.

As a result of these trends in society and in nursing regulation, practice at both the generalist and specialist levels have become more consistent nationwide.

Nursing practice and unlicensed assistive personnel

Increasing numbers of people needing health care, combined with increasing complexity of therapies, create a tremendous demand for nursing care. The ability to delegate, assign, and supervise unlicensed assistive personnel (UAP) is a critical competency to be developed by the RN. State nurse practice acts define the legal parameters for nursing practice. For years, hospitals and extended-care facilities have employed nurses' aides and assistants; both of these groups fall into the category of UAP. However, educational requirements and on-the-job responsibilities for UAP are not uniformly defined by statutes. Thus, RNs may not have a clear understanding of what UAP are capable of doing or how to utilize them.

To avoid liability, the nurse must understand the state's position

regarding delegation. If the nurse practice act doesn't address the topic, the nurse must rely on the employer's policy. At a minimum, the employer should have a policy dictating criteria for such delegation. Typically, the criteria mandate that the nurse understand the UAP's level of skill. The RN assigns and delegates tasks based on the needs and condition of the patient, potential for harm, stability of the patient's condition, complexity of the task, predictability of the outcomes, abilities of the staff to whom the task is delegated, and the context of other patient needs. The nurse must understand that the responsibility for the task can be delegated but not the accountability.

The ANA has defined UAP as individuals trained to function in an assistive role to the professional RN in the provision of patient care activities, as delegated by, and under the supervision of, that nurse. The decision of whether or not to delegate or assign is based on the RN's judgment concerning the condition of the patient, the competence of all members of the nursing team, and the degrees of supervision that will be required of the RN if a task is delegated. The RN uses critical thinking and professional judgment when following the five rights of delegation, to be sure that the delegation or assignment is 1) the right task, 2) under the right circumstances, 3) to the right person, 4) with the right directions and communications, and 5) under the right supervision and evaluation.

Take, for instance, the case of Bernard Travaglini, who was admitted to Ingalls Memorial Hospital in Harvey, Illinois, on February 22, 2002. He had a history of strokes that had resulted in difficulty swallowing. At home his wife assisted with his eating and observed him closely for chocking.

On admission to the hospital, his admitting physician placed a written order in the medical record to monitor Mr. Travaglini while he was eating and to assist him with his food. The physician also had a conversation with the patient's nurse, advising her of his concern. At approximatley 10 p.m. on the night of Mr. Travaglini's admission, the physician was notified that the patient had died.

The wife of Mr. Travaglini brought a wrongful death suit against the hospital, alleging nursing negligence. During the trial, Mr. Travaglini's hospital roommate, Mr. Carrell, testified that a nurse's aide brought a sandwich to Mr. Travaglini and left the room. Mr. Carrell testified that he witnessed the patient chocking on the sandwich and he pushed the emergency button on his call light system.

Mr. Carrell further stated that a nurse came into the room "within several minutes." He stated that he said to the nurse, "The guy next to me is chocking" and that the nurse ran out of the room. Several other hospital personnel came in and worked on Mr. Travalini but he didn't survive.

The nurse assigned to Mr. Travaglini admitted that failure to monitor the patient while eating would have been a deviation from the standard of care had there been an order to do so, but the hospital admission notes didn't contain instructions to assist him while eating. She also denied that the admitting physician had given these instructions verbally. However, she did admit that Mr. Travaglini's wife did speak with her about his eating and swallowing problems, which is why she asked the nursing assistant to monitor the patient.

A pathologist who performed the autopsy testified at trial that he had seen foreign particles in the most distal parts of the decedent's tracheobronchial tree that were consistent with his finding of food particles higher up in the lungs. He testified that the patient would have had to breathe these particles into his lungs and they could not have been driven there during vomiting as a result of resuscitative efforts. He stated the cause of death was acute aspiration of partially digested food particles.

After hearing the testimony, the jury deliberated and returned a verdict in favor of the plaintiff for $500,000.00. The defense failed in an attempt to have the decision reversed.

There were several deviations from the standard of care in this case example. However, for the purpose of this discussion, focus will be on the delegation of duties to a nursing assistant. It is the nurse's responsibility to make certain those to whom safety measures are delegated understand what specific actions are required. Professional nurses may be held responsible for failing to adequately instruct and monitor nursing assistants. All members of the team must understand the care plan, and nursing assistants must function under the direct supervision of the licensed nurse.

In addition, the health care facility should have documentation of the training unlicensed personnel have received for duties for which they have been assigned. A nurse who has concerns about a nursing assistant's abilities should document such concerns in writing so management can address any deficiencies (see *Supervising unlicensed assistive personnel*).

Legal risks in diverse clinical settings

Nurses work in a wide range of clinical settings. Although most nurses work in the hospital setting, many

LEGAL TIP **Supervising unlicensed assistive personnel**

If you supervise unlicensed assistive personnel (UAP), you're responsible and liable for their performance. Limit your liability by educating yourself and advocating that your employer establish policies that clearly delineate the responsibilities of RNs, LPNs, and UAP.

■ Attend all educational programs your employer sponsors with respect to supervising UAP.

■ Encourage your supervisors to establish a written policy that defines the actions UAP may take.

■ Work cooperatively with UAP. It's in your patients' best interest for you to establish a solid working relationship with them.

■ Educate your patients about what UAP can and can't do for them during your assigned work time. This will help them ask the appropriate individuals to assist them with their needs.

■ If problems or disagreements arise over the appropriate functions for UAP, report to your nurse-manager for immediate resolution.

■ Review your state nurse practice act for provisions about delegation to UAP. Follow all criteria for proper delegation set forth in the act.

■ Stay current with your state nursing board's recommendations about working with UAP.

others work as private-duty nurses or in long-term care facilities, home health care, schools, or freestanding clinics. The law affects these nurses in different ways, which is why it's important to know the subtleties of your particular field.

Nursing in correctional facilities

The United States is the world leader in incarcerated population; there are approximately 2.2 million people in US prisons or jails. This represents a 500% increase since 1980. Similar to the rest of society, the incarcerated population is aging and developing chronic illnesses associated with poor nutrition and aging.

There are two other trends that impact health care in correctional institutions. Based on a case from 1976, *Estelle v. Gamble*, inmates in correctional facilities have constitutional rights to health care that cannot be denied.

The U.S. Supreme Court case *Estelle, Corrections Director et al. v. Gamble*, 429 U.S. 97 (1976), underpins inmate rights to medical treatment in all correctional facilities. This case, generally referred to as *Estelle v. Gamble*, established for the first time that prison and jail inmates have a constitutional right to medical treatment under the Eighth Amendment. J. W. Gamble, an inmate at the Texas Department of Corrections, was injured while performing prison job–related duties after a bale of cotton fell on top of him while he was loading a truck. Gamble continued to work the rest of the day despite complaining of pain and tenderness in his back. He was diagnosed with lower back strain and prescribed pain medication.

Over the next 3 months, he complained of back and chest pains, was subject to administrative segregation for refusing to work, and ultimately was treated for an irregular heartbeat.

Gamble initiated his lawsuit by submitting a handwritten document complaining of inadequate medical treatment. The court found for the defendant's prison because it viewed his failure to receive proper medical care as "inadvertent." The case nevertheless established the principle that the deliberate failure of prison authorities to address the medical needs of an inmate constitutes "cruel and unusual punishment." It held that "deliberate indifference to serious medical needs of prisoners constitutes the 'unnecessary and wanton infliction of pain'…proscribed by the Eighth Amendment"(Wells).

The other trend that impacts health care in correctional settings is the outsourcing of correctional health care to private, for-profit companies and decreasing budgets for corrections. In many states such as Virginia, care at correctional facilities is provided by a private company, which says it saves prisons and jails an average of 15% on medical services and has an excellent record of fighting inmate lawsuits.

Staffing varies from prison to prison, but Virginia, for example, has 40 doctors to care for 30,000 prisoners. It depends day to day on about 700 nurses, many of whom are LPNs, not RNs.

Ethical and legal issues in correctional nursing

Nurses in a correctional setting walk a fine line between maintaining security and delivering optimal nursing care. Staying true to professional nursing values while practicing in the correctional setting can create a unique set of ethical, legal, and professional issues for the nurse.

ETHICAL CONCERNS

Unlike the nurse in a traditional medical setting, the correctional nurse may face ethical situations on a daily basis. The correctional nurse makes ethical decisions about care delivery, caring and patient advocacy in planning and providing safe patient care, and it is imperative that the nurse is familiar with nursing's ethical principles; the nurse can refer to the ANA's Code of Ethics, which delineates the ethical standards across all settings, levels, and roles, setting expectations as well as providing guidance.

There are six ethical principles that arise frequently for the nurse who works in the correctional setting:
1. Respect for persons (autonomy and self-determination)
2. Beneficence (doing good)
3. Nonmaleficence (avoiding harm)
4. Justice (fairness, equitability, truthfulness)
5. Veracity (telling the truth)
6. Fidelity (remaining faithful to one's commitment)

One common area of ethical concern is the nurse's responsibility for ensuring that patients have access to care. The goal of the corrections officer is security and public safety, while the goal of professional nursing is to provide compassionate quality health care, in this case, for an incarcerated population. At the same time, care must be provided in a secure environment, and many supplies used in providing health care would be considered contraband if obtained by an inmate. There are controls in the correctional setting on many things nurses don't often consider in other settings—for example, maintaining counts for lancets used for glucose monitoring and securing the alcohol-based hand sanitizer.

The values associated with nursing practice include nurse advocacy, respect for humans, and elimination of barriers to care. The correctional nurse is in a unique position to evaluate the quality and effectiveness of patient care. He or she works with corrections officers to ensure that the health needs of inmates are respected and responded to in a timely manner. When priorities of corrections officers differ from those of the health care needs of inmates, it falls to the nurse to advocate for inmates' needs and not be swayed by those priorities. For example, in a 2007 case (*Comeau v. Volusia County, Inc.* et al), a female inmate of a jail had verbally threatened self-harm and was placed on suicide precautions that necessitated constant observation by a correctional officer. At change of shift, the correctional officers told the nurse that they were short staffed. The nurse discontinued the constant observation, gave her back her belongings, and allowed the officers to move her to a regular cell with bunk beds, from which she hanged herself with shoelaces. A civil lawsuit brought by the family is still pending in 2014.

End-of-life care is another ethical concern for the nurse who works in a corrections setting. Patients die while incarcerated, and the nurse has a role in helping the patient to die with dignity and comfort.

LEGAL ISSUES IN CORRECTIONAL NURSING

The basis for litigation in health care can relate to negligence, that is, failing to exercise the level of care that a reasonable, prudent nurse would under similar circumstances. Acts of omission and commission will also subject the nurse to litigation and professional license review.

Nurses in correctional settings can be especially vulnerable to litigation because the correctional patient population has a constitutional right to health care. Compounding this, inmate patients encounter nurses more than any other type of health care provider.

Failure to provide inmates with access to health care to meet their serious medical needs can be litigated under the Eighth Amendment as deliberate indifference or under the 14th Amendment as a civil rights violation.

Inmates have several ways to access health care, such as by submitting a request slip or form. Another way is through oral communication, for example, by telling a correctional officer of a need to be seen by a medical assistant, or mentioning a health concern to the nurse during medication administration.

Regardless of the method, the nurse has a legal and ethical obligation to respond to the request for care. On the basis of the information provided, the nurse determines the type and level of nursing intervention required and then implements an action. The nurse may determine that the patient's health needs can be managed within his or her scope of practice, or determine that a higher level of care is needed and refer the patient to an APRN, physician assistant, or physician, or, in emergent situations, refer for transfer to a health facility that can provide the care that is needed.

WORKING IN A LONG-TERM CARE FACILITY

The United States Census Bureau estimates that the US population aged 65 years and older is expected to double in size within the next 25 years. By 2030, almost 1 out of every 5 Americans—some 72 million people—will be 65 years or older. The age group 85 and older is now the fastest-growing segment of the US population. This trend means that more patients will be cared for in long-term care facilities such as nursing homes.

The rapid growth in the number of nursing homes and nursing home

Helping your patient select a long-term care facility

Your elderly or disabled patient may need the care provided at a long-term care facility. Help the patient and his family choose a facility by explaining the three types of long-term care facilities available and what type of care each offers.

Residential care / assisted living facility

Best for a patient who needs minimal medical attention, a residential-care facility provides meals, modest medical care, and assistance with housekeeping responsibilities. Some offer recreational and social programs as well.

Intermediate-care facility

Best for a patient who can't manage independently, an intermediate-care facility provides room, board, and daily nursing care. The cost may be covered by government subsidy programs. An example is an intermediate care facility for mentally retarded or other developmentally disabled persons.

Skilled nursing facility

Best for a patient who needs constant medical attention, a skilled nursing facility provides 24-hour nursing care, medical care when needed, and such rehabilitation services as physical and occupational therapies. Depending on the patient's eligibility, Medicare or Medicaid may subsidize the cost.

patients began in 1965, when Congress passed the Medicare and Medicaid amendments to the Social Security Act. These amendments provided government reimbursement for long-term care of elderly and disabled patients.

The Medicare and Medicaid amendments also provided reimbursement for skilled nursing care in extended-care facilities. These facilities were initially planned to deliver short-term nursing care to elderly patients who no longer needed intensive medical and nursing care in a hospital. Today, most patients admitted to long-term care facilities come directly from hospitals or other health care facilities.

Scope and limits of long-term care nursing

Nurses in long-term care facilities provide skilled nursing, such as administering medications and patient teaching. They must be familiar with geriatric and rehabilitative medicine. The majority of the long-term care workforce includes nursing assistants, home health care aides, personal care workers, and personal care attendants. It's important for the nurse to work with these health care workers effectively and delegate responsibilities efficiently.

LIABILITY

Although the focus of long-term care nursing is on caring for those who are recovering from an illness (short-term) and providing supervision and medical care for those who have chronic medical problems (long-term), all patients in such facilities must be under the care of a physician. However, the fact that a patient is under a physician's care doesn't absolve the nurse from sharing in the responsibility for his care. If a patient's medical condition becomes emergent and goes unnoticed or if a patient's care doesn't meet reasonable standards, the nurse may be held liable.

SUBSTANDARD CARE

Many long-term care facilities come under attack by state licensing and certification agencies for providing substandard care. (See *Helping your patient select a long-term care facility.*) One major problem is that long-term care facilities employ only a small number of RNs.

Aware of these trying circumstances, many RNs and LPNs working in long-term care facilities are greatly concerned about their legal rights and responsibilities. Areas of concern include staffing ratios and patterns, quality of care, and patients' rights.

STAFFING PATTERNS

In most long-term care facilities, RNs hold administrative positions, shouldering supervisory responsibility for the quality of care. LPNs in many facilities work as charge nurses, performing most nursing procedures and supervising nursing assistants. Patients may depend on nurses' aides for a substantial amount of care. This arrangement, created by minimal licensed-personnel staffing, may lead to legal problems concerning both supervision and the scope of nursing practice. (See *Minimal licensed-personnel staffing.*)

Legally, a supervisor is responsible for her supervisory acts and decisions. Suppose a supervisor knows—or should know—that a subordinate is inexperienced, untrained, or unable to perform a task safely. A court may indeed find that supervisor liable in a malpractice lawsuit for delegating such a task to the subordinate. To limit liability, a supervisor must determine that the individual to whom tasks are delegated is competent to perform the tasks. Even then, the supervisor must evaluate the outcomes of the performance of the tasks.

> ## Minimal licensed-personnel staffing
>
> Health care professionals use the term *minimal licensed-personnel staffing* to describe the staffing situation in many long-term care facilities. Consider the following statistics:
> - Only about 1 of every 20 nursing home employees is an RN.
> - Only about 1 licensed health care professional is employed for every 100 nursing home patients.
> - Physicians spend only about 2 hours per month with their nursing home patients.
> - In some extended-care facilities, about 6 of 10 charge nurses on the 3 p.m. to 11 p.m. shift and about 7 of 10 charge nurses on the 11 p.m. to 7 a.m. shift are LPNs.

If the subordinate performs a task negligently, she'll also be liable. Furthermore, if the court finds that the supervisor and the subordinate were working within the scope of their employment, the nursing home may share liability under the doctrine of *respondeat superior.*

In determining whether the defendant nurse's actions met professional standards for her position, the courts may review details of the staffing situation. For example, a New York court found that nurses were negligent when an unsupervised patient jumped from a balcony (*Horton v. Niagara Falls Memorial Medical Center* [1976]). The court reached this conclusion after reviewing evidence detailing how many patients were on the unit, how many staff members were there, and what each staff member was doing. During this review, the court discovered that a charge nurse had permitted the only available nurses' aide to go to supper when she had the authority to prevent it, leaving the disoriented patient unsupervised.

As an RN or LPN working in a long-term care facility, you must practice within the legal limits set by your state's nurse practice act, meet professional standards for your position, and be familiar with state regulations for the type of facility in which you work.

If you're an RN, make sure you possess the management and supervisory skills required by your job. Keep in mind that if you're sued for malpractice, you'll be judged according to how a reasonably prudent nursing supervisor would act in similar circumstances. You can't defend yourself by claiming that you weren't trained to supervise.

If you're an LPN working in a long-term care facility, remember that no person or facility can force you to practice beyond the limits outlined in your state's nurse practice act. If you exceed the legally permissible scope of nursing practice in your state, your state board of nursing can suspend or revoke your license. You won't be able to use your employer's expectations to excuse your actions.

Under the law, an LPN who performs a nursing function legally restricted to RNs will be held to the RN standard if she's sued for malpractice. *Barber v. Reinking* (1966) involved an LPN who had performed an RN function. The court stated, "In accordance with public policy of this state, one who undertakes to perform the services of a trained or graduate nurse must have the knowledge and skill possessed by the registered nurse."

QUALITY OF CARE

Centers for Medicare & Medicaid Services (CMS) has conditions of participation that are minimally met by having one RN in-house. There is much written about the decline of RN staffing in long-term care facilities

and the effects on pressure sores, urinary tract infections, etc. The site "Nursing home compare" emphasizes that, in general, the not-for-profit facilities rank better than the for-profit ones. See http://www.ncbi.nlm.nih.gov/pmc/articles/PMC2442239/

Many nurses working in long-term care facilities are particularly concerned about the fragmentation of the nursing process. Although an RN remains responsible for overall patient assessment and evaluation, an LPN decides on the daily assessments, planning, and evaluation, and a nurses' aide implements the assessment plan.

Fragmenting the nursing process can greatly reduce the quality of patient care. It can also have legal consequences if nursing actions are performed improperly—or not performed at all. This list describes poor nursing practices that plague long-term care facilities:

- Failing to make a nursing diagnosis
- Being careless in the observation of a patient's condition
- Failing to document
- Writing illegibly when documenting
- Failing to keep up with current nursing knowledge required to care for elderly and disabled patients
- Failing to use nursing consultants such as certified wound, ostomy, continence, and foot care nurses
- Delegating improperly
- Failing to insist on clear facility policies
- Failing to question an order
- Taking a dangerous patient care shortcut
- Excluding the patient's family from communication, decision making, and education regarding patient care
- Failing to call the physician when the patient's condition changes

Consider the case of an RN named Adams who reported unsafe staffing levels at his facility in Massachusetts. He was harassed by the management and then fired in 1996. Mr. Adams filed a lawsuit and a complaint with the National Labor Relations Board (NLRB), and both a judge and the NLRB ruled that he was wrongfully terminated (NLRB case 1-CA-34663[1-2] and 1-CA-34699). Mr. Adams filed a complaint with the Massachusetts Board of Nursing against his former nursing supervisor, alleging unprofessional and unethical conduct. The complaint stated that, on the basis of her actions, she condoned the unsafe staffing levels that may have contributed to a patient's death. Massachusetts Board of Nursing members said the allegations were either lacking in sufficient evidence or had been resolved.

PATIENTS' RIGHTS

Many states have enacted patients' rights legislation patterned after the Patient's Bill of Rights published by the American Hospital Association. Most of these states have passed laws that make reporting maltreatment of patients a legal responsibility. Some states have even established an ombudsman's office that has the authority to investigate complaints of abuse and the obligation to post complaint procedures in all geriatric facilities.

On the federal level, the Omnibus Budget Reconciliation Act of 1987 markedly strengthens the rights of nursing home residents. The law says that nursing home residents have the right to choose a personal attending physician, to participate in planning their own care and treatment, and to be free from physical or mental abuse, corporal punishment, and physical or chemical restraints imposed for purposes of discipline or convenience. The law also imposes new requirements for additional nursing staff. In 1989, the Department of Health and Human Services, in an effort to carry out the 1987 law, issued new rules governing Medicare and Medicaid reimbursement for nursing homes.

STEPS YOU CAN TAKE

If you work in a long-term care facility, you should request that your facility:

■ require a patient's signature for any release of information

■ clearly specify who has access to medical records and impose penalties for unauthorized disclosure of patient information

■ foster a patient's right to know about his condition and provide for informed consent for his treatment

■ help combat drug abuse and misuse by requiring nurses who administer drugs to know the effects of the drugs and know how to assess each patient's changing needs.

■ ensure prompt, effective communication between physicians and nurses

■ acknowledge and respect a patient's right to refuse treatment

■ encourage nurses to evaluate the quality of nursing services

■ encourage nurses to work cooperatively with patient representatives and accreditation agencies

■ restrict the use of chemical and physical restraints; restraints should be used only when the patient's physical or mental status gives evidence that they're necessary (and even then only with a physician's order) and solely for the patient's safety.

PROTECTING YOUR JOB

Most health care professionals are patients' rights advocates, but advocating your patient's rights may lead to conflicts with your coworkers and employers. This is one paradox of nursing practice: You have a professional obligation to protect your patients' rights—but doing so could cost you your job. Unfortunately, your legal protection in this situation is limited. If you're an employee working without a contract, also known as *employee-at-will,* you can be dismissed for any reason your employer wants to give. You do have legal grounds to protest your dismissal if:

■ your contract clearly states that you can't be fired on these grounds
■ your facility guarantees you the right to notice and a hearing before dismissal
■ your state's laws prevent your employer from retaliating if you report violations to the appropriate agency
■ you're a government employee and can claim the First Amendment right to free speech.

PROFESSIONAL CHALLENGES

You'll encounter many challenges working in a long-term care facility, including those related to time management, a patient's quality of life, declining functional and cognitive status, chronic health conditions, interactions with a patient and his family over an extended period, and end-of-life issues. It's important to handle these challenges with care that's based on your nursing practice act and your board of nursing rules and regulations; doing so ensures you solid legal standing.

OPPORTUNITIES

In a long-term care facility, in which physicians' involvement with patients is limited, RNs and LPNs have an opportunity to grow professionally and to influence the quality of patient care. If you're an RN, you'll learn not only geriatric nursing but also good management. If you're an LPN, you may have the chance to fill a charge nurse position and to expand your nursing skills. Depending on your nurse practice act, you may also learn how to perform nursing assessment and patient teaching. However, keep in mind that along with opportunity comes responsibility—for practicing within legal limits and for continuing your education to meet professional standards.

WORKING IN AN ALTERNATIVE PRACTICE SETTING

Practicing nursing outside of traditional settings—such as hospitals, clinics, and nursing homes—dates back to the 19th century. Back then, most nurses worked outside hospitals: in physicians' offices, in patients' homes, and on battlefields. Today, many nurses practice in alternative settings. Their employers include factories, schools, the military, insurance companies, and claims review agencies. (See *Other areas for providing nursing care.*)

When working in an alternative setting, you may not have the legal services of a hospital's administration to provide assistance during a dispute. You must take on the special challenge of knowing your legal responsibilities.

Scope and limits of alternative practice nursing

Most states' nurse practice acts don't discuss professional standards for nurses working in alternative settings. However, you still must meet the same practice standards as for a hospital nurse. If you violate those standards, your state board of nursing may suspend or revoke your license, just as it would if you were a hospital nurse, and your patient may sue you for malpractice.

Historically, courts have held nurses who work in alternative settings to state standards for nursing practice. A California malpractice case, *Cooper v. National Motor Bearing Co.* (1955), concerned an occupational health nurse who failed to diagnose suspected cancer and didn't refer the patient for further evaluation and treatment. At the trial, the court ruled that the only point of law to be considered in deciding the case was whether the nurse met the standards of nursing practice in her area. When expert testimony showed that she had breached those standards, the court found her negligent. Her occupational setting was irrelevant to the court's decision. Similar court cases illustrating this principle include *Planned Parenthood of Northwest Ind. v. Vines* (1989), *Barber v. Reinking* (1966), and *Stahlin v. Hilton Hotels Corp.* (1973).

The Canadian approach to such cases is similar to the American approach. In *Dowey v. Rothwell* (1974), a nurse who worked in a physician's office knew that an epileptic patient was about to have a seizure, yet she failed to stay with the patient. This patient did have a seizure, fell, and fractured an arm. The court found that the nurse failed "to provide that minimum standard of care which a patient has a right to expect in an office setting." The court based its findings on testimony about the expected performance standards of experienced RNs in many settings.

LIABILITY

In certain cases, if you work in an alternative setting, you may be protected from a liability suit. For example, if you work for a government agency, you may be protected from lawsuits because of the doctrine of sovereign immunity. Depending on the state in which you're working, this immunity may be complete or partial. To determine the extent of the immunity, check with your personnel office or agency attorney. (See *Understanding sovereign immunity.*)

If you work for a privately owned business, such as an insurance company or a small medical practice group, you're still vulnerable to malpractice suits. In some states, however, you can't be sued by a fellow employee you've treated for a job-related injury. State workers' compensation laws, which protect the employer from excessive business costs, also protect you.

FINANCIAL BURDENS

If you choose to make your career in an alternative setting, take time to investigate your benefits as an employee. Your benefits and liability coverage may be somewhat different than if you had chosen to work in a hospital setting.

(Text continues on page 66.)

Other areas for providing nursing care

Nurses choose to practice in alternative settings for many reasons: to take on greater challenges and achieve more responsibility, for a change of pace, to increase their earning power, or to make an impact on public health policy.

The list that follows describes some of the important options for nurses today: school nursing, occupational health nursing, air rescue nursing, and hospice nursing. You'll also find descriptions of nursing opportunities in the business world: working as a case coordinator for an insurance company, making it on your own as an entrepreneur, or working in the legal arena.

School nurse

As a school nurse, your responsibilities include providing nursing care for sick or injured students and giving first aid in emergencies. When authorized, you also administer medications to students. Other tasks include:

■ assisting in examinations
■ giving annual screening tests—for example, vision, audiometry, and scoliosis tests—and referring students for further testing or treatment when appropriate
■ counseling parents and students
■ meeting with teachers and other staff members about health problems and health education programs
■ enforcing state immunization policies for school-age children
■ visiting sick or injured students at home when necessary
■ helping identify and meet special needs of disabled students.

Occupational health nurse

As an occupational health nurse, your primary responsibility is to provide nursing care for sick or injured employees. Other responsibilities include:

■ giving first aid in emergencies
■ performing medical screening tests or helping the physician perform them
■ referring sick or injured employees for appropriate treatment

■ counseling employees on health matters
■ meeting with management regarding health-related issues
■ developing and maintaining employee medical records
■ maintaining records for government agencies such as workers' compensation agencies, the Occupational Safety and Health Administration, and state or federal labor and health departments
■ alerting management to potential health and safety hazards.

Flight nurse

As a flight nurse, either on fixed-wing transport or helicopter, you have a job that's glamorous, challenging, and hazardous. Many of the dilemmas that you and your fellow flight-nurses face are unique, and as a small group, you don't have much power to exact change. Dilemmas include:

■ scheduled 24-hour shifts for nurses and pilots, which cause concerns for quality work and safety for everyone on board the helicopter
■ right to refuse an assigned flight because of personal safety concerns
■ applying patient restraints unnecessarily or risking patients with borderline behavior becoming violent during flight and jeopardizing all on board
■ safety concerns related to loading and unloading while rotor blades are in motion
■ protective equipment for the helicopter and protective gear for crew members, which are lacking in most helicopters
■ familiarity of the air rescue nurse with aircraft-specific emergency procedures and equipment.

Hospice nurse

As a hospice nurse, your most important responsibility is to provide skilled nursing care to the terminally ill patients. Expect to focus on providing pain relief and symptom control. Patients and their families rely heavily on you for emotional and psychosocial support. Professional satisfaction typically comes from knowing that

(continued)

Other areas for providing nursing care *(continued)*

you've helped the dying patient maintain dignity and make the most of the time he has left. The most significant means of limiting your liability is to review advance directives and living wills that have been prepared on behalf of the patients. If these documents haven't been drafted, you need to consider reviewing these issues with the patient to prepare for the ultimate care and treatment. Before your patient becomes unconscious, review options with him so his wishes are carried out.

Nursing case coordinator for an insurance company

When working for an insurance company, your responsibilities may include reviewing records and assessing insurance claims by talking with the patient, his physician, his family, and his employer. You may be asked to help design patient care plans. These care plans typically include medical, nursing, social service, and payment goals. You may also monitor the patient's progress and prognosis by talking with the patient and his physicians. Other tasks include:

- helping to coordinate medical, rehabilitation, and other services
- supervising other nursing case reviewers
- developing and maintaining insurance company records.

Nurse entrepreneur

Nurse entrepreneurs provide services such as continuing education seminars, serve as health care navigators for patients encountering the complex system, or may have a private practice of psychotherapy. As an entrepreneur, you must organize and manage your own business undertaking. You take on the risk of failure for the sake of potential profit. Your opportunity

to apply nursing skills as an entrepreneur is limited only by your own imagination. For example, legal nurse consultants have established successful businesses providing such services as reviewing medical records and performing research for insurance companies and attorneys; finding medical experts for testimony in medical malpractice actions, personal injury litigation, and workers' compensation matters; and developing educational programs for use inside hospitals.

Other tasks include:

- Conducting medical literature searches and assist in other research
- Identifying applicable standards of care in medical malpractice cases
- Identifying, screening, and facilitating review by expert witnesses
- Evaluating case strengths and weaknesses
- Drafting or analyzing medical portions of legal documents
- Evaluating causation and damages issues
- Educate attorneys and clients regarding relevant medical issues
- Identifying plaintiff's future medical needs and associated costs
- Participating in case management and case strategy discussions
- Attending independent medical examinations
- Serving as a nurse expert witness
- Performing cost of care estimates for long-term care treatment and catastrophic case management scenarios
- Locating or preparing demonstrative evidence for trial
- Assisting with preparation for and support during deposition, trial, or alternate dispute resolution.

LEGAL TIP — Legal considerations in hospice care

If you work in a hospice care, be aware of these special legal responsibilities.

Standing orders
A hospital staff nurse can follow standing orders for pain medication. When working in a hospice, however, never rely on standing orders as authorization to administer pain medication. Always obtain specific orders signed by the patient's physician.

Advice on making a will
In a hospice, never give the patient advice concerning his will. If he asks for advice, tell him you aren't allowed to provide such advice. Suggest that he discuss the matter with his attorney or his family.

Living wills
Unlike the hospital nurse, whose duty with respect to living wills varies from state to state, the nurse who works in a hospice care must respect the patient's living will. Don't violate it in any way, unless a court order instructs you to do so.

Understanding sovereign immunity

The doctrine of sovereign immunity goes back to the days when a person couldn't sue a sovereign or his agents unless the sovereign consented. In the United States, the courts transferred this privilege, applicable in most circumstances, to the elected government and its appointed agents–government employees. So government employees ordinarily can't be sued for their on-the-job mistakes.

Unfair results
In the past, this immunity has had some unfair results. A patient harmed in a private hospital could sue the hospital and its employees, but a patient harmed in a municipal or state hospital couldn't.

Perhaps because of this immunity, public hospitals gained a reputation for substandard practice; the public suspected that because public hospitals couldn't be sued for malpractice, their standards of care were lax.

Legislative action
In recent decades, most state legislatures have recognized the unfairness of this system. Many have passed laws that allow patients to sue public hospitals and other government agencies on a full or limited basis. In some states, legislatures have created special courts–usually called courts of claims–in which such lawsuits must be heard. Many state legislatures have set dollar limits on the amount a patient can recover from a government agency if he wins his suit.

PURCHASING PROFESSIONAL LIABILITY INSURANCE

Most private medical employers have coverage that includes the nurses they employ, but private industrial employers, especially small companies, may not. Check your employer's coverage thoroughly: If you have a doubt about whether you're fully protected, consider buying your own insurance.

You may also need your own professional liability insurance if you work for a peer review organization or a state or federal government agency, unless the law grants you complete immunity from job-related lawsuits.

UNION ELIGIBILITY

You usually retain the right to join a union. In fact, if you work as an occupational health nurse in a factory with a closed shop, you may be required to join a union. In a "right to work" state, however, you cannot be required to join a union; in fact, unions may have little influence on working conditions in such states.

If you work for a state or local government, state laws may permit you to join a union but may forbid your union to strike. Remember that the National Labor Relations Act exempts state and local governments and doesn't protect government nurses—such as community health nurses and public school nurses—in unionization disputes.

TERMINATION OF EMPLOYMENT

Whether you work in an alternative setting or a hospital, nothing but a contract clause, a union agreement, or a civil service law can legally protect you from being fired. Even if you have such protection, you may be vulnerable to discretionary firing until the end of an initial probationary period. After this period, any of these forms of protection guarantees you the right to appeal your employer's decision.

WORKERS' COMPENSATION

If you work in an alternative setting, you should know what coverage your employer and your state, federal, or Canadian jurisdictional government provide for on-the-job injuries. Workers' compensation will usually cover you—but not always.

Most states and jurisdictions require many privately owned businesses to participate in workers' compensation plans. If you work for such a business, you'll probably receive workers' compensation for job-related injuries. However, you should be aware that, if the money you receive from this fund is inadequate, workers' compensation laws prevent you from suing your employer for additional compensation.

IF YOU WORK FOR A SMALL OFFICE

Some states don't require employers with few employees or limited income (for example, a physician with a small practice) to participate in the workers' compensation plan; so if you work in such a setting, be aware that you may not be covered by workers' compensation for job-related injuries. In the event that you are injured on the job, keep in mind that you can sue your employer directly.

Most small employers buy their own insurance to cover workers' injuries. If your employer doesn't have such insurance, you can buy your own insurance.

IF YOU WORK FOR THE GOVERNMENT

If you work for a state or federal government agency, you may receive compensation from the state workers' compensation plan or by filing a claim under a state or federal tort claims act, depending on the applicable laws. However, if the sovereign immunity doctrine applies, you may not be eligible for compensation.

If you're eligible for workers' compensation, it usually covers any on-the-job injury. For example, if you're a school nurse and a student kicks you, workers' compensation will normally cover you. You also usually have the legal right to sue the person who caused the injury. If you win your lawsuit, the court, depending on state or territory statute, may consider any money you've already received, either from workers' compensation or from other insurance, in deciding the amount of damages you should receive. Because lawsuits are costly and can take years to resolve, most nurses don't sue.

PROFESSIONAL CHALLENGES

Nurses working in an alternative health care setting will face many challenges unlike those faced in the traditional hospital setting. Depending on the setting the nurse has chosen, she will have to meet and overcome these challenges. She will have to understand and meet the needs of culturally and ethnically diverse clients, stay current with emerging trends, and be responsible in continuing her professional education.

WORKING IN HOME HEALTH CARE

More patients are receiving nursing care in their homes. What's more, nursing care measures implemented in the patient's home are becoming more sophisticated. Whereas every hospital has similar characteristics, every home is unique. Each represents a different pattern of legal risks and an unknown constellation of interpersonal relationships.

Scope and limits of home health care nursing

Home health care nursing makes it possible for patients to obtain nursing care in their own homes. Unlike what patients receive with home health care aid service, RNs can provide skilled nursing care for all patients, regardless of their age or disease state. However, it's important for the home health care nurse to follow the federal and state laws that regulate home health care nursing as well as her state's nurse practice act.

LIABILITY

One factor that clearly affects your potential liability as a home health care nurse is your degree of control over the home environment, which is much less controlled than the hospital environment. For example, situations such as safety hazards that result in liability in the hospital may have a different outcome in home health care litigation because the health care provider has little control over the home setting.

If you work for a home health care agency and your responsibilities include managing other home health care workers, keep in mind that it's more difficult to evaluate personnel who work in the patient's home. Negligent training of a home health care worker may form the basis for a legal action. In *Loton v. Massachusetts*

Paramedical Inc. (1989), a personal care worker employed by a home health care company left the patient unattended in a shower. The worker left the apartment to go to another part of the building to do laundry. While the patient was alone, the temperature of the water became very hot. As the patient tried to readjust the water, she fell from the shower seat and inadvertently moved the temperature control to the hot zone. Because of her underlying disability, she was unable to move away from the scalding water. When the worker returned, she was unable to reach her supervisor. She then applied ice to the burns and waited before calling an ambulance. The patient suffered third-degree burns over a large portion of her body, requiring numerous operations and skin grafting.

The plaintiff alleged that the home health care agency was negligent in failing to educate personnel in managing patients with disabilities and also in not training staff for the appropriate response in emergency situations. The jury rejected the agency's defense and awarded the plaintiff $1 million.

Along with civil claims for malpractice and negligence, a home health care provider or agency may be held liable for criminal actions in cases of serious neglect. In one case involving neglect, a patient had been receiving home health care service. She was admitted to the hospital with numerous pressure ulcers, some of which extended to the bone. The woman looked unwashed and had a necrotic odor. An indictment was brought against the home health care agency, the administrator of one of its offices, a visiting nurse employed by the company, and an LPN in the agency's nursing and supportive care program. The charge involved knowingly and willfully neglecting the patient, causing serious mental and physical injuries. After a jury trial, the company was convicted of a Class A misdemeanor and fined more than $8,000.

FINANCIAL BURDENS

Most home health care nurses must own their own vehicle or provide their own transportation to their clients' homes; however, most home health care agencies reimburse nurses for gas and mileage.

PROFESSIONAL CHALLENGES

In the late 1990s, home health care had many changes stemming from widespread abuses of the Medicare benefit. The major outcome has been increased government regulation and the cuts in Medicare reimbursement. For example, Medicare pays for skilled services such as wound care in the home, but not for long-term care for the chronically ill. Home health care nurses must also continually prove the "cost-effectiveness" of their services and care to the government and to the insurers. Much of a nurse's time is spent on paperwork, proper billing and coding, and getting reimbursed for supplies and services.

The challenges for home health care nurses aren't all financial. When the nurse enters a patient's home, she must assess the patient's living situation, the physical environment, and family support, and figure how it affects her care and the patient's activities of daily living. She alone must assess the patient's status at home, his well-being, and his ability to stay at home or his need for acute care, and she's usually the first person to assess a patient following discharge from a hospital or after a surgical procedure.

The home health care nurse is also required to keep up with technological advances in nursing care and provide the patient with appropriate patient teaching.

WORKING FOR A STAFFING AGENCY AND TRAVEL NURSING

One of the expected outcomes of the Affordable Care Act will be an increase in the number of insured who will seek health care for the first time rather than wait for an emergency. Facilities will look for ways to staff flexibly rather than add permanent staff. At the same time, there are pockets of shortages of needed staff so recruitment will range farther.

Temporary nursing service agencies represent an innovative approach to the delivery of nursing services—one response to the constant demand for practical, efficient, and cost-effective nursing care. Many nurses decide to work for a temporary nursing service agency to achieve greater work schedule flexibility and the right to choose their own hours. What's more, most agencies pay higher salaries than hospitals.

Nurses who sign on with a company that provides nurses to hospitals needing more staff or a flexible staff can travel the country and further their careers in diverse settings. Besides getting to experience life in other areas of the country, there are numerous benefits to choosing travel nursing. Some of these include higher pay and free housing. Because certain areas of the country are in such high demand for qualified staff, nurses typically receive higher wages than a full-time permanent employee, and travel nursing companies pay for clean, quality housing that is close to the work site.

The areas most often recruiting for nurses are critical care areas, both adult and neonatal; the operating room; labor and delivery; and the emergency department. Another area is in psychiatry. And these positions are not limited to generalist RNs. Advance practice nurses are finding temporary positions as travel nurses as both clinicians and managers.

Scope and limits of agency nursing

Agency nurses work for a health care agency. The agency contracts with a health care facility to provide RN coverage in a capacity that fulfills the facility's needs. As an agency nurse, you may work in a hospital as a staff nurse, in a home as a home health care nurse, in a clinical research study for a university or pharmaceutical company, or wherever else the agency places you. Your scope is that of an RN, and the agency can't contract you for a job that's beyond your credentials. For example, if you haven't been certified in telemetry, you can't work on a telemetry floor. Keep in mind that you're obligated by your state's nurse practice act and the contractual agreement between you and your employer-agency. Although agency and travel nurses work within the structure of a health care facility, it is imperative to have sufficient experience in the area of nursing. At the same time, nurses should research the agency thoroughly to avoid problems. Some questions to ask either the agency or the facility for which you are being recruited:

■ Is the assignment guaranteed by contract? What about pay and hours?

■ Who is the employer: the agency or the facility? Who will pay me and how often?

■ Will there be insurance coverage? (liability, life, health)
■ Who will be the contact person during the assignment?
■ What happens if the facility cancels the assignment?

FEW CLEAR-CUT POLICIES

Learning the policies and procedures of the temporary facility is the most important way to avoid legal problems. There is no place for "We've always done it this way" attitude. At the same time, if the nursing practice of the assigned unit does not follow the written policy and procedure manual, it is imperative that the temporary RN speak to the manager and request clarification. For example, in one facility, structured patient assessments were done on every patient on each shift. The agency nurse was asked to cosign the assessment done by an LPN on the unit; she refused, citing the policy manual that since assessment is an element of the nursing process, it is outside the scope of LPN practice and that signing something she had not done would be falsification of records. The agency nurse spoke with the unit manager, who was not aware that LPNs were actually doing the assessments rather than contributing data such as vital signs to them. The manager issued a clarifying statement to the staff. Since it changed their practice, they were not pleased and the agency nurse had to work to regain a good working relationship with her peers.

A nurse's professional responsibilities as an agency worker are typically vague. No set of uniform policies and procedures has been formally identified or administratively defined. For example, if an RN and an LPN are assigned to care for the same patient in his home but on different shifts, what responsibility does the RN have for the LPN's work? Is the RN responsible for supervising home health care aides? Also, should communication between the RN and the patient's physician be direct or channeled through an agency supervisor?

Large agencies, especially those with nationwide placement, may have specific policies to deal with situations like these. But smaller, more regional agencies may not. Without clear-cut guidelines, you may have to rely heavily on your professional nursing judgment. However, remember that the courts apply the same legal principles governing staff nurse malpractice cases to agency nurse malpractice cases.

LIABILITY

A nurse is liable for her own wrongful conduct. However, if an agency nurse is judged to have been working within the legally permissible scope of her employment, then the agency may be held vicariously liable and may be required to pay any damages awarded to the plaintiff. The court may use the doctrine of *respondeat superior* to interpret the nurse's legal status. This doctrine makes an employer responsible for the negligent acts of his employees—so the agency is responsible for the actions of the nurses it employs. If the court finds that the nurse exceeded the scope of her employment, she may be solely responsible for any damages.

As an agency employee, you may be assigned to work in a patient's home, to care for a single patient in a hospital or other health care facility, or to temporarily supplement a facility's staff. These different practice circumstances can influence how a court determines liability. A malpractice lawsuit that involves an agency nurse will probably name as defendants the nurse, the temporary nursing service agency, and, if applicable, the health care facility in which the alleged malpractice happened. When you work as an agency nurse in a patient's home, your agency-employee status is usually clear-cut. The same is true when you care for a single patient in a health care facility.

The courts have more difficulty assigning legal liability in cases that involve agency nurses working as supplemental facility staff. In this situation, you're still an agency employee, but you're also in the "special service" of another "employer"—the facility.

Courts may apply the borrowed servant (or *ostensible agent*) doctrine, holding that the regular employer (the agency) isn't liable for injury negligently caused by the nurse-employee (the "servant") while in the special service of another employer (the hospital). Although the legal liability shifts from the agency to the hospital or facility when a court interprets a case this way, the nurse may be held to be the agent of both the agency and the hospital, under the doctrine of dual agency, making both potentially liable.

PROFESSIONAL GUIDELINES

To help protect yourself against a lawsuit, make sure you fully understand what's expected of you when you accept an agency job. Be prepared to adjust to different policies and procedures. This requires review of policy manuals and a clear understanding of what they contain. When you work in a patient's home, for example, your agency's policies and procedures govern your actions. Make sure you understand them thoroughly and follow them carefully. How competently you follow procedure may affect such matters as whether a claim for workers'

compensation is allowed or whether your agency will be included as a defendant with you in a malpractice suit. Don't perform any nonnursing functions when you work in a patient's home or arbitrarily change his nursing regimen policies and procedures from what your agency has specified. If you do and the patient or his family decides to sue, you may find yourself solely liable.

The last point is particularly important if an agency assigns you to work in a hospital or other health care facility. As always, you must make sure you understand the policies and procedures of the facility for the nursing tasks you're expected to perform. Get to know the head nurse or unit supervisor, and seek clarification from her whenever you're in doubt.

The hospital or facility, in turn, is obligated to supply any equipment you need for patient care and to keep its premises and equipment in safe condition.

FINANCIAL BURDENS

Although agency nurses are paid a higher salary because of the flexibility and skill they're willing to offer, agencies don't have to offer benefits (such as health, pension, and savings plans) because these nurses are temporary employees. To obtain such benefits, agency nurses must either bear the cost on their own (for example, by purchasing private health insurance) or seek additional, part-time employment with an employer that offers such benefits.

PROFESSIONAL CHALLENGES

Agency nurses must have years of acute care experience and be comfortable and confident with their acute care skills. You must be flexible with where you work and be willing to travel or work in different capacities (such as a home health care nurse, a staff nurse, or a critical care nurse) and in different settings. As an agency nurse, you're expected to keep up with the most current information and technology. Although the agency for which you're working may offer additional classes, it's up to you to keep up with certifications and continuing education.

Also, because new graduate nurses typically don't receive an "orientation" period, you must quickly adjust to your working environment, almost as soon as you start your first shift. You must be able to work well with others with whom you haven't yet built a rapport. Lastly, because of the nursing shortage crisis, many health care facilities are turning to agency nurses to help solve their staffing problem. You, as an agency nurse, will have to be prepared for whatever challenges you may face: heavy patient loads, the absence of more experienced nurses to whom you may turn for support, and low morale.

Despite the challenges that agency nursing presents, many agency nurses find their role fulfilling because it offers them flexibility as well as the opportunity to put their wide range of nursing skills to use.

WORKING WITH AN AGENCY NURSE

If you're a hospital staff nurse and an agency nurse is assigned to your unit, your responsibilities as a coworker are the same as those when you're working with a nonagency nurse. For example, if you see the agency nurse performing a procedure in a way that may harm the patient, you have a responsibility to stop the procedure, just as you would if you saw a nonagency nurse performing that same procedure. If you see an agency nurse performing a procedure incorrectly but without potential harm to the patient, simply report your observation to your nursing supervisor.

CONTROVERSY OVER AGENCY NURSING

When a nursing shortage exists, many health care facilities suffer imbalances in the number of nurses available to work regularly scheduled shifts. Temporary nursing service agencies provide a valuable service by supplying skilled nurses on short notice. However, use of agency-provided RNs and LPNs as supplemental staff in hospitals, nursing homes, and extended-care facilities is a fairly new and controversial practice.

On the one hand, critics point out that inequities in salaries between hospital and agency nurses performing the same functions can lead to morale problems. Proponents of agency-based supplemental staffing, on the other hand, stress the cost-effectiveness of the practice and believe that its flexibility helps to keep nurses working and prevents nurse burnout. Proponents and critics urge that nursing administrations plan supplemental staffing programs instead of bringing in agency nurses on a few hours' notice before a shift begins. Adequate planning helps to maintain quality and continuity of patient care.

POTENTIAL LEGAL PRECEDENT

Although no plaintiff has ever charged a hospital with inadequate staffing caused by a failure to obtain available supplemental staff from an agency, observers of the nursing profession believe that this may happen soon. In a Louisiana case, *McCutchon v. Mutual of Omaha Insurance Co.* (1978), a court required an insurance company to pay the agency fees of two LPNs recruited to care for a critically ill patient whose physician had ordered RNs (and whose insurance policy allowed payment for only RNs). The court reached its decision after reviewing evidence that neither the temporary nursing service agency, nor the hospital, nor the insurance company could locate any available RNs at the time the LPNs were assigned. The court also considered the fact that the assigned LPNs were closely supervised by an RN at all times.

Working as a legal nurse consultant

Legal nurse consultants apply knowledge acquired during their professional education and clinical experiences to the evaluation of the standards of care, causation, damages, and other medically related issues in medical-legal cases or claims. The work of the legal nurse consultants involved critical analysis of health care records and medical literature, as well as relevant legal and other documents pertinent to the evaluation and resolution of a medical-legal case or claim.

Whether working from a home office as an independent legal nurse consultant or working within a law firm, government agency, health care facilities (risk management department), insurance company, or other, legal nurse consultants are uniquely qualified and valuable members of the legal team. The legal team will utilize the legal nurse consultant to translate complex medical issues into clear, simple terms understandable by non-medical professionals such as attorneys, judges, mediators, and others.

In addition to analyzing medical records, evaluating case strengths and weaknesses, preparing attorney reports, conducting medical literature searches, and preparing support during depositions and trials, many legal nurse consultants serve as expert witnesses when appropriate.

Nurses who serve as expert witnesses support good nursing practices and help to protect the health, safety, and well-being of patients. After reviewing the medical case file and investigating the standards of nursing care, the nurse expert witness will be expected to testify at a deposition or trial if needed.

If serving as an expert witness, many states limit the percentage of time or percentage of income that comes from serving in this capacity. For both legal and ethical reasons, legal nurse consultants and expert witnesses cannot take cases that involve a current employer. Additionally, contingency-based fees are barred because of the appearance that the expert witness or legal nurse consultant is willing to alter her professional opinion or testimony based on the successful outcome of the case. Rather, both groups should bill for their services on an hourly or daily basis.

If the legal nurse consultant works in a law firm or other professional agency, the salary and benefits will be determined by the employer. The legal nurse consultant working from a home office will not receive health insurance or other benefits as an independent contractor. All legal nurse consultants should have a professional liability insurance policy.

SELECTED REFERENCES

Aiken, L., et al. "Supplemental Nurse Staffing in Hospital and Quality of Care," *The Journal of Nursing Administration* 37(7–8): 335–42, July–August 2007.

Bosworth, M. *Encyclopedia of Prisons & Correctional Facilities*. Thousand Oaks, CA: Sage, 2007.

Bowers, B.J., et al. "How Nurses Manage Time and Work in Long-term Care," *Journal of Advanced Nursing* 33(4):484–91, February 2001.

Brous, E. "Lessons Learned from Litigation: The Case of Bernard Travaglini. Did the Nurse's Improper Delegation of a Task Lead to the Patient's Death?," *American Journal of Nursing* 114(5):68–70, May 2014.

Cashin, D., et al. "The Complex Role of the School Nurse. Promoting Who We Are and What We Do," *School Nurse News* 20(3): 24–27, May 2003.

Chornick, N. "NCSBN Focus: APRN Licensure Versus APRN Certification: What Is the Difference?," *JONA's Healthcare Law, Ethics, and Regulation* 10(4):90–93, December 2008.

"Did Nurse Call Dr. Twice: Did Dr. Have Duty to Check Pt.? Case on Point: *Stubbs v. Ray*, 2000 WL 125325 S.E.2d-GA (2000)," *Nursing Law's Regan Report* 41(4):4, September 2000.

"Dr. Fails to Leave Post-op. Orders: Nurses Fail to Timely Call Dr. Case on point: *Lupinacci v. Med. Center of Delaware*, 2002 WL 31006263 N.E.2d-DE (2002)," *Nursing Law's Regan Report* 43(4):2, September 2002.

Dumpel, H. "Critical Patient Advocacy Issues Facing Correctional RNs in California, Part III," *California Nurse* 102(2):22–7, March 2006.

Dyck, M.J. "A Public Policy Problem: Access to Long-term Health Care," *Journal of Gerontological Nursing* 27(7):13–22, July 2001.

Ericksen, A.B. "10 Things Every Traveler Should Know," *Healthcare Traveler* 14(2): 18–20, 22–4, 26–30, August 2006.

Gadow, S. "Restorative Nursing: Toward a Philosophy of Postmodern Punishment," *Nursing Philosophy* 4(2):161–7, July 2003.

Hausman, S. "30,000 Inmates, 40 Doctors: Health Care Remains a Concern at Virginia Prisons," *WAMU News*, January 9, 2014.

Horn, S.D., Buerhaus, P., Bergstrom, N., and Smout, R.J. "RN Staffing Time and Outcomes of Long-stay Nursing Home Residents: Pressure Ulcers and Other Adverse Outcomes Are Less Likely as RNs Spend More Time on Direct Patient Care," *Am J Nurs* 105(11):58–70, November 2005.

"In Cases of Malpractice, Are Nurse Practitioners Held to the Same Medical Standard of Care When Prescribing Medications for Clients, or Would They Be Held to a Standard of Care Applicable to Advanced Practice Nurses?" *JONAS Healthcare, Law, Ethics & Regulation* 3(1):9, March 2001.

Institute of Medicine. The Future of Nursing: Leading Change, Advancing Health, October 5, 2010.

International Council of Nurses. "Codes and Declarations. The Nurse's Role in the Care of Prisoners and Detainees: International Council of Nurses, 3 Place Jean Marteau, 1201 Geneva, Switzerland," *Nursing Ethics* 9(4):448–9, July 2002.

Joint Statement on Delegation American Nurses Association (ANA) and the National Council of State Boards of Nursing (NCSBN). Retrieved from: https://www.ncsbn.org/Delegation_joint_statement_NCSBN-ANA.pdf, 2005.

Klein, C. "Care is Care No Matter Where the Nurse Practitioner," *The American Journal of Primary Health Care* 28(7):45, July 2003.

Konetzka, R.T., et al. The Staffing–Outcomes Relationship in Nursing Homes. Retrieved from: http://www.ncbi.nlm.nih.gov/pmc/articles/PMC2442239/

Moak, A. Defining a Correctional Nurse. Retrieved from: http://www.corrections.com/news/article/24280-defining-a-correctional-nurse, May 17, 2010.

Morrison, C.A. "Unlicensed Personnel Issues," *Advanced Practice Nurse* 9(8):29, August 2001.

Mueller, C. "A Framework for Nurse Staffing in Long-term Care Facilities," *Geriatric Nursing* 21(5):262–67, September–October 2000.

Parker-Conrad, J.E. "A Century of Practice. Occupational Health Nursing. 1988," *AAOHN Journal* 50(12):537–41, December 2002.

Patterson, M., and McMullen, P. "So You Want to Be a Legal Nurse Consultant or an Expert Witness," *The Journal for Nurse*

Practitioners, 3(1):29–32. Retrieved from: http://www.medscape.com/viewarticle/551033, January 2007.

Randolph, L.B. "Settling Down. Nursing Management," Nursing Management 35(supp 1):10–11, April 2004.

Reising, D.L., and Allen, P.N. "Protecting Yourself from Malpractice Claims," *American Nurse Today,* 2(2):39–43, February 2007.

"RNs Accused of Negligence: Must Panel Interview Pt.? Case on Point: *Gerber v. Juneau Bartlett Memorial Hospital,* 2000 W. 641057-AK (2000)," *Nursing Law's Regan Report* 40(12):4, May 2000.

Russell, K.A. "Nurse Practice Acts Guide and Govern Nursing Practice," *Journal of Nursing Regulation* 3(3):36–40, October 2012.

Salazar, M.K. "Applying Research to Practice. Practical Guidelines for Occupational Health Nurses," *AAOHN Journal* 50(11):520–27, November 2002.

Saver, C. "Nursing Today and Beyond," *American Nurse Today,* 1(1):18–25. Retrieved from: http://www.americannursetoday.com/archive/october-2006-vol-1-num-1, October 2006.

Schipske, G. "The Difference Between Negligence and Malpractice," *Advance Practice Nurse* 10(5):26, May 2002.

"Spotlight on Transport/Flight Nursing," *Nursing* 32(7):78, July 2002.

Turkoski, B.B. "Home Care and Hospice Ethics: Using the Code for Nurses as a Guide," *Home Healthcare Nurse* 18(5):308–16, May 2000.

Wells, M.L., and Eaton, T.A. *Constitutional Remedies: A Reference Guide to the United States Constitution.* Westport, CT: Praeger, 2002, 84.

Twenty-four Nurse Licensure Compact (NLC) States (2014)

CHAPTER 3

Patients' rights

Kelli M. Hansen, BSN, RN, CMCN, LNC, CSA

At one time, nurses were forbidden to give patients even the most basic information about their care or health. Only physicians could answer questions about a patient's condition.

In the 1960s, attitudes changed. Patients began demanding more information about their care and turned to nurses to assist them in getting the information.

This chapter will help you apply sound legal principles when confronted with questions about patients' rights in everyday nursing practice. It begins with a discussion on the evolution of patients' rights and goes on to outline your responsibilities in ensuring informed consent, the patient's right to refuse treatment, and upholding the patient's right to privacy. You'll find summaries of major US Supreme Court rulings on the right to die and issues surrounding reproductive rights. You'll learn the legalities of disclosing confidential information, what steps to take when the patient leaves the health care facility against medical advice (AMA), and how to avoid false imprisonment charges. Finally, you'll learn how to take responsibility for upholding the patient's dignity regarding decisions about death.

Documents upholding patients' rights

The Patients' Bills of Rights and Responsibilities was issued in 1998 by the Clinton administration to promote and assure health care quality and value and protect consumers and workers in the health care system. These documents define a person's rights while receiving health care.

For years, hospitals and extended-care facilities have had their own published patients' bills of rights and those of the American Hospital Association (AHA) to inform consumers of some of their rights in the health care setting. These privately drafted bills of rights are designed to protect such basic rights as human dignity, privacy, confidentiality, and refusal of treatment. They also assert the patient's right to receive a full explanation of the cost of medical care, to be fully informed, and to be required to give consent before participating in experimental treatments because the patient exercises control over his own health care. These bills emphasize the patient's right to acquire information about *all aspects* of care provided.

Early beginnings of patients' rights

The concept of a formal document setting forth patients' rights has been around since 1959, when the National League for Nursing (NLN) issued its position paper, which outlined seven key points to help patients better understand nursing care. It was entitled "What People Can Expect of Modern Nursing Practice" and referred to the patient as a partner in health care, whose ultimate goal was self-care. Patients' rights received increasing public support during the 1960s as more people became aware of their rights as consumers. In a 1962 message to Congress, President John F. Kennedy further heightened this awareness when he outlined four basic consumer rights: the right to safety, the right to be informed, the right to choose, and the right to be heard.

The AHA, in 1973, issued its "Statement on a Patient's Bill of Rights." The statement—the result of a study the AHA had conducted with consumer groups—listed 12 patient rights, which helped form the patient rights we know today. Also in that year, Minnesota became the first state to enact a law protecting a patient's rights. That law requires all state health care facilities to post Minnesota's patients' bill of rights conspicuously and to distribute it to their patients.

Since these early milestones, all states, many advocacy groups, and health care organizations have developed their own patients' bills of rights. In 1990, the Advisory Board of Directors of the Hospice Association of America approved a bill of rights for hospice patients.

Congressional action

In 1973, Congress passed the Rehabilitation Act. This act guarantees the physically or mentally disabled person the right to any service available to a nondisabled person. In 1990, an expanded version of this act, called the Americans with Disabilities Act (ADA), was passed. The act prohibits discrimination on the basis of disability by employers with 15 or more employees, and restricts employers' medical testing of employees and job applicants. In 2010, the ADA was revised to include its American Disabilities Standards for Accessible Design of buildings. The revision provides small business owners guidance to understand how those regulations should be applied. This new update not only applies to the built environment of businesses, but also to policies and procedures of how a business should provide services and goods to its customers.

Other laws passed by Congress to protect the rights of the disabled include the Community Mental Health Amendment of 1975, the Rehabilitation Comprehensive Services and Development Disability Amendment of 1978, the Personal Responsibility and Work Opportunity Reconciliation Act of 1996, and the Individuals with Disabilities Education Act of 1997.

In 1980, Congress enacted the Mental Health Systems Act (MHSA), a comprehensive federal law on mental health services. Although much of this statute was later repealed, the MHSA Patients' Bill of Rights, recommended that states review their mental health laws in light of patients' rights, survived. Since then, several states have used the bill as a model when revising their laws concerning the rights of patients suffering from mental illness.

(Text continues on page 79.)

Landmarks in the evolution of patients' rights

A spirit of paternalism dominated health care until the 1970s and severely limited the rights of patients. More attention is being paid to the rights of health care consumers due to the growth in consumer activism. It's interesting to note that despite the progress that has been made, nowhere in the United States is a person guaranteed an absolute right to health care.

1959: The National League for Nursing issues the first patients' bill of rights, outlining seven points to help patients understand nursing care.

1973: The American Hospital Association (AHA) draws up a patients' bill of rights, listing 12 patient "rights."

That same year, Minnesota passes a patients' bill of rights, modeled after the AHA bill, becoming the first state to establish a bill of rights as law.

1973 to 1978: Congress enacts a series of laws designed to protect the rights of the disabled. These laws include the Rehabilitation Act of 1973, the Community Mental Health Amendment of 1975, the Education for Handicapped Children Act of 1975, the Developmentally Disabled Assistance and Bill of Rights Act, and the Rehabilitation Comprehensive Services and Development Disability Amendment of 1978.

1976: The New Jersey Supreme Court rules in the *Quinlan* case, granting the parents of Karen Ann Quinlan, who was in a persistent vegetative state, permission to remove her ventilator. This is the first court case to use the constitutional right to privacy as a basis for withdrawing life support.

1980: The US government passes the Mental Health Systems Act, which includes a bill of rights for patients receiving mental health services. Although much of this statute is later repealed, several states adopt recommendations found in the act.

1990: The US Supreme Court rules in the *Cruzan* case. The parents of Nancy Cruzan requested their daughter's feeding tube be removed after she spent several years in a persistent vegetative state. The Court refuses, saying that under the Constitution, a state has the right to require clear and convincing evidence that the patient wanted life-sustaining treatment withheld. The ruling implies that when such evidence exists, the patient's desires will be respected.

1991: The Patient Self-Determination Act goes into effect. This federal law calls for hospitals, nursing homes, health maintenance organizations (HMOs), hospices, and home health care agencies that participate in Medicare and Medicaid to inform patients of their right (under state law) to draft advance directives, such as living wills, durable powers of attorney for health care, and any other document that states the patient's wishes with regard to health care should he become incapacitated. Facilities must honor the directives within the limits of existing state law.

1992: The American Hospital Association (AHA) revised the Patients' Bill of Rights. In 2003, this document evolved into "The Patient Care Partnership: Understanding Expectations, Rights, and Responsibilities."

This document is often given to patients on admission and read or explained to them.

1996: HIPAA (American Health Insurance Portability and Accountability Act) was enacted to create a set of rules for health care providers, physicians, and hospitals to follow. These regulation ensures that a patient's medical records, medical billing, and patient accounts meet certain ongoing standards in regard to documentation requirements, handling of information, and maintaining a level of privacy for the patient.

Landmarks in the evolution of patients' rights *(continued)*

1999 to 2004: The US House of Representatives and the US Senate, unable to come to bipartisan agreement, pass differing versions of a patients' bill of rights. None are enacted into law, but Congress continues working toward a national patients' bill of rights. Despite this setback, many states enacted patients' bill of rights laws.

2010 to 2014: In March 2010, The Affordable Care Act (ACA) was signed into law by President Obama. Six months after the ACA was signed, a Patients' Bill of Rights was enacted to put consumers in control of their own health care and given the ability to make informed choices about their health.

In 1987, Congress enacted the Omnibus Budget Reconciliation Act, which included provisions that imposed dozens of new requirements on extended-care facilities and home health agencies, to protect the rights of residents receiving long-term care. This law established minimum standards for the presence of registered nurses (RNs) and the training of nursing assistants. Patients were also granted the right to immediate access to relatives, and to federal and state officials who investigate complaints of abuse or neglect. Under the law, nursing homes can be fined up to $10,000 a day for violating a patient's rights.

Legal status

Patients have certain legal rights within the health care system. Some of those rights are guaranteed by federal laws that have been enacted, such as the right to get a copy of the medical records, and to keep them private. Informed consent is also an important patient right. Health care providers are required by law to provide a patient with appropriate information to make a decision regarding their health care.

HIPAA (American Health Insurance Portability and Accountability Act) was enacted in 1996 to create a set of rules for health care providers, physicians, and hospitals to follow. These regulations ensure that a patient's medical records, medical billing, and patient accounts meet certain ongoing standards in regard to documentation requirements, handling of information, and maintaining a level of privacy for the patient. As of 2014, HIPAA requirements include a clause indicating that any health care provider that electronically stores, processes, or transmits medical records, medical claims, remittances, or certifications must comply with the new regulations. This law provides a requirement that all patients be able to access their own medical records, correct errors or omissions, or be informed how their personal health information will be shared with others. A provider must now inform patients regarding privacy procedures implemented within their organization. HIPAA regulations are divided into five rules: Privacy, Security, Transactions, Identifiers, and Enforcement rules. For more information on HIPAA, visit the HIPAA

(Text continues on page 81.)

AHA patients' bill of rights

This document outlines the rights of the hospitalized patient as defined in 1992 by the American Hospital Association (AHA). Although this bill of rights had no enforcement mechanism, many hospitals have used it as a model when establishing guidelines for patient care. In 2003, this document evolved into "The Patient Care Partnership: Understanding Expectations, Rights, and Responsibilities." The plain language brochure replaces AHA's Patients' Bill of Rights and informs patients about what they should expect during their hospital stay with regard to their rights and responsibilities. The brochure is available in multiple languages. The brochure contains information in the following categories:

1. High-quality hospital care
2. A clean and safe environment
3. Involvement in your care
4. Protection of your privacy
5. Help when leaving the hospital
6. Help with your billing claims

In 2010, The Affordable Care Act (ACA) was enacted by President Obama; six months later, a new Patients' Bill of Rights was established to assist the general public consumers to be involved and in control of their own health care to make more informed decisions.

A new patients' bill of rights

Under this new Bill of Rights signed into existence, new protections for the average consumer were added. These protections include the following:

1. Ban on Discriminating against Kids with Preexisting Conditions

As of 2014, no one seeking insurance coverage can be discriminated against because of preexisting conditions, including children.

2. Ban on Insurance Companies Dropping Coverage

With this new Bill of Rights, insurance companies are now banned from dropping a consumer's coverage due to an unintentional error made on the application for coverage.

3. Ban on Insurance Companies Limiting Coverage

Prior to this enactment, consumers would often go without treatment for illnesses such as cancer because of the limited lifetime coverage that was imposed by insurance companies. They can no longer put a lifetime max coverage on insurance policies. As of 2014, insurance companies can no longer place annual dollar limits or lifetime limits on individual health insurance plans.

4. Ban on Insurance Companies Limiting Choice of Doctors

Consumers now have the right to choose their own doctor in the insurer network. Prior to this law, insurance companies could mandate the doctor that a consumer had to use.

5. Ban on Insurance Companies Restricting Emergency Room Care

Insurance companies are now banned from charging a consumer more money for an emergency service performed out of network; prior to that, consumers were charged a larger fee to use out-of-network emergency rooms when switching plans.

6. Guarantee You a Right to Appeal

Consumers now have the added benefit of being able to appeal a decision made by their insurance company with obtaining a decision from a third party.

7. Covering Young Adults on Parent's Plan

Coverage is now in effect for young adult who remain on their parent's insurance plan until their 26th birthday, unless coverage is offered at their place of work.

8. Covering Preventive Care with No Cost

When a consumer joins or purchases a new insurance plan, they will receive preventative care that is recommended with no additional out-of-pocket expenses. Services such as colonoscopies, mammograms, immunizations, prenatal, and new baby care will now be covered. This prevents insurance companies from charging co-payments, coinsurance, or deductibles.

Reprinted with permission from The American Hospital Association.

Guidelines page—see *References page.*
If a patient believes a health care facility has violated his legal rights, the
patient can report the violation to the
appropriate legal authority, usually the
state health or licensing department.
Most organizations now have HIPAA
compliance officers in charge of investigating any privacy concern violations
that need to be addressed. If a patient
is concerned that an organization may
have violated his or her privacy rights,
or if he or she disagrees with a decision the organization made regarding
access to their health information, or
in response to a request the patient
made to amend or restrict the use or
disclosure of their records, they can
now submit a written complaint to the
US Department of Health and Human
Services. If an investigation shows that
the facility violated the patient's rights,
the state will demand that the facility
modify its practices to conform to state
law; in addition to that, organizations
and facilities may now face a large fine
for such violations or possible jail time.

Bills of rights issued by health care
facilities and professional associations
aren't legally binding. However, facilities
may jeopardize federal funding, such as
Medicare and Medicaid reimbursement
or research funding, if they violate federal regulations or the standards of the
Joint Commission on Accreditation of
Healthcare Organizations.

You should regard bills of rights for
patients as professionally binding where
they exist as a facility's stated policy
in addition to those mandated by the
federal government. You are required
to uphold those rights. You're also
expected to uphold the bills of rights
published by professional organizations.
When those rights aren't upheld, you
may face legal fines, licensure issues,
and regulatory issues within the organization for which you are employed.

Interpreting patients' rights

The theory of patients' rights is clear,
but the practice is inherently full of
conflict. Questions arise of whose
duty is it to inform the patient of their
rights, potential complications from
procedures, alternative therapies, etc.
The line can often blur between the
legal obligations as a nurse and providing quality patient care as an advocate
for patients. The court system has been
very clear on the responsibilities and
duties of a nurse. Educating yourself
on those obligations and knowing
the rights that every patient has will
prevent unknowingly violating those
duties and responsibilities.

GUIDELINES FOR UPHOLDING PATIENTS' RIGHTS

The best guideline you can follow to
protect your patient's interests is to
become familiar with your employer's
stated policy on patients' rights, the
current laws implemented for protection of patient rights such as HIPAA
and the Affordable Care Act (ACA),
and any additional rights that patients
may have such as *Hospice Patients' Bill
of Rights.*

The AHA encourages you to view
your patient as a partner in the health
care process. In planning your patient's
care, recognize his or her right to participate in decisions, and their right to
refuse treatment. As an advocate for
your patient, encourage the patient
to set realistic health care goals for
themselves and teach them how those
goals can be achieved. Throughout
the decision-making process, continue
assessing the patient's understanding
of their diagnosis and aspects of their

(Text continues on page 83.)

Hospice patients' bill of rights

In 1990, the Hospice Association of America issued a bill of rights for hospice patients that remains current today.

Introduction

Patients have a right to be notified in writing of their rights and obligations before their hospice care begins. Consistent with state laws, the patient's family or guardian may exercise the patient's rights when the patient is unable to do so. Hospice organizations have an obligation to protect and promote the rights of their patients, including the following:

Dignity and respect

Patients and their hospice caregivers have the right to mutual respect and dignity. Caregivers are prohibited from accepting personal gifts and borrowing from patients, families, or primary caregivers.

Patients have the right to

■ have relationships with hospice organizations that are based on honesty and ethical standards of conduct;
■ be informed of the procedure they can follow to lodge complaints with the Hospice organization about the care that is, or fails to be, furnished and regarding a lack of respect for property (to lodge complaints with us, call _____);
■ know about the disposition of such complaints; and
■ voice their grievances without fear of discrimination or reprisal for having done so.

Decision-making
Patients have the right to

■ be notified in writing of the care that is to be furnished, the types (disciplines) of caregivers who'll furnish the care, and the frequency of the services that are proposed to be furnished;
■ participate in the planning of care, be advised of any changes in the care, and be advised that they have the right to do so;
■ refuse services and to be advised of the consequences of refusing care; and

■ request a change in caregiver without fear of reprisal or discrimination.

Privacy
Patients have the right to

■ confidentiality with regard to information about their health, social, and financial circumstances and about what takes place in the home; and
■ expect the hospice organization to release information only when required by law, consistent with internal policies of the organization, or when authorized by the client.

Financial
Patients have the right to

■ be informed of the extent to which payment may be expected from Medicare, Medicaid, or any other payer known to the hospice organization;
■ be informed of any charges that won't be covered by Medicare;
■ be informed of the charges for which the patient may be liable;
■ receive this information, orally and in writing, within 15 working days of the date the hospice organization becomes aware of any changes in charges;
■ have access, upon request, to all bills for the service the patient has received regardless of whether they are paid out-of-pocket or by another party; and
■ be informed of the hospice's ownership status and its affiliation with any entities to whom the patient is referred.

Quality of care
Patients have the right to

■ receive care of the highest quality;
■ be admitted by a hospice organization only if it's assured that all necessary palliative and supportive services will be provided that are necessary to promote the physical, psychological, social, and spiritual well-being of the dying patient. However, an organization with less-than-optimal resources may nevertheless admit the patient if a more appropriate hospice

Hospice patients' bill of rights *(continued)*

organization is not available, but only after fully informing the patient of its limitations and the lack of suitable alternative arrangements; and
■ be told what to do in case of an emergency.

The Hospice organization will assure that
■ all medically related hospice care is provided in accordance with doctors' orders and that a plan

of care developed by the patient's doctor and the hospice interdisciplinary group specifies the services to be provided and their frequency and duration; and
■ all medically related personal care is provided by an appropriately trained homemaker–home health aide who is supervised by a registered nurse.

Credit line: Reprinted with permission from the Hospice Association of America.

illness. If the patient requests additional information, first determine whether this information would be an appropriate intervention within the scope of nursing or if this request should be discussed with the physician initially. Certain information such as potential complications from a procedure and recovery time should be only discussed by the physician. Should the nurse decide to inform the patient of those potential issues without the physician first discussing them with the patient, the nurse could potentially face future litigation if the patient was misinformed by the nurse prior to signing an informed consent document. The nurse should allow the patient input into their own plan of care so that the patient's needs specific to them will be addressed as well as the rights of the patient in being aware, knowledgeable, and included in their medical cares.

Added benefits
Upholding patients' rights provides additional benefits such as opening health care to new ideas. For example, nurse-midwives and other maternity nurses have acted as advocates for

patients who challenge traditional childbirth practices. As a result, many health care facilities have introduced changes, such as
■ using birthing rooms as an alternative to traditional delivery rooms
■ using less intervention and medication during delivery
■ allowing patients to use a birthing chair or walk at will during labor
■ encouraging the company and support of a "coach"—husband, other relative, or friend—during labor and delivery
■ allowing families, including other children and grandparents, to participate in or attend the delivery.

Hospitals employ full-time patient advocates, or ombudsmen, to mediate between the patient and the hospital when a patient is dissatisfied with care. Patient advocates may help you uphold your responsibilities to your patient, but advocates don't diminish those responsibilities. The term "patient advocate" is a word that most nurses are aware of. At the core of a nurse is the intent to advocate and provide the level of care that every patient deserves. Recently, a new career path has opened for those in the medical field and surrounding disciplines, which is that of a patient advocate. A patient advocate is someone who works on behalf of the patient and their families, oftentimes, during a moment of medical situations and/or stressful decision-making processes during an illness. Patient advocates can be employed in a variety of settings from those you meet at the hospital as "nurse navigators" working with patients diagnosed with cancer, to those advocates that are considered independent and focus solely on the needs of their clients and their family's needs. Patient advocate roles vary from providing education, care coordination for a patient in the home to assisting with providing all the necessary information that a patient may need to make a decision on moving to a specific assisted living or long-term care facility. Currently, there is not a nationally recognized credential for these patient advocates; however, there are several programs throughout the United States that provide additional education and professional networking for this field of practice. Several of those organizations are currently working toward creating a nationally recognized certification for these individuals to provide a code of ethics, bylaws, and an expectation of education to be called a patient advocate. Advocates are beginning to be an essential part of the health care team to ensure that all the patient's needs are met in all aspects and to be the liaison between other providers and the patient and family. Whether you're an RN, licensed practical nurse (LPN), or licensed vocational nurse (LVN), you must respect and safeguard your patient's rights. It's the law. When these rights are violated, the patient can perceive harm, even if an unintentional

violation was made, thus resulting in further legal implications.

Informed consent

Being adequately informed about proposed treatment, procedures, surgery, alternative treatments, or research in order to properly consent is a patient's legal right. This information should also include probable results and potential complications that may occur. Without this information being provided, a patient's rights are violated with regard to informed consent with the exception of some medical emergency situations. So, it isn't surprising that the topic of informed consent appears in all current medical and nursing texts and must be evidenced in the patient's records when invasive or experimental procedures, treatment, or surgery are contemplated. Violations of those rights can be seen in court cases across the United States.

In the 1960s, physicians were primarily responsible for obtaining the patient's consent. Since then, nurses have also come to play a role in obtaining informed consent. It's a basic rule that the responsibility for obtaining a patient's informed consent rests with the person who'll carry out the procedure. This procedure may be delegated to an appropriate person under certain circumstances (for example, to another physician who'll participate in the procedure).

Informed consent basically involves the patient—or someone acting on his behalf—having enough information to know what the patient is risking should he or she decide to undergo the proposed treatment or surgery or the anticipated consequences should consent to the treatment be refused or withdrawn. Nurses may provide patients and their families with information that's within a nurse's scope of practice and knowledge base. However, a nurse can't substitute her knowledge for a physician's input. Nurses should never provide education about a procedure, potential complications, and alternative therapies if the knowledge base is not there; in addition, alternative therapies should be discussed with the providing physician first as those decisions to pursue other therapies lie with the plans of treatment recommended and carried out by the patient's physician.

Under certain circumstances, people with mental disorders may be held competent to consent. When there's a question about an individual's capacity to give consent, a legal determination may be sought from the appropriate court (for example, probate court) or an ethics committee of the facility.

The bottom line in determining capacity must be whether the person giving consent is impaired in mental capacity or judgment so as not to be fully aware of the treatment, potential complications, and outcomes before the treatment begins.

To assess a patient's capacity to consent, a nurse may need to rely on his or her instincts as well as professional judgment. If the nurse believes that the patient doesn't understand, the nurse should reassess the patient's level of knowledge and understanding of the proposed treatment. Discussion on the consent issues should include the patient, the legal guardian if applicable, or the durable power of attorney, and the physician before the treatment begins.

INFORMED CONSENT STANDARDS

Generally, informed consent can be viewed legally from two different perspectives. The first, from the physician's standpoint, is known as the majority rule, or malpractice model: what a reasonable physician would have disclosed to the patient regarding proposed treatment under normal circumstances. If a nurse has a patient sign a consent form for surgery or a procedure to be done under the direction of a physician, the consent form essentially becomes invalid without the physician explanation regarding the procedure, potential complications, and alternative options. Also, the consent form can also become invalid if the named physician is "et al.," unless there is a specific explanation provided that another physician may actually be completing the procedure. The patient has a right to refuse treatment if the identity of the physician performing the procedure is unknown, or if the patient objects to the physician delegating parts of the procedure to another physician. The physician is responsible to explain the language that is contained within a surgical or treatment procedure consent, not the nurse. Patients can sue and have sued physicians for procedures done without their informed consent. In the 1996 case of *Grabowski v. Quigley*, the Superior Court of Pennsylvania ruled that a patient can sue a physician who fails to explain to the patient what is going on and passes off this responsibility to a nurse to get the patient's signature on a confusing or ambiguous surgical consent form that the patient has difficulty understanding. In the 1999 Alabama Supreme Court case of *Wells v. Storey*, published in 2001, it was determined by the Supreme Court that nurses in hospitals where surgery is performed have no legal responsibility to see that a patient's consent is truly informed consent. Only the physician can be sued after the fact for lack of informed consent.

The second perspective, known as the minority rule, looks at disclosure of the material information that a *reasonable patient* in the situation *would deem significant to know* in making a decision to undergo the proposed treatment. Based on this court case, the Supreme Court of Alabama ruled that a patient cannot sue the hospital or its nurses if the patient did not give informed consent for surgery. All of the US states have ruled the same way on this issue. In this case, the nurse admitted the patient but was not a clinical specialist nurse in labor and delivery. The patient signed the standard consent for "Vaginal Delivery/Epidural Anesthesia" as the procedure to be performed that was already stamped on the form. The delivery was uncomplicated. After discharge several days later, the patient had to return to the emergency room due to progressive symptoms of paraplegia below the waist. The issue was traced back to a lumbar epidural abscess from the epidural procedure. The patient sued the physicians, hospital, and the nurse, claiming lack of informed consent. The courts determined she had valid grounds for the lawsuit based on not understanding potential complications, but that it only applied to the physician.

Negligent nondisclosure

One of the most dramatic court cases to consider is *Warren v. Schecter* (1997), in which the plaintiff won a $9.6 million judgment against the physician for failure to disclose the risk of osteoporosis. Dr. Schecter performed gastric surgery on Janet Warren for peptic ulcer disease and had warned the patient on the risks of bowel obstruction, dumping syndrome, and anesthetic death. The physician did not believe bone pain, osteoporosis, or osteomalacia were risks of the surgery,

so this was not discussed with the patient. The plaintiff testified at trial that if she had been warned of the risk of metabolic bone disease, she would not have consented to the surgery.

A second operation was undergone by this same patient due to the development of postoperative dumping syndrome and alkaline reflux gastritis. The surgeon again failed to advice of the potential bone disease on her consent. The plaintiff later developed severe osteoporotic fractures and filed a lawsuit under the informed consent law due to the negligent nondisclosure of information regarding those additional complications that was not presented by the physician attending to her care.

So, what should the patient be told? First, it's well accepted that a duty of reasonable disclosure of risks, incident to the medical diagnosis and treatment, is required. The patient must be given an opportunity to evaluate the options, alternatives, and risks, and then exercise his or her choice. In medical malpractice cases that involve consent issues, expert testimony is usually required to establish whether or not the information given to the patient was reasonable, understandable, presented at a time when the patient was functionally able to process the information (as opposed to being sedated or medicated), and complete enough to allow the patient to knowledgeably agree to proceed. However, not every single or remote risk or benefit must be raised or addressed. It's generally agreed that the risks and benefits that arise frequently or regularly need to be discussed with the patient or the decision-maker for the patient. Alternatively, if the health care practitioner knows that specific consequences are particularly significant to this patient, those must be discussed before true informed consent may be obtained.

Professional judgment must be exercised by all health care practitioners involved at this point.

A 1974 landmark case from Texas, *Karp v. Cooley*, is a good example of how informed consents are raised and added to other allegations in malpractice cases. Mr. Karp was offered a mechanical heart transplant when it was obvious that his medical condition was deteriorating and he was near death. Many consultants evaluated Mr. Karp. One Dr. Beasley wrote in Mr. Karp's chart that he did not recommend the procedure; he felt that the patient wasn't a suitable candidate for the surgery. Dr. Cooley, the surgeon, admitted at trial that he didn't tell Mr. Karp of Dr. Beasley's note, which was made during initial workups and was actually directed and related to Beasley's reservation about the patient's psychological or emotional acceptance of a less-than-perfect outcome.

Mrs. Karp testified to what Mr. Karp's physicians said in her presence. However, Mr. Karp also spoke with his physicians on several occasions about the proposed treatment when his wife wasn't present, and it was Mr. Karp who signed the consent form. The consent form matched the details Dr. Cooley testified to as being the basis of discussions with Mr. Karp before he signed the form.

No expert testimony was offered to indicate that what Dr. Cooley discussed with Mr. Karp was inadequate or breached Dr. Cooley's duty to obtain informed consent.

The court dismissed the informed consent issue on that basis and also raised the issue that the plaintiff, the estate of Mr. Karp, didn't present substantial evidence that there was any causal connection between their claimed lack of informed consent

and Mr. Karp's death. To address this proximate cause relationship, the court looked at Texas case law (previous cases on this issue) and noted that for a finding of proximate causation between the alleged omissions of informed consent and injury (in this case death), certain factors must be present:

- A hidden risk that should have been made known, and wasn't, must materialize.
- The hidden risk must be harmful to the patient.
- Causality exists only when disclosures of significant risks incidental to treatment would have resulted in the patient's decision against the treatment.

What the court relied upon, then, in discussing the case on the proximate cause issue was testimony that Mr. Karp was near death before the wedge excision operation to which he gave consent. There was no dispute by Mrs. Karp about the validity of that consent. After the excision, Mr. Karp was also near death. Therefore, no one testified that to a reasonable degree of medical certainty the mechanical heart caused Mr. Karp's death. Finally, no proof was offered at trial that Mr. Karp wouldn't have agreed to proceed with the mechanical-heart surgery had alleged undisclosed material risks been disclosed. On appeal, the dismissal on the informed consent issue was upheld. A request for an additional appeal hearing was denied.

Basic elements of informed consent

There are federal, state, and facility regulations and policies regarding the extent of informed consent requirements in various health care settings. In 2007, CMS regulations were revised for informed consent. (See *Selected References* for additional information.) Per regulations,

482.13(b)(2) The patient or his or her representative (as allowed under state law) has the right to make informed decisions regarding his or her care. The patient's rights include being informed of his or her health status, being involved in care planning and treatment, and being able to request or refuse treatment. This right must not be construed as a mechanism to demand the provision of treatment or services deemed medically unnecessary or inappropriate.

482.51(b)(2) A properly executed informed consent form for the operation must be in the patient's chart before surgery, except in emergencies.

482.24(c)(2)(v) Properly executed informed consent forms for procedures and treatments specified by the medical staff, or by federal or state law if applicable, to require written patient consent.

Informed consent should include the following:

❑ A description of the treatment or procedure

❑ A description of inherent risks and benefits that occur with frequency or regularity or specific consequences known by the health care practitioner to be particularly significant to this patient or his designated decision-maker

❑ An explanation of the potential for death or serious harm (such as brain damage, stroke, paralysis, or disfiguring scars) or for discomforting adverse effects during or after the treatment or procedure

❑ An explanation and description of alternative treatments or procedures

❑ The name and qualifications of the person who'll perform the treatment or procedure

❑ A discussion of the possible effects of not having the treatment or procedure

Patients must also be told that they have a right to refuse the treatment or procedures without having other care or support withdrawn and that they can withdraw consent after giving it. (See *Informed consent: A landmark ruling.*)

If you witness a patient's signature on a consent form, you attest to three things:

■ The patient voluntarily consented. In addition, an assessment indicating that the patient fully understand the consent and what they are signing should be included as part of this voluntary consent in your documentation.

■ The signature of the patient or the patient's designated decision-maker is authentic.

■ The patient appears to be competent to give consent.

However, there are many more consent and privacy issues now, particularly because of such procedures as human immunodeficiency virus (HIV) testing, drug and alcohol treatment, and sterilization. Your facility's risk manager should define your responsibilities, your employer's policies, and your state's legal requirements. Each state has specific statutes governing informed consent issues that are subject to change as tort reform evolves and as case law interprets existing statutes or legal concepts.

Informed consent under state law

Many state legislatures have passed laws supporting the standards of informed consent set by the courts. States have procedural laws on informed consent—laws that describe, for example, the tort of negligent nondisclosure. A few states have laws that are *substantive*, meaning they actually define what

COURT CASE   Informed consent: A landmark ruling

The right of informed consent didn't exist at the beginning of the century. A patient had no legal right to information about his medical treatment. If a physician performed surgery without the patient's consent, the patient could sue for *battery*–legally defined as one person touching another without consent. A patient could claim battery only if he had refused consent or wasn't asked to give it, but not if he didn't have enough information to make an appropriate decision.

Rare exceptions
Most battery lawsuits were unsuccessful because courts usually took the physician's word over the patient's. Two cases in which patients did win were *Mohr v. Williams* (1905), in which the patient consented to surgery on one ear but the physician performed it on both, and *Schloendorff v. Society of New York Hospitals* (1914), in which the patient consented to an abdominal examination but the physician performed abdominal surgery.

Establishing a patient right
The right to receive informed consent wasn't expressed legally until 1957, when the California Supreme Court introduced the theory in the case of *Salgo v. Leland Stanford, Jr., University Board of Trustees.* This case involved a patient who had acute arterial insufficiency in his legs. The physician recommended diagnostic tests but failed to describe the tests or their risks. The day after the patient underwent aortography, his legs became permanently paralyzed. The court found the physician negligent for failing to explain the potential risks of aortography.

This decision established a basic rule: A physician violates "his duty to his patient and subjects himself to liability if he withholds any facts that are necessary to form the basis of an intelligent consent by the patient to the proposed treatment."

Since this landmark ruling, a patient can sue for negligent nondisclosure if his physician fails to provide enough information to enable him to make an informed decision.

must be present for informed consent to have been established. These laws define who can give consent and for what, and what type of documentation is required. These laws define exemptions to documented consent and when consent becomes invalid. Although the physician or practitioner is primarily involved with explaining the treatment, the nurse plays an important role in documenting the patient's decision.

Exceptions to informed consent

Exceptions exist to informed consent like any established basic rule.

Exceptions to obtaining informed consent include the following: no duty to obtain informed consent, in an emergency situation, or if it's not medically feasible to get the informed consent. In a Louisiana case in 1991, a nurse performed an insertion of an in-dwelling catheter over the objections of the patient. Because this was not an emergency situation, the court argued that the nurse committed battery. This procedure was performed absent the informed consent. A Supreme Court of Massachusetts ruled in 1999 in the case of *Shine v. Vagas*, rejected the notion that in an emergency situation competent persons may be treated despite their refusal for treatment. The Court considered the emergency conditions under which consent is not required based on the doctrine of *presumed consent*: "If, and only if, the patient is unconscious or otherwise incapable of giving consent, and either time or circumstances do not permit the physician to obtain the consent of a family member, may a physician presume that the patient, if competent, would consent to life-saving medical treatment."

INABILITY TO CONSENT

Informed consent relies on an individual's capacity, or ability, to make decisions at a particular time under specific circumstances. To make medical decisions, people must possess not only the capacity to make such decisions, but also the competence to make decisions. Consider these three elements of decision-making:

- The ability to understand and communicate information relevant to the decision (if the patient speaks a foreign language, an interpreter must be obtained in order for the patient to have full understanding on the information that is being provided to them and the potential complications, as well as what they are signing). If the consent form is written in the patient's language, this is the form that should be signed. It is best to have a paid interpreter involved in the patient communication for validity purposes in case of potential legal issues that may arise in the future.
- The ability to reason and deliberate concerning the decision
- The ability to apply a set of values to the decision.

If you have reason to believe that a patient is incompetent to participate in giving consent because of medication or sedation, you have an obligation to

---

LEGAL TIP

When a patient doesn't understand

Suppose you're caring for a patient scheduled for surgery. He has talked to his physician and signed the consent form. However, the night before surgery, he doesn't seem to understand the implications of the procedure. What should you do?

As the nurse assigned to the patient, you should page the physician who's scheduled to perform the surgery and express your concern that the patient isn't properly informed. Also, if your facility provides institutionally approved guidelines or pamphlets on the procedure, you may review these with the patient before the patient talks to the physician.

---

call that to the practitioner's attention immediately. If you learn that the practitioner discussed consent issues with the patient at a time when the patient was heavily sedated or medicated, you need to bring your concerns to the attention of the practitioner. If the practitioner isn't available, discuss your concerns with your supervisor. Document attempts to reach the practitioner and attending physician in the medical record before allowing the patient to proceed with the surgery or invasive procedure.

Along with discussing the matter with the practitioner and the supervisor, you must assess the patient's understanding of the information provided by the practitioner. Nurses are trained to make professional assessments about patient understanding, and this is the proper time and place to use those professional skills, without, of course, interfering with the practitioner-patient relationship in the process.

The nurse needs to understand that his or her role with informed consent is limited to acting as a patient advocate and witnessing the patient's signature. The main focus of the nurse should be that the patient is giving consent voluntarily and not under duress, that the patient appears lucid and competent to give the consent for a procedure, and that the patient's signature is authentic. If any of these three are not felt to be met, then the nurse should not witness the signature. The nurse should then document the concerns in the patient's documented medical record and notify their immediate supervisor that the informed consent may be inadequate for the procedure to be performed. The nurse and/or supervisor should then inform the primary provider of the concerns over informed consent before a procedure should take place.

However, if you do nothing, and the patient undergoes the procedure without giving proper consent, you might find yourself as a codefendant in a battery lawsuit. The patient's attorneys, judges, and juries will look closely at the medication records to see when, in relation to the signing of the consent form, the patient was last medicated, and the patient's response to the medication as documented in the record. You could be held jointly responsible for the patient undergoing a procedure that he didn't consent to if

■ you took part in the battery by assisting with the treatment
■ you knew it was taking place and didn't try to stop it.

If the practitioner fails to provide adequate information for consent because of the patient's medicated status, the patient may sue the practitioner for lack of informed consent due to temporary incapacitation. The courts might hold you responsible if, knowing the practitioner hasn't

provided adequate information to a patient, you fail to try to stop the procedure until proper consent can be obtained.

So, if you see that a patient is confused or medicated, you can't provide the information the patient needs, or you assess that the patient wasn't competent to provide consent when speaking with the practitioner because of medication or sedation, notify the practitioner in a timely manner. Document your observations in the patient's chart, and make sure the patient gets information from his practitioner or another appropriate source. Your actions and documentation will be key evidence in the case of a lawsuit. What's more, by briefly delaying the surgery, you just might be saving the practitioner from a battery claim, as well.

Consent discrepancies

Just how far does the nurse's duty to protect the patient's interest in informed consent cases extend? Consider the following two cases.

In a 1988 Georgia case, later settled in 1994, Charlotte Butler sought relief for chronic pain, which she believed to be caused by breast cancer treatments. Her oncologist referred her to an anesthesiologist, who was working as an independent contractor at the South Fulton Medical Center in East Point, Georgia. The anesthesiologist, Dr. Kim, used epidural steroid injections on several occasions. Because the patient failed to obtain long-term relief, he administered a neurolytic block injection. At one point, the medication was injected too close to the spinal cord, and the patient became quadriplegic.

The patient sued and settled with Dr. Kim, but the patient also pursued litigation against South Fulton Medical Center, alleging that the nursing staff was negligent for filling out the consent form incorrectly and not noticing the error—that the procedure listed on the form was an epidural steroid injection, not a neurolytic block.

The court found in favor of the hospital (and its staff nurses) in a 6-to-3 decision, holding that the direct cause of her injury was the physician's negligence, not the nurses'. The patient's deposition testimony played a key role. She acknowledged that she didn't understand the difference between the treatments she received. Further, although she had signed consent forms for the steroid injections and for a prior neurolytic block, "*she had never read any of them.*" The court reasoned that she probably would have signed no matter what procedure had been listed. The court also held the physician solely responsible for failing to tell the patient what he was doing and what risks were involved. The dissenting judges felt the nurses had violated their duties to the patient because they violated their own policies, which required them to check that the consent form was complete and accurate and, if it wasn't, to notify the physician or administration, before the procedure was administered.

This case (*Butler v. South Fulton Medical Center* [1994]) highlights the importance of communicating with the patient. A few simple questions to the patient would have revealed that she didn't understand the complicated procedure or its risks.

In a Wisconsin case (*Mathias v. St. Catherine's Hospital* [1997]), the court held that simply notifying the physician that there was no signed consent form was enough for the nurses to fulfill their duty. In that case, a physician performed a postdelivery tubal ligation on a patient after being told by the nurses that there was no signed consent form in the patient's

chart. The physician reportedly replied, "Oh, okay," then performed the surgery. A few days after the tubal ligation had been performed, one nurse approached the patient with a consent form for the procedure and told the patient that the form was "just to close up our records." The nurse with the form then signed another nurse's name and backdated the form to the date of the procedure.

When the patient sued the physician and the hospital, claiming that the nurses should have stopped the physician from performing the surgery, the appeals court disagreed. It held that the nurses' only duty under these circumstances was to make the physician aware that there was no signed consent. The reason behind the decision apparently was that the court believed the nurses had no way of knowing the physician hadn't obtained the patient's consent and had no reason to think the absence of a signed form in the chart was anything more than a clerical error. The court wasn't swayed by the nurse's forging of another's signature, by the backdating of the form, or by the circulating nurse's testimony that she was an "advocate" for the patient.

Not all courts, however, would have reasoned as the Wisconsin Appeals Court did. Some courts would have taken the actions of the nurses in obtaining the patient's signature on the consent form several days after the procedure as evidence of "consciousness of guilt," fraud, or as a betrayal of the patient's trust. Some courts would have considered the nurse's conduct unethical, illegal, and unconscionable.

Even in cases in which the patient says he understands, this must be documented because it could save you from assault and battery charges for violating the patient's rights, should you participate in the procedure without consent being properly obtained. You also should document any teaching you do, in conjunction with answering questions the patient asks.

If special circumstances exist, such as a patient speaking a different language or being unable to read (and the form was read to the patient), they should be documented as well. If the patient can't sign his or her name, have the patient make an X on the form and note on it by whom the mark was made. Also, record the patient's verbal consent in the chart.

Incompetent patients

A patient is deemed mentally incompetent if they are unable to understand the explanations given regarding the procedure, or if the patient is unable to comprehend the results of making decisions. For minor children or those unable to make decisions for themselves, a parent or legal guardian is legally responsible for obtaining the information, making the decision, and signing the consent form. That doesn't mean that the patient who is mentally incompetent is always left out of the process. Some of those patients may still be able to understand the medical situation and procedure and make their wishes known to the legal guardian. A durable power of attorney for health care once established can choose to become legally responsible to make medical decisions on the patient's behalf. This person can often be referred to as a *proxy*, *agent*, *or surrogate*. Another option is a *court-appointed* surrogate or proxy who is someone a judge chooses to make medical decisions for the patient. If the patient is unable to appoint someone to act on their behalf for medical decisions, a family member, friend, doctor, or facility may petition the court to request the judge to appoint someone to act on

a patient's behalf. The process of how this is done varies from state to state.

However, that isn't always possible in the case of a potentially dangerous or deadly medical condition. Under those circumstances, the courts will look to the reasonableness of the actions by the health care providers, before proceeding with the treatment, in determining if there was informed consent by a proper party, or whether the informed consent requirement was properly waived.

Mental illness isn't the same as incompetence. People suffering from mental illness have been found competent to consent because they are alert and, above all, able to understand the proposed treatment, risks, benefits, and alternatives as well as the consequences of refusing the treatment. Consider a patient who has been hospitalized involuntarily but remains alert and oriented. His mental status and education enable him to understand the information presented by the practitioner, but he lacks freedom from incarceration. Should this patient be allowed to make medical decisions that will affect his life or future health? Why should a court-appointed person assume this authority? On the other hand, shouldn't the patient have the right to refuse treatment even if it might ease his mental illness (for example, electroconvulsive therapy)?

Since the late 1980s, practitioners have had to reexamine medical restraint issues that involve elderly, confused, and infirm patients. It's now well established that a confined patient, mentally or physically disabled, may be forcibly medicated only in an emergency when he may cause harm to himself or others. In such cases, documentation in the patient record regarding the actual mental status of the patient and competency to give consent is critical.

Minors

Over the past 25 years, as nurses, we've witnessed a great social and legal challenge involving the rights of minors, especially their right to seek health care. As concerns for the rights of minors regarding consent to health care have developed, all states have looked at the issue of just who can give consent for minors to receive what care and what information a minor may keep confidential in regard to that care. Certain rules have evolved.

Usually, the person giving consent for care and treatment of a minor is a parent or other designated adult. This isn't always the case, however, as you'll see here. The practitioner must disclose all relevant information to the person giving consent to ensure that the consent is informed.

States vary on the rights and limitations governing when minors can and can't consent to health care. For example, a teenage mother who is still a minor by state law must give consent before her baby can receive treatment but in general isn't permitted to determine the course of her own health care. Under federal law, adolescents can be tested and treated for HIV without parental involvement. However, parental consent is required to set an adolescent's broken arm in most cases.

Every state will allow an emancipated minor to consent to his own medical care and treatment. So far, state definitions of emancipation vary, but it's generally recognized that to be emancipated, the individual must be a minor by state definition (less than the legal age of majority in that state) and must have obtained a legal declaration of freedom from the custody, care, and control of his parents.

Most states allow teenagers to consent to treatment, even though they haven't been determined emancipated, in cases involving pregnancy and sexually transmitted diseases. Privacy issues are involved as well, so the nurse must understand the specific circumstances allowing a minor to consent and when to contact the parent or legal guardian. Your risk manager should be able to help you. Contact with a parent or legal guardian and disclosure of confidential information has resulted in lawsuits for breach of confidentiality.

Right to refuse treatment

It's generally held that parents have the right to refuse life-sustaining medical treatment for unemancipated children who lack the capacity or statutory criteria for maturity to make such decisions for themselves.

Decisions to limit, withhold, discontinue, or forgo treatment must be carefully documented and must be specific in nature. The collaborative process must occur between patient, parent (or legal guardian), and practitioner. Young children deserve to hear the general conclusions of a decision that will affect their survival, especially when the clinician believes treatment will no longer benefit the patient and should be withdrawn.

Emancipated or mature minors are presumed to have the capacity to give consent. Regarding younger children, however, it might be helpful to consider what the Tennessee State Supreme Court did in a 1987 case. It used the "Rule of Sevens." The court presumed that up to age 7 the child lacked capacity to consent. From ages 7 to 14, the presumption of incapacity can be rebutted (by evidence demonstrating that the child, in fact, possesses maturity); age 14 and older, the individual should be presumed to have capacity.

Remember that informed consent is a process, not a document. Hospitals generally address informed consent in policy and procedure manuals to ensure consistency and thorough implementation and documentation. Regarding informed consent issues, evidence is required that the consent is voluntary and that sufficient information regarding the treatment was given. This includes an explanation of alternatives, differences in effectiveness of alternatives, consequences of not having the proposed treatment, risk and benefits, impact on daily living, likelihood of success, responsible practitioners, and any possible conflicts of interest. In addition, this information must be presented in a manner that the patient understands, including appropriate language, reading level, cognitive ability, and ethnic orientation. Lastly, the appropriate documentation must be completed properly.

EVIDENCE OF CONSENT

Nurses need to be aware that there is a difference between informed consent and an informed consent document. The process of informed consent includes the previous discussions on the physician informing the patient or legal guardian of the treatment or proposed procedure and potential complications. Oftentimes, these discussions also include alternative options for treatment for consideration. The nurse has the responsibility to obtain the written informed consent that can be demonstrated by a signed, witnessed document; a note in the medical record detailing communications between the physician and patient; or the patient willfully undergoing the procedure by appearing at the appointed time and place. Some states (such as Georgia) have statutes stating that a signed consent form disclosing the treatment in general terms is deemed conclusive proof of a valid consent. Of course, the validity of the signature may be challenged. However, if the patient is legally competent to sign the form and does so, he waives the right to a later claim that he didn't. He also waives the right to a later claim that he didn't understand the medical treatment or that the physician didn't explain to him information in the consent form.

Other states take the position that a signed consent form is evidence of informed consent, but that may be refutable if the patient offers sufficient evidence to the contrary. The patient may challenge his consent by arguing the substance of the consent form. He may claim the practitioner didn't explain the medical terms in a manner that a patient could understand or (given the medical diagnosis, the patient's condition or the surgery contemplated) that relevant information significant to the patient wasn't provided.

A signed consent form may not be required in your state; most states have implemented this requirement; however, check with your local state requirements. However, there must still be evidence that the patient has been provided with the required information and that he has demonstrated his consent to proceed. This may be done by a physician's notation in the progress notes indicating that the patient has been told of specific risks, benefits, and alternatives; has had an opportunity to have questions answered; and understands and agrees to the procedure. The evidence of informed consent is further enhanced if the medical record documents other family members who were present with the patient when the consent was obtained, such as "Wife present and concurs with patient's decision to proceed with the surgery."

If you work in a facility that uses investigational drugs or engages in research (RI.1.2.1.1), your policies and procedures must state that the patient or surrogate receives a clear explanation of experimental treatment. This includes the procedures to be followed (RI.1.2.1.4), a clear description of potential discomforts and risks (RI.1.2.1.2), a list of alternative treatments (RI.1.2.1.3), and a clear explanation that patients may refuse to participate in the research project without compromising their access to care and treatment (RI.1.2.1.5). The nurses' notes or progress notes must also include an entry that the health care practitioner has discussed these issues with the patient or surrogate decision-maker and that he understands and gives consent or refuses it.

EXCEPTIONS TO OBTAINING INFORMED CONSENT FIRST

Emergency treatment (to save a patient's life or to prevent loss of organ, limb, or a function) may be done without first obtaining consent in specific circumstances. If the patient is unconscious or a minor who can't give consent, emergency treatment may be performed. The presumption is that the patient would have consented had he or she been able, unless there's reason to believe otherwise. For example, to sustain the life of unconscious patients in the emergency department, intubation has been held to be appropriate even if no one is available to consent to the procedure.

Children brought to the emergency department after serious injury in school whose parents can't be located in time may be provided with emergency medical care without consent while attempts are made to locate the parents. Even though consent can be legally presumed in these cases, health care facilities may still face lawsuits. For example, if blood is given to a severely injured, unconscious person, the patient or family could still sue if such an action were against their religious convictions. Courts will uphold emergency medical treatment as long as reasonable effort was made to obtain consent and no alternative treatments were available to save life or limb. The courts won't uphold treatment in the absence of informed consent if the practitioner has had prior contact and has been told that such treatment would be refused. If the practitioner has time to locate family members or to obtain proper consent from the patient, the courts will require the practitioner to do so.

Before proceeding, a prudent nurse will make certain that medical record documentation includes the medical emergency, attempts made to obtain proper consent, and any information that has been conveyed to the patient. If the practitioner wants to provide care to the patient without consent, but you feel the care could wait, discuss this with the practitioner. If the practitioner insists on proceeding anyway, evaluate the situation. If your refusal to help would harm the patient or create an unsafe situation (a practitioner caring for a patient without assistance), you should assist. If you refuse to participate, make sure you notify your nursing supervisor. The incident should also be reported to hospital administration.

Patients may also waive their rights to additional information by appointing someone else as their medical decision-maker. Advance directives are one way

Right to consent: from birth to adulthood

From birth, everyone has medical rights to
- confidentiality concerning medical records
- privacy during treatment
- reasonable and prudent medical care.

A person attains more medical rights as he reaches the age of majority, defined as the age when a person is considered legally responsible for his activities and becomes entitled to the legal rights held by citizens generally.

Minors

Anyone younger than the age of majority (18 or 21 depending on the state in which he lives) has the right to consent to treatment for sexually transmitted diseases, serious communicable diseases, and drug or alcohol abuse (although state law may require that the minor's parents be notified).

Mature minors

In certain instances, a physician or judge may decide that a minor is sufficiently mature—has a sufficiently developed awareness and mental capacity—to consent to medical treatment. If so, the minor has the right to make decisions about medical care.

Adults

Anyone who has reached the age of majority or who is a legally emancipated minor has the right to
- consent to or refuse medical treatment
- consent to or refuse medical treatment for his children (in most circumstances).

to have another person participate and be responsible for one's medical care and treatment. If this has been decided beforehand, proper documentation must appear in the medical record.

WHEN INFORMED CONSENT BECOMES INVALID

Informed consent can become invalid if a change in the patient's medical status alters the risks and benefits of treatment. In such situations, the practitioner must explain the new risks and benefits to make sure the patient will consent to the treatment.

THERAPEUTIC PRIVILEGE

The controversy over informed consent centers on medical and surgical treatments and procedures that are invasive, risky, experimental, or have low likelihood for a successful outcome. We've come a long way since the concept of silence, or therapeutic privilege. In that situation, the physician was allowed to withhold information from a patient at the sole discretion of the physician and the patient's family, who believed that the information would jeopardize the patient's health. In some instances, patients weren't told that they were dying or that the treatment would have no benefit. Now, therapeutic privilege is viewed narrowly because withholding significant information from patients or their designated decision-makers is frowned upon by the courts as a violation of a patient's right to self-determination, a right that the nurse is charged with protecting. (See *Right to consent: From birth to adulthood.*)

The patient who refuses treatment

Any mentally competent adult may legally refuse treatment if he or she is fully informed about their medical condition and about the likely consequences of refusing treatment. As a professional, you must respect that decision.

When your patient refuses treatment, you must understand more than patient rights and your responsibilities. (See *When a patient says no.*)

RIGHT TO REFUSE TREATMENT

Most court cases related to the right to refuse treatment have involved patients with a terminal illness, or their families, who want to discontinue life support. In one of the best known cases, Karen Ann Quinlan's parents argued that unwanted treatment violated their comatose daughter's constitutional right to privacy. *In re Quinlan* (1976), the Quinlans successfully petitioned the New Jersey Supreme Court to discontinue her life support.

In another landmark case, *Cruzan v. Director, Missouri Department of Health* (1990), the parents of Nancy Cruzan petitioned to have their comatose daughter's tube feedings discontinued. In 1990, the US Supreme Court held that the state of Missouri has the constitutional right to refuse to permit termination of life-sustaining treatment *unless "clear and convincing evidence" exists about a patient's wishes.* Because this standard wasn't met, the Court didn't allow removal of the feeding and hydration tube. Significantly, the Court implied that when

clear and convincing evidence exists, the patient's wishes will be respected.

Two months after the Supreme Court ruling, the Cruzans petitioned the local court with new evidence. A Missouri judge granted them the right to remove Nancy's feeding and hydration tube. She died shortly thereafter. Publicity about Nancy Cruzan's legal ordeal heightened the awareness of millions of Americans to the need to prepare ahead for critical medical decisions.

More and more, health care providers consider quality end-of-life care as an ethical obligation. But what does end of life mean, and how do you measure it? Some researchers have viewed decisions from the patient's perspective based on five domains, or focal points, that study participants viewed as end-of-life issues. By understanding these domains from the patient's perspective, nurses can improve the quality of end-of-life care.

■ The problem with pain and other symptoms is still of concern for some patients. Therefore, greater attention may be warranted to attitudes of nurses toward pain and symptom control and skill in delivering it. Clearer guidelines that separate appropriate pain management from euthanasia (thus alleviating the concerns of health care providers as well) are needed.

■ Many patients fear "being kept alive" after life could no longer be enjoyed and loss of "dignity in death." This indicates health care providers need to focus not only on specific treatment decisions but also on consent issues.

■ Sense of control is also critical, and some patients are adamant about controlling their end-of-life-care decisions.

■ Patients tend to focus more on psychological outcomes rather than precise treatment decisions. For example,

LEGAL TIP **When a patient says no**

A patient must give his or her consent before you can perform any treatment. If the patient refuses, take these steps:

1. Explain the risks involved in not having the treatment performed.

2. If the patient understands the risks but still refuses, notify your supervisor and the physician.

3. Record the patient's refusal in your nurses' notes.

4. Ask the patient to complete a refusal of treatment form, like the one shown below. The signed form indicates that appropriate treatment would have been given had the patient consented.

5. If the patient refuses to sign the release form, document this in your nurses' notes and write "refused to sign" on the patient's signature line. Initial it with your own initials and date it.

6. For additional protection, facility policy may require you to get the patient's spouse or closest relative to sign a refusal of treatment form. Document whether or not the spouse or relative does this in the same manner as above.

Refusal of treatment release form

I, [patient's name], refuse to allow anyone to [insert treatment].

The risks attendant to my refusal have been fully explained to me, and I fully understand the results for this treatment and that if the same isn't done, my chances for regaining my normal health are seriously reduced and that, in all probability, my refusal for such treatment or procedure will seriously affect my health or recovery.

I hereby release [name of hospital] its nurses and employees, together with all physicians in any way connected with me as a patient, from liability for respecting and following my expressed wishes and direction.

_____   _____
Witness   Patient or legal guardian

_____   _____
Date   Patient's date of birth

some patients feel their loved ones will be relieved of the burden that difficult end-of-life-care decisions entail.

■ Many patients express an overwhelming need to communicate with loved ones at this stage of their life. Dying offers important opportunities for growth, intimacy, reconciliation, and closure.

Nurses can use these domains of end-of-life care to clarify treatment goals and provide a conceptual framework for teaching the care of dying patients to others. The domains can also serve as a checklist to review the adequacy of the care being provided. Clinicians may ask themselves: Am I adequately treating pain and other symptoms? Am I inappropriately prolonging life? Am I helping patients achieve a sense of control, relieve burdens on their families, and strengthen relationships with loved ones?

ADVANCE DIRECTIVES

The Patient Self-Determination Act of 1990 ensured the rights of patients to author or execute *advance directives*—written or verbal instructions by the patient about his wishes for medical treatment in the event he or she becomes "incapacitated." The act encourages everyone to decide about the types and extent of medical care that they want to accept or refuse if they become unable to make those types of decisions due to an illness. Examples include living wills, durable powers of attorney for health care, and any document that states the patient's wishes.

A living will is a type of advanced medical directive that specifies what type of medical treatment is desired by the patient if they are incapacitated and unable to make that decision known. The living wills can be worded very specifically or very generalized. Most living wills include a patient's wishes regarding services such as antibiotics, pain relief, hydration, nutrition, ventilator use, cardiopulmonary resuscitation, and the use of blood products. The most common type of statement within living wills pertains to when a patient suffers an incurable, irreversible disease or condition, and the physician determines that the condition is terminal and that life-sustaining measures would serve to prolong death; these statements may request that type of treatment to be withheld or discontinued.

A durable power of attorney for health care is a document that specifically designates an agent to make health care decisions on behalf of the patient when he or she is no longer able to make them. This person is able to make decisions regarding all treatment, including the ability to make the final decision about discontinuing treatment.

Joint Commission on Accreditation of HealthCare Organizations (JCAHO) standard RI.1.2.4 mandates that each hospital assure patients older than age 18 the opportunity to initiate an advance directive. The hospital must also honor the directives within the limits of the law and their capabilities.

Consider the following tips for implementation:
- Information about the patient's rights and the opportunity to draft an advance directive should be initiated during the admission process and documented on the admission form.
- Regular audits of medical records should ensure that an advance directive has been completed; if not, a statement should be included that indicates the patient was told about his or her right to draft such an advance directive is included in the medical record.
- All employees of the facility must be told, during orientation and annual updates, that patients have rights to an advance directive.
- Policy and procedures must be drafted to include processes to resolve advance directive conflicts such as directing referral to the bioethics committee to assist with resolutions.

Not all advance directives are black and white and may not address all contingencies or medical situations that a patient may encounter. For example, the patient may not realize that advanced life support may only be necessary for a brief time to help him or her regain sufficient strength or to support breathing during surgery.

Although the health care proxy (that is, one authorized to act for another) is supposed to be the ultimate decision-maker, the physician has a legitimate role in the decision-making process and may refuse to comply with any decision that is believed is contrary to the patient's wishes or best interests. If that happens, the proxy may ask that the patient be transferred to a physician who will honor the patient's or the proxy's requests. Alternatively, the proxy may request the ethics committee of the hospital to mediate. As a last resort, the proxy may seek a court order to stop the unwanted care or treatment.

FREEDOM OF RELIGION

Jehovah's Witnesses may refuse treatment on the grounds of freedom of religion. Members from this denomination oppose blood transfusions, based on their interpretation of a biblical passage that forbids "drinking" blood. Some sect members believe that even a lifesaving transfusion given against their will deprives them of everlasting life. The courts usually uphold their right to refuse treatment because of the constitutionally protected right to religious freedom. In the case of *Harvey vs. Strickland* (2002), the court respected a Jehovah's Witness' right to refuse consent. The Jehovah's Witness patient explicitly rejected blood transfusions during surgery. While in surgery, the need for blood arose. The patient was unconscious due to being in surgery, so the surgeon sought the consent of the patient's mother. Consent was obtained based on the physician's claim that it was an emergency. The court disagreed with that claim based on the well-known knowledge that the patient did not want the blood transfusions and made it very clear before going into surgery.

Most other religious freedom court cases involve Christian Scientists, who oppose many medical interventions, including medicines in favour of

relying on prayer to treat illnesses. The First Amendment guarantees freedom of religion, so that anybody able to give their own consent may refuse medical treatment. However, when parents make those decisions on behalf of their children, it raises questions as to whether or not this is still a protected freedom under the constitution. Typically refusing medical care for a child would be considered neglect, but many states have created exemptions under the law based on religious grounds. However, if the condition is considered life-threatening, a physician must be consulted. Parents can still be found criminally liable if their child dies of a medically treatable condition.

Besides court rulings, most patients' bills of rights support the right to refuse treatment, starting with the bill of rights adopted by the AHA.

When a Jehovah's Witness refuses blood because of religious beliefs, health care professionals are challenged to provide optimal care without using standard medical treatment. Health care, legal, ethical, and management issues of how to treat blood loss when it occurs must be carefully considered. For example, some strategies are currently available that minimize blood loss during cardiac surgeries, as well as methods to increase endogenous production. With more than 7.9 million Jehovah's Witnesses worldwide and about 1.2 million in the United States, more health care providers are facing situations in which blood transfusion isn't a treatment option.

Using a cardiac-surgery example, some suggested blood-conserving strategies as effective treatments include the following:

■ Preoperative adequacy of hemoglobin levels, administration of erythropoietin, and use of iron and folic acid supplements

■ Intraoperative hemodilution to decrease blood viscosity and to improve systemic and pulmonary circulation, preservation of clotting factors and platelets to reduce the likelihood of postoperative bleeding, hypothermia to reduce tissue oxygen requirements, administering desmopressin to control bleeding in the presence of platelet defects and in patients with decreased level of factor VIII, and aprotinin to reduce blood loss by inhibiting fibrinolysis and the turnover of coagulation factors
■ Postoperative use of protamine sulfate to bind with heparin and to neutralize the anticoagulant effect; use of aminocaproic acid to enhance fibrinogen activity and clot formation; erythropoietin, iron, and folic acid to accelerate erythropoiesis; and the use of blood reservoir devices and the smaller collection tubes for blood sampling in children, to minimize the volume of blood lost with phlebotomy and to preserve the hemoglobin level

The use of blood-conserving techniques during surgery has been validated by several investigations and allows patients to adhere to their religious beliefs while resolving the dilemmas associated with the unacceptability of standard, accepted treatments. Of course, physicians would have the ethical and legal rights to refuse to care for any patient in a nonemergency situation when standard medical care isn't acceptable to the patient. Court orders can also be obtained, requiring the patient to undergo the standard treatment against the patient's wishes. Health care providers could also honor the patient's request under all circumstances. By looking at the available alternatives and trying to honor the patient's wishes, nurses may be able to comply with the Code of Nurses of the American Nurses Association (ANA), which specifies that nurses are obligated to support and protect each patient's right of self-determination, to respect the patient's individuality, to adhere to standards of care, and to maintain the patient's safety.

RIGHT TO DIE

Most states have enacted right-to-die laws (also called *natural death laws, Death with Dignity Acts,* or *living will acts*). These laws recognize the patient's right to choose death by refusing extraordinary treatment when he or she has no hope of recovery. These legal principles outline the patient's right to refuse life supports.

Whenever a competent patient expresses wishes concerning extraordinary treatment, health care providers should attempt to follow them. If the patient is incompetent or unconscious, the decision becomes more difficult.

In some cases, the next of kin may express the patient's desires on their behalf, but whether this is an honest interpretation of the patient's wishes is sometimes uncertain.

Written evidence of the patient's wishes provides the best indication of what treatment would be consented to if the patient was still able to communicate. This information may be provided through the following:
■ A living will—This is an advance directive document that specifies a person's wishes with regard to medical care if they should become unable to communicate. (See *Living will.*) In some states, living wills don't address the issue of discontinuing artificial nutrition and hydration.
■ A durable power of attorney for health care—In this document, the patient designates a person who will make medical decisions on their behalf

if they are incapacitated and unable to do so. This differs from the usual power of attorney, which requires the patient's ongoing consent and deals only with financial issues. (See *Durable power of attorney for health care*.)

Most states recognize living wills as legally valid and have laws authorizing durable powers of attorney for initiating or terminating life-sustaining medical treatment.

REQUIREMENTS OF THE SELF-DETERMINATION ACT

The Patient Self-Determination Act of 1990 requires that health care facilities ask whether the patient has completed an advance directive. This law includes the following requirements:

■ Each patient must be given written information about his or her rights under state law to make decisions concerning medical care, including the right to accept or refuse medical or surgical treatment and to formulate advance directives.

■ The patient's decision whether to execute an advance directive must be documented in the medical record.

■ The facility must ensure that the patient's decision about the execution of an advance directive doesn't influence the provision of care. Furthermore, health care providers can't discriminate against a patient in any way based on his decision.

■ The health care facility must provide education to the staff and community on issues concerning advance directives.

CHALLENGING THE PATIENT'S RIGHT TO REFUSE TREATMENT

There are two grounds for challenging a patient's right to refuse treatment: You can claim that the patient is

incompetent, or you can claim that compelling reasons exist to overrule his or her wishes. (See *Overruling the patient*.)

The courts consider a patient incompetent when he or she lacks the mental ability to make a reasonable decision such as when a patient experiences delirium.

Compelling circumstances

The courts also recognize several compelling circumstances that justify overruling a patient's refusal of treatment. These include the following:

■ When refusing treatment endangers the life of another—for example, a court may overrule a pregnant woman's objection to treatment if it endangers her unborn child's life.

■ When a parent's decision to withhold treatment threatens a child's life—for example, a court may overrule the parents' religious objections to their child's treatment when the child's life is endangered. When the child's life isn't in danger, the courts are more likely to respect the parents' religious convictions.

■ When, despite refusing treatment, the patient makes statements indicating that he or she wants to live—for example, some Jehovah's Witnesses who oppose blood transfusions say or imply that they won't prevent the transfusions if a court takes responsibility for the decision. In *Powell v. Columbia-Presbyterian Medical Center* (1965), the court authorized transfusions when a Jehovah's Witness indicated that she wouldn't object to receiving blood, although she refused to give written consent. In the 1996 Connecticut case of *Stamford Hospital v. Vega*, the court upheld the right of the Jehovah's Witness patient to have the right to refuse treatment. The patient

(Text continues on page 105.)

Living will

The living will is an advance care document that specifies a person's wishes with regard to medical care, should he or she become terminally ill, incompetent, or unable to communicate. The will is commonly used in combination with the patient's durable power of attorney.

All states and the District of Columbia have living will laws that outline the documentation requirements for living wills. The sample document below is from Ohio.

Living will

If my attending doctor and one other doctor who examines me determine, to a reasonable degree of medical certainty and in accordance with reasonable medical standards, that I am in a terminal condition or in a permanently unconscious state, and if my attending doctor determines that at that time I no longer am able to make informed decisions regarding the administration of life-sustaining treatment, and that, to a reasonable degree of medical certainty and in accordance with reasonable medical standards, there is no reasonable possibility that I will regain the capacity to make informed decisions regarding the administration of life-sustaining treatment, then I direct my attending doctor to withhold or withdraw medical procedures, treatment, interventions, or other measures that serve principally to prolong the process of my dying, rather than diminish my pain or discomfort.

I have used the term "terminal condition" in this declaration to mean an irreversible, incurable, and untreatable condition caused by disease, illness, or injury from which, to a reasonable degree of medical certainty as determined in accordance with reasonable medical standards of my attending doctor and one other doctor who has examined me, both of the following apply:

1. There can be no recovery.

2. Death is likely to occur within a relatively short time if life-sustaining treatment is not administered.

I have used the term "permanently unconscious state" in this declaration to mean a state of permanent unconsciousness that, to a reasonable degree of medical certainty, is determined in accordance with reasonable medical standards by my attending doctor and one other doctor who has examined me, as characterized by both of the following:

1. I am irreversibly unaware of myself and my environment.

2. There is a total loss of cerebral cortical functioning, resulting in my having no capacity to experience pain or suffering.

Nutrition and hydration

I hereby authorize my attending doctor to withhold or withdraw nutrition and hydration from me when I am in a permanent unconscious state if my attending doctor and at least one other doctor who has examined me determine, to a reasonable degree of medical certainty and in accordance with reasonable medical standards, that nutrition or hydration will not or no longer will serve to provide comfort to me or alleviate my pain.

_____

[Sign here for withdrawal of nutrition or hydration]

(continued)

Living will *(continued)*

I hereby designate [print name of person to decide] as the person who I wish my attending doctor to notify at any time that life-sustaining treatment is to be withdrawn or withheld pursuant to this declaration.

_____   _____

[Sign your name here]   [Today's date]

Witness by:

[Living will person's name] voluntarily signed or directed another individual to sign this living will in the presence of the following who each attests that the declarant appears to be of sound mind and not under or subject to duress, fraud, or undue influence.

_____

[First witness signs here]

_____

[Second witness signs here]

refused a blood transfusion that was necessary due to heavy bleeding following a vaginal delivery. The patient's husband maintained that his wife would not want the treatment due to religious beliefs, even if to save her life. The hospital asked for an emergency hearing; the judge ruled that the hospital could proceed to give the blood transfusion. The patient recovered and was in good health. The patient, her spouse, and the parent organization of Jehovah's Witnesses asked the court to review this case and make a precedent for the future, no civil claim was made. The Supreme Court of Connecticut ruled that it came down in favor of the patient's right to medical self-determination, even when the patient's refusal of a relatively safe and effective intervention could lead to a patient's demise. The Court ruled that a health care facility does not have the right to substitute its judgment for that of the patient being treated. The Court did state that it would honor the right of a health care facility to be able to go to Court to seek guidance before going ahead and making a decision in such a life-and-death situation.

■ When the public interest outweighs the patient's right—for example, the law requires school-age children (with few exceptions) to receive a polio vaccine before they can attend classes.

RESPONDING TO THE PATIENT'S REQUEST TO STOP TREATMENT

When a patient plans to refuse treatment, you may be the person told first. Whether he or she tells you they're going to refuse treatment or the patient simply refuses to give consent, stop preparations for any treatment at once. Immediately notify the physician and report your patient's decision to

(Text continues on page 108.)

Durable power of attorney for health care

The sample document below is an example of a durable power of attorney, which allows a competent patient to delegate to another person the authority to consent to or refuse health care treatment. This helps the patient ensure that their wishes will be carried out if he or she should become incompetent.

Each state with a durable power of attorney for health care law has specific requirements for executing the document. The sample form below is from Nebraska.

Power of attorney for health care

I appoint _____

whose address is _____

and whose telephone number is _____

as my attorney in fact for health care. _____

I appoint _____

whose address is _____

and whose telephone number is _____

as my successor attorney in fact for health care. _____

   I authorize my attorney in fact appointed by this document to make health care decisions for me when I am determined to be incapable of making my own health care decisions. I have read the warning that accompanies this document and understood the consequences of executing a power of attorney for health care.

   I direct that my attorney in fact comply with the following instructions or limitations (optional):

   I direct that my attorney in fact comply with the following instructions on life-sustaining treatment (optional):

   I direct that my attorney in fact comply with the following instructions on artificially administered nutrition and hydration (optional):

   I have read this power of attorney for health care. I understand that it allows another person to make life-and-death decisions for me if I am incapable of making such decisions. I also understand that I can revoke this power of attorney for health care at any time by notifying my attorney in fact, my physician, or the facility in which I am a patient or resident. I also understand that I can require in this power of attorney for health care that the fact of my incapacity in the future be confirmed by a second physician.

_____   _____
[Signature of person making designation]   [Date]

Overruling the patient

Even when a patient's decision to refuse treatment rests on constitutionally protected grounds, such as religious beliefs, the court will intervene in certain circumstances. Becoming familiar with court rulings in this area will help you better cope if you're ever caught between a patient, family, and the court. Here are some delicate legal situations the courts have ruled on. Keep in mind that each case is binding only in its own jurisdiction. A court where you practice may hold differently.

Incapacitated patient

If an adult patient becomes physically or mentally incapacitated, a relative can't always refuse treatment for him. The court reserves the right to overrule even a spouse on the patient's behalf if the decision seems to be medically unreasonable. For example, a well-known case in Florida involving Terri Schiavo's spouse made news headlines beginning in 2000. Terri Schiavo had been determined by the Florida circuit court to be in a persistent vegetative state and at the request of her spouse, Michael Schiavo, her feeding tube was to be removed in April 2001, but was later reinserted 2 days later on appeal of her parents. The courts of Florida went back and forth with appeals and legislature review. The final decision was made on February 25, 2005, when the Judge ordered Schiavo's feeding tube be removed in March of 2005. Because of this case, court systems have continued the debate about the removal of artificially provided nutrition and hydration in a patient in a persistent vegetative state that did not have an advance directive in place indicating a patient's wishes. Because of this case, the awareness to the need for advance directives was spread throughout the United States.

Patient responsible for child

If a patient who's responsible for the care of a child refuses lifesaving treatment, the court may reverse the patient's decision. In *Application* of the President and Directors of Georgetown College, Inc. (1964), the New York Supreme Court ordered a blood transfusion for a Jehovah's Witness who was the mother of an infant and who refused to give consent for her own transfusion.

Pregnant patient

If a patient who's pregnant refuses treatment, thereby threatening not only her own health but also that of her unborn child, the courts can reverse the patient's decision. In *Jefferson v. Griffin Spalding County Hospital Authority* (1981), the court awarded temporary custody of an unborn child to a state agency. The mother had a complete placenta previa but had refused to consent to a cesarean birth. The court's custody award included full authority to give consent for a surgical delivery. There is also a controversial case currently in the state of Texas. Marlise Munoz was determined to be brain-dead after collapsing on her kitchen floor in November of 2013 due to an apparent blood clot in her lungs. As her parents and her spouse prepared to say goodbye, the hospital informed them that they were not going to comply with their wishes as she was 14 weeks pregnant. As of January 2014, she continued to remain on life support. More than 31 states have adopted laws restricting the ability of doctors to end life support for terminally ill pregnant women, regardless of the wishes of the patient or the family. Texas is among 12 of those states with the most restrictive laws, which require that life-support measures continue no matter how far along the pregnancy is.

Patient who's a minor

If a patient is a minor, the court will allow the parents or legal guardian to consent to medical treatment, but it will not allow them to deny him lifesaving treatment. Many court systems will allow a state child protection agency to make medical decision for a child if the medical

Overruling the patient *(continued)*

community is in agreement about the appropriate course of treatment for the child, if the child would die without such treatment, if the parent is refusing to consent to treatment, or if the expected outcome of the treatment would allow the child to live a relatively normal life with a reasonably good quality of life. Parents or legal guardians who deny such treatment to a child may face loss of custody in that state due to neglect, or the child may be placed in state custody for their own protection. The parent/legal guardian may also face criminal charges for failing to obtain medical treatment for the child.

your supervisor. Never delay informing your supervisor, especially if a delay could be life-threatening. Any delay you're responsible for will greatly increase your legal risks.

The physician and hospital have the responsibility to take action, such as trying to convince the patient to accept treatment or asking him or her to sign a release form. This form relieves the hospital and the health care team of liability for any consequences the patient suffers by refusing treatment. It doesn't, however, release the health care team from its obligation to continue providing other forms of care. For complex cases, the hospital may seek to obtain direction from the legal court system within that jurisdiction.

Don't ignore the patient

Never ignore a patient's request to refuse treatment. A patient can sue you for battery—intentionally touching another person without authorization to do so—for simply following physician's orders. (See *Is this nurse liable?*)

To overrule the patient's decision, the physician or your hospital must obtain a court order. Only then are you legally authorized to administer the treatment. No matter how serious the patient's condition, refusing treatment doesn't constitute evidence of incompetence.

If the physician or hospital tries to convince the court to overrule the patient on the grounds of incompetency, they'll need proof that the patient lacks the mental ability to make a reasonable decision. Your documented observations about your patient's mental status may be used as evidence. In the 1991 Louisiana case of *Roberson v. Provident House*, a nurse inserted an in-dwelling catheter over the objections of a patient. Because this was not an emergency situation, the court argued that the nurse committed battery. The procedure was performed absent informed consent. If a patient refuses treatment, as a nurse you need to document this refusal and notify your supervisor and the ordering physician. Ignoring your patient's wishes could result in you being a defendant in a lawsuit against you and the organization that you represent.

RIGHT TO REFUSE EMERGENCY TREATMENT

A competent adult has the right to refuse emergency treatment. His or her family can't overrule the patient's decision. The physician may not administer the expressly refused treatment, even if the patient becomes unconscious.

If there are no grounds for overruling your patient's decision, you have an ethical duty to defend the patient's rights to refuse treatment in the face of all opposition, including family's. Try to explain the patient's choice to family members. Emphasize that the decision is a personal patient choice as long as they are determined to be competent.

Respecting the patient's autonomy

A patient may refuse any treatment—whether ordinary or extraordinary. However, the decision to refuse ordinary treatment presents an especially complex ethical dilemma. This dilemma hinges on the conflict between beneficence and autonomy. If a patient can make an informed decision, the right to refuse treatment is included. But what if the patient's decision doesn't serve their best interests? Which moral principle, autonomy or beneficence, should take precedence? (See *Saying "no" to rehabilitation*.)

AUTONOMY AND ITS LIMITS

One of the cornerstones of ethical decision-making, autonomy refers to the right to make decisions about one's health care. However, external and internal pressures can limit the patient's autonomy.

External pressures

Family members and health professionals can exert appreciable influence over the patient. Typically, this influence takes the form of persuasion or encouragement. Infrequently, it takes the form of coercion, in which the patient comes to believe they have no free choice.

Physician-patient relationships are inherently imbalanced. The physician

Is this nurse liable?

In the course of providing daily care, you may easily overlook the potential legal consequences of ignoring a patient who refuses treatment. Consider the fictional case below.

A battle of wills

Albert Proxmire, age 69, is hospitalized with a GI disorder. He's also depressed and uncooperative. His day-shift nurse, Bernice Bransted, reads on his chart that the physician ordered an enema.

Disgruntled and surly, Mr. Proxmire has other ideas. He bluntly tells the nurse, "Leave me alone. I'm not getting an enema now!"

Despite his protests, Ms. Bransted insists. She gently turns him in his bed and administers the enema.

Later, Mr. Proxmire's son becomes angry when his father tells him what happened. The son confronts the nursing supervisor and warns her that he intends to pursue the matter.

A battle in the courts?

Does Mr. Proxmire have a case for battery against the nurse? Yes. As a conscious, coherent adult, even though depressed, Mr. Proxmire has the right to refuse treatment. After he–or any other adult patient–refuses any nursing treatment, giving it will make the nurse liable for battery.

possesses knowledge and skill; the patient, a need for care. Because the patient has a need, he or she assumes a dependent and potentially vulnerable position. The patient must trust the caregiver. In doing so, he or she may think that assertiveness is inappropriate. You, however, can counteract this thinking by encouraging the patient to be informed and to ask questions.

Internal pressures

Doubt and illness itself can sap autonomy. For instance, the patient may see themselves as too ignorant to make crucial decisions about their own health. Encourage the patient to take an active role in decision-making, and support their efforts. Dyspnea, pain, and other symptoms may be distracting the patient from making important decisions. If they do, implement interventions to try to relieve them so that the patient can make thoughtful decisions.

BENEFICENCE

When dealing with children or patients who can't make informed decisions, beneficence outweighs autonomy. Young children, for instance, don't understand the implications of not being vaccinated for measles or mumps and would simply prefer to avoid the pain of an injection.

For patients who can make an informed decision, though, the burden of proof for beneficence lies with the health care provider. Typically, a health care provider can advance these arguments in support of beneficence:

■ The patient is under excessive stress and can't think rationally.

■ The patient may change his or her mind later, when little or nothing can be done to restore the patient's previous health status.

■ The patient needs to be protected from acting irrationally.

Underlying all of these arguments is a spirit of paternalism, of possessing superior or clearer knowledge than the patient. Of course, the patient could and might change decisions made, but this uncertainty doesn't constitute grounds for overruling a competent patient's decision.

FUTILITY

Medical futility refers to treatment that can't benefit a patient, not necessarily because the treatment itself has no merit but more commonly because the condition of the patient makes the medical action futile. A futile intervention differs from one that's harmful, ineffective, or impossible, and it shouldn't be equated with hopelessness. Hope may be maintained by patients even in impossible situations.

A futile treatment differs from an ineffective or a highly improbable treatment in that it may achieve a short-term gain (such as improving carbon dioxide excretion in a ventilated patient who has chronic obstructive pulmonary disease), but it remains futile because it doesn't lead to a true personal benefit (restoration of health).

Often, health care teams don't render care they deem futile, but with the growing importance of patient autonomy and self-determination, such choices aren't so readily made. Patients believe that they have a right to determine what constitutes a "benefit" to them. At the same time, nurses and physicians should be able to decide when a treatment is futile based on their knowledge of the treatment and its probable effect on the patient's quality of life. The patient's right to

(Text continues on page 112.)

Saying "no" to rehabilitation

One reward of rehabilitation nursing is watching a patient with severe injuries come to terms with an altered body image and eventually go on to live a fulfilling life with a disability. But what happens when a patient turns down the help that nurses and therapists offer? Nurses may experience a bitter ethical conflict between the principle of patient autonomy–which includes the right to refuse treatment–and the principle of beneficence. Consider the case of Philip Munson, a young quadriplegic who refused rehabilitative treatment, deciding that he preferred to die.

Wanting to die

Mr. Munson, age 30, was left a C3 quadriplegic after he broke his neck in an automobile accident. First admitted to the intensive care unit (ICU), Mr. Munson was totally dependent on others for all activities and all aspects of his care. His only relatives were a brother and a sister-in-law, who visited regularly and planned to have him live with them after rehabilitation.

During his month in the ICU, Philip told the nurses that he wanted to live. Shortly after being transferred to the rehabilitation unit, however, he changed his mind. He wanted to die and insisted on discontinuing his rehabilitation program. His brother made it clear that he wanted Mr. Munson's wishes respected. A psychiatrist evaluated Mr. Munson and concluded that he was competent and showed no evidence of psychosis or thought disorder.

Mr. Munson understood his condition and his prognosis; he was aware that after rehabilitation he would be able to operate a wheelchair and a computer. He also understood that he would be paralyzed from the neck down and would always need assistance with activities of daily living. Mr. Munson said that he wasn't afraid of death and wanted no heroic measures taken. His brother helped him draft an extensive legal statement establishing the right to refuse specific

treatments, including antibiotic and IV therapy. Plans were made to discharge him to a nursing home.

Ethical considerations

Many of the nurses and therapists on the rehabilitation unit were distressed by the decision to stop Mr. Munson's program. Depression, anger, and refusal of treatment are common among young accident victims, and these health care professionals were skilled at encouraging, bargaining with, and even coercing patients to comply. They argued that Mr. Munson's decision was misguided and that there was justification for intervention based on the principles of paternalism and beneficence.

Jim DiFrancesco, RN, a nurse on the rehabilitation team, pointed out that there was a significant difference between a young, recently injured quadriplegic and a terminal cancer patient who finally decides to "pull the plug." He believed that Mr. Munson was under too much stress from the initial impact of the injury and would probably later change his mind and view life as worth living once again. He pointed out to members of the health care team that there are many examples of patients reversing their decision to die. Elizabeth Bouvia, a young woman incapacitated by cerebral palsy, received national publicity when she requested that the hospital discontinue her tube feedings and allow her to starve herself to death, but she later changed her mind and stated that she wanted to live.

Mr. DiFrancesco pointed out that many factors, such as depression, fear of treatment, hidden family dynamics, and ambivalence, complicated Mr. Munson's ability to make an autonomous decision. Furthermore, Mr. Munson was clearly ambivalent about his desire to die. His behavior wasn't always consistent with his expressed wish for death. For example, Mr. Munson was cheerful on many days and took

(continued)

great interest in the positioning of his joints and measures taken to prevent joint contractures.

In fact, for a brief period, Mr. Munson backed out on his wish to die. His best friend from high school learned about the accident and decided to devote a long visit to helping Philip. When he learned his friend would be arriving soon, Mr. Munson asked to start full therapy again. Although his high school buddy helped out tirelessly and offered to stay even longer, Mr. Munson quickly became overwhelmed by the pain and hardship of his existence and requested that his previous statement outlining his wish to die be reactivated.

Respecting patient autonomy

Another nurse on the unit, Christina Walsh, RN, pointed out that the rehabilitation unit's mission was to serve the patient's best interest, not meet the emotional needs of the staff. She believed that members of the health care team had their own vested interest in keeping Mr. Munson alive. For example, the occupational therapist was excited about experimenting with the latest wheelchair control devices. Many of her coworkers, accustomed to seeing their patients readjust to life, couldn't accept that they would inevitably fail some of their patients. It wasn't right, asserted Ms. Walsh, to pursue every

technological intervention regardless of the cost or burden to the patient.

An ethical struggle

During the time Mr. Munson remained on the rehabilitation unit, the nurses who cared for him experienced an intense ethical struggle. It was difficult to agree not to perform routine tracheostomy care or range-of-motion exercises or to care for the pressure ulcer that developed on the back of Mr. Munson's head. It also was difficult, however, to do these things in good conscience for a patient who asked that they not be done. It seemed like a total usurpation of what little power and control Mr. Munson still had. Each nurse had to struggle with questions about the rights of a patient who doesn't have the ability to leave the hospital against medical advice, protest his treatment, or even complain without the assistance of another person.

Mr. Munson's ordeal finally came to an end when he was transported to a nursing home near the residence of his brother's family. After 2 months, he slipped into a coma and died. His existence was a lesson to the rehabilitation team: Most patients are grateful for the opportunity for a second chance at life; for some, however, the pain is too great. Ultimately, the decision to accept treatment belongs to the patient.

choose is limited by the nurses and physicians whose duty it is to provide quality care and practice medicine responsibly.

Ethicists argue that patient self-determination offers a right to refuse treatment or to choose from medically justifiable options. It isn't, they argue, a right to demand treatment. Furthermore, with growing emphasis on cost containment, it's probable that futile treatment won't even be a patient

option in the future. Treatment options may become a function of statistical measurement of probable benefits to a patient.

Helga Wanglie represents a classic case in futility. This 85-year-old woman was unconscious and ventilated at a hospital after suffering a heart attack at the nursing home where she resided. The physicians wanted to withdraw the life-sustaining support they deemed to be futile, but her husband objected and had her transferred to another medical center, where she was diagnosed as being in a persistent vegetative state. The physician at the second facility concurred and suggested that the ventilator be removed.

The family ultimately asked the courts to decide if the physicians should be compelled to provide treatment they believed to be nonbeneficial and inappropriate. The courts appointed the husband conservator and decided in his favor. The judge's decision wasn't based on medical values and principles but, rather, on the fact that the husband was the proper surrogate and the surrogate's decisions about the patient's wishes were reliable.

Society's values of freedom to choose and autonomy held precedence over the physicians' professional judgment of futility. "Self-benefit," as determined by a patient or their decision-maker, is subjective and can be decidedly different from the medical view of benefit, which consists of restoration of health, cure, pain relief, improved well-being, and quality of life.

Confidentiality and the right to privacy

The American Nurses Association (ANA) Code of Ethics for Nurses states that you must safeguard "the patient's right to privacy. The need for health care does not justify unwanted intrusion into the patient's life. The nurse advocates for an environment that provides for sufficient physical privacy, including auditory privacy for discussions of a personal nature and policies and practices that protect the confidentiality of information." "Maintaining confidentiality is essential to preserving the trust necessary to provide effective nursing care. A patient must often reveal sensitive or embarrassing information during an assessment if an accurate diagnosis is to be made. The patient must have confidence that this information will be shared in a professional manner only with those who require it for his care. (See *Right to privacy*.). The rights, well-being, and safety of the individual patient should remain the priority and the primary factor in making decisions and utilizing professional judgment concerning the disposition of confidential information received from or about the patient, whether the information is written, electronic, or oral.

UNDERLYING PRINCIPLES

Underlying confidentiality are two key ethical principles: autonomy and fidelity. *Autonomy* includes the patient's right to maintain control over their own life; this extends to the right to maintain control over personal information. *Fidelity* refers to one's faithfulness to agreements that one has accepted. The temptation to gossip is strong. To maintain confidentiality, the nurse's ethical belief in the patient's right to maintain autonomy must outweigh the temptation to gossip. If a nurse pledges to keep a confidence, he or she must recognize the seriousness of this obligation. After all, it's normal to share confidential information in the course of developing a therapeutic relationship. Without fidelity and respect for confidentiality, meaningful nurse-patient relationships can't survive.

BREACHES OF CONFIDENTIALITY

Confidential information can ethically be disclosed in certain circumstances such as when failure to disclose

(Text continues on page 115.)

Right to privacy

When entering the hospital, most patients tacitly agree to sacrifice a considerable amount of privacy to enable physicians and nurses to plan and provide care. Occasionally, however, a patient refuses to cooperate. If this resistance hampers your ability to give good care, you may face an ethical dilemma, as the following case study shows.

Hidden medicine bottle

John Gordon is admitted to the hospital with chronic diarrhea. All diagnostic test results have come back normal. His physician, Marvin Stein, suspects that Mr. Gordon is causing the diarrhea by taking laxatives—a charge Mr. Gordon vehemently denies.

Mr. Gordon's nurse, Susan Morrison, is starting to think that Dr. Stein may be right. Yesterday, Mr. Gordon put a medicine bottle in his satchel as she walked into his room. When she asked him what was in the bottle, he became defensive and refused to answer.

Dr. Stein asks Ms. Morrison to "do a little detective work" by searching Mr. Gordon's room for laxatives the next time he receives visitors in the lounge. "After all," he tells her, "we can't help Mr. Gordon until we know for sure what's going on."

Ethical considerations

At first, Ms. Morrison is willing to conduct a search of Mr. Gordon's room. Later, she begins to have doubts about whether such a search would be ethical. She decides to write down her concerns.

■ Do we know Mr. Gordon is lying when he denies taking laxatives? Several possible explanations exist for his defensive behavior. Perhaps he doesn't know what a laxative is and is reluctant to reveal his ignorance. Why did he hide the medicine bottle? He might be embarrassed to admit that he's taking a home remedy. There

may be several other reasons. What appears to be a medicine bottle could contain any number of things.

■ Even if Mr. Gordon is lying, is a search justified? Can one person's unethical behavior justify another's? Dr. Stein, after all, is a medical authority, not a moral authority.

■ Even if conducting an investigation is necessary, wouldn't openly searching Mr. Gordon's room without his permission be more ethical than conducting a search behind his back?

■ What about Dr. Stein's role in this incident? Should I allow him to delegate this distasteful duty to me?

■ Even if Mr. Gordon is indeed lying and is taking laxatives, who—besides himself—is he harming? Doesn't he have the right to treat himself with an over-the-counter medication against his physician's advice?

■ How would a search affect my nurse-patient relationship with Mr. Gordon? If he thinks that I violated his trust, it will probably destroy it forever.

■ Will the search really help us to accomplish our goal—to help Mr. Gordon get better? Unless we find out why he's taking a laxative, he'll probably continue taking it.

Presenting alternatives

Ms. Morrison decides that she has too many ethical misgivings to cooperate with the search. Before telling Dr. Stein her decision, she outlines the ways in which she's willing to help. Her first recommendation is to call a conference with the patient. She's willing to discuss with Mr. Gordon the need for the health care team to know about all of his medications, including over-the-counter medications and home remedies, and to again ask him to identify the medication he takes. If Mr. Gordon still refuses to discuss the problem, she'll make it clear that she's willing to listen if he should change his mind.

Right to privacy *(continued)*

She's also willing to arrange to be in Mr. Gordon's room during morning care. If, for example, she opens his drawer to get his toothbrush and finds a medicine bottle, she can then ask about it. However, that's as far as she will go. She won't participate in a search without the patient's consent, even in his presence. She realizes that, as Dr. Stein said, this might limit the ability of the health care team to help Mr. Gordon, but a competent patient has the right to forgo help.

---

information could cause serious physical harm to the patient, his family, facility staff, or another third party. However, knowing when confidentiality may be appropriately breached isn't always easy. Consider the three case studies here. For each case, decide whether you agree with the ethical decision made by the nurse.

Preventing harm to the patient

Kitisha Jefferson, RN, was caring for Will Cooke, a 33-year-old electrician who fractured his femur in a fall at a construction site. She had established a good nurse-patient relationship with him. However, Mr. Cooke had seemed bored and edgy for the past day or so. When Ms. Jefferson checked his room, she found his curtain drawn halfway around his bed. She walked to the open side and saw Mr. Cooke hurriedly closing a plastic bag that contained white powder. "What are you doing?" she asked him.

"All right," Mr. Cooke replied. "Because you're a good nurse, I'll level with you. I was doing cocaine. I know I shouldn't, but it gets boring when you're in traction with nothing to do but watch the tube. Please, don't tell anybody. If my wife finds out, I'm finished."

Ms. Jefferson patiently explained that cocaine can have severe effects,

especially when taken with other drugs. She advised Mr. Cooke to discontinue using cocaine—at least while he's hospitalized.

After taking these measures, Ms. Jefferson still faced ethical dilemmas. What should she write in the patient's chart? Should she tell Mr. Cooke's physician? Should she recommend that Mr. Cooke tell the physician?

After careful consideration, Ms. Jefferson decided to tell Mr. Cooke that she had an obligation to let the physician know about his cocaine use—unless Mr. Cooke wanted to tell the physician himself. Her decision was based on the ethical principle of beneficence; she believed that the risk of cardiac arrest caused by the combination of cocaine and other medications was an overriding factor.

Protecting staff

Steve Walcott, RN, was reviewing Tamara Smith's chart before giving her a preoperative sedative when he realized that one of his colleagues had been discussing her at lunch the day before. This colleague, who worked in the laboratory, didn't mention Ms. Smith by name, but the age and admission date gave away the patient's identity. She had said that Ms. Smith tested positive for HIV infection but that the results weren't being noted on the chart. Should Mr. Walcott inform the surgical team of Ms. Smith's test results?

Mr. Walcott felt a strong temptation to protect his coworkers as the first consideration. However, he also realized that his colleague was remiss in discussing Ms. Smith's test results. Therefore, he reasoned that he would be remiss in further violating the confidentiality of this information. He also feared stigmatizing the patient. He further reasoned that the surgical team should use standard precautions for all patients, not just those who test positive for HIV. After all, patients who haven't had the test can also carry the antibody.

Protecting the patient's family

Jenny Chu, RN, was caring for Susan Schaffer, a 32-year-old mother of five scheduled for a tubal ligation. She wanted to make sure her patient understood the effects of this surgery, so she asked Mrs. Schaffer to explain the procedure. Mrs. Schaffer did so eagerly and added, "I'm so happy I won't have to worry about getting pregnant again. Five kids is more than I can handle as it is."

Satisfied, Ms. Chu left Mrs. Schaffer and continued her rounds. Later that day, she met Mrs. Schaffer's husband, Matt, at the nurses' station. He asked for a box of tissues and said, "I hope the surgery fixes Susan's problem. Did she tell you we've been trying to have another baby for over 1 year? I really want to have a few more kids."

What should Ms. Chu do: protect Mrs. Schaffer's confidentiality or tell Mr. Schaffer the truth? Ms. Chu believed that her first obligation was to protect Mrs. Schaffer's confidentiality. The urge to tell Mr. Schaffer about his wife's deception was compelling, but

he wasn't in danger of physical harm from her action. Ms. Chu felt badly that Mr. and Mrs. Schaffer couldn't talk to each other frankly, but she also believed that this wasn't an excuse for breaching confidentiality. Nonetheless, Ms. Chu decided to discuss the matter with the surgeon, especially because hospital policy required a spouse's signature on the consent form for a sterilization procedure.

Patients' right to privacy

Obtaining highly personal information from a patient can be uncomfortable and embarrassing. Reassuring the patient that you'll keep information confidential may help to put you both at ease. But stop to think about the legal complexities of this responsibility. What do you do when your patient's spouse, other health care professionals, the media, or public health agencies ask you to disclose confidential information? Refer back to the section on HIPAA under *Legal Status*.

IS THERE A CONSTITUTIONAL RIGHT TO PRIVACY?

Privacy and confidentiality were first proposed as basic legal rights in 1890 in a *Harvard Law Review* article titled "The Right to Privacy."

The US Constitution doesn't explicitly sanction a right to privacy. But in several court cases, including *Roe v. Wade* (1973), the US Supreme Court cited several constitutional amendments that imply the right.

The right to privacy essentially is the right to make personal choices without outside interference. In the landmark case of *Griswold v. Connecticut* (1965), for example, the Supreme Court recognized a married couple's right to privacy in contraceptive use. In *Eisenstadt v. Baird* (1972), the

Supreme Court extended the right to privacy in contraceptive use to include unmarried people. In *Carey v. Population Services International* (1977), the Supreme Court said a state law that prohibited the sale of contraceptives to anyone younger than age 16 was unconstitutional.

The US Department of Health and Human Services tried to modify the *Carey* ruling by publishing a regulation, "Parental Notification Requirements Applicable to Projects for Family Planning Services." Also known as the "squeal rule," this regulation proposed that any federally funded clinic or health agency giving contraceptives to a minor be required to inform the minor's parents or guardian. A New York federal district court, however, declared that divulging such confidential information invades the minor's privacy and is unconstitutional.

Right to privacy and abortion law

The Supreme Court ruling in *Roe v. Wade* (1973) protects a woman's right to privacy in a first-trimester abortion. After the first trimester, a state may regulate abortion to protect the mother's health and prohibit an abortion if the fetus is judged viable. However, state legislators have complicated access to abortion services in different ways. In 1999 alone, President George W. Bush, then governor of Texas, passed several laws affecting abortion rights. One law mandates parental notification and a 48-hour waiting period for minors. Another prohibits licensed medical professionals from performing third-trimester abortions. Another law excludes organizations that offer abortion procedures from receiving family planning funding and mandates that funds for prescription contraceptives for minors be given only with parental consent; another

denies tax exemption to nonprofit organizations that perform, refer for, or assist other organizations that perform or refer for abortion. Yet another law prohibits the state Child Health Plan from covering any services that prevent conception or birth. Another prohibits school-based health centers from providing reproductive services, counseling, or referrals if they receive certain grants. Other states have passed similar laws, including Virginia, Arizona, Iowa, and Florida.

In *Stenberg v. Carhart* in 2000, Nebraska along with many other states passed a law to ban "partial birth abortions". The court struck down this Nebraska law by a 5-4 vote and therefore rendered the other state laws unenforceable as well. In 2007, the court reversed their decision from the 2000 decision, thus placing a nationwide ban on the use of this method.

Restrictions on the right to abortion

Since *Roe v. Wade* (1973), the Supreme Court has handed down more than 20 major opinions related to the abortion issue.

A 1989 Supreme Court decision, *Webster v. Reproductive Health Services*, placed certain aspects of *Roe v. Wade* into doubt. Although viability of the fetus remains the guideline, the Supreme Court now appears more willing to allow states to regulate abortion. For example, in 1992, in *Planned Parenthood of Southeastern Pennsylvania v. Casey*, the Supreme Court let stand Pennsylvania's Abortion Control Act of 1989. This act requires that a woman wait 24 hours between consenting to and receiving an abortion, except in narrowly defined medical emergencies, and that a woman seeking an abortion be given state-mandated abortion information and offered state-authored materials on fetal development. The Supreme Court struck down the requirement that a married woman inform her husband of her intent to have an abortion. Overall, the decision reaffirmed a woman's right to abortion, but suggested that the Court had revised its long-standing definition of that right as fundamental.

In May 1991, antiabortion groups won a victory on another front. In *Rust v. Sullivan* (1991), the Supreme Court upheld federal regulations prohibiting health care workers at more than 4,000 government-subsidized family planning clinics from providing any information about abortion. Under the regulations, if you work in a subsidized clinic you may not advise a pregnant woman that abortion is a possibility, nor may you help her find a private abortion clinic. You are obligated to refer pregnant women for prenatal care. (See *Money and contraception*.)

Twenty-seven states have effective informed consent laws protecting a woman's right to know the medical risks associated with abortion, the positive alternatives to abortion, and to be provided with nonjudgmental, scientifically accurate medical facts about the development of the unborn child before making the permanent and life-affecting decision. States with this law currently in place are Alabama, Arizona, Arkansas, Florida, Georgia, Idaho, Indiana, Kansas, Kentucky, Louisiana, Michigan, Minnesota, Mississippi, Missouri, Nebraska, North Carolina, North Dakota, Ohio, Oklahoma, Pennsylvania, South Carolina, South Dakota, Texas, Utah, Virginia, West Virginia, and Wisconsin.

Abortion rights for minors

Roe v. Wade (1973) played an important role in extending abortion rights to minors. In *Planned Parenthood of Central Missouri v. Danforth* (1976), the Supreme Court overruled a law that prevented first-trimester abortions for minors without parental consent. This decision was based on *Roe v. Wade*.

In *Bellotti v. Baird II* (1979), the Supreme Court acknowledged that the privacy rights of a minor aren't equal to those of an adult. The Court held, however, that a state law requiring a minor to obtain parental consent for an abortion infringed on the minor's rights.

In *H.L. v. Matheson* (1981), the Supreme Court upheld a Utah law requiring a physician to notify the parents of an unemancipated minor before an abortion. However, in *Hodgson v. Minnesota* (1990), a Minnesota statute that required notification of both biological parents before a minor's abortion, after a wait of at least 48 hours, was held unconstitutional. The chief difference between the two cases is that the Utah law required notification of only one parent, where feasible; the Minnesota law required notification of both parents, even if they were divorced or separated. In *Hodgson*, the Supreme Court decreed that the rule requiring notification of both parents was too burdensome on the right to abortion because it could create exceptional difficulties for one-parent families. The Court also stated that the 48-hour waiting period required under the Minnesota law would not, by itself, render the statute unconstitutional.

By letting stand Pennsylvania's Abortion Control Act in 1992, the Supreme Court allowed the state to require that one parent or guardian give consent in person for a minor seeking an abortion, unless the minor obtains a judicial waiver.

In *Hodgson* and *Ohio v. Akron Center for Reproductive Health* (1990), the Supreme Court set forth its position on judicial bypass statutes. Judicial bypass statutes allow a minor to avoid notifying parents or obtaining consent for an abortion by going before a judge. The Court stated that judicial bypass satisfies the requirement that parents or other third parties can't have an absolute veto over the minor's abortion decision.

Each state within the United States has enacted different laws pertaining to the abortion laws for minors. For more specific state information, refer to *Witmer, D.* on the *References* page.

PRIVILEGE DOCTRINE

The state courts have been strong in protecting a patient's right to have information kept confidential. Even in court, your patient is protected by the privilege doctrine. People who have a protected relationship, such as a physician and patient, can't be forced (even during legal proceedings) to reveal communication between them, unless the person who benefits from the protection agrees to it. This means that the patient must agree before confidential information is revealed in court. The purpose of the privilege doctrine is to encourage the patient to reveal confidential information that may be essential to his treatment. State law determines which relationships are protected by the privilege doctrine. Most states include husband-wife, lawyer-client, and physician-patient relationships.

Nurse-patient relationships

Only a few states (including New York, Arkansas, Oregon, and Vermont) recognize the nurse-patient relationship as protected. This means that the nurse has a right to refuse to testify against a former patient in a court of law. However, some courts have said that the privilege exists when a nurse is following a physician's orders. Whether the privilege applies to LPNs and LVNs as well is uncertain.

Money and contraception

Contraception and abortion are heavily restricted through legislation. A federal directive issued on July 2, 1998, by the Clinton administration specifically mandates payment by Medicaid and insurance companies for the drug sildenafil (Viagra), which treats impotence. However, there were previously no laws mandating any type of payment for birth control, and about 50% of large insurance companies won't pay for it. According to recent information, 85% of large employers were already offering contraception coverage before the Affordable Care Act (ACA) required it. As of 2014, controversy surrounds the ACA that also requires that most businesses provide their employees with health care coverage that includes the full range of contraceptive approved by the Food and Drug Administration. Some businesses have objected to this law requiring them to offer contraception coverage because it conflicts with the owner's religious beliefs. In June 2014, the Supreme Court in Washington ruled in a 5-4 decision that profit-seeking businesses can hold religious views under the federal law. Two of the cases are *Burwell v. Hobby Lobby* and *Conestoga Wood Specialties v. Burwell.* Hobby Lobby is operated by the owners based on biblical principles, and Conestoga Wood is owned and operated by a Mennonite family. This decision allows companies the ability to refuse to fund health plans that cover "abortion-inducing" contraceptives.

Extent of privilege

State laws also determine the extent of privilege in protected relationships. In *Hammonds v. Aetna Casualty and Surety Co.* (1965), the court reinforced the privilege doctrine by declaring that protecting a patient's privacy is a physician's legal duty. It further ruled that a patient could sue for damages any unauthorized person who disclosed confidential medical information about him. Similarly, a patient can sue for invasion of privacy any unauthorized personnel such as student nurses who observe him without his permission. The only hospital personnel who have a right to observe a patient are those involved in his diagnosis, treatment, and related care.

Exceptions

In some states, a patient automatically waives his right to physician-patient privilege when he files a personal injury or workers' compensation lawsuit.

A hospital or physician can't invoke the privilege doctrine if the motive is self-protection. In *People v. Doe* (1978), a nursing home was being investigated for allegedly mistreating its patients. The court ruled that the nursing home's attempt to invoke patient privilege was unjust because the issue at hand was the patients' welfare. Federal courts do not recognize a physician-patient or hospital-patient privilege. If asked, physicians and the underlying organization must comply with federal requests for information. One such case is the 2011 court case of *Cleveland Clinic Foundation v. United States of America*. Cleveland Clinic objected to the civil investigative demands out of concern for compliance that they would violate the privacy of their patients and expose them to civil liability under Ohio's

physician-patient privilege status. The court found that they must comply with the two civil investigative demands.

Patient privilege and Canadian law

In all Canadian jurisdictions, privilege doctrine applies only to solicitor-client communications. Physicians and nurses are bound by codes of ethics as well as legislation concerning confidentiality. Cases that suggest the physician-patient privilege include *Dembie* (1963), *Re SAS* (1977), and *Geransy* (1977). The Canadian Nurses Association has its own code of ethics, which has been largely adopted in nurse practice acts in Canadian jurisdictions. The code requires nurses to keep confidential any personal information they receive from a patient during nursing care. Consequently, although violation of a patient's right to privacy isn't subject to criminal prosecution in Canada, it's deemed professional misconduct. A nurse who violates a patient's right to privacy could lose her nursing license.

YOUR RESPONSIBILITIES IN PROTECTING PATIENT PRIVACY

Despite legal uncertainties regarding your responsibilities under the privilege doctrine, you have a professional and ethical responsibility to protect your patient's privacy, whether you're an RN or a LPN.

This responsibility requires more than keeping secrets. You may have to educate your patients about their privacy rights. Some of them may be unaware of what the right to privacy means, or that they even have such a right. Explain to the patient that he or she can refuse to allow pictures to be taken of his or her disorder and its treatment, for example. Tell the patient that they can choose to have information about their condition withheld from others, including family members. Make every effort to ensure that the patient's wishes are carried out.

WHEN YOU MAY DISCLOSE CONFIDENTIAL INFORMATION

Under certain circumstances, you may lawfully disclose confidential information about your patient. For example, the courts allow disclosure when the welfare of a person or a group of people is at stake. Consider the patient who's diagnosed as an epileptic and asks you not to tell family. Depending on the circumstances, you may decide that this isn't in the patient's and family's best interest, particularly in terms of safety. In that situation, inform the patient's physician, who may then decide to inform the patient's family to protect the patient's well-being. In most states, the physician is required to inform the Department of Motor Vehicles of uncontrolled epilepsy.

You're also protected by law if you disclose confidential information about a patient that's necessary for continued care or if your patient consents to the disclosure.

Be careful not to exceed the specified limit of a patient's consent. Taking pictures is the largest single cause of invasion of privacy lawsuits. In *Feeney v. Young* (1920), a woman consented to the filming of her cesarean birth for viewing by medical societies, but the physician incorporated the film into a generally released movie titled *Birth*. The court awarded damages to the woman under the state's privacy law.

In 2009, Kaiser Permanente's Bell-flower Hospital was fined $250,000 for failing to keep employees from snooping in the medical records of Nadya Sulemann, the mother who gave birth to octuplets that set off a media frenzy. Between 2003 and 2009, the US Department of Health and Human Services received nearly 44,000 complaints of privacy violations, since federal law prohibits unauthorized access of patients' medical records.

Protecting the public

The courts have granted immunity to health care professionals who, in good faith, have disclosed confidential information to prevent public harm. In *Simonsen v. Swenson* (1920), a physician who thought that his patient had syphilis told the owner of the hotel in which the patient was staying about the patient's contagious disease. The court ruled that physicians are privileged to make disclosures that will prevent the spread of disease.

A controversial California case established a physician's right to disclose information that would protect any person whom a patient threatened to harm. In *Tarasoff v. Regents of the University of California* (1976), a woman was murdered by a mentally ill patient who had told his psychotherapist that he intended to kill her. The victim's parents sued the physician for failing to warn their daughter. The Supreme Court found the physician liable because he didn't warn the intended victim. The Court ruled similarly in *McIntosh v. Milano* (1979).

Various states have adopted special statues to deal with the issues related to HIV and disclosure of that information. Continuing to maintain privacy and confidentiality of patients is required; however, in some situations, it may warrant disclosing this information to a third party which is ethically and legally acceptable. In the state of Virginia, the law allows the disclosure of HIV status to the patient's spouse. In Virginia it is also a physician's duty to notify public health authorities when caring for an HIV-positive patient. Other laws also exist that are similar for hepatitis B/C. The Federal Centers for Disease Control (CDC) has issued other sets of guidelines for dealing with HIV confidentiality in health care workers based on risk of virus transmission.

WHEN YOU MUST DISCLOSE CONFIDENTIAL INFORMATION

In some situations, the law requires you to disclose confidential information.

Child abuse

All 50 states and the District of Columbia have disclosure laws for child abuse cases. Except for Maine and Montana, all states also grant immunity from legal action for a good faith report on suspected child abuse. In fact, there may be a criminal penalty for failure to disclose such information. The United States, Canada, Australia, and many other countries have some form of mandatory reporting. Mandated reporters typically include teachers, health care workers, and child care providers among others. The United States has 48 states that have mandatory reporting laws in place. As of 2012, 18 states require "everyone" to report suspected child maltreatment. (*Go to Children's Bureau in References* to review specific state mandates and disclosure of confidential information in these instances.)

Courts may also order you to disclose confidential information in cases of child custody and child neglect. One case involving such an order was *D. v. D.* (1969). Despite the physician-patient privilege, the court ordered the physician to turn the mother's medical records over to the court for a private inspection. The mother had a history of illness, and the court said that the inspection would help to decide which parent should be granted custody. The courts made a similar ruling in *In re Doe Children* (1978). The court stated that the children's welfare outweighed the parents' right to keep their medical records private.

Criminal cases

Some laws create an exemption to the privilege doctrine in criminal cases so that the courts can have access to all essential information. In states where neither a law nor an exemption to the law exists, the court may find an exemption to the doctrine in criminal cases.

Government requests

Certain government agencies can order you to reveal confidential information, including federal agencies such as the Internal Revenue Service, the Environmental Protection Agency, the Department of Labor, and the Department of Health and Human Services. State agencies that may order you to reveal confidential information include revenue or tax bureaus and public health departments. For example, most state public health departments require reports of all communicable diseases, births and deaths, and gunshot wounds.

Public's right to know

The newsworthiness of an event or person can make disclosure acceptable. In such circumstances, the public's need for information may outweigh a person's right to keep his or her medical condition private. For example, newspapers routinely publish the findings of the President's annual physical examination in response to the public's demand for information. Even the

First Lady's health may become a matter of public record.

Other events for which the public's right to know may outweigh the patient's right to privacy include breakthroughs in medical technology (the first successful hand transplant) and product tampering cases, for example. In 1999, the national media gave wide exposure to an incident in New York State in which nine people died after being bitten by a mosquito that transmitted a flavivirus that causes St. Louis encephalitis.

Even when the public has a right to know about a confidential matter, the courts won't allow public disclosure to undermine a person's dignity. In *Barber v. Time, Inc.* (1942), *TIME* magazine was sued by a woman whose name and photograph were published in an article that revealed she suffered from an illness that caused her to eat as much food as 10 people could eat. The court ruled that publishing the patient's name and picture was an unnecessary invasion of her privacy, and that ethics required keeping such information confidential.

Doe v. Roe (1977) is a similar case. A patient sued his psychiatrist for publishing the patient's biography and thoughts verbatim. Even though the physician didn't use the patient's name, the court stated that the patient was readily identifiable by the article. It found the physician liable for violating the physician-patient privilege.

When the patient demands to review the chart

Suppose the patient says to you, "I'm paying for the tests; I have a right to know the results." Does the patient have the legal right to know what's in their medical records?

Yes—and because patients increasingly want explanations about what's being done to them and why, you should know how to respond when your patient asks to see their medical records.

Disclosure debate

For years, health care experts have debated the merits of letting a patient see his medical records. Proponents argue that knowing the information helps the patient to better understand his condition and care and makes him a more cooperative patient.

Opponents, usually physicians and hospitals, argue that the technical jargon and medical abbreviations found in medical records may confuse or even frighten a patient. In addition, opponents claim that opening medical records to a patient will increase the risks of malpractice lawsuits. No evidence exists to support this contention.

The "right to access" issue has spawned an important legal debate. The first issue the courts had to answer involved ownership.

Determining ownership

The hospital owns the hospital medical records, and the physician owns the office records, according to court decisions. Most courts have decided that a patient sees a physician for diagnosis and treatment, not to obtain records for personal use.

Right to access

The second issue the courts had to resolve involved access. While granting ownership of medical records to physicians and hospitals, the courts have expressed their rights to get a patient's records anytime they need to have them for a case review.

For this reason, any patient in any state can file a lawsuit to subpoena their own medical records. However, some court decisions and some states' laws have given patients the right to direct access. Many states guarantee a patient's right to their own medical information.

In *Cannell v. Medical and Surgical Clinic* (1974), the court ruled that a physician had the duty to disclose medical information to his patient. The court also ruled, however, that physicians and hospitals need not turn over the actual files to the patient. Instead, they need only to show the complete medical record—or a copy—to the patient. With the most recently enacted HIPAA privacy laws, patients now have the right by federal law to have access to their medical records. *Refer to HIPAA section.*

The court based the patient's limited right to access on two important concepts:

■ A patient has a right to know the details about their medical treatment under common law.

■ A patient has a right to the information in their records because of payment for the treatment.

Roadblocks to information

Despite the laws and court decisions, hospitals don't always make access to records easy. Some hospitals discourage a patient from seeing his medical records by putting up bureaucratic barriers. For example, requiring the patient to have an attorney make the request can stifle a patient's attempt to gain access and encourage visits to malpractice lawyers. Other hospitals charge high copying fees to discourage patient record requests.

Some states, such as Pennsylvania, have laws setting maximum fees that can be charged for copying a patient's medical records.

HOW TO RESPOND TO YOUR PATIENT'S REQUEST

If a patient requests to see his medical record you may want to question "Why? The patient may simply be curious, or the request may reflect hidden fears about proposed treatments. Many hospitals have established policies that deal with this issue. These policies may include notifying your nursing supervisor that the patient has asked to see their medical records and notifying the risk manager, if your facility has one, to alert administrative staff and legal counsel, if necessary.

After your patient gets approval to see medical records, stay with the patient while the records are reviewed. Explain to the patient that state laws prohibit changing or erasing information on patient records, even information the patient considers incorrect. Ask the patient to show you any information felt to be incorrect. Offer to answer any questions; assure him or her that the physician will answer questions, too. In fact, encourage the patient to write down specific questions for the attending physician, and offer to contact the physician on their behalf if necessary.

While your patient reads, help him to interpret the abbreviations and jargon used in medical charting. One patient hospitalized for hypertension was greatly relieved when her nurse explained that the "malignant hypertension" notation on her chart had nothing to do with cancer.

Observe how the patient responds while information is read. Some patients want to read their records just to make sure you and the physicians aren't hiding information. For example, one patient who demanded to see her medical records merely flipped through the pages. The hospital's willingness to share information about her treatment apparently satisfied her.

WHEN A RELATIVE REQUESTS MEDICAL RECORDS

A relative may see a patient's medical records under any of these conditions:

■ The relative or next of kin is the patient's legal guardian, and the patient has been deemed as incompetent by a court of law.

■ The relative has the patient's approval. Document this approval received whether by written permission received from the patient or received verbally. It's a good idea to have a second witness to note in the records.

Patient discharge against medical advice

The patients' bill of rights and the laws and regulations based on it give a competent adult the right to refuse treatment for any reason without being punished or having his liberty restricted.

Some states have turned these rights into law. And the courts have cited the bill of rights in their decisions.

The right to refuse treatment provides patients with the right to leave the hospital AMA any time, for any reason. As a nurse, all you can do is try to talk the patient out of it.

When a patient discharges AMA, a nurse has the option to contact the patient's family to inform them. The nurse should make sure to explain the AMA procedure and make sure the patient signs the AMA form. As a nurse, provide the appropriate discharge care to the patient prior to their leaving.

RECOGNIZING A POTENTIAL PATIENT WALKOUT

Because you have more contact with your patient than any other health care

professional, you're likely to be the first person to suspect that a patient is contemplating leaving AMA.

Complaints or hostile behavior may indicate the patient's extreme dissatisfaction with hospital routine or with care being received. By carefully observing, listening, and talking with the patient, you may be able to resolve the problems by offering a fresh perspective and perhaps change the patient's mind about leaving. Eliminating communication barriers can often prevent the final patient decision to leave AMA.

If you discover that a specific problem has caused the patient to become dissatisfied, try to resolve it. If the problem lies outside the scope of your practice, call the patient's physician.

A patient may tell you that he or she has changed their mind about leaving just to divert your attention. If you suspect this, check on the patient more often and ask colleagues to do the same. Stay with the patient when escorting to another part of the hospital.

WHEN THE PATIENT INSISTS ON LEAVING

If your patient still insists on leaving AMA and your hospital has a policy on managing the patient who wants to leave, follow it exactly. Following policy will help to protect the hospital, coworkers, and you from charges of unlawful restraint or false imprisonment. If your employer doesn't have such a policy, take these steps:

■ Contact the patient's family (if he or she hasn't already called them), and explain that the patient is getting ready to leave. If you can't reach the family, contact the person listed in the patient's records responsible for him or her or for their body and valuables should the patient die.

■ Explain the hospital's AMA procedures to the patient if hospital policy delegates this responsibility to you.

■ Give the patient the AMA form to sign. (See *Documenting a patient's decision to leave AMA*, page 127.) The patient's decision to leave is the same as a refusal of treatment. Inform the patient of medical risks if he or she leaves the hospital, and explain the alternatives available at the hospital and at other locations, such as regular visits to the hospital's outpatient clinic or admission to another facility. The patient signature on the AMA form is evidence for refusal of treatment. You should witness the signature.

■ Provide routine discharge care. Even though your patient is leaving AMA, the patient has rights to discharge planning and care. They are the same as those for a patient who's signed out with medical advice. So if the patient agrees, escort them to the door (in a wheelchair, if necessary), arrange for medical or nursing follow-up care, and offer other routine health care measures. These procedures will protect the hospital as well as the patient.

WHEN THE PATIENT REFUSES TO SIGN OUT

If the patient refuses to sign the AMA form, you should document the refusal in a note stating that all risks have been explained to the patient. One innovative nurse routinely told emergency department patients that she would like them to indicate their refusal to sign by signing the back of the form. Most patients complied with her request.

Dealing with an escape

If you discover that a patient is missing from the hospital, notify the

nursing supervisor and security immediately. If the patient was in police custody or poses a threat to anyone outside the hospital, the administration should contact the police. The hospital administration subsequently may ask you to notify the patient's family or friends, collect the patient's belongings, and document the escape in the patient's medical chart and incident report.

FALSE IMPRISONMENT

Never attempt to detain a competent adult who has a right to leave. Any attempt to detain or restrain the patient may be interpreted as unlawful restraint or false imprisonment, for which you can be sued or prosecuted.

Your hospital's policy should reflect state law. It should specifically answer such questions as follows:

■ How long and for what reasons may a patient be detained?
■ When can you use forcible restraints?
■ Who may order the use of restraints?
■ Who may apply the restraints?

Knowing the policies will reduce your liability exposure.

Court cases

Most courts disapprove of detaining a patient arbitrarily or for an unreasonably long time, which may be ruled false imprisonment.

One such case involved Joseph Wheeler's claim against Prince George's Hospital alleging false imprisonment. The 46-year-old man was admitted to the hospital following injuries sustained from a car accident in July 2010. He states that he woke up the next day and was told by the nurse that he couldn't eat because he

(Text continues on page 128.)

LEGAL TIP

Documenting a patient's decision to leave AMA

An against-medical-advice (AMA) form is a medical record as well as a legal document. It's designed to protect you, your coworkers, and your facility from liability resulting from the patient's unapproved discharge or escape.

To document an AMA incident, begin by getting your facility's AMA form. The form may look like the one shown below. The form clearly states that the patient

■ knows they are leaving AMA
■ has been advised of, and understands, the risks of leaving
■ knows they can come back.

Discuss this form with the patient and ask for a signature. Don't try to force the patient to sign, if they're unwilling to do so. You should sign as a witness.

Add the AMA form to the patient's medical chart. Then write a detailed description of how you first learned of the patient's plan to leave AMA, what you and the patient said to each other, and what alternatives to the patient's action were discussed.

Also, check facility policy concerning incident reports. If the patient leaves without anyone's knowledge or if he or she refuses to sign the AMA form, you'll probably be required to file an incident report. Be sure to include the names of any other employees involved in the discovery of the patient's absence. The administration or your nurse-manager also may want to solicit corroborating reports from other employees, including other registered nurses, licensed practical nurses, nurses' aides, orderlies, and clerical staff.

Responsibility release

This is to certify that I, _____,

a patient in _____,

am being discharged against the advice of my doctor and the hospital administration. I acknowledge that I have been informed of the risk involved and hereby release my physician and the hospital from all responsibility for any ill effects that may result from such a discharge. I also understand that I may return to the hospital at any time and have treatment resumed.

_____   _____
[Patient's signature]   [Date]

_____   _____
[Witness' signature]   [Date]

RE: _____   _____
[Name of patient]   Patient #

had to undergo surgery. The ID bracelet from the hospital was for a female born 13 years earlier than Mr. Wheeler. Based on this bracelet, it identified him as having a potentially cancerous mass that needed to be removed from his chest. Mr. Wheeler and his wife tried to leave, but security detained him. Apparently, the security supervisor acknowledges the ID mix-up but told the guards to prevent the patient from leaving unless the bracelet was returned. He claims that the hospital security cursed at him and pushed him into a wall and metal railing. He was later admitted to St. Mary's hospital for 3 days where he was then treated for a concussion, sprained shoulder, and a ruptured spleen. Joseph Wheeler filed a lawsuit seeking $12 million—$9.5 million in punitive damages and $3.2 million in compensatory damages.

Court cases that involve false imprisonment charges have occurred when facilities threatened to hold patients or their personal belongings until bills were paid. In most cases, the courts ruled against the facilities.

A hospital or nursing home can delay a patient's discharge, for a reasonable period of time, until routine paperwork is complete. *Bailie v. Miami Valley Hospital* (1966) was a case in which the court ruled in favor of a hospital.

An exception

In a few cases, because of extenuating circumstances, the courts have ruled against patients who sued on grounds of false imprisonment. The case of *Pounders v. Trinity Court Nursing Home* (1979) is one such example.

Mrs. Pounders, age 75, was a disabled widow. When her niece and nephew no longer wanted her to live with them, the niece arranged for her

to move to Trinity Court Nursing Home. Mrs. Pounders didn't object.

During her 2 months at Trinity Court, Mrs. Pounders complained only once to a nurses' aide that she wanted to leave. Unfortunately, the aide failed to report the complaint to anyone in authority at the home.

Mrs. Pounders was finally released, through the aid of an attorney, into another niece's care. She eventually sued the nursing home.

However, because Mrs. Pounders couldn't prove she had been involuntarily detained, the court absolved the nursing home of the false imprisonment charges.

LAWFUL DETENTION

The right to leave the hospital AMA isn't absolute. Certain patients who pose a threat to themselves or to others can't legally leave the hospital. Restraint through the use of physical means or medication, when necessary, is lawful with psychiatric patients, prisoners, and violent patients.

Patients from psychiatric hospitals or prisons

If a patient transferred to your hospital for medical care from a prison or psychiatric hospital threatens to escape, notify the custodial facility immediately. They're responsible for sending personnel to guard the patient and for making new arrangements for providing care. Restrain the patient only if the medical condition warrants it or if the police or psychiatric hospital authorities instruct you to do so.

If the prisoner or psychiatric patient escapes, you or your hospital or nursing administration should call the authorities at the custodial facility or the police.

Violent patients

If you suspect that a patient with a history of violence or violent threats is planning to leave AMA, notify hospital and nursing administrators immediately. If state law allows it, your hospital administrators may decide to get police assistance to restrain the patient.

If the violent patient has escaped, notify your nursing or hospital administration immediately. They'll contact the police and mental health authorities. If the patient ever expressed an intention to harm a known person, the administration also should contact that person.

When a patient dies

When a patient dies, his or her rights are transferred to their estate. However, in recent years, legally determining when death occurred has become difficult. That, in turn, complicates your role.

How can you be sure a patient is legally dead? Who has the right to pronounce death? What are your responsibilities after the patient dies?

CONTROVERSY OVER THE DEFINITION OF DEATH

Determining death used to be simple—when a person's circulation and respiration stopped, a determination of death was made. However, advances in medical technology have made death pronouncements more complicated. Because medical equipment, such as ventilators, pacemakers, and intra-aortic balloon pumps, can maintain respiration and circulation, patients may continue to "live" even after their brains have died.

Criteria for brain death

To help physicians determine death in such cases, an ad hoc committee

at Harvard Medical School published a report in 1968, establishing specific criteria for brain death, including the following:

- Failure to respond to the most painful stimuli
- Absence of spontaneous respirations or muscle movements
- Absence of reflexes
- Flat EEG

The committee recommended that all these tests be repeated after 24 hours, and that hypothermia and the presence of central nervous system depressants such as barbiturates be ruled out.

In 1981, the American Medical Association, the American Bar Association, and the President's Commission for the Study of Ethical Problems in Medicine and Behavioral Research collaborated to derive a working definition of brain death. The result of this effort, the Uniform Determination of Death Act (UDODA), has gained wide acceptance among the health care and legal communities.

In general terms, the UDODA defines brain death as the cessation of all measurable functions or activity in every area of the brain, including the brain stem. This definition excludes comatose patients as well as those in a persistent vegetative state. Current debate centers on whether to expand the definition to include certain patients who still have brain stem function such as anencephalic infants.

Court cases

Several court decisions have been based on such definitions.

In the case of *State v. Brown* (1971), an Oregon court was among the first to recognize brain death. In this case of second-degree murder, the defendant argued that he hadn't caused the victim's death by inflicting a gunshot wound to the brain. Instead, he claimed, a physician killed the victim by removing artificial life support. The court ruled that the defendant caused the victim's death because the gunshot wound resulted in brain death.

Various court cases have existed over this definition of brain death. In some circumstances, physicians' battle over whether to consider a patient as "brain dead," giving them an official diagnosis. This can often lead to much conflict, court battles, and heartache for the families involved. Even physicians can at times disagree on whether or not brain death has occurred. A recent case involving Terry Schiavo gained national news attention when the battle over withdrawing or withholding treatment was considered appropriate given Mrs. Schiavo's diagnoses. The courts in Florida along with legislature and Congress became involved in the case which previously had been handled in similar cases as a private family matter between a physician and families.

Know your state's law

A person who is defined as having a brain-death diagnosis is based on the inability for the patient to breathe on their own and is legally dead; this is recognized in all 50 states. However, in New York and New Jersey, hospitals are required to consider the family's religious and moral views when deciding on whether or not to terminate care. In other states including Texas and California, hospitals are not required to consult with the families before making such decision as to how to terminate care. A recent case out of Texas is the case of Marlise Munoz. She collapsed in her home after suffering a blood clot in her lungs. She was taken to the hospital and placed on a ventilator and diagnosed as brain dead. During examination the hospital determined that

she was 14 weeks pregnant. The John Peter Smith Hospital cited a state law refusing to remove the ventilator as it would harm the fetus, now in its 20th week, despite the family's wishes that the ventilator be turned off and their daughter be allowed the right to die." The decision went before the court and the judge ruled that Mrs. Munoz had been brain dead since admission and her fetus, now 24 weeks, was not viable. Despite the legal documentation of both the spouse and the patient on not wanting to remain alive by artificial means, Texas law had prevented withdrawing of the life-sustaining treatment from a pregnant woman until this specific ruling was made by the judge. According to the Texas state law under the Texas Health and Safety Code Section 166.049, it states that "a person may not withdraw or withhold life-sustaining treatment under this subchapter from a pregnant patient." If you're likely to be involved with patients on life-support equipment, protect yourself by finding out how your state defines death.

Canadian law

In Canada, pinpointing the moment of death has traditionally been left to medical professionals. Human tissue gift legislation may vary from one jurisdiction to another, although generally the state of death is determined by accepted medical practice.

PRONOUNCING DEATH

Only a physician or a coroner can legally pronounce a person dead. In some health care facilities, such as nursing homes, nurses pronounce death when a physician isn't available. Several states permit nurses to pronounce death only if two nurses are present, or if the nurse has a signed physician order permitting the nurse to do so, or in some states, it is permissible if the death of the patient is anticipated due to situations such as hospice care. Know your state board of nursing regulations for those states in which you are licensed to practice. The state board must indicate that this is an appropriate nursing practice. If you work in such a facility, you should understand that pronouncing death typically isn't a nursing responsibility.

The attending physician is usually responsible for signing the death certificate, unless the death comes under the jurisdiction of a medical examiner or coroner. State laws specify when this occurs. The coroner or medical examiner usually has jurisdiction over deaths with violent or suspicious circumstances. These include suspected homicides and suicides, and deaths after accidents.

Canadian law

The Canadian provincial laws on autopsies are similar. Any death that occurs in violent or suspicious circumstances comes under the jurisdiction of a medical examiner or coroner. Depending on the province, other types of death—including a prisoner's death, a sudden death, or a death not caused by a disease—come under the jurisdiction of a medical examiner or coroner.

Your responsibility when a patient dies

When a patient dies, you're responsible for accurately and objectively charting all of the patient's signs and any actions you take. For example, an appropriate entry in the nurses' notes would be "12:00PM. No respirations or pulse, pupils fixed and dilated. Dr. York notified." Don't write a conclusion that borders on a medical diagnosis such as "patient seems dead." Whenever in question about what to write, stick to

the facts; those can be defended in a court of law; subjective opinions cannot.

You're also responsible for notifying the physician who can be reached most quickly. If this is the physician on call, he or she should notify the patient's physician, who should notify the family. Find out who will be notifying the family, and document it.

At the appropriate time, you should prepare the body for removal to the morgue, according to facility procedure. When doing this, carefully identify the body. In one specific case example from years ago, a nurse mistagged two bodies, causing a Roman Catholic to be prepared for an Orthodox Jewish burial and an Orthodox Jew to be prepared for a Roman Catholic burial. The court found the nurse liable in *Lott v. State of New York*. In cases such as this, the courts are not so much concerned about the extent of mishandling of the physical body, but rather how that improper handling affects the emotions of the surviving family.

Obtaining consent for an autopsy

If a death comes under the jurisdiction of a medical examiner or coroner, the decision to perform an autopsy rests solely with him or her, despite the family's wishes. In all other cases, the patient's family has a right to give or withhold consent. In some states, the patient can give preplanned written consent to an autopsy.

When a physician or other hospital representative seeks consent from a patient's family, you can help by explaining why the autopsy is needed and how autopsy arrangements are made.

Who may give consent?

Most states have laws that specify who has the right to give consent to autopsies. Some state laws list which relatives can give consent. Others list relatives in descending order, according to their relationship to the deceased. The usual order is spouse, adult children, parents, brothers or sisters, grandparents, uncles or aunts, and cousins. The person with the right to consent may withhold consent or impose limits on the autopsy. If the autopsy exceeds these limits, the consenting relative may sue.

The relative with the right to consent may also sue if an autopsy is performed without any consent. The grounds for such lawsuits are usually mental or emotional suffering.

OBTAINING CONSENT FOR ORGAN DONATION

Depending on the facility where you work and the patient's physical condition at the time of death, you may be asked to assist with obtaining consent for organ donation from the deceased's next of kin. This can be a delicate procedure. Carefully explain to the next of kin what can be donated and how the organs are distributed. Alleviate fears by providing reassurance that organ donation doesn't disfigure the body or cost anything. Also, ensure that the next of kin knows that they won't receive financial compensation for giving consent because it's illegal to sell human organs or tissues.

It's important to remember that in most states, a donor's card or a driver's license with the donor box checked isn't a legally binding document. (In December 2002, Minnesota passed a law stating otherwise.) Consent must still be obtained from the next of kin, unless the deceased had made it perfectly clear of the intent to donate their organs, such as through a living will, an advance directive, and a donor registry. Check with your local organ procedure organization for more details and procedures specific to your area. (See *Organ/tissue donor card.*)

Organ/tissue donor card

In recent years, various governmental and nonprofit organizations have developed programs to raise awareness about the importance of organ and tissue donation. One of their initiatives has been to promote organ/tissue donor cards (such as the one shown below), which people can keep on their person to signify their willingness to donate their organs in the case of an accident. While not a legally binding document, donor cards are helpful in getting a victim's next of kin to consent to donation.

I wish to donate my organs and tissues. I wish to give

■ Any needed organs and tissues   ■ Only the following organs and tissues:

Donor signature: _____   Date: _____

Witness: _____

Witness: _____

EXPERIMENTAL PROCEDURES

The family has a right to give or withhold specific consent to practice medical procedures on a corpse. In teaching hospitals, residents and medical students practice such procedures as intubation on corpses. However, if a hospital doesn't obtain proper consent, the family member responsible for consent may sue. In many states, the hospital may even face criminal charges.

RESPONSIBILITY FOR BURIAL

In the United States, the family member who has the right to consent to autopsy usually has the responsibility to bury the body as well. The regulations vary by jurisdiction in Canada. If no one claims the body despite the hospital's effort to contact the person responsible, a state or county official must dispose of it. Laws in many states direct this official to deliver unclaimed bodies to an appropriate educational or scientific facility unless the person is a veteran or has died of a contagious disease. In these situations, the state pays for burial or cremation.

SELECTED REFERENCES

American Hospital Association. The Patient Care Partnership [PDF file]. Retrieved from: http://www.aha.org/advocacy-issues/communicatingpts/pt-care-partnership.shtml, August 2014.

American Nurses Association. Code of Ethics for Nurses with Interpretative Statements [PDF file]. Retrieved from: http://nursingworld.org/MainMenuCategories/EthicsStandards/CodeofEthicsforNurses/Code-of-Ethics.pdf, 2015.

American Cancer Society. Informed Consent. American Cancer Society. Retrieved from: http://mstage.qa.cancer.org/treatment/findingandpayingfortreatment/understandingfinancialandlegalmatters/informedconsent/informed-consent-legal-requirements-of-consent, August 2014.

Barnes, R. "Supreme Court Sides with Employers over Birth Control Mandate," *The Washington Post.* Retrieved from: http://www.washingtonpost.com/national/supreme-court-sides-with-employers-over-birth-control-mandate/2014/06/30/852e5c84-fc61-11e3-b1f4-8e77c632c07b_story.html, June 30, 2014.

Blood Transfusion: Court Upholds Jehovah's Witness's Right to Refuse, *Legal Eagle Eye Newsletter for the Nursing Profession.* Retrieved from: http://www.nursinglaw.com/blood3.pdf, July 1996.

Butler v. South Fulton Medical Center, 215 Ga. Ap. 809, 452 SE2d 768 (Geor, 1994).

Carey, B., and Grady, D. "At Issue in 2 Wrenching Cases: What to Do After the Brain Dies," *The New York Times.* Retrieved from: http://www.nytimes.com/2014/01/10/health/the-science-behind-brain-death.html?_r=0, January 9, 2014.

Case summaries: Informed Consent (1991). *Lack of Consent and Battery Claims: Roberson v. Provident House.* Retrieved from: http://www.lawandbioethics.com/demo/Main/LegalResources/C5/background01.htm

Case summaries: Informed Consent (1999). *Consent and Emergencies: Shine v. Vagas.* Retrieved from: http://www.lawandbioethics.com/demo/Main/LegalResources/C5/background01.htm

Case summaries: Informed Consent (2002). *Exceptions to Informed Consent: Harvey v. Strickland.* Retrieved from: http://www.lawandbioethics.com/demo/Main/LegalResources/C5/background01.htm

Child Welfare Information Gateway, Children's Bureau. Disclosure of Confidential Child Abuse and Neglect Records [Pdf file]. Retrieved from: https://www.childwelfare.gov/systemwide/laws_policies/statutes/confide.pdf, June 2013.

Cleveland Clinic Foundation et al. v. United States of America, 1:11MC14 (Ohio, 2011). Retrieved from: http://law.justia.com/cases/federal/district-courts/ohio/ohndce/1:2011mc00014/172900/3

Department of Health & Human Services. *Center for Medicaid and State Operations/Survey and Certification Group.* (Memorandum regarding Informed Consent). Retrieved from: http://www.cms.gov/Medicare/ Provider-Enrollment-and-Certification/ SurveyCertificationGenInfo/downloads/ scletter07-17.pdf, April 13, 2007.

Fernandez, M., and Eckholm, E. "Pregnant, and Forced to Stay on Life Support". *The New York Times.* Retrieved from: http:// www.nytimes.com/2014/01/08/us/ pregnant-and-forced-to-stay-on-life-support.html?_r=0, January 2014.

Grabowski v. Quigley, 684 A. 2d 610 (Penn, 1996).

Harris, J. "Consent and End of Life Decisions," *Journal of Medical Ethics* 29(1):10–15, February 2003.

HIPAA-HITECH Guidelines. Retrieved from: http://www.hipaaguidelines.com, October 2014.

Hospice Association of America. *The Hospice Patients' Bill of Rights.* Retrieved from: http://www3.nahc.org/haa/attachments/ BillOfRights.pdf, 1990.

Informed Consent: Nursing Getting Patient's Signature Judged Improper, Doctor Faulted By Court. *Legal Eagle Eye Newsletter for the Nursing Profession.* Retrieved from: http:// nursinglaw.com/informed.pdf, February 1997.

Informed Consent: Court Throws Out Lawsuit Filed Against Hospital and Nurse. *Legal Eagle Eye Newsletter for the Nursing Profession.* Retrieved from: http://www .nursinglaw.com/informed4.pdf, December 2001.

Karp v. Cooley, 493 F.2d 408 (Tex. 1974).

LaDuke, S. "Nurses and the Attorney-Client Relationship", *JONAS Healthcare, Law, Ethics & Regulation* 2(4):117–23, December 2000.

LaMance, K. *Christian Scientists and Children's Medical Care Lawyers.* Retrieved from: http://www.legalmatch.com/law-library/ article/christian-scientists-and-childrens-medical-care.html, September 2012.

Lebowitz & Mzhen LLC. Man Files $12 Million Maryland Personal Injury Lawsuit Against Prince George's Hospital Alleging False Imprisonment [Web log post]. Retrieved from: http://www.marylandacci-dentlawblog.com/2010/08/man_files_12_ million_maryland.html, August 2010.

Lott v. State of New York, 32 Misc. 2d 296 (New York, 1962).

Luce, J.M. "Three Patients Who Asked that Life Support be Withheld or Withdrawn in the Surgical Intensive Care Unit", *Critical Care Medicine* 30(4):775–780, April 2002.

National Right to Life Committee, Inc. *The State of Abortion in the United States.* Retrieved from: http://www.nrlc.org/ uploads/communications/stateofabor-tion2014.pdf, January 2014.

Ornstein, C. Kaiser Hospital Fined $250,000 for Privacy Breach in Octuplet Case. *Pro Publica.* Retrieved from: http://www .propublica.org/article/kaiser-hospital-fined-250000-for-privacy-breach-in-octuplet-case-515, May 2009.

Rock, M., and Hoebeke, R. "Informed Consent: Whose Duty to Inform?" *Medsurg Nursing* 23(3):189–194, May–June 2014.

Shah, R. "Judge Rules that Pregnant Brain Dead Woman in Texas Can Be Removed from Life Support," *National Monitor.* Retrieved from: http://natmonitor. com/2014/09/03/judge-rules-that-preg-nant-brain-dead-woman-in-texas-can-be-removed-from-life-support/, September 2014.

Tan, S.Y. "Informed Consent: Disclosure of Risks," *Internal Medicine News*, pp. 54–55, April 15, 2010.

The White House. A New Patient's Bill of Rights. Retrieved from: http://www .whitehouse.gov/files/documents/health-care-fact-sheets/patients-bill-rights.pdf, 2014.

U.S. Department of Justice, Civil Rights Division, Disability Rights. ADA Update: A Primer for Small Business. Retrieved from: http://www.ada.gov/regs2010/smallbusi-ness/smallbusprimer2010.htm, 2011.

University of Virginia. Patient Confidentiality for Health Care Workers-HIV Confidenti-ality. Retrieved from: http://www.med-ed .virginia.edu/courses/rad/confidential-ity/3/hiv.html, 2013.

Wells v. Storey, 792 so. 2d 1034 (Alab. 1999).

Witmer, D. Abortion Laws for Teens by State. About.com. Retrieved from: http:// parentingteens.about.com/od/ teenpregfact/a/abortion_laws.htm, 2007.

Understanding malpractice liability

Rebecca F. Cady, Esq., BSN, CPHRM, DFASHRM

No legal issue sparks as much anxiety among nurses as malpractice, which can be emotionally harrowing and financially devastating. Unfortunately, more nurses are being named in lawsuits, and this trend shows no sign of changing. The most recent data from the National Practitioner Data Bank indicate that, for the time period from 2003 to 2012, medical malpractice payments on behalf of nurses have increased about one and a half times, from 483 payments in 2003 to 711 payments in 2012. Nurses also represent a growing percentage of the medical malpractice payments reported to the Data Bank, from 2.6% of payments in 2003 to 5.9% of payments in 2012 (see http://www.npdb.hrsa.gov/resources/annualRpt.jsp). Several reasons for this phenomenon exist:

- Patients are more knowledgeable about health care, and their expectations are higher.
- The health care system is more reliant on nurses and providers other than physicians to help contain costs.
- Nurses are more autonomous in their practice.
- The courts are expanding the definition of liability, holding all types of medical professionals to higher standards of accountability.
- Attorneys representing patients are seeking to maximize the potential sources of insurance dollars available to pay their claims by naming more individual defendants.

Losing a malpractice lawsuit can jeopardize your nursing career. Prospective employers and insurance companies will ask if you've been found liable for nursing malpractice, been named a defendant in a lawsuit, or been disciplined by your state's board of nursing. If you answer "yes" to any of these queries, you may find job hunting more difficult or have an extended probationary period or restrictions placed on your nursing practice. Also, your insurance company may refuse to renew your professional liability coverage. Other insurance carriers may refuse to insure you or require you to pay higher premiums for coverage. If you are an advanced practice nurse, a history of litigation activity may also impair your ability to get privileges to practice in a hospital, as review of litigation history is part of the credentialing process.

Fortunately, you can take steps to help limit your risk of malpractice litigation. Your best protection against malpractice litigation is giving your patients the best possible nursing care, according to the highest professional standards. To do this, you must be

(Text continues on page 137.)

National practitioner data bank

In 1990, the National Practitioner Data Bank began operation. As a result, physicians, dentists, nurses, and other health care practitioners who are forced to pay malpractice judgments are going to have a much harder time concealing their professional histories from potential employers. The data bank, which stores malpractice data on a nationwide scale, was created under the Health Care Quality Improvement Act of 1986 and the Medicare and Medicaid Patient and Program Protection Act of 1987.

Reporting requirements

The National Practitioner Data Bank collects information about practitioners who have paid judgments, had payments made on their behalf in settlement, entered into settlements, or have adverse action against their license or privileges to practice. All hospitals and health care facilities, professional health care societies, state licensure boards, and insurance companies are now required to report the following information about nurses to the data bank:

■ a nurse's malpractice payments (including judgments, arbitration decisions, and out-of-court settlements)

■ actions taken against a nurse's clinical privileges

■ adverse licensure actions, including revocations, suspensions, reprimands, censure, or probation.

Failure to report a nurse's malpractice payment of any amount–no matter how small–carries a $10,000 fine. However, the filing of a suit isn't, by itself, reportable; only the making of a payment is. Adverse clinical privilege actions against nurses may be reported at the discretion of the reviewing health care agency.

Federal agencies

Under the law, federal agencies aren't required to report to the National Practitioner Data

Bank. However, the Department of Defense, the Drug Enforcement Administration, and the Department of Health and Human Services have voluntarily agreed to observe the regulations.

Availability of information

The information in the data bank isn't available to the general public, nor is it available to attorneys, except in a specific context. If a practitioner is sued and it's determined that the employer didn't check the data bank, the attorney can send verification that the employing institution didn't check, along with the pending charges. If a similar case against the provider is in the data bank, notification will be sent. State licensing boards, hospitals, professional societies, and health care facilities involved in peer review may access the data bank. Individual nurses have access to records that pertain to themselves.

All hospitals must check the data bank when a nurse applies for clinical privileges. The hospital must request information on the nurse again every 2 years. The courts will presume that the hospital is aware of any information the data bank contains on any nurse or other practitioner in its employ. If knowledge of the information contained in the data bank would have resulted in denial of clinical privileges, the hospital could be held vicariously liable for negligence committed by the nurse as well as negligence in hiring the nurse in a malpractice lawsuit.

Information in the data bank

Reports made to the data bank typically include:

■ the nurse's full name, home address, date of birth, professional schools attended and graduation dates, place of employment, Social Security Number, and license number and state

■ name, title, and phone number of the official submitting the report

■ relationship of the reporting official to the practitioner

National practitioner data bank (continued)

- dates of judgment or settlement or amount paid
- description of judgment, settlement, or action.

Disputing a report

If a report about you is submitted to the data bank, you'll receive a copy for your review. If you believe the report is in error, ask the official submitting the report to correct it. The official making the report must submit corrections to the data bank.

If you fail to get satisfaction from the reporting official, you'll have to follow a detailed procedure for disputing the report. This must be done within 60 days of the initial processing of the report. Ultimately, you may request review from the Secretary of Health and Human Services.

---

familiar with and follow the standards of care that apply to your specific area of nursing as well as state and federal regulations, accreditation standards promulgated by the Joint Commission on Accreditation of Healthcare Organizations or the Community Health Accreditation Program, standards adapted by the American Nurses Association (ANA), standards of clinical specialty nursing organizations, and policies set forth by your employer.

You can further protect yourself by becoming familiar with malpractice law. This chapter describes malpractice issues, defines key legal terms, and explains legal doctrines that may arise in a malpractice lawsuit. You'll find extensive information on steps to take to avoid malpractice suits and advice on how to shop for professional liability insurance.

Even if you're meticulous in your practice and carefully avoid unnecessary legal risks, you can't completely escape the risk of being named in a lawsuit. In most jurisdictions, a patient can sue you without having a legitimate claim. To prepare you for this reality, you'll find guidelines in this chapter for

facing a malpractice lawsuit and a court appearance with less anxiety.

Understanding malpractice law

Our legal system's view of malpractice evolved from the premise that each person is responsible, or *liable*, for the consequences of his or her actions. Malpractice law deals with a professional's liability for negligent acts, omissions, and intentional harms.

CASE LAW

Case law, or *judicial precedent*, may set a standard of care in nursing or may impact the outcome of a specific malpractice case. Case law arises when a lawsuit has gone to trial and someone, either the plaintiff or the defendant, has been unhappy with the verdict and filed an appeal. After the appeals court has rendered a decision about the issues raised in the appeal, the written decision of the court may be published; cases are typically only

(Text continues on page 139.)

Understanding tort law

Most lawsuits against nurses fall into the tort category. If you're ever a defendant in a lawsuit, understanding the distinctions in this broad category may prove especially important.

A tort is a civil wrong or injury resulting from a breach of a legal duty that exists by virtue of society's expectations regarding interpersonal conduct or by the assumption of a duty inherent in a professional relationship (as opposed to a legal duty that exists by virtue of a contractual relationship). More generally, you may define a *tort* as "any action or omission that harms somebody." Malpractice refers to a tort committed by a professional acting in his or her professional capacity.

Unintentional vs. intentional torts

The law broadly divides torts into two categories: unintentional and intentional. An *unintentional* *tort* is a civil wrong resulting from the defendant's negligence. If a patient sues you for negligence, he or she must prove four things in order to win:

■ You owed a specific duty to the patient. (In nursing malpractice cases, this duty is equivalent to the standard of care.)
■ You breached this duty.
■ The patient was harmed. (The harm can be physical, mental, emotional, or financial.)
■ Your breach of duty caused the harm.

An *intentional tort* is a deliberate invasion of someone's legal right. In a malpractice case involving an intentional tort, the plaintiff doesn't need to prove that you owed him or her a duty. The duty at issue (for example, not to touch people without their permission) is defined by law, and you're presumed to owe this duty. The plaintiff must still prove that you breached this duty and that this breach caused harm.

Tort claim	Nursing actions that may lead to claims
Unintentional torts	
Negligence	■ Leaving foreign objects inside a patient after surgery because you did the instrument count incorrectly or you failed to do it at all ■ Failing to observe a patient as the physician ordered ■ Failing to be sure that the informed consent paperwork matches the procedure being done ■ Failing to report a change in a patient's vital signs or status ■ Failing to report another staff member's negligence that you witnessed ■ Failing to provide for a patient's safety by keeping the side rails up on the bed or stretcher ■ Failing to provide the patient with appropriate teaching before discharge ■ Giving the patient the wrong amount or type of medication
Intentional torts	
Assault	■ Threatening a patient
Battery	■ Assisting in nonemergency surgery performed without consent ■ Forcing a patient to ambulate against his wishes ■ Striking a patient ■ Inappropriately restraining a patient

Understanding tort law *(continued)*

Tort claim	Nursing actions that may lead to claims
Intentional torts *(continued)*	
Invasion of privacy	■ Releasing private information about a patient to third parties ■ Allowing unauthorized persons to read a patient's medical records ■ Allowing unauthorized persons to observe a procedure ■ Taking pictures of the patient without consent
Slander	■ Making false statements about a patient to a third person, which causes damage to the patient's reputation
False imprisonment	■ Inappropriately restraining a patient ■ Confining a patient in a psychiatric unit without a physician's order ■ Refusing to let a patient return home

published when they represent landmark decisions or represent an important clarification of the underlying law. The majority of appeals court decisions are not published. If an appeals case is published, it then becomes case law.

Generally, the case law that applies to an individual nurse's practice is the case law for the state in which he or she practices and any applicable federal case law. A seminal case from another state may also establish a standard of care because of the national acceptance of its ruling.

HOSPITAL AND CORPORATE LIABILITY

Employers have the overall responsibility and liability for the actions of their employees under the doctrine of vicarious liability or *respondeat superior*. This means your employer may be responsible for your actions, even if you weren't following its policies and procedures.

Because of the potential for corporate liability, health care facilities and agencies must be especially diligent in their hiring processes. They have to verify identity, training (including certificates, diplomas, transcripts, and licensure), and references, and they have to perform a background check (with the applicant's permission). Employers also have to thoroughly interview applicants, test basic nursing skills that are applicable to the open position, and check driving records. Then they must make sure that their findings are properly documented.

PHYSICIAN LIABILITY

As a nurse, you're responsible for following the nursing process in the care and treatment of your patients and for recognizing deviations from the standard of care. Furthermore, you're a patient advocate who is expected to question the appropriateness of every order you receive. For orders that you know to be potentially detrimental to your patient, you must question the order, seek alternative treatment, and seek advice or intervention from your nursing supervisor, in addition to documenting the actions you took. For example, if a physician orders a drug that your patient is allergic to, you must question the physician's order and obtain an order for a different drug, one that the patient isn't allergic to. Doing otherwise puts you and the physician at risk of liability. This is known as *joint responsibility.*

A classic example of joint responsibility would be that of a foreign object (such as a sponge) being left in a patient during surgery. The surgeon is responsible for not leaving a foreign object in the patient during surgery; the nurses assisting in the operating room are responsible for making sure that all equipment, supplies, and sponges used are accounted for before the surgeon closes. If the surgeon and the nurses fail in their responsibilities and the patient is harmed, then the surgeon as well as the nurses are responsible for their negligence. (Keep in mind that there have been a few cases in which only the nurses doing the surgical counts were held liable for a foreign object being left in the patient. Typically these would be cases where the nurse was aware of a count discrepancy but did not inform the surgeon.)

NURSE LIABILITY

Educational and licensing requirements for nurses increased after World War II. Nursing tasks became more complex, which led to specialization.

These changes meant that nurses began to make independent judgments and were viewed as clinicians. Although this increased responsibility provides a sense of autonomy and a more rewarding working environment, it also makes nurses more liable for errors and increases their likelihood of being sued.

Advance nurse practitioners are at the forefront of a paradigm shift occurring in today's health care industry. Ten years ago, nurse practitioners did not assume a prominent role in patient care. However, as policymakers address the goal of making health care accessible in all of our communities, they increasingly focus upon the nurse practitioner.

Nurse practitioners now occupy a central role in malpractice litigation. A threshold in such litigation often is the express regulatory authority of a nurse practitioner to render certain types of patient care. State Nurse Practice Acts differ dramatically in the professional activities that nurse practitioners may perform as well as in the policies, procedures, and/or protocols promulgated by their employers. Nurse practitioners will benefit from taking a proactive risk management approach to their clinical practice.

Causes of lawsuits against nurses

Nurses at one time were considered custodians of patients and few claims were made against nurses in this role. Negligence in patient care was attributed to the attending physician. While *nurse-as-custodian* claims continue to be asserted, plaintiff's lawyers have now begun to pursue claims that focus on the nurse as clinician, responsible for using professional judgment in the course of treatment.

In these claims, nurses are perceived as highly skilled and educated professionals who are charged with making clinical observations, exercising discretion and taking appropriate treatment actions based on a patient's changing clinical picture. This shift reflects, to some extent, the increasing number and importance of specialties and areas of expertise within the profession. The following are examples of the new paradigm of nursing claims:

■ Following a fall by a geriatric patient, the nurse is sued for failure to change the care plan despite increasing problems with gait and behavior.

■ A child is born with profound brain damage, and the nurse is alleged to have failed to properly interpret fetal monitoring strips.

■ A lawsuit charges the nurse with failure to appreciate a patient's risk for skin breakdown and to take appropriate preventive measures.

■ After a patient experiences adverse drug reactions, the family alleges that the nurse failed to properly administer and provide the correct dosage.

■ A patient in the emergency department (ED) has a cardiac arrest, and a lawsuit is filed alleging that the triage nurse failed to appreciate acute cardiac symptomatology.

This shift from viewing nurses as custodians to clinicians has afforded increasing opportunities for attorneys to name nurses as defendants in medical malpractice suits.

Negligence vs. malpractice

The courts' view of nursing liability has changed significantly over the years. At one time, nurses were charged only with negligence. Today, however, all courts recognize nursing negligence as a form of malpractice.

Negligence is the failure to exercise the degree of care that a reasonable person of ordinary prudence would exercise under the same circumstances. A claim of negligence requires that there be a duty owed by one person to another, that the duty be breached, and that the breach of duty results in injury. Although nurses always have

a duty to their patients, *malpractice* is a more restricted, specialized kind of negligence, defined as a failure to meet a standard of care, which typically means failure to act as a reasonable professional with the same education, training, and experience would act in similar circumstances.

Courts recognize nursing as its own profession. This professional status may affect the statute of limitations applicable in a particular case. The *statute of limitations* defines the time period in which a lawsuit may be filed. Many states have statutes of limitations specifically pertaining to medical malpractice claims, which may be shorter than those for ordinary negligence actions. Generally, one statute of limitations applies to adults (usually 2–3 years) and one applies to minors (up to 21 years of age depending on the state). However, additional statutes may limit or extend the statute of limitations, depending on the claim, the entity being sued, and the state where the harm was done.

Nurse practitioners

Nurse practitioners also represent a growing category of defendants in liability actions. According to the Nurse Service Organization's 2012 closed claim study (see NSO 2012), from the period of January 1, 2007 to December 31, 2011, the most common allegations against nurse practitioners are failure to diagnose and delay in making the correct diagnosis, failure to provide the proper treatment, and medication-prescribing errors. The study also showed that nurse practitioners who worked in the areas of adult medical/primary care and family practice were more likely to have claims. In terms of indemnity payments on behalf of NPs, this study showed a 19% increase in the average *(Text continues on page 144.)*

Liability in special practice settings

Although errors can be made in virtually any practice setting, nurses who work in certain settings are more vulnerable to malpractice charges because their patients are more complex, and their errors usually prove more costly for patients. Also, the courts may expect a higher standard from a nurse who practices a specialty. In specialty areas, the nurse will be judged by what a specialty nurse would do in a similar situation, not what a generalist nurse would do.

Critical-care nursing

Compared with nurses in other units, critical-care nurses spend more time in direct contact with their patients, thus increasing the opportunity for errors and the number of potential lawsuits. Because of the many invasive and potentially harmful procedures performed in this setting, critical-care nurses are especially vulnerable to charges of negligence and battery. Furthermore, if they perform duties or procedures that are outside their scope of practice, they may be accused of practicing medicine without a license.

Additional tort claims that may be filed against critical-care nurses include:
- abandonment–the unilateral severance of a professional relationship with a patient without adequate notice and while the patient still needs attention (a critical-care nurse who fails in her duty to observe the patient closely for any subtle changes in condition or who leaves her shift without giving adequate report to the oncoming nurse is vulnerable to this charge)
- invasion of privacy, intentional infliction of emotional distress, or battery–such cases usually involve a patient who was placed on or removed from life support against their or the family's wishes
- failure to validate informed consent–this is more likely to occur in a critical-care setting because of the inherent pressure and urgency for immediate treatment (a critical-care nurse who denies a competent patient the right to refuse treatment–even if lack of treatment would result

in the patient's death–exposes the nurse to charges of various intentional torts).

ED nursing

Many day-to-day practices of ED nurses fall into a legal gray area because the law's definition of a *true emergency* is open to interpretation–for example, health care workers who treat a patient for what they regard as a true emergency may be liable for battery or failure to obtain informed consent if the court ultimately concludes that the situation wasn't a true emergency. The provider usually must have a reasonable belief that death or permanent harm will come to the patient if treatment is not given.

One of the most common charges filed against ED nurses is failure to assess and report a patient's condition. Inadequate triage may be considered negligence.

Other tort claims made against ED nurses include:
- failure to instruct a patient adequately before discharge
- discounting complaints of pain from a patient who is mentally impaired by alcohol, medication, or injury
- failure to validate informed consent, giving rise to claims of battery, false imprisonment, and invasion of privacy.

Psychiatric nursing

Malpractice cases involving psychiatric care usually involve failure to validate informed consent. A nurse may wrongly assume that informed consent is not required, especially if the patient's condition interferes with his or her awareness or understanding of the proposed treatment or procedure. Violation of a patient's right to refuse treatment may stem from the mistaken belief that all mentally ill patients are incompetent. The right to refuse treatment isn't absolute, however, and can be abrogated if a drug or treatment is required to prevent serious harm to the patient or others. Generally, a physician, not a nurse,

Liability in special practice settings *(continued)*

makes this decision, and in many cases, a court makes the decision.

A nurse who reveals personal information about a patient to someone not directly involved in the patient's care also is vulnerable to malpractice charges. Violation of a patient's right to privacy and confidentiality is a common complaint in lawsuits against psychiatric health care workers, probably because of the stigma associated with mental illness.

Malpractice allegations may also stem from failing to protect a patient from inflicting foreseeable harm to self or others. Protecting a patient or potential victims from harm may include a duty to warn the patient's family that the patient is a threat to her/himself or a duty to warn a potential victim. This duty to warn is a standard of care in mental health practice that has been incorporated as either case law, statutory law, or both in many states.

If a nurse fails to report information given by the patient, even in confidence, that could have prevented the harm, he or she may be held liable for breaching the duty to appropriately assess the patient and for failing to comply with the duty to warn.

Obstetric nursing

Cases involving labor and delivery may have at least two plaintiffs: mother and infant. Monetary damages may be substantial, especially if the neonate sustained permanent and long-term injuries and is expected to live a long or near-normal life expectancy despite the injuries. An obstetric nurse may be held liable for:

■ negligence through participation in transfusion of incompatible blood, especially in relation to rhesus factor incompatibility
■ failure to attend to or monitor the mother or the fetus during labor and delivery
■ failure to recognize labor symptoms and to provide adequate support and care

■ failure to monitor contractions and fetal heart rate, particularly in obstetric units that have internal monitoring capabilities
■ failure to recognize high-risk labor patients who show signs of preeclampsia or other labor complications
■ abandonment of a patient in active labor
■ failure to exercise independent judgment, such as knowingly carrying out medical orders that will harm the patient
■ failure to validate that a patient has given informed consent for various procedures or treatments, including physical examinations, administration of a medication, type of delivery method, sterilization, and postdelivery surgical procedures.

Other common sources of malpractice suits filed against obstetric and neonatal nurses include failure to attend to the infant in distress, failure to monitor equipment, use of defective equipment, failure to monitor oxygen levels, and failure to recognize and report neonatal jaundice during the immediate postnatal period.

In some states, parents can file a *wrongful birth* lawsuit if a nurse failed to advise them of contraceptive methods or the methods' potential for failure, potential genetic defects, the availability of amniocentesis to detect defects, or the option of abortion to prevent birth of a defective child. A child with a genetic defect can file a *wrongful birth* lawsuit if a nurse failed to inform the parents of amniocentesis and the option of abortion. Failure to provide adequate genetic counseling and prenatal testing when the mother has a history of Down syndrome can also result in a wrongful birth or wrongful life lawsuit. (Keep in mind that many states don't allow recovery for wrongful birth.) Wrongful birth/wrongful life cases are usually brought against physicians or advanced practice nurses, as registered nurses (RNs) do not typically provide this scope of care to women.

indemnity payment since the previous study in 2009.

Criminal liability

Although most legal actions arising out of nursing practice are civil actions, nurses occasionally face criminal charges. There are several types of crimes for which a nurse may be charged as a result of nursing care.

Criminal negligence is more than ordinary carelessness, in other words, recklessness. Carelessness can be a crime when a nurse recklessly disregards a substantial and unjustifiable risk. In this situation, the nurse's conduct is evaluated according to community standards to determine if the carelessness is serious enough to demonstrate criminal conduct.

Criminal neglect is an act, omission, or course of conduct that because of the failure to provide adequate care creates a significant danger to the mental or physical health of a patient.

Negligent homicide is the negligent killing of one human being by the act or omission of another.

Criminal homicide is when a person purposely, knowingly, recklessly, or negligently causes the death of another. Murder and manslaughter are both examples of criminal homicide.

Assault is a crime that occurs when one person tries to physically harm another in a way that makes the person under attack feel immediately threatened. Actual physical contact is not needed; threatening gestures that would alarm any reasonable person can constitute an assault.

Battery is a crime consisting of physical contact that is intended to harm someone.

Other crimes for which nurses have been charged include elder/dependent adult abuse, drug possession/use, and breach of privacy (in some states this is indeed a crime).

Crimes can be classified as felony (serious crime) or misdemeanors/ infractions (less serious crimes). The exact definition and seriousness of the crime will depend on the law of the state in which the care was delivered. Usually a felony is punishable by a prison term of more than 1 year or, in some cases, by death; a misdemeanor is usually punishable by no more than 1 year in jail.

An example of failing to take the necessary actions might involve an RN ignoring the observations of a licensed practical nurse (LPN) regarding the severity of a patient's condition and failing to appropriately observe and assess the patient, ensure the necessary intervention, and follow up. If the RN's inaction leads to a severe worsening of the patient's condition, she could face criminal action for criminal negligence.

An example of intentionally acting to harm the patient would include a violent act that caused either physical or mental harm to a patient such as wrongfully restraining the patient in a way that caused injury. Another example is abuse that causes the patient physical or mental harm. One of the most extreme examples is when a nurse intentionally causes a patient's death, such as by administering a purposeful overdose or administering medications designed to stop the heart. Fortunately, these kinds of cases are rare. The more common situation is when a nurse's negligence is deemed so outrageous that it becomes a crime. One of the most well-publicized cases like this from 2006 involved a Wisconsin labor and delivery nurse who accidentally hung a bag of epidural anesthesia medication on the patient's IV line instead of the antibiotics she intended. She was charged with criminal "neglect of a patient causing great bodily harm" as a result of the patient's death.

Nurses have also been charged with crimes for what most of us would simply consider "unprofessional" conduct. In 2007, a group of New York nurses were indicted for endangering the welfare of pediatric patients at a nursing home. The 11 defendants were charged with misdemeanor endangering the welfare of children and physically disabled persons when they resigned en masse without giving notice. The nurses were recruited to this New York nursing home from the Philippines and brought to the United States under a contract that required them to honor a 3-year work commitment or pay $25,000 to the nursing home. A dispute developed between the nurses and the facility over working conditions. The indictment charged that the defendants agreed to resign en mass knowing that doing so would make it hard for the facility to find skilled replacement nurses in a timely manner. Ultimately these charges were dropped, but the nurses suffered the stress, embarrassment, and cost of defense for a number of years before being cleared. Not surprisingly, they filed a federal lawsuit against the prosecutor who pursued these charges despite the fact that both the board of nursing and the department of health determined that no patients had been harmed and that the open shifts created by their resignations had been covered by other staff, alleging that the prosecution was unconstitutional.

It's important for nurses to understand the differences between the criminal and civil systems. In the civil system, cases are decided by a judge or a jury, the penalties are limited, you must get your own attorney, and you may have a right to sue the other party if they sued you frivolously. In the criminal system, only a jury will decide the case, you may be penalized via fines or jail time, the state must provide you with an attorney if you can't afford one, and you have little recourse if you are wrongfully charged/prosecuted.

If a nurse is involved as a criminal defendant, it is important to understand that conviction of a crime is a basis for nursing license discipline (even if the crime is not related to patient care, for example drunk driving or drug use/possession can result in losing your license in most states). It is also important to understand that professional malpractice insurance does not cover criminal charges and the resulting legal costs, and your employer may or may not choose to pay your legal expenses even if the charge arose from work done in the course and scope of your employment.

Understanding the statute of limitations

The statute of limitations specifies the number of years within which one person can sue another. For malpractice lawsuits, the statute of limitations is specified in each state's medical malpractice law. These limits vary widely from state to state, so you should know the limits in your state. In the United States, the time limits are usually up to 3 years for an adult patient and up to age 21 for a patient who is a minor when the malpractice occurs.

Recognizing its purpose

As time passes, evidence vanishes, witnesses' memories fail, and witnesses die. A time limit for bringing a lawsuit ensures that enough relevant evidence exists for a judge or jury to decide a case fairly.

The statute of limitations for general negligence usually gives a person 3 years to sue another for damages. Defendants may invoke these limits as a defense in general personal-injury lawsuits. However, in response to pressure from medical and insurance groups, many states have established shorter statutes of limitations for professions that require independent judgments and frequent risks. The statutes of limitations of medical malpractice laws, for example, may give the adult patient 2 years or less to sue for damages.

DETERMINING WHICH STATUTE APPLIES

In some states, only physicians and dentists are expressly subject to medical malpractice statutes of limitations. These states view the nurse as someone carrying out orders, not making independent, risk-taking judgments.

If a nurse in one of these states alleges that a patient's claim is invalid because the suit was not filed until after the statute of limitations expired, the court must determine whether the statute of limitations for state medical malpractice law or the statute of limitations for general personal-injury lawsuits applies. (The statute of limitations for malpractice law is usually shorter.) The court will likely base its decision on two considerations:

■ *The amount of limitation protection the court believes the defendant-nurse's job warrants.* If the nurse's job requires many independent patient-care judgments, the court may apply a strict, or short, statute of limitations. A short time limit offers more protection for the nurse because the patient has less time to seek damages.

■ *The type of negligent act the plaintiff-patient claims the nurse committed.*

An injured patient may sue a nurse for one or several charges that constitute negligence or malpractice. The patient's attorney determines which charge has the best chance of winning the most damages for the patient and structures his case accordingly. Then, if a statute of limitations is used as part of the nurse's defense, the court decides which statute of limitations to apply in relation to the patient's charges.

Court case

In a California case, *Benun v. Superior Court* 123 Cal. App. 4th 113 (2004), the physician defendant argued that the statute of limitations applicable to professional negligence cases should be applied where a physician is being sued for any professional action including those in violation of the elder abuse statutes. The court held that a cause of action for custodial elder abuse against a health care provider is a separate and distinct cause of action from one for professional negligence against a health care provider. It follows that egregious acts of elder abuse are not governed by laws applicable to negligence. Specifically, Cal. Welf. & Inst. Code § 15657.2 was enacted to make sufficiently clear that "professional negligence" was to be beyond the scope of Cal. Welf. & Inst. Code § 15657. Cal. Welf. & Inst. Code § 15657.2 specifies that actions for professional negligence as defined in Cal. Code Civ. Proc. § 340.5 are governed by laws specifically applicable to actions for professional negligence (e.g., § 340.5), so it would seem to follow that § 340.5 has no application to actions brought under Cal. Welf. & Inst. Code § 15657. What this case illustrates is that the specific facts of the allegations against the defendant will drive which statute of limitations applies. Courts will not usually allow a plaintiff's attorney to attempt to create a breach of contract case (which has a longer statute of limitations) from facts that very clearly demonstrate a simple medical malpractice case.

APPLYING THE STATUTE OF LIMITATIONS

Even if a patient files suit long after the statute of limitations has expired, that statute may not necessarily protect you from liability. Remember that the patient's attorney knows about the statute of limitations, and the suit is being filed anyway. That means he or she believes that the court may set aside the statute of limitations because of some special circumstances.

Normally, the statute begins to run on the date the plaintiff's injury occurred. However, what if the plaintiff doesn't know that he was injured or doesn't find out that he has grounds for a suit until after the normal limitation period expires? Determining when the applicable statute begins to run becomes the pivotal question whenever a defense attorney invokes the statute of limitations as a bar to the plaintiff's case.

Legislatures and the courts, which are continually struggling with this question, have devised a series of rules to help decide, in individual malpractice cases, when a statute should begin to run. A court can apply these rules, when a plaintiff-patient's attorney requests that it do so, to extend the applicable statute of limitations beyond the limit written in the law. That means that the nurse's use of a statute of limitations as a defense may be invalidated, and the plaintiff-patient would still be allowed to sue. It is also important to understand that all the rules may not apply in each state; legislatures are free to pass laws

determining that only one of these rules will apply in that state, so it's important to check with your facility's risk management office if you have any questions about what the rules are in the state in which you practice. If you are involved in a potential lawsuit, your attorney can explain to you what rules may apply to your particular case.

Occurrence rule

Under the occurrence rule, the statute of limitations begins to run on the day the patient is injured. The occurrence rule generally leads to the shortest time limit. In several states, the courts have interpreted the occurrence rule strictly, so that even badly injured patients have been prevented from bringing suit after the applicable statute of limitations had expired.

Termination-of-treatment rule

The courts may apply the termination-of-treatment rule when a patient's injury results from a series of treatments extended over time, rather than from a single treatment. The termination-of-treatment rule (also known as the continuing treatment doctrine) states that a statute of limitations begins on the date of the last treatment. In devising this rule, the courts reasoned that for the patient, a series of treatments could obscure just how and when the injury occurred.

The Supreme Court of Virginia applied this rule in *Justice v. Natvig* 238 Va. 178, 381 S.E.2d 8, 1989 Va. Lexis 114, 5 *Va. Law Rep.* 2895 (1989). In this case, a patient filed a lawsuit 8 years after an allegedly negligent operation. The patient had continued to receive treatment during this interval. The defendant-physicians argued that the statute of limitations had lapsed. The court ruled, however, that the statute didn't begin to run until the treatment had ended, so the patient's lawsuit was allowed. However, subsequent decisions have clarified this ruling such that it would probably be hard for a plaintiff to use this rule against a nurse, especially if that nurse is employed by a hospital. In the case of *Castillo v. Emergency Medical Associates*, 372 F.3d 643, (2004), the U.S. Court of Appeals for the Fourth Circuit held that while the continuing treatment doctrine could apply to care provided by a corporation, the patient's emergency room visits (which were the alleged source of the negligent care) were discreet and isolated, and thus didn't meet the doctrine's requirement for a "continuous and substantially uninterrupted course of examination and treatment" for a particular ailment.

Constructive-continuing-treatment rule

The constructive-continuing-treatment rule is essentially the same as the termination-of-treatment rule, but it applies even after the patient leaves a nurse's or a physician's care. For example, suppose a patient you cared for is injured later, in someone else's care, and sues. Under the constructive-continuing-treatment rule, if the subsequent health care providers relied on decisions you made earlier in caring for the patient, the court may extend the statute of limitations in malpractice cases.

Discovery rule

Under the discovery rule, the statute of limitations begins to run when a patient discovers the injury. This may take place many years after the injury occurred. The discovery rule considerably extends the time a patient has to file a malpractice lawsuit. In some states this rule is modified to state

that the statute begins to run when a patient discovers or through reasonable diligence should have discovered the injury.

Two types of cases in which the discovery rule is usually applied are foreign object and sterilization cases. When a nurse or a surgeon leaves a scalpel, sponge, or clamp inside a patient, the patient might not discover the error until long after the surgery. Under the discovery rule, the applicable statute of limitations wouldn't begin to run until the patient found out about the error.

A court's decision to apply the discovery rule depends on whether it believes the patient could have discovered the error earlier. If evidence indicates that the patient should have recognized that something was wrong (for example, if he had chronic pain for months after the surgery but didn't take action to discover the reason for the pain until long afterward), the court could apply the termination-of-treatment rule instead. Time limits for applying the discovery rule in foreign-object cases also vary from state to state.

In lawsuits involving tubal ligations or vasectomies, the courts have sometimes allowed the discovery rule to apply when a subsequent pregnancy occurs. In these cases, the courts' reasoning is that a patient can't discover the negligence until the procedure proves unsuccessful, no matter how long after the surgery this proof appears.

Because the discovery rule is so generous to plaintiffs, some states, notably Texas, have restricted its application. A number of states have adopted separate statutes of limitations, one for readily detected injuries and one for injuries discovered later. Other states permit statute of limitations extensions only in foreign-object cases.

Proof of fraud

Courts, in most states, will extend the limitation period indefinitely if a plaintiff-patient can prove that a nurse or physician used fraud or falsehood to conceal from the patient information about the injury or its cause. In most cases, the law says that the conceal-ment must be an overt act, not just the omission of an act. The most flagrant frauds involve concealing facts to pre-vent an inquiry, elude an investigation, or mislead a patient.

Consider, for example, *Christy v. Miulli*, 692 N.W.2d 694 (2005). In this case, the family of a patient who died during a brain tumor biopsy sued the surgeon performing the biopsy. The court held that the doctor was not entitled to a dismissal based on the statute of limitations because the fam-ily had evidence that the doctor lied; he told the patient's wife that the cause of death was due to a disease, when actually an error during the procedure caused the death.

Minor or mentally incompetent patients

In most states, laws give special con-sideration to minors and mentally incompetent patients because they lack the legal capacity to sue. Some states postpone applying the statute of limitations to an injured minor until he or she reaches the age of majority, which may be age 18 or 21, depending on the state. Other states have specific rules about how statutes of limitations apply to minors.

Cases involving mentally incompe-tent patients who file after the statute of limitations has expired usually follow the discovery rule or a special law. Most special laws state that a stat-ute of limitation doesn't begin until the patient recovers from the mental incompetence or until a competent legal guardian is appointed for that patient.

USING THE STATUTE OF LIMITATIONS AS A DEFENSE

When a defendant-nurse uses a stat-ute of limitations as a defense, they're making, in legal terms, an affirmative defense. The defendant must prove that the statute of limitations has run out. If the court decides that the statutory time limit has expired, the plaintiff-patient's case is dismissed.

RETAINING MEDICAL RECORDS

Because a patient may file a malprac-tice suit years after he claims his injury occurred—and because you may be called on to recall specific clinical facts and procedures—accurate medical records are quite important in defend-ing a malpractice suit. If you are an independent practitioner, you should be sure to keep your records securely stored in a safe location through the period of any reasonable statute of limitations in your state. You should consult with your own attorney for specific advice on this issue and should keep in mind any regulatory records retention requirements. Complete documentation of your care is usually found only in these medical records. These records provide your best defense. Without them, you're legally vulnerable.

Few states have laws setting precise time periods, but many legal experts urge hospitals and other health care facilities to maintain medical records long after patients are discharged.

Some states have adopted the Uniform Business Records Act. This act calls for keeping records for no less than 3 years. Some states allow microfilm copies of medical records to be admitted as evidence in malpractice cases, but other states insist that only the original records can be used in court. If you work for a facility, be sure that you do not keep separate copies of patients' medical records; removing them from the facility is a breach of patient privacy laws and will likely violate your facility's medical records policies. You can inquire of your medical records department how long records are stored if you have concerns. You should also immediately report any patient-care event that you think may result in litigation so that the facility can investigate the issue as well as preserve any potential evidence including medical equipment, records, or other documents.

Avoiding malpractice liability

You can take steps to avoid tort liability by using caution and common sense and by being aware of your legal responsibilities.

MAKE A FAVORABLE FIRST IMPRESSION

The patient's first impression of a nurse is lasting and can set the tone for the nurse-patient relationship. Because a patient is less likely to sue someone he likes and trusts, a favorable first impression can help prevent a malpractice suit. Convey a caring attitude, give your full attention to the patient, try to avoid interruptions, and create a trusting relationship.

ESTABLISH YOUR BASELINE

Nurses frequently find themselves in trouble because they fail to obtain adequate information about a patient before attempting to provide care. To avoid problems caused by lack of knowledge, each nurse should establish her own baseline for each of her patients by:

■ reviewing each patient's medical records and noting significant information

■ reading all pertinent information contained in the care plan

■ discussing the care plan and past and current problems with the patient

■ revising the care plan as needed

■ appropriately reporting and documenting the patient's condition.

KNOW YOUR STRENGTHS AND WEAKNESSES

Don't accept responsibilities for which you aren't prepared. For example, if you haven't worked in pediatrics for 10 years, accepting an assignment to a pediatric unit without orientation only increases your chances of making an error. If you do make an error, claiming that you weren't familiar with the unit's procedures won't protect you against liability.

As a professional, you shouldn't accept a position if you can't perform as a reasonably prudent nurse would in a similar setting. Courts may, however, be more lenient when dealing with nurses who work in emergency settings, such as in a fire or a flood. However, simply being told "We need you here today" doesn't constitute an emergency.

EVALUATE YOUR ASSIGNMENT

You may be assigned to work on a specialized unit, which is reasonable, as long as you're assigned duties you can perform competently and as long as an *(Text continues on page 152.)*

Everyday situations that can trigger lawsuits

Everyday nursing situations can present legal hazards. These examples of nursing liability, based on actual court decisions, show how deviating from accepted standards can harm a patient and result in lawsuits. By being aware of how certain common situations can cause you legal entanglements, you can avoid making similar mistakes.

Failing to perform a proper assessment

When a man traveling between cities began having chest pain and numbness in his left shoulder and arm, he and his companion stopped at a small hospital for help. The nurse on duty in the ED advised him to travel to a larger hospital 24 miles away. She failed to perform a physical assessment or to obtain a formal history. On his way to the other hospital, the man had a massive myocardial infarction and died.

Clearly, the nurse failed to accurately assess her patient. Her mistake cost the patient his life and resulted in a landmark decision that established a nurse's independent relationship with her patient.

The court held the nurse responsible and accountable for her omissions, stating that she had failed to meet her duty to protect the patient from harm.

Federal law (Emergency Medical Treatment and Active Labor Act) also prohibits an ED from refusing treatment or discharging a patient without medical screening and stabilization. Hospitals are subject to fines and liability for failure to comply. Moreover, the plaintiff-patient may file suit under federal law as well as state negligence law for any injury that occurred as a result of the nurse's failure to screen the patient and stabilize his condition prior to discharge.

Failing to take appropriate precautions

An elderly senile patient with a history of falling down was left in bed with the side rails down. She fell out of bed and hurt herself.

Another patient, an alert 28-year-old, was instructed by a nurse to call for help before getting out of bed. After the nurse left the room, the patient got herself out of bed and fell.

In the first case, the nurse was found liable for failing to raise the side rails. When a patient is at clear risk for injury, the nurse must take extra measures to protect her.

In the second case, the nurse wasn't held liable for the patient's injuries. Her patient, a competent adult, had received appropriate instructions and chose to ignore them. In such circumstances, a court will likely hold the patient responsible.

Neglecting to document and communicate information

A mother took her two sons to an ED with head and chest rashes and high fevers. The mother gave the nurse an accurate history, which included the recent removal of two ticks from one of the boys.

The nurse didn't tell the physician about the ticks or record the information in the chart. The physician diagnosed measles in both boys and sent them home.

Two days later, one boy died of Rocky Mountain spotted fever, which is transmitted by ticks.

Although neither the hospital nor the physician was held responsible for the boy's death, the nurse's omission was found to be a contributing cause of death.

Performing nursing procedures incorrectly

A nurse administered an IM injection in the wrong quadrant of a patient's buttocks. He later developed footdrop from sciatic nerve damage.

In this case, both the nurse and the hospital were found negligent. Nurses are expected to administer drugs and treatments without injuring patients by following set standards of care. (Drug errors are one of the most common sources of negligence claims against nurses.)

(continued)

Everyday situations that can trigger lawsuits *(continued)*

The hospital's liability was established under the legal doctrine *respondeat superior*, which holds an employer responsible for an employee's errors.

Failing to report another's mistakes

While delivering a patient's baby, an obstetrician made an incision in the patient's cervix to relieve a constrictive band of muscle. After delivery, he failed to suture the incision.

The patient was sent to the postpartum unit for care and observation. The patient's nurse, noticing that the patient was bleeding heavily, called the obstetrician three times. He assured the nurse that the bleeding was normal. Within 2 hours, the patient went into shock and died.

Even though the nurse contacted the patient's physician, the court held the nurse negligent for failing to intervene further. The courts expect nurses to exercise professional, *independent* judgment and to object when a physician's orders are inappropriate. In this case, the nurse should have escalated her concerns using the facility's chain of command in order to ensure that the patient receive proper care.

Being involved in a surgical team's error

During a cholecystectomy, the surgical team accidentally left a sponge in the patient's body. When the sponge was discovered later, the patient needed another operation to remove it.

When the court awarded damages, both the surgeon and the nurse paid. At one time, the surgeon would have been fully responsible under the "captain of the ship" doctrine. Today, all members of the surgical team are responsible for their actions.

---

experienced nurse on the unit assumes responsibility for the specialized duties. Assigning you to perform total patient care on the unit is unsafe if you don't have the skills to plan and deliver that care.

Therefore, before you accept an assignment, make sure that you're competent to complete the assignment. If you're in the process of being oriented to a new unit or a new facility, don't take an assignment that puts you in over your head. Whenever an assignment requires skills that you don't have, make sure that another nurse with the necessary skills is available to help you with that portion of the care.

Nurses working in acute-care facilities are sometimes asked to float to units on which they aren't qualified to work. For example, a medical-surgical nurse might be asked to float to an orthopedic unit. If the nurse knows nothing about orthopedic nursing, she should insist that she be paired with an experienced orthopedic nurse and that she work alongside that experienced nurse in caring for orthopedic patients. However, if a nurse is asked to work in a critical-care area or an ED, it may not be feasible to pair her with another nurse in that type of setting; therefore, the nurse should refuse to be floated to that unit.

DELEGATE CAREFULLY

An RN may delegate patient-care responsibilities to another RN, an LPN, or an unlicensed assistive person (UAP), such as a nursing assistant or a medical technician. However, before the nurse delegates a given responsibility, he or she must know the skills and abilities of the delegate and which patient-care needs may be met by LPNs and UAPs and which require the intervention of an RN.

For example, if a nurse wants a nursing assistant to take a blood pressure reading on a patient who has an arteriovenous fistula, the state's nursing practice act must allow it. The nurse must also make sure that the assistant knows how to properly take and record the blood pressure reading and understands special considerations that must be observed.

Nurses can be held liable if they fail to appropriately delegate responsibilities. It's important for every delegating nurse to remember to:

- make sure staff members are competent
- teach and direct staff members
- evaluate staff members on an ongoing basis
- rectify any incompetent actions
- reassess patients
- take responsibility for all delegated tasks
- ensure accurate documentation.

A delegating nurse should check the state's nurse practice act to learn which tasks may and may not be delegated. The nurse should then delegate nursing tasks only to individuals who are appropriately trained. It's also important to report incompetent health care personnel to superiors through your facility's chain of command.

CARRY OUT ORDERS CAUTIOUSLY

Never treat any patient without orders from a physician, except in an emergency. Don't prescribe or dispense any drug without authorization. In most cases, only physicians and pharmacists may perform these functions legally.

Don't carry out any order from a physician if you have any doubt about its accuracy or appropriateness. Follow your facility's policy for clarifying ambiguous orders. Document your efforts to clarify the order, and whether or not the order was carried out.

If, after you carry out an order, the treatment adversely affects the patient, discontinue it. Report all unfavorable signs and symptoms to the patient's physician. Resume treatment only after you've discussed the situation with the physician and clarified the orders. Document your actions.

Keep in mind that a physician can change orders at any time, including while you're off duty. A patient may know something about his prescribed care that no one has told you. If a patient protests a procedure, drug dosage, or drug administration route—saying that it's different from "the usual" or that it has been changed—give the patient the benefit of the doubt. Question the physician's orders, following your facility's policy.

If you're an inexperienced nurse, you should take steps to clarify all standing orders. Contact the prescribing physician for guidance, or tell your supervisor that you're uncertain about following the order, and let him or her decide whether to delegate the responsibility to a more experienced nurse.

ADMINISTER DRUGS CAREFULLY

Drug errors are the most common type of nursing error. They typically occur because nurses fail to appropriately check the drug order or are unfamiliar with the drug they're giving.

Nurses can avoid drug errors by using the "rights" of medication

Who is looking for litigation?

Patients who are more likely to file lawsuits against nurses share certain personality traits and behaviors. Furthermore, nurses who are more likely to be named as defendants also have certain common characteristics.

Beware of these patients

Although not all persons displaying the behaviors listed here will file a lawsuit, a little extra caution in your dealings with them won't hurt. Providing professional and competent care to such patients will lessen their tendency to sue.

A patient who is likely to file a lawsuit may:
- persistently criticize all aspects of the nursing care provided
- purposefully not follow the care plan
- overreact to any perceived slight or negative comment, real or imagined
- unjustifiably depend on nurses for all aspects of care and refuse to accept any responsibility for his or her own care
- openly express hostility to nurses and other health care personnel
- project anxiety, or anger onto the nursing staff, attributing blame for all negative events to health care providers
- have filed lawsuits previously.

Nurses at risk

Nurses who are more likely to be named as defendants in a lawsuit display certain characteristic behaviors. If you recognize these attributes in yourself, changing your behavior will reduce your risk of liability.

A nurse who is likely to be a defendant in a lawsuit may:
- be insensitive to the patient's complaints or fail to take them seriously
- fail to identify and meet the patient's emotional and physical needs
- refuse to recognize the limits of their own nursing skills and personal competency
- lack sufficient education for the tasks and responsibilities associated with a specific practice setting
- display an authoritarian and inflexible attitude when providing care
- inappropriately delegate responsibilities to subordinates
- fail to advocate for the patient.

---

administration: right patient, right drug, right dose, right time, right route, right documentation, right reason, and right response. Also, when a nurse is unfamiliar with a drug to be administered, the nurse has the duty to look up the drug to understand its intended effects, any contraindications, the appropriate dose and route of administration, and potential adverse effects or drug interactions. Finally, the nurse needs to be able to evaluate and document the patient's response to the drug administered.

MAINTAIN RAPPORT WITH THE PATIENT

Trial attorneys have a saying: "If you don't want to be sued, don't be rude." Failing to communicate with patients is the cause of many legal problems.

Always remain calm when a patient or family becomes difficult. Patients must be told the truth about adverse outcomes, but this information should be communicated with discretion and sensitivity. You should never have a discussion with a patient about an adverse outcome without speaking to the risk management department in your facility. Many hospitals have specific policies on disclosure of adverse events to patients, and you need to be aware of and follow your facility's policy. Most of the time, the attending physician will lead this discussion with the patient.

THINK BEFORE YOU SPEAK

Avoid offering your opinion when a patient asks you what you think is the matter with him or her. If you do, you could be accused of making a medical diagnosis, which would be practicing medicine without a license. Don't volunteer information about possible treatments for the patient's condition or about possible choices of physicians, either.

Avoid making any statement that could be perceived by the patient as an admission of fault or error. Don't criticize other nurses or health care practitioners, or the care they provide, if the patient or family can hear you. Don't discuss with the patient or visitors which members of the health care team are covered by malpractice insurance. Gossiping with the patient about other staff is a recipe for disaster, and it's not fair to your coworkers. If you have real concerns about the care provided by other staff, you have a professional obligation to raise those issues according to your facility's policy.

Be careful not to discuss a patient's confidential information with anyone except when doing so is consistent with proper nursing care. Also, avoid such discussions in public areas, such as waiting areas, elevators, or cafeterias.

DOCUMENT CARE ACCURATELY

From a legal standpoint, documented care is as important as the actual care. If a procedure wasn't documented, the courts assume that it wasn't performed. Contemporaneous documentation of observations, decisions, and actions is considered to be more solid evidence than oral testimony given after the fact.

The patient's chart, when taken into the jury room, is a nurse's "best evidence" of the care given. The chart should follow the FACT rule—that is, it should be factual, accurate, complete, and timely.

Use incident reports to identify and report accidents, errors, or injuries to a patient. A long period may elapse between an incident and subsequent court proceedings, and this documentation may contain pertinent facts of the incident that may have been left out of the patient's medical record. Don't ever mention in the medical record that you have completed an incident report. In most states, incident reports are considered protected peer review and/or quality improvement materials and they are not subject to discovery by a patient's attorney in the course of a lawsuit. If you mention the incident report in the medical records, however, the attorney may be able to make a case with the judge to require that the report be shared.

Don't ever correct, destroy, or revise a patient's medical record after a bad event happens or after you become aware of a pending lawsuit. Altering the records will in most cases result in a presumption that the original evidence would have supported the patient's case; it will also likely subject the nurse to termination from employment and to administrative discipline by the board of nursing. In the case of *Morrison v. Rankin* 305 Wis.

2d 240 (2008), a medical malpractice suit, a directed verdict was entered by the court against the doctor, his insurer, and the Wisconsin Patients Compensation Fund as a sanction under Wis. Stat. §§ 804.12(2)(a), 805.03 for the doctor's spoliation of evidence as the doctor attempted to affect the outcome of the litigation by destroying medical records.

In many states, a rebuttable presumption of negligence arises if a health care facility's records are unavailable to a plaintiff and the plaintiff can demonstrate that the missing records are necessary to prove his or her negligence claim.

EXERCISE CAUTION WHEN ASSISTING IN PROCEDURES

Don't assist with a surgical procedure unless you're satisfied that the patient has given proper informed consent. Never force a patient to accept treatment he has expressly refused. Don't use equipment that you are unfamiliar with or aren't trained to use or that seems to be functioning improperly. And, if you're an operating room nurse, always check and double-check to ensure that no surgical equipment, such as sponges or instruments, are unaccounted for after an operation is completed. Be sure that all surgical specimens are accounted for and are appropriately labeled and taken to the laboratory after the procedure is completed.

DOCUMENT THE USE OF RESTRAINTS

Restraints need to be applied correctly and checked according to your facility's policy. Documentation must be exact about the reason for restraint, the need for restraint, the amount and kind of restraint used, and the status of the restrained patient. Generally, there must be a physician's order for restraints to be used. Restraining patients without a proper order may be a claim for patient abuse or false imprisonment. An omission or failure to properly monitor a restrained patient may also result in a malpractice claim.

TAKE STEPS TO PREVENT PATIENT FALLS

Patient falls are a common area of nursing liability. Patients who are elderly, infirm, sedated, confused, agitated, or mentally incapacitated are the most likely to fall. Often, there's no way to predict if and when a patient is going to fall. However, if the nurse has any reason to suspect that a patient is at an increased risk for falling, he or she must take appropriate measures to safeguard the patient. Most facilities have a fall risk assessment that must be completed on each patient upon admission. Be sure that you are completing this assessment and that you appropriately address any risks identified.

COMPLY WITH LAWS ABOUT ADVANCE DIRECTIVES

The Patients Self-Determination Act, a federal law, requires that every competent adult patient, upon admission to a hospital, be given information about living wills and durable power of attorney. In most facilities, this is done by administrative staff in patient registration. Follow your facility's policy for providing the required information. Don't, as one of the patient's health care providers, become a witness to a living will or a durable power of attorney. You should also be aware of state laws concerning living wills and advance directives. If the patient has an advanced directive, be sure that there is a copy of it available in the chart for providers to review; a patient may have a viable claim for battery if providers give care in violation of the patient's wishes as described in the advanced directive.

ADHERE TO YOUR FACILITY'S POLICIES

You have a responsibility to adhere to your facility's policies. If they're sound and you follow them carefully, they can protect you against a malpractice claim. Courts routinely hold that hospital policies are admissible as standards of care for the treatment of its patients.

Inexperienced nurses are at high risk for liability. The RN must be able to recognize his or her limitations and admit to them, especially if the safety of the patient is at issue. If the nurse doesn't know how to perform a nursing function or doesn't understand the reason for a particular treatment, it's his or her duty to obtain assistance that's timely and appropriate.

KEEP POLICIES UP TO DATE

As the nursing profession changes, so should a health care facility's policies. As a professional, you're responsible for keeping these policies up to date. For example, does your facility have a written policy on dealing with emergency situations? "We've always done it this way" isn't an adequate substitute for a clearly written, officially accepted policy. At the same time, it's important that the policies be realistic and evidence based. If the policies will be impossible to follow, they are not appropriate and should be revised.

PROVIDE A SAFE ENVIRONMENT

When providing care, avoid using faulty equipment. If you believe a piece of equipment is not working properly, clearly mark the equipment as defective and unusable. Even after repairs are done, don't use the repaired equipment until technicians demonstrate that the equipment is operating properly. Document the steps you took to handle problems with faulty equipment via your incident reporting system to show that you followed the proper procedure.

Maintaining professional liability insurance

In any work setting, you're at risk for malpractice suits, and the risk may increase if you work in an area that requires a high level of skill, specialized knowledge, or independent functioning. Many nurses choose to obtain their own nursing malpractice policy. Doing so can provide you with an extra layer of security should you find yourself on the wrong end of a lawsuit and alleviates the stress of having to worry whether or not your employer is making a change in its coverage or failing to maintain adequate coverage.

Many nurses mistakenly believe that purchasing an individual malpractice policy invites lawsuits. Unfortunately, this false belief deters some nurses from obtaining individual insurance coverage. The reality? A plaintiff's attorney won't know if a nurse has malpractice insurance unless he has begun a lawsuit and asked questions about insurance coverage via interrogatories or at a deposition. You should have a clear understanding of what coverage your employer provides for you and what the policy limits are.

Importantly, many facilities will not cover you for costs of defense in a disciplinary situation involving the board of nursing, so you may want to obtain a separate policy for this coverage alone even if you feel the facility's malpractice coverage is adequate.

UNDERSTANDING LIABILITY INSURANCE

When you buy professional liability insurance, you get protection under contract for a designated period from the financial consequences of certain professional errors. The type of insurance policy you buy determines the amount that the insurance company will pay if the judgment goes against you in a lawsuit. If you want coverage for board of nursing disciplinary actions, you need to be sure that your policy specifically includes this coverage as it is not automatically included in a professional liability policy.

You may purchase a policy designated with "single limits" or "double limits." In a single-limits policy, you buy protection in set dollar increments—for example, $100,000, $300,000, or $1,000,000. The stipulated amount will shield you if a judgment, arising out of a single nursing malpractice occurrence, goes against you.

In the double-limits policy, you buy protection in a combination package, such as $100,000/$300,000, $300,000/$500,000, or $1,000,000/$3,000,000. The smaller sum is what your insurance company will make available to protect you from any one injury arising out of a single nursing malpractice occurrence. The larger sum is the maximum amount that will be paid for all claims under that policy in a given year. Although the single-limits policy will also protect you against injuries to more than one patient, the double-limits policy makes considerably more money available to protect you if you're involved in multiple lawsuits. You need to be sure that you understand whether the policy limits include cost of defense (i.e., the cost of your attorney will be deducted from the limit available to pay a judgment) or whether defense costs are separate from the indemnity coverage limits provided.

Occurrence policies and claims-made policies

The two main types of insurance policies available to nurses are occurrence policies and claims-made policies. If you purchase an occurrence policy that begins on January 1, 2015, and ends on December 31, 2015, you're covered for any incident that occurs in this period that later results in a malpractice suit, regardless of when it's reported. When you cease to practice nursing for any reason, you don't have to purchase additional coverage.

If you purchase a claims-made policy that begins on January 1, 2015, and goes through December 31, 2015, you're covered only for the incidents that both occur and are reported during the indicated time period. However, if you continue your claims-made coverage with a new policy the following year and in the subsequent years during which you're practicing, you'll be covered for any incident that occurs and is reported during any consecutive policy period. If you retire from nursing or if you don't renew a claims-made policy, you need to purchase a reporting endorsement, commonly referred to as "tail" coverage, so that you'll be able to later report and have coverage for an incident that occurred when the policy was in effect. If you change insurance carriers and go from one claims-made

(Text continues on page 160.)

Choosing liability insurance

To find professional liability coverage that fits your needs, compare the coverage of a number of different policies. Make sure your policy provides coverage for in-court and out-of-court malpractice suits and expenses and for defense of a complaint or disciplinary action made to or by your board of nursing. Understanding insurance policy basics will enable you to shop more aggressively and intelligently for the coverage you need. You should work with an insurance agent who is experienced in this type of insurance. If you already have professional liability insurance, the information below may help you better evaluate your coverage.

Type of coverage

Ask your insurance agent if the policy covers only claims made before the policy expires (claims-made coverage) or if it covers any negligent act committed during the policy period, regardless of when it's reported (occurrence coverage). Keep in mind that the latter type offers better coverage.

Coverage limits

All malpractice insurance policies cover professional liability. Some also cover representation before your board of nursing, general personal liability, medical payments, assault-related bodily injury, and property damage.

The amount of coverage varies, as does your premium. Remember that professional liability coverage is limited to acts and practice settings specified in the policy. Be sure your policy covers your nursing role, whether you're a student, a graduate nurse, or a working nurse with advanced education and specialized skills.

Options

Check whether the policy would provide coverage for these incidents:
- negligence on the part of nurses under your supervision
- misuse of equipment

- errors in reporting or recording care
- failure to properly teach patients
- errors in administering medication
- mistakes made while providing care in an emergency, outside your employment setting.

Also, ask if the policy provides protection if your employer sues you.

Definition of terms

Definition of terms can vary from policy to policy. If your policy includes restrictive definitions, you won't be covered for actions outside those guidelines. Therefore, for the best protection, seek the broadest definitions possible and ask the insurance company for examples of actions the company hasn't covered. Be forewarned, however, that only the language in the policy governs your coverage—verbal or other representations from the company are not part of your contract.

Duration of coverage

Insurance is an annual contract that can be renewed or canceled each year. Most policies specify how they can be canceled—for example, in writing by either you or the insurance company. Some contracts require a 30-day notice for cancellation. If the company is canceling the policy, you'll probably be given at least 10 days' notice.

Exclusions

Ask the insurer about exclusions—areas not covered by the insurance policy. For example, "this policy doesn't apply to injury arising out of performance of the insured of a criminal act" or "this policy doesn't apply to nurse anesthetists."

Other insurance clauses

All professional liability insurance policies contain "other insurance" clauses that address payment obligations when a nurse is covered by more than one insurance policy, such as

(continued)

Choosing liability insurance *(continued)*

the employer's policy and the nurse's personal liability policy:

■ The *pro rata* clause states that two or more policies in effect at the same time will pay any claims in accordance with a proportion established in the individual policies.

■ The *in excess* clause states that the primary policy will pay all fees and damages up to its limits, at which point the second policy will pay any additional fees or damages up to its limits.

■ The *escape clause* relieves an insurance company of all liability for fees or damages if another insurance policy is in effect at the same time; the clause essentially states that the other company is responsible for all liability.

If you're covered by more than one policy, be alert for "other insurance" clauses and avoid purchasing a policy with an escape clause for liability.

Additional tips

Here's some additional information that will guide you in the purchase of professional liability insurance.

■ The insurance application is a legal document. If you provide false information, it may void the policy.

■ If you're involved in nursing administration, education, research, or advanced or nontraditional nursing practice, be especially careful in selecting a policy because many policies don't cover these activities.

■ After selecting a policy that ensures adequate coverage, stay with the same policy and insurer, if possible, to avoid potential lapses in coverage that could occur when changing insurers.

■ No insurance policy will cover you for acts outside of your scope of practice or licensure, nor will insurance cover you for intentional acts that you know will cause harm.

■ Be prepared to uphold all obligations specified in the policy; failure to do so may void the policy and cause personal liability for any damages. Remember that an act of willful wrongdoing on your part renders the policy null and void and may lead to a breach of contract lawsuit.

■ Check out the insurance company by calling your state division of insurance to inquire about the company's financial stability.

---

policy to another, you need to obtain prior-acts coverage, which allows you to report incidents that occurred during a previous policy period and have resulted in a lawsuit or board of nursing complaint during your new policy period with your new insurance carrier.

Excess judgment

A judgment that exceeds policy limits is known as *excess judgment*. However, if you've purchased your own policy to supplement the coverage your employer is providing, it's unlikely that there will be an excess judgment. Also, if the insurance carrier or carriers

providing coverage think that a verdict in excess of your policy limits is possible, they're obligated to try to get the case settled within your policy limits.

If your attorney has told you that the case might result in an excess judgment and the insurance company isn't moving to get it settled, your attorney should write a letter to your insurance company demanding that the case be settled within your policy limits. Once such a letter is written, the insurance carrier may become responsible for any excess judgment if it fails to make a good faith effort to settle the case. If a good faith effort to settle the case is unsuccessful and there's an excess judgment, then you may end up being personally responsible for the amount of the excess judgment.

Depending on the laws in your state, almost everything you own, except for a limited portion of your equity in your home and the clothes on your back, can be taken to satisfy the uninsured portion of a judgment.

SUBROGATION

Subrogation is defined as the act of substituting another (that is, a second creditor) with regard to a legal right or claim. Employers (or other defendants such as physicians) who have been found liable for damages can subsequently sue another person involved in the incident to recoup their losses.

In a Pennsylvania case, *Mutual Insurance Company of Arizona v. American Casualty Company of Reading* (1997), a patient underwent angioplasty and had a complication, which was treated. However, during nurse-to-nurse report, the incident wasn't mentioned. The patient went into cardiac arrest and died within 12 hours. The patient's family sued the hospital and the physician, but the nurses weren't named in the lawsuit. After the hospital was found liable, the hospital's insurer filed suit against the nurses involved, saying that the patient would have been more closely monitored if the staff had known that it hadn't been a routine angioplasty. The court ruled that the suit was permissible. Cases like this are rare, however. Remember that the hospital is always liable for the acts of its employees under respondeat superior. This is one instance in which having your own malpractice insurance may be a detrimental thing as it might give the employer a reason to seek contribution from you for a case in which you were involved but where

you were not named as a defendant by the patient.

INSURANCE COSTS

Fortunately, premiums for insurance coverage of $1 million aren't much more than they are for smaller limits. The reason is that a substantial part of the premium pays for the insurance company's assumption of risk; higher limits don't increase the premium disproportionately.

General duty RNs usually pay less for coverage than critical-care nurses, operating room nurses, ED nurses, postanesthesia care nurses, and advanced practice nurses. In recent years, nurses specializing in obstetrics have typically paid the highest insurance premium rates, in part because of the large number of lawsuits filed against obstetricians.

Insurance companies offer various liability insurance policies. If possible, choose an agent who is experienced in professional liability coverage. Organizations such as the ANA and your state nurses' association offer group plans at attractive premiums. You need to review the extent of coverage with your agent to make sure it's adequate for your needs.

INSURER'S ROLE IN A LAWSUIT

Professional liability insurance can supply you with more than just financial protection. The insurance company may also provide a defense counsel to represent you for the entire course of litigation if it's included in your insurance contract. Remember that insurance companies aren't in business to lose money; they'll retain highly experienced attorneys with considerable experience in defending malpractice lawsuits.

When preparing your defense, attorneys will investigate the subject of the lawsuit, obtain expert witnesses, handle motions throughout the case, and prepare medical models, and other court exhibits, if necessary. The cost incurred in preparing a defense and defending you through trial and appeals maybe covered by your insurance policy.

Out-of-court settlements

During litigation—and even before a lawsuit is filed in court—your insurance company may seek an out-of-court settlement from the plaintiff's attorneys. Although this saves time and money, it may not be in your best interest professionally. In the United States, if you believe your professional reputation is at stake, you may be able to refuse to agree to an out-of-court settlement. If your policy contains a threshold limit, your insurer can't settle a case out of court for an amount greater than the threshold limit without your permission. Without a threshold limit, your insurer has control over out-of-court settlements. Be aware, however, that most policies include what is called a "hammer clause," which requires you to cooperate with the defense and settlement of the case; if you refuse to give your permission to settle the case and the jury awards more than the amount of the proposed settlement you rejected, you could be personally responsible for the entire verdict as well as your defense costs.

If the lawsuit against you goes to court and the insurance company is defending you, the insurer has the right to control how the defense is conducted. The insurer's attorney, however, makes all decisions regarding the case's legal tactics and strategy.

You have a right to be kept informed about every step in the case because you, not the insurance company, are the client, so the attorney must perform his legal duties

according to what's in your best interest, not the insurance company's. After all, the insurer knows that a successful defense depends in part on the defendant's cooperation. Also, you can sue the insurance company if it fails to provide a competent defense.

If you lose a malpractice lawsuit, the insurance company will cover you for jury-awarded general and special damages. Typically damages include but aren't limited to:
- medical expenses
- lost wages
- loss of earning potential
- other related expenses, such as:
  - ❏ modifications that need to be made to a home or vehicle
  - ❏ equipment that needs to be purchased or leased
  - ❏ homemaker or housekeeping services.

Other monetary damages that also may be added to the settlement or verdict value of a case include damages awarded for pain and suffering; loss of consortium; or emotional harm, now and in the future. In states where tort law has undergone tort reform, there may be caps on the amount of recovery legally allowable for such things as pain and suffering or loss of consortium.

Punitive damages

Some states allow a plaintiff-patient to recover punitive damages from a defendant-nurse (or other health care provider) if that defendant did something to intentionally harm the patient or knowingly failed to take steps to prevent harm to the patient.

Some insurance carriers have provisions in their policies that specifically state that they won't indemnify a policy holder for punitive damages if the policy holder is shown to have acted with malice or reckless disregard. Why? Punitive damages are meant to punish the defendant, and the defendant isn't really being punished if such damages are paid. However, many insurance carriers have decided to indemnify their insured health care provider for punitive damages that have been included in a settlement or verdict. Such decisions are generally made on a case-by-case basis. Additionally, if an insurance carrier doesn't have a specific exclusion in the policy for punitive damages, they may be responsible for payment of any and all damages up to the limits of liability in any given policy.

Multiple insurers

If you have more than one insurance policy—for example, malpractice coverage through your employer as well as your individual insurance policy—both insurance companies might well become involved in defending or settling a patient's claim against you. Determining who pays is complex. Generally, the coverage provided by your employer would be the primary policy if the lawsuit involves actions you performed at your place of employment within your scope of practice. The coverage provided by your individual policy would be secondary and would take effect only after the primary policy was exhausted.

Your secondary policy would cover you up to its policy limits for any excess verdicts or settlements that weren't covered by your primary policy. However, you must promptly notify each insurance company you have a policy with that you're the target of a malpractice lawsuit. If you fail to notify your insurance companies of this or if you delay in notifying them, they can use such policy defenses to avoid responsibility for providing coverage.

Indemnification suits

If several insurance companies are representing different parties in a malpractice lawsuit, they'll typically file counteractions against the other parties, seeking compensation, or *indemnification,* for all or part of any damages the jury awards.

Many states now permit damages to be apportioned among multiple defendants, the extent of liability depending on the jury's determination of each defendant's relative contribution to the harm done. This is called comparative negligence. For example, suppose you were the nurse responsible for the instrument count during surgery in a foreign-object case, and the court found you to be 75% responsible. Your insurance company would pay 75% of the total award. The other insurance companies would be held liable for the remaining 25%, in proportion to the percentage of harm attributed to each remaining defendant.

Also, a plaintiff's acts or omissions (for example, failure to follow a physician's order) may be considered by a jury in determining where liability lies. This is known as contributory negligence. A judgment would be reduced by the plaintiff's own negligence. Still other jurisdictions subscribe to a rule of joint and several liability. This means that if there are multiple defendants, any one of them can be held liable to the patient for the entire amount of the verdict, regardless of the proportion of fault. So if you were the only defendant who had insurance, you could be held responsible for paying the patient if none of the other providers had the ability to pay the verdict. In most joint and several liability states, the defendants evenly split the verdict among themselves or they privately negotiate proportional shares after a verdict has been reached.

LIABILITY COST CONTAINMENT

Many states are taking steps to decrease malpractice litigation and the size of potential jury verdicts. Besides establishing special statutes of limitations, some states have imposed a maximum limit on the monetary sums a jury can award for certain damages, such as loss of consortium, wrongful death, and pain and suffering. The federal government has also been debating a proposed award cap of $250,000 for pain and suffering, but the proposal has met stiff resistance; it has been called unconstitutional by certain members of Congress and various special-interest groups.

Medical associations and insurance companies are trying to limit malpractice awards by forcing malpractice claims into arbitration, thus removing them from the province of lay juries, and by requiring that claims be screened by a medical malpractice screening panel. A few states, such as Ohio, provide for submission to non-binding arbitration panels if all parties agree. State laws may also provide for binding arbitration if specified by a written contract between a patient and the physician or hospital.

In some states, if a malpractice screening panel decides that the plaintiff's claim is invalid, the plaintiff can't file suit unless he posts a bond to cover his defense costs in advance. These panels have been criticized by consumer groups and plaintiffs' attorneys and challenged in court as being unconstitutional.

YOUR EMPLOYER'S INSURANCE

Virtually all health care facilities carry insurance to protect against their liability for an employee's mistakes. Without professional liability insurance, the facility would have to pay damages awarded in a lawsuit out of its own funds, which could lead it to bankruptcy.

To help you to more wisely assess your own professional liability insurance needs, find out the degree of professional and financial protection you're entitled to under your employer's liability insurance. To do this, consider obtaining and reviewing a copy of your employer's insurance policy. If you don't understand something in the policy, contact the insurer.

Coverage limits

Although each health care facility's professional liability insurance policy has a maximum dollar coverage limit, your employer can purchase coverage that exceeds the basic limit. Many hospitals do so for extra protection.

Deductible limit

Most hospitals also have a deductible provision that makes them responsible for damages under a certain figure. The higher the deductible limit, the lower the premium the insurer charges. You should pay careful attention to the deductible limit because your employer may be able to settle a claim against you, for which they may be held financially responsible, under that figure without ever consulting you or the insurer. Because you won't have a chance to defend yourself and because many people interpret a settlement as an admission of guilt, such an action could tarnish your professional reputation. A tarnished reputation, in turn, could jeopardize your ability to obtain your own professional liability insurance or a new job. Therefore, in the event of a lawsuit where you are individually named as a defendant, you should maintain close contact with your employer's legal staff and insist on being informed about every step in the case.

Provisions for your defense

If you're sued and your employer's insurance covers you, the insurer may have a duty to provide a complete defense, including assigning an attorney to handle the entire case. The insurer will pay attorney fees as well as any investigation costs and expert witness fees.

If there's ever a conflict between your best interest and your employer's best interest, you should obtain your own attorney who will be concerned with your defense. This attorney may work closely with hospital counsel, but his loyalty is to you. He'll provide you with an opportunity to confer with him and give your side of the story.

If your employer grants written consent to settle the case, the insurer may do so or it may decide to try the case in court if its legal advisors overrule the employer. If the plaintiff wins the lawsuit, the insurer is obliged to pay damages awarded to the patient up to the insurance policy's coverage limit.

Stipulations for denying coverage

Insurance companies that provide professional liability coverage for hospitals and other health care facilities reduce the risk they assume under *respondeat superior* in several ways. One way is by stipulating a precise coverage period, typically 1 year. Another way is by defining the type of coverage they provide, whether, for example, it's an occurrence policy or a claims-made policy. A third way is by putting exclusions into malpractice policies. These exclusions vary considerably from policy to policy, but all list specific acts, situations, or personnel that the insurance doesn't cover.

Besides exclusions, insurers may deny coverage to you or your employer because of other circumstances, including:

■ The insurance policy lapses because your employer failed to pay the premiums.

■ Your employer refuses to cooperate with the insurance company, for whatever reason.

■ The insurer discovers that your employer made misstatements on the insurance application.

In some malpractice situations, an insurer could agree to provide you with a defense but refuse to pay damages awarded to a patient. The insurer agrees to defend you in this situation because he doesn't want to be accused of breach of contract. However, he must notify you of his intention not to pay damages in a reservation-of-rights letter. This letter informs you and your employer that the insurer believes the case falls outside what's covered by the insurance policy.

When your employer and the insurer disagree about whether insurance coverage exists, the dispute may have to be resolved through separate legal action. Similarly, you have the right to bring such action against your employer's insurance company if it refuses to cover you.

Most hospitals maintain their insurance coverage by way of a captive insurance company; this way the hospital is in essence self-insured for the lower layers of insurance coverage designed to capture most run-of-the-mill claims. The facility then purchases commercial excess coverage to protect against large claims or batch claims involving one event that impacts a large number of patients. As such, most cases in which a nurse may be involved will in essence be managed directly by the hospital's risk or insurance staff.

This is a good thing for the employed nurse because the facility's interest is in keeping a unified defense among all the employees who may be defendants in the case, which reduces the likelihood of finger pointing among the providers.

Special considerations

Keep in mind a few more concerns when reviewing your employer's policy. First, is the policy purchased for you as an employee benefit? In that case, the insurer protects you and not the hospital. Second, the policy may provide coverage only for incidents that occur while you're on the job. You may be held liable for nursing actions off the job, unless your actions are covered under a Good Samaritan act, a state law that protects health care professionals who act in an emergency.

Third, many employers provide only a claims-made policy. If a suit is filed against you for work you performed while working for a *former* employer, you probably won't be covered by your former employer's insurance plan.

Fourth, if you're an independent contractor such as a private-duty nurse, the court likely won't consider you to be under the hospital's direct supervision and control. Consequently, the hospital won't be considered responsible for your actions, and its insurance probably won't cover you. However, if the policy is yours with the hospital paying the premiums as an employee benefit, you're still covered.

Finally, with regard to intentional acts of harm, such as striking a patient, you would be responsible for any criminal or civil penalties levied against you. Simply keep in mind that intentional acts of harm usually aren't covered by any professional liability policy.

SELECTED REFERENCES

American Hospital Association's Quality Agenda, American Society of Health-System Pharmacists, and Hospital & Health Networks. "Medication Safety Issue Brief: A Fully Stocked Toolkit. Series II, part 1," *Hospitals & Health Networks* 77(6, supp 2): 24, June 2003.

Berwick, D.M. "Errors Today and Errors Tomorrow," *New England Journal of Medicine* 348(25):2570–2572, June 2003.

Cady, R. "Criminal Prosecution for Nursing Errors," *JONA's Healthcare Law, Ethics, and Regulation* 11(1):10–16, January-March, 2009.

Clark, A.P. "Malpractice Prevention and Technology Expertise," *Clinical Nurse Specialist* 17(3):126–127, May 2003.

Clement, R. "Liability Awards and Nurses," *Hospitals & Healthcare Networks* 77(1):12, January 2003.

Denney, C. "Safe, Secure Staff Provides Better Care," *Nursing Management* 34(3):18, March 2003.

Elbow S. St. Mary's Nurse Is Charged with Neglect: Medication Error Led to Teen's Death. Madison, WI: The Capital Times, November 2, 2006. Retrieved from: www.madison.com/tct/mad/topstories/index.php?ntid=105800&ntpid=1

Haugh, R. "Surviving Medical Malpractice Madness," *Hospitals & Healthcare Networks* 77(5):46–50, 52, May 2003.

Mello, M.M., et al. "The New Medical Malpractice Crisis," *New England Journal of Medicine* 348(23):2281–2284, June 2003.

Nurse Service Organization. Nurse Practitioner 2012 Liability Update: A Three-Part Approach, NSO, 2012.

U.S. Department of Health and Human Services, Health Resources Services Administration, Bureau of Health Professions, and Division of Practitioner Data Banks. 2012 Annual Report, February 2014.

"Professional Liability Insurance. Myth vs. Fact," *Colorado Nurse* 102(1):18, March 2002.

Rosenbaum, S. "Medical Errors, Medical Negligence, and Professional Medical Liability Reform," *Public Health Reporter* 118(3):272–274, May-June 2003.

Walsh, P. "We Must Accept That Health Care Is Risky Business," *British Medical Journal* 326(7402):1333–1334, June 2003.

CHAPTER 5

Lawsuits and the legal process

Kristopher T. Starr, RN, MSN, JD, CEN, CPEN

Before the early 1970s, health care providers seldom thought about their potential for being sued for medical malpractice because patients and their families were generally unaware of their legal rights within the health care system. Patients didn't know their civil law options when dealing with less-than-satisfactory outcomes. However, the malpractice crisis that erupted in the late 1970s—spurred on by greater patient awareness of disorders (and their specific treatments) and higher patient awards—quickly taught all health care providers that patients now expect higher quality of care and will sue if they feel they don't receive Trial lawyers in the 1980s also increased the marketing of their services to coordinate with increased mass tort lawsuits.

The medical malpractice lawsuit

Most malpractice lawsuits against nurses are filed under the auspices of tort law. *Torts* are personal, civil injuries that reside outside a contractual relationship. *Malpractice* is a type of tort that's defined as a professional person's unsafe or inadequate actions, improper discharge of professional duties, or failure to meet or adhere to the standards of care that results in harm to a patient under the care of the professional.

Patients typically file malpractice lawsuits against nurses when they perceive their nursing care to be substandard or the proximate cause of foreseeable injuries. It is important to note, though, that malpractice is more than an undesired outcome. An aggrieved patient has to mount a significant burden of proof in order to *successfully* file a malpractice lawsuit against a nurse. First, there must be evidence that some action or inaction (errors of commission or omission) that the nurse was obligated to perform resulted in harm to the patient. If the patient doesn't have compelling evidence, they may still file suit, but the court may dismiss the suit outright. If the case was permitted to continue, the plaintiff is unlikely to prevail.

Any person can file a lawsuit for a perceived wrong, but not every lawsuit is a winner.

THE FOUR ELEMENTS

In a civil lawsuit, a plaintiff must prove, by a preponderance of the evidence (51% or more likely than not), that the nurse owed a duty to the patient, the nurse then breached that duty owed the patient, and said breach was the cause of injury to the patient, which resulted in calculable damages.

Duty owed the patient
The patient-plaintiff must show that the nurse-defendant owed him a specific duty and to what level the duty was owed. The nurse-patient relationship, showing that the patient was relying on the professional judgment of the nurse to deliver safe and competent care, forms the basis for this element. Standards of care become the main issue. The patient's attorney and the nurse's attorney will both present their views of what a reasonably prudent nurse, with like training and experience, would have done under similar circumstances. The nursing standard of care is a professional standard, not that of an ordinary prudent person, but, instead, that view of a reasonably prudent professional.

Breach of duty owed the patient
Attorneys for the patient-plaintiff will present testimony concerning the nurse-defendant's failure to meet a nursing standard of care. Attorneys for the nurse will present contradictory testimony. This portion of the lawsuit can be lengthy and usually involves the use of expert witnesses.
(See *Courtroom controversy: nurses as expert witnesses.*)

Causation
Causation, the concept that certain events may reasonably be expected to cause specific results, is usually the most difficult element to prove at trial. Most state laws command that the specific outcome must be foreseeable before there can be malpractice liability.

Causation may be further divided into cause in fact and proximate cause. Cause in fact involves the concept that what the nurse does or fails to do must be directly attributable to the harm that the patient incurs. It isn't enough that a patient is harmed; there must be a direct and usually uninterrupted relationship to the harm and what the nurse did or failed to do. This element, like breach of duty owed the patient, is commonly argued at court through the use of expert witnesses.

Finally, there can be proximate cause for which nurses are held liable. Proximate cause actually builds on foreseeability and attempts to determine how far the liability of the individual extends for consequences following negligent actions. If a nurse administers an overdose of a known nephrotoxic medication and the patient develops renal failure 2 years later, is the nurse liable for the renal failure? Under the concept of proximate causation, the answer could be yes. However, if a patient is deemed partially responsible for her injury, proximate causation may not apply. (See *Proximate causation*.). Plaintiff's lawyers will often attempt to stretch the concept of proximate causation to its limits to establish a meritorious claim.

Injury and damages
In order for a nurse to be held liable for malpractice, the patient must prove physical injury and calculable monetary damages. Although courts allow some award of damages for pain and suffering, damages are generally awarded to compensate the patient for economic expenses incurred (actual and projected) as a direct or indirect

(Text continues on page 170.)

Courtroom controversy: nurses as expert witnesses

Testimony by experts is an essential ingredient in malpractice cases for both plaintiff and defendant. In lawsuits against nurses, the court's position is that a nurse is the appropriate expert witness when dealing with the actions or decisions of a nurse. Before 1980, it was common for physicians to testify about the standards for nursing care.

No double standard

In the case of *Sullivan v. Edward Hospital 806 N.E. 2d 645 (Ill. 2004)*, the court concluded that physicians may not determine nursing standards of care. Per the court, the physician, not being a nurse, is no more qualified to opine on a nursing standard of care, than a nurse is to opine on a physician standard of care (quoting the amicus curiae brief of the American Association of Nurse Attorneys). The court also concluded that professional registered nurses are unable to opine on advanced practice nurses standards of care. The expert witness nurse can explain technology or nursing care in the language jurors can understand. This type of testimony is crucial to dispel common misconceptions or to explain scientific facts as they pertain to nursing care and the care at hand.

Qualifications of an expert

A nurse expert witness testifying for the plaintiff in a malpractice case must be able to describe the relevant standard of care, describe how the nurse deviated from the acceptable standard, and explain how failure to meet acceptable nursing standards caused or contributed to the patient's injury. Defense counsel will also provide a nurse expert who will testify to the standard and whether the defendant nurse met the standard.

A nurse must meet certain criteria to be considered an expert witness. The first and only absolute criterion is current licensure to practice nursing. Also, the expert witness' credentials must match or exceed the defendant's. This includes clinical expertise in that specialty area, certification in the clinical specialty, and recent education relevant to the nursing specialty at issue. However, the expert witness may hold licensure in another state. Another criterion is a lack of bias; the expert witness must not have any relationship, professional or personal, with any parties involved in the suit.

Expert witness or legal consultant?

There's a difference between being a "behind-the-scene" legal nurse consultant and an expert nurse witness. A legal nurse consultant working behind the scenes will generally review the medical records and all pertinent standards of care and offer opinions to the attorney on issues of concern to the case. Her written report and any other work product is considered privileged and confidential attorney work product; it is not given to the opposing counsel. However, when a nurse agrees to become an expert witness, her name is given to opposing counsel and she may have to testify in court. Also, any comments, notes, or reports she makes may be discovered and reviewed by opposing counsel.

The nurse expert witness faces two dilemmas: the changing standard of care and being trapped into saying that only one opinion is correct. A nurse expert witness must consider the possibility that the standard of care may have changed by the time the case goes to trial, and thus, it's crucial to know what was acceptable at the time of the incident.

On occasion, a nurse may testify as an expert about a physician's care, when the physician performs an act that's also a nursing function, such as drawing blood or inserting a nasogastric tube. The nurse expert must be cautious, however, that the testimony stays on topic to the shared nursing function and does not stray into the physician functional role or physician standard

(continued)

Courtroom controversy: nurses as expert witnesses *(continued)*

Testimony exception

There are certain cases where expert testimony is not necessarily needed to establish a breach of the standard of care. In *Hubbard ex rel. Hubbard v. Reed*, 774 A. 2d 495, 500-01 (N.J. 2001), the New Jersey Supreme Court held that something as obvious as "pulling the wrong tooth" does not require an expert showing of negligence. The "common knowledge exception" is generally used when the negligence is so clear that any reasonable person would note it as obvious. As the Tennessee Court of Appeals noted, the common knowledge exception is applicable when the negligence of a health care provider is as "obvious as a fly floating in a bowl of buttermilk so that all mankind knows that such things are not done absent negligence." *Patterson v. Arif*, 173 S.W. 3d 8, 12 (Tenn. Ct. App. 2005).

COURT CASE — Proximate causation

In *Floyd et al. v. United States of America*, 2010 US Dist. LEXIS 125247 (2010), the federal district court determined that a nurse practitioner's (NP) malpractice in prescribing Prozac for a 15-year-old girl was the proximate cause of her later death from anoxic brain damage due to the patient's attempted suicide by hanging. In this case, the court explained that, while the teen's attempted suicide by hanging was the direct cause of her anoxic brain injury and later death, the NP was negligent in creating an increased likelihood of suicidality in prescribing the psychotropic against the known prescribing recommendations for the medication and was, therefore, a proximate cause of the plaintiffs' demise.

punish the nurse or other health care provider for harms that were the result of malicious or wanton disregard for the patient's safety. For example, in *Manning v. Twin Falls Clinic and Hospital* (1992), a decision was made to move a terminally ill patient to another room on the same unit. The patient, who was projected to have less than 24 hours to live, was on oxygen. His family requested that supplemental oxygen be given during the transfer. His nurses declined the request because "the patient was a no-code." The patient went into cardiac arrest about 15 feet from his original room and was pronounced dead by the attending physician.

BURDEN OF PROOF

The plaintiff in a medical malpractice lawsuit has to meet a burden of proof in order to collect damages. This statement means that he must not only prove the four above-mentioned elements exist but also that they meet an evidentiary standard called the *preponderance of the evidence*. The preponderance of the evidence standard (the least stringent of the evidentiary standards)

result of the injury sustained. These damages may be apportioned among the various health care providers that are named as defendants in the case, if all the defendants are found to be liable to some degree.

Sometimes the court awards punitive damages, which are meant to requires that the fact finder—the judge in a bench trial or jury—believe that the evidence presented to prove each of the four elements is more than 50% likely to be true. If the fact finder believes that the plaintiff's attorney has proved the four required elements to be true by a preponderance of the evidence, then the fact finder should rule in favor of the plaintiff.

Another evidentiary standard that's used in civil litigation is *clear and convincing evidence*, which requires that there be substantial proof that the evidence presented is true. In states that require this level of evidence, a plaintiff's attorney would have to convince the fact finder that there's about a 75% chance that the evidence is true for each required element for him to prevail at trial. A third standard of evidence, beyond a *reasonable doubt*, is used in criminal cases and requires the fact finder to believe that each element of the prosecution's case has a 90% or greater chance of being true.

In a malpractice case, the only time that the plaintiff doesn't have the burden of proof is when evidence important to the plaintiff's case has been destroyed (or *spoliated*). For example, if a malpractice case involved issues related to the appropriate management of a patient in labor, and it was shown that the fetal monitor strips taken during labor were missing from the medical record, this would be considered spoliation of evidence; the burden of proof would then shift from the plaintiff to the defendant. Although this doesn't happen often, it's just another reason why you should try to carefully preserve the medical record. Spoliation of evidence is actionable in a malpractice case by means of sanctions, which is a way to punish the defendant for destroying evidence of negligence in addition to reversing the burden of proof.

MALPRACTICE DEFENSES

Over the years, the law has developed special doctrines, or theories, to apply to cases involving subordinate-superior relationships. These doctrines may be used in a nurse's defense during a lawsuit. Exactly how much protection they offer, however, depends on the circumstances of the case and the development of the law in the nurse's state or province.

Respondeat superior

One of the most important malpractice defenses or abilities to point to a wealthier or better-insured defendant is the doctrine of *respondeat superior* (Latin for "let the master answer"), also called *the theory of vicarious liability*. This doctrine, developed from agency law, holds that when an employee is found negligent, the employer must accept responsibility if the employee was acting within the scope of his employment. The doctrine applies to all occupations, not just health care—a utility company, for instance, is liable for injuries that result if one of its on-duty truck drivers negligently hits a pedestrian.

To the extent that a nurse is working as the hospital's functionary or agent, she can claim some protection under this theory. This doctrine is attractive to plaintiffs as well as employees because hospitals usually have much more money available to pay claims than nurses do (a reality facetiously known as the "deep-pocket" theory).

Consider, for example, *Tisdale et al. v. Toledo Hospital*, No. L-11-1005 (Ct. App. Ohio 2012). A nurse delayed in placing pneumatic compression boots on a patient ordered by the surgeon after surgical repair of an abdominal hernia. The patient developed deep vein thrombi and, later, pulmonary emboli and sustained severe brain injury. Patient sued the hospital and the doctors, but the nurses were dismissed from the suit. The trial court dismissed the hospital. On appeal, the appellate court reversed indicating that liability for the employer hospital was proper based on the negligence of its employee/agent nurses.

A concept closely related to *respondeat superior* is the borrowed-servant or captain-of-the-ship doctrine. It's still applied in malpractice lawsuits, but not as often as it was in the past. The borrowed-servant doctrine might apply when you, as a hospital employee, commit a negligent act while under the direction or control of someone other than your supervisor such as a physician in the operating room. Because the physician is an independent contractor and you're responsible to him during surgery, you're considered his borrowed servant at the time. If you're sued for malpractice, his liability is vicarious, meaning that even though the physician didn't direct you negligently, he's responsible because he was in control.

Many states have moved away from strict application of the borrowed-servant theory. One reason for this shift is that operating room procedures are becoming so complex that they're beyond the direct control of any one person, thus making it too difficult for courts to determine responsibility under the borrowed-servant doctrine. However, some states, like Texas, still employ borrowed-servant liability and ostensible agency to have legal responsibility for negligent acts reach those

not employed directly by the main hospital or institutional defendant. These include nurses in an operating room acting under orders of a surgeon not employed by the hospital. There is also the concept of extended liability for those who are truly independent contractors under a "locum tenens" analysis, which offers that liability may indeed lie with those temporarily employed by the defendant hospital employer in a contractor capacity, who are relying on their own skill and training to serve in a professional capacity.

Res ipsa loquitur

In some cases, injured parties who aren't fully able to meet the element of causation may still be successful in a subsequent lawsuit. Res ipsa loquitur, literally "the thing speaks for itself," is a rule of evidence that's applied when patients are injured in such a way that they can't show how the injury occurred or who was responsible for the injury. Malpractice may be inferred from the fact that the injury occurred. The principle underlying this doctrine is that the injury wouldn't have occurred in the absence of malpractice. The importance of applying the doctrine lies in the fact that expert witnesses aren't needed to assist the jury in understanding the facts of the case. Essentially, the rule of res ipsa loquitur allows a plaintiff to prove negligence with circumstantial evidence, when the defendant has the primary, and sometimes the only, knowledge of what happened to cause the plaintiff's injury.

Res ipsa loquitur derives from a 19th-century English case, *Byrne v. Boadle* (1863). In this case, the injured person had been struck by a flour barrel that fell from a second-floor window of a warehouse, but the plaintiff wasn't able to show which warehouse employee had been negligent in allowing the barrel to fall. The court applied the concept of res ipsa loquitur to the warehouse owners, who were found liable in the absence of proof that the employees weren't responsible for the plaintiff's injury.

Application of res ipsa loquitur

In most medical malpractice cases, the plaintiff has the responsibility for proving every element of his case against the defendant; until he does, the court presumes that the defendant has met the applicable standard of care. However, when a court applies the res ipsa loquitur rule, the burden of proof shifts from the plaintiff to the defendant. The defendant must prove that the injury was caused by something other than his negligence.

The case that set the precedent for this doctrine, *Ybarra v. Spangard* (1944), concerned a patient who suffered a permanent loss of neuromuscular control in his right shoulder and arm after an appendectomy. At trial, the patient's attorney was able to show that this wasn't the type of injury that normally occurs during an appendectomy but was unable to show how the injury occurred or who was responsible for it. The court in that case established three criteria that must be shown for res ipsa loquitur to apply:

- The injury must be the kind that ordinarily doesn't occur in the absence of some type of negligence.
- The injury must be caused by an action within the exclusive control of the defendant.
- The injury must not be the result of any voluntary action or contribution on the part of the plaintiff.

Usually, res ipsa loquitur is applied in lawsuits where the patient was unconscious and had no means of asserting any level of control in the situation such as a case involving an anesthetized surgical patient. Examples of court cases where res ipsa loquitur was successfully applied include those in which a foreign object was left in a surgical patient, infection was caused by unsterile instruments, surgical burns occurred, or a surgical operation was performed on the wrong part of a patient's body.

A recent case allowing for the application of res ipsa loquitur was *Babits v. Vassar Brothers Hospital* (2001). In that case, a patient awoke from surgery with third-degree burns on the back of her thighs. Although it wasn't clear how the burns got there, an expert witness gave two different hypothetical explanations. The court, acknowledging that the expert witness' theories were speculative, ruled that such an injury wouldn't have happened in the absence of negligence and applied the doctrine of res ipsa loquitur.

For and against res ipsa loquitur

Not all states that allow res ipsa loquitur apply this doctrine in the same manner. Some states limit its application, especially in cases where more detail is needed to assure the jury's understanding of the issues of the case, such as in instances of secondary infection. Other states have totally rejected the doctrine on the premise that negligence and malpractice must be proven, not presumed. *Frazier v. Angel Medical Ctr.,* 308 F.Supp.2d 671, 77 (W.D.N.C. 2004) illustrates this point. In *Frazier*, the court determined that plaintiff could not rely on the doctrine of res ipsa for complications from a severe heel fracture and the alleged complications from the subsequent orthopedic care. In *Bak v. Cumberland County Hosp. Sys. Inc.,* No. COA03-994 (N.C. Ct. App. 2004),

Challenging a malpractice suit

If your attorney can establish one of the following malpractice defenses, the court may either dismiss the allegations or reduce the damages for which you're liable.

Defense	Rationale
Insufficiency	Does the plaintiff have legally sufficient proof that your actions caused his injuries? If he doesn't, the court may rule that the allegations against you lack sufficient evidence and dismiss the case.
Contributory	Did the plaintiff, through recklessness or carelessness, contribute to his injury? If he did, some states permit the court to charge the plaintiff with failing to meet the standards of a reasonably prudent patient. Such a ruling may prevent the plaintiff from recovering damages. Many states permit the court to apportion liability, which prevents the plaintiff from recovering some, but not all, of the damages he claims.
Comparative	Does the patient share a percentage of the blame for his injuries? If so, damages may be proportionately reduced.
Assumption	Did the plaintiff understand the risk involved in the treatment, procedure, or action that allegedly caused his injury, especially if the treatment is experimental or a clinical trial? Did he give proper informed consent and so voluntarily expose himself to that risk? If so, the court may rule that the plaintiff assumed some of the risk by knowingly disregarding the danger, thus relieving you of some or all of the liability, depending on your state's laws.

the court determined that res ipsa could not be applied easily to medical negligence cases because, due to the nature of evolving technology and scientific evidence in medical care, medical negligence is not as obvious without an expert showing of liability.

Other malpractice defenses

Nurses and other health care providers aren't the only people who may have accountability for injuries that befall patients. Various circumstances may help to mitigate a health care provider's negligence and malpractice liability. (See *Challenging a malpractice suit*.) The three most commonly known

mitigating defenses are contributory negligence, comparative negligence, and assumption of the risk.

Contributory negligence and comparative negligence are essentially variations of the same concept. Both hold injured parties responsible for their own actions in creating or augmenting an injury. Examples of how patients contribute to injuries include failure to take prescribed medications, failure to keep follow-up appointments with health care providers, both under an expectation of treatment compliance, and giving misinformation to health care providers.

Contributory negligence, which is the older of the two doctrines, states that a patient who had any part in the adverse consequences of his medical or nursing care is barred from receiving compensation. Today, more states follow the comparative negligence concept, which reduces monetary awards by the percentage of harm that the injured party caused. For example, in a case in which $750,000 is the total monetary award and the patient's actions account for 20% of the harm, the final settlement to the patient would be $600,000. Some states disallow compensation for the injured party if he's found more than 50% accountable for the ultimate injury.

The third defense is assumption of the risk, which states that patients are partially responsible for consequences if they understood the risks involved at the time they proceeded with the action. Many medical therapies, surgical interventions, and drug protocols have risks involved, and patients are made aware of these risks during the informed consent process. The doctrine of assumption of risk assists in allocating liability if untoward outcomes result.

Defending yourself in a lawsuit

Imagine you're at the nurses' station, catching up on paperwork, when a stranger approaches and asks for you. He thrusts some legal papers into your hands and starts to walk away. Baffled, you ask, "What's this all about?" He replies, "You've just been served with a summons."

As you look over the papers, you recognize the name of a former patient listed as the plaintiff, and you see your name listed as the defendant. You learn that you've been accused of "errors and omissions." A nagging worry for most nurses has just become

reality: You've been sued for nursing malpractice.

When and how should you respond? You should act on this summons immediately. Failing to respond to the complaint within 20 to 30 days in most jurisdictions could result in a default judgment against you. However, how you respond depends on whether or not you have professional liability insurance. (See *Responding to a malpractice summons.*)

NOTIFYING APPROPRIATE PERSONNEL

If you're covered by your employer's insurance, immediately contact your risk management or legal department at your place of employment. These administrative people will coordinate yours and the facility's response.

If you have your own professional liability insurance, consult your policy and read the section that tells you what to do when you're sued. Every policy describes whom you should notify and how much time you have to notify your claims representative or give official notice to your insurer. Immediately telephone this representative, and tell him you've been sued. Document the time, his name, and his instructions. Then hand-deliver the lawsuit papers to him, if possible, and get a signed, dated receipt. Alternatively, send lawsuit papers by certified mail, return receipt requested, so you're assured of a signed receipt.

If you don't contact the appropriate representative within the specified time, the insurance company may refuse to cover you. In this case, you may have to sue your insurer in an action called a "declaratory judgment"

(Text continues on page 177.)

Responding to a malpractice summons

If you receive a summons notifying you that you're being sued, your immediate response can significantly affect the suit's outcome.

If you're contacted by the plaintiff, family members or friends of the plaintiff, or his attorney, do not speak to them. You should respond only through your attorney. If you're insured, you should politely insist to the insurer that your claim be handled by an attentive, experienced claims adjuster (the insurance company representative who investigates your claim and makes estimates for settlement) and a qualified attorney.

Be prepared to maintain your separate file on the case. Ask for copies of all relevant documents and reports from the claims adjuster, your attorney, and reports your attorney gets from the patient's attorney. Check the status of your case regularly with your attorney.

Selecting a defense attorney

One of your first concerns will be finding a qualified attorney to represent you.

If the patient names your hospital in the lawsuit, the hospital's insurance company may supply an attorney to defend you as the hospital's employee. If the hospital's attorney is representing the hospital's interest in the lawsuit, you should have a separate attorney to represent your interest. If you're sued alone, your insurance carrier may appoint a defense attorney to represent you. If you're uninsured, you'll have to find an attorney on your own.

If the dollar amount for which you're being sued exceeds your insurance coverage, consider hiring a private lawyer. This attorney will work exclusively for you. He'll notify your primary defense attorney and your insurer that, should the judgment exceed your coverage, the carrier may be held liable.

Shopping around

When seeking a qualified attorney, consider the following:

■ Consulting with your hospital's legal services department

■ Consulting with your state nurses' association or other appropriate professional organization

■ Asking friends or relatives with legal experience whose judgments you can trust

■ Calling your local bar association

When you meet with a prospective attorney, ask him about his experience with malpractice cases. If he has little experience or if too many of his cases were decided for the plaintiff, you have the right to ask your insurance carrier for another attorney.

Working with your attorney

Establishing a good working relationship with your attorney is crucial. It's your job to educate the attorney about the medical information he needs to defend you. Be prepared to spend many hours reviewing charts, licensing requirements, hospital policies and procedures, journals, and texts as well as your professional qualifications and the details of the case. Here are some pointers:

■ Provide your attorney and claims adjuster with all the information you can about the case, including anything relevant you remember that may not appear in the record.

■ Supply your attorney with the nursing practice standards for your specialty and facility.

■ Discuss with your attorney how you feel about settling out of court versus litigating to judgment.

■ Develop a list of experts qualified to testify on the standards of care in your specialty, and present it to your attorney. Avoid recommending friends, because the jury may believe them to be less objective. These can include nurses who you've heard present at professional seminars in your practice area.

■ Review all available records, including those obtained by your attorney that are normally inaccessible to you such as the records of the patient's private physician.

to force the insurer to defend you. To protect yourself, act quickly, document your actions, and get a receipt.

In addition, contact the National Nurses Claims Data Bank established by the American Nurses Association. Provide a full report of the incident in question, including the date, time, and persons involved. This contact will give you access to national data that may support your case, and your data will, in turn, help other nurses who are involved in lawsuits. Your name and address will be kept confidential.

Insurance company considerations

When you notify your insurance company that you've been sued, it will first consider whether it must cover you at all. The insurer does this by checking for policy violations you may have committed. For example, your insurance company will check whether you gave late notice of the lawsuit, gave false information on your insurance application, or failed to pay a premium on time. If the company is sure you've committed such a violation, it will use this violation as a policy defense, and it can simply refuse to cover you. If the company thinks you've committed such a violation but isn't sure it has evidence to support a policy defense, it will probably send you a letter by certified mail informing you that the company may not have to defend you, but that it will do so while reserving the right to deny coverage later, withdraw from the case, or take other actions. Meanwhile, the company will seek a declaration of its rights from the court. If the court decides the company doesn't have to defend you, the company will withdraw from the case.

Usually, however, an insurance company takes this action only after careful consideration because denying coverage may provide you with grounds for suing the company. If you receive such a letter, find your own attorney to defend you in the lawsuit and to advise you in your dealings with the insurance company. If your case against the insurance company is sound, he may suggest that you sue the insurer.

If your insurance company doesn't assert a policy defense, your company representative will select and retain an attorney or a law firm specializing in medical malpractice cases as your attorney of record in the lawsuit. When so designated, this attorney is legally bound to do all that's necessary to defend you. Even though this attorney is named and paid for by your insurance company, their ethical and legal obligation is to defend you, the client.

Your employer will almost certainly be named as a codefendant in the lawsuit. Even if that isn't the case, notify your employer that you're being sued. Your insurance company may try to involve your employer as a defendant.

FINDING AN ATTORNEY

If you don't have insurance—either your own or your employer's—you'll have to find your own attorney. Do not, under any circumstances, consider defending yourself. You need an attorney who's experienced in medical malpractice because the case will be complex and experienced medical negligence attorneys will be the opposition.

Make appointments with a few attorneys who seem qualified to defend you. In most cases, you likely will not be charged for this initial consultation. When you meet with each attorney, ask how long he thinks the lawsuit will take and how much money he will charge. Also, try to appreciate the attorney's understanding of the issues in your case. Then choose one as your attorney of record. Do this as soon as possible after you are served with legal summons.

PREPARING YOUR DEFENSE

Your attorney will file the appropriate legal documents in response to the papers you were served. He will ask you for help in preparing your defense. He should give you a chance to present your position in detail. Remember that all discussions between you and your attorney are *privileged communication*, meaning that your attorney can't disclose this information without your permission. Your attorney will also obtain complete copies of the pertinent medical records and other documents he or you feel are important in your defense.

Interrogatories, depositions, and examinations

Your attorney will use discovery tools to uncover every pertinent detail about the case against you. *Discovery tools* are legal procedures for obtaining information and may include the following:

■ *Interrogatories*—questions written to the other party that require answers under oath
■ *Depositions*—oral cross-examination of the other party under oath, either taken before a court reporter or recorded on videotape
■ *Defense medical examination*—a medical examination of the injured party by a physician selected by your attorney or insurance company

The plaintiff-patient's attorney will also use discovery tools, so you may have to answer interrogatories and

appear for a deposition as well. Your attorney will carefully prepare you for these procedures.

Neither the interrogatories nor the deposition should be taken lightly. Do not speculate when answering a question. Work closely with your attorney in preparing your written answers to the interrogatories, and never submit interrogatories or other documents directly to the plaintiff's attorney; your attorney must review everything and submit the final copies to the opposing counsel.

That doesn't mean, however, that you must say or do anything your attorney asks. If you feel he's asking you to do or say things that are not in your best interest, tell him so. You have the right to change attorneys at any time. If you believe an attorney selected by your insurance company is more interested in protecting the company than in protecting you, discuss the problem with a company representative. Then, if you still feel that he is not properly defending you, hire your own attorney. You may have grounds for subsequently suing the insurance company and the company-appointed attorney.

PREPARING FOR COURT

Plan on spending a considerable amount of time preparing your case before you appear in the courtroom. Make sure you dress nicely and present yourself professionally. This time can be stressful, and you need to be prepared.

Do not talk about the case

Do not try to placate the person suing you by calling him and discussing the case. Every word you say to him can be used against you in court. In fact, before the trial, don't discuss the lawsuit with anyone except your attorney.

That will help prevent information leaks that could compromise your case. To protect your professional reputation, don't even mention to your colleagues that you've been sued.

Study copies of the medical records

Your attorney will ask you to study relevant medical records as soon as possible. Examine the complete medical chart, including nurses' notes, laboratory reports, and physicians' orders. If you must, on a separate sheet of paper, make appropriate notes on key entries or omissions about the records, but don't make any changes on the records. Such an action will undermine your credibility and hurt your case. Remember that you aren't the only person with a copy of these records. Also, remember that once the plaintiff acquires your notes they may be used as evidence against you. Only your attorney's notes are safe from discovery.

Create your own legal file

Ask your attorney to send you copies of all documents and correspondence pertaining to the case. Try to maintain a file that's as complete as your attorney's. Also, make sure you understand all the items in your file. If you receive a document you don't understand, ask your attorney to explain it. Maintaining such a file should keep you current on the status of your case and prevent unpleasant surprises in court.

Take steps to protect your property

Many states have homestead laws that protect a substantial part of the equity in your house, as well as other property, from any judgment against you. Ask your attorney about the law in your state or province. If you don't have

malpractice or professional liability insurance or if damages awarded to the plaintiff exceed your insurance coverage, you'll probably want to mount as aggressive a defense as possible.

NAVIGATING PRETRIAL EVENTS

While your attorney prepares your legal defense, he'll also explore the desirability of reaching an out-of-court settlement. If he decides an out-of-court settlement is in your best interest, he'll try to achieve a compromise before your trial date. (See *Settling out of court.*)

If your case goes to trial, your attorney will participate in selecting the jury. During this process, attorneys for both sides will question prospective jurors, and your attorney will ask your opinion on their suitability. Either attorney may reject a small number of prospective jurors without reason (a peremptory challenge). Either attorney may reject an unlimited number of jurors for specific reasons. For example, an attorney may reject someone who knows the plaintiff or someone who has a personal interest in the lawsuit (*challenge for cause*).

To help prepare you to testify, your attorney will ask you to review the complete medical record, your interrogatory answers, and your deposition. You should also review the entire legal file you've been keeping, to make sure you understand all aspects of the case.

Deposition

Before the trial, you'll probably be called to testify at a deposition. (If you're called to testify as an expert witness at another defendant's trial, you should be aware that some states don't permit expert witnesses to give pretrial depositions.) The deposition can take place in an attorney's office or in a special room in the courthouse

Settling out of court

Only a small number of malpractice suits that are filed actually go to trial; of those that do go to court, even fewer end with a final judgment. The rest are settled out of court.

Making a compromise

Settling your case out of court isn't an admission of wrongdoing. The law regards settlement as a compromise between two parties to end a lawsuit and to avoid further expense. You may choose to pay a settlement rather than incur the possibly greater expense, financial and emotional, of defending yourself at trial.

Determining your settlement rights

If you're covered by professional liability insurance, the terms of your policy will determine whether you and your attorney or the insurance company can control the settlement. Most policies don't permit the nurse to settle a case without the consent of the insurance company. In fact, many policies, especially those provided by employers, permit the insurance company to settle without the consent of the nurse involved.

Review your policy to determine your settlement rights. If the policy isn't clear on this point, call the insurance company representative and ask for clarification.

Evaluating a possible settlement

Offer your attorney and your insurance company's representative all the information you can about the case so they can evaluate not only your liabilities but also a possible settlement with the plaintiff.

---

set aside for that purpose. Although the deposition takes place in a less formal atmosphere than a courtroom, don't forget that every word you and the attorneys say will be recorded and sets the basis of the reliability of your recollection of event at time of the incident. In a way, it's a rehearsal for the actual trial. At the trial, the plaintiff and the defendant's attorneys have the right to use your pretrial testimony to bolster their respective cases, which is why you should work with your attorney to thoroughly prepare for your deposition.

PARTICIPATING IN THE TRIAL

Keep in mind that your trial may last several days or even weeks. After all witnesses have given their testimony,

the jury, not the judge, will decide if you're liable unless both sides agree not to have a jury trial. If the jury finds you liable, it will also assess damages against you. (See *The trial process: step by step*, page 181.) In some instances, an arbitration proceeding is used instead of a jury trial, but that's the exception and not the rule.

Testifying in court

When you're called to testify in a malpractice lawsuit, as a defendant or as an expert witness in another defendant's trial, you may be expected to respond quickly to a confusing presentation of claims, counterclaims, allegations, and contradictory evidence. You can use various techniques to help reduce

(Text continues on page 182.)

The trial process: step by step

This list summarizes the basic trial process from complaint to execution of judgment. If you're ever involved in a lawsuit, your attorney will explain the specific procedures that your case requires.

Pretrial preparation
1. Complaint
Plaintiff files a complaint stating his charges against the named defendants, injuries sustained, and demand for award.

2. Summons and service
Court issues defendant a summons for service of the complaint stating plaintiff's charges.

3. Answer or counter-/cross-claim
Defendant files an answer and may add a counterclaim to plaintiff's allegations or cross-claim against other defendants. A motion for judgment may also be filed.

4. Discovery
Plaintiff and defendant's attorneys develop their cases by gathering information by means of depositions and interrogatories and by reviewing documents and other evidence.

5. Pretrial hearing
Court hears statements from both parties and tries to narrow the issues.

6. Negotiation by settlement
Both parties meet to try to resolve the case outside the court and try to reach settlement.

7. Jury selection
Attorneys from both sides question prospective jurors and select a final panel of jurors.

8. Opening statements
Plaintiff and defendant's attorneys outline for the jury what they intend to show during the trial.

9. Plaintiff presents case
Plaintiff's witnesses testify, explaining what they saw, heard, and know. Expert witnesses review any documentation and give their opinions about specific aspects of the case.

10. Cross-examination
Defendant's attorney questions plaintiff's witnesses.

11. Plaintiff closes case
Defendant's attorney may make a motion to dismiss the case, claiming plaintiff's evidence is insufficient.

12. Defendant presents case
Defendant's witnesses testify, explaining what they saw, heard, and know. Expert witnesses review any documentation and give their opinions about specific aspects of the case.

13. Cross-examination
Plaintiff's attorney questions defendant's witnesses.

14. Defendant closes case
Defendant's attorney may claim the plaintiff hasn't presented an issue for the jury to decide. Either side may move for a direct verdict.

15. Closing statements
Each attorney summarizes his case for the jury, making a final argument for the jury to consider.

16. Jury instruction
Judge instructs the jury in points of law that apply in this particular case and the specific charges.

17. Jury deliberation and verdict
Jury reviews facts and votes on verdict. Jury announces verdict before the judge and both parties. After the verdict is known, the losing side may request a new trial.

18. Appeal (optional)
Attorneys review transcripts. The party against whom the court ruled may appeal if he feels the judge didn't interpret the law properly, instruct the jury properly, or conduct the trial properly.

19. Execution of judgment
Appeals process is completed, and the case is settled.

stress and enhance the value of your testimony.

Maintaining proper courtroom demeanor

How you present yourself from the witness stand is very important. The jury may form its first, and sometimes final, impression of your credibility while you're testifying.

Your attorney will help prepare you to testify at the trial. He'll tell you how to dress—conservatively, as if you were going to an important job interview—and how to act. Your attorney may recommend, for example, that you sit with both feet on the floor and with your hands folded in front of you and pay polite attention to other speakers. He'll also tell you to look at the jurors while you testify to help you appear more credible to them. Keep in mind that the purpose of these instructions is to help you win the case. Remember also, that if you fail to cooperate with an attorney provided by an insurance company, the insurance company can use that information to deny coverage.

Malpractice lawsuits are notoriously slow-moving. Interruptions occur in the form of recesses, attorneys' lengthy arguments in the judge's chambers, and the calling of witnesses out of turn. Be patient regardless of what happens. When you're asked to appear, be prompt. You may not score points with your punctuality, but you'll definitely lose a few if you aren't in court when you're called to testify.

When you testify, the jury doesn't expect you to be letter-perfect or to have instant or total recall. If you don't know the answer, say so. You may also refer to your prior deposition for answers that are specific, such as what the patient's blood pressure was at the time of the incident or how many milliliters of a drug you administered to the patient. Listen closely to questions, and answer only what the questioner has asked. Always answer the questions simply and in lay terms, and never elaborate or volunteer information. If you're going to be describing a piece of equipment that's unfamiliar to a lay audience, get your attorney's approval to bring it to the courtroom and show it to the jury.

Above all, be honest. When your testimony must be critical of a colleague or of your hospital's policies, you may be tempted to bend the truth a little—but don't.

During the trial, your professional reputation will be at stake. Project a positive attitude at all times, suggesting that you feel confident about the trial's outcome. Never disparage the plaintiff inside or outside the courtroom. Characterizing him as a gold digger, for example, can only generate bad feelings that may interfere with a possible settlement. If you happen to speak to him during the trial, make sure you are polite and dignified.

Undergoing cross-examination

During cross-examination, the opposing attorney will try to discredit your testimony. This may take the form of an attack on your credentials, experience, or education—especially if you're testifying as an expert witness. Don't take the attacks personally or allow them to fluster you.

Another way of discrediting expert testimony is the "hired gun" insinuation. The cross-examining attorney may imply that because you accept payment for your testimony, you're being unethical and biased. Remember that as an expert witness you have the right to expect compensation for the time you spend on behalf of the case in and out of the courtroom, just as the attorney does. Say so if necessary.

Another ploy the opposing attorney can use to discredit your testimony is the "hedge." He may try to get you to change or qualify an answer you gave previously on direct examination or at the deposition. He may also try to confuse the issue by asking you a similar, but hypothetical, question with a slightly different—but significant—slant. Just remember that a simple but sincere "I don't know" can reinforce a jury's belief in your honesty and competence. You may also state that you don't understand a question and ask the attorney to clarify it. Your best protection against cross-examination jitters is adequate preparation and honest answers.

Understanding the judgment

The final stage of a lawsuit is the execution of the judgment, which occurs after all appeals have been exhausted. Two conclusions are possible: Monetary damages are awarded to the injured party, or all causes of action are dismissed against the defendant-nurse. If the injured party has prevailed, the individual will request that the award of damages be executed. This request is necessary because it gives legal relief if a losing defendant chooses to ignore the court order. In certain states, such a request allows for the garnishing of wages or for property to be confiscated and sold to pay the amount of the award. Because states vary greatly with regard to such measures, attorneys guide their clients at this stage of the trial process.

Res judicata

Nurses may wonder, because there are different courts in which a lawsuit may be filed, if an injured party may attempt to bring a second lawsuit based on the

same facts as an unsuccessful lawsuit. The doctrine of res judicata, literally "a thing or matter settled by judgment," prevents the same parties in a lawsuit from retrying the same issues as were involved in the original lawsuit, thus preventing duplication of litigation and the possibility of contradicting decisions. However, a word of caution about this doctrine is it doesn't apply to appeals, to parties not named in the original lawsuit, or to issues that weren't part of the original lawsuit. Therefore, it's possible for a losing party to file a second lawsuit if the issues at hand weren't part of the original trial.

SELECTED REFERENCES

Ashley, R.C. "The Anatomy of a Lawsuit: Part 1," *Critical Care Nurse* 22(4):68–69, August 2002.

Ashley, R.C. "The Anatomy of a Lawsuit: Part 2," *Critical Care Nurse* 22(5):82–83, October 2002.

Brous, E. "Lessons Learned from Litigation: The Case of Eric Decker," *American Journal of Nursing* 114(2):58–60, February 2014.

Brous, E. "Lessons Learned from Litigation: The Nurse's Duty to Protect," *American Journal of Nursing* 114(11):68–70, November 2014.

Culley, C.A., Jr., and Spisak, L.J. "So You're Being Sued: Do's and Don'ts for the Defendant," *Cleveland Clinical Journal of Medicine* 69(10):752, 755–756, 759–760, October 2002.

Jenkins, R. "Defensive Medicine: The First Sixteen Years of North Carolina Medical Negligence Litigation under NCRCP 9(j) and NCRE 702," *Charlotte Law Review* 3:375–467, Summer 2012.

King, J. "The Common Knowledge Exception to the Expert Testimony Requirement Establishing the Standard of Care in Medical Malpractice," *Alabama Law Review* 59(1):51–105, November 2007.

McCarter, W.D., and Hayek, T.J. "Expert Medical Testimony is Generally Required to Prove Medical Negligence," *Missouri Medicine* 98(10):488–489, October 2001.

Miller, K. "Nurse Practitioners and Claims Reported to the National Practitioners Data Bank," *The Journal for Nurse Practitioners* 7(9):761–763, 773, October 2011.

Miller, K. "The National Practitioner Data Bank: History and Data," *The Journal for Nurse Practitioners* 8(9):698–701, 2012.

Miller, L. "Scope of Practice and Scope of Employment: What's the Difference?" *Journal of Perinatal and Neonatal Nursing* 27(4):284–285, 2013.

Olson, D. "Wrongful Death Cases Based upon Suicide: The General Rule has Exceptions," *EPIC: The Journal of the Georgia College of Emergency Physicians* 15:17, Spring 2011.

Painter, L., Dudjak, L., Kidwell, K., Simmons, R., and Kidwell, R. "The Nurse's Role in the Causation of Compensable Injury," *Journal of Nursing Care Quality* 26(4): 311–319, 2011.

Ramos, F., Jr. "Reducing Malpractice Exposure," *Advance Nurse Practitioner* 11(2):20, February 2003.

Regan, J.J., and Regan, W.M. "Medical Malpractice and Respondeat Superior," *Southern Medical Journal* 95(5):545–548, May 2002.

Thornton, R. "Responsibility for the Acts of Others," *Baylor University Medical Center Proceedings* 23(3):313–315, 2010.

Tingle, J. "The Professional Standard of Care in Clinical Negligence," *British Journal of Nursing* 11(19):1267–1269, October 2002.

Tingle, J. "Clinical Negligence and the Need to Keep Professional Updated," *British Journal of Nursing* 11(20):1304–1306, November 2002.

Wood, C. "The Importance of Good Recordkeeping for Nurses," *Nursing Times* 99(2):26–27, January 2003.

CHAPTER

6

Legal risks on the job

Samantha M. Steiner, JD, RN

Harried and tense, you're struggling through your shift in an intensive care unit (ICU). You're already caring for more patients than one nurse can possibly handle, when the emergency department (ED) calls and says two more patients will be arriving soon. You know that there's no way you can provide safe care. Your supervisor turns down your pleas for additional staff. Your first impulse is to walk out. How can you remedy this situation?

You're caring for a patient with a criminal record and a reputation for narcotics dealing. You're nervous enough as it is, but the situation gets worse when a stranger stops you in the hallway, flashes a detective's badge, and asks for articles of the patient's clothing and a blood sample. He says that you're legally obligated to turn over this evidence. Should you do what he tells you?

A prestigious civic leader who's a candidate for local political office recently has made several trips to the ED. She has brought her daughter, whom she calls "Miss Clumsy." The child has had multiple hematomas. You think that it *might* be child abuse. Fearful of wrongfully damaging the woman's reputation, you hesitate to make a report. What should you do?

Your patient has told you repeatedly that he doesn't want any "heroic measures" taken or "means" used to preserve his life if there's no reasonable chance of recovery. However, one evening after the patient has experienced a massive stroke, five members of his family march into your office demanding that everything be done to preserve his life. Should you fight to have the patient's wishes respected?

The situations described above are examples of the complex legal dilemmas you may encounter in daily practice. As the nursing profession grows and you take on greater responsibilities, you'll inevitably face increased legal vulnerability. Hardly any aspect of nursing practice is untouched by legal risk. It's important that you know how to avoid possible litigious or legally damaging situations. (See *Taking steps to prevent lawsuits,* pages 186 and 187.)

Reading this chapter will enable you to identify the legal responsibilities and risks of your profession. You'll find information on the legal consequences of violating your health care facility's policies and suggestions to help you cope with understaffing. You'll read about your responsibilities for witnessing and signing documents, maintaining patient safety, administering drugs (one of the riskiest aspects of nursing practice), and upholding a patient's

(Text continues on page 187.)

Taking steps to prevent lawsuits

Anytime you provide care that falls short of current legal and nursing standards, you make yourself a target for a malpractice suit.

In most situations, you can prevent this from happening to you by following these guidelines in your daily practice.

Defend the patient

Your first duty is to protect your patient, not his physician. If your judgment says that your patient's condition warrants a call to his physician, don't hesitate—in the middle of the day or in the middle of the night—to fully communicate your concerns to the physician. If your judgment says to question a physician's order because you can't read it, don't understand it, think that it's incomplete, or think that it may harm your patient, don't hesitate.

If your hospital doesn't already have a policy covering nurse-physician communications, ask for one and keep asking until you get one. Meanwhile, for your own protection, carefully record all contacts with physicians, including the date, time, and the substance of the communication.

Stay current

Here are some effective ways to stay up-to-date on nursing practices: join a professional nursing organization in your area of nursing, read nursing journals, attend clinical programs, attend in-service programs, and seek advice from nurse specialists. If your hospital doesn't offer needed in-service programs, ask for them. Check the Internet for online continuing education courses.

Remember, ignorance of new techniques is no excuse for substandard care. If you're ever sued for malpractice, your patient care will be judged against current nursing standards, regardless of whether your employer has offered

you the necessary training. This is especially true if you're certified in a specialty area.

Use the entire nursing process

Taking shortcuts increases risks to your patient's well-being and your own. If you're charged with malpractice, and the Court finds that you took a dangerous patient-care shortcut, the court may hold you liable for causing harm to your patient.

Document thoroughly

Document every step of the nursing process for every patient. Chart your observations as soon as possible, while facts are fresh in your mind; express yourself clearly; and always write legibly. When using charting forms, make certain that they're complete and have no omissions or blank spaces. If you're ever involved in a lawsuit, a complete patient-care record could be your best defense.

Make sure to document conversations with other providers regarding the patient's care. Be sure to clearly document who was notified, what orders were given, and what actions were taken when communicating a change in your patient's status to another provider.

Audit your nursing records

Audit your records consistently and comprehensively, using specific criteria to evaluate the effectiveness of patient care. Ask for a charting class—or start one yourself—to encourage staff nurses to chart patient care correctly, uniformly, and legibly. Use problem-oriented charting (to be sure that you're documenting all parts of the nursing process) and flow sheets (to record large volumes of data). Encourage other nurses to use these documenting aids. If certain charting forms, such as admission or evaluation forms, need the counter-signature of a supervisor or physician, be sure to have the form signed.

Taking steps to prevent lawsuits *(continued)*

Use what you know

Use your nursing knowledge to make nursing diagnoses and give clinical opinions. You have a legal duty to your patient not only to make a nursing diagnosis, but also to take appropriate action to meet his nursing needs. Doing so helps protect your patient from harm and you from malpractice charges.

Delegate patient care wisely

Know the legal practice limits of the people you supervise, and caution them to act only within those limits. If your delegation of skilled tasks to an unskilled person harms a patient, you can be held liable for violating your state or jurisdiction's nurse practice act.

Know your nursing department policy manual

Review the policies at least yearly. If you think that policies need to be added, amended, or omitted, ask for them. If you're ever involved in a malpractice lawsuit, a well-prepared manual and your knowledge of nursing policies could be important in your defense.

Show kindness and respect

Treat your patient and his family with kindness and respect. When you help relatives cope with the stress of the patient's illness and teach them the basics of home care, they'll more likely remember you with a thank-you card than with a legal summons.

---

living will (advance directive). You'll also learn about your responsibility under the law when you encounter victims of child abuse, are forced to use restraints on a psychologically disturbed patient, or are asked by police to turn over a patient's belongings or fluid and tissue samples for evidence. This chapter also covers the special legal risks incurred when working in the ED, operating room, ICU, and other special care units.

Basic principles of nursing liability

To hold someone liable for negligence it is up to the claimant to prove that they were owed a duty by someone, there was a breach of that duty, and that the breach of that duty caused them harm.

As a nurse you owe a duty to your patient. A nurse's duty to their patient is not only to appropriately care for their patient but also to advocate for the patient's health needs, safety, and rights. When a nurse breaches her duty to care for and/or advocate for her patient, and it causes harm to the patient, the nurse may be held liable.

Basic standards

Whether you're an advanced practice nurse (APN), registered nurse (RN), licensed practical nurse (LPN), or licensed vocational nurse (LVN), you're always legally accountable for your nursing actions. In any practice setting, your care must meet minimum legal standards. Your care also should:
■ reflect the scope of your state's nurse practice act

- measure up to established practice standards
- consistently protect your patient.

Upholding these standards should provide a base for sound legal practice no matter where you practice nursing.

Hospital policies

Every hospital and health care facility has *policies*—a set of general guidelines and principles by which it manages its affairs. You're obligated to know these policies and to follow the established procedures that flow from them.

However, never do this blindly. As a nurse, you're also obligated to maintain your professional standards, and these standards may sometimes conflict with your employer's policies and procedures. At times, you may be forced to make decisions and take actions that risk violating those policies and procedures. You must do what's best for your patient. If it's unsafe to follow the policy, then don't. Document the reasons you didn't follow policy and inform your nurse-manager and the nursing supervisor of your actions.

At times such as these, you may need help balancing your duty to your patient with your responsibility to your employer. Your best help is a nursing department policy manual that states relevant, clear guidelines based on up-to-date standards of care that are generally accepted by the profession. A typical problem with policies is that they aren't practical, are too restrictive, or involve standards too difficult to meet. In addition, there may be so many policies that nurses aren't familiar with all of them.

A policy manual that states relevant, clear guidelines based on the most up-to-date standards of care is the

mark of a successful nursing department—one whose first concern is delivering safe, high-quality patient care.

QUALITIES OF A GOOD NURSING DEPARTMENT MANUAL

Although nursing department manuals will differ, they should:

- show how general policies apply to the nursing department
- outline the nursing department's roles and responsibilities, internally and in relation to other departments
- identify the expected limits of nursing action and practice
- offer guidelines for handling emergency situations
- contain procedures that show compliance with state and federal laws such as patient antidumping laws
- give standing orders for nurses in special areas, such as ICU and coronary care unit (CCU)
- show the steps to be taken before—and after—arriving at nursing care decisions. These steps provide the basis for the facility's nursing care standards. The manual itself will be used as evidence in malpractice cases.

However, policies are typically:

- too specific
- too restrictive
- too idealistic
- irrelevant
- so voluminous that nurses don't know them
- not reviewed or discussed in regular staff meetings
- not updated or reviewed on a regular basis
- not communicated to the staff when changes are made.

Today, hospitals are rapidly revising and expanding their basic policies and procedures. Any good nursing department manual should undergo regular revision. Some of these procedure and policy changes result from efforts to streamline and standardize patient care. Others result from efforts to comply with new state, jurisdictional, territorial, and federal regulations or to implement recommendations of The Joint Commission or the Canadian Council on Health Services.

HOW HOSPITAL POLICIES AFFECT COURT DECISIONS

Policies aren't laws, but courts generally have ruled against nurses who violated their employers' policies. Courts have also held hospitals liable for poorly formulated—or poorly implemented—policies. As previously discussed in Chapters 1 and 2, other sources that describe nurses' duties include:

- nurse practice acts
- licensing board regulations
- state and federal laws
- case law
- professional organization standards.

Legally, if you practice within the scope of your job description and are sued for malpractice, the hospital will have to assume secondary responsibility under the theory of *respondeat superior.* Whether or not you've acted properly is determined, in court, by the patient's condition on admission, the hospital's nursing service policy, and the standard of care reasonably expected in your community.

How policy is applied in court

In *Utter v. United Hospital Center* (1977), nurses failed to report a patient's deteriorating condition to the department chairman after the physicians they notified failed to act, causing a critical 24-hour delay in the patient's treatment. A provision in the hospital's nursing manual said that

if ever a physician in charge—after being notified—did nothing about adverse changes in a patient's condition or acted ineffectively, the nurse was to "call this to the attention of the Department Chairman."

The judge told the jury that it could label the nurses' failure to follow this provision as the proximate cause of the patient's injury. Because they failed to follow hospital policy, the nurses shared blame for the physicians' inaction.

HOW LAWS AFFECT HOSPITAL POLICIES

Many hospital policies and procedures are mandated by state or jurisdictional licensing laws or by such federal regulations that are the conditions for participation in Medicare or Medicaid.

Many such mandatory requirements exist. In the United States, for instance, the Patient Self-Determination Act, 42 U.S.C. § 1395 cc(f), is a federal law that requires hospitals, nursing homes, home health care agencies, and health maintenance organizations (HMOs) that are Medicare providers to inform patients about their rights to execute "advance directives," which includes written instructions such as a living will and a durable power of attorney for health care. The Freedom of Information Act requires hospitals to give consumers and patients access to certain data previously considered privileged. In addition, U.S. Department of Health and Human Services regulations require that hospitals observe strict guidelines when using patients in research studies.

Canadian law

In Canada, each jurisdiction has its own laws governing hospitals.

Although health care is the responsibility of the jurisdictions, the federal government outlines requirements for receiving federal funding. Since passage of the Canada Health Act of 1984, health care facilities are considered public institutions in Canada.

The jurisdictional legislatures also pass laws governing hospitalization in psychiatric facilities. Matters of criminal law, however, are in the hands of the federal parliament, so hospital policy makers look there for guidance on such issues as opioids and abortions.

COMPARING U.S. AND CANADIAN POLICIES

Hospital policies in the United States and Canada are similar in many ways; however, the differences are sometimes important. Always check the laws that prevail in your region.

Under English common law, people usually aren't obligated to help each other—not even in emergencies. However, where hospitals are concerned, Canadian legislatures in several jurisdictions have departed from this tradition. For example, the Nova Scotia Hospitals Act states that if a qualified medical practitioner makes application for a patient and the hospital has room, it must admit the patient, even if he can't pay for his care.

Antidumping laws

In 1986, the U.S. Congress amended the Social Security Act to prevent hospitals from turning away uninsured or financially strapped patients. Called *patient anti-dumping laws,* the amendments require that hospitals participating in Medicare provide screening and stabilizing treatment for anyone who has an emergency condition or is in labor. Furthermore, the Act gives guidelines and requires

documentation for transfers or for hospital discharge.

Failure to comply can lead to fines, loss of Medicare provider status, or both. This legislation has expanded regularly since 1989 and is currently known as the Emergency Treatment and Active Labor Act.

HOW HOSPITAL POLICIES AFFECT YOUR JOB

Hospital administrators write policies to guide workers in the hospital's daily operations. These policies stem from the hospital's philosophy and objectives and are part of the hospital's planning process, so they affect your job directly.

If you're considering employment at a hospital, you can ask to see its policies. Study its policies carefully; if they're well defined, they may give you an indication of how satisfied and secure you can expect to be in your job.

If you're working in a specialized nursing area, such as the ICU or CCU, pay special attention to any policies that directly or indirectly apply to you. Make sure that your specialty is clearly defined in keeping with your state or jurisdictional nurse practice act—and with the standards recommended by accrediting agencies and professional medical and nursing associations.

Besides reading policies—the general principles by which a hospital is guided in its management—read the hospital's rules too. These describe the actions that employees should or shouldn't take in specific situations. "No healthcare worker that has direct contact with patients is permitted to wear artificial fingernails," for example, is a rule that should be enforced without exception for infection prevention purposes.

If you feel reasonably comfortable with the hospital's philosophy, objectives, policies, rules, and quality of care, you'll probably feel comfortable on the job. However, if the hospital's policy calls for nursing procedures that conflict with your personal nursing standards or ethics, then you should consider looking elsewhere for employment.

WHEN HOSPITAL POLICY AND YOUR NURSE PRACTICE ACT CONFLICT

You must refuse to follow hospital policy when it conflicts with your nurse practice act. A willful violation of rulings passed by the board of nursing, even with your hospital's knowledge and encouragement, could result in suspension or revocation of your nursing license.

The case of *O'Neill v. Montefiore Hospital* (1960) illustrates the dilemma a nurse faces when she must choose between hospital policy and her professional standards. This case involved a nurse who, following hospital policy, refused to admit a patient because he belonged to an insurance plan her hospital didn't accept. The man returned home and died. Although the trial court ruled in favor of the nurse, the New York Supreme Court reversed the decision and ruled the hospital and the nurse negligent for refusing to admit the patient.

A conflict affecting many nurses right now is knowing how much help they can lend to a physician or mid-level provider. In some hospitals it is written in their policies that nurses can push a local anesthetic or nerve block. Often times these medications are drawn up by a physician, nurse practitioner, or physician assistant, not labeled, and handed to the nurse to administer. In this situation, the nurse remains liable for the administration of the medication including any adverse effects or outcomes it may cause. In this case it is important for the nurse to push back when asked to administer such a medication and to notify their manager of the request. The bedside nurse should work with management to get the hospital policy changed in order to help shield the nurses from liability.

HOSPITAL POLICIES THAT APPLY TO LPNS AND LVNS

LPNs and LVNs shouldn't be coerced to exceed limits that the law places on their practice, although practice may extend beyond the nurse's academic training. State law and national health commissions have recognized the rights of LPNs and LVNs to perform in an expanded role—for example, to administer drugs and intravenous (IV) fluids—if the LPN or LVN is properly trained for the task and it's one that other LPNs and LVNs perform in the hospital.

Get it in writing

Be careful to protect yourself. Make sure that the conditions for your doing this work are included in your hospital's written policies and that the policies have been established by a committee representing medical staff, nursing staff, and administration. The written version should be available to all medical and nursing staff members. If, for example, the policy that allows LPNs and LVNs to administer IV drugs isn't stated in writing, you better not administer IV drugs. If you're sued on this basis and can't back up your actions with written hospital policy or state regulation, you may be found liable.

CHANGING HOSPITAL POLICY

When seeking to bring nursing policy problems to your hospital administration's attention, you can involve your health-team colleagues by discussing policy problems at committee meetings, conferences, and interdepartmental meetings. Many health care facilities require policy implementation to follow the chain of command. Your charge nurse or manager should be able to give you direction on where to start on a particular issue. Alternatively, you can communicate directly with your hospital administration via the grievance procedure, counseling, attitude questionnaires, and formal and informal unit management committees.

Legal risks caused by understaffing

Understaffing occurs when the hospital administration fails to provide enough professionally trained personnel to meet the patient population's needs. If you're like most nurses, you're familiar with understaffing and the problems it can cause.

Plaintiffs' attorneys frequently argue that understaffing is widespread and that it results in substandard bedside care, increased mistakes and omissions, and hasty documentation—all of which increase nurses' (and their employers') liability. For example, if during hospitalization a patient is harmed and can demonstrate that the harm resulted from the hospital's failure to provide sufficient qualified personnel, the hospital may be held liable.

WHAT CONSTITUTES ADEQUATE STAFFING?

You won't find many legal guidelines to help you answer this question unless you work in a nursing home or skilled nursing facility. Determining whether your unit has too few nurses or too few specially trained nurses may be difficult. The few guidelines that do exist vary from state to state and are limited mainly to specialty care units (such as the ICU). Even The Joint Commission offers little help. Its staffing standard sets no specific nurse-to-patient ratios. It just states generally that "The organization provides an adequate number of staff whose qualifications are commensurate with defined job responsibilities and applicable licensure, law and regulation, and certification."

Lawmakers have taken note of this issue. In October 1999, California passed a bill that requires hospitals to meet minimum nurse-to-patient ratios in all units, mandates additional staffing based on patient acuity, and prohibits nurses from being assigned to areas for which they lack adequate orientation or clinical training. In September 2002, the California Department of Health Services developed standardized nurse-to-patient ratios. The predetermined nurse-to-patient ratios went into effect in 2004. Most recently, in late 2014, Massachusetts enacted a law mandating a nurse-to-patient ratio of one-to-one in all ICUs across the state. The courts have had no reliable standard for ruling on cases of alleged understaffing. Each case has been decided on an individual basis.

Important court rulings

The decision in the landmark case *Darling v. Charleston Community Memorial Hospital* (1965) was based partly on the issue of understaffing. A young man broke his leg while playing football and was taken to Charleston's ED, where the on-call physician set and cast his leg. The patient began to complain of pain almost immediately. Later, his toes became swollen and dark, then cold and insensitive, and a stench pervaded his room. Nurses checked the leg only a few times per day, and they failed to report its worsening condition. When the cast was removed 3 days later, the necrotic condition of the leg was apparent. After making several surgical attempts to save the leg, the surgeon had to amputate below the knee.

After an out-of-court settlement with the physician who had applied the cast, the court found the hospital liable for failing to have enough specially trained nurses available at all times to recognize the patient's serious condition and to alert the medical staff.

Since the Darling case, several similar cases have been tried—for example, *Cline v. Lun* (1973), *Sanchez v. Bay General Hospital* (1981), and *Harrell v. Louis Smith Memorial Hospital* (1990). Almost every case involved a nurse who failed to continuously monitor her patient's condition—especially his vital signs—and to report significant changes to the attending physician. In each case, the courts have emphasized:

■ the need for sufficient numbers of nurses to continuously monitor a patient's condition

■ the need for nurses who are specially trained to recognize signs and symptoms that require a physician's immediate intervention.

HOSPITAL LIABILITY

Courts have held hospitals primarily liable in lawsuits in which nursing understaffing is the key issue. A hospital can be found liable for patient injuries if it accepts more patients than its facilities or nursing staff can accommodate. The hospital controls the purse strings and, in the courts' view, is the only party that can resolve the problem.

Defending understaffing

Hospitals accused of failing to maintain adequate nursing staffs have offered various defenses. Some have argued that they acted reasonably because their nurse-to-patient ratio was comparable to other area hospitals. This argument fails if any applicable rules and regulations contradict it.

Other hospitals have defended understaffing by arguing that no extra nurses were available. The courts have hesitated to accept this defense, however, especially when hospitals have knowingly permitted an unsafe condition to continue for a long period. One possible future scenario—a hospital may be held liable for failing to use the nursing personnel available from temporary-nursing service agencies or nurses' registries.

Still other hospitals have excused understaffing by pleading lack of funds. The courts have repeatedly rejected this defense.

Emergency defense

Hospital liability for understaffing isn't automatic. If the hospital couldn't have provided adequate staff by any reasonable means—because, for example, a nurse suddenly called in sick and no substitute could be found quickly—the hospital may escape liability. This is known as the *sudden emergency exception* when used as a defense during a trial. The emergency couldn't have been anticipated—in contrast to chronic understaffing.

Except for the sudden emergency exception defense, a hospital has only two alternatives for avoiding liability for understaffing: either hire sufficient personnel to staff an area adequately or else close the area (or restrict the number of beds) until adequate staff can be found.

CHARGE NURSE'S LIABILITY

A nurse put in charge of a unit, even temporarily, may find herself personally liable in understaffing situations, including these examples:

■ She knows understaffing exists but fails to notify the hospital administration about it.

■ She fails to assign her staff properly and then also fails to supervise their actions continuously. (See *When coworkers put you at risk,* page 195.)

■ She tries to perform a nursing task for which she lacks the necessary training and skills.

Court cases

In *Horton v. Niagara Falls Memorial Medical Center* (1976), the charge nurse, 1 LPN, and 1 nurses' aide were responsible for 19 patients on a unit. During their shift, one patient became delirious and tried to climb down from a balcony off his room. The attending physician, when notified, ordered that someone stay with the patient at all times to keep him from going out on the balcony again.

The charge nurse, instead of calling for additional help from within the hospital or notifying the administration, called the patient's wife and summoned her to the hospital. The wife agreed to send her mother but said it would take time before her mother could arrive. During the interim, the charge nurse provided no supervision of the patient, who went out on the balcony again, jumped, and sustained injuries. In the lawsuit that followed, the court held the charge nurse liable.

In *Norton v. Argonaut Insurance Co.* (1962), a temporary staff shortage led the assistant director of nurses to volunteer her nursing services on a pediatric floor. Because she had been an administrator for several years and was unfamiliar with pediatric care,

she proceeded to give a neonate 3 ml of digoxin in injectable, rather than elixir, form. The infant died of cardiac arrest, and the court held the assistant director liable. (See *Floating: understanding your legal responsibility,* page 196.)

Viable defenses

A charge nurse isn't automatically liable for mistakes made by a nurse on her staff. Most courts won't hold the charge nurse liable unless she knew, or should have known, that the nurse who made the mistake:

■ had previously made similar mistakes

■ wasn't competent to perform the task

■ had acted on the charge nurse's erroneous orders.

Remember, the plaintiff-patient has to prove two things: that the charge nurse failed to follow customary practices, thereby contributing to the mistake, and that the mistake actually caused the patient's injuries.

COPING WITH A SUDDEN OVERLOAD

Like other nurses, you're probably all too familiar with understaffing. You begin your shift and suddenly find yourself assigned more patients than you can reasonably care for. What can you do to protect yourself?

First, make every effort to protest the overload and get it reduced. Begin by asking your supervisor or director of nursing services to supply relief. If they can't or won't, notify the hospital administration. If no one there will help either, write a memorandum detailing exactly what you did and said and the answers you received. Don't walk off the job (you could be held liable for abandonment); instead, do the best you can. After your shift is

When coworkers put you at risk

To help you avoid legal dangers when working with a health care team, here are some questions and answers to clarify legal responsibilities.

Can I be held liable for mistakes made by a student nurse under my supervision?

Yes, if you have primary responsibility for instructing the student and correcting her mistakes.

If a student performs tasks that only a licensed nurse should perform and does so with my knowledge but without my supervision, am I guilty of breach of duty?

Yes, because as a staff nurse, you should know that a student nurse can perform nursing tasks only under the direct supervision of a nurse licensed to perform those tasks.

What should I do if I see another health-team member perform a clinical procedure incorrectly?

If the incorrect procedure can harm the patient, you have a legal duty to stop the procedure–tactfully, when possible–and immediately report your action to your nursing supervisor. If the incorrect procedure doesn't threaten to harm the patient, don't stop the procedure–but report your observation to your supervisor.

Can I face legal action if I ask a hospital volunteer to help me give patient care and she does something wrong?

Yes. Don't ask a volunteer to participate in a task she isn't trained and professionally qualified to perform.

Here is an example of legal action taken based on a nurse delegating her role.

In *Travaglini v. Ingalls Health System* (2009), a family brought a wrongful death lawsuit against a hospital alleging nursing negligence. The family alleged that the nurses taking care of Mr. Travaglini departed from the standards of practice and this led to his death.

It was known that Mr. Travaglini was at high risk for aspiration and needed assistance with meals. This was allegedly communicated by the physician to the nurse and was documented in the medical record as having been communicated. One evening the nurse asked a nursing student to bring Mr. Travaglini a sandwich and monitor his eating. Mr. Travaglini's roommate in the hospital testified that the nursing student dropped off the sandwich and left the room instead of monitoring Mr. Travaglini. Mr. Travaglini was found to have aspirated and died as a result. Mr. Travaglini's family won their wrongful death lawsuit against the hospital based on nursing negligence.

over, prepare a written report of the facts and file it with the director of nursing.

Keep in mind that filing a written report isn't guaranteed to absolve you from liability if a patient is injured during your shift. You may still be found liable, especially if you could have foreseen and prevented the patient's injury; however, a written report will impress a jury as a sincere attempt to protect your patients. The report could also provide you with a defense if the alleged malpractice involves something you should have done but didn't because of understaffing.

Refusing to work

If conditions become intolerable and you refuse to work, you may be suspended from duty without pay.

Floating: understanding your legal responsibility

For many nurses, an order to float to an unfamiliar unit triggers worry and frustration. It may cause worry about using skills that have grown rusty since nursing school or frustration at being pulled away from familiar or enjoyable work.

Unavoidable

Unfortunately, floating is necessary. Hospitals must use it to help solve their understaffing problems. The courts sanction it as being in the public's best interest.

Exceptions

Legally, you can't refuse to float simply because you fear that the skills you need for the assignment have diminished or because you're concerned about legal risks in the assigned unit. You'll have to go along with an order to float unless:
■ you have a union contract that guarantees you'll always work in your specialty
■ you can prove you haven't been taught to do the assigned task.
Tell your supervisor if you haven't been taught a task she's assigned you. Usually, she'll accommodate you by changing your assignment. However, if she insists that you perform the task that you don't know how to do, refuse the assignment. If the hospital reprimands or fires you, you may be able to appeal the action taken against you in a court of law.

Consider the Canadian case, *In re Mount Sinai Hospital and Ontario Nurses Association* (1978).

This case involved three nurses in the hospital's ICU. Because they were already caring for many critically ill patients, they refused to accept still another from the ED. The nurses argued that admitting the new patient would endanger the patients already under their care. The hospital disagreed and suspended them for three shifts without pay.

The case was settled in favor of the hospital, on the premise that a hospital is legally obligated to provide care for patients it admits and can insist that certain instructions be carried out. If the hospital had to defer to its employees' opinions, the decision stated, it would be placed in an intolerable legal position.

CHRONIC UNDERSTAFFING

Chronic understaffing, if it occurs on your unit, presents you with a dilemma. On the one hand, your conscience tells you to try your best to help every patient. On the other hand, you feel compelled to protect yourself from liability.

Collective action

The best protection, as you might expect, is prevention—action taken to remedy the understaffing situation. Try to work with your institution to develop creative, workable solutions. The law will protect you in several important ways as long as you and your colleagues act responsibly and collectively to try to bring about institutional change.

A case in point is *Misericordia Hospital Medical Center v. N.L.R.B.* (1980), which involved a charge nurse who was discharged from her job because her employer found her activities "disloyal."

She belonged to a group of hospital employees called the Ad Hoc Patient Care Committee. The committee was formed after The Joint Commission, which intended to survey the hospital, had invited interested parties—including hospital staff—to submit at a public meeting information on whether accreditation standards were being met. One complaint lodged by the nurse and her committee was insufficient coverage on many shifts—a situation the hospital had failed to remedy.

Even though Joint Commission examiners approved the hospital, the nurse was fired shortly afterward. When the National Labor Relations Board (NLRB) ordered the hospital to reinstate the nurse, the hospital appealed. The appeals court upheld the NLRB order, citing a U.S. Supreme Court ruling that employees don't lose protection "when they seek to improve terms and conditions of employment or otherwise improve their lot as employees through channels outside the immediate employee-employer relationship."

Though this decision offers nurses some protection in conflicts with employers, especially those in which working conditions directly affect the care given patients, persons involved in the hiring, firing, scheduling, disciplining, or evaluation of employees are considered management and may not be included in the collective bargaining unit if a nurses' union exists in the hospital. Therefore, a nurse may be covered, depending on the court's interpretation of whether she's management.

Make sure you follow the appropriate channels of communication. If you can't get help to remedy a dangerous understaffing situation, first go through all hospital channels. Simply report what the problem is, the number of hours you've been forced to work without relief, the number of consecutive days you've been forced to work, and any other relevant facts.

Then if you still can't get help and if your complaint involves an alleged unfair labor practice, consider contacting the NLRB.

Legal risks in special care units

In special care units, such as the ED, operating room, postanesthesia care unit (PACU), ICU, and CCU, nurses regularly perform tasks that only physicians used to perform. Here, patient care offers exciting nursing challenges, increased nursing responsibilities and extra risk of liability.

For example, if you're an ED nurse, you'll have to employ triage—classifying patients according to the seriousness of their medical problems. If you make a mistake and a patient's treatment is needlessly delayed, you may be liable.

If the PACU, ICU, or CCU is your assignment, you know you must watch your patients for signs and symptoms of adverse anesthetic effects, of postoperative cardiac and pulmonary complications, and of shock caused by hypoxia, hemorrhage, or infection. In these units, you may also have to administer sophisticated drugs or perform difficult procedures such as operating an intra-aortic balloon pump. In these special care units, the patient's survival may depend on your judgment.

WHERE YOU STAND LEGALLY

If you work in a special care unit, take your increased liability seriously. Remember, even though hospital policy requires that you perform certain tasks, or you perform them under a physician's orders as a physician's borrowed servant or ostensible agent, your individual liability continues.

If a patient sues for malpractice, all the persons involved can be held separately and jointly liable. That suggests that you carefully evaluate the jobs you're asked to do. If a task is beyond your training and expertise, don't attempt it. Even if you can do it, make sure you're permitted to do it according to hospital policy and your state or jurisdictional nurse practice act. (See *Self-protection for nurses in special care units*, page 199.)

Role expansion and the law
In general, a nurse can't legally make a medical diagnosis or prescribe medical, therapeutic, or corrective measures, *except as authorized by the hospital and the state where she's working*. This means that if you intubate a patient with an endotracheal tube while working on a postoperative orthopedic floor, you may be liable for performing a medical function, especially if you could have called a physician. However, you probably wouldn't be liable if you had been trained in Advanced Cardiac Life Support and performed endotracheal intubation in the ED during a disaster.

In Canada, several jurisdictions, including Ontario and Quebec, have passed medical practice acts that permit the delegation of specific medical functions to nurses. Some jurisdictions require that a nurse obtain special training or certification to perform these functions. In the United States, however, current laws provide little guidance for nurses who regularly face situations such as these.

Suppose, for example, you're working in an ICU and so must usually act on standing orders and without a physician's supervision. How can you be sure when you perform quasi-medical functions, even with standing orders, that you aren't violating your nurse practice act?

You can't be sure, of course, because nurse practice acts don't provide specific guidelines. They were written in general terms, probably to give discretion to the practitioner. The hospital needs to write specific, practical policies that comply with the nurse practice act.

Treating patients based on standing orders is a matter of judgment. In such situations, be sure you're qualified to recognize the problem; then follow established medical protocol.

HOW NURSING STANDARDS APPLY
In general, a nurse working in a special care unit is subject to the same general rule of law as her staff nurse colleagues: she must meet the standard of care that a reasonably well-qualified and prudent nurse would meet in the same or similar circumstances.

However, in a malpractice lawsuit, when deciding whether a specialty nurse has acted reasonably, the court won't consider what the average LPN, LVN, RN, or APN would have done. Instead, the court will seek to determine the standard of care that an LPN, LVN, RN, or APN specifically trained to work in the special care unit would have met. Thus, the law imposes a higher standard of conduct on persons with superior knowledge, skill, or training.

Courts' view of standards
Hunt v. Palm Springs General Hospital (1977) illustrates how the courts evaluate the reasonable nurse standard in light of prevailing practices.

The patient, Mr. Hunt, was rushed to the ED with seizures. When he was examined, his physician concluded that Mr. Hunt, a known drug addict, was experiencing seizures because he had

Self-protection for nurses in special care units

If you're working in a special care unit of a hospital–the ED, ICU, operating room, or PACU–your expanded responsibilities make you especially vulnerable to malpractice lawsuits. To protect yourself, follow these precautions.

Know your role
Request a clear, written definition of your role in the hospital. Your hospital should have an overall policy and an individual, written job description for you that specifies the limits of your nursing role. You will be better protected if guidelines for advanced nursing competencies are formally established.

Document thoroughly
Document everything you do, so there's no question later about your actions. Your nurses' notes, of course, should reflect the nursing process: document your assessment of the patient, your care plan, your actual care, and your evaluation

of the plan's effectiveness. Be sure to accurately document the date and time.

Maintain skills
Make sure of your own competence. If your role expands, your skills have to grow, too. If that requires advanced courses and supervised clinical experience, make sure you get both.

Insure yourself
Damages awarded to patients can be very high, and high legal fees may mean you can't afford even to defend yourself in a lawsuit. If you don't have your own professional liability insurance, and your hospital doesn't help defend you against a lawsuit, you could face a startling bill even after all claims against you are proved groundless and dropped. (You might never even get to court–but you could still find yourself with a large bill for legal consultation.)

gone without drugs for several days. The physician advised the hospital administration that the patient's condition wasn't critical, but he nevertheless requested hospitalization.

The hospital refused to admit Mr. Hunt because of a history of unpaid bills. During the next 4 hours, Mr. Hunt waited in the ED while the physician tried to find hospitalization for him elsewhere in the city. Eventually, Mr. Hunt was admitted to a neighboring hospital. He lived for 26 hours before dying of brain damage caused by prolonged seizures.

During the lawsuit that followed, the court examined the practice of ED nurses elsewhere and found that the Palm Springs General Hospital nurses had acted unreasonably. Their duty

was to monitor Mr. Hunt's condition periodically while he awaited transfer to another hospital. If this duty had been carried out, the court concluded, the nurses would have noted his elevated temperature—a clear indication that he needed immediate hospitalization.

Similarly, in *Cline v. Lund* (1973), the patient, Ms. Cline, was sent to a coronary care stepdown unit when problems developed after she underwent a hysterectomy on July 10. Except for one episode with nausea, she appeared to be making satisfactory progress. At about 2:30 p.m. on July 11, a nurse dangled Ms. Cline's legs from the side of her bed. The nurse charted that the patient tolerated the dangling well. By 3:30 p.m., Ms. Cline was unresponsive, her blood pressure was rising, and she was vomiting.

At 9 p.m., when Ms. Cline's blood pressure reached 142/90 mm Hg, the attending nurse notified her supervisor, who at 9:40 p.m. notified the attending physician. He came to the hospital, examined the patient, and—suspecting an internal hemorrhage—ordered blood work and vital signs taken every 30 minutes. At 11:45 p.m., the patient's blood pressure was 160/90 mm Hg. Her arms and legs were stiff and her fists were clenched.

Instead of summoning the physician again, the attending nurse once more notified her supervisor. At 12:15 a.m. on July 12, when Ms. Cline's blood pressure had reached 230/130 mm Hg, the physician was called. The patient stopped breathing at 12:40 a.m., suffered a cardiac arrest at 12:45 a.m., and died at 4:45 a.m.

In the ensuing lawsuit, the court found the nurse liable, stating that her care had fallen below that of a reasonably prudent nurse in the same or similar circumstances. "Nurses," the court decision said, "should notify the physician of any significant change or unresponsiveness."

Another case involving critical care nurses failing to respond to a deteriorating patient is the case of *Decker v. Rochowiak* (2010). Eric Decker was born on July 17, 1996, via vacuum extraction at a rural hospital in Michigan. At birth his Apgar scores were normal but the next day his bilirubin was elevated and he was not feeding well. Despite these changes he was discharged home.

On July 19th, Eric was airlifted to the pediatric ICU of a second hospital. When his glucose levels were checked they were found to be dangerously low. A central line was inserted for glucose administration; however, his glucose levels remained low and Eric began having seizures. On July 20th, a CT scan of Eric's brain showed that Eric had suffered extensive hypoxic ischemia with hemorrhage. Eric continued to deteriorate and went into cardiac arrest. During resuscitation efforts the medical team determined that the central line was not in the right place and had caused cardiac tamponade and a large pneumothorax. Eric was stabilized after a second central line was inserted. On September 3rd, Eric was discharged home with developmental delays, blindness, and sensory deficits as a result of the anoxic brain injury he suffered while in the hospital.

Eric's mother brought a lawsuit against both hospitals involved in Eric's care based on nursing management. Specifically, she alleged that the nurses failed to monitor Eric's glucose levels and the status of his central line. She also alleged that the nurses failed to record changes in Eric's condition and report them to physicians in a timely manner. In the medical record it shows that an order for hourly glucose checks was ordered, yet there was a 3-hour window on the 19th where no glucose tests were completed. It also showed that multiple medications weren't administered as ordered, in a timely fashion. Additionally, the medical record showed that Eric suffered instances of bradycardia, low oxygen saturation, and drastically low blood glucose levels, yet there was no documentation that a physician was notified of these changes.

Eric Decker's case settled out of court for an undisclosed amount. There are several lessons a nurse can take away from this case. First, is the need for strong communication between nurses, physicians, and the entire interdisciplinary medical team.

The nurses here did not properly communicate changes in the patient to the physician. Second, is the need for robust documentation. The nurses failed to document if they communicated changes to a physician. Third, is the need to carefully monitor patients for complications. There are several examples in this case where the nurses did not notice that the central line was not in the right place and that Eric's blood glucose continued to drop despite receiving IV glucose.

Canadian nursing standards

A Canadian nurse's performance is also measured against the appropriate standard of care. For example, in *Laidlaw v. Lions Gate Hospital* (1969), the court held that both the PACU nurse who left for a coffee break and the supervisor who permitted her to leave should have anticipated an influx of patients from the operating room.

When the nurse left on her break, only two patients and the nurse supervisor were in the PACU. In a short time, however, three more patients arrived—including the plaintiff, Mrs. Laidlaw. Because only one nurse was on duty to care for five patients, Mrs. Laidlaw didn't receive appropriate care and suffered extensive, permanent brain damage as a result of anesthesia-related hypoxia.

When the resulting lawsuit came to trial, another nursing supervisor testified that usually two nurses were present in the PACU and that nurses weren't permitted to take breaks after new patients arrived. Other testimony revealed that PACU nurses should know the operating room schedule and so should anticipate when new patients will arrive.

The court found the nurse who left and her supervisor negligent in leaving only one nurse on duty in the PACU.

STAYING WITHIN NURSING PRACTICE LIMITS

When you work in special care units, you must not presume that your increased training and broadened authority permit you to exceed nursing's legal limits. That's especially important in an area such as medical diagnosis, in which you can easily cross the legal boundary separating nursing from medicine.

One place where this sometimes happens is in the ED, where an on-call physician may refuse to see a patient himself, instead ordering care based on a nurse's observations of the patient. In another common ED situation, a patient asks an ED nurse for advice over the telephone. In such a case, she should respond carefully, telling the patient to come to the ED or see his physician if he has questions or his symptoms persist. Similar situations may occur in the PACU, ICU, and CCU, where split-second patient-care decisions are sometimes made based on nurses' phone calls to attending physicians.

Keep in mind that all state and jurisdictional nurse practice acts prohibit you from medically diagnosing a patient's condition. In addition, the nurse is prohibited from deciding which of the physician-ordered medical treatment to administer. This is considered practicing medicine without a license, and the nurse will be held liable for any harm that comes to the patient based on these actions for harm to the patient that results.

In *Methodist Hospital v. Ball* (1961), a young man, Mr. Ball, was brought to the ED with injuries sustained in an automobile accident. Because of a sudden influx of critically ill patients, the ED staff was unable to care for him immediately. While lying on a stretcher in the hospital hallway, Mr. Ball became boisterous and demanded care. Apparently, the attending nurse decided he was drunk. Instead of being treated, Mr. Ball was put into restraints and transported by ambulance to another local hospital. There, 15 minutes after arriving, he died from internal bleeding.

An autopsy revealed no evidence of alcohol in Mr. Ball's system. In the resulting lawsuit, the court found the attending nurse and medical resident negligent because they failed to diagnose Mr. Ball's condition properly, to give supportive treatment, and to alert personnel at the second hospital about Mr. Ball's critical condition.

A few precautions

If you practice in a special care unit, be sure you know—and follow—hospital policies and procedures. Know your own limitations—never perform a procedure you feel uncertain about. Remember, admitting to inexperience is never improper. However, performing a procedure that may exceed your capabilities could be, especially if it results in injury or death.

If you're an LPN or LVN working in a special care unit, the same precautions apply. As you help RNs care for acutely ill patients and carry out physicians' orders, remember that you assume a significant legal risk when you perform a task ordinarily assigned to an RN. If you injure the patient in the process and he sues you for malpractice, your care will be measured against what a reasonably competent RN would do in the same or similar circumstances.

If you work in an ED, remember to reassess the patient after treatment. It's both sound nursing care and a requirement of Joint Commission to note and document a patient's response to care.

If the patient hasn't had the expected response to treatment, you'll need to also document your subsequent intervention.

Legal responsibility for patient safety

One of your most important responsibilities is your patient's physical safety. To prevent falls, for example, you have to make sure bedside rails are up for a debilitated, elderly, confused, or medicated patient. You also have to help a weak patient walk, use proper transfer methods when moving a patient, and sometimes use restraining devices to immobilize a patient.

In the interest of patient safety, you also have to keep an eye on your hospital's facilities and equipment. If you spot loose or improperly functioning side rails, water or some other substance on the unit floor, or an improperly functioning ventilator, you have a duty to report the problem and call for repairs or housekeeping assistance. Failure to do so may not only endanger patients, but also make you—and the hospital—liable if injuries occur.

PATIENT-SAFETY STANDARDS OF CARE

In a malpractice lawsuit against a nurse, she's judged on how well she performed her duty as measured against the appropriate standards of care. The court will analyze whether the defendant-nurse gave the plaintiff-patient care equal to that given by a reasonably well-qualified and prudent nurse in the same or similar circumstances.

With regard to patient safety, your duty includes anticipating foreseeable risks. For example, if you're aware that the floor in a patient's room is dangerously slippery, you must report the condition to the appropriate hospital department and place caution signs on the floor to warn of the dangers. If you don't, and a patient falls and is injured, you could be held liable.

In fact, you might be held liable even if you didn't know the floor was slippery. Using accepted standards of care, a court might reason that part of your duty as a reasonable and prudent nurse was to check the floor of your unit regularly and report any patient hazard immediately.

The standards of care that you meet will vary with your job and the training you've had. A staff nurse's actions, for example, will be measured against staff nurse standards, and a gerontologic nurse's actions will be measured against standards that gerontologic nurses must meet.

National patient safety goals

In July 2002, Joint Commission approved its first set of National Patient Safety Goals, which have been reviewed and updated yearly. Joint Commission established these goals to help accredited organizations better address patient safety. Current goals include:

- improving the accuracy of patient identification
- improving the effectiveness of communication among caregivers
- improving the safety of medication administration
- eliminating wrong-site, wrong-patient, wrong-procedure surgery
- improving the effectiveness of clinical alarm systems
- improving the identification of patient safety risks such as suicidal patients.
- Using proven guidelines to prevent infection

Failure to implement these safety goals will result in a special Type I recommendation.

THE CANADIAN PATIENT SAFETY INSTITUTE

In 2003, the Canadian Patient Safety Institute was established with the purpose of ensuring the safety of health care in Canada. The Canadian Patient Safety Institute set out four priority areas. Currently, the four priority areas are (1) medication safety, (2) surgical care safety, (3) infection prevention and control, and (4) home care safety.

One key strategy the Canadian Patient Safety Institute has come up with to make health care safer in Canada is the development of Interprofessional Competency Domains. The competencies are a way to identify the knowledge, skills, and attitudes required by all health care professionals in order to maintain patient safety. The competencies were designed to be relevant to all disciplines in health care. The seven domains are brief statements of components needed by a health care team to ensure patient safety. The seven domains are:

1. contribute to a culture of patient safety

2. work in teams for patient safety

3. communicate effectively for patient safety

4. manage safety risks

5. optimize human and emotional factors

6. recognize, respond to, and disclose adverse events.

SPECIAL SAFETY CONCERNS

In your practice, you need to recognize special safety concerns, such as patient falls, the use of restraints, the prospect of suicide attempts, the safety of equipment, and the risk of transmitting disease.

Patient falls

Almost anything can cause a patient to fall, particularly if he's elderly or receiving medication. Elderly patients are, in many instances, confused, disoriented, and weak. Medications can cause or increase confusion and lessen a patient's ability to react in situations in which he might fall. Here are some ways you can protect your patient from falls:

■ Make sure the bed's side rails are kept up, when indicated.
■ Orient him to where he is and what time it is, especially if he's elderly.
■ Monitor him regularly—continually, if his condition makes this necessary.
■ Offer a bedpan or commode regularly.
■ Provide adequate lighting and a clean, clutter-free environment.
■ Make sure that someone helps and supports him whenever he gets out of bed and that he wears proper shoes when walking.
■ Make sure adequate staff are available to transfer him, if necessary.
■ Make sure the call light is within his reach and in working order.

Elderly patients and patients taking medications that cause orthostatic hypotension, central nervous system depression, or vestibular toxicity need special nursing care when physicians' orders require them to be "up in chair for 15 minutes × 3 daily" or "up in chair for meals." If you can't supervise such a patient while he's sitting up, at least make sure another member of the health care team is available.

Restraints

Usually prescribed to ensure a patient's safety, restraints unfortunately can also endanger the patient. When a physician prescribes a restraining device, keep in mind that such devices don't remove your responsibility for the patient's safety. In fact, they increase it.

For example, when a patient wears a restraining belt, you have to make sure he doesn't undo it or inadvertently readjust it; if he does, it could choke or otherwise injure him. You also have to make sure the belt fits properly; if it's too tight, it could restrict the patient's breathing or irritate his skin. You may have to decide when the belt is no longer necessary. Check the governing laws and protocols for an automatic expiration of restriction orders. If you fail to handle patient restraints properly, you may be accused of false imprisonment.

Suicide prevention

Suicide prevention is another important aspect of patient safety. Keep in mind that self-destructive, suicidal patients are found in medical as well as psychiatric wards.

Your first obligation is to provide close supervision. A suicidal patient may require one-on-one, 24-hour-a-day supervision until the immediate threat of self-harm is over. Take from him all potentially dangerous objects, such as belts, bed linens, glassware, and eating utensils. Make sure he swallows pills when you give them; otherwise, he may retain them in his mouth, to save them for later.

Assess the hospital environment carefully for possible dangers. If he can easily open or break his room windows, or if escape from your unit would be easy, you may have to transfer him to a safer, more secure place—if necessary, to a seclusion room.

Remember, whether you work on a psychiatric unit or a medical unit, you'll be held responsible for the decisions you make about a suicidal patient's care. If you're sued because he harmed himself while in your care, the court will judge you based on:

■ You knew (or should have known) that the patient was likely to harm himself; and

■ You knew he was likely to harm himself, if you exercised reasonable care in helping him avoid injury or death.

In *Woodword v. Myers, Dean, and Correctional Medical Services of Illinois* (2001), a nurse evaluated a jail detainee and documented "yes" to an intake question asking him if he had expressed thoughts about killing himself. Despite the affirmative answer, the nurse did not obtain suicide precautions. Later, the man committed suicide while in custody. The nurse was sued on a claim that she deprived the detainee of his right to due process under the Fourteenth Amendment.

Equipment safety

You're responsible for making sure that the equipment used for patient care is free from defects. You also need to exercise reasonable care in selecting equipment for a specific procedure and patient and then helping to maintain the equipment. Here again, your patient care must reflect what the reasonably well-qualified and prudent nurse would do in the same or similar circumstances. This means that if you know a specific piece of equipment isn't functioning properly, you must take steps to correct the defects and document the steps you took. If you don't and a patient is injured because of the defective equipment, you may be sued for malpractice.

Selecting proper equipment and maintaining it also means making sure it isn't contaminated. When cleaning equipment, always follow hospital procedures strictly, and document your actions carefully. This will decrease the possibility that you could be held liable for using contaminated equipment.

You can also be held liable for improper use of equipment that's functioning properly. This liability frequently occurs with equipment that can cause burns—for example, diathermy machines, electrosurgical equipment, and flash sterilized instruments. When using such equipment, carry out the procedure or therapy carefully, observe the patient continually until finished, and ask the patient frequently (if awake) whether he's experiencing pain or discomfort.

Disease transmission

Be careful not to cause contamination or cross-infection of patients. In *Widman v. Paoli Memorial Hospital* (1989), the hospital was found negligent because a preoperative patient was assigned to the same room as a patient infected with the *Klebsiella* organism. The court found that the hospital didn't make sure that personnel assigned to care for the patient followed established infection control procedures.

HOSPITAL'S RESPONSIBILITY FOR PATIENT SAFETY

Your hospital shares responsibility for the patient's safety. This institutional responsibility for patient safety rests on the two most frequently used doctrines of malpractice liability.

The first doctrine, *corporate liability,* holds the hospital liable for its own wrongful conduct—for breach of its duties as mandated by statutory law, common law, and applicable rules and regulations. The hospital's duty to keep patients safe includes the duty to provide, inspect, repair, and maintain reasonably adequate equipment for diagnosis and treatment. The hospital also has a duty to keep the facility reasonably safe. Thus, if a patient is injured because the hospital alone breached one of its duties, the hospital is responsible for the injury.

Over time, the courts have expanded the concept of an institution's liability for breaching its duties. In a landmark case, *Darling v. Charleston Community Memorial Hospital* (1965), the Illinois Supreme Court expanded the concept of hospital corporate liability to include the hospital's responsibility to supervise the quality of care given to its patients.

In *Thompson v. The Nason Hospital* (1991), the courts went even further and discussed four general areas of corporate liability. These include:

■ a duty to use reasonable care to maintain adequate and safe facilities and equipment

■ a duty to staff the hospital with only competent physicians

■ a duty to oversee all individuals practicing medicine within the hospital

■ a duty to develop and enforce policies and procedures designed to ensure quality patient care.

The second doctrine of institutional malpractice liability is *respondeat superior*. Under this doctrine, the facility is liable for an employee's wrongful conduct. This means that both the employee and the health care facility can be found liable for a breach of duty to the patient—including the duty of ensuring his safety.

DETERMINING LIABILITY

In a lawsuit involving failure to ensure patient safety, the hospital alone may be held liable or the nurse may share in the liability. The outcome depends on the facts involved.

If, for example, a court can determine that the duty to monitor patient-care

equipment and to repair any discovered defects rests with the hospital and the nurse, then both could be held liable for a breach of that duty. In *May v. Broun* (1972), the plaintiff-patient sued the hospital, the circulating nurse, and the physician for burns she sustained when an electric cautery machine's electrode burned her during a hemorrhoidectomy.

Although the machine had been used successfully earlier in the day, when the physician began to use it on the plaintiff, he noticed that its heat wasn't sufficient to cauterize blood vessels. He asked the circulating nurse to check the machine. She did, and after that it apparently worked properly. Nevertheless, the plaintiff was burned where the electrode had touched her body. She later sued the hospital, the circulating nurse, and the physician.

Because the hospital and the nurse settled with the plaintiff out of court, the physician was the only one to stand trial. The court held the physician not liable for the patient's injuries because the hospital had the duty to monitor the equipment and to provide trained personnel to operate it. This meant that the hospital had to bear responsibility for the defective equipment and wrongful conduct by the nurse. In this case, the hospital and the nurse were liable for the plaintiff's injury.

In *Story v. McCurtain Memorial Management, Inc.* (1981), the outcome was different. This case involved the delivery of one twin by the mother herself when she was left unattended in a shower room. The patient continuously called for help, but her calls went unanswered and the baby the mother delivered herself died.

The mother sued the hospital and the nurse on duty at the time. The court found the nurse not liable, but it held the hospital liable (under the doctrine of corporate liability) for failing to provide safeguards in the shower room and adequate supervision on the unit. Here, then, the hospital alone was liable for breaching its duty to protect patients from harm.

DECREASING YOUR LIABILITY

As a nurse, you have an important duty to ensure your patient's safety. Remember, all your actions directed toward patient safety must be in line with your hospital's policies and procedures, so be sure you know what these are. If no policies exist, or if they're outdated or poorly drafted, bring this to your supervisor's or head nurse's attention. Consider volunteering to help write or rewrite the policies. By getting involved in efforts to improve patients' safety, you may decrease your potential liability and, at the same time, improve the quality of patient care.

Legal risks when administering drugs

Administering drugs to patients continues to be one of the most important—and, legally, one of the most risky—tasks nurses perform.

Over time, nurses' responsibilities with regard to drug administration have increased. For many years, U.S. and Canadian nurses were permitted to give drugs only orally or rectally. Today, nurses give subcutaneous and intramuscular injections, induce anesthesia, and administer IV therapy. In some states, nurses may even prescribe drugs, within certain limitations.

U.S. and Canadian laws continue to strictly guard the nurse's role in drug administration. Within this limited

scope, however, the law imposes exceptionally high standards.

EIGHT RIGHTS FORMULA

When administering drugs, one easy way to guard against malpractice liability is to remember the eight rights formula:
- the right drug
- to the right patient
- at the right time
- in the right dosage
- by the right route and
- the right documentation.
- the right reason
- the right response

DRUG-CONTROL LAWS

Legally, a drug is any substance listed in an official state, jurisdictional, or national formulary. A drug may also be defined as any substance (other than food) "intended to affect the structure or any function of the body…(or) for use in the diagnosis, cure, mitigation, treatment, or prevention of disease." N.Y. Educ. Law.

A *prescription drug* is any drug restricted from regular commercial purchase and sale. A state, jurisdictional, or national government has determined that this drug is, or might be, unsafe unless used under a qualified medical practitioner's supervision.

Federal laws

Two important federal laws governing the use of drugs in the United States are the Comprehensive Drug Abuse Prevention and Control Act and the Food, Drug, and Cosmetic Act. The Comprehensive Drug Abuse Prevention and Control Act (incorporating the Controlled Substances Act) seeks to categorize drugs by how dangerous they are and regulates drugs thought to be most subject to abuse. The Food, Drug, and Cosmetic Act restricts interstate shipment of drugs not approved for human use and outlines the process for testing and approving new drugs.

State laws

At the state and jurisdictional level, pharmacy practice acts are the main laws affecting the distribution of drugs. These are state and jurisdictional laws that mirror federal laws. Through these, criminal penalties attach under state or jurisdictional law for similar violations. These laws give pharmacists (in Canada, sometimes physicians as well) the sole legal authority to prepare, compound, preserve, and dispense drugs. *Dispense* refers to taking a drug from the pharmacy supply and giving or selling it to another person. This contrasts with administering drugs—actually getting the drug into the patient. Your nurse practice act is the law that most directly affects how you administer drugs.

Most nursing, medical, and pharmacy practice acts include:
■ a definition of the tasks that belong uniquely to the profession
■ a statement saying that anyone who performs such tasks without being a licensed or registered member of the defined profession is breaking the law.

In some states and jurisdictions, certain tasks overlap. For example, both nurses and physicians can provide bedside care for the sick and patient teaching.

In many states, if a nurse prescribes a drug, she's practicing medicine without a license; if she goes into the pharmacy or drug supply cabinet, measures out doses of a drug, and puts the powder into capsules, she's practicing pharmacy without a license. For either action, she can be prosecuted or lose her license, even if no harm results. In most states and Canadian jurisdictions, to practice a licensed profession without a license is, at the very least, a misdemeanor.

Court case

In *Stefanik v. Nursing Education Committee* (1944), a Rhode Island nurse lost her nursing license in part because she had been practicing medicine illegally: She had changed a physician's drug order for a patient because she didn't agree with what had been prescribed. No one claimed she had harmed the patient. However, to change a prescription is the same as writing a new prescription, and Rhode Island's nurse practice act didn't consider that to be part of nursing practice.

LAWSUITS RELATED TO MEDICATION ERRORS

Unfortunately, lawsuits involving nurses' drug errors are common. The court determines liability based on the standard of care required of nurses when administering drugs. In many instances, if the nurse had known more about the proper dose, administration route, or procedure connected with giving the drug, she might have avoided the mistake that resulted in the lawsuit.

In *Derrick v. Portland Eye, Ear, Nose and Throat Hospital* (1922), an Oregon nurse gave a young boy a pupil-contracting drug when the physician had ordered a pupil-dilating drug. As a result, the boy lost his sight in one eye; the nurse and the hospital were found negligent.

Getting the dose right is also important. In a Louisiana case, *Norton v. Argonaut Insurance Co.* (1962), a nurse inadvertently gave a 3-month-old infant a digoxin overdose that resulted in the infant's death. At the malpractice trial that followed, the nurse was found liable, along with the hospital and the attending physician.

Similarly, in *Dessauer v. Memorial General Hospital* (1981), an ED physician ordered 50 mg of lidocaine for a patient. However, the nurse, who normally worked in the hospital's obstetrics ward, gave the patient 800 mg. The patient died, the family sued, and the hospital was found liable.

In *Moore v. Guthrie Hospital* (1968), a nurse made a mistake in the administration route, giving the patient two drugs intravenously rather than intramuscularly. The patient suffered a seizure, sued, and won.

When reviewing these cases, one point becomes clear: The courts won't permit carelessness that harms the patient.

EMERGENCY DOSES

Some hospitals and extended care facilities have written policies that permit a nurse under special circumstances to go into the pharmacy and dispense an emergency drug dose. In the ED, physicians frequently write emergency orders for one to three doses—just enough to hold the patient until he can go to the pharmacy and have his prescription filled. If there's no pharmacist on duty, hospital policy may allow the nurse to obtain the required drug, bottle it, and label it.

Regardless of whether her employer has such a policy, a nurse who dispenses drugs is doing so unlawfully— unless her state's pharmacy practice act specifically authorizes her actions. If she makes an error in dispensing the drug and the patient later sues, the fact that she was practicing as an unlicensed pharmacist can be used as evidence against her.

Your options

If you need to dispense an emergency drug dose, you may choose to disregard the laws that govern your practice for the benefit of your patient's well-being. You do so at your own risk, however. Even if you don't harm your patient, you can still be prosecuted and you can still lose your license. When ethics and the law conflict and you have to weigh concern for your patient's life or health against concern for your license, you must make up your own mind about what action to take.

If your hospital policy requires you to dispense emergency medications and is in clear violation of your state's nurse practice act, consider taking steps to have your hospital policy changed. Start by approaching your nurse-manager with a copy of the nurse practice act and relevant hospital policies. Point out the inconsistencies and the professional risk nurses in the ED are taking. Then offer to accompany your nurse-manager when she approaches nursing administrators and the policy and procedure committee. Hospital administrators may designate an ED pharmacist, hire additional pharmacy staff, or prevail upon pharmacists or staff to take greater responsibility for distribution of ED medications.

YOUR ROLE IN DRUG EXPERIMENTATION

At times, you may participate in administering experimental drugs to patients or administering established drugs in new ways or at experimental dosage levels. Your legal duties don't change, but if you have any questions, you'll get your answers from the experimental protocol—not your usual sources (such as books and package inserts). Also, an institutional review board (IRB) probably reviewed and accepted the protocol before it was instituted. This is another resource for the nurse, especially if ethical concerns regarding the treatment develop. You'll also need to make sure no drug is given to a patient who hasn't consented to participate. (Note that if it's a federally funded experiment, consent should be in writing.)

YOUR RESPONSIBILITY FOR KNOWING ABOUT DRUGS

When you have your nursing license, the law expects you to know about any drug you administer. If you're an LPN or LVN, you assume the same legal responsibility as an RN once you've taken a pharmaceutical course or obtained authorization to administer drugs. More specifically, the law expects you to:

■ know a drug's safe dosage limits, toxicity, potential adverse reactions, and indications and contraindications for use
■ refuse to accept an illegible, confusing, or otherwise unclear drug order
■ seek clarification of a confusing order from the physician and not to try to interpret it yourself.

Increasingly, judges and juries expect nurses to know what the appropriate observation intervals are for a patient receiving medication. They expect you to know this even if the physician doesn't know or if he doesn't write an order stating how often to check on the newly medicated patient. A case that was decided on this basis is *Brown v. State* (1977). After a patient was given 200 mg of chlorpromazine, the nurses on duty left him largely unobserved for several hours. When someone finally checked on the patient, he was dead. The hospital and the nurses lost the resulting lawsuit.

QUESTIONING A DRUG ORDER

If you question a drug order, follow your hospital's policies. Usually, they'll tell you to try each of the following actions until you receive a satisfactory answer:

■ Look up the answer in a reliable drug reference.
■ Ask your charge nurse.
■ Ask the hospital pharmacist.
■ Ask your nursing supervisor or the prescribing physician.
■ Ask the chief nursing administrator, if she hasn't already become involved.
■ Ask the prescribing physician's supervisor (service chief).
■ Get in touch with the hospital administration and explain your problem.

WHEN YOU MUST REFUSE TO ADMINISTER A DRUG

All nurses have the legal right not to administer drugs they think will harm patients. You may choose to exercise this right in a variety of situations:

■ when you think the dosage prescribed is too high
■ when you think the drug is contraindicated because of possible dangerous interactions with other drugs, or with substances such as alcohol
■ because you think the patient's physical condition contraindicates using the drug.

In limited circumstances, you may also legally refuse to administer a drug on grounds of conscience. Some states and Canadian jurisdictions have enacted right-of-conscience laws. These laws excuse medical personnel from the requirement to participate in an abortion or sterilization procedure. Under such laws, you may, for example, refuse to give a drug you believe is intended to induce abortion.

When you refuse to carry out a drug order, make sure you do the following:

■ Notify your immediate supervisor so she can make alternative arrangements

(assigning a new nurse, clarifying the order).
■ Notify the prescribing physician if your supervisor hasn't done so already.
■ If your employer requires it, document that the drug wasn't given, and explain why.

PROTECTING YOURSELF FROM LIABILITY

If you make an error in giving a drug, or if your patient reacts negatively to a properly administered drug, immediately inform the patient's physician, and protect yourself by documenting the incident thoroughly. Besides normal drug-charting information, include information on the patient's reaction and medical or nursing interventions taken.

In the event of error, you should also file an incident report. Identify what happened, the names and functions of all personnel involved, and what actions were taken to protect the patient after the error was discovered.

LPN/LVN ROLES IN ADMINISTERING DRUGS

Most nurse practice acts now permit LPNs and LVNs *with the appropriate educational background or on-the-job training* to give drugs under the supervision of an RN, physician, or dentist. What constitutes appropriate training or educational background? No clear-cut definitions exist, but most courts probably would be satisfied if an LPN or LVN could prove that her supervising RN or physician had watched her administer drugs and had judged her competent. For tasks that require instruction and experience beyond the nurse's academic training, health care facilities usually develop didactic training with goals and proficiency tests. Additionally, skills testing should

be documented through proficiency checklists. This provides objective documentation in case of a lawsuit. (Note, however, that some states prohibit LPNs and LVNs from inserting IV lines.)

Telephone triage

Telephonic medical advice traditionally has been a part of most primary care practices. This type of service, which has become known as telephone triage, generally operates with a clinician taking calls and processing requests for medical advice. As health care costs continue to rise, more managed care organizations, HMOs, and EDs are using these systems as a cost-saving and case management measure.

Most telephone triage systems are staffed with fully trained nurses who use computerized algorithms and their clinical judgment to analyze a patient's complaints and give advice. The algorithms, which are designed in a systematic, question-and-answer format, indicate what advice the nurse should give. The nurse may provide self-care instructions, or she may tell the caller to come to the emergency room or make an appointment with his primary care physician or a specialist.

If you dispense advice over the phone, keep in mind that a legal duty arises the minute you say, "OK, let me tell you what to do." You now have a nurse-patient relationship, and you're responsible for advice you give. After you start to give advice by telephone, you can't decide midway through that you're in over your head and simply hang up; that could be considered abandonment. You must give appropriate advice or a referral—for example, "After listening to you, I suggest that you go to the emergency department."

You also need to ensure that you complete the proper documentation for every call you take. Every telephone call that the unit receives should be logged in. The log should include the date and time of the call, the caller's name and address, the caller's chief complaint or request, the disposition of the call, and the name of the person who made the disposition. Make sure that you document this information properly. Take thorough notes during the call, and complete the call log immediately after the call has been completed—when the information is still fresh in your mind. That way, you're ensuring its completeness and accuracy.

As a telephone triage nurse, you'll run into challenges that don't exist in other units of your facility. A telephone call doesn't allow you to visually assess the caller. In addition, a caller may be reluctant to provide personal details over the phone. Language and cultural differences can also make evaluating a caller's symptoms difficult. Finally, processes to follow up with the caller's physician may not be adequate.

Standards

The Emergency Nurses Association (ENA) and the American Accreditation HealthCare Commission (URAC) have established guidelines and standards for telephone triage programs. ENA guidelines require telephone triage nurses to be experienced professional RNs with specialized education in triage, telephone assessment, and communication and documentation skills. Included in the ENA guidelines are mandatory continuing education requirements; defined protocols, policies, and procedures; and a continuous quality improvement program.

URAC's Health Call Center Standards apply to managed care organizations providing triage and health information services to the public when conducted by telephone, via Web site, or other electronic means. The standards assure that RNs, physicians, or other validly licensed individuals perform the clinical aspects of triage and other health information services in a manner that's timely, confidential, and medically appropriate. URAC also mandates that each telephone triage unit must have a continuous staff management program, including orientation and training, written job descriptions, performance evaluations, and verification of licenses.

Health Insurance and Portability and Accountability Act

The Health Insurance and Portability and Accountability Act (HIPAA), passed by Congress in 1996, was designed to provide safeguards against the inappropriate use and release of personal medical information, including all medical records and identifiable health information in all forms (electronic, on paper, or oral). The telephone triage nurse needs to follow HIPAA's policies and procedures and inform callers of the scope of confidentiality that exists within the telephone triage program. Although the telephone triage nurse isn't likely to be in a position to violate HIPAA regulations, she must be made aware that protecting personal health information is a serious duty.

Case law

In *Shannon v. McNulty and HealthAmerica Pennsylvania* (1998), the court held HealthAmerica, an HMO, vicariously liable for the of its nursing telephone triage staff when it failed to quickly refer Mrs. Shannon to her physician or hospital when she called complaining of signs and symptoms of preterm labor. Mrs. Shannon lost her child. The Shannons also alleged that HealthAmerica was liable for its lack of appropriate procedures and protocols when dispensing telephonic medical advice to its subscribers.

In a Texas case, *Norman v. Good Shepard Medical Center* (2001), the court held the hospital liable for the actions of one of its LVNs who improperly performed telephone triage when Mrs. Norman called the ED looking for medical advice regarding her 10-year-old daughter's rash. The evidence established that the LVN disobeyed a hospital policy stating that LVNs were not to give medical advice in non–life-threatening situations. The LVN gave incorrect medical advice, which caused a delay in diagnosis and forced the child to undergo several limb amputations.

AVOIDING LIABILITY

To avoid liability while working as a telephone triage nurse, you need to know the policies and procedures of your telephone triage unit and uphold the privacy of protected health information. Proper training that includes orientation to protocols, proper documentation and follow-up communication, continuing education, and quality improvement monitoring is paramount for your own—and your patient's—protection.

Patient teaching and the law

Anytime you give a patient information about his care or treatment, you're involved in patient teaching—a professional nursing responsibility and a potential source of liability.

Patient teaching has taken on increased significance, largely because patients are routinely discharged much earlier from hospitals. Patients and their families need more understanding of patients' illnesses and how to manage them at home.

Patient teaching may be formal or informal. You teach formally when, for example, you prepare instructions on stoma care for a colostomy patient. When giving the patient this detailed information, you should follow these steps:

■ assessing what the patient wants or needs to know
■ identifying goals that you and the patient want to reach
■ choosing teaching strategies that will help reach the goals
■ evaluating how well you've reached the goals.

You teach informally when, for example, you calm a patient's fears by explaining an upcoming diagnostic test or when you answer a friend's questions about how to treat her child's fever.

For best results, patient teaching should include the family and others involved in the patient's care. If family members understand the reason for a patient's treatment, they may be more willing to provide emotional support.

PATIENT-TEACHING STANDARDS

Most nurse practice acts in the United States and Canada contain wording about promoting patient health and preventing disease or injury. However, they don't specify a nurse's responsibility for patient teaching. Nurses can find this information in the practice standards developed by professional organizations, in nursing job descriptions, and in statements about nursing practice from national commissions.

Joint Commission requires that the "hospital provides patient education and training based on each patient's needs and abilities." Joint Commission requires patient teaching be done in an interdisciplinary manner, considering the patient's ability to learn and any cultural or emotional factors or any cognitive or physical limitations that would affect his ability to learn.

Patient teaching should be a dynamic process that changes to meet the patient's and his family's needs. It should include instruction in how to adapt to the illness as well as how to prevent future problems.

PATIENT'S RIGHT TO HEALTH CARE INFORMATION

Both statutory law and common law support the patient's right to have information about his condition and treatment. In fact, when a patient is admitted to a hospital, he may be handed a patient's bill of rights that clearly outlines his rights. The doctrine of informed consent further supports the patient's right to know.

Despite RNs' deep involvement in patient teaching, the courts have rarely addressed nurses' liability in this area of patient care. The issue typically arises in litigation when a patient sues and the defendant health care provider attempts to prove patient responsibility for the bad outcome. For example, a patient is seen in the ED for an infection, is prescribed an antibiotic, is told to follow up with a specialist, and is discharged. The patient doesn't follow instructions and his infection worsens. To rebut his own negligence, the patient will argue that he wasn't told the risks if he didn't follow the physician's advice. However, some legal experts believe that as nurses take on greater patient-teaching

responsibilities, they'll increasingly become the target of lawsuits dealing with the patient's right to information.

Suppose you're sued for malpractice, and your alleged wrongful act involves patient teaching. The court will consider whether patient teaching was your legal duty to the patient and whether you met or breached it.

Court case

The court in *Kyslinger v. United States,* 406 F Supp. 800 (W. D. Pa. 1975) addressed the nurse's liability for patient teaching. In this case, a veteran's administration (VA) hospital sent a hemodialysis patient home with an artificial kidney. He eventually died (apparently while on the machine), and his wife sued the federal government—because a VA hospital was involved—alleging that the hospital and its staff had failed to teach either her or her late husband how to properly use and maintain a home hemodialysis unit.

After examining the evidence, the court ruled against the patient's wife, as follows: "During those 10 months that plaintiff's decedent underwent biweekly hemodialysis treatment on the unit (at the VA hospital), both plaintiff and decedent were instructed as to the operation, maintenance, and supervision of said treatment. The Court can find no basis to conclude that the plaintiff or plaintiff's decedent weren't properly informed on the use of the hemodialysis unit."

If the patient doesn't want to be taught

Suppose you begin teaching a patient about the medications he's taking, only to hear him say, "Oh, just tell my wife; she gives me all my pills." When something like this happens, be sure to document the incident. Include the patient's exact words; then describe what you taught his wife, and how.

LPN/LVN ROLES IN PATIENT TEACHING

Unlike RNs, LPNs and LVNs aren't typically taught the fundamentals of patient teaching as part of their school curriculum—nor is patient teaching included in their scope of practice. RNs are primarily responsible for patient teaching and may delegate to LPNs or LVNs only the responsibility to reinforce what has already been taught. For example, if an RN is preparing a patient for a barium enema, she could ask an LPN or LVN to tell the patient about the X-ray room and what to expect. The RN could add to the information as necessary.

COOPERATING WITH COLLEAGUES

Physicians, nurses, and other health-team members sometimes disagree about how patient teaching should be done and who should do it. To avoid conflict, always consult physicians and other appropriate health-team members when you're preparing routine patient-teaching protocols. A team approach to patient teaching not only decreases conflicts, but also ensures continuity in teaching—and a better-educated patient.

You can also avoid conflicts by listening to the instructions that physicians, respiratory therapists, dietitians, and others give the patient. Then you'll know exactly what has already been said to him, and you can structure your teaching accordingly.

Candor and diplomacy, of course, also help reduce conflict. Everyone profits when health-team members share their patient-teaching approaches and work together to achieve patient-teaching goals.

Incident reports

An incident is any event that is inconsistent with the hospital's ordinary routine, regardless of whether injury occurs. In most health care facilities, an injury to a patient requires an incident report. Patient deteriorations, medication errors, and injuries to employees and visitors require incident reports as well.

An incident report serves two main purposes:
■ to inform hospital administration of the incident so that it can monitor patterns and trends, thereby helping to prevent future similar incidents (risk management)
■ to alert the administration and the hospital's insurance company to the possibility of liability claims and the need for further investigation (claims management).

Even when the incident isn't investigated, the report serves as a contemporary, factual statement of it. The report also helps identify witnesses if a lawsuit is started months or even years later.

To be useful, an incident report must be filed promptly and must be thorough and factual.

YOUR DUTY TO REPORT PATIENT INCIDENTS

Whether you're an APN, an RN, an LPN or LVN, a nursing assistant, a staff nurse, or a nurse-manager, you have a duty to report an incident of which you have first-hand knowledge. Not only can failure to report an incident lead to your being fired, it can also expose you to claims of malpractice—especially if your failure to report the incident causes injury to a patient.

If you're the staff member who knows the most about the incident at the time of its discovery, you should complete the incident report. When you do so, include only the facts: what you saw when you came upon the incident or what you heard that led you to believe an incident had taken place. If information is second-hand, place it within quotation marks and identify the source. After completing the incident report, sign and date it. You should complete it during the same shift the incident occurred or was discovered.

REPORTING AN INCIDENT

An incident report is an administrative report, and therefore does not become part of the patient's medical record. In fact, the record shouldn't even mention that an incident report has been filed because this serves only to deflect the medical record's focus. The record should include only factual clinical observations relating to the incident. (Again, avoid value judgments and subjective information.)

Entering your observations in the nurses' notes section of the patient's record doesn't take the place of completing an incident report. Nor does completing an incident report take the place of proper documentation in the patient's chart.

Once an incident report has been filed, the nursing supervisor, the physician called to examine the patient, appropriate department heads and administrators, the hospital attorney, and the hospital's insurance company may review it. (See *Filing an incident report: Chain of events.*) The report may be filed under the involved patient's name or by the type of injury, depending on the hospital's policy and the insurance company's regulations. Reports are rarely placed in the reporting nurse's employment file.

If you're asked to talk with the hospital's insurance adjuster or attorney about an incident, be cooperative, honest, and factual. Fully disclosing what you know early on will help the hospital decide how to handle legal consequences of an incident and it also preserves your testimony in case you're ever called to testify in court.

What to include

An incident report should include only the following information:
- the names of the persons involved and witnesses
- factual information about what happened and the consequences to the person involved (supply enough information so that the hospital administration can decide whether the matter needs further investigation)
- other relevant facts (such as your immediate actions in response to the incident; for example, notifying the patient's physician).

What not to include

Never include the following types of statements in an incident report:
- opinions (such as a reporter's opinion of the patient's prognosis or who's at fault)
- conclusions or assumptions (such as what caused the incident)
- suggestions of who was responsible for causing the incident
- suggestions to prevent the incident from happening again.

Including this type of information in an incident report could seriously hinder the defense in a lawsuit arising from the incident.

Remember, the incident report serves only to notify the administration that an incident has occurred. In effect, it says, "Administration: Note that this incident happened, and decide whether you want to investigate it further." Such items as detailed statements from witnesses and descriptions of remedial action are normally part of an investigative follow-up; don't include them in the incident report itself.

Filing an incident report: chain of events

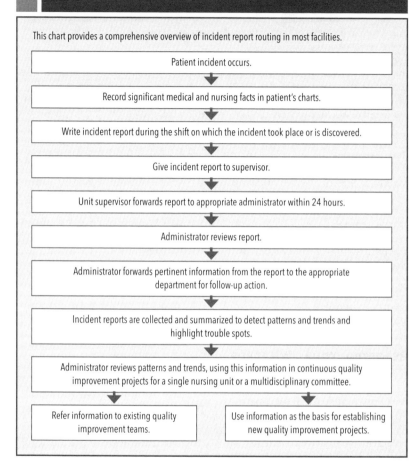

This chart provides a comprehensive overview of incident report routing in most facilities.

Patient incident occurs.

↓

Record significant medical and nursing facts in patient's charts.

↓

Write incident report during the shift on which the incident took place or is discovered.

↓

Give incident report to supervisor.

↓

Unit supervisor forwards report to appropriate administrator within 24 hours.

↓

Administrator reviews report.

↓

Administrator forwards pertinent information from the report to the appropriate department for follow-up action.

↓

Incident reports are collected and summarized to detect patterns and trends and highlight trouble spots.

↓

Administrator reviews patterns and trends, using this information in continuous quality improvement projects for a single nursing unit or a multidisciplinary committee.

↓   ↓

Refer information to existing quality improvement teams.

Use information as the basis for establishing new quality improvement projects.

Potential pitfalls

Be especially careful that the hospital's reporting system doesn't lead to improper incident reporting. For example, some hospitals require nursing supervisors to correlate reports from witnesses and then file a single report. Also, some incident report forms invite inappropriate conclusions and assumptions by asking, "How can this incident be prevented in the future?" If your hospital's reporting system or forms contain such potential pitfalls, alert the administration about them.

USING INCIDENT REPORTS AS COURTROOM EVIDENCE

Controversy exists over whether a patient's attorney may "discover" (request and receive a copy of) an incident report and introduce it into evidence in a malpractice lawsuit. The law on this issue varies from state to state. To avoid discovery, the hospital may send copies of the incident report to its attorney, or the hospital attorney may write a letter stating that the report is being made for his use and benefit only, or the hospital may make the incident report an integral part of the quality assurance process and label it as such.

Concern about incident report discovery should be minimal if an incident report contains only properly reportable material. The information in a properly completed incident report is readily available to the patient's attorney through many other sources. Only when an incident report contains second-hand information, opinions, conclusions, accusations, or suggestions for preventing such incidents in the future does discovery of the incident report become an important issue for attorneys and the courts.

REPORTING YOUR OWN ERROR

If an incident results from your error, you still have the duty to file an incident report immediately. Making a mistake is serious and may invite corrective action by your hospital, but the potential consequences of attempting to cover it up are worse.

For one thing, the likelihood that an incident report will be used against you is slight. A hospital wants its nurses to report incidents and to keep proper records. Nurses may not do this consistently if they're always reprimanded for even small errors. Most hospitals, in fact, will reprimand a nurse for not filing an incident report if injury is done to the patient.

If an incident results from your act of gross negligence or recklessness or

is one of a series of incidents in which you've been involved, then the hospital may take action against you; that possibility increases if the patient sustains injury because of your error.

Reporting a coworker's error

If a fellow employee's error causes a reportable incident, your safest course is to be factual and objective in reporting what you observed. This allows institutional review to be unbiased in its investigation. Remember, the truth isn't libel. If corrective action is taken, remember that the person who made the error is responsible, not the person who made the report. By properly fulfilling your duty to your patient and your hospital, you'll also minimize potential liability if the employee files a lawsuit against you.

Here's another point to remember: Most states have laws granting "qualified privilege" to those who have a duty to discuss or to evaluate coworkers, employees, or fellow citizens. This privilege means that no liability for libel exists unless the person giving the information knows it's false or has acted with a reckless disregard for the truth.

RISK MANAGEMENT STRATEGY

How can you minimize the chances that a patient will sue after an incident? And how can you protect yourself and your hospital in case he does? The best way is to follow the "three R's" of risk management strategy: rapport, record, and report.

Maintain rapport with the patient

Answer his questions honestly. Don't offer an explanation if you weren't personally involved in the incident; instead, refer the patient to someone who can supply answers. If you try to answer his questions without direct knowledge of the incident, inconsistencies could arise and the patient could interpret these as a cover-up.

If you feel uncomfortable talking to the patient or family, ask your supervisor, hospital patient-relations specialist, or an administrator for advice on how to answer questions or to participate and help you provide answers. Remember that patients usually respond favorably if they know you're being honest and show that you care about their well-being.

Don't blame anyone for the incident. If you feel someone was at fault, tell your charge nurse or supervisor—not the patient.

If an incident changes the patient's care plan (such as medication orders), tell the patient about it and clearly explain the reasons for the change.

Record the incident

Be sure to note the facts of the incident in the medical record. Remember, truthfulness is the best protection against lawsuits. If you try to cover up or play down an incident, you could end up in far more serious trouble than if you had reported it objectively. Never write in the medical record that an incident report has been completed. An incident report isn't clinical information but rather an administrative tool.

Report every incident

Some nurses think incident reports are more trouble than they're worth and, furthermore, that they're a dangerous admission of guilt. That's false. Here's why incident reports are important:

■ Incident reports jog our memories. The medical chart is client-focused, and facts pertinent to the incident—but not the patient—may be left out. Much time may pass between an incident and when it comes to court. We

simply can't trust our memories—but we can trust an incident report.

■ Incident reports help administrators to act quickly to change the policy or procedure that seems to be responsible for the incident. An administrator can also act quickly to talk with patients' families and offer assistance, explanation, or other appropriate support. Sometimes helpful communication with an injured patient and his family can calm a family's anger and prevents a lawsuit.

■ Incident reports provide the information hospitals need to decide whether restitution should be made. One example is tracking "lost" belongings.

Caring for a minor

A minor is a person under the age of majority, which is usually 18 or 21, depending on state or jurisdictional law. When you care for a minor, you should keep in mind the way minors' legal rights are structured. What legal rights a minor has depends largely on his age. He may also have special legal status.

MINOR'S RIGHTS

A minor's rights fall into three categories:

■ *Personal rights that belong to everyone from birth*. Examples include the right to privacy and the right to protection against crimes.

■ *Rights that can be exercised as a minor matures.* These fall into two groups. The first includes the right to drive a car, to work at a paying job, and to have sexual relations—as long as both partners are of legal age. These rights are granted at certain ages, according to state laws, whether or not the minor is mature enough to exercise the right intelligently.

The second group includes rights granted by the courts rather than by statutory law. These are given to a minor who shows the mental and emotional ability to handle them.

■ *Rights that belong to adults and can be exercised only by adults and by emancipated minors.* Examples include many financial and contractual rights, such as the right to consent to medical treatment.

The law provides special protection for minors so that they may exercise certain rights after reaching the age of majority. For example, because a minor can't sue in court, most states give minors a grace period after they reach the age of majority to bring any lawsuit relating to when they were minors. This includes suing persons their parents could have sued earlier on the minor's behalf but chose not to. Because this can include a lawsuit for medical malpractice, the law generally requires that hospitals keep the records of pediatric patients longer than the records of adults.

MATURE MINOR

A mature minor is a nonemancipated minor in his middle to late teens who shows clear signs of intellectual and emotional maturity. A mature minor may be able to exercise certain adult rights, depending on laws in his state.

EMANCIPATION

Emancipation is the legal process whereby children may obtain freedom from the custody, care, and control of their parents before the age of majority. Under most state statutes, an emancipated minor loses his right to financial support from his parents in exchange for the ability to govern his own affairs. Emancipation may also

enable a minor to enter into binding contracts and to sue and be sued in his own name. Some statutes also give an emancipated minor the ability to consent to medical, dental, or psychiatric care without parental consent.

Depending on the jurisdiction, emancipation may be addressed by common law or statutory law. Most state statutes require a hearing in emancipation cases.

Standards for emancipation may include:

■ *best interests of the minor* (Many state statutes contain a provision allowing judges to use the best interests of the child as a standard for emancipation.)

■ *ability to manage financial affairs* (Many state statutes have a provision requiring that a minor demonstrate the ability to manage financial affairs before becoming emancipated.)

■ *living separate and apart from parents* (Many statutes require that minors who wish to be emancipated live separate and apart from their parents. Some require parental consent for separate living arrangements.)

■ *parental consent* (Many states require parental consent for an emancipation petition; others ignore this requirement altogether.)

■ *age* (Most states require that children be at least age 16 before initiating emancipation proceedings. A few states don't have an age requirement.).

Under most circumstances, you should treat an emancipated minor the same as if he were an adult.

Restrictions on rights

Note that even an emancipated minor may not exercise some rights. If he's 18 and the drinking age in his state is 21, he can't legally buy an alcoholic beverage. Some states set a minimum age for making a will (usually the age of majority). In those states, even if the minor is married or has a child, a will he draws up won't be valid.

Guardians *ad litem*

A *guardian ad litem* is a person appointed by the court to protect the interest of a minor in a legal proceeding. The court may appoint a guardian *ad litem* when these conditions coexist:

■ A decision is needed for the minor.
■ A "diversion of interest" exists. (The court possesses evidence that the interest of the minor's parents or legal guardians probably doesn't coincide with the minor's welfare.)

The court may appoint a guardian ad litem even if one or both parents are still living and interested in the minor's welfare or if the minor already has a guardian.

Obtaining consent

By far the most common problem with minors is obtaining proper consent for their medical care. Although the physician bears the legal responsibility for this, you'll commonly be involved in the process. Here are 11 different situations you may face in helping to obtain a minor's consent.

Nonemancipated minor

If the minor isn't emancipated, his mother, father, or legal guardian has the right to refuse or consent to treatment for him. Whenever possible, consent should be obtained from both parents or both guardians when joint guardians have custody of the minor.

If the parents are divorced or separated, the policy is to obtain consent from the parent who has custody.

If the minor's parents are incompetent or dead and he has no legal guardian, the court will usually appoint a legal guardian. The guardian can consent or refuse, just as if he were a parent.

Mature, nonemancipated minor

In some Canadian jurisdictions under certain circumstances, mature, nonemancipated minors may consent to medical treatment themselves. Where legislation exists, common law provides that if nonemancipated minors understand the nature and consequences of treatment, they may give their own consent. In the United States, nonemancipated but mature minors' rights aren't as broad. However, in some jurisdictions, parental consent is no longer necessary for various types of medical and psychiatric care. In California, for example, nonemancipated minors age 15 and older, who live separate from their parents and manage their own finances, may consent to their own medical care. Ask your hospital attorney to check your state's statutes in this area.

Emancipated minor

An emancipated minor can usually refuse or consent to treatment himself. However, if he can't do so (for example, he's unconscious after an accident), you have to try to find someone who can give consent for him. Talk to the hospital attorney to determine if there are laws in your state that designate surrogate decision makers when the patient becomes incompetent. Possibilities, in descending order of preference, include his spouse, parents or guardians, and nearest living relative. You may waive this requirement for consent only in an emergency situation when your failure to treat a minor immediately could result in further injury or in death.

When parents or joint guardians disagree

Problems can arise when parents (whether married, divorced, or separated) or joint guardians disagree about consenting to treatment for a nonemancipated minor. The hospital's only recourse may be to go to court, where a judge either decides or assigns responsibility to one parent or guardian. If you find yourself in a situation in which a minor's parents or guardians can't agree on consenting to his treatment, tell the hospital administrators immediately so that they can talk to the parents or guardians and, if necessary, and alert the hospital's attorney.

When a minor needs emergency care

The legal rule to follow when a minor needs emergency care is the same as that for adults: Treat first and get consent later. Some courts have held that a mature minor, emancipated or not, may give valid and binding consent to emergency treatment. For example, in *Younts v. St. Francis Hospital and School of Nursing* (1970), a nonemancipated but mature 17-year-old was held able to consent to surgical repair of a severed fingertip.

When a minor requests an abortion

Several U.S. Supreme Court rulings, including *Ohio v. Akron Center for Reproductive Health* (1990) and *Hodgson v. Minnesota* (1990), indicate that state laws can't prevent a minor from seeking and obtaining a legal abortion; however, states can impose conditions on consent. The law in some states (such as Virginia, in which abortion-consent laws have been upheld by the Supreme Court) may require a minor seeking an abortion to notify her parents or to bypass this consent requirement by going before a judge, a procedure called *judicial bypass.*

For the rules your state requires you to follow when verifying consent for a minor's abortion, check with your facility's attorney.

When a minor asks for a contraceptive

In *Carey v. Population Services International* (1977), the U.S. Supreme Court ruled unconstitutional a state law prohibiting the sale of contraceptives to anyone younger than age 16. The court held that the decision to bear a child is a fundamental right and that state interference can be justified only if it protects a compelling state interest. As a result, a minor can obtain contraceptives without parental consent.

Again, consult the hospital's attorney if you have questions regarding restrictions on distributing contraceptives to minors. For example, your state may require you to notify a parent or guardian about the matter.

When a minor needs treatment for a communicable disease

Most states and Canadian jurisdictions have laws that permit minors to consent to treatment for serious communicable diseases, including sexually transmitted diseases, without parental approval.

If you must deal with a minor who's refusing diagnosis or treatment for a communicable disease, check your state's laws. Most states permit public health authorities to deal with a nonconsenting minor as an adult, including deciding whether he should be quarantined.

When a minor needs treatment for drug abuse

State and federal laws generally permit minors to consent to take part in drug-abuse treatment and rehabilitation programs just as though they were adults. Like adults, minor patients in drug treatment programs are entitled to have their records kept confidential.

When religious beliefs conflict with a minor's treatment

If your patient or his parents or guardians are Jehovah's Witnesses or Christian Scientists, you may have special problems getting consent to treatment.

Although competent adults or emancipated minors may refuse treatment for religious reasons, nonemancipated minors may not. In most states in which the question has come before the courts, judges have ruled that parents and guardians can't stop a hospital from treating their child solely on religious grounds if a reasonable chance exists that the treatment will help the patient.

In some situations a judge may grant a court order for treatment to be rendered. Note, however, that in some situations a court will have to appoint a guardian *ad litem* for the sick minor. This may take some time, so to avoid delaying the minor's treatment unnecessarily, notify your hospital administration as quickly as possible.

When a minor seeks or receives mental health care

Minors, like adults, may be treated at private and state-run mental health facilities. When the minor and his parents agree to seek such treatment for the minor, the facility will follow its normal medical guidelines and procedures in deciding whether to admit him. This usually involves informing the patient and his parents or guardian of their rights and then obtaining their informed consent for admission.

In many states, however, the rules controlling admission of minors to inpatient mental health facilities are more rigorous. The rules may call for a full-scale hearing, with attorneys present, within a set time after admission (if not concurrent with admission).

Caring for an abused patient

In the course of your career, you're likely to encounter victims of abuse. Sometimes abuse is physical battering such as when a son regularly beats his aging father. At other times, abuse involves verbal, sexual, or emotional attack, or neglect and abandonment.

PROFILE OF THE ABUSER

People who abuse others come from all socioeconomic levels and all ethnic groups. No specific psychiatric diagnosis encompasses the abuser's personality and behavior. However, many abusers have a history of being abused themselves when young or of having witnessed abuse of parents or siblings. (Such childhood experiences are usually profound and can influence a person's behavior throughout his adult life.) In many cases, abusive persons lack self-esteem and the security of being loved—qualities that help nonabusive persons cope with stress.

In times of crisis, abusers resort to the behavior learned in childhood. They abuse just as they were abused—all in an attempt to restore their own feelings of self-control and self-esteem. After all, if abuse was an acceptable behavior for their parents, why can't it be the same for them now?

Abusers are usually unable to tolerate personal failure or disapproval from spouses, children, or friends. When an abuser's self-esteem is low, he expects rejection and will act in ways that cause others to reject him. Rejection in turn provokes the abuser to commit further verbal or emotional abuse.

Abusers commonly have unrealistic expectations of the people they abuse. When an individual fails to live up to those expectations, the abuser feels a stronger compulsion to control, mortify, reject, and, if necessary, physically injure that individual.

Cycle of abuse

Low self-esteem may prompt an abuser to choose a partner much like himself. Each will then feed into the other's forms of abuse. If the couple has children, in many cases they become targets of their parents' abusive behavior. What the children witness and suffer often begins another cycle of abused child-to-child abuser.

CHILD ABUSE

U.S. government studies indicate that abused children who die from their injuries are most likely to die before age 4. Studies have indicated that the majority of maltreatment fatalities occur in children younger than age 5. (See *Responding to suspected child abuse.*) Children with behavior problems are particularly vulnerable to abuse, as are malformed or developmentally disabled children and children born prematurely or to unmarried parents. From the abusive parent's perspective, such a child represents an unplanned disruption or a stress-producing crisis. If the child has mental or physical defects, the parent may see this as reaffirming his own inadequacy and weakness. If the child has severe defects, the parent may be unable to accept that the child is his: He may pour on abuse in an effort to be rid of the child.

Parents may also view children as extensions of persons they hate. Sometimes this results from similarities in physical appearance or similarities in behavior. If a child resembles a spouse who deserted the family, he may be blamed for the spouse's failures and abused accordingly.

ADULT ABUSE

Spouses, disabled persons, and elderly parents or relatives are the most common victims of adult abuse.

The abused spouse in many cases suffers from lack of self-esteem. An abused spouse's parents may have abused each other, or one parent may have abused the other. Having witnessed these attacks as a child, the present-day abused spouse accepts that she too will be abused. By behaving passively, spouses make it easy for their partners to abuse them repeatedly without fear of retaliation.

Like children, adults can become abuse victims if they're viewed as too dependent, too sickly, or too much like a hated person. Ill or elderly persons who make financial, emotional, or personal demands in many cases will end up injured when the stress they create becomes intolerable for their abusers. (See *Elder abuse,* page 226.)

Among abusers of adults, men who abuse women predominate, but sometimes the opposite happens. Abused men, married or not, in most cases show the same low self-esteem and passivity as abused women. Sometimes an abused man is the less aggressive and more subservient member of the relationship and accepts a certain level of abuse in the hope that it won't get worse. At other times, he may be so ashamed by his inability to provide adequately that he invites abuse to give himself a feeling of atonement.

LEGAL TIP

Responding to suspected child abuse

Suppose you're on duty in the ED when Mrs. Firth comes in with her son Billy, age 4. She tells you, "Billy was riding in a friend's car and they had an accident. I didn't think he was hurt at first, but later on his knee swelled up. I decided I'd better have a doctor look at it."

You examine Billy closely for head and neck injuries. You don't see any, but you do notice some bruises on his left arm and on his legs that look several weeks old. You question Mrs. Firth about the accident, but she offers few details. Then, when you ask her about Billy's injuries, she gets defensive. Although his injuries look painful, Billy sits quietly while you examine him.

How to respond

You suspect Billy has been abused. What should you do next? Follow these guidelines:

■ Tell the physician your reasons for suspecting child abuse and ask him to order a total-body X-ray, especially if you detect multiple old and new fractures or suspicious-for-age fractures. Also, inform your supervisor of the situation.

■ If you suspect the child has been forced to ingest drugs or alcohol, get an order for toxicology studies of the child's blood and urine.

■ Document the location, size, and appearance of all bruises and wounds (old or new) on

an intake form with a body profile, making sure to sign and date it.

■ Pictures may be taken of the patient's injuries and placed in the medical record. If photos are taken, be sure they include proper identification of the patient, date, and time. Be sure to take the photographs with a unit camera and not on a personal smart phone.

■ If the child is severely bruised, get an order for a blood coagulation profile.

■ If X-rays or other studies suggest that the child has been abused, talk with the physician about confronting the parents. Ask how you might help him do this.

■ If a parent admits to abusing the child and appears to want help, give the address and telephone number of a local group, such as a local chapter of Parents Anonymous (PA), and encourage the parent to call.

■ Whether or not the parent admits to abusing the child, report all suspected abuse to the state-designated agency empowered to investigate the situation.

■ Keep in mind that in many states, failure to report suspected abuse is a crime. Nurses are considered mandated reporters in many states and therefore must report suspected abuse.

Also be aware that abuse occurs in same-sex relationships, but the abused person may fail to report it out of fear of discrimination.

ABUSE AND THE LAW

In 1874, grossly battered "Mary Ellen," age 9, was found chained to her bed in a New York City tenement. Etta Wheeler, a church worker, tried to find help for Mary Ellen, but she quickly discovered

that New York had no laws to protect children. Her only recourse was the American Society for the Prevention of Cruelty to Animals, which agreed to intervene on Mary Ellen's behalf.

One year after Mary Ellen's case reached the courts, New York state adopted the country's first child-protection legislation. This gave child-protection agencies a legal base, and it proved a breakthrough for other disadvantaged groups as well.

Elder abuse

According to the best available estimates, between 1 and 2 million American age 65 or older have been injured, exploited, or otherwise mistreated by someone on whom they depended for care or protection. A study by the Administration on Aging and the Administration for Children and Families estimates that more than 500,000 older persons in domestic settings were abused or neglected during 1996 and that for every reported incident, about 5 went unreported.

The greater an elderly person's disabilities, the more vulnerable he is to abuse or neglect by caregivers–usually his relatives. Family members provide about 80% of all care given to older people, and about 85% of all reported abuse involves a family member's behavior.

Defining abuse and neglect

Nearly every state has laws mandating that suspected elder abuse be reported to the authorities. However, not all states define elder abuse. Instead, they leave its diagnosis to health care professionals. One definition of abuse and neglect is as follows:

- *Elder abuse* is destructive behavior that's directed at an older adult, carried out in a context or relationship of trust, and occurring intensely or frequently enough to produce harmful physical, psychological, social, or financial suffering and a decreased quality of life.
- *Elder neglect* is harm caused by failure to provide prudently adequate and reasonable assistance to meet the elderly person's basic physical, psychological, social, and financial needs.

Detecting abuse

As a nurse–especially if you're in an outpatient or acute care setting–you have more contact with patients than most other members of the health care team. You may be the first to notice or suspect mistreatment of an elderly patient. In fact, in hospitals with special Elder Assessment Teams, most abuse referrals are generated by nurses–especially those in the ED. If you suspect elder abuse, report it according to hospital or agency policy or as mandated by state law.

Signs and symptoms

Detecting abuse in a frail, elderly person with multiple health problems can challenge your assessment skills. A situation or condition that suggests mistreatment may actually represent the progression of disease. For example, you may suspect that an elderly woman covered with bruises is battered when in fact she has a coagulation disorder caused by the medication she takes for heart disease.

The following signs and symptoms, though not definitive for abuse, call for further investigation and reporting:

- unexplained bruises, fractures, or burns
- poor hygiene or nutritional status
- pressure ulcers or other evidence of skin breakdown or infection
- dehydration
- fear of a family member or a caregiver
- indications of overmedication or undermedication, such as grogginess or decreased level of consciousness
- unusual listlessness or withdrawal
- signs and symptoms of sexually transmitted disease.

Since then, child abuse has gained increasing attention from the public, from legislators, and from concerned health care professionals. In 1946, for example, radiologists reported that subdural hematomas and abnormal X-ray findings in the long bones were commonly associated with early childhood traumatic injuries. In 1961, an American Academy of Pediatrics symposium on child abuse introduced the term "battered child."

The first statutes requiring mandatory reporting of child abuse resulted from a 1963 report by the Children's Bureau of the U.S. Department of Health, Education, and Welfare (now the Department of Health and Human Services). Most states, using the model in the report, developed protective legislation by the early 1970s. Unfortunately, the diversity of these laws made uniform interpretation impossible.

To help remedy this, Congress passed the Child Abuse Prevention and Treatment Act in 1973. This act requires states to meet certain uniform standards to be eligible for federal assistance in setting up programs to identify, prevent, and treat the problems caused by child abuse. The act also established a National Center on Child Abuse and Neglect.

The act was amended in 1984 in response to "Baby Doe" cases. These cases involved parents who refused lifesaving treatment for mentally and physically handicapped infants. The amendments require the states to respond to reports of a child's medical neglect. States must respond to reports that medically indicated treatment (including appropriate nutrition, hydration, and medication) has been withheld from an infant. The law allows three exceptions under which treatment may be withheld:

■ when the infant is chronically ill and irreversibly comatose

■ when treatment would only prolong dying

■ when treatment itself would be inhumane and futile in terms of survival.

According to interpretive guidelines to the regulations (which don't have the force of law), even when one of these exceptions is present, the infant must still receive appropriate nutrition, hydration, and medication.

State law

Two common features characterize most state child abuse legislation:

■ empowering of a social welfare or law enforcement bureau to receive and investigate reports of actual or suspected abuse

■ granting of legal immunity from liability, for defamation or invasion of privacy, to a person reporting an incident of actual or suspected abuse.

Laws protecting abused spouses are still being written. Although many domestic relations laws exist, additional legislation is required to help protect victims of domestic violence.

YOUR LEGAL DUTY TO REPORT ABUSE

As a nurse, you play a crucial role in recognizing and reporting incidents of suspected abuse. While caring for patients, you can readily note evidence of apparent abuse. When you do, you must pass the information along to the appropriate authorities. In many states, failure to report actual or suspected abuse constitutes a crime.

Protection from liability

If you've ever hesitated to file an abuse report because you fear repercussions, remember that the Child Abuse Prevention and Treatment Act protects you against liability. If your report is bona fide (that is, if you file it in good faith), the law will protect you from a suit filed by an alleged abuser.

FILING A REPORT

Make your report as complete and accurate as possible. Be careful not to let your personal feelings affect either the way you make out a report or your decision to file the report.

Abuse cases can raise many difficult emotional issues. Remember, however, that not filing a report can have more serious consequences than filing one that contains an unintentional error. It's better to risk error than to risk breaching the child abuse reporting laws—and, in effect, perpetuating the abuse.

RECOGNIZING ABUSE

Learn to recognize the events that trigger abuse and the signs and symptoms that mark the abused and the abuser. Early in your relationship with an abused patient, you'll need to be adept to spot the subtle behavioral and interactional clues that signal an abusive situation.

Examine the patient's relationship with the suspected abuser. For example, abused people tend to be passive and fearful. An abused child usually fails to protest if his parent is asked to leave the examining area. An abused adult, on the other hand, usually wants his abuser to stay with him.

Abused persons may react to procedures by crying helplessly and incessantly. They tend to be wary of physical contacts, including physical examinations.

Many facilities have a policy, procedure, or protocol that establishes criteria to help nurses and other health care providers make observations that will help identify possible victims of abuse. Learning these criteria will make spotting victims of abuse more objective and prevent cases from going unrecognized.

Assessing the abuser

Sometimes the abuser will appear overly agitated when dealing with health care personnel; for example, he'll get impatient if they don't carry out procedures instantly. At other times, he may exhibit the opposite behavior: a total lack of interest in the patient's problems.

Patient history

When you take an abuse victim's history, he may be vague about how he was injured and tell different stories to different people. When you ask directly about specific injuries, he may answer evasively or not at all. Sometimes he'll minimize or try to hide his injuries.

Physical examination

Look for characteristic signs of abuse. In most cases of abuse, you'll find old bruises, scars, or deformities the patient can't or won't explain. X-ray examinations may show the presence of many old fractures.

Documenting abuse

Always document your findings objectively; try to keep your emotions out of your charting. One way to do this is to use the SOAP technique, which calls for these steps:

- In the subjective (S) part of the note, record information in the patient's own words.
- In the objective (O) part, record your personal observations.
- Under assessment (A), record your evaluations and conclusions.
- Under plan (P), list sources of hospital and community support available to the patient after discharge.

OFFERING SUPPORT SERVICES

Many support services have become available for both abusers and their victims. For example, if a female victim is afraid to return to the scene of her abuse, she may find temporary housing in a women's shelter. If no such shelter is available, she may be able to stay with a friend or family member.

Social workers or community liaison workers may also be able to offer suggestions for shelter. Another possibility is a church, synagogue, or mosque, which may have members willing to take the patient in. If no shelter can be found, the patient may have to stay at the hospital for her safety.

Alert the patient to state, county, or city agencies that can offer protection. The police department should be called to collect evidence if the patient wants to press charges against the abuser. If the patient is a child, the law will probably require filing a report with a government family-service agency.

Help for the abuser

You need to evaluate the abuser's ability to handle stress. He'll probably pose a continued threat to others until he gets help in understanding his behavior and how to change it. In such a situation, you may attempt to refer him to an appropriate local or state agency that can offer help.

For abusive fathers or mothers, a local chapter of PA may be helpful. (See *Help for the abused and the abuser.*) PA, a self-help group made up of former abusers, attempts to help abusing parents by teaching them how to deal with their anger.

Besides helping short-circuit abusive behavior, a self-help group takes abusing parents out of their isolation and introduces them to individuals who can empathize with their feelings. It also provides help in a crisis, when members may be able to prevent an abusive incident.

Telephone hot lines to crisis intervention services also give abusers someone to talk with in times of stress

Help for the abused and the abuser

These organizations offer support and counseling for the abuse victim and the abuser. Also, check the "Guide to Human Services" section of your phone directory under "Abuse" and "Child & Youth" for local or state agencies.

Childhelp USA
1-800-4-A-CHILD
Web site: *www.childhelpusa.org*

National Court Appointed Special Advocate Association
1-800-628-3233
Web site: *www.nationalcasa.org*

National Domestic Violence Hotline
1-800-799-SAFE
Web site: *www.ndvh.org*

National Sexual Assault Coalition Resource Sharing Project
3030 Merle Hay Road c/o Iowa Coalition Against Sexual Assault
Des Moines, IA 50310
Web site: *www.resourcesharingproject.org*

Rape, Abuse and Incest National Network
1-800-656-HOPE
Web site: *www.rainm.org*

and crisis and may help prevent abuse. Typically staffed by volunteers, telephone hot lines provide a link between those who seek help and trained counselors.

These and other kinds of help are also available through family-service agencies and hospitals. By becoming familiar with national and local resources, you'll be able to respond quickly and authoritatively when an abuser or his victim needs your help.

TEACHING THE PUBLIC

Besides your duty to report abuse, you also have the opportunity to teach the public about abuse. The Child Abuse Prevention and Treatment Act encourages health care facilities to develop programs to identify, report, and ultimately prevent abuse. You can help reduce the incidence of abuse by teaching people about its signs and symptoms, diagnosis, and treatment, not just in the workplace, at health fairs, at school presentations, or other interactions with the public.

Caring for a mentally ill or developmentally disabled patient

Despite his usually dependent condition, a mentally ill or developmentally disabled patient has most of the same rights as other members of society. In fact, usually the law covers such a patient's rights in extra detail to ensure that he receives proper care and treatment. If you violate these rights, even unwittingly, you could face serious legal complications.

Much of today's concern for the rights of the mentally ill and developmentally disabled stems from attempts to correct past abuses. Under the U.S. Constitution, a person's rights can't be limited or denied merely because of his mental status. Many health care professionals still don't realize that the courts have generally interpreted the Constitution to mean that mentally ill and developmentally disabled persons have a right to fair and humane treatment, including during hospitalization. Under most circumstances, such

a patient can't be kept in a hospital against his will, for example. Nor can he be denied the right to refuse treatment or to receive information, so he can give informed consent to a proposed surgery.

GOVERNMENT ACTION

State governments have tried to ensure the rights of this special population by enacting legislation specifically addressing the problems of the mentally ill and developmentally disabled. This legislation describes and authorizes specific services and provides the necessary funding.

The federal government also provides for the mentally ill and developmentally disabled. The Rehabilitation Act of 1973, for example, earmarked funds specifically for rehabilitative programs. It provides cash assistance for persons who, because of their disabilities, aren't able to provide adequately for themselves or their families. The act also outlines 14 patient's rights to ensure high standards of health care. Facilities that participate in Medicare must comply with these 14 rights and make sure that the patient, his guardian, next of kin, or sponsoring agency knows about them, too.

The Americans with Disabilities Act of 1990 (P.L. 101-336) further ensures a disabled citizen's rights by providing a "national mandate for the elimination of discrimination against individuals with disabilities." This act addresses discrimination in employment, public accommodations, and public services, programs, and activities.

Canada makes similar provisions for mentally ill and developmentally disabled persons. As in the United States, Canadian legislation seeks to prevent maltreatment and to fund programs that help these persons to function successfully in society.

ESTABLISHING LEGAL RESPONSIBILITY

When a mentally ill or developmentally disabled child is admitted to a hospital, legal responsibility for him must be established immediately. If a parent accompanies the patient, usually the parent will be legally responsible.

If the child has been institutionalized before entering the hospital, the institution may have responsibility. However, this is true only if the parents have waived responsibility and the institution has written evidence to prove it.

If the courts have found the parents unfit or unable to care for the child, a legal guardian will have been appointed. This person has the legal right to assume responsibility for the child.

When no guardian has been appointed for the child, the state may act as a guardian under the doctrine of *parens patriae*. This doctrine also applies to mentally ill or developmentally disabled adults, who must have guardians.

Adult guardianship

If your mentally ill or developmentally disabled patient is an adult, check his chart to see if he requires a legal guardian and to establish whom it is. It may be a parent. Or if the patient is married, it may be the patient's spouse.

Sometimes an adult patient and his guardian will seriously disagree about the patient's care. When this happens, get clarification by going through proper hospital channels.

Remember, you have no right to control the life of a mentally ill or developmentally disabled patient. Restricting his liberty for any reason is almost never legally permissible, except when he may otherwise harm himself or others. You must analyze each situation carefully to determine at what point the patient needs help in making health care decisions.

OBTAINING INFORMED CONSENT

When consent is required from a patient who's mentally ill or developmentally disabled, consider the following three questions:
- Can consent for treatment or a special procedure be obtained the same way it is from any other patient?
- Does the patient fully understand the procedure that he is about to undergo, including the risks, benefits, and alternatives?
- Does the patient have the authority to give his own consent, or must someone else give it?

The answers to these questions will vary with each patient. Clearly, if the patient is of unsound mind and can't understand the nature, purpose, alternatives, and risks of the proposed treatment, he cannot legally consent. In such a case, consent must be obtained from the patient's legal guardian.

If the legal guardian is unavailable, a court authorized to handle such matters may authorize treatment.

Questioning a patient's ability to give consent

Sometimes a physician or nurse may doubt a patient's capacity to consent, even though he hasn't been judged incompetent. This commonly happens during an illness that causes temporary mental incompetence. In such a situation, you must follow your state laws to determine who can make health care decisions for the patient. Typically, the nearest relative's consent is often obtained or, if none can be found, the court must authorize treatment.

In the New York case of *Collins v. Davis* (1964), a hospital administrator sought a court order to permit surgery on an irrational adult whose life was considered to be in danger. The patient's wife had previously refused to give consent, allegedly for reasons she felt served the patient's best interest. The court, after considering the entire situation—especially the patient's prognosis if surgery wasn't performed—agreed that the hospital and the physician had only two choices: either let the patient die, or perform the operation against his wife's wishes. The court overruled the wife's refusal, holding that the patient had sought medical attention and that treatment normally given to a patient with a similar condition should be provided.

Nurse's role

You can best protect the mentally ill or developmentally disabled patient's legal rights to informed consent by making sure that a physician has provided him or his guardian with information. Find out if the patient's and guardian's questions have been answered to their satisfaction.

Unless your absence would place the patient in danger, you should refuse to assist with procedures on a patient whose informed consent hasn't been obtained. If you do participate, you can be held liable along with the physician and the hospital. In fact, if your patient is a minor, you could face double liability: his parents could sue you now, and he could sue you when he comes of age.

FORCED HOSPITALIZATION AND USE OF RESTRAINTS

Mentally ill or developmentally disabled persons may be involuntarily

kept in hospitals if they're at risk of taking their own lives or if they pose a threat to other persons' property or lives. However, mental illness alone isn't a sufficient legal basis for detaining a patient.

Similar restrictions apply to physical restraint of patients. Most states require a physician to write the restraint order and place it in the patient's medical record before applying restraints.

Restraint (or seclusion) may be used only to prevent a patient from seriously injuring himself or others— and only when all other physical and psychological therapies would likely fail to prevent such injuries. Whenever possible, use minimal restraint—only that amount necessary to protect patient and safeguard the staff and others. Restraint should never be used for punishment, for the convenience of staff, or as a substitute for treatment programs. Use of restraints is usually limited to a specific period. (See *Caring for a patient in restraints or seclusion*.)

If you make a decision to apply restraints, you should immediately request that a physician examine the patient and write an order to restrain him. In an emergency situation—such as a violent outburst with actual or potential harm to persons or property—a person may apply restraints to the patient. However, in such a situation one must obtain an order for the restraint as soon as possible, and document the incident carefully.

Potential liability

As a nurse, you may be held liable in a lawsuit if you can't verify that—in your judgment—a patient needed to be restrained and that he was restrained only as long as necessary. If you restrain or seclude a patient simply for shouting obscenities, for example, you risk a lawsuit for false imprisonment.

LEGAL
TIP **Caring for a patient in restraints or seclusion**

Before you can keep a patient in restraints or in seclusion, you must get an order from the patient's physician authorizing it. The Joint Commission standards are specific regarding restraint and seclusion.

situation the physician must write an order for the restraints as soon as possible and evaluate the patient in-person within 1 hour. Joint Commission regulations state that PRN or "as needed" orders for restraints are not to be used.

Guidelines

The Joint Commission requires that when restraints or seclusion are initiated there must be:
■ documented evidence that such interventions are clinically justified
■ less restrictive interventions were attempted
■ the patient's current condition has been considered.

Orders are to be time-limited and written for a specific episode, with start and end times, rather than for an unspecified time in the future. JCAHO, state law, and established hospital policy should specify the maximum length of time that each intervention may be used.

In an emergency, specially trained staff may initiate the use of restraints or seclusion. In this

Care requirements

When you're caring for a patient in restraints or seclusion, periodic monitoring and observation is essential (as required by your facility's policy).

For patients who require frequent or pro-longed restraint or seclusion, the treatment team should meet to consider alternatives and changes in the care plan. Generally, 72 hours of continuous restraint or more than four episodes in 7 days is considered prolonged or frequent.

Document such items as the patient's hydra-tion, feeding, toileting, and range of motion and condition of limbs. The facility should have policies or procedures for addressing these con-cerns; they should be followed and documented accurately.

You should also be sure you know how to use restraining devices safely and effectively. You may be held liable if your restraints don't prove effective and the patient is injured as a result. (See *Use of restraints and nursing liability,* page 234.)

How to apply restraints

When applying restraints, follow these guidelines:
■ Restraint is a form of imprisonment, so it should only be used as a last resort. Before restraining a patient, consider alternatives, such as constant observa-tion or walking with the patient.
■ Take care to avoid undue force; oth-erwise, you may invite a lawsuit

for battery. Even threatening to use force may be sufficient cause for legal action.
■ When a physician isn't immediately available, you're responsible to see that restraints and seclusion are used only to the extent necessary to prevent injury. Make sure the staff contacts the physician as soon as possible.
■ Most states follow the *least restrictive principle,* which holds that no more restraint should be used than neces-sary. For example, a restraining vest shouldn't be used when simple wrist restraints will suffice.
■ To avoid allegations of false impris-onment, document carefully the deci-sion-making process that led to the use

Use of restraints and nursing liability

Improperly restraining a patient can leave the nurse vulnerable to a host of legal charges, such as negligence, professional malpractice, false imprisonment, and battery. This case provides an example of nurses who failed to use restraints effectively.

The patient who escaped

In *Rohde v. Lawrence General Hospital* (1993), police brought the patient into the hospital at 1 a.m. following an auto accident. The patient assaulted a clinician in the ED and was diagnosed as having an "acute psychotic episode." The physician ordered leather restraints.

Around 6 a.m., the patient escaped from four-point restraints, went into the parking lot, found a car that had been left running, and drove off. He crashed the car and was seriously injured.

The patient sued the hospital, the ED physician, and two nurses for medical malpractice, claiming that the staff didn't supervise him properly and that his restraints weren't securely fastened.

RIGHT TO PRIVACY

The law has tried to protect all citizens from unwarranted intrusion into their private lives. Unfortunately, mentally ill and developmentally disabled patients' rights to privacy are easily violated. A good definition of privacy, first presented at the International Commission of Justice in 1970, reads: "Privacy is the ability to lead one's life without anyone:

- interfering with family or home life
- interfering with physical or mental integrity or moral and intellectual freedom
- attacking honor and reputation
- placing one in a false light
- censoring or restricting communication and correspondence, written or oral
- disclosing irrelevant or embarrassing information
- disclosing information given or received in circumstances of professional confidence."

Keep this definition in mind as you work with mentally ill and developmentally disabled patients, and do all you can to protect their right to privacy.

of restraints, and review the continuing need for restraints on a regular basis.

- Bedside rails are a form of restraint, and shouldn't be raised indiscriminately. The patient's age alone isn't a justification for raising the side rails.
- Tranquilizing drugs may provide an alternative to restraints. However, use them sparingly, with caution, and only with a physician's order. The patient's right to the least restrictive treatment or to an open-door policy that allows patients to move about "freely" means little if accompanied by indiscriminate drug use as a substitute for restraints.

RIGHT TO WRIT OF *HABEAS CORPUS*

Institutionalization may, at times, breach a patient's rights, giving him cause to petition for a writ of *habeas corpus*. This writ seeks to ensure the timely release of a person who claims that he's being detained illegally and deprived of his liberty.

RIGHT TO TREATMENT

In *Wyatt v. Stickney* (1972), the court upheld the legal right of a mentally ill person hospitalized in a public institution to receive adequate psychiatric treatment. This decision suggests that when a patient is involuntarily committed because he needs treatment, his rights are violated if he doesn't receive proper care. Furthermore, if the underlying reason for a patient's commitment is that he's dangerous to himself or others, treatment must be provided to make him less so.

In the Wyatt decision, the court outlined a complete bill of rights for the mentally ill patient. Among the key points, the court said treatment should be given:

- by adequate staff
- in the least restrictive setting
- in privacy
- in a facility that ensures the patient a comfortable bed, adequate diet, and recreational facilities
- with the patient's informed consent before unusual treatment
- with payment for work done in the facility, outside of program activities
- according to an individual treatment plan.

If possible, ensure that a mentally ill or developmentally disabled patient knows what treatment he needs and how he'll get it. You must know what his major problems are and what he can do for himself—or what others must do for him—to help him get ready for discharge. You should also involve him in formulating his treatment plan, unless you have a documented reason why he can't or won't be involved.

SEXUAL RIGHTS

The U.S. Supreme Court has upheld the rights of mentally ill or developmentally disabled patients:

- to marry
- to have children
- to employ contraception, abortion, or sterilization, if desired
- to follow a lifestyle of their own choosing.

Several cases, such as *Sengstack v. Sengstack* (1958), *Wyatt v. Stickney* (1972), and *O'Connor v. Donaldson* (1975), have used the U.S. Supreme Court decisions as a basis for their rulings.

Involuntary sterilization

Involuntary sterilization of developmentally disabled patients isn't employed today as it was in the past. Although the U.S. Supreme Court upheld the constitutionality of involuntary sterilization in *Buck v. Bell* (1927), if a similar case were to come before the Supreme Court today, the precedent would likely be overturned.

In *Buck v. Bell,* the court held that the state has the right to sterilize a developmentally disabled or mentally ill person provided that:

- the sterilization isn't prescribed as punishment
- the policy is applied equally to all
- a potential child's interest is sufficient to warrant the sterilization.

Courts today can authorize such a procedure but only within specific guidelines. Generally, it must be shown that sterilization is the only workable means of contraception. In some cases, the court orders a separate, independent presterilization review of the case. (In New York state, unlike California, for example, an independent medical review board must review and approve every planned involuntary sterilization before it can be performed.) Even though the patient's guardian has requested sterilization, if the patient refuses to submit to surgery, the court may call for use of a less permanent birth control method.

PARTICIPATION IN RESEARCH

Another troublesome area involves using mentally ill and developmentally disabled persons as subjects for medical or other research—especially if risks are involved. Guidelines for consent to experimentation and drastic, questionable, or extreme forms of treatment are complicated and raise many unresolved questions. The so-called Willowbrook decision, *N.Y. State Association for Retarded Children, Inc. v. Carey* (1977), however, decreed that both voluntary and involuntary residents of a mental health facility have the constitutional right to be protected from harm. The proper authority (usually an IRB) should allow the patient to participate in the research only if it's relevant to his needs and the needs of others like him and its potential benefits outweigh its potential risks. For example, a depressed patient shouldn't be asked to participate in research involving anxiety and schizophrenia.

Strict federal regulations guide how experimental treatment can be carried out. Such treatment must be given with extreme caution to mentally ill or developmentally disabled patients.

RESPONDING TO PATIENT REQUESTS

"Ordinary" requests made by mentally ill or developmentally disabled patients may require special consideration.

For example, a patient may demand to smoke a cigarette. His physician hasn't written an order for the request. If the patient should smoke only under supervision because of the danger of fire, you may decide to stay with him while he does so. If you have a duty to be elsewhere, you should refuse his request, explaining why and telling him when he'll be able to smoke.

If you know a refusal will agitate and anger him, you can also ask another nurse to supervise the patient while he smokes.

Perhaps the patient is well aware that he's violating the hospital's no-smoking policy and his request is really a challenge to authority. If so, you may decide to refuse the request, explaining the need to follow the hospital's social and safety policies.

If the patient's behavior is part of a pattern that includes, for example, refusing to shower, refusing to go to bed by a certain time, and demanding to make an immediate phone call, then you need to refer the situation to the treatment team for a well-thought-out decision—one that serves the best interests of both the patient and the hospital. Once it's made, ask all the health-team members to enforce this decision consistently.

Caring for a suspected criminal

Suppose you're asked to care for an injured suspect who's accompanied by police. Because the police need evidence, they ask you to give them the patient's belongings and also a sample of his blood. Should you comply? The answer to this question isn't simple. If you're ignorant of the law and fail to follow proper protocol, the evidence you turn over to police may not be admissible in court. Worse still, later on, the patient may be able to sue you for invasion of privacy.

CONSTITUTIONAL RIGHTS

The Fourth Amendment to the U.S. Constitution provides that "the right of the people to be secure in their persons, houses, papers and effects, against unreasonable searches and seizures shall not be violated, and no warrants shall issue, but upon probable cause." This means that every individual, even a suspected criminal, has a right to privacy, including a right to be free from intrusions that are made without search warrants. However, the Fourth Amendment doesn't absolutely prohibit all searches and seizures, only unreasonable ones.

Further, under constitutional law, when a magistrate issues a warrant authorizing a police officer to conduct a search, the warrant must be specific about the places to be searched and the items to be seized.

Probably the exclusionary rule is the most common rule affecting nurses in relation to suspected criminals and their victims. This rule stems from the Fourth Amendment's prohibition of unreasonable searches and seizures. In the landmark case of *Mapp v. Ohio* (1961), the U.S. Supreme Court held that evidence obtained through an unreasonable or unlawful search can't be used against the person whose rights the search violated.

Searches without a warrant

Under certain circumstances, a police officer may lawfully conduct a search and obtain evidence without a warrant:
- If an accused person consents to a search, any evidence found is considered admissible in court (*Schneckloth v. Bustamonte* [1973]).
- A search incidental to an arrest may be conducted without a warrant. Usually, such a search shouldn't extend beyond the accused person's body or an immediate area where he could reach for a weapon. However, in *Maryland v. Buie* (1990), the U.S. Supreme Court ruled that a search incidental to an arrest could extend to adjoining rooms and closets of

a private residence from which an accomplice could attack. Police may even conduct a sweep of an entire area if they have reason to think they may be in danger. Although this Supreme Court case dealt with searches in a private home, the ruling could apply to searches conducted in a hospital.
- Police may search an area, even out of arm's reach, to recover a weapon that could pose a threat to their safety (*New York v. Class* [1985]).
- Police may enter a private area and seize items in plain view if they're in "hot pursuit" of a criminal suspect (*Warden v. Hayden* [1967]).

Evidence obtained as part of a blood test

Opinions differ as to whether a blood test, such as a blood alcohol test, is admissible in court if the person refused consent for the test. In *Schmerber v. California* (1966), the U.S. Supreme Court said that a blood extraction obtained without a warrant, incidental to a lawful arrest, isn't an unconstitutional search and seizure and is admissible evidence. Many courts have held this to mean that a blood sample must be drawn *after* the arrest to be admissible.

Further, the blood sample must be drawn in a medically reasonable manner. In *People v. Kraft* (1970), a suspect was pinned to the floor by two police officers while a physician drew a blood sample. In *State v. Riggins* (1977), a suspect's broken arm was twisted while a policeman sat on him to force consent to a blood test. In both cases, the courts ruled the test results inadmissible. The courts have also ruled as inadmissible—and as violative of due process rights—evidence gained by the forcible and unconsented insertion of a nasogastric tube into a suspect to remove stomach contents (*Rochin v. California* [1952]).

Courts have admitted blood tests as evidence when the tests weren't drawn at police request but for medically necessary purposes such as blood typing (*Commonwealth v. Gordon* [1968]). Some courts have also allowed blood work to be admitted as evidence when it was drawn for nontherapeutic reasons and voluntarily turned over to police.

Be careful, though. A physician or nurse who does blood work without the patient's consent may be liable for committing battery, even if the patient is a suspected criminal and the blood work is medically necessary.

Blood alcohol tests and drunk driving arrests

Many states have enacted so-called implied consent laws as part of their motor vehicle laws. These laws hold that by applying for a driver's license, a person implies his consent to submit to a blood alcohol test if he's arrested for drunken driving. Many of these laws state specifically that if an individual refuses to submit to the chemical test, it may not be given, but the driver then forfeits his license. Check to see whether such laws exist in your state.

Evidence obtained during a surgical procedure

A Massachusetts case, *Commonwealth v. Storella* (1978), involved a bullet that a physician removed during a medically necessary operation. After the operation, the physician turned the bullet over to the police. The court allowed the bullet to be admitted as evidence because the physician was acting according to good medical practice, and not as a state agent, in removing the bullet.

In 1985, the U.S. Supreme Court ruled that the constitutionality of

such court-ordered surgery to acquire evidence must be decided on a case-by-case basis. The interest in individual privacy and security must be weighed against the societal interest in collecting evidence. Therefore, you should be wary if asked to assist in a highly invasive procedure to help the state obtain evidence if the suspect doesn't consent. If necessary, consult an attorney.

Swallowed contraband

Drug couriers have been known to carry contraband by swallowing it in small balloons, which can be recovered after elimination. As a nurse, you may become involved in efforts to detect and recover swallowed contraband. In *United States v. Montoya de Hernandez* (1985), the U.S. Supreme Court ruled that the police could lawfully detain drug couriers until swallowed items could be recovered and seized.

Searches by a private party

In *Burdeau v. McDowell* (1921), the U.S. Supreme Court said that the Fourth Amendment protections applied only to governmental (such as police) action and not to searches conducted by private parties. Although several courts have criticized this rule, it has been repeatedly upheld.

In *State v. Perea* (1981), a nurse took a suspect's shirt for safekeeping, then turned it over to the police even though they hadn't requested it. A New Mexico court allowed the shirt to be admitted as evidence. The reason is that because no governmental intrusion was involved, the suspect's Fourth Amendment right wasn't violated.

The case of *United States v. Winbush* (1970) produced a similar result. In this case, the court ruled that evidence found during a routine search of an unconscious patient's pockets was admissible because the purpose of the search was to obtain necessary identification and medical information.

Evidence in plain view

As a nurse, if you find a gun, knife, drug, or other item that the suspect could use to harm himself or others, you have a right to remove it. You should, however, notify the administration immediately and maintain control over the evidence until you can give it to an administrator or law enforcement official.

When the suspect may sue

In general, searches that occur as part of medical care don't violate a suspect's rights. However, searches made for the sole purpose of gathering evidence—especially if done at police request—very well may. Several courts have said that a suspect subjected to an illegal private search has a right to seek remedy against the unlawful searcher in a civil lawsuit. One such case was *Stone v. Commonwealth* (1967). (See *Conducting a drug search,* page 240.)

Canadian law

The major difference between U.S. and Canadian law regarding searches is that, in Canada, evidence obtained during an illegal search may still be admissible in court. However, a police officer should have a search warrant before searching a suspected criminal to protect his rights.

A word of caution

The laws of search and seizure are complex and subject to change by new legal decisions. Consult with the administration or an attorney before complying with a police request to turn over a patient's personal property. Some state laws require that police obtain a warrant before they're legally entitled to this evidence.

DOCUMENTING YOUR ACTIONS

Be careful and precise in documenting all medical and nursing procedures when you care for a suspected criminal. Note the blood work done, and list all treatments and the patient's response to them.

If you turn anything over to the police or administration, record what it was and the name of the person you gave it to. Record a suspect's statements that are directly related to his care. If a suspect says, "I shot a cop in the arm tonight," that isn't related to his care. However, if he says, "I think I was shot in the leg by a cop," that relates directly to his medical care.

SAFEGUARDING EVIDENCE

Before any evidence can be admissible in court, the court must have some guarantee of where—and how—it was gathered. Someone must account for the evidence from the moment you collect it until it appears in court, a continuum known as the *chain of custody.* Evidence can't be left unattended because it might be tampered with.

If you discover evidence, use your facility's chain of custody form. First used when evidence is taken from the patient, this form should remain with the evidence until the trial. It documents the identity of each person handling the evidence as well as the date and times it was in their possession. In effect, the form should serve as an uninterrupted log of the evidence's whereabouts.

If your facility doesn't have a chain of custody form, keep a careful note as to exactly what was taken, by whom, and when. Give this information to the administrator when you deliver the evidence. Until such time as the evidence can be turned over, it should be kept in a locked area.

LEGAL TIP **Conducting a drug search**

If you suspect your patient is abusing drugs or alcohol, you have a duty to do something about it. If such a patient harms himself or anyone else, resulting in a lawsuit, the court may hold you liable for his actions.

When you know about drug abuse

Suppose you know for certain that a patient is abusing drugs–if you're an ED nurse, you may find drugs in a patient's clothes or handbag while looking for identification. Your hospital policy may obligate you to confiscate the drugs and take steps to ensure that the patient doesn't acquire more.

When you suspect drug abuse

When a patient's erratic or threatening behavior makes you suspect he's abusing drugs or alcohol, your hospital's policy may require that you conduct a search. Is your search legal? As a rule of thumb, if you strongly believe that the patient poses a threat to himself or others and you can document your reasons for searching his possessions, you're probably safe legally.

Guidelines for searches

Before you conduct a search, review your hospital's guidelines on the matter. Then follow these guidelines carefully. Most hospital guidelines will first direct you to contact your supervisor and explain why you have legitimate cause for a search. If she gives you her approval, ask a security guard to help you. Besides protecting you, he'll serve as a witness if you do find drugs. When you're ready, confront the patient, tell him you intend to conduct a search, and tell him why.

Depending on your hospital's guidelines, you can search a patient's belongings as well as his room. If you find illegal drugs during your search, confiscate them. Depending on your hospital's guidelines, you may be obligated to report the patient to the police.

If you find alcoholic beverages during your search, hospital guidelines may require you to take them from the patient. Explain to the patient that you'll return them when he leaves the hospital.

Maintaining written records

After you've completed your search, record your findings in your nurses' notes and in an incident report. Your written records will be an important part of your defense (and your hospital's) if the patient decides to sue.

When a suspect dies, most states provide that the coroner can claim the body. Police are free to gather any evidence that won't mutilate the body. A dead body has no constitutional rights, so no rights are violated by a search.

NURSING BEHIND BARS

Even after conviction, an individual doesn't forfeit all constitutional rights. Among those retained is the Eighth Amendment's proscription against cruel and unusual punishment. This implies that prison officials and health care workers must not deliberately ignore a prisoner's medical needs.

The U.S. Supreme Court, in *Estelle v. Gamble* (1976), stated that the Eighth Amendment prohibits more than physically barbarous punishment. The amendment embodies "broad and idealistic concepts of dignity, civilized standards, humanity, and decency against which we must evaluate penal measures."

Right to medical care

The state has an obligation to provide medical care for those it imprisons. The Supreme Court has concluded that "deliberate indifference to serious medical needs of prisoners constitutes the unnecessary and wanton infliction of pain proscribed by the Eighth Amendment. This is true whether the indifference is manifested by prison physicians in response to a prisoner's needs or by prison personnel in intentionally denying or delaying access to medical care or intentionally interfering with the treatment once prescribed."

In *Ramos v. Lamm* (1980), the court outlined several ways in which prison officials show deliberate indifference to prisoners' medical needs:

■ preventing an inmate from receiving recommended treatment

■ denying access to medical personnel capable of evaluating the need for treatment

■ allowing repeated acts of negligence that disclose a pattern of conduct by prison health staff

■ allowing such severe deficiencies in staffing, facilities, equipment, or procedures to exist that inmates are effectively denied access to adequate medical care.

Providing care

Working daily with prisoners is difficult and demanding, both professionally and emotionally. Along with exhibiting a host of other unpleasant behaviors, prisoners can be abusive, manipulative, and angry. In spite of this, health care professionals can't forget their ethical and legal duty to provide quality care.

Nurses working in a prison setting should be aware that the doctrine of *respondeat superior* doesn't apply to prison cases when the prisoner sues for violations of his constitutional rights. The nurse supervisor or manager can't be held responsible for accusations of "cruel and unusual punishment" unless she has personally acted to deprive the prisoner of medical care *Vinnedge v. Gibbs* (1977).

When a prisoner refuses treatment

Several courts have stated that individuals have a constitutional right to privacy based on a high regard for human dignity and self-determination. That means any competent adult may refuse medical care, even lifesaving treatments. For instance, in *Lane v. Candura* (1978), an appellate court upheld the right of a competent adult to refuse a leg amputation that would have saved her life.

A suspected criminal may refuse unwarranted bodily invasions. However, an arrested suspect or convicted criminal doesn't have the same right to refuse lifesaving measures. In *Commissioner of Correction v. Myers* (1979), a prisoner with renal failure refused hemodialysis unless he was moved to a minimum security prison. The court disagreed, saying that although the defendant's imprisonment didn't divest him of his right to privacy or his interest in maintaining his bodily integrity, it did impose limitations on those constitutional rights.

As a practical matter, anytime a patient refuses lifesaving treatments, inform your facility's administration. In the case of a suspect or prisoner, notify law enforcement authorities as well.

Upholding a patient's living will

When a legally competent person draws up a living will, he declares the steps he wants or doesn't want taken when he's incompetent and no longer able to express his wishes. The will applies to decisions made after a patient is incompetent and has no reasonable possibility of recovery. Generally, a living will authorizes the attending physician to withhold or discontinue certain lifesaving procedures under specific circumstances.

The will is called *living* because its provisions take effect before death. By clearly stating his wishes regarding lifesaving procedures, the patient also helps relieve guilt his family and the health care team might otherwise feel for discontinuing life support.

A living will is considered a legal statement of the patient's wishes. Most states have statutes authorizing living wills and the appointment of a health care agent. The exceptions are states with legislation authorizing only the appointment of a health care agent (Massachusetts, Michigan, and New York) or authorizing only living wills (Alaska).

A patient may also choose to execute a durable power of attorney for health care. Should the patient become incompetent, this document designates a surrogate decision maker with authority to carry out the patient's wishes regarding health care decisions. Most states have laws authorizing only durable power of attorney for the purpose of initiating or terminating life-sustaining medical treatment.

CONTENT OF LIVING WILL LAWS

Living will laws usually include provisions, such as:

- who may execute a living will
- witness and testator requirements
- immunity from liability for following a living will's directives
- documentation requirements

- instructions on when and how the living will should be executed
- under what circumstances the living will takes effect.

WHEN LIVING WILLS DON'T APPLY

When the patient's condition is such that the living will isn't applicable, or in cases in which the patient hasn't executed a living will, the patient's surrogate will need to make decisions regarding the removal of life support systems and treatment.

The Supreme Court's ruling in *Cruzan v. Director, Mo. Dept. of Health* (1990) may influence future court rulings in this area. The U.S. Supreme Court held that the state of Missouri has the constitutional right to refuse termination of life-sustaining treatment unless "clear and convincing evidence" exists about a patient's wishes, implying that the patient's wishes will be honored. Because states differ on what they consider "clear and convincing evidence," consult your facility's ethics committee or attorney in cases of this type.

INTERPRETING THE WILL

A physician may also face real difficulties in determining when a living will should apply. Wording in many living wills is vague. What, for example, is a "reasonable expectation of recovery?" And what's a "heroic" or an "extraordinary" measure? When a patient actually enters a coma, it may be difficult to precisely interpret the intentions expressed in his living will. That's one reason why legislatures have been slow to make living wills binding.

States have tried to relieve patients and families from the burden of judicial involvement in medical decisions, encouraging decision making by the patient, family, and physician. Unfortunately, the more latitude provided for decision makers, the less protection for the patient. For instance, the original Illinois Health Care Surrogate Act, effective January 1, 1998, expanded the boundaries of surrogate decision-making legislation to include general medical decisions, permitting the patient to remain uninformed about his loss of decision-making status and subsequent decisions. It's important to note that the Act applies to those who lack a living will or a chosen health care agent as well as to those with a living will that doesn't address the specific condition of the patient. This Act would allow a surrogate decision maker to refuse an abortion for a pregnant minor, for instance. The surrogate decision maker, a close family member, could be an abusive spouse, a child abuser, or another person that the patient would deem unacceptable, if he were informed. Because of the uncertainty in the judicial system today, it's important that a patient clearly state in his living will exactly what medical treatments he'd choose to receive and which he'd forgo to ensure that his wishes are honored.

Patients should be encouraged to review their living wills with their families and physicians, so that unclear areas can be discussed. Living wills also need to be reviewed periodically to keep pace with changes in technology. Some living wills are detailed, multipage documents; some, a simple paragraph.

Immunity

If physicians, nurses, and other health care providers follow the wishes expressed in a living will authorized by law, they're generally immune from civil and criminal liability. No matter which state you work in, check your facility's policy and procedures manual and seek advice from the legal department as needed.

CHILDREN AND LIVING WILLS

Although minors can't make valid testamentary wills, and adults can't make such wills for them, living wills are another matter. In a few states, adults are authorized to make living wills for their minor children.

Parents don't normally plan for their child to die, so most are unlikely to make a living will before a child's terminal illness is diagnosed. Even then, a living will is usually legally unnecessary. If the parents and the child agree that no extraordinary means should be used to prolong life, or if the child is too young to understand, the parents have the legal right to act for the child. They can require that the health care team not use extraordinary means to prolong his life. The same principle also applies in reverse: if the child wants to die but his parents want him treated, the parents' wishes prevail.

If a terminally ill adolescent doesn't want extraordinary treatment but his parents do, and the adolescent has written a living will, a physician or health care facility may use the will to petition a court on his behalf. Even though the will itself is legally invalid because it was written by a minor, its existence may prompt the court to consult the adolescent and, in its ruling, grant the patient his wishes.

LIVING WILL FROM ANOTHER STATE OR COUNTRY

U.S. law applies to foreign citizens treated in the United States. That means a foreign citizen may execute a living will while in the United States, and it must be honored if executed in a state with a living will law.

What if a patient produces a living will executed in a foreign country? What about a patient who executes a living will in one state and later finds himself terminally ill in another state? The law of the state where the living will decision will be carried out prevails. Therefore, if a patient has an out-of-state living will, you should determine whether it matches the criteria required by the laws of the state you're in. When dealing with an out-of-state living will, consult your facility's legal counsel.

The same general legal principle applies to U.S. citizens in Canada or in another foreign country. A foreign country's law applies to all persons, whether citizens of that country or not, and determines the extent to which a living will be honored. Check with your facility's attorney.

WHEN A LIVING WILL BECOMES INVALID

A living will needn't be honored if it has been revoked or is out of date. State law may mandate that a living will is valid only for a limited number of years. If the patient's family and attending medical personnel find that the patient made the living will many years ago and his life circumstances have changed substantially since then, they may have legal justification for disregarding the will. For this reason, publishers of living will forms suggest reviewing the living will yearly, revising it if necessary, and redating and re-signing it.

If the patient asks that the will be disregarded, or if a patient tells his physician to proceed with treatment that contradicts the will, such action effectively revokes the will.

WHEN THE FAMILY'S WISHES CONTRADICT THE WILL

The patient's family can't revoke a patient's living will unless they can prove the will is invalid. Some states provide penalties for concealing a patient's living will or for falsely reporting that it has been revoked.

DRAFTING A LIVING WILL

Like all legal documents, a living will must be written, signed, and witnessed. State laws specify the execution requirements. If the patient asks for help drafting a living will, refer him to your facility's legal department or the local legal aid agency.

Although it isn't required, a patient should be encouraged to file copies of his living will with his physician and with family members who would attend him in the event of a terminal illness.

You may be asked to witness a living will. Check to see if your state law allows this. If it doesn't, ask your nursing supervisor for the procedure you should follow.

If the patient drafts a living will while under your care, document this in your nurses' notes, describing factually the circumstances under which the will was drawn up and signed.

ORAL STATEMENTS

Patients may make oral statements expressing their wishes about further medical treatment before or during a terminal illness.

Before terminal illness

When a patient has made his treatment wishes known to his family and physician in advance, they'll usually respect his wishes even if he later becomes comatose or otherwise incompetent. If the physician and the family disagree about what's best for the terminally ill incompetent patient, they may have to settle the dispute in court.

During terminal illness

Every competent adult has the right to refuse medical treatment for himself, including the use of extraordinary means. If a competent terminally ill patient tells a physician or nurse to discontinue extraordinary efforts, his wishes are binding.

If a patient tells you his wishes about dying, first write what he says in your nurses' notes, using his exact words as much as possible. Next, describe the context of the discussion—for example, was the patient in pain, or had he just been informed of a terminal illness? Be sure you also tell the patient's physician about the discussion. Remember, *oral statements aren't legally enforceable,* although a patient's stated refusal of treatment is binding. Oral statements *should* be respected, however, as guidelines to how the patient feels about his treatment.

Dealing with living wills

Federal legislation, the Patient Self-Determination Act of 1990, requires hospitals, extended care facilities, HMOs, hospices, and home health care agencies that participate in Medicare and Medicaid to provide patients with written information about their rights under state law regarding living wills and durable power of attorney (together called *advance directives*) as well as about the facility's procedure for implementing them. The law also requires the health care facility or agency to document whether the patient has a living will or durable power of attorney.

If your patient has a living will, review your nursing or facility manual for directions on what steps to take. For instance, you may need to inform the patient's physician about it. Or you may need to ask your nursing supervisor to inform the administration and the legal department. With the patient's permission, make sure that the family knows about the will; if they don't, show them a copy.

If the patient is able to talk, discuss the will with him, especially if it contains terms that need further definition. As always, objectively document your actions and findings in the patient's record.

Beyond these actions, your responsibilities for a patient's living will are determined by the circumstances involved—including the family's and physician's responses to the will. If there's conflict among the parties, work with family members and colleagues to come up with a unified care plan.

Personal conflicts over a living will

If implementing a living will conflicts with your personal ethics or beliefs, you may wish to discuss the matter with a clinical nurse specialist, your nursing supervisor, a nursing administrator, a chaplain, an administrator at your facility, or an ethics committee member. If you're still unable to accept the idea after talking over your feelings with one of them, you can ask for reassignment to another patient. Chances are that your request will be honored and no disciplinary action will be taken against you.

Working as a quality management nurse

Quality management (QM) or continuous quality improvement focuses on processes of care delivery and not on individual blame. As a QM nurse, it's your job to monitor, evaluate, and correct potential quality of care issues—a complicated task, indeed. You have to make sure that your facility follows appropriate federal and state laws, complies with its own internal set of rules and regulations, and meets the accreditation requirements of various accrediting agencies, such as the Joint Commission and the National Committee for Quality Assurance. If you fail to perform your duties properly, you put yourself and your facility at professional and legal risk.

CONFIDENTIALITY

Confidentiality is every nurse's responsibility, but as a QM nurse, it's more than a responsibility—it's a mission. Usually, you're dealing with sensitive, privileged information. Withholding this information from friends and colleagues can be a burdensome duty, especially when you're dealing with adverse events, peer review, incident reporting, and record review for investigational purposes or focused quality improvement studies. Although various state and federal statutes for peer review afford some protection from liability, the legal realities of discovery and the absence of immunity put you at risk to testify, should a lawsuit arise.

SELECTED REFERENCES

American Nurses Association. Code of Ethics for Nurses with Interpretative Statements. Retrieved from: http://www .nursingworld.org/MainMenuCategories/ EthicsStandards/CodeofEthicsforNurses/ Code-of-Ethics.pdf, November 2010.

Brous, E. "Lessons Learned from Litigation: The Case of Bernard Travaglini," *American Journal of Nursing* 114(5):58–60, May 2014.

Brous, E. "Lessons Learned from Litigation: The Case of Eric Decker," *American Journal of Nursing* 114(2), February 2014.

Canadian Patient Safety Institute. Patient Safety Forward with Four. Retrieved from: http://www.patientsafetyinstitute.ca/ English/About/PatientSafetyForwardWith4/ Pages/default.aspx

Johnson, R.W., et al. "Reasons for Noncompletion of Advance Directives in a Cardiac Intensive Care Unit," *American Journal of Critical Care* 21(5):311–20, September 2012.

Joint Commission on Accreditation of Healthcare Organizations. 2014 Hospital Accreditation Standards. PC25, PC60-65. Retrieved from: http://www .jointcommission.org/accreditation/ hospitals.aspx

Joint Commission on Accreditation of Healthcare Organizations. National Patient Safety Goals. Retrieved from: http:// www.jointcommission.org/standards_ information/npsgs.aspx

King, J., and Anderson C. "The Canadian Interprofessional Patient Safety Competencies: Their Role in Health-Care Professional's Education," *Journal of Patient Safety* 8(1):30–5, March 2012.

Smalls, H.T. "Nursing Liability and Chain of Command," *Neonatal Network: The Journal of Neonatal Nursing* 28(6):401–402, November-December 2009.

Tevington, P. "Mandatory Nurse-Patient Ratios," *Medsurg Nursing* 20(5):265–8, September-October 2011.

Wilmont, S. "Massachusetts Nurses Achieve Safe-Staffing Victory," *American Journal of Nursing* 114(10):15, October 2014.

7

Legal aspects of documentation

Patricia Iyer, MSN, RN, LNCC

Just how important is good nursing documentation? Ask nurses at Tipton Hospital in Indiana who were involved in caring for a woman after she underwent a laparoscopic Nissen fundoplication operation. Shortly after surgery, the patient had constant and persistent pain. She became tachycardic; her oxygen saturation and white blood cell count dropped, and her hemoglobin rose. Her surgeon was informed of this and sent her to ICU. The next morning, X-rays showed free air in her abdomen. Her surgeon took her back to the operating room, where he found a perforation of the stomach, which had occurred in the original surgery. The patient developed septic shock and died. The plaintiff claimed that the surgeon had delayed the post-surgical diagnostic workup and that the hospital staff had failed to assess the patient's symptoms and update the physicians on her declining condition. The defendants denied any negligence. The jury returned a verdict against the hospital for $2.5 million, but returned a defense verdict for the surgeon. The verdict was reduced to $1.25 million in compliance with the state's cap on awards. (*Estate of Rich v. Tipton Hospital*, reported in April 2014.)

In this chapter, you'll learn about the legal significance of the patient's medical record—the confidential principal tool used by the health care team to plan, coordinate, and document the care given to each patient. You'll also read about the importance of good nursing documentation, examine several court cases in which documentation quality affected the litigation outcome, and review guidelines for avoiding documentation errors. You'll find a discussion of handwritten, hybrid, and electronic medical records and their advantages and disadvantages.

Purpose of accurate documentation

The trends in health care mean that patients are being assessed, cared for, and treated by more health care professionals than ever before. They receive care from nurses in hospitals, clinics, ambulatory surgery centers, assisted living, nursing homes, school, homes, day care, jails, prisons, and other settings. Complete, accurate, and timely documentation is crucial to the continuity of each patient's care. The medical record is also a legal and business record with many uses. A well-documented medical record:

- reflects the patient care given
- demonstrates the results of treatment

- helps to plan and coordinate the care contributed by each professional
- allows interdisciplinary exchange of information about the patient
- provides evidence of the nurse's legal responsibilities toward the patient
- supplies information for analysis of cost-to-benefit reduction
- reflects professional and ethical conduct and responsibility
- furnishes data for a variety of uses—continuing education, risk management, diagnosis-related group assignment and reimbursement, continuous quality improvement, case management monitoring, and research
- demonstrates fulfillment of standards, rules, regulations, and laws of nursing practice.

Consider this case. A seventy-nine-year-old woman was examined by a physiatrist while the patient was hospitalized at Kingston Hospital in New York. She had undergone hip replacement. The physician attempted to treat the patient, but the patient fainted. Her condition declined; she developed pneumonia and died several weeks later. The plaintiff claimed the pneumonia was due to dehydration, vomiting, aspiration, and syncope related to the doctor's treatment. The plaintiff argued that the physician and nursing staff failed to monitor intake and output of fluids. The physician claimed that as a physiatrist, monitoring of intake and output was not required and that the hospital staff approved the start of rehabilitation. The defendant also denied that the patient aspirated vomitus during her treatment. The jury found the physician 20% negligent and the hospital 80% negligent. They awarded $189,066.78 in Eileen Rosman as the Adminx of the Estate of Jerod Rosman and Eileen Rosman, Indiv. v. Kingston Hospital and Srivani Karra MD reported in August 2014.

As you can see in this case, the medical record was used to determine whether the nurses monitored intake and output, which the plaintiff argued should have been done.

LEGAL TIP **Documentation tips**

If you're ever involved in a malpractice lawsuit, how you documented, what you documented, and what you didn't document will heavily influence the jury and the outcome of the trial. Following these tips can ensure that your records don't tip the scales of justice against you.

How to document

- Document the care given in a timely manner. Avoid waiting until the end of your shift before starting your documentation. Delaying documentation for several hours may affect its accuracy.
- Include patient statements in quotations when significant.
- Be specific. Avoid general terms and vague expressions.
- Use standard abbreviations only.
- Use a medical term only if you're sure of its meaning.
- Document symptoms by using the patient's own words.
- Document objectively.
- Follow the standards of your employer and specialty area to include the expected components of documentation.
- Avoid use of abbreviations on TJC "do not use" list.

Documentation tips *(continued)*

What to document

■ Document all nursing actions you take in response to a patient's problem. For example, "8 p.m. medicated for incision pain." Be sure to include the medication name, dose, route, and site.

■ Document the patient's response to medications and other treatment.

■ Document safeguards you use to protect the patient. For example, "raised side rails" or "applied safety belts."

■ Document an incident in two places: in your progress notes and in an incident report. Don't mention the incident report in the patient's record, unless your facility or state requires it.

■ Document each observation. Failure to document observations will produce gaps in the patient's records. These gaps will suggest that you neglected the patient.

■ Document procedures after you perform them, never in advance.

■ Avoid including your work sheet or work list as part of the medical record. Always make sure you shred it and do not remove it from your workplace.

■ Chart an omission as a new entry. Never back-date or add to previously written entries. Within the body of the note, reference the time and date of omission.

■ Correct errors according to your facility's policies and procedures.

■ Verify that you carried out interventions specified on the patient's care plan critical pathways,

and protocols. (See *Managed care: implications for documentation.*)

■ Document only the care you provide. Never document for someone else.

■ Understand and follow the documentation standards of your facility and your state or province. These standards are usually defined in state or provincial nurse practice acts (the statutes governing nursing practice) and in state or provincial administrative codes (the rules and regulations governing nursing practice).

■ Document discharge instructions and your evaluation of the patient's comprehension of the instructions.

■ Record attempts to reach other health care providers; whom you called, when you called, and how the provider responded.

■ Consistently record details about the patient's pain, the effectiveness of pain reduction measures, and what you did if a plan in the pain management was warranted.

■ Details of the patient's condition when you hand off (transfer the care of the patient) to another person.

■ If the patient refuses care or to follow your instructions, document the patient's reason, explanations you offered, and whom you notified about the refusal. A patient who refuses needed care or does not follow instructions may have some responsibility if an injury occurs later. This is called contributory negligence and affects how plaintiff's attorney views a case.

CONTENTS OF THE MEDICAL RECORD

Federal regulations, such as those governing Medicare and Medicaid reimbursement, partially determine the form and content of the medical record. Although state laws vary in their stringency and specificity, all states require health care facilities to maintain the medical record in sufficient detail.

Managed care: implications for documentation

Because managed care balances the importance of a medical procedure or treatment against its cost, it requires greater standardization of care plans as well as continuous monitoring of health care outcomes. To improve outcomes, several tools have been developed.

Clinical practice guidelines are standards developed to help practitioners and patients make decisions regarding appropriate care in specific clinical circumstances.

Practice parameters are educational tools that enable physicians to obtain the advice of clinical experts, keep abreast of the latest clinical research, and assess the clinical significance of often conflicting research findings.

Clinical pathways and *critical paths* are clinical management tools that help to organize, sequence, price, and time the major interventions of nurses, physicians, and other health care providers for a particular case type, subset, or condition.

Care maps are elaborate critical pathways that show the relationships of sets of interventions to sets of intermediate outcomes along a time line. They merge standards of care with standards of practice in a cause-and-effect relationship.

The following documents are usually included in the hospital medical record:
- patient admission form
- history and physical
- advance directives
- provider orders (written by interns, residents, nurse practitioners, attending physicians, fellows, and physicians assistants)
- progress notes written by each treating discipline
- nursing admission assessment
- risk assessments (skin breakdown, falls, etc.)
- nursing plan of care
- medication administration record
- medication reconciliation form
- nurses' notes and flow sheets
- patient education
- diagnostic and laboratory test results
- X-ray and other radiologic reports
- preoperative checklists, operative, anesthesia, intraoperative nursing, and postanesthesia care unit reports
- graphic sheets for vital signs
- assessments and progress notes of case management, dietary and physical, occupational, respiratory, and speech and language therapists
- consultations
- consents
- discharge summary
- clothing and valuables lists.

Long-term care records consist of these components:
- minimum data set and care area assessments
- nursing admission assessment
- risk assessments (falls, skin breakdown, elopement, pain, bowel and bladder continence, need for side rails, etc.)
- behavioral assessments
- provider orders
- provider progress notes
- care plan
- interdisciplinary team meeting notes
- dental consults
- treatment administration records
- medication administration records
- monthly summaries
- wound documentation flow sheets
- weight and vital signs
- transfer records from another facility

- intake and output
- diagnostic studies
- history and physical
- nursing notes
- nursing assistant flow sheets of activities of daily living
- consents
- restorative nursing records
- assessments and progress notes of activities, dietary, physical, occupational, respiratory, social services, and speech and language therapists
- pharmacist consults and other consults.

Sources of documentation duties and standards

Factors that influence nursing documentation standards include:
- federal statutes and regulations
- state regulations and statutes, including licensing statutes and nurse practice acts
- custom
- accrediting bodies
- standards of practice issued by professional organizations
- institutional policies and procedures.

The federal government defines charting requirements in some settings such as long-term care, for example. OBRA (42 C.F.R. 483.75 (1)) provides that the long-term care facility must maintain clinical records that are complete, accurately documented, readily accessible, and systematically organized.

The Joint Commission (TJC) sets standards that are used to accredit inpatient and outpatient facilities. Documentation should reflect the collaborative planning and provision of care and treatment. TJC doesn't specify a format for medical record documentation. Thus, patient care, treatment, and rehabilitation may involve many forms, from preprinted forms

to handwritten reports to electronic formats, which may include decision algorithms and care maps.

Professional organizations have developed and refined recommendations and standards of practice for nursing documentation. Sometimes these standards are more stringent than those required by state law. The American Nurses Association (ANA) has included documentation in its Standards of Nursing Practice. The ANA says documentation must be systematic, continuous, accessible, communicated, recorded, and readily available to all health care team members.

Many of the professional specialty societies, such as the American Association of Critical Care Nurses, the Association of Operating Room Nurses, and the Emergency Nurses Association, have developed guidelines, standards, or recommendations concerning content and technique of nursing documentation.

Typically, a health care facility has integrated the appropriate laws, regulations, and standards into its own policy and procedure manual. Your best assurance of following the law may be to adhere to the facility's policy, which usually describes who's to maintain each portion of a patient's record and by which technique.

NURSING DOCUMENTATION

With a large number of health care professionals involved in each patient's care, nursing documentation must be complete, accurate, and timely to foster continuity of care. It should cover the following:
- initial assessment using the nursing process and applicable nursing diagnoses
- plan of care
- nursing actions

- ongoing assessment, including the frequency of assessment
- variations from the assessment and plan
- accountability information, including forms signed by the patient, location of patient valuables, and patient education
- notification of other providers about important elements of care
- collaboration with other clinicians
- notation of care by other disciplines, including physician visits, if practical
- health teaching, including content and response
- procedures and diagnostic tests
- evaluation of patient response to therapy, particularly to nursing interventions, drugs, and diagnostic tests
- statements made by the patient
- any refusals of medication or treatment or not following instructions of nurse
- incidents
- patient comfort and safety measures.

Types of medical records

Handwritten, hybrid, and electronic medical records currently simultaneously exist—and often in the same medical record. Let's look at these different methods of charting.

HANDWRITTEN MEDICAL RECORDS

The outcome of nursing care is often rooted in the information found in a medical record. The legibility and completeness of the record is crucial. Handwritten notes are easy to create, can be faster than entering data into the electronic medical record, and are a familiar method of charting to many health care providers.

Drawbacks of handwritten records

Handwritten information may be illegible, creating the potential for errors in patient treatment or medication orders. It is costly to maintain them and uses up valuable space. A medical record that is maintained in paper form has limitations. Of great concern is the lack of access to the record. Only one person at a time may use the chart, and the chart has to be in a single location. Staff needing access to the record must wait until it is available for their use. Delayed access to the chart negatively affects coding, billing, and reimbursement processes. Fragmentation of the patient's record occurs as the result of multiple encounters with different health care providers. Owing to disparate patient documentation and billing systems, there is often minimal or no exchange of information that contributes to compiling a medical history for the patient. Each provider or facility has only a limited portion of the patient's overall health information.

It is difficult to locate information in a handwritten record. A thick chart may need to be thinned, which results in removal of information that may be critical for understanding the patient's course.

METHODS OF CHARTING: HYBRID

Today's medical records are likely to be a combination of handwritten and computer-generated records. Certain sections of a chart may be handwritten, and others may be computer generated. This results in a hybrid chart—part handwritten, part electronic. Hybrid medical records result from:
- funding gaps
- delays in full implementation of electronic medical records

- other institutional priorities
- allowing staff to choose which system they prefer to use to document
- the need to combine medical records from more than one source
- incomplete staff education.

There are pieces of the medical record that even today can be handwritten, such as consent forms, immunization records, physician office records, physician orders, physician progress notes, and histories and physicals. These records may be scanned and included in an electronic medical record. Many nursing home records and home health records are still handwritten. Hybrid records may be part of the transition to electronic medical records. They may be generated if the computer has downtime and becomes unavailable for real-time documentation.

Drawbacks of hybrid records

Since hybrid records encompass handwritten records, all of the drawbacks of handwritten records apply. The quality of the actual documentation varies according to the health care provider's documentation skills and knowledge level. While standardization of the documentation has improved over the years, not all providers use the same abbreviations, terminology, format, or chart organization. This can result in incomplete or inaccurate health care data collection. For example, there are handwritten orders, computer-generated orders, and standard order sets. If the computer system goes down, there may be handwritten documents generated while the staff are unable to chart. Hybrid records may create further confusion because of the lack of consistency between paper and electronic records or in format. Some of the information can be retrieved from a computer, and other pieces

have to be obtained by a search of handwritten information.

Consider these errors:

- A provider wrote an order for Toradol 30 mg on the patient's chart. The nurse administered the medication and documented it in the electronic medical record, but not on the paper emergency department chart. A second nurse also saw the order and administered the medication again.
- Orders in a paper chart were not transferred to the electronic medical record. These included "NPO till procedures completed, Ancef 1 Gm on call to operating room and vital signs every 15 minutes × 4." None of the orders were carried out.
- Heparin was ordered for a patient with a pulmonary embolism. The order was written on the assessment order sheet and entered into the pharmacy information system, but not transcribed to the Kardex or the medication administration record. The patient did not receive the dose.

Unless a facility can fully implement electronic medical records, they must be keenly aware of the potential for workarounds that may result in medical errors.

Consider how this medication error led to a patient's death:

In a March 2014 Alabama case, a 62-year-old man went to the emergency department because of extreme weakness, fever, and a dry hacking cough. He was diagnosed with pneumonia. He had a typed list of medications he was taking. The list was made part of his hospital record. He took lithium carbonate for a total of 900 mg per day in two doses. He took 300 mg in the morning and 600 mg at night. At the time of his admission, his lithium level was normal.

When the patient's medications were transcribed by a nurse, the lithium was written as three 300 mg tablets three times a day for a total of 2,700 mg instead of the 900 mg the patient had been taking. His doctor (Dr. Meka) checked the form, but failed to recognize the error. The patient received 11 days of 2,700 mg of Lithium. He deteriorated and died.

The family reached a settlement with the doctors and the nurse for $1 million, leaving Dr. Meka as the only defendant in a trial. The jury awarded $1.85 million and subtracted the $1 million already received in settlement. (*Estate of Haralson v. Meka*.)

METHODS OF CHARTING: ELECTRONIC MEDICAL RECORDS

An *electronic health record* (EHR) brings together legible information about a patient collected from outpatient and inpatient settings. It is ideally available from any setting where the patient may receive care, such as an emergency department, hospital, or clinic. For this to happen, systems need to be integrated and built on a common platform. An *electronic medical record* contains information from one provider, such as a physician's office or a hospital admission. EHRs allow providers to immediately access and share information, reduce duplicate testing, and provide information more readily within a facility. Recognizing the savings and efficiency associated with electronic medical records, both President Bush and President Obama supported legislation to encourage adoption of electronic medical records. Financial and legislative incentives spurred rapid adoption of electronic medical records in both inpatient and outpatient settings.

Electronic medical records have many advantages. They are more than automated paper records; they take advantage of the unique ability to use drop-down menus, collate data from monitoring equipment, and avoid having to write long free-form notes. The use of computer technology to prescribe medications, in combination with other software applications, is a means of decreasing medication errors. Bar code scanning of medications at the bedside helps to ensure that the right patient receives the right medication. EMRs allow the nurse to enter the information once and reuse it many times. Data entry may be driven by the patient's care plan, policies and procedures, standards of care, and patient safety.

EMRs minimize the risk of lost information, which may occur if a handwritten chart or handwritten papers are mislaid. Each person who enters information in the record is identified by name, eliminating the need to guess at the identity of the author of the entry. Electronic medical records promote patient safety through the use of alerts, prompts, and timely transfer of test results. They are legible, which replaces the labor-intensive task of transcribing orders or contacting providers asking for clarification of illegible handwriting.

Electronic medical records can promote standardized documentation when used with templates. Nurses don't need to remember the important elements of care to document; the software prompts them to enter the data. EMRs are useful for generating work lists to help nurses organize and prioritize their time. Patient monitoring equipment may feed data directly into the electronic medical record, thereby eliminating the need to manually input it. They may incorporate built-in safety mechanisms and clinical alerts, although providers must pay attention to them for them to be effective.

For example, a nephrologist wrote a prescription for potassium for a woman who was on dialysis. The order was not clear. Originally, he wrote it as 10 mEq and then changed his mind and attempted to write a 2 over the 1. The hospital computer provided a notation for the need for confirmation. The nurses and pharmacists misinterpreted the order and believed it was 120 mEq, which was a fatal dose. The nurse started an infusion of 120 mEq. The woman died 4 hours later. The hospital settled for a confidential amount before trial.

At trial, the plaintiffs argued that the physician set the chain of events in motion, although the nurses and pharmacists should have recognized the error. The physician admitted that the prescription was not clearly written, but argued that it was unforeseeable that such a high dose would be administered without being questioned. The hospital's computer had tagged the potassium order for confirmation, but it was not confirmed. The defendant also argued that the patient had a limited life expectancy of 6–12 months. The defendant also pointed out the orders for "do not resuscitate" and "do not intubate" were in place. The jury assigned 90% of the fault to the hospital and 10% to the physician and awarded $379,122.39. The verdict was reduced to $37,912.24. (*Martha G. Garcia, Judith Rocha, et al v. Baptist Health System, d/b/a VHS San Antonio Partners L.P. d/b/a Northeast Baptist Hospital and Flavio Alvarez MD,* reported in April 2014.)

Research has focused on how nurses benefit from EHRs by improving nursing documentation, reducing medical records, and improving legibility. Do electronic medical records improve patient outcomes? A University of Pennsylvania study found that nurses from hospitals with fully implemented EHRs were significantly less likely to report unfavorable outcomes compared with nurses working in hospitals without fully implemented EHRs. The outcomes included less frequent medication errors, improved quality of care and confidence that the patient was ready for discharge, and an increased emphasis on patient safety. There were fewer incidences of things being overlooked when the patient was transferred between units.

Audit trails permit investigation of how the electronic medical record was generated and viewed. This information may be essential in a lawsuit, and could affect determinations of whether the provider followed the standard of care. It is difficult to determine whether a health care provider picked up a handwritten chart and looked at it. There is no tracking system that creates a log of such activities. However, EMRs provide accurate logging of health care providers who accessed a medical record. This may complicate the provider's defense.

In *Roben Carter and Timothy Carter v. U.S.A.,* reported in June 2014, in June 2008, a woman from Tennessee went to a clinic as part of a hospital when she had a lump in each of her breasts. The nurse practitioner ordered a mammogram and ultrasound, which were done in July 2008. The radiologist reported not seeing a solid or cystic mass in the right breast and saw multiple benign-appearing lesions in the left breast. The Chief of Mammography Services wrote a letter recommending the patient see her primary care provider for a referral to a surgeon because there was a palpable lump. The letter was placed in her mammography file and not her treatment file; the patient did not receive this letter. In November 2008, the patient saw another nurse practitioner; a second mammogram and ultrasound was ordered and then cancelled. The patient had an ultrasound done on the left breast in January 2009; it was interpreted as benign.

The patient returned to the clinic in March 2010. An image of the right breast led to a needle biopsy that showed cancer. The patient was diagnosed with Stage III cancer and underwent surgery and chemotherapy. She claimed there was a delay in diagnosis of her cancer and that her prognosis would have been better if her cancer was diagnosed earlier. Her attorney was able to show through expert evaluation of the electronic medical records that the mammogram and ultrasound reports had been signed off on by a nurse practitioner at the clinic. The jury awarded $5.2 million dollars.

In this case, analysis of the EMR was interpreted as showing that the nurse practitioner viewed the concerning reports. In another case, the EMR showed that a health care provider did not view the medical records. A 64-year-old man involved in a car collision was taken to Suburban Hospital. He complained of right arm weakness, left shoulder pain, right hand weakness, and neck pain. A CT scan showed a neck fracture, but it could not be determined whether it was from the collision or from a neck injury the patient had as a teenager. The trauma surgeon ordered a neurological exam and instructed a resident to see that it was performed. The resident told the trauma surgeon he had spoken to the neurosurgeon; the trauma surgeon said the patient could be discharged if he

was "at baseline." The plaintiffs claimed that the neurological exam was not performed. The neurosurgeon testified during trial that he was not called to see the patient. The defendants claimed that the neurological consultation occurred but was not documented. The plaintiff argued that there was no record of the neurosurgeon even accessing the patient's medical records.

A nurse performed some testing on the patient and determined he was "close to baseline," but did not examine his right arm and hand. The patient was discharged a few hours after arrival, and woke up the next day paralyzed from below his midchest. A magnetic resonance imaging (MRI) showed a large herniated disc that was caused by the collision. Despite emergency surgery, the patient remained paralyzed. The plaintiff alleged negligence in the failure to have a neurosurgical examination, as was the hospital's policy for persons with spinal fractures. The jury returned a verdict of $3,587,687.44. (*Buttrey, et ux v. Suburban Hospital et al,* reported in August 2014).

Drawbacks of electronic medical records

Electronic medical record systems are expensive to purchase and implement, with large investments in training and maintenance. The system has to be reliable and protected from power outages, electrical storms, and air conditioning failures. Information technology employees must be available to troubleshoot and restore a system that has "gone down" or become inoperable. Nurses and other clinicians need to enter data into the record once the system is restored.

Until electronic medical records are fully integrated, there will be inefficiencies and lack of information with redundant testing and data entry. While drop-down menus organize information about the patient, the choices may not accurately capture what the nurse wants to document about the patient. Misinformation about a patient is easily disseminated and difficult to eradicate. A nurse may get into a pattern of rote clicking of fields and thus enter information that is nonsensical.

Consider these real entries:

- The call bell was within reach of a woman with contracted arms and who was in a coma.
- The nurse recorded she gave hair care to a man who was bald.
- A nurse documented that a man, who was a paraplegic, was walking in the hall.
- A nurse documented that a woman who was NPO consumed 100% of her breakfast.
- A nurse documented that a patient who was incontinent was voiding without difficulty.
- A physician documented that he explained to a patient that she should call the office if he developed fever, redness of her incision, or death.

Recent studies have focused on additional drawbacks of electronic medical records. ECRI Institute compiles a database of patient safety events. With more than 300,000 event reports, ECRI is in an ideal position to spot trends. One of the top 10 concerns is data integrity failures with health information technology systems—errors caused by electronic medical records. ECRI points out that the integrity of data in health IT systems can be compromised by

- data entry errors
- missing or delayed data delivery
- inappropriate use of default values
- copying and pasting older information into a new report

- use of both paper and electronic systems for patient care (hybrid records)
- patient/data association errors (patient data from a medical device is mistakenly associated with another patient's record).

An insurance company called CRICO collects data in a large database of 275,000 open and closed claims. In a study released in 2014, it found 147 cases in which EHRs were a contributing factor in a year's worth of medical malpractice claims. These were the top issues:

- incorrect information in the EHR 20% of cases
- hybrid health records/EHR conversion issues 16%
- systems failure—electronic routing of data 12%
- pre-populating/copy and paste 10%
- failure of system design to meet the need 9%
- EHR (user) training and/or education 7%
- lack of integration/incompatible systems 7%
- EHR-related user error (other than data entry) 7%.

Nurses use text messages and e-mails to contact physicians or notify them of pertinent clinical information. This raises questions about how that information is safeguarded and incorporated into the medical record.

Software designed without input from nurses may result in cumbersome, user-unfriendly programs that do not build on the workflow and clinical processes nurses use.

Consider how the plaintiff asserted the nurse should have used the electronic medical record in this case:

In *Pilarski v. Huran Valley-Sinai Hospital, Inc,* reported in August 2014, the plaintiff had a history of back problems and went to an orthopedic spine surgeon for an elective lumbar decompression surgery. After surgery, the postoperative hospital nurse found an order under "activity" for weight bearing as tolerated, and stood the patient up for 3 minutes unassisted. He allegedly stumbled. There was an order written later in time for "absolute bed rest." After the patient was discharged, he was readmitted 5 days later with constipation, incontinence, urine retention, and pain. An MRI of the lumbar spine revealed an epidural hematoma compressing the cauda equina nerve roots. The plaintiff claimed that this hematoma was caused by the nurse standing him on the day of surgery. The plaintiff contended that the hematoma caused permanent nerve injury and resulted in bowel, bladder, and sexual dysfunction.

The plaintiff argued that the EMR reflected that the order for bed rest was several orders removed from the weight-bearing order in the chart. The plaintiff claimed that the nurse was required to scroll through all of the orders. The defendant claimed that the order category of "activity" is the only place where the nurse was required to look for postoperative movement orders and that the 3-minute period of standing was not enough to cause the injuries alleged by the plaintiff. The hospital maintained that the plaintiff's injury was related to the surgery. The jury returned a defense verdict.

Confidentiality of medical records

The legal implications of computerized medical records are evolving. The most pressing legal questions concern the threat to patient privacy and confidentiality. With traditional records, information is restricted simply by keeping the record on the unit; EMRs can be called up at any terminal in the facility. The primary safeguard is the signature code, limiting access to the records. For example, a nurse's code would call up a patient's entire record, but a technician's code would produce only a part.

Various laws protect the privacy of a patient's medical records. The Federal Privacy Act of 1974 protects the confidential medical information of patients in veterans' hospitals. The Health Insurance Portability and Accountability Act (HIPAA) of 2003 protects the privacy, confidentiality, and security of medical information. (Under HIPAA, only those who have a need to know patient information for the care of the patient and those authorized by the patient to have access to his medical information can lawfully enter a patient's medical record.) Some state practice acts impose an ethical duty to guard patients' privacy. However, no one can fully guarantee that unauthorized persons won't gain access to computerized records.

Care also must be taken to safeguard patient information sent by fax machines. In particular, policies and procedures should be established to prevent confidential patient information such as a positive result on a human immunodeficiency virus test from being transmitted by fax machine—especially one that's centrally located and easily seen by staff members or the general public. HIPAA requires that procedures be in place to reduce the exposure of patient information to anyone who doesn't have a need to know the patient's private information.

In addition, hospitals must show that their computer systems are trustworthy enough to be used in court. For example, they should use software that automatically records the date and time of each entry and each correction, as well as the name of the author or anyone who modifies a record. When an error is corrected, the software should preserve both the original and the corrected versions and identify each author.

EMRs may be lost or stolen.

■ A resident left a laptop on a Boston Subway and lost confidential medical records.

■ A Maryland internist's office was broken into; he realized the next day that his backup files of patient records were gone.

■ The medical records of veterans were hacked into.

These real incidents highlight concerns about privacy and confidentiality of electronic medical records (Refer to *Tips for documenting with electronic medical records*.).

Medical records in litigation

Patients or their families who have concerns about the medical or nursing care they received may seek the assistance of a plaintiff's attorney. To win a medical malpractice case, the plaintiff has to prove four things:

■ The provider had a duty to give the patient care. (There was a relationship between the patient and the provider.)

■ The provider breached this duty by not following the standards of care or what a reasonably prudent person would do in the same or similar situation.

■ The patient was injured.

Tips for documenting with electronic medical records

■ Know your state's rules and regulations and your facility's policies and procedures regarding privileged data, confidentiality, and disclosure. To learn about state rules and regulations, consult your facility's policy and procedure manual, check with your facility's attorney, or consult your state board of nursing or the state statutory and administrative codes.

■ Know the requirements of the HIPAA concerning privacy, confidentiality, and security of medical information.

■ Be sure you are entering information into the correct patient record.

■ Be aware of the need to communicate with patients while entering information into the computer so the patient does not feel ignored.

■ Know the risks associated with cutting and pasting information. It may be outdated or not applicable to the patient's condition.

■ Use the opportunity to enter narrative notes when you need to clarify or amplify on your documentation.

■ Check your narrative entries to be sure your spelling is correct.

■ Be sure to sign out of the computer when you have completed entering information so someone else cannot document under your name.

■ Recognize the risk of relying on technology instead of using critical thinking skills. Not everything recorded in a computer may be accurate.

■ Never share your user name and password with anyone else.

■ Inform your supervisor if you suspect that someone is using your code.

■ Be aware that, increasingly, patients are asking to access their electronic medical records and to add to, amend, or correct information.

- The injuries are causally connected to the actions of the provider.

As a first step, the patient or family may obtain medical records from the providers. At this point, the providers do not know they are going to be sued. The patient or family pays the fee and receives the records and may read them or turn them over to a plaintiff's attorney. The attorney determines whether the case falls within the statute of limitations, or the time frame in which the plaintiff is allowed to file a claim. In most states, the time frame is 2 years from when the plaintiff knew or should have known there was an error. For example, a state has a 2-year statute of limitations.

- A woman fell out of a window of a nursing home and died. Her family has 2 years to file a claim.
- A man underwent surgery for a bowel obstruction. Five years later, he learned he had a towel in his abdomen. He has 2 years from the time he learned of this in which to file a claim.

The attorney may use a legal nurse consultant or other health care provider to review the records to make a preliminary decision about whether the claim is viable. Ultimately, in most cases, a physician needs to evaluate the causation part of the claim. For example, in the case of the man cited above, who developed the epidural hematoma, part of the defense was to dispute there was a causal connection between standing and the development of the hematoma.

Plaintiff's attorneys usually accept very few cases because they have to meet these four criteria. Malpractice cases are expensive to litigate and often difficult to win. If the attorney decides the case might have merit, the next step is typically to retain an expert witness to review the medical record and form an opinion about whether the health care providers met the standard of care. Many states have regulations that govern who is qualified to act as a liability expert. A combination of recent or current clinical practice that matches the clinical setting where the fall occurred, excellent communication skills, and analytical ability make a strong expert. Plaintiff's attorneys most often use nursing experts from the same specialty as the nurse defendant to reach this conclusion. Many states require this.

If the plaintiff's attorney decides to put the case into a suit, the nurse defendant is notified of the lawsuit. A defense attorney designated to assist the nurse will review the medical record and may meet with the nurse to go over the case facts and medical records. A defense nursing expert witness reviews the medical record.

As the case proceeds, the plaintiff's attorney may take the deposition of the nurse defendant (questioning under oath) and ask the nurse to explain the medical record entries. Often, the nurse has no recollection of the patient and must rely on the medical record. If the case is not settled, it may go to trial, where again the nurse is questioned about the medical record entries. The jury makes the decision about whether they believe the nursing defendant and the medical record are credible and whether the nurse followed the standards of care.

High-risk aspects of nursing care

These are a few of the types of cases that put nurses at risk and may prompt a patient or family to ask questions about the outcome.

FALLS WITH SERIOUS INJURY

Falls may result in paralysis, major fractures, and intracranial bleeding. Consider how an expert witness reviews the medical record to ask these kinds of questions. (See *How expert witnesses evaluate liability for falls.*)

In this case, the medical record helped the plaintiff win. The ninety-year-old nursing home resident suffered from several ailments upon admission to the defendant's facility. She was deemed to be at significant fall risk due to muscle weakness, lethargy, and difficulty walking. She required constant assistance in all aspects of mobility. In July 2009, the decedent was found on the floor of her room. She was bleeding profusely from her forehead. It was assumed she had fallen out of bed. The woman was transported to a hospital and diagnosed with a subdural hematoma. She died several days later. The medical records indicated that proper precautions were not in place to prevent the fall. The plaintiff claimed that the defendant was

---

How expert witnesses evaluate liability for falls

There are very many factors that could cause a fall, but from a liability perspective, the issue that is of high concern for attorneys, risk managers, expert witnesses, and insurance carriers is which of those falls could have been prevented. The questions below assume the fall occurred within a health care facility. Which falls should have been prevented by the actions of either the health care providers or the people who designed the environment in which the fall occurred?

■ Was the patient identified as being at risk for falls?

■ How was that risk communicated to others?

■ Were measures implemented to prevent the fall?

■ Was the call light at the bedside utilized to call for assistance?

■ Was the patient capable of using the call bell?

■ Was the bed in its lowest position?

■ Were lights on in the room or under the bed to help light the area at night?

■ Was the new plan implemented to minimize the opportunity for other falls to occur?

■ Was the patient given antiskid slippers?

■ Is it possible to determine how soon the individual was found after he had sustained a fall?

■ What was done at the time of the fall?

■ Was the patient appropriately monitored after the fall to detect injuries?

■ What did the assessment reveal?

■ Did the nurse communicate the findings to the physician?

■ Were X-rays ordered and performed?

■ Was there an injury, and how soon was that injury treated?

■ If the patient fell and hit his head, was the chart reviewed to determine if the individual was on anticoagulation blood thinner such as heparin or Coumadin?

■ Was this communicated to the physician so that head scans could be performed to see if there was some type of bleed in the head?

■ Was there a change in mental status after the fall?

■ What were the vital signs?

■ Were there specific conditions that contributed to the fall?

■ Was the person assessed and monitored?

■ What medications had the patient received prior to the fall? Did they have side effects that could have contributed to the fall?

■ Was the patient's risk for falls identified after the fall and the plan of care changed?

negligent in failing to have side rails placed on the patient's bed to avoid the fall. The plaintiff also argued that the facility was understaffed. A $175,000 settlement was reached. (*Estate of Anonymous Ninety Year Old Woman v. Anonymous Nursing Home* reported in August 2014.)

FAILURE TO RESCUE

Patients rely on nurses to get them assistance when they develop a change in condition. This concern cuts across all aspects of nursing. Rapid response teams (RRTs) are saving lives in hospitals. A key factor in their success is a nursing staff who knows when to request their help. A sudden deterioration in a patient's condition should stimulate activation of emergency efforts. The goal of a RRT is to avert a cardiac arrest. Here are some generally accepted reasons to call a team of professionals to the bedside:

- staff worried about patient
- acute change in heart rate
- acute change in systolic blood pressure
- acute change in respiratory rate
- acute drop in O_2 saturation
- acute change in mental status
- drop in urine output
- new, repeated, or prolonged seizures
- fractional inspired oxygen of 50% or greater
- failure to respond to treatment for an acute problem/symptoms.

Failure to rescue is a term that describes the outcome when a patient's condition deteriorates before the changes are recognized and acted upon. Failure to rescue is a nursing-sensitive performance measure on the list of 15 identified by the National Quality Forum in 2004 to be collected by CMS (Centers for Medicare and Medicaid Services). A 2009 study performed by HealthGrades showed that patient safety incidents with the highest incidence rates were failure to rescue. There were 92.7 incidents (per 1,000 population). Starting June 1, 2010, CMS began collecting data about a facility's failure to rescue rates.

The expert witness uses the medical record to identify the symptoms of deterioration and determine how quickly the nurse and other staff reacted. In this case, one of the issues was an alleged delay in contacting the RRT.

The patient developed colon cancer and underwent a partial colectomy with a colostomy at a Veterans Administration Hospital. He underwent further treatment for a wound infection, incisional hernia, and additional surgery. Three days after surgery he vomited, but the reason for it was not investigated. The next day, he had an episode of hypotension that was treated with lisinopril. A little later, he had an episode of oxygen desaturation that was treated with bronchodilators and respiratory therapy. He also had an episode of severe back pain treated with Dilaudid. Later that same day, the day he was to be discharged, he suffered oxygen desaturation, vomited and aspirated blood, and died. An autopsy found the cause of death to be "acute vomiting of melanotic emesis and aspiration." The plaintiff claimed that as the patient's condition deteriorated, he continued to receive care primarily from a first-year resident and that monitoring from an attending surgeon would have resulted in the recognition of the decedent's condition earlier. The plaintiff also claimed that the RRT and Code Blue Team were not timely called. A confidential settlement was reached. (*Catherine Vincler Richards, as PR and o/b/o statutory beneficiaries of Estate of Stephen Vincler v. U.S.A. August 2014.*)

PROVIDER ORDERS

Provider orders fall into three groups: correct as written, ambiguous, and apparently erroneous. Follow your health care facility's policy for clarification of orders that are vague or possibly in error. If your facility lacks a policy, contact the provider, and always document your actions. Then ask your nursing administrator for a step-by-step policy to follow in this situation, so that if it happens again, you'll know what to do.

An order may be correct when issued but improper later because of changes in the patient's status. When this occurs, delay the treatment until you've contacted the provider and clarified the situation. Follow your facility's policy for clarifying an order. Always remember that your role is that of an advocate for the patient to protect him or her from errors.

Nurses have been named in suits when they make errors in taking telephone or verbal orders. A misunderstood order may result in a medical error. As a general rule, verbal and telephone orders are acceptable only under acute or emergency circumstances, when the physician can't promptly attend to the patient, or according to facility policy. If possible, have another nurse listen to the verbal order with you to avoid miscommunication and to ensure accurate interpretation. Communication errors can be avoided, and proof or evidence of the verbal order is more easily established. Record the order on the physician's order sheet, note the date and time of the order, and record the order verbatim. On the following line, write "v.o." for verbal order or "t.o." for telephone order, and record the physician's name, followed by your signature and the time. Read the order back to the provider to be sure you have heard it correctly.

Preprinted standing orders or protocols and standing order admission sheets are usually checkmarked and signed by the provider, cosigned by the nurse, and retained in the chart according to your facility's policy.

Here's what can happen if you don't document verbal orders:
- You could face disciplinary measures by your employer and state board of nursing for failing to document.
- You could damage your defense or your employer's in a malpractice suit.
- Other nurses, not knowing what orders have been given, may follow prior orders that result in harm to the patient.
- If controlled substances are given, suspicions could be raised that you're diverting drugs for your own use.

PRESSURE SORES

Many states and regulatory agencies target the development of pressure sores as a quality-of-care indicator. Your documentation should contain your assessment of the patient's risk for developing a pressure sore and the measures you carried out to prevent one. If one develops, it is vital to quickly institute measures to reduce the risk of the sore progressing to become deeper and larger. Accurate recording of the actual dimensions and depth of the wound helps others to determine whether the treatment is or is not working. Use a consistent method of measuring wounds, and document how you measured the wound as well as its dimensions in centimeters. Identify the length and width and depth. Be sure you understand the differences between the stages of pressure sores, and correctly document the stage.

Your facility may require weekly or more frequent recording of pressure sore measurements. Some facilities also require the use of photographs. Your policies and procedures may cover:

- how often the photos are taken
- how they are taken
- how they are stored and retrieved
- what information should be contained along with the photograph, such as the anatomical location, date and time, and the patient's name and identification number.

In a California case, the plaintiff alleged that the patient did not receive appropriate care to prevent the progression of a pressure sore. The patient was 85 when she was admitted to a nursing home for long-term care. The staff found a Stage I pressure sore on her coccyx in April 2011. A care plan was put in place to treat, observe, and document the condition. The sore progressed to Stage IV with bone exposure and necrosis. The patient was hospitalized on seven occasions due to infections related to the pressure sore. It remained at Stage IV for a year until the patient died. The plaintiff claimed that prior to admission to the defendant's facility, the patient had three separate episodes of developing pressure sores (in 2007, 2009, and 2010) and that all three sores were completely resolved. The plaintiff claimed that there was no charting of care for 12 days during which the ulcer progressed from Stage I to Stage IV. The defendant claimed that proper care and treatment had been provided and that the pressure sore was due to her preexisting condition. The parties engaged in arbitration. The family received an arbitration award for $975,000, which included awards for negligence, elder abuse, wrongful death, and violation of the patient bill of rights. (*Estate of Sui Mee Chiu v. Arcadia Convalescent Hospitals, Inc. d/b/a Arcadia Health Care Center et al,* reported in June 2014.)

Avoiding documentation errors

In addition to their potential impact on patient care, charting errors or omissions, even if seemingly harmless, will undermine your credibility in court. Especially avoid the following.

OMISSIONS

Include all significant facts that other nurses will need to assess the patient. Otherwise, a court may conclude that you failed to perform an action missing from the record or tried to hide evidence.

CHANGE IN TREATMENT

When an ordered treatment is no longer appropriate, which may occur after a change in the patient's condition, document why the treatment wasn't administered and any communications with the patient's physician regarding the need for new orders.

PERSONAL OPINION AND CRITICISMS

Don't enter personal opinions. Record only factual and objective observations and the patient's statements. Avoid words that reveal that you have labeled the patient's behavior, with terms such as "obnoxious" or "rude." Don't criticize other providers or cast blame on them. This is unprofessional, affects the team atmosphere, and is damaging in the event of a lawsuit.

VAGUE ENTRIES

Instead of "Patient had a good day," state why "Patient didn't complain of pain." Avoid slang, such as "hung a banana bag" or "emergency department frequent flier."

LATE ENTRIES

If a late entry is necessary, identify it as such, and make a new entry into the medical record. An EMR will automatically record the date and time of your entry. Reference the date and time you're relating back to.

ERRONEOUS OR VAGUE ABBREVIATIONS

Use only standard abbreviations, and follow your facility's policies.

ILLEGIBILITY AND LACK OF CLARITY

If you are handwriting an entry, write so that others can read your entry. Use a dictionary if you're unsure of spelling or usage.

Avoiding suspicious changes and potential legal traps

In the event of a legal challenge, or if the medical record has been requested for examination in a trial, avoid making changes, corrections, or additions. To do so would raise suspicion, even if you have legitimate reasons and the best intentions. Do not give in to pressure put upon you to alter or destroy medical records. Tampering with medical records can have far-reaching consequences, including loss of your job, reputation, nursing license, and even the possibility of criminal charges and prison time.

In addition, many lawyers advise against keeping personal notes about a questionable patient care incident. Often those notes are written when the nurse is less than objective and may convey a far different message than was intended. Also, a plaintiff's attorney can obtain personal notes you use to prepare for a deposition or trial; in a trial, if you deny using them—or a source of information other than the patient's record—to refresh your memory, you're perjuring yourself. If you admit you did use personal notes, the notes may be used to incriminate you or other defendants. Simply put, avoid written or oral statements without first consulting your attorney.

CONTROLLED SUBSTANCES

You're responsible for proper storage of controlled substances in the nursing unit as well as for maintaining detailed records of each dose dispensed and the remaining quantities.

The legal consequences of improper charting are especially significant when administering opioids and other controlled substances and maintaining controlled substance records. Be familiar with your facility's policy when you dispense these drugs. Also, be aware of *controlled substance acts*—federal and state laws that control the distribution, classification, sale, and use of drugs. Consult your facility's policies or contact your state board of nursing for information about these laws. If you have a specific question about the propriety of a policy or procedure in your facility, talk to your facility's attorney or write to the state board of nursing and request a formal board opinion or a declaratory ruling.

Administering opioids

For proper, accurate documentation of opioids, use the special opioids records—the control sheet and the check sheet—provided by the pharmacy, and follow the procedure described below.

Before you give an opioid:
- Verify the count in the opioids drawer.
- Sign the opioid control sheet to indicate you removed the drug.
- Get another nurse to sign the control sheet if you waste or discard all or part of a dose.

At the end of your shift:
- Record the amount of each opioid in the drawer on the opioid sheet while the nurse beginning her shift counts the opioids out loud.
- Sign the opioid check sheet only if the count is correct. Have the other nurse countersign.
- Identify and correct discrepancies before nurses leave the unit.

For your own protection, conform to all facility, nursing department, and pharmacy policies and procedures if an ordered dose of a controlled substance isn't administered, or if it's wasted or discarded.

Witnessing and signing documents

As a nurse, you may be asked to witness the signing of documents, such as deeds, bills of sale, powers of attorney, contracts, and wills. You may also participate in witnessing oral statements made by patients and others that may have legal significance. Your actions at these times can influence whether what you witnessed has the force of law, and they can also expose you to legal consequences. Later, you may have to testify in court about the signing and the circumstances surrounding it.

SIGNIFICANCE OF YOUR SIGNATURE

When you sign as a witness, you're usually certifying only that you saw the person, known to you by a certain name, place his signature on the document. You're not necessarily certifying the presence or absence of duress, undue influence, fraud, or error. Also, keep in mind that you aren't validating that the patient has been told the significant risks, benefits, and options for treatment, which constitute informed consent. When you witness consent forms in a nursing capacity, your signature merely attests to the signer's:
- authenticity
- voluntariness
- capacity.

If you're called to testify about the signing, don't underestimate the importance of your testimony. A court looking into charges of fraud or undue influence used in executing a document will usually give great weight to a nurse's perception. You may be asked about the patient's physical and mental condition at the time of the signing, and the court may ask you to describe his interactions with his family, his attorney, and others.

RELEVANT LAWS

In the United States and Canada, nurse practice acts establish nurses' scope of professional and legal accountability. When you witness a document, other laws also apply. For example, all states have laws setting out the legal requirements for written and oral wills, dying declarations, living wills, powers of attorney, and gifts in expectation of death.

Wills

State laws establish requirements for wills, including:

- format requirements
- the number of witnesses needed
- who can be a witness
- what makes a will valid or invalid
- how to make a will inoperative
- how to contest a will.

Usually, an individual must be age 18 or older and have two witnesses present to make a valid will. In about two-thirds of all states, the will may be handwritten—such a document is called a holographic will.

In many states, your signature on a will certifies that:

- you witnessed the will signing
- you heard the maker of the will declare it to be his will
- all witnesses and the maker of the will were actually present during the signing.

By attesting to the last two facts, you help ensure the authenticity of the will and the signatures. Your signature doesn't certify, however, that the maker of the will is competent.

Precautions

If a patient asks you to serve as a witness when he draws up his will, follow these precautions:

- Don't forget to notify the patient's physician and your supervisor before you act as a witness.
- Don't give the patient any legal advice.
- Don't offer to assist him in phrasing the document's wording.
- Don't allow yourself to be named as a recipient in the will.
- Don't comment on the nature of his choices.
- Don't forget to document your actions in your nurses' notes.

The laws also cover dying declarations and gifts in expectation of death, specifying when they're valid and when they aren't.

In the case of a living will, your state law may prohibit you from acting as a witness because of your role in executing the instructions in a living will.

YOUR LIABILITY

You can be held liable and in violation of the prevailing standard of care if the signature you witness is false or if you sign knowing the patient is incompetent or has given uninformed consent. You can also be held liable if you knowingly allow a minor, nonguardian, or other ineligible person to sign a document.

If you're the only person who informs a patient about a planned medical procedure and you then witness his signature, you can be liable for practicing outside your nurse practice act, for practicing medicine without a license, or both. Your hospital may be liable for negligence under the doctrine of respondeat superior. If you give the patient false information in an attempt to deceive him, you may be guilty of fraud or misrepresentation.

READ BEFORE YOU SIGN

Before you sign any document, read at least enough of it to make sure it's the type of document the primary signer represents it to be. Usually, you won't have to read all the text, and legally that isn't necessary for your signature to be valid as a witness only. You should, however, always examine the document's title and first page and give careful attention to what's written immediately above the place for your signature. (The place for your signature should be clearly labeled.)

HOW TO SIGN

When signing a document, write legibly and use your full legal name. When signing on hospital forms, add your title. On other documents, the title is optional, but adding it will establish why you're in the hospital.

WHEN TO SIGN

When you're asked to sign as a witness, do so only if you believe the patient to be mentally and physically competent. Legally, you don't need to have knowledge of exactly what's contained in the documents you witness. However, professionally, you should be aware of the content, just as you should be aware of the content when witnessing the patient's signature to an informed consent form.

WHEN TO REFUSE

Here are some instances when you shouldn't witness a document:

■ when the patient isn't legally able to give consent—for example, when he's a minor or a nonguardian

■ when the patient isn't who he says he is, or you can't be sure

■ when the patient has no power of free choice—for example, when he's being blackmailed or otherwise pressured into signing

■ when the patient is uninformed about what he's consenting to because he has been given misleading information, doesn't understand the information given, or hasn't been told of the risks involved. (Clarify with the physician why known risks haven't been disclosed.)

■ when a patient is obviously incompetent—for example, when he's suffering from advanced dementia and is being pressured to sign a deed transferring a real estate title to someone else or if he's received a sedating medication

■ when you feel uncomfortable about signing.

Keep in mind that you have no legal obligation to witness a will or other document. In such situations, simply explain that you choose not to act as a witness. Then record the incident in your nurses' notes, using a chronological format. Chart the setting, the patient's mental and physical condition, the reason for the refusal, what you saw and heard, and what happened after your refusal (for instance, that someone else witnessed or someone else gave consent).

Finally, report the incident to other staff members concerned—for example, your supervisor and the patient's physician.

WRITING THE NURSES' NOTES

When you record in your notes that you've witnessed a patient's signature on a document, always include something about his apparent perceptions of his health and general circumstances.

When you witness a written will, document that it was signed and witnessed, who signed it, who else was present, what was done with it after signing, and the patient's condition at the time.

When you witness oral statements, such as dying declarations and oral wills, document the names of other witnesses, the patient's physical and mental condition at the time, and the patient's reaction to the statements afterward. Make your notes carefully: remember, they could be used in court for probating the will, for resolving creditors' claims, or for prosecuting alleged criminals. The notes will also refresh your memory if you're called to testify in court.

CANADIAN PROCEDURES

Formalities of signing and witnessing documents in the United States and Canada may differ. Both countries, however, have legal systems based primarily on English common law, and both have essentially the same rules governing how a witness should sign legal documents.

SELECTED REFERENCES

Austin, S. "Stay Out of Court with Proper Documentation," *Nursing* 41(4):25–29, April 2011.

Gardner, L., and Sparnon, E. "Work-Arounds Slow Electronic Health Record Use," *American Journal of Nursing* 114(4):64–67, April 2014.

Huryk, L. "Information Systems and Decision Support Systems," *American Journal of Nursing* 112(1):62–65, January 2012.

Kelley, T., Brandon, D., and Docherty, S. "Electronic Nursing Documentation as a Strategy to Improve Quality of Patient Care," *Journal of Nursing Scholarship* 43(2):154–162, June 2011.

Kutney-Lee, A., and Kelley, D. "The Effect of Hospital Electronic Health Record Adoption on Nurse-Assessed Quality of Care and Patient Safety," *Journal of Nursing Administration* 41(11):466–472, November 2011.

McBride, S., Tietze, M., and Delaney, J. "Health and Information Technology and Nursing," *American Journal of Nursing* 112(8):36–42, August 2012.

Menon, S., Singh, H., Meyer, A., Belmont, E., and Sittig, D. "Electronic Health Record-Related Safety Concerns: A Cross-Sectional Survey," *Journal of Healthcare Risk Management* 34(1):14–26, 2014.

8

Legal risks while off duty

Taralynn R. Mackay, RN, JD

When you are on duty, numerous guidelines define the legal limits of your nursing practice. They include hospital policies, standards issued by nursing organizations, and state or jurisdictional nurse practice acts. Statutory law and common law provide additional direction. When you are off duty, however, you have few specific guidelines. Your legal responsibilities are not as clear-cut.

For example, you probably would not hesitate to perform an abdominal thrust maneuver to save a choking victim. However, what if you panic, make a mistake, and injure the patient? Can you be sued by the victim or his estate? Can your nursing license be suspended or revoked? Does the law protect you because of your good intentions? Is a nurse ever really off duty according to the state nursing board?

Fortunately, thus far, lawsuits resulting from off-duty nursing actions have been extremely rare. However, many disciplinary actions have been taken by state boards of nursing on the basis of actions of nurses while off duty. Whether you frequently provide off-duty care or give free advice to a neighbor, it's important to act on a sound legal footing.

Legal issues covered

This chapter discusses legal issues related to off-duty nursing. You'll find information on:

■ acting as a Good Samaritan—your liability when you give emergency care at an accident scene or in a disaster

■ giving free health care advice—legal ramifications of giving advice to family members and friends

■ donating nursing services— protecting yourself legally when you volunteer your nursing skills

■ acting during disasters—legal aspects of providing nursing services during emergencies and declared disasters, and suggestions to prepare you for a disaster.

Legal basics

PROVING MALPRACTICE

Normally, to bring a malpractice suit to a jury trial, the patient must establish the following:

■ you owed a duty, based on a nurse-patient relationship

■ you breached that duty

■ the patient was harmed

■ your breach of duty caused the harm.

BREACH OF DUTY

Once you have stopped at an accident scene to help, you can avoid breaching your duty by utilizing appropriate medical techniques when assisting the injured person, and by utilizing your nursing knowledge and skills when treating the injured party. A breach of duty occurs when your performance falls below the standard of care expected of a reasonably prudent nurse in a similar situation. In most states, your action or inaction has to be grossly negligent, intentional, or reckless for there to be a cause of action. If your act didn't make the victim measurably worse, the court may find that the harm committed doesn't warrant damages. Your act must cause measurable harm for the court to consider you legally responsible.

Causation

Causation means your negligent act caused the injury to the individual or increased the degree of injury the injured person already had. For example, if you improperly move an injured person, you may not be responsible for the initial injury from the accident, the head, neck, and back injury, but you could be responsible for the individual's paralysis resulting from your moving the person inappropriately. Some states consider the fact that an injured person may have difficulty in proving causation and will allow an "increased risk of harm standard"; that is, your action or inaction increased the risk of harm and was a substantial factor in causing damages. The victim must prove that the probability is better than 50% that your error (whether an act of commission or omission) caused his injuries. Historically, the courts have recognized the 50% figure as the standard. Because the typical victim

already has suffered injuries from the accident, he's likely to have a hard time proving that your error caused or worsened his injuries.

In making it hard for the accident victim to prove you negligent, the courts must balance the victim's right to justice with society's need to encourage trained professionals to assist in emergencies.

Common Law

Common law, also known as case law, is the cumulative court decisions. These decisions may provide guidelines for acting in a similar situation since courts look to precedent when determining actions. State courts typically rely upon their state's previous decisions, because those decisions are binding on the court. Decisions rendered in other states' courts may be persuasive in a lawsuit.

Good Samaritan Law

Imagine yourself driving in heavy traffic. Not far ahead, you see an automobile accident and a bloodied motorist gesturing for help. Nearby, another victim lies sprawled at curb. What should you do? Your conscience and compassion prompt you to help the victim in any health care emergency. Your common sense prompts you to ask if helping out means courting legal trouble.

Your options

You have three options. You can:
- help the accident victim(s) at the scene
- leave the scene but call 911 for an ambulance or other rescue service
- pass the scene and make no attempt to call for help.

In most states, you have the legal right to choose any of these options, but there are a few states with laws requiring specific actions in the case of an accident or an injury to a victim of a crime. Even though there may not be a legal duty to act, it is generally thought that a nurse would have an ethical and moral duty to provide assistance. The public, including most nurses, would be shocked if a nurse failed to provide assistance to the degree of that nurse's ability.

Good Samaritan acts were enacted to encourage people to voluntarily help someone in need without the fear of being sued for any reasonable care rendered—even if some mistake in treatment might occur. Every state has enacted a Good Samaritan act, but each state's statute varies. Some may apply specifically to nurses or other health care professionals, while others may apply to anyone who offers assistance.

Your legal duty

As long as you pass the accident scene—whether you stop down the road to call for help—you owe the victim no legal duty unless you reside in a state that has a duty-to-rescue law. The injured individual is not your patient, and thus has no legal claim to your professional services.

However, depending on your state's laws, just by stopping your car at the scene, you may incur a legal duty. From that point on, you must intervene appropriately, and you cannot leave the victim until he is being cared for by another health care professional with at least as much training as you have or if the scene becomes too dangerous to remain or if you are unable to continue providing care or until the police order you away from the scene.

The rationale for this duty is that when you stop your car at the scene, you give the appearance to other potential rescuers that you will take care of the victim. At that point, you establish a nurse-patient relationship for that particular emergency. You owe the victim the normal duty you owe any patient—treatment that meets the standard of care of a reasonably prudent nurse in a similar situation.

Good Samaritan acts do not prevent an accident victim from filing a malpractice suit, but they may limit your liability for any service you render at an accident or emergency scene unless it is proved that your care was grossly negligent or intentionally harmful or you were the person who initially caused the emergent situation. Most states require your services to be performed in good faith, meaning you sincerely intended to help. A few states specifically require consent for the services you render; however, if someone is unconscious or unable to communicate, implied consent is assumed.

Determining gross negligence

No law can protect you if you commit an act of gross negligence, which is an extremely careless act or omission that seriously violates the applicable standard of care. Whether your negligent error constitutes "ordinary" negligence or "gross" negligence is up to the judge or jury. To make this distinction, they measure your error against the local standard of care, which may vary from place to place. For example, what may qualify as ordinary negligence in rural Georgia may be gross negligence in metropolitan New York. However, as more nurses take certification examinations that are national in scope, members of the profession are held increasingly accountable to a national standard, like physicians.

Additionally, the court considers your training and experience to decide whether you have breached the standard of care and, if so, to what

LEGAL
TIP
Care tips for Good Samaritans

When you stop at an emergency scene to offer assistance, always observe professional standards of nursing care, regardless of the setting. To reduce your malpractice risk, consider these tips:

- Ask the injured person, or family member, if available, for permission to help.
- Care for the victim in the vehicle or at the exact site, if you can do so safely.
- Assess the possibility of fractures.
- Move the victim if he is in danger and if conditions permit. Avoid moving him needlessly, and don't try to straighten his arms and legs.
- Let him lie or sit quietly. Do not carry him or force him to walk.
- Keep his airway open.
- Stop his bleeding.
- Keep the victim warm.
- Determine his level of consciousness.
- Ask the victim where he feels pain.
- Avoid speculating about who or what caused the accident.
- Allow only skilled personnel to attend or treat the victim.
- Stay at the accident site until skilled personnel arrive to assume care of the victim; the relieving personnel need to be at your skill/knowledge level or above.
- Provide a complete picture of the care given to the first responders.
- Guard the injured person's personal property. Try not to handle the personal property; instead, watch over the property, and release it to the police or members of his family.

degree. This means that the court holds registered nurses (RNs)—even as Good Samaritans—to a higher standard than it holds licensed practical nurses (LPNs)/licensed vocational nurses (LVNs). (See *Care tips for Good Samaritans.*) In addition, a court will hold a nurse responsible for what another nurse would be expected to know and do if that nurse had been put in the same situation. For example, if you undertake an intervention for a child accident victim and you do not have the required education or training for that intervention since you have cared for only adults in your entire nursing career and an injury results, you will be held to the same standards as a pediatric nurse.

Compensated care
Keep in mind that most Good Samaritan acts apply only to uncompensated emergency care. If you charge or accept money for your services, you typically forfeit the special protections afforded by such acts. Likewise, if a person is in your work place and requires care and it is part of your job to provide such care (like in an emergency room), the Good Samaritan acts would not apply.

INVOKING GOOD SAMARITAN LAW
Regardless of the kind of Good Samaritan act your state or jurisdiction has, accident victims rarely sue "Good Samaritans." Although nurses have been sued, when the Good Samaritan defense has been raised, no nurse has been found responsible. In addition, common law so far has served as a deterrent. Ironically, although auto accident victims sometimes claim that a Good Samaritan act *requires* a nurse or physician to respond at an accident scene, to date, the courts have accepted this argument only in those states that have enacted duty-to-rescue laws.

In some states, physicians have invoked a Good Samaritan act as a defense against malpractice suits, claiming the act protects them from liability for emergency services they provided in a hospital. In Illinois, a physician responded to an in-hospital emergency in which both parties (mother and fetus) later died, and the estate brought suit. The physician successfully invoked, as part of his defense, the Illinois Good Samaritan Act. The appellate court found the Act protected the physician from liability for a true hospital emergency in which the service was provided in good faith and without fee. The same argument would not hold for nurses in California because the Good Samaritan act specifically covers nurses only during emergencies "outside both the place and course" of employment. Therefore, you must check your state's Good Samaritan Act in order to determine where you are covered and when are you considered to be performing acts within your employment scope.

LAW Q&A — Understanding Good Samaritan acts

Am I covered by a Good Samaritan act if I respond to an emergency outside the hospital while I'm officially on duty?

That depends on two things: the wording of the act in your state and court decisions, if any, interpreting that act. All Good Samaritan acts cover aid at the scene of an emergency, accident, or disaster. If an emergency occurs just outside your hospital and you provide care, this could be considered providing care in an emergency setting and, therefore, would be covered under Good Samaritan law. Note that some states' Good Samaritan statutes specifically cover emergencies outside of the hospital, physician's office, and other places that have medical equipment.

I live and work in Kansas. Every year, I go skiing in a different state. What if I help an accident victim while I'm vacationing? Does the Good Samaritan act of the state I'm in apply to me?

It does if that state's act says it applies to "any person." It may not, however, if the act specifically states that it applies only to "nurses." The designation "nurses" in a law or act may mean a registered nurse, licensed practical nurse, or licensed vocational nurse licensed in that state.

Does the Good Samaritan act apply if I accept money from the person I've helped?

Not usually. By accepting money in such a situation, you establish a professional relationship with the person you have helped. Remember the minute you accept compensation, monetary or otherwise, for your help in an emergency, you most likely destroy the Good Samaritan act's protection from liability.

For how long am I responsible to the person I've helped?

Statutory law does not address this subject, but common law does. The courts say your responsibility ends:

■ when the emergency ends (when you're certain that the victim is no longer in danger)
■ when an authorized rescuer or other qualified medical service takes over for you
■ when you are unable to continue physically or the scene becomes too dangerous to remain
■ when the victim is pronounced dead.

If a physician and I respond to the same emergency, does the Good Samaritan act cover us equally?

Not necessarily. In some states, the Good Samaritan act for nurses differs completely from the Good Samaritan act for physicians.

USE OF AUTOMATED EXTERNAL DEFIBRILLATORS (AEDs)

If a person uses an AED, federal law 42 U.S. Code §238q protects him from liability for injury caused by the use of the AED or the attempted use of the AED. The law takes protection a little further and applies it to anyone who obtains an AED for use if certain provisions are met: notifying local emergency responders of the AED, properly maintaining and testing the device, and providing appropriate training.

A nurse is not covered under the federal law if the nurse is grossly negligent, reckless, shows willful or criminal misconduct, or shows a conscious, flagrant indifference to the person's rights or safety. In addition, a nurse is not covered if the AED was used while acting within the nurse's scope of employment.

DUTY TO RESCUE

In general, the only people who may have a legal duty to rescue others are individuals who perform rescues as part of their jobs—firefighters, police officers, emergency medical technicians, and a few others such as public transportation workers. However, in a few states, such as Vermont, Rhode Island, Minnesota, and Wisconsin, "duty-to-rescue" laws may apply to nurses. Unless you're covered by a duty-to-rescue law, your decision to help remains voluntary and personal.

Four states and most Canadian jurisdictions (as well as most European countries) have taken the Good Samaritan principle a step further by requiring potential rescuers to help a victim. Vermont's law, the first of its type in the United States, defines a *rescuer* as a person who knows that another is exposed to grave physical harm. The Vermont law requires that anyone (Vermont resident or not) who can help a victim must do so, provided he will not endanger himself or interfere with important duties he owes to others. Minnesota has a similar law, as do Rhode Island and Wisconsin (which has a "duty to rescue crime victims" law). These duty-to-rescue statutes also carry criminal implications including fines for a failure to comply.

In contrast, some other states have duty-to-rescue statutes that apply specifically to criminal events causing injury. The statutes generally provide for liability if someone on the scene fails to report the crime or call for assistance for the victim of the crime, but they do not specifically address the requirement to render aid to the victim.

Giving free health care advice

"You are a nurse, what does this look like to you?" or "I do not want to call my pediatrician over the weekend, what do you think my son has?" At some point, almost every nurse is asked something similar. Friends and family members rely on you for advice on health matters. This is an area where you can easily let your guard down and forget you must respond cautiously, even though this may seem unnatural when speaking with individuals you know well. Although you were not working as a nurse at the time and you did not receive compensation for your advice, you can be sued for giving inappropriate advice and not acting as a reasonably prudent nurse. If you decide not to give advice at all, be reassured, there is no legal requirement for you to answer all medical/nursing questions asked of you when off duty. The person suing you for harm caused by inappropriate advice must prove that you owed him a specific duty, that you breached that duty, that he was harmed, and that the harm was a result of the breach of duty.

If you choose to offer advice, be aware of positions on the issue taken by your state's nurse practice act, common law, professional organizations, and your malpractice insurance coverage. (See *Minimizing legal risks when giving advice.*)

Establishing breach of duty

For a duty to exist, you must have a nurse-patient relationship with the person asking for your advice. This rarely occurs in everyday, short-lived conversations with other people. Suppose, for example, that you're a guest at a cocktail party. Another guest finds out that you are a nurse and bombards you with questions about his health. If you decide to answer, you have a duty to answer as correctly as a reasonably prudent nurse would, but you do not have a duty to follow up after the party is over or to monitor the outcome of your advice. The person who is asking your advice has not established (or clearly indicated to you that he intends to establish) an ongoing nurse-patient relationship with you.

Some state nursing boards consider a nurse-patient relationship to be established as soon as you provide nursing advice or care even if it is an informal action. So the moment you provide the advice or care, you will be held to your state nursing board's rules, your state nurse practice act, and any established nursing standards.

Establishing probable reliance

The situation may be different if you decide to give advice to a neighbor.

For instance, imagine that your neighbor calls across the yard and asks you about her child's fretfulness. You observe honestly that the child's activity does not appear to warrant a call to the physician. A day later, you see the mother and child together outdoors, and the child appears particularly listless. If you discover that the child has a fever or other signs and symptoms of illness, you are legally and professionally responsible for telling the mother to take the child to a physician as soon as possible. This holds true regardless of your original advice.

You must respond to the mother's probable reliance on you for further advice, even though your original intention wasn't to form a nurse-patient relationship with her and her child.

Again, if you realize your neighbor now relies on you for further advice, you have an obligation—a legal and professional duty—to keep your advice current as the situation changes. Or you may opt to take formal steps to break off the relationship by telling the mother to look elsewhere for help.

Keep in mind that the principles and standards that apply to your on-duty work also apply to off-duty advice. The help and advice you give your patient on a Monday morning may have to be changed by Tuesday afternoon. Furthermore, if a person's questions reveal that his problem may be beyond the scope of nursing practice, you have a clear duty to advise the individual to seek the care of a physician, and you should inform the person the questions are beyond your knowledge/scope as a nurse. (See *Neighborly advice: some legal safeguards,* page 276.)

(Text continues on page 278.)

LEGAL TIP Minimizing legal risks when giving advice

The *best* step to take is *not* to give advice; however, since this can be difficult to adhere to, here are some steps to take to minimize your risk when giving health care advice to friends or family.

What to do

■ Be sure that your advice reflects accepted professional and community standards.

■ Check whether your (or your employer's) professional liability insurance covers such off-the-job nursing activities as giving advice. Note that most employer-based professional liability insurance policies will not cover any actions outside the scope of employment, while a nurse's personal malpractice insurance will most likely cover the actions (another reason for a nurse to have his/her own malpractice insurance).

■ Remember that Good Samaritan acts exclude gratuitous actions not associated with an emergency. However, keep in mind that some state statutes specifically include illnesses.

■ Know what–if anything–your state's nurse practice act says about giving advice to friends.

Also research the nurse practice act and/or the board of nursing's rules in order to determine when the nurse-patient relationship is established.

■ Give advice only within the confines of your nurse practice act, education, and experience.

■ Make sure that the advice you give is up-to-date. You will be judged on current nursing standards if your advice results in a lawsuit. Remember you will be held to the knowledge a reasonable nurse would have about the issue of the free advice.

What not to do

■ Do not charge a fee or accept money for your advice.

■ Avoid speculating about your friends' or family's illnesses or ailments.

■ Never suggest friends or family members change or ignore their physicians' orders.

■ Steer clear of giving a medical diagnosis, medical opinion, or advice about medical care.

■ Avoid giving directions that, if wrong or misinterpreted, could result in serious or permanent injury.

LAW Q&A Neighborly advice: some legal safeguards

My best friend Sara and I have babies the same age. Sara isn't a nurse, and I know she relies on my judgment a lot. How should I answer her when she asks questions? For instance, yesterday, she asked, "If your Richie had a rash like Tommy's, would you take him to the doctor?"

If you answer "yes" or "You need to call or see your son's doctor," no harm will result from your advice, and you will be on safe legal ground. If you answer "no," and if following your advice results in harm to the child, you may be liable. In such situations–best friend or not–conservative advice is legally safer, especially if you have doubts.

(continued)

Neighborly advice: some legal safeguards *(continued)*

I seem to be the neighborhood ear piercer. Of course, with children I require a parent's permission, and I warn everyone about the risks of infection and how to reduce the risk of infection. Still, I'm worried: If someone got an infection and sued me, would this verbal warning protect me from malpractice liability?

Some states have legislation or regulations governing ear piercing, so check your state laws or rules both for nurses and specifically for ear piercing. If your state doesn't have regulations on ear piercing, your warnings about possible infection protect you only if infection results from piercing done according to accepted standards. The warning does not protect you if the infection results from your negligence. Since verbal consent may be difficult to prove, written confirmation of the warning provides a little better protection.

One of my neighbors comes to see me whenever one of her family members gets sick or enters the hospital. She is a good friend, and I am glad to help, but I think she is making a habit of asking for my advice. I feel especially uncomfortable when she asks me to explain everything the physician tells her. Once she said, "The doctor says my husband might have adhesions from a previous operation. What does that mean? Is that common?" How can I answer her questions and protect myself too? Should I say, "I can tell you only what I know from my own experience?"

You would be better off saying, "I can tell you what those terms usually mean, but not what they mean in your husband's case." You can best serve your neighbor, though, by encouraging her to write all of her questions and then ask the physician to explain anything she doesn't understand.

PROFESSIONAL STANDARDS

Whenever you establish a professional relationship with an individual seeking advice, you must provide an answer as good as any reasonably prudent nurse would give in similar circumstances.

Do this by applying the same standards you are expected to apply in your regular work. If you feel confident that you know the answer—and your education and experience support you—you're legally free to give it. Naturally, you must make sure your answer is correct and that giving it falls within your scope of nursing practice.

To protect yourself, you might say something such as, "I think your problem sounds like arthritis, but it could be something more serious, and I'm not sure. You should ask a physician."

Remember, you are legally protected if you refer the questioner to his or her physician. However, the law does not require you to make that suggestion if you are honestly convinced that it is not necessary and that a reasonably prudent nurse would not make it either.

Guard against the temptation to say, "Don't worry," when family members or friends ask for advice. Try to imagine that an inquiring family member or friend is a complete stranger, consider the professionally considered answer you would give to the stranger, and then give that advice to your friend or family member.

Giving health care advice can lead to legal problems if the advice can be interpreted as giving medical advice, which may put you at risk for practicing medicine without a license. Instead, urge the person seeking advice that seems to be outside of your nursing scope of practice to seek medical attention, either at a hospital or with a physician.

Donating nursing services

Many health care professionals, including nurses, donate their professional services to community organizations or activities.

You might donate your nursing services to family members, friends, or such community organizations and activities as the following:
- a community ambulance service
- a bloodmobile or hypertension outreach program
- a home and school association panel discussion on child health issues
- a community or sporting event
- a summer camp.

As a nurse, your responsibilities to patients do not change when you donate your services; however, your legal status does. It may become less defined than when you are paid. In some states, nurse practice acts specify only the legal limits of paid nursing practice.

DONATED SERVICES AND THE LAW

The Federal Volunteer Protection Act of 1997 provides liability protection for volunteers and specifically addresses licensed volunteers. If the volunteer is properly licensed and is practicing within the volunteer's scope of responsibilities within the nonprofit organization for whom the volunteer is providing nursing services, there is liability protection. The same exclusions

apply for willful, reckless, or criminal harm, gross negligence, or a conscious disregard for the injured individual's rights or safety. The Act also does not apply if the volunteer accepts payment except for reimbursement for expenses.

If you volunteer and are accused of negligence, the court can use the provisions of your state nurse practice act—together with expert witness testimony and applicable standards of nursing care—to determine whether you acted as a prudent nurse would have acted in similar patient-care circumstances. If the court finds your care did not conform to the requirements of your state's nurse practice act or established nursing care standards, you may be facing paying a settlement arising out of a malpractice suit. In addition, your malpractice insurance may or may not cover your voluntary services. Any insurance you have at work through your employer will not cover your volunteer activity, which is why your malpractice insurance policy must be a personal policy. Because insurance is a contract, you should review your insurance policy's language to determine its application and coverage. (See *Minimizing legal risks when volunteering,* page 280.)

Even if no lawsuit results, you may be subject to discipline by your state nursing board if the board finds your nursing services fall below the accepted standard of care. In such a situation, the board may discipline your license including suspension or revocation.

Volunteering out of state

If you travel to a state in which you are not licensed to practice, you are not prohibited from donating your nursing services as long as that state's nurse practice act covers only paid nursing care. However, if the state's nurse

LEGAL TIP

Minimizing legal risks when volunteering

When offering your time and skills for free, observe the same standards of care you observe in your paid job. Consider these guidelines:

Have necessary orders

Obtain a physician's order or a standing order before giving any treatment or medication that requires such an order. Remember every medical act requires a physician order of some type since your nursing scope of practice only covers nursing care acts.

Document your actions

Document your donated care as carefully as you document the care you give on the job. Keep a copy of your nurses' notes so you have a permanent record of your actions should a question ever arise. Make sure you redact/mark out completely any identifying information regarding the patient in order to protect confidentiality, and keep these records in a locked location. You may leave a medical record number or use initials, but no one should be able to obtain the records, and if they do, the patient's identify should not be obtainable.

Check your coverage

Check your professional liability insurance and its limitations from every angle before agreeing to donate your services to any organization. Also check the coverage provided by the organization that receives your volunteer services. Does your or the organization's coverage include the volunteer nursing duty that you are considering? Is the coverage adequate in light of the potential damages and legal fees that you might have to pay if sued?

practice act does not limit the practice of nursing to paid positions, you could be found to be practicing nursing in that state without a license. If you are sued for negligent acts that occurred while volunteering in another state, the court will probably evaluate your actions and their consequences against whatever standard of nursing care would apply in that state rather than your home state.

Good Samaritan acts

Good Samaritan acts won't cover you in day-to-day situations in which you donate nursing services. These acts apply only to accidents or other emergency situations. In addition, remember not all state Good Samaritan acts extend coverage to all nurses.

Acting during a disaster

A tornado levels a part of your community. Spring floods take life and property at the south end of town. A freight train derails, blanketing the community with toxic vapor. The brakes fail on an airplane carrying 137 passengers, and the craft careens off the runway. Any of these disastrous events can overload local medical and nursing resources. In situations such as these, nurses have special responsibilities and legal rights.

CONTRACT DUTIES

When you give nursing care during a disaster, professional, ethical, and legal concerns figure heavily in every decision you make. In general, with the exception of declared emergencies, a nurse's responsibilities in a disaster do not differ legally from her everyday responsibilities. You may have specific duties to perform in specific kinds of disasters, and you may be legally bound to perform those duties, but that is likely to be based on your employment contract and not on laws or precedent-setting legal cases.

If you work in a city hospital, for example, your employment contract may contain a provision that you can be called to work whenever a government official declares a state of emergency. If you refuse to come in, you can be disciplined, suspended, or fired. This rule applies even if the work you are assigned to do is not normally part of your job description.

If you are already on the job when a disaster occurs, the same contractual provisions may be invoked to keep you from going home at the end of your shift. And the same penalties apply if you refuse to cooperate.

Similarly, if you are an unpaid volunteer for a community service, such as the Red Cross or an ambulance unit, you may be expected to report for duty in any local disaster as long as your reporting does not conflict with your regular employment. If you refuse, the service can drop you from its roster; if you are a paid, part-time worker for such an organization, you can be dismissed. These duties apply even if your work arrangements are unwritten but are part of an oral agreement. The American Nurses Association has drafted a position statement that contains guidelines for RNs who need a release from work in order to perform relief work during a disaster. The guidelines cover steps an RN should take, and there are also guidelines for employers.

CONTRACT DEFENSES

Because reporting for work in an emergency, including a disaster, is usually a contract matter, specific contract defenses apply if you're disciplined for failing to fulfill your duties. One such contract defense is impossibility. If reporting is impossible for you and you can prove it—even if you are contractually required to do so and would be paid for the work—you cannot be disciplined or prosecuted. For example, if a blizzard absolutely prohibits travel from your home to the job or disastrous flooding causes the governor to ban all travel in your area, what your contract says does not apply. In addition, if you are disciplined at work, you have a legal defense. However, watch for exceptions to travel bans—for example, a ban may be announced for all but "required personnel" or "persons with medical or nursing training." In those situations, obviously, you must report for duty.

Other considerations

If you are at work or scheduled to work when a disaster occurs, you will be held to abandonment laws. State nursing boards have disciplined nurses for leaving their workplace when a disaster occurred and also for failing to come in to work when a disaster is occurring. For example, nurses who left work during a hurricane, abandoning their patients and leaving them with no provider were disciplined. Likewise, a nurse who refused to come in to work because a hurricane was on the way to the city was disciplined by her state nursing board.

It is critical that you know what you will be required to do if a disaster occurs while at work or if you are scheduled to work. Also, you must know what steps to take if it is impossible for you to remain at work or if you are unable to make it to your workplace. In view of this heightened burden placed on nurses because they are critical health care providers, it is very important that you have a personal disaster plan in place. You need to set up a plan of action for your family, pets, and property in the event you have to stay at work or have to go in to work. For example, who will pick up your children from school or stay with them? Where will your family go during an emergency, and how will you reconnect with them? Do you have extra clothes, toiletries, and medications in your car in case you have to stay at work?

During a disaster, people turn to the frontline health care providers for guidance, and nurses are part of that front line. You are not going to be able to focus on your nursing care during a disaster if you are worrying about your family, pets, property, or trying to coordinate their evacuation, and so on, while you are still caring for patients. You must know your facility's disaster plan in case communication is compromised and you are suddenly the person in charge of coordinating the disaster relief or care where you are located.

VOLUNTEERING DURING A DISASTER

No law prevents you from voluntarily donating your services; however, if your nursing license is under disciplinary sanctions or probation, you may be restricted from volunteering during a disaster. Specific statutory or common laws may provide protection if you volunteer during a disaster rather than during normal times. This is another area you need to plan for ahead of time—whether you will volunteer during a disaster, are there any scenarios you will not volunteer for, and whether you are allowed to volunteer your services. (See *Minimizing legal risks during a disaster,* page 283.)

Suppose you are working in a hospital that does not have a policy mandating health care personnel to report to work when a disaster occurs. You can still volunteer to stay for extra shifts or to perform services outside your normal scope of employment. If you do volunteer to remain at work, you will be held to the same abandonment issues as if you were scheduled to work. You can necessarily expect your pay to reflect the extra work performed during a disaster. Most facilities will try to pay for the overtime, but some may not. If you are curious, find out what your facility's policy is before a disaster occurs. The policy may depend on union rules, state fair labor employment laws, or, if you work in a city or state hospital, on city ordinances or state regulations.

Volunteering in another state

Nurse practice acts do not legally restrict you from volunteering during a disaster in an out-of-state location. For instance, suppose you are licensed in California, and while you are on vacation in Oregon, a disaster occurs. You can give your nursing services during the disaster without concern that you are breaching California's or Oregon's nurse practice act. That is because most nurse practice acts have a special exemption for care given in emergencies that usually includes disasters. However, if you are under disciplinary stipulations or probation in your home state, you need to verify with the appropriate monitoring staff member at your home state's nursing board that you are allowed to volunteer in the other state. Some state statutes specifically address nurses with out-of-state licenses.

Right to refuse

If you do not want to volunteer and your hospital policy or contract does not require it, in most states you have the

Minimizing legal risks during a disaster

By taking a few precautions, you can help assure protection from liability when working under disaster conditions.

Be prepared
Do not wait for a disaster to happen before you ask your charge nurse what you will be required to do during a disaster. Keep equipment you are likely to need available and in working condition.

Be personally prepared with a family disaster plan and by having needed personal supplies ready in your locker or vehicle.

Follow instructions
In any disaster, public officials and other authorities–such as medical personnel, public health workers, or municipal staff–will probably issue orders. Even if these people are not normally your superiors, follow their directions as much as possible. Offer advice only when you think necessary.

If at home, pay attention to the media since advisories to health care providers is often distributed through media sources.

Do not assume you will not be required to work. Check with appropriate personnel to avoid charges of abandonment.

Know your limits
Do not work beyond the point of effectiveness. If you're so tired you cannot make correct decisions, no one will benefit from your care. Describe your fatigue to the person in charge, and ask for a break.

Do not leave the workplace just because you have worked a full shift. If there is no one to accept responsibility for your patients, most nursing boards and courts expect you to remain because a tired nurse is better than no nurse. You would be sure to put a protest verbally and in writing to your supervisor immediately (keep a copy) informing the supervisor you are unable to give report due to a lack of staff or whatever the causation is. You may want to do this even if you understand why you must stay at work and you know there is nothing that can be done at the time, but putting your protest in writing may protect your license if an issue arises.

---

right to refuse. Most nurse practice acts do not require you to provide emergency care in disasters, any more than they require you to perform care during a disaster. Similarly, Good Samaritan acts provide some legal immunity for giving emergency care but do not require you to provide that care—except in states with duty-to-rescue laws.

Civil defense laws, also known as disaster relief laws, do not apply in most states to nurses who are not already involved in civil defense work—although in a declared national emergency, nurses (like anyone else) can be drafted. Alternatively, martial law may be imposed, which makes all citizens subject to public authority. Many civil defense laws authorize state or federal governing bodies to enforce special regulations dealing with the duties of medical and nursing personnel in a declared emergency. Some states already have such plans ready for use in a sufficiently serious disaster.

Deciding whether to volunteer
When deciding whether to help out in a disaster, assess your actual ability to help. Caring for the disaster victims may require particular skills, for example, knowledge of a special area such as toxicology. Alternatively, the skill required may be as simple as rowing a boat in a flood or applying a bandage to a cut.

Consider whether you can get to the disaster site or to the place where care will be provided. If an airliner crashes, for example, and emergency departments throughout the city are treating victims, your ability to get to your hospital or another hospital quickly may figure in whether you decide to volunteer. What if, for example, the disaster involves a riot occurring during a total blackout in your city, and the mayor decrees, "Don't travel to work unless you're within walking distance?" If you try to drive into the city from your suburban home, you will only complicate driving conditions—and you probably will not get to your hospital in time to be helpful. However, you must check with your hospital if possible to be sure the travel ban applies to staff who are not already at the hospital.

You may also consider whether volunteering in the disaster will keep you from working and earning your regular salary. Find out, too, whether your professional liability insurance covers services provided in a disaster or other off-the-job activities.

WORKING OUTSIDE YOUR SCOPE OF PRACTICE

In a disaster, you may find yourself performing duties outside your usual scope of practice. If you are an LPN or an LVN, you may be asked to perform duties that ordinarily would be restricted to RNs, and nurses' aides may be asked to do work you usually do. If you are an RN, you may find yourself doing tasks usually reserved for medical residents. Provided you have the knowledge and skill to meet minimum safety requirements, you may be permitted to give such substitute care in disasters based on the same exemption in nurse practice acts that lets an out-of-state nurse volunteer his services in a disaster. This exemption may be construed as letting you expand the scope of your practice in a disaster. You will want to check your state's nurse practice act to determine such exemption. Even if it cannot be construed this way, statutory or common laws usually permit regulatory authorities

to place the public welfare above strict enforcement of the letter of the law.

SELECTED REFERENCES

42 U.S. Code § 238q.

American Nurses Association. American Nurses Association Position Statement on Registered Nurses' Rights and Responsibilities Related to Work Release During a Disaster - Guidelines for Employers. Retrieved from: http://www.nursingworld.org/MainMenuCategories/Policy-Advocacy/Positions-and-Resolutions/ANAPositionStatements/Position-Statements-Alphabetically/Work-Release-During-a-Disaster-Guidelines-for-EEmployersEmlpoy Employers.html, 2014.

Federal Volunteer Protection Act of 1997, Pub. L. 105-19, at 42 USC § 14506.

Hampshire, M. "Aftershock," *Nursing Standard* 14(29):16–17, April 2000.

Howie, W., Howie, B., and McMullen, P. "To Assist or Not Assist: Good Samaritan Considerations for Nurses Practitioners," *The Journal of Nurse Practitioners* 8(9):688–692, October 2012.

Ohio Nurses Association. The Nurse as a Volunteer, Nursing Practice Statement NP 81, Approved on March, 2005.

Romohr, P. "A Right/Duty Perspective on the Legal and Philosophical Foundation of the No-Duty-To-Rescue Rule," *Duke Law Journal* 55:1025, March, 2006.

Sbaih, L.C. "Dilemma — Volunteering Help," *Accidental Emergency Nursing* 9(4):222–224, October 2001.

Scordato, M. "Understanding the Absence of a Duty to Reasonably Rescue in American Tort Law," *Tulane Law Review* 82:1447, March, 2008.

Sullivan, W. "Good Samaritan Statutes: When Do They Protect You?" *Emergency Physicians Monthly*. Retrieved from: http://www.epmonthly.com/archives/features/good-samaritan-statutes-when-do-they-protect-you/, February 2010.

Tumolo, J. "To the Rescue: Considering the Risks and Rewards of Being a Good Samaritan," *Advanced Nurse Practitioner* 10(2):68–70, February 2002.

Walker, M. "To Stop or Not: Good Samaritan 2001," *Journal of Christian Nurses* 18(3):34–35, Summer 2001.

9

Nurses' rights as employees

Lanette L. Anderson, MSN, JD, RN

Decent wages mean financial security for you and your family. Optimal working conditions can mean improved job security, enhanced job satisfaction, and the opportunity to deliver the best possible care to your patients.

However, to achieve the wages, benefits, and working conditions you deserve, you need to understand your rights as an employee. You also need to be prepared to take appropriate action if your employee rights are violated.

Becoming familiar with the information in this chapter will help you assert your employee rights. The focus of this chapter is on two crucial issues: strategies for reading and understanding an employment contract, and the pros and cons of joining a union.

You'll learn about types of contracts and implied conditions as well as what to do if your employer breaches your employment contract. You'll also learn about the strategies unions use to protect the rights of their nurse members, including collective bargaining, grievance procedures, arbitration, and strikes, and how these strategies may affect you.

Understanding employment contracts

Most nurses are hired without the benefit of a written employment contract. Usually, an application or a résumé is submitted and an agreement is reached as to the start date, position, benefits, and starting pay. This arrangement is no less legal than a written contract. It does, however, present certain problems if, at a later date, some portion of the employment agreement is disputed by either party.

If you sign an employment contract, read it carefully to make sure it adequately defines your duties, authority, and benefits. Knowing what to look for in a contract will help you decide if a particular job is right for you. Learning to interpret contract terms will help you function within the contract's specified limits. Also, be sure to carefully read the procedure for terminating the contract.

Labor attorneys try to draft most employment agreements as *at-will contracts*, meaning that either party can end the agreement for any reason or for no reason. These contracts are in contrast to the less common just cause agreements, in which the employer must have just cause to fire you or risk penalties if a court finds that you were wrongfully terminated. Although the at-will contract has benefits for the employer, the employer risks having the employee quit at any time, without a reason. If you are currently employed, look at the documents that you received from your employer as well as any contract that you may have signed, as well as policy manuals, and so on. Unless otherwise stated, you can assume that your employment is at will.

RESTRICTIONS OF AT-WILL CONTRACTS

There are some important restrictions on an employer's ability to terminate an employee at will. Primarily, these restrictions arise if an employer's decision to terminate an employee violates a law—for example, firing someone based on race, religion, sex, or other factors addressed by antidiscrimination laws. The scope of these laws differs depending on the state. Firing based on race, for example, is illegal in all states as well as under federal law. Firing someone based on sexual orientation, on the other hand, is illegal in some states, but not in others. As of 2013, 20 states and the District of Columbia have laws that prohibit discrimination based upon sexual orientation for both public and private sector employers. Other states prohibit it only in public sector workplaces. There has been federal legislation introduced, which would prohibit discrimination based upon sexual orientation and gender identity. The Employment Non-discrimination Act of 2009 was introduced in Congress but to date it has not passed, so it is not prohibited by federal law.

In some states, legislation has recently been enacted that prohibits health care employers from firing nurses (and, in many cases, other employees) who act as whistle-blowers by reporting unsafe conditions or illegal activities to state or federal agencies. Workers who are considering blowing the whistle can feel supported in knowing that there are a variety of laws that protect bona fide whistle-blowing. These include the Americans with Disabilities Act, the Age Discrimination in Employment Act, and the Civic Rights Act of 1964. In addition, on the federal level the Whistleblower Protection Enhancement Act of 2012 was signed into law by the President in November of that year. It provides protection only to federal employees.

Employers also can't fire someone for exercising her legal right to join a union or to engage in collective bargaining.

In addition to situations where terminating an employee violates an existing law, 42 states (except Alabama, Florida, Georgia, Louisiana, Maine, Maryland, New York, and Rhode Island) and the District of Columbia recognize a "public policy" exception to at-will employment. Under the public-policy exemption, an employer wrongfully terminates an employee when said termination violates a state's well-established public policy, which can be found in the state's constitution, statutes, administrative rules, common laws, and any expansion thereof. For example, it would be against public policy if an employer fired an employee for filing a worker's compensation claim after being injured on the job or for refusing to break the law at the employer's request. However, states differ in terms of how they define them.

Some states also recognize an *implied covenant of good faith and fair dealing,* meaning that an employer can't fire an employee maliciously or in bad faith. This concept is the general assumption in contract law that parties to the contract will not deceive each other and will act in good faith. Even among those states that recognize this exception to "at-will" employment there are differences in how far it extends and how to apply it.

TYPES OF CONTRACTS

A *contract* is a legally binding promise between two parties that can be enforced in court. Contracts can be either express (stated in written or verbal words) or implied (demonstrated by actions). According to U.S. and Canadian law, an employment contract is legally binding if all of these provisions apply:

■ You've accepted an offer, verbally or in writing, to perform in a certain capacity.

■ You and the other person are legally competent, of legal age, and without mental impairment.

■ You both understand the agreement and enter into it voluntarily.

■ The terms and conditions for performance of the agreement are lawful.

■ You receive something of value such as money for fulfilling the agreement or, in some cases, you give up something of value.

In general, agreements about conscience, morals, and social activities aren't legally binding. If you break a lunch date, you can't be fined or taken to court. If you violate any term in a legally binding contract, however, you might face consequences.

Written contract

Sometimes an employment contract is a formal, written contract. It may be an individual contract, which you

negotiate, or a collectively bargained contract that was negotiated by a nurse negotiation committee and a labor organization or union. In either contract, wage increases may be awarded automatically or may be linked to merit or experience.

Oral express contract

Contracts need not be in writing to be legally binding; most oral contracts are legally enforceable with few exceptions. An employment agreement can be and is usually an oral contract, offered and accepted orally. Most states allow parties to orally agree to employment relationships, and those contracts are legal and enforceable in court (assuming state law allows them). However, because the judge and jury won't have a written contract to consider if a dispute about the terms of employment arises, other documents (such as an employee handbook, a notice of a physical examination, a welcoming letter, or pay stubs) would play a major role in proving that such an oral contract existed and outlining its terms.

Finally, witnesses who may have overheard the offer extended to the nurse and the nurse's acceptance may be called to testify at a hearing, deposition, or trial to prove the existence of an oral employment agreement.

Pitfalls of oral contracts

An oral contract can be problematic if the parties involved disagree about its terms. Memories fail and witnesses move away or may become otherwise unavailable. Consequently, if the original agreement isn't in writing, the subjective and fallible memories of the parties may have to reconstruct it. If the matter must be litigated, more time and money will be spent to prove what simply could have been put into writing.

If an employer doesn't offer you a written contract, you can write a letter to the person with whom you spoke, confirming that you accept the offer and repeating the terms you heard. Confirm the start date and say that you look forward to working with that person. Be sure to put all important, agreed-to terms and conditions in the letter. At the end, write that if they have anything to add or disagree with the matters in your letter, they should contact you in writing at their earliest convenience. Send the letter, but first make a copy for your file. Hopefully, you'll never need to refer to it but just as documentation is important in our nursing practice it is also important in our employment relationships.

IMPLIED CONDITIONS

Most contracts contain *implied conditions*—elements that aren't explicitly stated but are assumed to be part of the contract. For example, your employer assumes that you'll practice nursing in a safe, competent manner as defined by your nurse practice act and the health care facility's standards and policies. You assume, based on implied conditions, that the employer will provide you with resources, supplies, and equipment necessary for you to perform your work and that the employer will ensure a safe working environment.

OFFER AND ACCEPTANCE

In any contract, there must be an offer and an acceptance. An offer must be definite and communicated by words or actions. If you fail to respond, the employer can't interpret your silence as acceptance, but can withdraw the other without penalty at any time before it has been accepted.

Although you may orally accept an offer or simply report for duty, a written acceptance is generally best. The employment contract should be as specific as possible about wages, hours, and the terms and conditions of the relationship. (See *Components of an employment contract*.)

BREACH OF CONTRACT

Unjustified failure to perform all or part of your contractual duty is considered a breach of contract. If the breach is substantial, the entire agreement may have been broken and legal damages may result. (In the case of at-will employment, a likely consequence is that the employment relationship will terminate.) If only part of the agreement has been breached, the remaining contract may still be effective and both parties may want to continue the relationship, with some clarification. Breaches can be avoided if both parties carefully consider the terms and conditions of the contract and know what they're promising each other.

Employee breach of contract

When you agree to do (or not to do) something in an employment contract, and you don't perform as promised, you may be in breach of the contract and subject to litigation forcing you to perform as promised. You may even be required to reimburse your employer for the cost of hiring someone else to do the job that you were supposed to do.

It's rare, except in unusual circumstances, for a court to order an employee to perform services against his will. If the employment relationship is at-will, failure to perform may simply terminate the agreement. However, in other employment contracts—especially those involving

Components of an employment contract

For an employment contract to be legally binding, it must include the following components:

A promise
Two or more legally competent parties must promise each other to do or not do something.

Mutual understanding
The parties involved must clearly understand the terms and obligations the contract imposes on them.

Compensation
The parties involved must agree that, to fulfil the contract, lawful actions will be performed in exchange for something of value.

Commonly, misunderstandings can be cleared up by talking with the proper people in the chain of command (always in a professional and unemotional manner). If documents are involved, they're important proof. If you have a union contract, tell your representative as soon as you're aware of a breach.

If you exhaust all channels of appeal, you may need to discuss the problem with an attorney with contract and employment law expertise, using a written log of your attempts to rectify the situation, including statements made, with dates and times. As stated previously, documentation of events can be very beneficial to your case.

Canadian law
Because the law varies by jurisdiction, it's best to check with local legal counsel about procedures and deadlines.

INVALID CONTRACTS

A nursing employment contract is considered invalid when the agreement concerns actions that are illegal or impossible to carry out, or when any of the following applies:

- An applicant has lied about qualifications.
- A nurse is forced into signing a contract.
- The agreement involves unlawful activity—for example, it requires you to bill for services that weren't actually performed.
- A minor or mentally incompetent person signs the contract.

Physical or mental inability to carry out the agreement may be a basis to set the agreement aside but not always. Both parties expect, from the start, that the nurse will be able to physically carry out the agreement.

specialized services—failure to perform as agreed may result in legal consequences, which may require the person to perform as agreed in the contract.

Of course, the terms and conditions of a contract can be changed or modified by oral or written agreement—certainly, it's far better to change a contract than to breach it. Good communication may prevent a perceived breach, and renegotiation is cheaper than litigation.

Employer breach of contract
An employer may also breach a contract. If, for example, he fails to give you the vacation time agreed to, he has breached the contract. If you discover a breach, follow procedures outlined in your employee handbook.

If your health status changes, you may feel that your agreement no longer stands. If litigated, your obligation will be determined on an individual basis by the judge. Mere physical or mental disability won't void the contract. However, you may be protected under the Americans with Disabilities Act, which requires reasonable accommodations in certain instances.

TERMINATING A CONTRACT

When you terminate a contract, you've fulfilled or absolved yourself of all obligations. Because most employment contracts don't specify termination dates, you can end them at any time if you follow proper notification procedures. You can also end contracts with termination dates if your employer agrees to the date. Follow the contract's procedures for giving written notice (most require 2–4 weeks) or, if your contract has an automatic expiration date, don't renew it.

Your employer can terminate your contract if he determines that you're incompetent or have behaved unprofessionally on the job. Before discharging you, he'll probably give you several warnings about the quality of your work. Then he might confront you with several examples of your shortcomings from previous written evaluations of your performance. If you don't want to lose your job, you should discuss areas of improvement with him in a timely and professional manner.

If you disagree with your employer's complaints, you can request an evaluation by someone else who supervised your work, or you can request a transfer to another unit where you would be reevaluated after an agreed-upon length of time. However, your employer isn't obligated to agree to either request unless these steps are

part of a disciplinary process stated in an employment contract or an employee manual. If he doesn't agree, you may seek written support from your coworkers who can refute your employer's complaints. You can also seek support from your union, if you have one. The union may file a grievance on your behalf.

Most hospitals operate on an employment-at-will basis, in which there's either no employment contract or the existing contract fails to specify the job's duration. However, the hospital can't violate a union bargaining agreement that mandates proof of just cause for discipline or discharge.

Unions

Although individual contracts provide significant legal protection, employees in many areas—from farm workers, laborers, and truck drivers to actors, teachers, and musicians—have found that they're better off signing a contract negotiated for them as a group. Their union representatives engage in collective bargaining for contract conditions. When necessary, they use arbitration, strikes, and threats of strikes to enhance their terms of employment and enforce contracts.

Before 1974, nurses' rights to form labor unions were limited primarily to employees of nursing homes, for-profit hospitals, and many public hospitals and health care agencies. Also, some state laws allowed for labor unions in nonprofit hospitals, and some private nonprofit hospitals voluntarily recognized nurses' unions. Nonprofit hospital workers were covered by the original Wagner Act in 1935, but were excluded in 1947 with the Taft-Hartley amendments. When the new legislation was considered in 1974 by the

Senate Committee on Labor and Public Welfare, it was determined that labor relations in the health care industry required special considerations so that patients could be protected. In 1974, Congress extended the National Labor Relations Act (NLRA) to cover private, nonprofit health care facilities and agencies. Since then, the number of unionized nurses has increased dramatically.

The NLRA now applies to employees of hospitals and other health care facilities with annual revenues of at least $250,000 and to nursing homes, visiting nurses' associations, and related nursing facilities with annual revenues of at least $100,000. Also, many states now have collective bargaining laws patterned after the NLRA that controls public sector bargaining in the state.

A new window of opportunity for nurses to unionize was opened in 1991, when the U.S. Supreme Court decided, in *American Hospital Association v. National Labor Relations Board* (NLRB), that the NLRB had acted properly in defining eight bargaining units in acute-care hospitals, including one unit composed of only registered nurses. After the 1991 decision, unions stepped up campaign efforts to organize nurses. Case law subsequent to 1991 has continued to reinforce the fact that hospitals cannot prevent union solicitation unless it interferes with patient care. In fact, the 7th Circuit U.S. Court of Appeals in 2008 determined that union solicitation is not different than solicitation by employees for other causes such as sales of Girl Scout Cookies or collecting money for charities.

THE SUPERVISORY ISSUE

Two U.S. Supreme Court cases— *NLRB v. Health Care & Retirement Corporation* (1994) and *NLRB v.*

Kentucky River Community Care (2001)—have addressed the issue of whether and when nurses who direct the work of others should be considered "supervisors" within the meaning of the NLRA. This is an extremely important issue because supervisors aren't covered by the NLRA, and thus they aren't protected by it—meaning, among other things, that they have no right to form or join unions or to bargain collectively. Furthermore, because many registered nurses (RNs) may "direct" the work of others (for example, licensed practical nurses, licensed vocational nurses, unit clerks, and nurses' aides) in the course of performing their own professional duties, the issue of where and how to draw the line in determining who is a "supervisor" has tremendous implications for the nursing community as a whole.

Before 1994, the NLRB generally found that nurses weren't considered supervisors because when they direct the work of others as an incidental aspect of providing patient care, they're acting in the interests of the patient and not of the employer. However, in *Health Care & Retirement Corporation,* the U.S. Supreme Court rejected this distinction, even though it didn't make a blanket decision as to whether nurses were supervisors. Instead, the Court found that the NLRB couldn't use this distinction to determine whether a nurse or a group of nurses worked in a supervisory role. After this case, the NLRB continued to examine each case individually, and RNs continued to organize despite disputes as to whether charge nurses (sometimes including nurses who are assigned charge duties on a rotating basis) were supervisors.

In 2001, the Supreme Court revisited the issue of nurses as supervisors in the case of *NLRB v. Kentucky River Community Care*. It rejected the NLRB's argument that nurses who direct other employees as part of their patient-care duties are exercising professional judgment, and that this differs from exercising independent judgment as supervisors. However, the Court didn't specifically rule that all RNs who direct the work of others are supervisors. It left open other avenues for finding that nurses who direct the work of others aren't supervisors and, once again, the NLRB continued to evaluate each case individually. The Court also ruled that employers and not employees have the burden of proof in demonstrating that a nurse is a supervisor.

Nurses' unions objected to the Supreme Court's decision but emphasized that it didn't eliminate nurses' rights to organize, whereas employer groups supported the decision. Thus far, organizing among nurses continues, but the issue of whether and when nurses are supervisors is still debated. (See *Nurses' unions and collective bargaining*.) In the case of *NLRB v. Oakwood Health Care* in 2006, the NLRB ruled that the permanent charge nurses employed by Oakwood Health Care exercised independent judgment, and therefore supervisory authority in assigning tasks to employees. The American Nurses Association (ANA) was opposed to this decision as it limited the rights of many nurses to basic protections under federal labor laws. In 2007 the Re-Empowerment of Skilled and Professional Employees and Construction Tradeworkers (RESPECT) Act was introduced in Congress. The purpose of this act is to clarify the definition of the term "supervisor," therefore limiting the ability of employers to take away union protections. The ANA supports the RESPECT Act. To date this legislation has not passed in Congress.

JOINING A UNION: PROS AND CONS

Union officials have targeted the hospital field as one of the last large industries ripe for organizing. Unionization continues to spark debate within the hospital setting and the nursing profession.

Pros

Union proponents argue that unionization gives nurses a strong voice in such issues as wages, benefits, and pensions. Unionization, they argue, assures fair grievance procedures and provides nurses with more influence in patient-care decisions. Unionization also gives nurses more control over working conditions, such as staffing and overtime, and equalizes bargaining power between employer and employee.

Cons

Critics argue that unionization tarnishes the image of the nursing profession by shifting emphasis away from patient care to economic advancement. Many nurses are reluctant to depend on an organization for their economic and professional well-being. Some nurses fear the potential disruption of picketing and strikes. Others argue that unionization creates antagonism between nurses and their employers, preventing effective cooperation.

Questions to consider

Before deciding whether to participate in collective bargaining, ask yourself these questions:

■ Am I eligible? (See *Joining a nurses' union*.)

Nurses' unions and collective bargaining

The question of whom nurses should choose as their collective bargaining representative has been a hot-button issue among nurses for years. In July 2001, the ANA addressed this issue when it published its *Code of Ethics for Nurses with Interpretive Statements*, which addressed collective bargaining in Provision 6. It states that nurses "participate in establishing, maintaining, and improving health care environments and conditions of employment conducive to the provision of quality health care and consistent with the values of the professional through individual and collective action." It also recommends that nurses address their concerns about the health care environment through the proper channels, preferably through a professional association such as their state nurses' association.

State nurses' associations

Many RNs choose their ANA-affiliated state nurses' association as their collective bargaining representative because they believe that their association can best advocate for them on practice and professional issues as well as wages and working conditions. Organizing through a state nurses' association may also mean that nurses are part of the ANA and, by extension, also part of the International Council of Nurses. In a small number of states including California, the state nurses' associations have chosen not to be affiliated with ANA. National Nurses United (NNU) is the largest union and professional organization for nurses in the United States. NNU was founded in 2009 when the California Nurses Association,

United American Nurses (UAN), and the Massachusetts Nurses Association joined together.

Not all state nurses' associations have chosen to engage in collective bargaining. Reasons for this vary. Association leadership may not want the association to get involved with collective bargaining activity, or the association may not possess the expertise or resources to effectively engage in collective bargaining.

Unionization

In 1999, the ANA formed the UAN, a union composed of state nurses' associations that engage in collective bargaining, those associations' labor programs, or both. The following year, UAN joined AFL-CIO, the federation to which most labor unions belong. The UAN also provides a mechanism for organizing nurses in states where the state nurses' association doesn't engage in collective bargaining.

In addition to the UAN, several large unions that represent a wide range of workers in different industries have been active in organizing nurses. These include the Service Employees International Union; the American Federation of State, County, and Municipal Employees; and the American Federation of Teachers. In some instances, nurses are represented by independent unions, which operate only at one or two hospitals. There are also state-specific nursing unions. For example, the California Nurses Association and the Massachusetts Nurses Association are statewide labor unions that were affiliated with the ANA but decided to become independent.

■ Will collective bargaining help my professional and economic status?
■ Can I address my professional concerns through collective bargaining?
■ Can I change my working conditions as an individual, or do I need to organize with other nurses?

If you believe that organizing a union is necessary to improve the professional or economic status of the nurses in your facility, the full force of the law will protect your efforts.

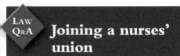

LAW Q&A

Joining a nurses' union

For most nurses, the decision to join a union is a difficult one. Here are some answers to frequently asked questions about unionization.

Can I join a labor union?

A nurse who works as an employee can join a labor union. However, under the National Labor Relations Act, some nurses may be excluded from the definition of "employee"–for example, nurses who are managers or supervisors. The courts and the National Labor Relations Board (NLRB) continue to wrestle with the circumstances under which a nurse is considered a "supervisor" because she responsibly directs the work of others. For the most part, the NLRB continues to examine this issue on a case-by-case basis.

Can I be forced to join a union?

If you're eligible to join the union and you work under a "union shop" contract, you must join the union within a specified time to remain employed. If the contract provides for an "open shop," you can choose not to join the union and still keep your job.

Can the hospital where I work fire me for helping to organize a union?

Federal regulations strictly forbid your employer from firing you or taking any other reprisal against you for helping to organize a union.

What consequences do I face if I refuse to participate in my union's strike?

As long as you continue working, your hospital or health care facility will pay your wages and benefits. Although no union can force you to strike, you might face some antagonism from those colleagues who do strike.

PROTECTING THE RIGHT TO UNIONIZE

In the United States, regulations governing union organizing among nurses in private sector employment come under the jurisdiction of the NLRB, the agency that enforces federal labor laws.

The NLRB protects eligible employees' rights to organize a union, join a union, or decertify a union (vote the union out), and may defend you against unfair labor practices. The NLRB also helps employers by enforcing regulations that control picketing and strikes, and by providing remedies for any unfair union practices.

If a nonsupervisor decides to organize a union, the NLRB supervises procedures for elections. These procedures enforce rules that both the union and management must follow. The NLRB works to investigate unfair labor practices that may arise during the election process. (See *Recognizing unfair labor practices.*)

INITIATING A UNION DRIVE

To organize a collective bargaining unit at your facility, begin by talking to a few of your coworkers about the possibility of unionizing. This small group may begin to discuss workplace issues and making plans to contact your state nurses' association if it engages in collective bargaining or the union of your choice. The union will assign a union staff member to help you organize your campaign. An organizing committee representing all major departments, shifts, and ethnic and racial diversity in the workplace should be established. The union may support your efforts by supplying stationery, printing, legal advice,

Recognizing unfair labor practices

If eligible, you have a legal right to participate in union activities. If your work involves supervising others, you may be ineligible to join the union. However, you still have some protection under Sections 7 and 8 of the National Labor Relations Act regarding the organization of a union in your facility and management's practice. If your employer infringes on that right–through interference, domination, discrimination, or refusal to bargain–you can charge unfair labor practices.

Interference

Employers may interfere with a union election by unilaterally improving wages or benefits to encourage votes against the union. This is considered an unfair labor practice. Other unfair practices include:

- helping employees withdraw from union membership
- making coercive statements about participation in union activities
- libelling or slandering union officials
- threatening to close down the facility
- questioning employees about union activities or organizers
- spying on–or implying the possibility of spying on–union meetings
- creating an atmosphere of fear.

Domination

The NLRB doesn't allow management to dominate a union by paying a union's expenses,

giving union leaders special benefits, or taking an active part in organizing a union.

Discrimination

Discrimination is an unfair labor practice that can involve discharging, disciplining, or threatening an employee for joining a union or for encouraging others to join. Other types of discrimination include:

- refusing to hire anyone who belongs to a union
- refusing to reinstate or promote an employee because she testified at an NLRB hearing
- enforcing rules unequally between employees who are involved in union activities and those who aren't.

Refusal to bargain

To weaken union participation, management may refuse to take part in collective bargaining. It's an unfair labor practice to take unilateral action to alter employment conditions that either are covered in an existing contract or are included among legally mandated areas of bargaining. Other unfair labor practices include:

- refusing to meet with a union representative
- refusing to negotiate a mandatory issue
- demanding to negotiate a voluntary issue.

---

organizational guidance, and encouragement. The union can also arrange for meeting halls and publicity, and can file the proper election petitions with the NLRB. Information about the workplace and decisions about the improvements that the union would

try to achieve (demands) should be clearly articulated.

Management's rights and limitations

During a union drive, the NLRB also protects the rights of management.

LEGAL TIP
The NLRB: protecting your right to organize a union

If your hospital punishes you solely because you're involved in organizing a union, the federal agency known as the National Labor Relations Board (NLRB) will protect you. This board enforces the National Labor Relations Act, the federal labor laws that explicitly set forth your rights to form and join a union.

An example
Suppose you're working as a hospital pediatric nurse, and you support unionization of the hospital's nurses. Union organizers ask you to distribute pro-union pamphlets to your colleagues. You begin giving out pamphlets in the nurses' lounge, but a hospital administrator orders you to stop. He says the hospital solicitation policy prohibits anyone from distributing literature inside the hospital. You remind him that the hospital has allowed nurses to distribute other information, such as literature to solicit volunteers for the local cancer society. You ignore the administrator's order and resume handing out pamphlets. You are suspended or intimidated by management staff.

You file an unfair labor practice charge with the NLRB. After a hearing, the board concludes that the hospital can't prevent you from distributing the pamphlets on your own time in a nonwork area. The board also concludes that the hospital was discriminatory in applying the non-solicitation policy.

A likely ruling
In this situation, the board would order the hospital to reinstate you, pay your back wages, and refrain from punishing you or any other nurse who was active in the union drive.

Under the law, management is allowed to:
- tell you the disadvantages of belonging to a union
- explain to you your election rights, such as your right to refuse to sign an authorization card
- encourage you to vote "no" in a union election (provided they don't use threats or coercion of any kind).

However, to protect your right to organize and belong to a union, the NLRB places the following limitations on management:
- Management can't interfere with your organizing activities.
- Management can't discriminate against you for participating in union activities, for testifying against management, or for filing a grievance.
- Management can't dominate a union by gaining undue influence over it, such as by paying union expenses or giving union leaders special benefits.
- Management can't refuse to bargain in *good faith* (an honest desire to reach an agreement).
- Management must assume responsibility for any unfair labor practice committed by a supervisor. (See *The NLRB: protecting your right to organize a union.*)

Union's rights and limitations
Neither management nor the union can interfere with your individual rights as guaranteed by federal or state law. However, just like management, the union must also comply with certain limitations. The NLRB ensures that the union:
- bargains in good faith
- assumes responsibility for any unfair labor practice committed by union officials

- doesn't threaten or force you to support the union
- doesn't demand that your employers do business only with companies that have unions.

ELECTING A UNION

In the initial step toward a union election, eligible nurses or union representatives distribute membership cards. Nurses who want a union election sign a membership card. In the United States, if at least 30% of eligible nurses sign the cards, the nurses or the union can ask the NLRB to authorize and supervise an election. If 50% or more of eligible nurses sign the cards, U.S. law allows the employer to forgo the election process and simply recognize the union, but this rarely occurs. In Canada, more than 50% of nurses must sign the cards to authorize an election. (See *What happens when nurses decide to unionize.*)

Union and management may disagree about which nurses are eligible to vote. Either side can challenge a nurse's eligibility. In the United States, the NLRB will settle an eligibility dispute by reviewing the individual nurse's job description, her duties and responsibilities, and her supervisory functions, if any.

What happens when nurses decide to unionize

The decision to unionize initiates a step-by-step process. First, organizers distribute leaflets and authorization cards. At least 30% of all proposed union employees must sign those cards to authorize a union election.

Steps in the election process
After the employees sign the membership cards, the following occurs:

1. The union notifies the NLRB, and an NLRB representative steps in to referee and organize the election.

2. The NLRB holds a hearing to decide who's eligible to join the bargaining unit. The employer may challenge any employee's eligibility. For example, the employer may argue that one or more employees are supervisors and are therefore ineligible.

3. The NLRB determines the place and election date. The employer and the union can then begin campaigning.

4. Within 7 days of the NLRB announcement of the election date and place, the employer provides the NLRB the names and addresses of all eligible employees. The NLRB gives this list to the union.

5. On election day, employees vote by secret ballot to accept or reject the union. If more than one union is on the ballot, employees can select one of the unions or vote for no representation at all.

6. The NLRB representative tallies the votes. The results depend on the majority of ballots cast, regardless of the percentage of eligible employees who actually vote. (If only a minority of eligible employees vote, those few employees will decide the question of unionization for all.)

The outcome
If most of the voting employees choose the union, that union is legally required to represent all eligible employees, even those who didn't vote. The NLRB will certify the union as the employees' collective bargaining representative.

If most of the voting employees reject the union, the law prohibits another election involving a union for 1 year.

To win the election, the union must get a majority of the votes of those nurses who actually voted, not those who are eligible to vote. If the union does not receive the majority of votes, you must wait at least 1 year before trying again.

In some cases, more than one union may be on the ballot. This can happen when, after the first petitioning, the union demonstrates that 30% or more of the eligible nurses want an election. If this occurs, other unions can get on the ballot provided they can obtain a show of interest from 10% of the nurse employees.

If elected, the union will negotiate a contract addressing mutually agreeable wages, benefits, and work rules and other professional issues. The contract will be devised by the negotiators and ratified by members of the bargaining unit.

Maintaining perspective

When making a commitment to a unionization drive, be prepared to continue to nurture good relations with supervisors and coworkers who oppose the union. Keep in mind that, regardless of the election's outcome, everyone will need to continue to work together. If the union wins, both management and labor will have to adjust to new rules spelled out in the contract. If the union loses, management should optimally correct the problems that led to the organizing campaign; otherwise, the same problems will resurface.

Legal issues in collective bargaining

In collective bargaining, the employer and the employees' representatives meet to confer about employment issues and put their agreements into writing. According to the NLRB, two or more people who share employment interests and conditions may constitute a bargaining unit. (See *Landmarks in the history of collective bargaining.*)

THE NLRB'S ROLE IN COLLECTIVE BARGAINING

In the United States, the laws governing collective bargaining are outlined in the NLRA and the Labor Management Relations Act (LMRA), also known as the *Taft-Hartley Act*, which was passed in 1947. The NLRB is the federal agency authorized to administer and enforce these laws. (See *Appealing to the NLRB.*)

The NLRB's responsibilities include determining appropriate bargaining units for employee groups, resolving disputes between labor and management, and conducting elections for employee bargaining representatives. The NLRB won't assert jurisdiction over labor laws for minimum wages, overtime pay, termination, or discrimination unless those issues have been written into the employees' labor contract and the contract doesn't provide for binding arbitration of alleged violations. If arbitration is provided for, the NLRB usually declines its jurisdiction and defers to the arbitrator.

Canadian law

In Canada, the provincial or territorial labor relations boards handle local labor issues, and the Canada Labour Relations Board deals with labor issues

(Text continues on page 300.)

Landmarks in the history of collective bargaining

The following is a summary of major legislative landmarks in the struggle for collective bargaining rights:

1935: Congress passes the National Labor Relations Act (NLRA). This act requires employers to bargain with employees and provides for the formation of the National Labor Relations Board (NLRB) to enforce the provisions of the act.

1946: The American Nurses Association (ANA) launches its Economic Security Program to establish national salary guidelines for nurses. ANA takes an active role in supporting nurses' rights to bargain collectively.

1947: The Labor Management Relations Act (LMRA), also known as the Taft-Hartley Act, says that nonprofit organizations, including nonprofit hospitals, don't have to bargain with their employees.

1962: An amendment to the LMRA gives federal employees, including nurses, the right to bargain collectively.

1974: Health care amendments to the NLRA explicitly grant employees of nonprofit health care facilities and agencies the right to bargain collectively.

1991: In *American Hospital Association v. NLRB,* the U.S. Supreme Court upholds NLRB regulations that make it easier for unions to organize nurses.

1994: In *NLRB v. Health Care & Retirement Corporation of America*, the U.S. Supreme Court rejects the NLRB's traditional grounds for finding that those nurses who direct the work of others aren't "supervisors." Because supervisors are excluded from the protections of the NLRA, this decision raises concerns that many registered nurses (RNs) would no longer be eligible to engage in collective bargaining. However, the Court states that the NLRB should evaluate this issue on a case-by-case basis, and the NLRB continues to recognize RNs' right to union representation.

2001: In *NLRB v. Kentucky River Community Care*, the U.S. Supreme Court rejects the NLRB's argument that says nurses who direct other employees as part of their patient-care duties are exercising professional judgment and not independent judgment as supervisors. However, the Court left open other avenues for finding that nurses who direct the work of others aren't supervisors, and the NLRB continues to evaluate each nurse on a case-by-case basis. The Court also rules that employers have the burden of proof in demonstrating that a nurse is a supervisor and thus excluded from the NLRA's protections.

State law

Before passage of the 1974 Health Care Amendments, several states had passed legislation requiring nonprofit hospitals to bargain with their employees. Consequently, nurses who worked for such hospitals in Connecticut, Idaho, Massachusetts, Michigan, Minnesota, Montana, New Jersey, New York, Oregon, Pennsylvania, and Wisconsin had some bargaining rights all along.

State legislatures have also passed laws defining the rights of nurses who work for state, county, and municipal health care facilities. Some states gave these government employees the right to organize and bargain, but not the right to strike. Other states assigned a specific arm of the state government to negotiate labor concerns or mandate pay scales for state-employed nurses.

Appealing to the NLRB

If you feel that management is engaging in unfair labor practices, begin by telling your union representative. If she believes your charges are valid, either you or the union can appeal to the NLRB. The NLRB receives approximately 25,000 charges per year from unions, employers, and employees alleging unfair or illegal labor practices.

NLRB response
The board will ask you for a sworn statement concerning the dates and times of the alleged events, the names and positions of management staff involved, and the names and addresses of other employee witnesses. Your statement will serve as a legal affidavit that will supply the NLRB with the information it needs to carry out an investigation.

Should the NLRB investigate and find that management is engaging in unfair labor practices, it will issue a formal complaint against your employer. The employer may appeal the NLRB's complaint, but if the court upholds it, the

employer must comply with the NLRB's decision on a penalty–usually reinstating employees, issuing back pay, or restoring other benefits. However, most charges are settled informally, withdrawn by the party who brought the charges, or dismissed.

An example
While nurses at Good Faith Hospital were organizing a union campaign, supervisors asked them for the names of nurses who attended meetings the organizers sponsored. Also, one supervisor suggested to her staff that if a nurses' union was organized, the union might try to force management to increase wages–which because of the hospital's precarious financial position, could result in layoffs. Several nurses complained about the supervisor's remarks at a subsequent union meeting. The union organizers agreed that management was interfering with union organization–an unfair labor practice–and consequently filed a complaint against the employer with the NLRB.

at the federal level, as in the case of military hospitals.

Bargaining units
Bargaining units usually represent different groups of workers in the same hospital. The NLRA empowers the NLRB to decide what an appropriate bargaining unit is. This gives the NLRB considerable power. It's much easier to unionize employees if there's a bargaining unit for each kind of job classification; employees in each bargaining unit typically have more shared interests.

In 1987, the NLRB issued rules permitting eight bargaining units for acute-care hospitals. Since its

establishment in 1935, this was the first time the NLRB had drafted rules defining permissible bargaining units for an entire industry. These bargaining units included:

- RNs in nonsupervisory positions
- physicians
- professionals other than RNs and physicians
- technical employees
- skilled maintenance employees
- business office clerical employees
- guards
- all other nonprofessional employees.

In response to these 1987 rules, the American Hospital Association (AHA) filed suit. In *AHA v. NLRB* (1991), the AHA claimed that the NLRB rules were illegal, arguing that the Taft-Hartley Act requires determination of appropriate bargaining units in each individual hospital.

The U.S. Supreme Court unanimously rejected the AHA's interpretation and ruled that the NLRB has the power to promulgate rules for all hospitals, not just on a hospital-by-hospital basis. This ruling made it easier for unions to organize nurses and was considered a blow to management's efforts to resist.

Also, in 2011 the NLRB overruled its 1991 decision and determined that certified nursing assistants (CNAs) also comprise an individual bargaining unit. This fragmentation of the workforce opened the door for even more such stand-alone bargaining units such as housekeepers, dietary workers, and so on.

Other NLRB functions

Along with rule making, the NLRB also resolves disputes by interpreting provisions of the LMRA. The NLRB hears cases on the supervisor's role and the employee's right to solicit new members or picket. The NLRB also determines whether labor or management has committed unfair acts during a campaign or the term of a contract. For example, in *NLRB v. Baptist Hospital* (1979), the NLRB upheld its rule against soliciting new members in upper-floor hospital halls and sitting rooms near patients, but upheld the employees' right to talk about the union in first-floor lobbies and other areas away from patients.

If a hospital or bargaining unit disagrees with an NLRB decision, either party can appeal in a federal appellate court.

Canada's courts are unlikely to interfere with a provincial labor relations board decision unless it acted outside its jurisdiction or violated common law.

Mandatory bargaining issues

The NLRB has interpreted the *mandatory bargaining issues* (issues an employer must address during bargaining) broadly to include wages and hours, seniority, leaves of absence, work schedules and assignments, benefits, promotion and layoff policies, grievance and discipline procedures, and breaks, holidays, and vacations. (See *Perils of not bargaining,* page 302.)

Voluntary issues

Bargaining on other issues may occur if both parties voluntarily agree. The NLRB considers voluntary bargaining issues to include all other possible legal employment issues. It excludes illegal issues, such as requiring new employees to join a union in less than 30 days or job discrimination. Because nurses can't force an employer to bargain over voluntary issues, negotiating or not negotiating with the employer usually depends on how committed nurses are to their professional concerns and on management's willingness to be flexible.

NEGOTIATIONS

Before bargaining begins, union negotiators should prepare for the procedure by understanding the beliefs and attitudes of the people they represent and developing a system of communication between negotiators and the bargaining unit. They should also consider in advance how management might respond to various issues.

The actual bargaining involves good-faith negotiations (an honest desire to reach an agreement) between the union's and the management's negotiating teams. Proposals may be

COURT CASE

Perils of not bargaining

A hospital can't avoid collective bargaining by refusing to recognize its nurses' union. The law, strengthened by court decisions, requires a hospital to bargain in good faith with duly elected unions. A key court case, *Eastern Maine Medical Center v. NLRB* (1981), illustrates this principle.

An antiunion stand
Nurses at Eastern Maine Medical Center voted 114 to 110 to be represented by the Maine State Nurses Association, the state's largest nurses' union. In response, the hospital administration adopted a strong antiunion stand, refusing to meet with the nurses for collective bargaining talks. Moreover, the administration gave substantial wage-and-benefit increases to nonunion employees and withheld the increases from the unionized nurses.

The administration's policy of not bargaining with the union made the nurses bitter and frustrated. The union filed unfair labor practice charges against the hospital administration.

NLRB ruling
The NLRB concluded that the hospital had violated the National Labor Relations Act by refusing to bargain in good faith and by discriminating against the unionized nurses. The board directed the hospital administration to negotiate with the union and to pay the wage-and-benefit increases withheld from members of the bargaining unit.

Appeals court ruling
In upholding the actions of the NLRB, an appeals court ruled that the hospital's refusal to negotiate violated the nurses' collective bargaining rights.

exchanged for study before the first session. Each proposal and counterproposal is discussed, and disagreements are debated in detail, sometimes with teams taking time-outs to privately reconsider positions. When disagreements persist and outside mediation fails, the union members may decide to strike. If all issues are resolved, however, the written agreement is taken to the union members with a recommendation that they ratify the terms.

DECISION TO STRIKE

Collective bargaining doesn't guarantee that the bargaining parties will reach an agreement. If the parties arrive at a stalemate, employees may decide to strike in hopes of forcing the employer to make concessions. Each union has its own rules about what percentage of the members must vote in favor of a strike before it occurs, but at least 80% is common. A strike decision is an extreme measure especially in a health care setting, so labor laws have established provisions that require any curtailment of services to be orderly.

In the United States, negotiating parties must follow this timetable—and series of steps—before a strike can be called:

- The side wanting to modify or terminate the contract must notify the other side 90 days before the contract expires (or labor or management proposes that changes take place).
- If, 30 days later, the two sides don't agree, they must notify the Federal Mediation and Conciliation Service (FMCS) and the corresponding state agency of the dispute.
- Within 30 days, the FMCS will appoint a mediator and, in rare cases, an inquiry board. Within 15 days, the mediator or inquiry board will give both sides its recommendations.

- If, after 15 more days, the parties don't agree, the employees may plan to strike. If the union didn't have employees vote earlier, a vote will be held to decide whether or not to send a strike notice.
- If most employees vote to send a strike notice, the union must send management the strike notice at least 10 days before the scheduled strike, specifying the exact date, time, and place of the strike. The strike can't be scheduled before the contract expires.

In most cases, union and management representatives, with the assistance of a mediator, schedule additional negotiations during this period. A strike vote is held before the walkout is scheduled to begin.

Note that, in many states, public sector employees are prohibited from striking. If an impasse occurs, labor and management must resolve their differences through binding arbitration.

Canadian law
Some Canadian jurisdictions prohibit health care employees from striking. In these jurisdictions, compulsory arbitration is imposed when employees and employer fail to reach an agreement. The arbitrator can then draft and impose contract terms.

Wildcat strikes
Employees who ignore the strike provisions and engage in illegal strikes lose the protection of the NLRA. They may be discharged by their employer. Unions that sanction or encourage illegal strikes may have their certification revoked by the NLRB.

Delaying a strike
Employees may delay a strike for up to 72 hours if they feel the extra time would enable them to come to terms with management.

To delay the strike, they must give management written notice at least 12 hours before the time the strike was scheduled to start. If the initial strike date passes during the negotiations, the union must issue another 10-day strike notice. If the contract expires during the negotiations, the employer and employees remain bound by the contract.

Grievances and arbitration

When an employee's dispute isn't resolved, tempers flare, morale declines, and apparent injustices smoulder. That's why union and management officials give grievance and arbitration procedures high priority when they negotiate collective bargaining agreements. Even if your workplace isn't unionized, understanding these procedures can help you create fair work rules and grievance procedures in your workplace.

RESOLVING DISPUTES
When unionized employees and management sign a labor contract, they agree to abide by certain rules and policies. A contract can't cite every potential dispute, so it includes grievance procedures—specific steps that both sides agree to follow. Usually, the process moves from discussions to formal hearings and written statements of times, dates, details, and even witnesses. If the matter can't be resolved, the aggrieved party requests arbitration.

Recognizing a grievance
The definition of *grievance* depends on the contract. Some contracts define the term as any complaint that reflects dissatisfaction with union or management

policies. However, most contracts define it as a complaint that involves contract violations.

As a staff nurse, you or your union representative can file a grievance against your employer. Your union can file a grievance against management. Management can file a grievance—usually called a disciplinary action—against any employee. Most grievances are filed against management because of management's decision-making role.

Distinguishing between gripes and grievances

Smooth labor relations require both sides to honor the contract's terms and to show good faith in using the grievance procedures. Both parties need to know when to compromise and when to retreat on a disputed issue.

Union representatives must typically defuse complaints before they become formal grievances. An effective union representative will be able to distinguish between a legitimate grievance and a gripe. A grievance is a substantive complaint that involves a contract violation and is usually a denial of a section of the contract.

Sometimes union or management representatives pursue a groundless grievance (that is, a gripe) for political or harassment purposes. A gripe may be something that you believe to be unfair but is not unlawful. Often a gripe may be the result of a personality conflict between employees. A nurse's self-interest or her resentment of authority can lead to a groundless grievance. So can a supervisor's poor decision or misuse of her authority.

TYPES OF LEGITIMATE GRIEVANCES

Most grievances fall into one of two classifications:

- unfair labor practices
- violations of a contract, a precedent, or a past practice. (See *Legitimate grievances.*)

Unfair labor practices are tactics prohibited by state and federal labor laws. For example, under federal law, an employer who discriminates against you because you're involved in union activities commits an unfair labor practice. Violations of a contract, precedent, or past practice are actions that break mutually accepted work rules. For example, suppose your contract says a supervisor must give you 2 weeks' notice before making you rotate to another shift. If a supervisor assigns you to another shift without giving you notice, you can file a grievance.

MOST COMMON GRIEVANCES

Grievances can involve an almost infinite number of complaints, but some are more common than others. Management usually takes disciplinary action against employees who:

- allow personal problems to interfere with their jobs
- fail to perform their assigned duties
- show poor work habits, such as tardiness or unreliability
- take an antagonistic attitude toward management in labor relations when serving in union positions.

Employees commonly file grievances against supervisors who dispense discipline inconsistently, show favoritism, or treat employees unfairly. Other common sources of grievances include management's selection policies for promotions, favored shift assignments, disciplinary actions, and merit salary raises. Staff nurses sometimes file grievances when they're temporarily assigned nurse manager responsibilities without getting commensurate pay.

Many grievances result from unwitting contract violations (such as poorly thought-out workload decisions) by first-level or midlevel managers. Personnel and labor relations departments can resolve many actions that would otherwise lead to grievances by answering labor questions and offering advice.

LEGAL TIP · Legitimate grievances

Not all complaints against an employer meet the definition of a "legitimate grievance." If your complaint fits into one of the following categories, chances are it's a legitimate grievance upon which your union can act.

Contract violations
Your employment contract is binding between you and your employer. If your employer violates it, you have a valid grievance. The following examples describe violations that would likely be prohibited by an employment contract:

■ You're performing the charge nurse's job 2 to 3 days a week but still receiving the same pay as other staff nurses.

■ You've had to work undesirable shifts or on Sundays more often than other nurses.

■ Your supervisor doesn't post time schedules in advance.

■ Your employer fires you without just cause.

Federal and state law violations
An action by your employer that violates a federal or state law would be the basis of a grievance, even if the employment contract permits the action. For example:

■ You receive less pay for performing the same work as a male nurse.

■ You don't receive the overtime pay to which you're entitled.

■ Your employer doesn't promote you because of your race.

Past practice violations
A past practice—one that has been accepted by both parties for an extended time but that's suddenly discontinued by the employer without notification—may be the basis for a grievance.

The past practice need not be specified in the contract. If the practice violates the contract, either party can demand that the contract be enforced. If the practice is unsafe, an arbitrator may simply abolish it. Examples of past practice violations might include:

■ Your employer charges you for breaking equipment when others haven't been charged.

■ Your employer revokes parking lot privileges.

■ Your employer eliminates a rotation system for float assignments.

Health and safety violations
Grievances pertaining to health and safety violations usually involve working conditions for which the employer is responsible. Legitimate grievances may be recognized even if the contract doesn't address the specific complaint. For example:

■ You're required to hold patients during X-rays.

■ You have no hand-washing facilities near patient rooms.

Employer policy violations
Employers have the right to establish *reasonable* work rules and policies. These rules and policies aren't usually specified in the employment contract. Your employer can't violate its own rules without being guilty of a grievance (note, however, that an employer can change rules unilaterally). For example:

■ You haven't received a performance evaluation in 2 years, though your employee handbook states that such evaluations will be done annually.

■ Your employer assigns you a vacation period without your consent, contrary to personnel policies.

GRIEVANCE PROCEDURES

The elements of a grievance procedure vary from contract to contract. Key elements always include:

■ reasonable time limits for filing a grievance and making a decision
■ procedures to appeal a grievance to higher union-management levels if the grievance is unresolved
■ assigning priority to crucial grievances (such as worker suspensions or dismissals)
■ an opportunity for both sides to investigate the complaint.

The first step is usually an informal discussion between the nurse and her supervisor. The nurse may then submit her complaint in writing. If the supervisor doesn't or can't resolve the grievance, the nurse can ask for a union representative, or *steward*, to assist her. The representative will meet with the supervisor to discuss the grievance's merits. If the supervisor stands firm, the nurse can then file a written complaint within a contract-specified time period. Subsequent hearings move to higher levels of management. The number of steps in a grievance procedure varies with each contract's provisions.

ARBITRATION

When neither side can work out a settlement on a substantive issue, arbitration is indicated. During arbitration, the parties present evidence to a neutral labor relations expert. Parties who have negotiated a collective bargaining agreement or are covered by one with an arbitration clause are required to arbitrate contract disputes. Parties with no bargaining agreement (non-unionized) may agree to independent arbitration, hoping to resolve a matter short of litigation or termination of the relationship.

The side requesting arbitration gives a written notice to the other party. The requesting party then contacts one of several national agencies that supply arbitrators, such as the FMCS or the American Arbitration Association. Both sides must agree on a specific arbitrator; the date, time, and place of the hearing; and the finality of the arbitrator's decision.

Arbitration hearing

An arbitration hearing resembles a courtroom proceeding, except that it's less formal. The party requesting arbitration has the burden of proof and must present evidence that the contract has been violated. (However, when a nurse challenges disciplinary action, management must prove its case first by presenting supporting evidence.) In an arbitration hearing, both sides may call and cross-examine witnesses. The requesting side makes a closing summary, followed by one from the opposing side. Each side can submit written briefs instead of making summary statements.

The arbitrator usually renders a written decision weeks or even months after the hearing. If both sides request an immediate response, the arbitrator can issue an oral decision and withhold a written explanation of the decision unless both parties request it.

In most cases, both sides prefer arbitration to a lengthy court fight because arbitration is speedier and less expensive, and may be conducted without attorneys. When a dispute goes to arbitration, both sides lose control of the outcome because, in the United States, the arbitrator's decision is binding. Although the losing party can challenge the decision in court, the court rarely overturns an arbitrator's decision.

In Canada, arbitrators' decisions are binding, and courts don't interfere with decisions unless there's a question of jurisdiction or the decision is patently unreasonable.

RESOLVING COMPLAINTS CAUSED BY UNFAIR LABOR PRACTICES

Most grievances arising from contract violations follow contract-stipulated grievance and arbitration procedures. The NLRB addresses allegations of unfair labor practices. If a nurse who isn't a member of a collective bargaining unit brings an allegation to the NLRB, the NLRB must determine if she's engaged in concerted action—that is, if her action is part of (or in concert with) a group effort. The NLRB will conduct a hearing to review evidence and then issue a decision. Either side can challenge an NLRB decision in court.

If a nurse has a complaint involving discrimination on the basis of race, religion, national origin, age, disability, or sex, she can file a charge of discrimination with the U.S. Equal Employment Opportunity Commission (EEOC) or a comparable state agency in addition to filing a grievance. The EEOC handles violations of:

■ the Equal Pay Act of 1963, which forbids wage discrimination based on an employee's sex

■ the Civil Rights Act of 1964, which forbids job and wage discrimination based on an employee's religion, race, sex, or ethnic background, and the Pregnancy Discrimination Act, which amended the Civil Rights act to include discrimination against a woman because of a pregnancy-related condition

■ the Age Discrimination in Employment Act of 1967, which forbids discrimination based on an employee's age

■ the Americans with Disabilities Act of 1990, which states that "no individual shall be discriminated against on the basis of disability in the full and equal enjoyment of the goods, services, facilities, privileges, advantages, or accommodations of any place of public accommodation...."

■ the Genetic Information Nondiscrimination Act of 2008, which makes it illegal for an employer to use genetic information such as the results of genetic tests in making hiring or other employment decisions.

The EEOC will also prosecute disputes involving sexual harassment. Employees don't have to be union members to file a complaint with the EEOC.

DISCIPLINARY PROCEEDINGS BY A BOARD OF NURSING

A complaint against your nursing license can be initiated by an employer, coworker, patient, their family, and so on. While most complaints are resolved informally after investigation by the Board, a disciplinary hearing may be needed. The hearing may be based on allegations of incompetence or alleged violation of the Nurse Practice Act of that state pertaining to nursing practice.

If you're ever served with notice that a state's licensing board is investigating you, seek legal counsel, plus emotional and professional support. Don't ignore the notice or approach these proceedings lightly or unprepared. The disciplinary process and the outcome can have a major impact on how you view yourself, how you practice nursing, and how you view your profession.

During the process do your homework, be aware of recent state laws, muster witnesses and evidence, and be prepared to stand up for your rights and your nursing license. If in fact you have violated the Board's Nurse Practice Act, be prepared to be honest and work with the Board to resolve the matter in everyone's best interests. Remember that the Board exists to protect the public, not the nurse. Learn everything you can from the experience. Finally, be prepared to support your colleagues who may also go through a disciplinary hearing.

SELECTED REFERENCES

American Nurses Association. 2002 Legislation: Whistleblower Protection. Retrieved from: www.nursingworld.org/gova/state/2002/whistle.htm, December 2002.

American Nurses Association. *Code of Ethics for Nurses with Interpretive Statements.* Washington, DC: American Nurses Publishing, 2001.

Burke, M.R. "Demystifying Common Terms in Employment Agreements," *Family Practitioner Management* 10(6):38–40, June 2003.

Crooks, L., and Rathbone, L. "Should Nurses Ever Strike?" *Nursing Times* 98(50):18–19, December 2002.

Forman, H., and Grimes, T.C. "Living with a Union Contract," *Journal of Nursing Administration* 32(12):611–614, December 2002.

Forman, H., and Kraus, H.R. "Decertification: Management's Role When Employees Rethink Unionization," *Journal of Nursing Administration* 33(6):313–316, June 2003.

Forman, H., and Merrick, F. "Grievances and Complaints: Valuable Tools for Management and for Staff," *Journal of Nursing Administration* 33(3):136–138, March 2003.

Gamroth, L., et al. "The Undergraduate Nurse Employment Project," *Canadian Nurse* 99(4):32–36, April 2003.

Haiven, L., and Haiven J. *The Right to Strike and the Provision of Emergency Services in Canadian Health Care.* Ottawa: Canadian Centre for Policy Alternatives, 2002. Retrieved from: www.policyalternatives.ca/publications/right-to-strike.pdf

Heitlinger, A. "The Paradoxical Impact of Health Care Restructuring in Canada on Nursing as a Profession," *International Journal of Health Services* 33(1):37–54, 2003.

Muhl, C.J. "The Employment-at-will Doctrine: Three Major Exceptions," *Monthly Labor Review* 124(1):3–11, January 2001.

Zimmerman, P.G. "Organizing in the Face of Increasing Demands on Nursing," *Journal of Emergency Nursing* 26(4):294–295, August 2000.

INTERNET RESOURCES

Congressional Research Services: www.loc.gov/crsinfo

National Nurses United: www.nationalnursesunited.org

U.S. Equal Employment Opportunity Commission: www.eeoc.gov

U.S. National Labor Relations Board: www.nlrb.gov

10

Ethical decision making

Frances W. Sills, MSN, APN, CLNC, RN

"Even the most rational approach to ethics is defenseless if there isn't the will to do what is right."

–Alexander Solzhenitsyn

Today's health care, with the scientific and technological advances, economic realities, and global communication, has brought to the forefront the many ethical issues that we face in the world community, our everyday lives, and our various work settings. More and more controversial and sensitive ethical issues continue to challenge all health care professionals, particularly nurses. It is no longer practical to look at ethics based on our personal opinions and beliefs, intuition (based on experience), and various definitions of ethics.

Overview of ethics, morals, and the law

Ethics is defined as a systematic approach to understanding, analyzing, and distinguishing matters of right and wrong, good and bad, and admirable and deplorable as they relate to the well-being of and the relationships among sentient beings. Ethical determinations are applied through the use of formal theories, approaches, and codes of conduct, such as codes that are developed for professions and religions (Butts et al., 2013). The ANA Code of Ethics for Nurses: Interpretation and Application is the guide that is used by the nursing profession as it gives a voice to who we are as nurses at our very core. This reflects our fundamental values and ideals as individual nurses and a member of a professional group (ANA Code of Ethics for Nurses with Interpretive Statements, 2015).

Morals are specific beliefs, behaviors, and ways of being derived from doing ethics. Morals are judged to be good or bad through systematic ethical analysis (Butts et al., 2013). Immorality, the reverse of morality, is when a person's behavior is in opposition to accepted societal, religious, cultural, or professional standards and principles. It is important to realize that when considering matters of ethics, one is looking at the freedom one has regarding personal choices, one's obligations to other individuals, and/or judgments about human behavior.

Billington (2003) delineated important features regarding the concepts of morals and ethics:

■ Probably the most important feature about ethics and morals is that no one can avoid making moral or ethical decisions because the social connection with others necessitates that people must consider moral and ethical actions

■ Moral decisions matter because every decision affects someone else's life, self-esteem, or happiness level

■ In the area of morals and ethics, people cannot exercise moral judgment without being given a choice; in other words, to make a sound moral judgment it is necessary to be able to choose from among a number of choices.

The *legal system* is founded on rules and regulations that guide society in a formal and binding way. It is mostly defined as a system of principles and processes by which people in a society deal with their disputes and problems, seeking to solve or settle them without resorting to force. Laws are general rules of conduct that are enforced by government, which imposes penalties when the law is violated (Pozgar, 2013).

Relationship between ethics and the law

The relationship between ethics and the law is one in which the issues become so intertwined that it becomes difficult to separate the two. The goal of both is similar, except for the fact that there is no system of enforcement for ethical guidelines. In health care, law and ethics overlap in many areas. In each interaction with a patient, there is the opportunity for an ethical and/or legal situation to occur. Legal and ethical issues assist nurses in decision making and in providing compassionate, competent, quality nursing care. Anyone can make a mistake at any given time; however, nurses who have a thorough understanding of the Code of Ethics for Nurses (ANA, 2015), who follow that code, and stay within The Scope and Standards of Practice for Nursing (ANA, 2010) and the Nurse Practice Act of their state are much less likely to find themselves named in a lawsuit.

Ethical theories

Ethics seeks to understand and determine how human actions can be judged right or wrong. Ethical judgments can be made on the basis of our own experiences or on the basis of the nature or principles of reason. Ethical theories and principles introduce order into the way people think about life. They are the foundations of ethical analysis and provide guidance in the decision-making process. Ethical theories help caregivers to predict the outcome of alternative choices, when following their duties to others, in order to reach an ethically correct decision (Pozgar, 2013).

Normative ethics is an attempt to determine values, behaviors, and ways of being that are right or wrong, good or bad. In using normative ethics as a method of inquiry, one asks how humans should behave, what ought to be done in certain situations, and what type of character one should have. The outcomes of using the method of normative ethics are accepted moral standards and codes such as common morality. It consists of normative beliefs and behaviors that members of society generally agree about and that are familiar to most individuals. It also provides society with a framework of ethical stability. One of the central questions of modern normative ethics is whether human actions are to be judged right or wrong solely according to their consequences.

There are particular moralities that are adhered to by specific groups and can be distinguished from the common morality.

The Code of Ethics for Nurses with Interpretive Statements (American Nurses Association, 2015) is a specific morality for professional nurses in the United States. Nurses have specific obligations toward recipients of their care that are different from the obligations of other people. As risks and dangers for nurses become more complex, the profession's morality must evolve and be continually reexamined (Butts et al., 2013).

Descriptive ethics is often referred to as a scientific rather than a philosophical ethical inquiry. It is the approach used when individuals want to describe what people think about morality or when they want to describe how people actually behave... that is what people believe to be right and wrong. An example of descriptive ethics is research that identifies nurses' attitudes regarding death with dignity.

Applied ethics is the application of normative theories to practical moral problems. It attempts to explain and justify specific moral problems such as abortion, euthanasia, and assisted suicide.

Consequential ethics emphasizes that the morally right action is whatever action leads to the maximum balance of good over evil. It revolves around the premise that the rightness or wrongness of an action depends on the consequences or effects of an action. It is based on the view that the value of an action derives solely from the value

of its consequences. The goal of a consequentialist is to achieve the greatest good for the greatest number. It involves asking such questions as:

- What will be the effects of each course of action?
- Who will benefit?
- What will do the least harm?

Utilitarian ethics is an approach to ethics that involves the concept that the moral worth of an action is determined solely by its contribution to overall usefulness. It is doing the most good for the most people. As a form of consequential ethics, its meaning is that the moral worth of an action is determined by its outcome, and that the ends justify the means.

Deontological ethics focuses on one's duties to others and others' rights. It includes telling the truth and keeping your promises. It is often referred to as duty-based ethics. It involves ethical analysis according to a moral code or rules, religious or secular. It differs from consequentialism in that consequences are not the determinant of what is right, so doing what is right may not always lead to an increase in what is good.

Nonconsequential ethics denies that the consequences of an action or rule are the only criteria for determining the morality of an action or rule. The rightness or wrongness of an action is based on properties intrinsic to the action, not on its consequences. Applying this theory to health care decision making, each situation will probably have a different fact pattern, which will result in moral decisions being made on a case-by-case basis. Values that are held ever so strongly in one situation may conflict with the same values given a different set of facts.

Bioethics was born out of the rapidly expanding technical environment of the 1900s. It is a specific domain of ethics that is focused on moral issues in the field of health care. Patients who would not have survived did so because of the new technology. These advances brought increased responsibility and distress among health care professionals, who were faced with the question of how to allocate newly developed, scarce medical resources. Eventually, health care policies and laws were enacted to address the questions "Who lives?" "Who dies?" and "Who makes the decision?"

Principles of health care ethics

Ethical principles are universal rules of conduct derived from ethical theories that provide a practical basis for identifying what kinds of actions, intentions, and motives are valued. They assist the caregivers in making choices based on moral principles that have been identified as standards considered worthwhile in addressing health care–related ethical dilemmas. They provide a framework where particular dilemmas can be analyzed and decisions made.

One will find, however, that difficult decisions often involve choices between conflicting ethical principles. When shocking information regarding serious ethical lapses began to surface, societies around the world became very conscious of the ethical dangers in conducting biomedical and behavioral research. In the United States, a commission was created to outline the underlying principles that must be supported during research involving human subjects (National Institutes of Health, 1979).

In 1978, the commission released its report, called the Belmont Report. The report outlined three basic principles for research on all human subjects:

respect for persons, beneficence, and justice (National Institutes of Health, 1979). In 1979, as an outcome of the Belmont Report, T.L. Beauchamp, an American philosopher specializing in moral philosophy and bioethics, and J.F. Childress, a philosopher and theologian whose main concern was biomedical ethics, published the first edition of their book, *Principles of Biomedical Ethics*, which described four bioethical principles: beneficence, nonmaleficence, autonomy, and justice.

The approach of ethical principlism using the four principles outlined by Beauchamp and Childress (2009) has become one of the most popular tools used today for decision making in resolving bioethical problems.

Beneficence describes the principle of doing good, being kind, showing compassion, and helping others. Health care workers demonstrate beneficence by providing benefits and balancing the benefits against risks. This principle requires one to do good, which requires knowledge of the beliefs, culture, values, and preferences of the patient. It is important to remember that what one person may believe to be good for a patient may in reality be harmful.

For example, you may decide to tell a patient honestly that "there is nothing more I can offer you in terms of treatment for your illness" when in fact what the patient really wants is encouragement and information about care options. A compassionate response would have been, "I am not aware of any new treatments for your illness, but I can help treat your symptoms and make you more comfortable while I continue to look for any significant research that may be helpful in treating your disease process."

Paternalism is a form of beneficence. It occurs when individuals and/or institutions, for example, political, military, organizational, religious, believe they know what is best for others, and so will make decisions for others.

Medical paternalism involves making choices for a patient by withholding medical information, preventing the patient from making a true informed decision. In situations of an individual's age, cognitive ability, or level of dependency, the decision made by the physician(s) and/or a legal *Living Will Directive* is justified. The problem that arises with paternalism involves a conflict between principles of beneficence and autonomy, each of which is conceived by different individuals as the overriding principle in case of conflict. Conflict between demands of beneficence and autonomy underlies a broad range of controversies.

Nonmaleficence—this principle requires health care providers to avoid causing patients harm. It is not concerned with improving others' well-being but with avoiding the infliction of harm. Medical ethics require every health care provider to ensure that he or she "first does no harm." This principle is broken when a physician faces the decision to end a life by removing respirators, giving lethal injections, or writing prescriptions for lethal doses of medication. Assisting patients to die violates many of the health care provider's duty to save lives. In the final analysis, the answer lies in finding an answer to the questions "what is the difference between killing patients and letting them die," "what is more important—the quality of life or the quantity of life." The principle of autonomy enters into the equation as health care providers struggle with the dilemma.

Autonomy—"No right is held more sacred, or is more carefully guarded, by the common law, than the right of every individual to the possession and control of his own person." (*Union*

Pacific Ry. Co, v. Botsford [141 U.S. 250,251 (1891)]). This definition of autonomy was stated in the above law case that dealt with the body of law known as right-to-die cases.

The principle of autonomy recognizes the right of a person to make one's own decisions. It simply means that an individual has the right to make his or her own decisions about what is best for him or herself. It is not an absolute principle as the autonomous actions of one individual must not infringe upon the rights of another.

This principle has been recognized in the Fourteen Amendment to the Constitution of the United States. The law upholds an individual's right to make his or her own decisions about health care. Patients have the right to refuse health care treatment, medications, blood or blood products, and invasive procedures even if the benefits may save their lives. They have the right to have their decisions followed by family members who disagree with the treatment plan or simply are unable to "let go." The caregiver must respect the mentally competent decision-making abilities of the individual to make his or her own decisions. The eminent Justice Cardozo, in *Schloendorff v. Society of New York Hospital,* stated:

> Every human being of adult years and sound mind has a right to determine what shall be done with his own body and a surgeon who performs an operation without his patient's consent commits an assault, for which he is liable in damages, except in cases of emergency where the patient is unconscious and where it is necessary to operate before consent can be obtained. [102 N.E. 92, 93 (N.Y. 1914)].

Justice—as a principle in health care ethics, it considers fairness, treating individuals equally and without prejudice. It is the obligation to be fair in the distribution of benefits and risks. Justice looks at how individuals are treated when their interests, wants, or needs compete with one another. Many ethical issues are involved in the day-by-day delivery of health care. There are several reasons for this, including limited or scarce resources as a result of remote geographic areas, the patient's inability to pay for services combined with health care providers who are unwilling to accept patients who are perceived as "no pays" with high risks for legal suits. Difficult health care resource allocation decisions are based on attempts to answer questions such as who has a right to health care, how much health care a person is entitled to, who is going to pay for health care, and how much responsibility an individual has regarding his or her own health. It is important to remember that justice is a broad concept in the field of ethics and is considered to be both a principle and a virtue.

In 1984, Kitchener identified a fifth moral principle that has been included in many of the ethical decision-making models.

Fidelity involves the notions of loyalty, faithfulness, and honoring of commitments. Patients and families must be able to trust and have faith in the therapeutic relationship between the physician, nurse, and other members of the health care team. It is important that the treating team takes care to see that the trust relationship is not threatened or the obligation is not left unfulfilled.

Ethical dilemmas

An ethical dilemma is a situation in which an individual is compelled to choose between two actions that will affect the welfare of an individual. Health care providers are constantly faced with complex ethical dilemmas in the delivery of patient care. One action must be chosen that creates a quandary for the group or person that has to make that choice. Kidder (1995) focused on one characteristic of an ethical dilemma when he described the heart of an ethical dilemma as "the ethics of right versus right." He proposed that individuals generally can judge wrong choices that are based on three criteria:

- Violation of the law
- Departure from the truth
- Deviation from moral integrity.

When faced with an ethical dilemma, it is important to reexamine the situation and see how each of the principles relates to that particular case. There will be times when this process will clarify the issues in the situation to the extent that the means for resolving the situation will become obvious. However, in more complicated cases, it becomes necessary to work through steps of an ethical, decision-making model, which will assist in clarifying which of the ethical/moral principles may be in conflict. There are several different models that can be used.

As a result of this, professional codes of ethics have been developed to provide guidance to those faced with ethical dilemmas. Health care professionals are governed by ethical codes that demand a high level of integrity, honesty, and responsibility. It is the direct caregiver who is confronted with complex ethical dilemmas in the delivery of patient care, and the Code of Ethics for each health care professional provides guidance for those faced with ethical dilemmas.

Ethics committees

Ethics committees first emerged in the 1960s in the United States as health care was experiencing rapid scientific and technological growth. They address legal-ethical issues that arise during the course of a patient's care and treatment. They serve as a resource for families, patients, and staff, and provide both educational and consultative services, but do not replace the important patient/family–physician/nurse relationship. To date, ethics committees do not have sole surrogate decision-making authority; however, they play an ever-expanding role in the development of policy and procedural guidelines to assist in resolving ethical dilemmas (Pozgar, 2012). The goals of the committee are to:

1. Promote the rights of the patient

2. Promote shared decision making between patients, families, and their clinicians

3. Assist the patient and family in coming to a consensus regarding the options that best meet the patient's goal for care

4. Promote fair policies and procedures that maximize the likelihood of achieving good, patient-centered outcomes.

The ethics committee should include a wide range of multidisciplinary health care professionals, which should include, but not be limited to, ethicists, clergy, physicians, nurses, educators, legal advisors, and a quality improvement manager. The emerging trend is that the committee should be structured to include a large range of community leaders in positions of respect and diversity. Too often the ethics committees are comprised of mostly hospital employees and members of the medical staff with one or two representatives from the community.

The functions of the committee are multifaceted and include development of policy and procedure guidelines that will assist in resolving ethical dilemmas that are presented to the committee. Other functions include:

■ Staff and community education
■ Conflict resolution
■ Case review
■ Consultation and support

It is important to remember that the ethics committee is not a decision maker but a resource that can provide advice and guidance in making a decision when there is really no right or wrong choice.

In the case of *Woods v. Commonwealth*, the Kentucky Supreme Court ruled that Kentucky's Living Will Directive, allowing a court-appointed guardian or other designated surrogate to remove a patient's life support system, was constitutional. The patient in this case had suffered a heart attack and was placed on a ventilator. He never regained consciousness, and it was generally agreed that he would die in 2–10 years. Following a recommendation from the ethics committee, the patient's guardian asked for approval to remove the life support. The court affirmed an appeals court decision and in their holdings in the case stated, "Life support will be prohibited, when there is clear and convincing evidence that the patient is permanently unconscious or in a persistent vegetative state and removal of life support is in the patient's best interest" (Pozgar, 2012).

ETHICAL DECISION-MAKING MODELS

As healthcare becomes more complex, ethical dilemmas are not always easily resolved through the use of the various codes of ethics. Ethics committees evolved a framework in which the issues could be reviewed and analyzed, and a decision or a recommendation could be made. There are several different ethical frameworks.

One of the models most frequently used in health care by the ethics committees is "The Four Topics Method," sometimes called the Four Box Approach, which was first published in 1982 in the book *Clinical Ethics: A Practical Approach to Ethical Decisions in Clinical Medicine*, now in its seventh edition (Butts et al. 2013).

This is a case-based approach that allows the health care professionals to look at the facts of the case in a structured manner that promotes critical thinking about the ethical problems. Individual cases are reviewed according to four topics. Members of the ethics committee gather information in an attempt to answer the questions contained in the four boxes. This model facilitates dialogue between the patient-family/surrogate and members of the health care team. In this way the health care providers are able to examine and evaluate the full scope of the patient's condition and the ethical dilemma they are facing.

a. MEDICAL INDICATIONS examines the principles of Beneficence and Nonmaleficence and asks such questions as: What is the patient's medical problem? What are the goals of the treatment? What are the probabilities of success with various options?

b. QUALITY OF LIFE examines the principles of Beneficence, Nonmaleficence, and Respect for Autonomy, and asks such questions as: What are the prospects, with or without treatment, for a return to normal life, and what physical, mental, and social deficits might the patient experience even if the treatment succeeds?

c. PATIENT PREFERENCES examines the principle of Respect for Autonomy and asks such questions as: Has the patient been informed of the benefits and risks, has he or she understood this information, and given consent?

d. CONTEXTUAL FEATURES examines the principles of Justice and Fairness and asks such questions as: Are there professional, interprofessional, or business interests that might create conflicts of interest in the clinical treatment of the patient? Are there religious or legal issues that might affect the clinical decision?

Two other model frameworks that are well worth reviewing are:

1. McDonald, Michael with additions by Rodney, Paddy and Rosalie Starzomski, School of Nursing, University of Victoria. A Framework for Ethical Decision-Making: Version 6.0, Ethics Shareware. The W. Maurice Young Centre for Applied Ethics, University of British Columbia, January 2001. Retrieved from: http://www.ryerson.ca/content/dam/ethics network/downloads/model_D.pdf)

This framework contains five major categories with subcategories that can also be used as a guide. Although it takes more time, it does have additional elements that may assist the committee in making a decision or recommendation.

2. Guo, L.K. "Decide: A Decision-Making Model for More Effective Decision Making by Health Care Managers," *The Health Care Manager* 27(2):118–127, April/June, 2008. http://www.ncbi.nlm.nih.gov/pubmed/18475113

This article describes a step-by-step process for decision making and a model that has been developed to aid health care managers in making more quality decisions, which ultimately determines the success of organizations. It presents a model that consists of six particular activities needed in the decision-making process.

CRITICAL THINKING AND ETHICAL DECISION MAKING

Day by day, minute by minute, ethical and moral issues arise, and we often make decisions without a conscious awareness of a process, but we have an innate sense of knowing what to do in the situation. It is fundamentally important that nurses and other members of the health care team have the systematic and investigative skills to respond to the many everyday decisions that must be made. Communication is probably one of the most important abilities that we possess. One of the most important components of communication is that of listening attentively to other individuals, and not making hasty conclusions. Our personal values and competencies, ethical principles, and knowledge of our professional code of ethics are variables that must be considered. The questions "What is the right thing to do?" "What ought I to do?" or "Whom do I go to for direction?" are ever present as we go about our work in the various settings of health care. In ethics, there are no easy answers, and often one cannot find any definable answer. Nurses using their critical thinking skills, ethical principles, and ethical issues that they have encountered will have more confidence in working through the decision-making process when confronted with difficult situations. "Be aware of how everyday life is full of ethical decisions and that the numerous ethical issues can arise when caring for patients." (Pozgar, 2012)

Ethical decision making is really the process of deciding the right thing to do when faced with a moral dilemma. It is not an easy task when there is more than one way of looking at the issue. Health care dilemmas occur when there are alternative choices, limited resources, and different values among the patient, family members, and the health care team. Consensus building happens only when the individuals involved can come to an agreement, and this requires a clear willingness to listen, learn, share your individual views and concerns, and eventually make a decision.

The following case study using the Four Topic Method will demonstrate the methodology.

CASE STUDY

D.C., age 25, is severely burned in a propane gas explosion. Upon arrival at the hospital, he was found to have severe burns over 65% of his body, his hand and face suffered 3% burns, and his eyes were severely damaged. After the initial period during which his survival was in doubt, he stabilized and underwent amputation of several fingers and removal of his right eye. During much of the 232 hospitalization days he spent in the intensive care unit, followed by a few weeks in a rehab facility, and then another 6 months in an acute care facility, he repeatedly insisted that the treatments be discontinued and he be allowed to die. Despite his demands, wound care was continued, skin grafts were performed, and nutrition and fluid support were provided. He was discharged totally blind, with minimal use of his hands, badly scarred, and dependent on others to assist in personal functions.

The discussion of the case begins with an orderly review under the four topics.

MEDICAL INDICATION

D.C.'s medical indications included the clinical facts necessary to diagnose the extent and seriousness of burns; make a prognosis for survival or restoration of function; and options for treatment including risk, benefits, and probable outcomes of each treatment modality. Note: After emergency treatment, D.C.'s prognosis for survival was approximately 20%. After months of intensive care, his prognosis was 100%, barring no complications.

PATIENT PREFERENCE (AUTONOMY)

In all medical treatment, the preferences of the patient, based on the patient's own values and personal assessment of benefits and burdens, are ethically relevant. In the early days of D.C.'s refusal of care, it was assumed that he lacked the capacity to make his own decisions. His mother's consent for treatment was accepted. During the last hospitalization, a psychiatric consult was requested, which affirmed his capacity to make decisions. The implications of his desire to refuse further care became central.

QUALITY OF LIFE

In all medical situations, the topic of quality of life must be considered. This topic is not well discussed in the literature because it is perilous as it opens the door for bias and prejudice. However, it must be considered in the analysis of clinical ethical problems.

Prior to the accident, D.C. was a popular, athletic young man, just discharged from the Air Force, after having served as a fighter pilot in Vietnam. Before the accident, his quality of life was excellent. After the accident, even with the best of care, he was confronted with significant physical deficits, including notable disfigurement, blindness, and limitation of activity. At some stage in his illness, he had the capacity to determine what quality of life he wished for himself. The meaning and importance of such considerations must be clarified in any clinical ethical analysis.

CONTEXTUAL FEATURES

Every medical case is embedded in a larger context of persons, institutions, and financial and social arrangements. Patient care is influenced, positively or negatively, by the possibilities and the constraints of that context. At the same time, the context itself is affected by the decisions made by or about the patient. These decisions have a psychological, emotional, financial, legal, educational, and religious impact on others. The relevance of the contextual features must be determined and assessed. They may be crucially important to the understanding and resolution of the case. In D.C.'s case, several of the contextual features were significant.

His mother was opposed to termination of medical care for religious reasons. The legal implications of honoring his demand were unclear at the time (they are much clearer today). The distress felt by the medical and nursing personnel by his refusal to cooperate with treatment could influence their attitudes toward him. These and other contextual factors must be made explicit and assessed for their relevance.

The four topics that make up the Four Topic Method are relevant to any clinical case. They serve as a useful organizing tool for teaching and discussion. What is more important is how a review of these topics can help to move a discussion of an ethical problem toward a resolution. The discussion of each topic raises certain common ethical or moral principles. These principles are best appreciated in the specific context of the actual circumstances of a case. The key issue in D.C.'s case is the patient's autonomy. The significance of autonomy in his case is derived not simply from the principle of autonomy, but from the confluence of considerations about preferences, medical indications, quality of life, and role of the mother, the treatment team, lawyers, and the hospital. When all of these are evaluated in relation to each other, the meaning of the principle of autonomy will be appreciated in this case.

Every ethical problem is a complex collection of facts. Good ethical judgment consists in appreciating how several of the ethical principles should be evaluated in the actual situation under consideration. The case study approach will assist nurses to understand the complexity of ethical decision making and be a valuable member of the ethics committee.

SELECTED REFERENCES

Aiken, T.D., and Catalano, J.T. *Legal, Ethical, and Political Issues in Nursing*. Philadelphia, PA: F.A. Davis Company, 1994.

ANA Code of Ethics with Interpretive Statements, January 2015. http://www.nursingworld.org/MainMenuCategories/EthicsStandards/CodeofEthicsforNurses/Code-of-Ethics-For-Nurses.html

ANA Nursing: Scope and Standards of Practice, 2010. http://www.nursesbooks.org/ebooks/download/NursingScope-Standards.pdf

Billington, R., *Living Philosophy: An Introduction to Moral Thought*. New York: Routledge, 2003.

Butts, J.B., and Rich, K.L. *Nursing Ethics Across the Curriculum and into Practice*, 3rd ed. Jones and Bartlett Learning: Sudbury, MA, 2013.

Davis, M. "Developing and Using Cases to Teach Practical Ethics", *Teaching Philosophy*, Volume 20, December 1997, pp. 353–385.

Fowler, M. (ed). ANA, Guide to the Code of Ethics for Nurses, Interpretation and Application, 2008. Retrieved from: Nursesbooks.org.

Gray, B. H., Cooke, R.A., and Tannenbaum, A.S. "Research Involving Human Subjects". *Science* 1978 Sept 22, 201 (4361); 1094–101.

Guido, G.W. *Legal Issues in Nursing*, 2nd ed. Stamford, CT: Appleton & Lange, 1988.

Guo, L.K. "Decide: A Decision-Making Model for More Effective Decision Making by Health Care Managers," *The Health Care Manager* 27(2):118–127, April/June, 2008. Retrieved from: http://www.nursing center.com/lnc/static%3Fpageid%3 D800371

Jonsen, A.R., Sergler, M., and Winslade, W. *Clinical Ethics: A Practical Approach to Ethical Decisions in Clinical Medicine*, 7th ed. New York, NY: McGraw-Hill, 2010.

Kidder, R. (1995). *How good people make tough choices: Resolving the dilemmas of ethical living*. New York, NY: Fireside Publications.

McDonald, Michael with additions by Rodney, Paddy and Rosalie Starzomski, School of Nursing, University of Victoria. A Framework for Ethical Decision-Making: Version 6.0, Ethics Shareware. The W. Maurice Young Centre for Applied Ethics, University of British Columbia, January 2001. Retrieved from: http://www.ryerson.ca/content/dam/ethics network/downloads/model_D.pdf

Pozgar, G.D. *Legal Aspects of Health Care Administration,* 11th ed. Sudbury, MA: Jones & Bartlett, 2012.

Pozgar, G.D. *Legal and Ethical Issues for Health Professionals*, 3rd ed. Sudbury, MA: Jones and Bartlett Learning, 2013.

Stanford, C.C., and Connor, V.J. *Ethics for Health Professionals*. Sudbury, MA: Jones and Bartlett, 2014.

Edith Brous, RN, BSN, MS, MPH, JD

"The first step in the evolution of ethics is a sense of solidarity with other human beings."

–Albert Schweitzer

Introduction

Nurses make ethical choices every day and may be unaware of the decision-making process that underlies those choices. To understand that process, it is necessary to review basic concepts in the study of ethics. In health care, nurses are exposed to conflicts around many issues such as the beginning and end of life, the use of technology, patient management, and allocation of finite resources. All of these arenas involve human suffering. All of these arenas involve painful decision making. And all of these arenas require nurses to evaluate their own values and beliefs.

ETHICS

Ethics is a branch of philosophy that asks what course of action should be taken. Unlike the study of science, there are no absolutes in patient-care decision making. There are always "what if" questions. Different cultures hold different views as to what is and is not an acceptable act. Different time periods view human conduct

differently. What was acceptable in the past might not be acceptable today. What is acceptable today might not be acceptable tomorrow. While the underlying values can remain constant, our interpretation of those values evolves.

The study of ethics is not the study of law. One can violate legal mandates while behaving ethically. Slavery was legal, but no one today would argue that it was an ethical institution. There is, however, a great deal of overlap between ethics and the law, and this chapter will discuss legal cases in which ethical issues were at the heart of the dispute.

The study of ethics is also not the study of religion. One can behave ethically in the absence of religious conviction. Conversely, one can have deeply held religious convictions yet behave in ways that are considered unethical. Personal morality is determined by both religious and secular interpretations.

Ethical study is fundamentally an investigation into the principles of right and wrong. It is an analysis of character and the process we use in asking the question "What should I do?"

NURSING AND ETHICS

Nurses are individuals. They are also employees of organizations, members of groups, societies, and cultures, and representatives of a profession. As an individual, decisions of right and wrong are made on a basis of personal values. As an employee, decisions and actions are made within a setting of organizational missions and policies. As a member of groups, societies, and cultures, decisions and actions are made in a context of commonly held norms. And as a representative of a profession, decisions and actions are made within acceptable standards and guiding principles of the nursing profession.

Health care is a field that applies a particular code of ethics referred to as *medical ethics* or *bioethics*. Bioethics addresses the medical issues of patients and the conduct of providers. The basic principles of bioethics encompass four main concepts:

Autonomy involves patient independence in health care decision making. Providers are expected to provide adequate information for patients to make informed choices and to refrain from coercing, misleading, or making decisions for them. A nurse might think one course of action is better than another, but cannot withhold or selectively provide information to persuade a patient to make that choice.

Justice involves issues of resource distribution. Which one of the three critically ill patients in the emergency

ANA code of ethics for nurses

1. The nurse, in all professional relationships, practices with compassion and respect for the inherent dignity, worth, and uniqueness of every individual, unrestricted by considerations of social or economic status, personal attributes, or the nature of health problems.

2. The nurse's primary commitment is to the patient, whether an individual, family, group, or community.

3. The nurse promotes, advocates for, and strives to protect the health, safety, and rights of the patient.

4. The nurse is responsible and accountable for individual nursing practice and determines the appropriate delegation of tasks consistent with the nurse's obligation to provide optimum patient care.

5. The nurse owes the same duties to self as to others, including the responsibility to preserve integrity and safety, to maintain competence, and to continue personal and professional growth.

6. The nurse participates in establishing, maintaining, and improving health care environments and conditions of employment conducive to the provision of quality health care and consistent with the values of the profession through individual and collective action.

7. The nurse participates in the advancement of the profession through contributions to practice, education, administration, and knowledge development.

8. The nurse collaborates with other health professionals and the public in promoting community, national, and international efforts to meet health needs.

9. The profession of nursing, as represented by associations and their members, is responsible for articulating nursing values, for maintaining the integrity of the profession and its practice, and for shaping social policy.

room gets the one available Intensive Care Unit bed?

Beneficence requires providers to take actions with the intent to do good for the patient. The nurse-patient relationship is for the sole benefit of the patient. The American Nurses Association (ANA) states that "[t]he nurse's primary commitment is to the patient, whether an individual, family, group, or community" [see ANA Code of Ethics for Nurses with Interpretive Statements (ANA, 2015)].

Nonmaleficence is the maxim that providers do no harm. Because many therapeutic or diagnostic procedures can result in complications or cause discomfort, the decision to engage in those procedures must be made with adequate analysis of risks, benefits, or alternatives. (Refer to select terms in ethics).

These four principles may be in conflict with each other. For example, it is in a postoperative patient's best interest (beneficence) to perform pulmonary toilet procedures. Doing so can prevent respiratory complications such as pneumonia. Coughing, deep breathing, incentive spirometry, chest physiotherapy, and suctioning, however, can cause incisional pain and discomfort, violating the principle of doing no harm (nonmaleficence). In this case, the nurse would be doing harm to avoid a greater harm.

MORAL DISTRESS

In some cases, personal ethics may conflict with organizational or professional values. Nurses can differ with their employer's view or with the profession's standards. They might be under-resourced and unable to fulfill their own or the institution's mission. They might be expected or required to act in a manner that violates their own values. Such conditions can lead to a condition identified as *moral distress*.

The American Association of Critical Nurses has noted with concern that "Moral distress is a serious problem in nursing which contributes to nurses feeling a loss of integrity and dissatisfaction with their work environment. Studies demonstrate that moral distress is a major contributor to nurses leaving the work setting and profession" (AACN, 2014).

Although most discussions of ethical issues focus on situational dilemmas, any analysis of those ethical issues must include a discussion of moral distress. As the ANA notes:

…[M]oral distress occurs when the internal environment of nurses—their values and perceived obligations—are incompatible with the needs and prevailing views of the external work environment. Traditional ethics education that focuses on ethical dilemmas and underlying principles is inadequate to address situations involving moral distress. Values clarification, communication skills, and an understanding of the system in which healthcare is delivered are the tools necessary to address conflicts between the internal and external environments (Epstein et al., 2010).

The areas of practice that are most often associated with moral distress involve the concepts of autonomy, justice, beneficence, and nonmaleficence. They have been identified as:

■ Continued life support even though it is not in the best interest of the patient; (beneficence/nonmaleficence)
■ Inadequate communication about end-of-life care between providers and patients and families; (autonomy)
■ Inappropriate use of health care resources; (justice)
■ Inadequate staffing or staff who are not adequately trained to provide the required care; (nonmaleficence)

(Text continues on page 324.)

Select terms in ethics

Autonomy: (auto/self + nomos/custom, law = independence) The principle of respect for persons and of individual self-determination. The American Nurses Association (ANA) defines autonomy as the agreement to respect another's right to self-determine a course of action and the support of independent decision making.

Beneficence: (bene/well + facio/to do, act = to do well) The principle that one should help others further their important and legitimate interests, either as those persons understand them (respecting autonomy) or as we conceive them (paternalism). The ANA defines beneficence as compassion, taking positive action to help others, the desire to do good, and the core principle of our patient advocacy.

Deontology: (deon/duty + ology/study = the science of duty) The theory that the morality of an action is determined by adherence to rules and duties, regardless of the consequences of following those rules or duties. The ANA identifies deontology as the theory that the ethics of an action are determined by the intentions behind the decisions rather than the outcomes that result from them.

Nonmaleficence: (non + mal/evil, wrong, bad + facio/to do, act = non-evildoing) Defined by the ANA as the avoidance of harm or hurt and the core of medical oath and nursing ethics. (Do no harm.)

Paternalism: (pater/father + ism/doctrine, action, condition = acting as a parent) The view that that it is justifiable to restrict a person's liberty to prevent self-harm, or to promote that person's own well-being. Paternalism is the practice of a person in authority restricting the freedom of subordinates in the belief that doing so is in the subordinate's best interest. The ANA identifies paternalism as an application of power over the patient based upon the health care professional's belief about what is in the best interest of the patient.

Relativism: (relativus, from relates- referre/carry back, ascribe + ism/doctrine, action, condition) The ANA defines ethical relativism as a theory holding that morality is relative to the norms of one's culture. Truth and moral values are not absolute but are relative to the persons or groups holding them. There are no absolute truths in ethics. What is morally right or wrong varies from person to person or from society to society. Culture and society influence whether an act is considered ethical, and what is right for one group may not be right for another. There is no universal truth, and decisions must be evaluated in a context.

Utilitarianism: (utilis/useful + + ism/doctrine, action, condition = acting in a useful manner) Reasoning in terms of means and ends such that the value of conduct is determined by the usefulness of its outcome to the most people. The ANA defines utilitarianism as a theory supporting what is best for most people–the value of the act is determined by its usefulness, with the main emphasis on the outcome or consequences. The theory examines what creates the most happiness for the most people.

Sources: American Nurses Association. Short Definitions of Ethical Principles and Theories Familiar words, what do they mean?, 2011. Retrieved from: http://www.nursingworld.org/mainmenucategories/ethicsstandards/resources/ethics-definitions.pdf

Cushman, R. Ethics Terms and Terminology, 2005. Retrieved from: http://www.lasalle.edu/~price/Hon%20365%20ethics%20terms.htm

Memidex. Online Dictionary & Thesaurus, 2013. Retrieved from: http://www.memidex.com/

■ Inadequate pain relief provided to patients; (beneficence/nonmaleficence) and

■ False hope given to patients and families (autonomy/nonmaleficence) (Epstein et al., 2010).

Nurses are generally aware of their duty to patients but might not be as mindful of the duties they owe to themselves. Provision five of the American Nurses Association Code of Ethics states, "[t]he nurse owes the same duties to self as to others, including the responsibility to preserve integrity and safety, to maintain competence, and to continue personal and professional growth" (ANA, 2010a).

When a nurse explores the beliefs, values, and actions that allow him or her to maintain a sense of personal integrity, it becomes possible to incorporate that personal philosophy into clinical practice. It is that self-examination that makes it possible to accomplish a genuine human connection to a patient. And only in experiencing that human connection does the practice of nursing become meaningful.

Reproduction and beginning of life

Every Night and every Morn Some
to Misery are born.
Every Morn and every Night Some
are born to Sweet Delight,
Some are born to Endless Night.
William Blake

Advances in reproductive technology have permitted previously infertile women to achieve conception. Assisted reproductive technology (ART) methods such as fertility enhancing drugs, intracytoplasmic sperm injections, and in vitro fertilization (IVF) can result in successful pregnancies that previously would have been impossible in cases of postmenopausal women, endometriosis, pelvic inflammatory disease, and male or female infertility (Stock, 2014).

Fertilized conceptus can be screened for genetic disorders. More than a single embryo can be implanted. Unused embryos can be destroyed or frozen. Frozen embryos can then be used for stem cell research. Ultrasound technology permits the diagnosis of congenital problems at a period in the gestation when the pregnancy can be terminated. Consequently, technological advances have created controversial ethical issues. Questions have been posed such as:

■ When does life begin? Fertilization? Conception? Viability? Birth?

■ Are fertilized embryos "people"? If so, what rights do they have?

■ Is abortion murder? If so, are there circumstances in which the decision to terminate a pregnancy is still acceptable? What are those circumstances? Who should make that decision?

■ Does the destruction of fertilized embryos constitute the destruction of human life?

■ Is it wrong to not use such tissue for research if the knowledge gained from it can potentially save lives, find cures for disease, and alleviate human suffering?

Newborns are screened for genetic, endocrine, and metabolic disorders. Mandatory screening laws differ by state, but are an attempt to be consistent with the view of the Centers for Disease Control that "[n]ewborn screening identifies conditions that can affect a child's long-term health or survival. Early detection, diagnosis, and intervention can prevent death or disability and enable children to reach their full potential" (Centers for Disease Control, N.D.). As Dr. Bailey notes, however, "[E]arly identification of an "untreatable" condition could lead to heightened anxiety about parenting, oversensitivity to development, alterations in parenting, or disrupted bonding (Bailey, 2011).

Such mandatory screening poses ethical issues:

- What is the cost of such screening? Who pays for it? Is that a responsible use of collective resources?
- Is there evidence that screening produces a clear benefit for each new test that is mandated?
- Is it ethical that testing for different disorders depends upon the state in which the newborn is born?
- Is it ethical to test a newborn against the parent's wishes? Are parents fully informed of the implications of positive results?
- Are there adequate resources for follow-up services?

Mary Ann Baily notes that "[m]any states already had difficulty providing adequate follow-up services for the conditions in their existing test panels, and for all states, expanding programs to cover so many conditions is a major managerial and financing challenge" (Baily, 2014).

The President's Council on Bioethics has concluded that "[T]he potential benefits of mandatory, population-wide newborn screening for diseases for which there is no current treatment are outweighed by the potential harms. These harms will be accentuated once new DNA technologies make it possible to expand screening to target additional diseases and to detect disease susceptibility as well (The President's Council on Bioethics, 2008).

Technical advances have also permitted fetal survival at earlier stages of gestation. Neonates who previously would not have survived outside the womb may now survive with the highly specialized care provided by a neonatal intensive care unit (NICU).

Some of these preterm infants can experience profound congenital defects as well as both short- and long-term clinical consequences. Some will present with intractable medical problems. NICUs may also care for full-term newborns with acute conditions, severe disabilities, or congenital anomalies for which providers find highly sophisticated medical care to be inappropriate or futile.

Barnum and Catlin have identified the phenomenon of *benevolent injustice*:

A benevolent injustice occurs when the well-intentioned treatment efforts of a physician or a medical team produce an outcome that limits the potential of a patient or renders them technologically dependent. … Many of these neonates are left with subsequent morbidities and disabilities that are a direct result of medical treatment. Thus, a paradox arises – attempts to save the neonate's life, correct malformations, or restore health can initiate new health problems, increase morbidities, or cause further harm to the health of the patient (Barnum et al., 2009).

Conflict can arise between providers and families and raise questions of quality versus quantity of life, compassion, and the appropriate utilization of scarce and expensive resources:

- Are nurses and doctors obligated to provide treatment they believe is medically inappropriate or futile?
- Who should bear the financial burden of providing such care?
- Is it right to provide treatment that imposes pain and suffering without the hope of potential benefit?
- Who is qualified to determine the quality of life?
- Is prolonging life more valuable than the relief of pain and suffering?
- When does the selection of a course of action among treatment options

become the denial of treatment or deprivation?

A lawsuit known as "the Baby Jane Doe case" addressed some of these questions. On October 11, 1982, Baby Jane Doe was born with multiple serious disorders. They included myelomeningocele (spina bifida), microcephaly, and hydrocephalus. Her life expectancy was a matter of weeks. Surgery to close the myelomeningocele and reduce the fluid in her skull could increase her life expectancy to 20 years, and she was transferred to a hospital for the procedures.

The parents had lengthy consultations with neurological experts, nurses, religious counselors, and a social worker. They understood that Baby Jane Doe would probably have severe intellectual disability and a seizure disorder. It was also likely that she would be paralyzed and bedridden and suffer from constant urinary tract infections. They decided not to consent to the surgery, preferring conservative care.

Their decision was challenged and a guardian *ad litem* was appointed. (A guardian *ad litem* is a person appointed by the court to represent the interests of someone without capacity, such as a minor, and given the authority to make legal decisions on the person's behalf, including medical decisions.) A hearing was held in which the judge determined that Baby Jane Doe was being deprived of adequate medical care and that her life was in imminent danger without the surgery. The guardian *ad litem* was authorized to consent to the surgery on Baby Jane Doe's behalf.

The parents challenged this decision. On appeal, the court disagreed with the hearing judge and found that the parents' choice of a course of conservative treatment instead of surgery was well within accepted medical standards and that there was no medical reason to disturb the parents' decision:

> [T]his is not a case where an infant is being deprived of medical treatment to achieve a quick and supposedly merciful death. Rather, it is a situation where the parents have chosen one course of appropriate medical treatment over another. These concededly concerned and loving parents have made an informed, intelligent, and reasonable determination based upon and supported by responsible medical authority. On this record, and in light of all the surrounding circumstances, we find the parents' determination to be in the best interest of the infant. Accordingly, there is no basis for judicial intervention (*Weber*, 1983).

An anonymous hotline complaint was placed with the U.S. Department of Health and Human Services (HHS). The complaint alleged that Baby Jane Doe was being discriminatorily denied indicated medical treatment. A lengthy legal battle ensued, in which HHS attempted to obtain Baby Jane Doe's medical records. The federal government argued that it needed to review them to determine whether the hospital denied treatment to Baby Jane Doe based on her handicap, in violation of the Rehabilitation Act of 1973. The court determined that the surgery was not performed because the parents refused to consent to it, not because of the infant's handicap. HHS appealed the decision, and another legal battle ensued. The issue was whether the Rehabilitation Act of 1973 was intended to give the government power to intervene in medical decision making. The Court determined that it did not and denied HHS's request for the medical records.

The case created discussion and commentary in the literature. George

Annas described the issues that remain unresolved:

Unless and until the state and federal governments are willing to provide the funding and support necessary to properly care for severely handicapped children, parents should retain the primary decision-making authority in the arena, subject, of course, to state child abuse laws and supported by factual information about their child's prognosis and the community resources available to them and their child (Annas, 1984).

In the Baby Jane Doe case, the parents did not want treatment that others wanted to have provided to the infant. The conflict can also be reversed, as in *Matter of Baby K* (1994). Baby K was born in October of 1992 with anencephaly. Her brain stem supported autonomic functions and reflexes, but she lacked a cerebrum. This rendered her permanently unconscious—unable to see, hear, or interact with her environment. She had no cognitive abilities or awareness. There was no medical treatment that would improve her condition, and she would remain in this state as long as she lived. She was placed on a ventilator for respiratory distress.

Physicians discussed the situation with Baby K's mother. They explained that most anencephalic infants die within a few days of birth due to breathing difficulties and other complications. They believed that aggressive treatment would serve no therapeutic or palliative purpose, and recommended that Baby K only be provided with supportive care in the form of nutrition, hydration, and warmth. They suggested a "Do Not Resuscitate" order.

The mother insisted that Baby K be provided with mechanical breathing assistance whenever she developed difficulty breathing on her own. The physicians maintained that such care was inappropriate, and the hospital tried to transfer Baby K to another hospital. All hospitals in the area with pediatric intensive care units declined to accept her.

In November of 1992, Baby K no longer needed acute care and was transferred to a nursing home. The mother wanted the hospital to provide respiratory support to Baby K whenever she needed it, and she was subsequently readmitted to the hospital three times with breathing difficulties. After the second admission, the hospital sought a *declaratory judgment* that, under the Emergency Medical Treatment and Active Labor Act (EMTALA), also known as the patient antidumping law, it was not required to provide treatment other than warmth, nutrition, and hydration (CMS, 2014). (A *declaratory judgment* is a legally binding judgment of a court that determines the rights or duties of the parties in a dispute.)

The court found EMTALA did require the hospital to provide respiratory support whenever Baby K presented to the hospital in respiratory distress, and treatment was requested. Baby K died on April 5, 1995, at 2 years and 174 days of age (see *EMTALA* box).

Some states permit causes of action called *wrongful birth* or *wrongful life*. Lawsuits filed in these cases are actions in malpractice and negligence. In *wrongful birth*, the parents allege that the providers did not advise them of the potential for severe disability. In the absence of that information, the parents were unable to make a decision to continue or terminate the pregnancy. The lawsuit is an attempt to recover the *child's* economic damage from the expenses of such things as medical bills, durable medical equipment, physical therapy, occupational therapy, speech

EMTALA

As stated by the Centers for Medicare and Medicaid Services:

> In 1986, Congress enacted the Emergency Medical Treatment & Labor Act (EMTALA) to ensure public access to emergency services regardless of the ability to pay.

> Section 1867 of the Social Security Act imposes specific obligations on Medicare-participating hospitals that offer emergency services to provide a medical screening examination (MSE) when a request is made for examination or treatment for an emergency medical condition (EMC), including active labor, regardless of an individual's ability to pay.

> Hospitals are then required to provide stabilizing treatment for patients with EMCs.

> If a hospital is unable to stabilize a patient within its capability, or if the patient requests, an appropriate transfer should be implemented.

Source: Centers for Medicare and Medicaid Services. The Emergency Medical Treatment & Labor Act, 2014. Retrieved from: http://www.cms.gov/Regulations-and-Guidance/Legislation/EMTALA/index.html?redirect=/EMTALA/

therapy, around-the-clock care, and special education.

Lawsuits filed in *wrongful life* are attempts to recover the *parents'* economic damages. These can include pregnancy expenses and psychiatric or psychological treatment for emotional distress. Some states also allow lawsuits for *wrongful pregnancy*. These lawsuits are attempts to recover damages from the medical expenses and the emotional distress of unwanted or unexpected pregnancies. They may also include the costs of raising the child. Wrongful birth, wrongful life, and wrongful pregnancy cases are controversial for all of the ethical questions they raise about abortion, eugenics, euthanasia, informed consent, and quality of life.

End of life

Death belongs to the dying and those who love them.

Sherwin B. Nuland

As in beginning-of-life issues, nurses are on the front line in conflicts over death and dying. High-profile cases such as Karen Ann Quinlan, Nancy Cruzan, and Terri Schiavo have highlighted the dilemmas that result from the use of sophisticated technology and artificial nutrition and hydration in cases of profound brain damage.

KAREN ANN QUINLAN

Karen Ann Quinlan was 21 years old when she experienced at least two 15-minute apneic periods. After ineffective resuscitative attempts, she was taken to a New Jersey hospital with unreactive pupils. She was unresponsive to deep pain and exhibited decorticate posturing. After her transfer to another hospital, an electroencephalogram demonstrated abnormalities consistent with her clinical presentation. She was ultimately determined to be in a persistent vegetative state (PVS). Although she had some brain stem function, it was ineffective for respiratory function. She required a ventilator, and a tracheotomy was performed. She continued to deteriorate, losing at least 40 pounds.

Despite excellent nursing care, her posture was described as fetal-like and grotesque, with extreme flexion-rigidity of the limbs and muscles. Her joints were severely rigid and deformed. There was no treatment that could improve or cure her condition, and it was determined that she could never be restored to cognitive or sapient life. Despite the irreversible nature of her condition, she did not meet the criteria for "brain death."

Ms. Quinlan's father, Joseph Quinlan, a devout Roman Catholic, sought the guidance of his church. Bishop Lawrence B. Casey took the position that "[T]he continuance of mechanical (cardiorespiratory) supportive measures to sustain continuation of her body functions and her life constitute extraordinary means of treatment. Therefore, the decision of Joseph … Quinlan to request the discontinuance of this treatment is, according to the teachings of the Catholic Church, a morally correct decision" (*Quinlan,* 1976, p. 32).

When the family requested withdrawal of life support, her physician, Dr. Morse, refused because he believed that the disconnection of the ventilator was unethical in the absence of cerebral death. Dr. Morse was also concerned that the discontinuation of life support was a violation of medical standards and would expose him to civil and criminal liability.

A complicated lawsuit ensued in which the Supreme Court of New Jersey analyzed the intersection of medicine, the law, religion, and ethics:

Medicine with its combination of advanced technology and professional ethics is both able and inclined to prolong biological life. Law with its felt obligation to protect the life and freedom of the individual seeks to assure each person's right to live out his human life until its natural and inevitable conclusion. ……Theology with its acknowledgment of man's dissatisfaction with biological life as the ultimate source of joy defends the sacredness of human life and defends it from all direct attacks. ……These disciplines do not conflict with one another, but are necessarily conjoined in the application of their principles in a particular instance such as that of Karen Ann Quinlan. Each must in some way acknowledge the other without denying its own competence (*Quinlan*, 1976, p. 32).

The Court noted that "[T]he subject has lost human qualities" (*Quinlan*, 1976, p. 28) and that:

[T]here is a real and in this case determinative distinction between the unlawful taking of the life of another and the ending of artificial life-support systems as a matter of self-determination. …We do not question the State's undoubted power to punish the taking of human life, but that power does not encompass individuals terminating medical treatment pursuant to their right of privacy (*Quinlan*, 1976, p. 52).

In a unanimous decision, the Court ruled that:

Upon the concurrence of the guardian and family of Karen, should the responsible attending physicians conclude that there is no reasonable possibility of Karen's ever emerging from her present comatose condition to a cognitive, sapient state and that the life-support apparatus now being administered to Karen should be discontinued, they shall consult with the hospital "Ethics Committee" or like body of the institution in which

Karen is then hospitalized. If that consultative body agrees that there is no reasonable possibility of Karen's ever emerging from her present comatose condition to a cognitive, sapient state, the present life-support system may be withdrawn and said action shall be without any civil or criminal liability therefore on the part of any participant, whether guardian, physician, hospital, or others (*Quinlan*, 1976, p. 54).

It was the first time a court in the United States had determined that the right to privacy permitted the discontinuation of life support. Ms. Quinlan was removed from the ventilator in 1976. Nine years later, after ten years in a PVS, she died on June 11, 1985.

NANCY CRUZAN

In January of 1983, Nancy Cruzan was 25 years old. She lost control of the car she was driving, and it overturned, throwing her into a ditch. She landed facedown in water and was found by paramedics to have no pulse or respirations. She was resuscitated after 12–14 minutes of oxygen deprivation and taken to a hospital in Missouri, where she was ultimately determined to be in a PVS. Her parents requested that the hospital discontinue her feeding and hydration but the hospital refused to do so unless they had the authority of a court. An 8-year legal battle ensued, which made its way to the United States Supreme Court (USSC) and received national attention.

The Missouri trial court had found that:

(1) her respiration and circulation are not artificially maintained and are within the normal limits of a thirty-year-old female; (2) she is "oblivious to her environment except for reflexive responses to sound and

perhaps painful stimuli"; (3) she suffered anoxia of the brain resulting in a "massive enlargement of the ventricles filling with cerebrospinal fluid in the area where the brain has degenerated" and that "cerebral cortical atrophy is irreversible, permanent, progressive and ongoing"; (4) "her highest cognitive brain function is exhibited by her grimacing perhaps in recognition of ordinarily painful stimuli, indicating the experience of pain and apparent response to sound"; (5) she is aspastic quadriplegic; (6) her four extremities are contracted with irreversible muscular and tendon damage to all extremities; (7) "she has no cognitive or reflexive ability to swallow food or water to maintain her daily essential needs" and that "she will never recover her ability to swallow sufficient [sic] to satisfy her needs" (*Cruzan*, 1988, p. 411).

The trial court ordered the employees of the State of Missouri to "cause the request of the coguardians to withdraw nutrition or hydration to be carried out" (Cruzan, 1988, p. 412).

The state and Ms. Cruzan's guardian *ad litem* appealed. The Supreme Court of Missouri reversed the trial court decision. It found that there was no expressed right to privacy in either the federal or the Missouri state constitution. It reasoned that "[T]he state's concern with the sanctity of life rests on the principle that life is precious and worthy of preservation without regard to its quality" (*Cruzan*, 1988, p. 419). The Court also stated that "[T]he state's interest in prolonging life is particularly valid in Nancy's case. Nancy is not terminally ill. Her death is imminent only if she is denied food and water. Medical evidence shows Nancy will continue a life of relatively normal duration if allowed basic sustenance" (*Cruzan*, 1988. p. 419).

Missouri law required "clear and convincing evidence" that Ms. Cruzan would have wanted life-sustaining treatment to be discontinued. The Supreme Court of Missouri held that the trial testimony did not amount to clear and convincing proof of Ms. Cruzan's desire to have hydration and nutrition withdrawn. In the absence of that clear and convincing evidence, the Court would not grant the parents' request. The state of Missouri had a strong interest in preserving life, and the Missouri Supreme Court held that this interest outweighed an individual's right to privacy or the right to refuse treatment.

Ms. Cruzan's parents appealed to the USSC. Although noting that "[T]he choice between life and death is a deeply personal decision of obvious and overwhelming finality," the USSC found the Missouri requirement to be constitutional and upheld the Supreme Court of Missouri's decision (*Cruzan*, 1990, p. 281).

The parents were later able to satisfy the clear and convincing standard, and nutrition and hydration were discontinued in December of 1990. Ms. Cruzan died 12 days later—8 years after the car accident that left her in a PVS.

TERRI SCHIAVO

On February 25, 1990, 27-year-old Theresa Marie Schiavo collapsed from a cardiac arrest. Her husband, Michael Schiavo, found her and called 911. Paramedics resuscitated her and took her to a local Florida hospital in a coma. Ms. Schiavo never regained consciousness, and the coma progressed to a PVS. A percutaneous endoscopic gastrostomy (PEG) tube was inserted, and artificial feeding was instituted. In 1998, after 8 years in a PVS, Michael Schiavo sought court approval to remove her PEG tube. As her husband, he was Ms. Schiavo's health care proxy under Florida law. Florida law also permitted health care proxies to withdraw artificial nutrition and hydration if doing so would be in the patient's best interest, or if it would be consistent with the patient's wishes. Ms. Schiavo's parents objected, expressing the belief that Ms. Schiavo would want the feedings and hydration continued.

The conflict went to trial, and on February 11, 2000, the court issued an order to remove her PEG tube. The parents appealed, but an appellate court confirmed the order on January 24, 2001. Legal battles continued, but the feeding tube was removed on April 24, 2001. On April 26, 2001, a circuit court ordered that the PEG tube be reinserted. Multiple court petitions and hearings ensued, resulting in a final order that it be removed on October 15, 2003. The PEG was removed again on that day (Cerminara, Part 1, 2014).

On October 20, 2003, the Florida House of Representatives passed House Bill 701 (HB 701), known as "Terry's Law," which permitted the governor to issue holds on orders for feeding tube withdrawals and even to order reinsertion of the feeding tubes after a court had ruled that they could be discontinued. The legislation also allowed guardian *ad litems* to be appointed and required "express and informed consent" for end-of-life decisions (Florida House of Representatives, 2005).

The following day, October 21, 2003, then Governor Jeb Bush issued an executive order directing that the PEG tube be reinserted and feeding resumed (Florida Office of the Governor, 2003). The actions of the Florida House of Representatives and of the Florida Governor were unprecedented and resulted in considerable legal, religious, ethical, and political debate.

Michael Schiavo challenged the law, and the Florida Bioethics Network issued an analysis of HB701:

House Bill 701 is a well-intentioned response to the tragic case of Theresa Marie Schiavo. We are, however, of unanimous and emphatic belief that the proposed measure:

- Would impose impossible burdens on physicians and patient surrogates, proxies, and guardians
- Would establish insurmountable barriers to Floridians' exercise of uncontroversial rights to refuse burdensome medical treatment
- Misjudges the medical nature of artificial nutrition and hydration and the ethical issues involved in withholding and withdrawing such interventions
- Misunderstands the nature and importance of disability in end-of-life care.

The bioethics network also noted:

Appropriate placement of a PEG tube is based on evidence that the intervention will assist the body until it recovers to a point at which it can function without such assistance. That is, PEG tubes, ventilators and the like are medically appropriate only when used as a "bridge to recovery," not as a way to prolong the dying process in the patient population that would be affected by HB701.

The Florida Supreme Court held that "Terri's Law" was unconstitutional, but the battle continued. The United States Congress petitioned for involvement, issued subpoenas for hearings, and held press conferences (Gennett, 2005). Governor Bush filed a petition with the U.S. Supreme Court, but the Court denied the petition, refusing to hear the case (Bush, 2004). On March 18, 2005, the PEG tube was removed for the third time. Terry Schiavo died 13 days later, on March 31, 2005 (Cerminara, Part 2, 2014).

An autopsy report was released on June 15, 2005 (Thogmorton, 2005). A neuropathologist described Ms. Schiavo's brain:

Brain weight is an important index of its pathologic state. Brain weight is correlated with height, weight, age, and sex. The decedent's brain was grossly abnormal and weighed only 615 grams (1.35 lbs.). That weight is less than half of the expected tabular weight for a decedent of her adult age of 41 years 3 months 28 days. By way of comparison, the brain of Karen Ann Quinlan weighed 835 grams at the time of her death, after 10 years in a similar persistent vegetative state (Nelson, 2005).

The legal battle over Terry Schiavo's end-of-life care had taken 12 years and consisted of 20 court proceedings. Its influence was considerable, and the ethical debate continues (Haberman, 2014).

As with all high-profile cases involving end-of-life controversies, Karen Ann Quinlan, Nancy Cruzan, and Terry Schiavo are remembered for their deaths. Little information is available about their lives. All of these cases raised questions that remain unresolved. Lois Shepherd poses the following questions:

- How much deference should be given to surrogate decision makers?
- How should the interests of family members, or others close to the patient, be weighed against respecting the preferences or best interests of the patient?
- In what condition must the patient be to warrant the withdrawal of life-sustaining treatment?
- How certain do we have to be that the patient is in that condition?

- Should we treat different conditions differently when making the decision to withdraw treatment?
- Should there be stricter rules for withdrawing feeding than other forms of treatment? (Shepherd, 2006)

ADVANCE DIRECTIVES

Quinlan, Cruzan, and *Schiavo* all demonstrate the need for advance directives. Advance directives outline an individual's wishes about treatment in the event that he or she becomes incompetent or loses the capacity to communicate those wishes. Advance directives can take the form of a *living will,* or the designation of a *health care proxy* or *health care power of attorney. Living wills* are documents that specify the treatments a person does or does not want and under what conditions. Different states have different requirements for honoring a living will, and nurses should be familiar with the law in the states in which they practice. A *health care proxy* is a person the individual has identified as the decision maker in the event that he or she can no longer make or communicate such decisions. A *health care power of attorney* is a document that gives the health care proxy the legal authority to make health care decisions on the individual's behalf. The presence of such advance directives can prevent conflict by providing clear and convincing evidence of the person's wishes.

In an effort to address the need for advance directives, the Patient Self-Determination Act (PSDA) was passed in 1990. The legislation was a direct response to the Nancy Cruzan case. It was enacted in 1991 and requires that patients be given written notice *upon admission* of:

- decision-making rights;
- policies regarding advance health care directives in their state; and
- policies regarding advance health care directives in the institution.

Under the PSDA, patients have the right to facilitate their own health care decisions, to accept or refuse medical treatment, and to make an advance health care directive. Facilities must inquire if the patient already has an advance health care directive and document it in the medical record. Health care organizations must maintain written policies and procedures concerning advance directives for all adults receiving care, and provide written information concerning the patient's right to accept or refuse treatment and to formulate advance directives, as well as the written policies of the facility regarding the implementation of those rights (101st Congress, 1990).

In 1995, the Government Accounting Office (GAO) issued a report to Congress on the effectiveness of the PSDA. The report indicated that there was general compliance with the law, but the issue of end-of-life decision making remained problematic:

> We also found that advance directives have been advocated more than they have been used. Surveys indicated that, in general, only 10 to 25 percent of Americans have documented their end-of-life choices or appointed a health care agent. Lack of communication between patients and physicians and misunderstandings about the appropriateness and purpose of advance directives may explain why completion rates remain low. The provider groups we spoke with generally support advance directives. Yet, advance directives may not always be implemented as patients intend. A variety of factors affects whether an advance directive actually controls end-of-life care decisions, including the availability or specificity of a

living will, family wishes, physicians' attitudes, and legal issues (GAO, 1995).

Nearly a decade after this report, the issue remains problematic, as the Institute of Medicine has noted:

Understanding and perceptions of death and dying vary considerably across the population and are influenced by culture, socioeconomic status, and education, as well as by misinformation and fear. Engaging people in defining their own values, goals, and preferences concerning care at the end of life and ensuring that their care team understands their wishes has proven remarkably elusive and challenging (IOM, 2014).

One approach is the "Five Wishes." Five Wishes is a document that meets the requirements of most states and is available in 27 languages. The wishes are:

■ Wish 1: The person I want to make health care decisions for me when I can't;

■ Wish 2: The kind of medical treatment I want or don't want;

■ Wish 3: How comfortable I want to be;

■ Wish 4: How I want people to treat me; and

■ Wish 5: What I want my loved ones to know (Aging with Dignity, 2014).

End-of-life wishes can take the form of standardized forms such as Physicians (or Providers) Orders for Life-Sustaining Treatment (POLST). POLST is a standardized form that is signed by the patient and the provider. Unlike living wills, POLST constitutes portable formal provider orders that are honored by prehospital personnel. POLST may also be referred to as "life with dignity orders."

The American Medical Association has committed to "intensified efforts to promote the use of advance directives" (AMA, N.D.). Advance directives can address "do not resuscitate (DNR)," "do not intubate (DNI)," and "allow natural death (AND)" requests to some extent, but in many cases, the quality of end-of-life care remains inadequate to meet palliative care needs.

THE EFFECT OF CULTURE

Culture strongly influences reactions to serious illness and decisions about end-of-life care. Religion, faith, and spirituality influence a person's perceptions and decisions. Western values are not necessarily consistent with other philosophical views. Because nurses care for patients from different backgrounds, it is important to have an understanding of the role those backgrounds play in the patient's experience of death and dying. Western cultural values include "truth telling" over nondisclosure, informed consent, open communication, autonomy in decision making, and patient-centered rights. These are not universal beliefs. As the United States becomes more culturally and ethnically diverse, nurses must develop the competency to care for patients whose core values might differ from those with which we are most familiar. Failure to do so can compromise care and result in health disparities.

All cultures do not share the Western belief that patients should be honestly told their prognosis when it involves death. Death may be a taboo topic, or may be considered disrespectful or inappropriate to discuss. Patients may come from cultures in which information is shared with family members or identified family leaders before or instead of the patient. Decision making may be collective, rather than individual. The physician may be viewed as an authority figure with whom it is disrespectful to disagree or ask questions and who is considered the appropriate person to make all decisions (Coolen, 2012).

Patients from different cultures have varying levels of assimilation into the dominant society in which they live. Some patients maintain their home culture views. Some patients adopt the new culture views. Some patients maintain some of the home culture views while adopting some of the new culture views. The ability to fully understand advance directives is affected by those cultural differences and the ability of the patient to trust Western medicine and its providers. Nurses cannot provide individualized and holistic care to patients in the absence of these considerations. (Refer to Coolen's Suggestions for advance directives discussions.)

EUTHANASIA/PHYSICIAN-ASSISTED SUICIDE

In 1997, Oregon became the first state to pass legislation permitting physician-assisted suicide. Oregon's Death with Dignity Act allows terminally ill patients to self-administer lethal medications, and it permits physicians to prescribe those medications for the purpose of allowing those patients to voluntarily end their lives. Washington state followed with similar legislation in 2008 (Washington *State Legislature*, 2008) as did Vermont in 2013 (Vermont *State Legislature*, 2013).

Unlike Oregon, Washington, and Vermont, Montana has permitted physician-assisted suicide not solely from legislation, but from a court decision interpreting such a statute. Four Montana physicians (Compassion & Choices) along with a 76-year-old man, Robert Baxter, brought the suit in 2008. Mr. Baxter, along with the physicians, asked the court to establish

a constitutional right "to receive and provide aid in dying" (*Baxter*, 2009).

Mr. Baxter was terminally ill with incurable lymphocytic leukemia. He had diffuse lymphadenopathy and experienced infections, chronic fatigue, weakness, anemia, night sweats, nausea, massively swollen glands, significant ongoing digestive problems, generalized pain, and discomfort. He was being treated with multiple rounds of chemotherapy, which typically becomes less effective over time. It was expected that these debilitating symptoms would increase in frequency and intensity as the chemotherapy became less effective. Because there was no chance of recovery, "Mr. Baxter wanted the option of ingesting a lethal dose of medication prescribed by his physician and self-administered at the time of Mr. Baxter's own choosing" (*Robert Baxter*, 2009, p. 5).

Mr. Baxter and the physicians (the plaintiffs) sought a court opinion to challenge the applicability of Montana's criminal homicide statute to the physicians in these circumstances. The plaintiffs cited the Montana state constitution, which said:

Section 4. Individual dignity. The dignity of the human being is inviolable. No person shall be denied the equal protection of the laws. Neither the state nor any person, firm, corporation, or institution shall discriminate against any person in the exercise of his civil or political rights on account of race, color, sex, culture, social origin or condition, or political or religious ideas.

Section 10. Right of privacy. The right of individual privacy is essential to the well-being of a free society and shall not be infringed without the showing of a compelling state interest.

(Text continues on page 337.)

Coolen's suggestions for advance directive discussions

■ Ideally, discussions on advance directive planning should be performed in advance of an impending health care crisis. For example, it should be part of the patient's routine care. It should also be a continuing discussion as patient's views change, they grow older, or their health status declines and their perspective on advance directives may change. Incorporating an advance directive discussion on a yearly basis is advisable.

■ When the family is the designated decision maker on health care issues, the discussion about advance directive planning must be done with the family. It is also important to determine the patient's preference for being present at the discussion.

■ Sufficient time must be allocated for the discussion. Setting up a separate time for the discussion allows for a more thorough discussion and question-and-answer session. Also, the patient may need to make arrangements for family members to attend the discussion.

■ The discussion should be done in private. The health care provider should encourage the patient and family to ask questions. The health care provider should reassure the patient and family that the advance directive will only be shared with those who are on the patient's health care team.

■ Determine whether the patient and family understand the purpose of an advance directive. Common misconceptions are that it is a will, that if the person signs the document he or she will lose their home, that it requires an attorney, and that it addresses funeral and burial arrangements.

■ Provide detailed information including the natural course of the disease, the prognosis, and chance of survival. Many family members will pursue less aggressive treatment if the chance of survival is poor. Help the patient and family understand that "doing everything" may also bring about additional pain and suffering. However, recognize that for some people, even in the face of a low survival rate, aggressive treatment is expected, and supporting those decisions is important. When the patient or family wants "everything possible done," an exploration of what that means can provide a greater understanding of what's behind the request. Consideration may be: denial of the illness or the progression of the illness, unrealistic goals, fear of dying, and loss of self-control, false hope, or a sense of familial duty (Braun, et al., 2008).

■ Patients and family members need to be assured that an advance directive that excludes curative treatment does not mean the patient will be abandoned by the health care system. The health care provider must provide reassurance that stopping curative or life-supporting treatment does not mean no treatment, but that the focus of the patient's treatment will be aggressive management of any pain and symptoms the person may experience.

■ For some cultures, the concept of present orientation is to "take each day as it comes." The health care provider may suggest having a trial intervention to help with the decision-making process. A trial intervention is time limited and takes the approach of "Let's see what happens to your mom's condition in the next few days, and we can then revisit the discussion on life-sustaining treatment. Meanwhile, if you have any questions for me, please feel free to ask them."

■ A religious leader can play an important role in facilitating the discussion and decision-making process in advance directive planning through clarification of how certain aspects of a religion's principles or beliefs may influence the decision on providing life-support measures. The religious leader can also act as a crucial intermediary in helping the patient connect with his or her faith or spiritual life.

■ When the discussion of death and dying is a taboo subject, the health care provider might initiate having the patient do a life review. Xiao et al.'s study on Chinese patients with advanced

Coolen's suggestions for advance directive discussions *(continued)*

cancer found that encouraging patients to do a life review prepared them for death (Xiao et al., 2011). Encouraging the patient to review and value his or her life experiences and complete unfinished business may enable the patient to work on advance directive planning.

■ More subtle, indirect, and implicit nonverbal communication may be preferred when discussing advance directive planning

(Matsumura, et al., 2002). Nonverbal communication includes active listening with pauses between sentences, silence, and holding the patient's hands.

■ Development of educational tools in collaboration with a targeted culture community can increase awareness of the value and usefulness of advance directive planning and end-of-life choices.

Source: Coolen, P., et al. "Culture Relevance in End-of-Life", *EthnoMED*, May 1, 2012. Retrieved from: http://ethnomed.org/clinical/end-of-life/cultural-relevance-in-end-of-life-care

---

Although the state argued that the Montana constitution did not give a person the right to end his life, the court ruled in favor of the plaintiffs. It held that patients do have the right to die with dignity and physicians had a right to assist them in those efforts. The decision held that the patient's right to die with dignity included protection of the patient's physician from prosecution under the state's homicide statutes. Mr. Baxter died the same day as the decision, but before learning of it.

Montana's Attorney General appealed the decision, and in hearing the case, the Montana Supreme Court concluded that "[W]e find no indication in Montana law that physician aid in dying provided to terminally ill, mentally competent adult patients is against public policy" (*Robert Baxter*, 2009, p. 8).

The Court further stated:

…[A] physician who aids a terminally ill patient in dying is not directly involved in the final decision *or* the final act. He or she only provides a means by which a terminally ill patient himself can give effect to his life-ending decision, or not, as the case may be.

Each stage of the physician-patient interaction is private, civil, and compassionate. The physician and terminally ill patient work together to create a means by which the patient can be in control of his own mortality. The patient's subsequent private decision whether to take the medicine does not breach public peace or endanger others (*Robert Baxter*, 2009, p. 12).

The Montana Supreme Court concluded that:

[T]he right of personal autonomy included in the state constitutional right to privacy, and the right to determine "the most fundamental questions of life" inherent in the state constitutional right to dignity, mandate that a competent terminally ill person has the right to choose to end his or her life. With regard to whether this includes the right to obtain assistance from a medical care provider in the form of obtaining a prescription for lethal drugs to be taken at a time of the patient's choosing, the Court concludes that it does.

The Court referenced Montana's "The Rights of the Terminally Ill Act"

(Montana, 2014) that provided terminally ill patients with autonomous, end-of-life decisions, "The Terminally Ill Act, in short, confers on terminally ill patients a right to have their end-of-life wishes followed, even if it requires *direct* participation by a physician through withdrawing or withholding treatment" (*Robert Baxter*, 2009, p. 15).

Similarly, a New Mexico suit has ruled that "[T]his court cannot envision a right more fundamental, more private or more integral to the liberty, safety and happiness of a New Mexican than the right of a competent, terminally ill patient to choose aid in dying" (NY Daily News, 2014). Although under New Mexico law, helping with suicide is a fourth-degree felony, the ruling does not consider physician assistance in dying as a form of suicide that can be prosecuted.

Four of the remaining 45 states have no specific statutory or common law (case law decisions) addressing euthanasia. Forty-two states prohibit provider-assisted suicide—39 by statute and 3 by common law. The classification of crime (misdemeanor or felony) and penalties vary by state (Pro Con, 2014).

Provider-assisted euthanasia is controversial. Proponents believe that terminally ill people who are suffering should have the right to a "quick, dignified, and compassionate death" (Pro Con, 2014). Supporters of these statutes argue that the constitution protects a person's right to die.

Opponents believe that providers cannot morally participate in euthanasia. Some opponents express concern about the potential for eugenics—ending the lives of people with disabilities or qualities considered undesirable. Opponents also worry about the potential for end-of-life decisions being made for financial gain and a "slippery slope" in application of laws that allow physician-assisted suicide.

The three states that permit provider-assisted suicide by law have addressed these concerns in their statutes. The Death with Dignity Acts contain multiple requirements to prevent the potential abuses that concern opponents. For example, patients must be mentally competent adults who are legal residents of those states; they must be suffering from a terminal illness with a life expectancy of 6 months or less; the request must be made voluntarily and twice in the presence of witnesses, and so on. It is important to note that each of these acts specifies that physicians and health care systems are not obligated to participate, see *Comparison of assisted suicide requirement.*

Debates about provider-assisted euthanasia will continue. Unanswered questions remain, such as:

■ Is there an ethical distinction between causing death and allowing death to occur—between withholding and withdrawing treatment; between stopping and not starting treatment?
■ Where is the line drawn between treatment and resuscitation?
■ Is nursing's ethical responsibility to prolong life or to facilitate a peaceful death?
■ Should we offer or insist on providing care that we ourselves would not want? (The IOM notes that "[W]hen it comes to their own care, many physicians choose much less aggressive treatments than they offer their patients" [IOM, 2014]).
■ Is it ever moral or ethical to participate in ending human life?

NURSING OBLIGATIONS

To assist patients with end-of-life wishes, nurses should examine their own views about mortality and

(Text continues on page 340.)

Comparison of assisted suicide requirements

Oregon
Patient eligibility
- 18 years of age or older
- Resident of Oregon
- Capable of making and communicating health care decisions for him/herself
- Diagnosed with a terminal illness that will lead to death within 6 months

Physician protocol
- The attending physician must be licensed in the same state as the patient
- The physician's diagnosis must include a terminal illness, with 6 months or less to live
- The diagnosis must be certified by a consulting physician, who must also certify that the patient is mentally competent to make and communicate health care decisions
- If either physician determines that the patient's judgment is impaired, the patient must be referred for a psychological examination
- The attending physician must inform the patient of alternatives, including palliative care, hospice, and pain management options
- The attending physician must request that the patient notify their next of kin of the prescription request.

Patient request timeline
- First oral request to physician
- 15-day waiting period
- Second oral request to physician
- Written request to physician
- 48-hour waiting period before picking up prescribed medications
- Pick up prescribed medications from the pharmacy

Other
- Use of the law cannot affect the status of a patient's health or life insurance policies

- The Department of Human Services – Health Services enforces compliance with the law. Compliance requires physicians to report all prescriptions to the state. Physicians and patients who comply with the law are protected from criminal prosecution
- Physicians and health care systems are not obligated to participate.

Vermont
Patient eligibility
- 18 years of age or older
- Resident of Vermont
- Capable of making and communicating health care decisions for him/herself
- Diagnosed with a terminal illness that will lead to death within 6 months.

Physician protocol
- The attending physician must be licensed in the same state as the patient
- The physician's diagnosis must include a terminal illness, with 6 months or less to live
- The diagnosis must be certified by a consulting physician, who must also certify that the patient is mentally competent to make and communicate health care decisions
- If either physician determines that the patient's judgment is impaired, the patient must be referred for a psychological examination
- The attending physician must inform the patient of alternatives, including palliative care, hospice, and pain management options.

Patient request timeline
- First oral request to physician
- 15-day waiting period
- Second oral request to physician
- Written request to physician
- 48-hour waiting period before picking up prescribed medications
- Pick up prescribed medications from the pharmacy

(continued)

Comparison of assisted suicide requirements *(continued)*

Other
- Use of the law cannot affect the status of a patient's health or life insurance policies
- Physicians and health care systems are not obligated to participate.

Washington
Patient eligibility
- 18 years of age or older
- Resident of Washington
- Capable of making and communicating health care decisions for him/herself
- Diagnosed with a terminal illness that will lead to death within 6 months

Physician protocol
- The attending physician must be licensed in the same state as the patient
- The physician's diagnosis must include a terminal illness, with 6 months or less to live
- The diagnosis must be certified by a consulting physician, who must also certify that the patient is mentally competent to make and communicate health care decisions
- If either physician determines that the patient's judgment is impaired, the patient must be referred for a psychological examination

- The attending physician must inform the patient of alternatives, including palliative care, hospice, and pain management options
- The attending physician must request that the patient notify their next of kin of the prescription request.

Patient request timeline
- First oral request to physician
- 15-day waiting period
- Second oral request to physician
- Written request to physician
- 48-hour waiting period before picking up prescribed medications
- Pick up prescribed medications from the pharmacy.

Other
- Use of the law cannot affect the status of a patient's health or life insurance policies
- The Department of Health enforces compliance with the law. Compliance requires physicians to report all prescriptions to the state. Physicians and patients who comply with the law are protected from criminal prosecution
- Physicians and health care systems are not obligated to participate.

Source: Pro Con. State-by-State Guide to Physician-Assisted Suicide, 2014. Retrieved from: http://euthanasia .procon.org/view.resource.php?resourceID=000132

---

end-of-life care. Nurses should also be familiar with professional organization standards and position papers on palliative care. Provision 8 of the ANA code of ethics states, "[T]he nurse collaborates with other health professionals and the public in promoting community, national, and international efforts to meet health needs" (ANA, 2010a). Toward that end it is helpful to be aware of the Institute of Medicine's

recommendations for improving end-of-life care in the United States (See *IOM recommendations*).

Nurses have an ethical obligation to respect patient autonomy and to maintain competency in having end-of-life conversations. As the ANA notes:

> The counseling a nurse provides regarding end-of-life choices and preferences for individuals facing

IOM recommendations

■ Government health insurers and care delivery programs as well as private health insurers should cover the provision of comprehensive care for individuals with advanced serious illness who are nearing the end of life.

■ Professional societies and other organizations that establish quality standards should develop standards for clinician-patient communication and advance care planning that are measurable, actionable, and evidence based. These standards should change as needed to reflect the evolving population and health system needs and be consistent with emerging evidence, methods, and technologies. Payers and health care delivery organizations should adopt these standards and their supporting processes, and integrate them into assessments, care plans, and the reporting of health care quality.

■ Educational institutions, credentialing bodies, accrediting boards, state regulatory agencies, and health care delivery organizations should establish the appropriate training, certification, and/or licensure requirements to strengthen the palliative care knowledge and skills of all clinicians who care for individuals with advanced serious illness who are nearing the end of life.

■ Federal, state, and private insurance and health care delivery programs should integrate the financing of medical and social services to support the provision of quality care consistent with the values, goals, and informed preferences of people with advanced serious illness nearing the end of life. To the extent that additional legislation is necessary to implement this recommendation, the administration should seek and Congress should enact such legislation. In addition, the federal government should require public reporting on quality measures, outcomes, and costs regarding care near the end of life (e.g., in the last year of life) for programs it funds or administers (e.g., Medicare, Medicaid, the Department of Veterans Affairs). The federal government should encourage all other payment and health care delivery systems to do the same.

■ Civic leaders, public health and other governmental agencies, community-based organizations, faith-based organizations, consumer groups, health care delivery organizations, payers, employers, and professional societies should engage their constituents and provide fact-based information about care of people with advanced serious illness to encourage advance care planning and informed choice based on the needs and values of individuals.

Source: Institute of Medicine. "Dying in America: Improving Quality and Honoring Individual Preferences Near the End of Life," *National Academies Press*, 2014. Retrieved from: http://www.iom.edu/Reports/2014/Dying-In-America-Improving-Quality-and-Honoring-Individual-Preferences-Near-the-End-of-Life.aspx

life-limiting illness, as well as throughout the patient's lifespan, honors patient autonomy and helps to prepare individuals and families for difficult decisions that may lie ahead. The overarching ethical precept of patient autonomy should guide all discussion regarding the end of life. ...It is essential that nurses acquire the necessary competencies, through their academic preparation and continuing education, to effectively guide and advocate for patients and families in end-of-life planning the dying process itself (ANA 2010b).

An IOM-guiding principle states that "[N]ear the end of life, clinical care is not a person's sole priority. Patients and families may be deeply concerned with existential or spiritual issues, including bereavement, and with practical matters of coping. Appropriate support in these areas is an essential component of good care (IOM, 2014, p. 107). Nurses are privileged to witness human death; most of the population is not. To meet the needs of dying patients and their loved ones, nurses must be capable of introspection and carefully examine their own values and beliefs.

NURSING IMPLICATIONS

- To discuss death and dying, one must be able to face his own mortality.
- Have and encourage others to have advance directives.
- Have and encourage others to have donor cards.
- Develop cultural competency.
- Examine our own values and biases.
- Develop familiarity with professional organizations' code of ethics and position statements. Read the ANA position paper on Euthanasia, Assisted Suicide, and Aid in Dying (ANA, 2013).
- Involve bioethics and pastoral care when appropriate.
- Address vicarious traumatization and moral distress.
- Know available palliative care options.

Involuntary confinement/treatment

Liberty exists in proportion to wholesome restraint.

Daniel Webster

Ethical issues can arise when there is a conflict between an individual's civil liberties and the good of the public at large. Persons thought to pose a risk to public health and safety can be hospitalized and treated against their will in certain circumstances. This raises issues of personal autonomy versus paternalism, and utilitarian/consequentialism versus deontology.

INFECTIOUS DISEASE

The epidemiological model of isolation, confinement, and quarantine can be at odds with a person's right to decline treatment. Persons who are noncompliant with treatment for multiresistant strains of tuberculosis, for example, have been subject to involuntary confinement and treatment. This has been done to protect the public from exposure and to contain potential epidemics. This public health measure, however, is enacted at the expense of the individual's personal liberty. The decision to restrict the freedom of a person should be made on the basis of scientifically sound principles using evidence-based criteria and only after exhausting less restrictive measures. The confinement must be restricted to the period in which the person is contagious. Often, infectious diseases create public anxiety and fear. High-profile diseases receiving a great deal of media attention can lead to emotional reactions and misinformation. Health professionals should respond with accurate information and education.

MENTAL HEALTH

People with psychiatric illnesses can also be subject to involuntary hospitalizations and treatment. This can involve restraint, seclusion, or chemical sedation against the person's will. Nurses must be familiar with their organization's policies. The decision to involuntarily confine a patient must be based upon the determination that the patient is at imminent risk of harm to himself or others and the determination that the person is lacking the capacity to make decisions on his own behalf. Court orders may be required in some circumstances. The deprivation of one's personal liberty and coercive treatment can compromise the trust the patient has in his providers.

OTHERS

There are many other circumstances in which patients have been treated against their wills. Providers must wrestle with the ethical conflicts posed in those circumstances. Antiandrogen therapy for sex offenders, forced feedings for eating disorders, involuntary sterilization, compulsory gay conversion therapy, and compelled medical treatment for pregnant women are some examples. Each of these circumstances poses ethical questions that are not easily answered and can create ethical conflict and moral distress for providers.

Professional boundaries

Professional boundaries are the spaces between the nurse's power and the patient's vulnerability.
National Council of State Boards of Nursing (NCSBN, 2011a).

Nurses have an ethical obligation to act in the best interests of their patients. Provision 3 of the ANA code states, "[T]he nurse promotes, advocates for, and strives to protect the health, safety, and rights of the patient" (ANA, 2010a). To act consistently with that standard, nurse-patient relationships must be professional and therapeutic, with the patient's best interests at the core. Nurses who engage in relationships with patients outside of the

therapeutic role risk violating ethical standards of the profession.

Personal, business, or posttherapeutic relationships with patients can be considered professional misconduct by nursing boards and lead to licensure discipline. Nurses who have sexual relationships with patients can even be criminally charged. Patient consent is not a defense to such charges. Boundary violations can undermine the therapeutic alliance, distort the provider-patient relationship, and cause patient harm.

NCSBN lists behaviors that can be considered boundary violations:

- Excessive personal disclosure—discussing personal problems, feelings of sexual attraction, or aspects of the nurse's intimate life with the patient;
- Secretive behavior—keeping secrets with the patient; becoming guarded or defensive when questioned about these interactions;
- "Super nurse" behavior—thinking one is immune from fostering a nontherapeutic relationship and that only he or she understands and can meet the patient's needs;
- Singling out patient treatment or patient attention to the nurse—spending inappropriate amounts of time with a particular patient, visiting the patient when off-duty, trading assignments to be with the patient;
- Selective communication—failing to explain actions and aspects of care, reporting only some aspects of the patient's behavior, or giving double messages;
- Flirtations—communicating in a flirtatious manner, employing sexual innuendo, off-color jokes, or offensive language;
- "You and Me Against the World" behavior—viewing the patient in a protective manner, tending not to accept the patient as merely a patient,

or siding with the patient's position regardless of the situation; and

■ Failure to protect—failing to recognize feelings of sexual attraction to the patient, to consult with a supervisor or colleague, or to transfer care of the patient when needed to support boundaries (NCSBN, 2011a).

Workplace environment

In the end we will remember not the words of our enemies, but the silence of our friends.

Dr. Martin Luther King Jr.

Provision 6 of the ANA Code of ethics states, "[T]he nurse participates in establishing, maintaining, and improving health care environments and conditions of employment conducive to the provision of quality health care and consistent with the values of the profession through individual and collective action" (ANA, 2010a). Employers and organizations have responsibilities to provide workplaces that are free from violence and hazardous conditions. Nurses also have a responsibility to provide safe practice environments.

BULLYING

Lateral or horizontal violence, also referred to as relational aggression or bullying, is a form of psychological abuse that is widespread in the nursing profession (ANA, 2011). Its effects are damaging and undermine patient safety. In some cases, it can rise to the level of professional misconduct and result in licensure discipline. Lateral violence takes the form of intimidation, gossip, exclusion, withholding information, harsh criticism, negativity, or other nonsupportive conduct. Such

behavior creates psychological pain and diminishes the well-being and confidence of its targets. It can cause insomnia, posttraumatic stress disorder, depression, or even suicidal ideation. Nurses who are targets of workplace bullying are also subject to physical health complaints.

Bullies reduce morale and intensify work dissatisfaction, resulting in accelerated turnover and staffing shortages. Such hostile conduct compromises clinical performance and productivity. Of greatest concern is that lateral violence compromises patient safety. As Christie and Jones note, "[T]he multiple effects of lateral violence ultimately both decrease a nurse's ability to deliver optimal patient care and also compromise patient safety" (Christie, 2014). Nurses, therefore, have an ethical obligation to all patients to refrain from such behavior and to intervene when others engage in it.

The use of social media platforms to ostracize or criticize coworkers, known as cyberbullying, is particularly problematic as noted by the NCSBN:

Online comments by a nurse regarding co-workers, even if posted from home during non-work hours, may constitute as lateral violence. Lateral violence is receiving greater attention as more is learned about its impact on patient safety and quality clinical outcomes. Lateral violence includes disruptive behaviors of intimidation and bullying, which may be perpetuated in person or via the Internet, sometimes referred to as "cyber bullying." Such activity is cause for concern for current and future employers and regulators because of the patient safety ramifications. The line between speech protected by labor laws, the First Amendment and the ability of an employer to impose expectations on employees outside of work is still being determined. Nonetheless, such comments can be detrimental to a cohesive health care delivery team and may result in sanctions against the nurse (NCSBN, 2011c).

The ANA recommends the following:

■ Zero tolerance toward violent or abusive behavior;

■ Protection from retribution if reported;

■ Utilize employee assistance program;

■ Interrupt the violence;

■ Assess the nursing unit and raise awareness;

■ Brainstorm solutions and encourage dialogue; and

■ Create unit-specific guidelines (ANA, 2011).

Positive work environments require healthy interpersonal relationships. Nurses have an ethical obligation to be collegial and respectful of their co-workers so optimal patient care can be provided. Nurses also have an ethical obligation to recognize destructive behavior and intervene.

IMPAIRMENT

Nursing practice involves high-risk activities that require focus and concentration. The ability to safely administer medications, assess patients, or intervene in clinical emergencies is compromised when nurses are impaired from sleep deprivation, substance abuse, alcoholism, or mental health problems. Because impaired providers cannot provide safe patient care, nurses have an ethical obligation to protect patients from the potential danger they pose.

Alcoholism or drug use can manifest with physical and behavioral signs; see *Recognition of impaired colleagues* table

(Thomas et al., 2011). Nurses should periodically take continuing education courses related to the recognition of and intervention for impaired colleagues. Ignoring poor performance can be considered complicity. Nurses must be aware of their own behaviors, which can enable impaired providers to remain unsafe. Altering assignments to accommodate an impaired nurse, for example, imperils patients and does not help the nurse who needs professional assistance.

Careful attention should be paid to controlled substance management. When counting is necessary, it must be performed by two nurses. The destruction or wasting of unused portions of controlled substances must be witnessed. Never sign for a count or a waste that you have not actually performed or witnessed. Be familiar with the organization's policies for the management of controlled substances, and do not diverge from them. Be aware of coworkers who request you to do so.

Nurses who divert narcotics for personal use expose themselves to civil, administrative, and criminal charges. The automation and computerization of medications has made such diversion easier to discover. Pyxis or Omnicell records that conflict with medication administration or medication order records can trigger discrepancy reports, as well as variances from the norm. Many medication rooms and patient-care areas have camera video surveillance—the footage of which can be damaging evidence against the nurse who diverts medications.

Nurses have an ethical obligation both to patients and to their colleagues to report suspicious behavior. Impaired nurses need intervention

Table 1 Recognition of impaired colleagues

Signs/symptoms	Physical signs	Behavior changes
Brief, unexplained absences from the nursing unit Rounding at odd hours	Shakiness and or tremors Fatigue	Frequent mood changes Outburst of anger Defensiveness
Medication errors	Slurred speech	Inappropriate laughter
Isolation from peers	Frequent use of mouthwash or breath mints	Hyperactivity or hypoactivity
Mood changes after meals or breaks	Watery eyes	Lack of concentration Blackout periods
Frequent reports of lack of pain relief from assigned patients	Constricted/dilated pupils	Justify the addiction to "relax," "need to escape reality"
Volunteers to count narcotics or offers to medicate coworkers' patients	Diaphoresis	Cold weather clothing in warm weather to hide track marks
Wasted narcotics attributed to a single nurse	Unsteady gait	Frequent accidents or emergencies
Increased narcotic sign-outs	Frequent runny nose	Personal relationship issues
Discrepancies with the narcotic record and/or the patient record	Frequent nausea, vomiting, and diarrhea	Insomnia Frequent complaints of pain
Altered verbal or telephone medication orders	Weight gain or loss	Denial of problem Frequent lying
Decreased quality of care, documentation, arriving late to work, and requesting to leave early	Changes in grooming	Decreased judgment in their own performance

Source: Thomas, C., and Siela, D. "The Impaired Nurse: Would You Know What To Do If You Suspected Substance Abuse?" American Nurse Today 6(8), 2011. Retrieved from: http://www.medscape.com/viewarticle/748598

and treatment. Most state boards of nursing have "alternative to discipline" programs that allow an addicted nurse to temporarily stop practicing nursing without formal disciplinary action against the license in the process. This alternative might not be available if there has been patient harm.

Nurses with mental health problems also need intervention and treatment both to protect the public and to professionally assist the nurse. Many psychiatric illnesses can be successfully treated, allowing the nurse to remain in practice. Coworkers need and deserve compassion and the respect of their colleagues. As the ANA notes, "a nurse's duty of compassion and caring extends to themselves and their colleagues as well as to their patients" (ANA, 2014a).

WHISTLE-BLOWING

Reporting the unlawful, unethical, or unsafe practices of other providers or of an organization can be complicated. Some nursing regulations or public health laws mandate that nurses report the unsafe actions of their colleagues or of other providers. Some states do not specifically mandate such reporting but still hold nurses accountable when patient harm results, for failing to have intervened to prevent the harm. Regardless of the legal requirements, there can be an ethical imperative not to "look the other way" if patients can be injured when doing so.

State laws vary regarding the protection nurses have for making reports to outside agencies. Nurses who engage in whistle-blowing can be subject to retaliation and adverse employment actions in states where "whistle-blower" protection is not in place. In making the decision, The ANA recommends the following:

- If you identify an illegal or unethical practice, reserve judgment until you have adequate documentation to establish wrongdoing.
- Do not expect those that are engaged in unethical or illegal conduct to welcome your questions or concerns about this practice.
- Seek the counsel of someone you trust outside of the situation to provide you with an objective perspective.
- Consult with your state nurses association or legal counsel if possible before taking action to determine how best to document your concerns.
- Remember, you are not protected in a whistle-blower situation from retaliation by your employer until you blow the whistle.
- Blowing the whistle means that you report your concern to the national and/or state agency responsible for regulation of the organization for which you work or, in the case of criminal activity, to law-enforcement agencies as well.
- Private groups, such as The Joint Commission or the National Committee for Quality Assurance, do not confer protection. You must report to a state or national regulator.
- Although it is not required by every regulatory agency, it is a good rule of thumb to put your complaint in writing.
- Document all interactions related to the whistle-blowing situation, and keep copies for your personal file, NURSING.
- Keep documentation and interactions objective.
- Remain calm and do not lose your temper, even if those who learn of your actions attempt to provoke you.
- Remember that blowing the whistle is a very serious matter. Do not blow the whistle frivolously. Make sure you

have the facts straight before taking action (ANA, 2014b).

Ethics committees

Many of the complex ethical issues in health care require a team approach. The assistance and advice of a formal committee can be invaluable in these cases. In 1992, the Joint Commission added to its accreditation standards a requirement that American hospitals establish a mechanism for hospital personnel to consider and educate its constituents on ethical issues in patient care (Joint Commission, 1992). Two years later, the American Medical Association issued an opinion paper providing guidelines on the establishment of ethics committees in health care institutions (AMA, 1994).

A multidisciplinary ethics committee or bioethics committee should be composed of individuals from a variety of backgrounds. Nurses should have an active role in these committees. The purpose of the committee is not to make decisions, but to provide education and advice for those who do. Ethics committees are concerned with patient rights, shared decision making, and the resolution of conflict. In addition to reviewing individual cases, ethics committees can also be involved in developing institutional policies and procedures for dealing with issues such as advance directives, withholding or withdrawing life support or nutrition and hydration, DNR or DNI orders, and organ donation.

Tips for practice

Familiarize yourself with professional principles of ethical practice as identified by international, national, and local associations. Official codes of ethics have been published by the International Council of Nurses, the ANA, and many professional nursing organizations. (Refer to The ICN Code of Ethics for Nurses box.)

■ Read a prospective employer's mission statement before applying for a position so you are familiar with the institution's philosophy. Accept employment in an organization whose philosophy is consistent with your own values.

■ Seek the advice of the institution's ethics committee with difficult cases.

■ Maintain clinical competence with continuing education, membership in professional organizations, and subscriptions to professional journals.

■ Educate yourself on cultural issues to attain cultural competency.

■ Familiarize yourself with the Nurse Practice Act or nursing regulations in every state in which you practice, and be particularly aware of the nursing board's definitions of moral character, practice guidelines, delegation, and nursing's scope of practice.

■ Anticipate and recognize situations that create moral distress, and develop strategies to cope with it. The AACN's workbook, The 4A's to Rise Above Moral Distress, offers much guidance in this area. (Refer to AACN box.)

Conclusion

Nurses enjoy a privileged position in the public eye. Gallup polls consistently rank the profession as the most trustworthy (Future of Nursing, 2013). That trust is based upon the view that nurses are honest and ethical. We owe it to our patients, the public, each other, and ourselves to be worthy of that trust.

The ICN code of ethics for nurses

Elements of the code

1. Nutrses and people

- ❑ The nurse's primary professional responsibility is to people requiring nursing care. In providing care, the nurse promotes an environment in which the human rights, values, customs, and spiritual beliefs of the individual, family and community are respected.
- ❑ The nurse ensures that the individual receives accurate, sufficient and timely information in a culturally appropriate manner on which to base consent for care and related treatment.
- ❑ The nurse holds in confidence personal information and uses judgment in sharing this information.
- ❑ The nurse shares with society the responsibility for initiating and supporting action to meet the health and social needs of the public, in particular those of vulnerable populations.
- ❑ The nurse advocates for equity and social justice in resource allocation, access to health care and other social and economic services.
- ❑ The nurse demonstrates professional values such as respectfulness, responsiveness, compassion, trustworthiness, and integrity.

2. Nurses and practice

- ❑ The nurse carries personal responsibility and accountability for nursing practice, and for maintaining competence by continual learning.
- ❑ The nurse maintains a standard of personal health such that the ability to provide care is not compromised.
- ❑ The nurse uses judgment regarding individual competence when accepting and delegating responsibility.
- ❑ The nurse at all times maintains standards of personal conduct which reflect well on the profession and enhance its image and public confidence.
- ❑ The nurse, in providing care, ensures that use of technology and scientific advances are compatible with the safety, dignity and rights of people.
- ❑ The nurse strives to foster and maintain a practice culture promoting ethical behavior and open dialogue.

3. Nurses and the profession

- ❑ The nurse assumes the major role in determining and implementing acceptable standards of clinical nursing practice, management, research and education.
- ❑ The nurse is active in developing a core of research-based professional knowledge that supports evidence-based practice.
- ❑ The nurse is active in developing and sustaining a core of professional values.
- ❑ The nurse, acting through the professional organization, participates in creating a positive practice environment and maintaining safe, equitable social and economic working conditions in nursing.
- ❑ The nurse practices to sustain and protect the natural environment and is aware of its consequences on health.
- ❑ The nurse contributes to an ethical organizational environment and challenges unethical practices and settings.

4. Nurses and co-workers

- ❑ The nurse sustains a collaborative and respectful relationship with co-workers in nursing and other fields.
- ❑ The nurse takes appropriate action to safeguard individuals, families and communities when their health is endangered by a co-worker or any other person.
- ❑ The nurse takes appropriate action to support and guide co-workers to advance ethical conduct.

AACN 4A'S to rise above moral distress

Ask

■ Am I feeling distressed or showing signs of suffering?
■ Is the source of my distress work related?
■ Am I observing symptoms of distress within my team?
Goal: You become aware that moral distress is present.

Affirm

■ Affirm your distress and your commitment to take care of yourself.
■ Validate feelings and perceptions with others.
■ Affirm professional obligation to act.
Goal: You make a commitment to address moral distress

Assess

■ Identify sources of your distress
■ Personal

■ Environment
■ Determine the severity of your distress
■ Contemplate your readiness to act
■ You recognize there is an issue but may be ambivalent about taking action to change it
■ You analyze risks and benefits.
Goal: You are ready to make an action plan

Act

■ Prepare to act
■ Prepare personally and professionally to take action
■ Take action
■ Implement strategies to initiate the changes you desire
■ Maintain desired change
■ Anticipate and manage setbacks
■ Continue to implement the 4A's to resolve moral distress.
Goal: You preserve your integrity and authenticity

SELECTED READINGS

101st Congress. H.R.4449 — Patient Self Determination Act of 1990, 1990. Retrieved from: http://thomas.loc.gov /cgi-bin/query/z?c101:H.R.4449.IH

Aging with Dignity. Five Wishes Resources, 2014. Retrieved from: http://www .agingwithdignity.org/forms/5wishes.pdf

American Association of Critical Care Nurses. The 4As to Rise Above Moral Distress, (N.D.). Retrieved from: http://www.aacn .org/WD/Practice/Docs/4As_to_Rise_ Above_Moral_Distress.pdf

American Association of Critical Care Nurses. Moral Distress, 2014. Retrieved from: http://www.aacn.org/wd/practice/ content/ethic-moral.pcms?menu=practice

American Medical Association. AMA Policy on Provision of Life-Sustaining Medical Treatment, (N.D.). Retrieved from: http://www.ama-assn.org/ama/pub/ physician-resources/medical-ethics/about- ethics-group/ethics-resource-center/ end-of-life-care/ama-policy-provision-life- sustaining-medical.page

American Medical Association. Opinion 9.11 — Ethics Committees in Health Care Institutions, 1994. Retrieved from: http:// www.ama-assn.org/ama/pub/physician- resources/medical-ethics/code-medical- ethics/opinion911.page

American Nurses Association. Guide to the Code of Ethics for Nurses: Interpreta- tion and Application, 2010a. Retrieved from: http://www.nursingworld.org/ MainMenuCategories/EthicsStandards/ CodeofEthicsforNurses

American Nurses Association. Registered Nurses' Roles and Responsibilities in Pro- viding Expert Care and Counseling at the End of Life, 2010b. Retrieved from: http:// www.nursingworld.org/MainMenu Categories/EthicsStandards/Ethics- Position-Statements/etpain14426.pdf

American Nurses Association. Lateral Violence and Bullying in Nursing, 2011a. Retrieved from: http://www.nursingworld.org/

Mobile/Nursing-Factsheets/lateral-violence-and-bullying-in-nursing.html

American Nurses Association. Short Definitions of Ethical Principles and Theories Familiar Words, What Do They Mean?, 2011b. Retrieved from: http://www.nursingworld.org/mainmenucategories/ethicsstandards/resources/ethics-definitions.pdf

American Nurses Association. Euthanasia, Assisted Suicide, and Aid in Dying, 2013. Retrieved from: http://www.nursingworld.org/euthanasiaanddying

American Nurses Association. Impaired Nurse Resource Center, 2014a. Retrieved from: http://www.nursingworld.org/MainMenuCategories/Workplace-Safety/Healthy-Work-Environment/Work-Environment/ImpairedNurse

American Nurses Association. Things to Know About Whistle Blowing, Nursing World, 2014b. Retrieved from: http://www.nursingworld.org/MainMenuCategories/ThePracticeofProfessionalNursing/workforce/Workforce-Advocacy/Whistle-Blowing.html

Annas, G. "The Case of Baby Jane Doe: Child Abuse or Unlawful Federal Intervention?" *American Journal of Public Health* 74(7), 727–729, July 1984. Retrieved from: http://ajph.aphapublications.org/doi/pdf/10.2105/AJPH.74.7.727

Bailey, D. Lessons Learned From Newborn Screening for Fragile X Syndrome, 2011. Retrieved from: https://acc.hhs.gov/non-iacc-events/2011/slides_elsi_don_bailey_092611.pdf

Baily, M. Newborn Screening, The Hastings Center Bioethics Briefing Book, 2014. Retrieved from: http://www.thehastingscenter.org/Publications/BriefingBook/Detail.aspx?id=2268

Barnum, B., and Catlin, A. "Ethical Issues in Newborn Care: Benevolent Injustice: a Neonatal Dilemma," *Advances in Neonatal Care* 9(3):132–136, June 2009. Retrieved from: http://www.nursingcenter.com/lnc/journalarticleprint?Article_ID=867162

Bush, J. Petition for Writ of Certiorari, 2004. Retrieved from: http://umshare.miami.edu/web/wda/ethics/documents/schivao/120104-schiavo-cert-docket.pdf

Centers for Disease Control. Newborn Screening, (N.D.). Retrieved from: http://www.cdc.gov/newbornscreening/

Centers for Medicare and Medicaid Services. The Emergency Medical Treatment & Labor Act, 2014. Retrieved from: http://www.cms.gov/Regulations-and-Guidance/Legislation/EMTALA/index.html?redirect=/EMTALA/

Cerminara, K., and Goodman, K. Schiavo Timeline. Part 1, University of Miami Ethics Programs, 2014. Retrieved from: http://www.miami.edu/index.php/ethics/projects/schiavo/schiavo_timeline/

Cerminara, K., and Goodman, K. Schiavo Timeline. Part 2, University of Miami Ethics Programs, 2014. Retrieved from: http://www.miami.edu/index.php/ethics/projects/schiavo/schiavo_timline2/

Christie, W., and Jones, S. "Lateral Violence in Nursing and the Theory of the Nurse as Wounded Healer," *Online Journal of Issues in Nursing* 19(1), 2014. Retrieved from: http://www.nursingworld.org/MainMenuCategories/ANAMarketplace/ANAPeriodicals/OJIN/TableofContents/Vol-19-2014/No1-Jan-2014/Articles-Previous-Topics/Lateral-Violence-and-Theory-of-Wounded-Healer.html

Coolen, P., et al. Culture Relevance in End-of-Life, EthnoMED, May 1, 2012. Retrieved from: http://ethnomed.org/clinical/end-of-life/cultural-relevance-in-end-of-life-care

Cushman, R. Ethics Terms and Terminology, 2005. Retrieved from: http://www.lasalle.edu/~price/Hon%20365%20ethics%20terms.htm

Epstein, E., and Delgado, S. "Understanding and Addressing Moral Distress," *Online Journal of Issues in Nursing* 15(3), 2010. Retrieved from: http://www.nursingworld.org/MainMenuCategories/EthicsStandards/Courage-and-Distress/Understanding-Moral-Distress.html

Florida House of Representatives. HB 0701, 2005. Retrieved from: http://www.myfloridahouse.gov/

Florida Office of the Governor. Executive Order No. 03-201, 2003. Retrieved from: https://umshare.miami.edu/web/wda/ethics/documents/schivao/Schiavo_Controversy_Fla_Gov_Exec_Order_No_03-201.html

Future of Nursing Campaign for Action. 2013 Gallup Poll: Nursing is the Most Trustworthy Profession, 2013. Retrieved from:

http://campaignforaction.org/
community-post/2013-gallup-poll-
nursing-most-trustworthy-profession

Gennett, G. Motion to Intervene of the Committee on Government Reform of the U.S.
House of Representatives, 2005. Retrieved
from: https://umshare.miami.edu/web/
wda/ethics/documents/schivao/
031805-USHouse_Motion_Intervene.pdf

Haberman, C. "From Private Ordeal to National Fight: The Case of Terry Schiavo,"
The New York Times, Retro Report, April
20, 2014. Retrieved from: http://www
.nytimes.com/2014/04/21/us/from-
private-ordeal-to-national-fight-the-case-
of-terri-schiavo.html?_r=0

Institute of Medicine. "Dying in America: Im-
proving Quality and Honoring Individual
Preferences Near the End of Life," *National
Academies Press*, 2014. Retrieved from:
http://www.iom.edu/Reports/2014/
Dying-In-America-Improving-
Quality-and-Honoring-Individual-
Preferences-Near-the-End-of-Life.aspx

International Council of Nurses. The ICN
Code of Ethics for Nurses, 2012. Retrieved
from: http://www.icn.ch/images/stories/
documents/about/icncode_english.pdf

Joint Commission. Accreditation Standard:
Mechanism for Considering Ethical Issues,
Patient Rights Standard R1.1.1.6.1 at 104,
1992.

Memidex. Online Dictionary & Thesaurus,
2013. Retrieved from: http://www
.memidex.com/

Montana State Legislature. Rights of the
Terminally Ill Act, 2014. Retrieved
from: http://leg.mt.gov/bills/mca_
toc/50_9.htm

National Council of State Boards of Nursing.
A Nurse's Guide to Professional Boundaries, 2011a. Retrieved from: https://www
.ncsbn.org/ProfessionalBoundaries_
Complete.pdf

National Council of State Boards of Nursing.
White Paper: A Nurse's Guide to the Use
of Social Media, 2011c. Retrieved from:
https://www.ncsbn.org/11_NCSBN_
Nurses_Guide_Social_Media.pdf

National Council of State Boards of Nurs-
ing. Substance Use Disorder in Nursing:
A Resource Manual and Guidelines for
Alternative and Disciplinary Monitoring

Programs, 2011b. Retrieved from: https://
www.ncsbn.org/SUDN_10.pdf

Nelson, S. Chief Medical Examiner, 10th Judicial Circuit, Neuropathology Report to Jon
R. Thogmartin, M.D., District 6 Medical
Examiner, 2005. Retrieved from: https://
umshare.miami.edu/web/wda/ethics/
documents/schivao/061505-autopsy.pdf

New York Daily News. New Mexico Judge
Rules Doctors Can Help Terminally Ill
Patients Commit Suicide Without Prosecution, 2014. Retrieved from: http://
www.nydailynews.com/news/national/
new-mexico-judge-rules-terminally-ill-pa-
tients-seek-suicide-article-1.1578854

Oregon Health Authority. Death with Dignity
Act, 2014. Retrieved from: http://public
.health.oregon.gov/ProviderPartner
Resources/EvaluationResearch/
DeathwithDignityAct/Pages/index.aspx

The President's Council on Bioethics. The
Changing Moral Focus of Newborn
Screening: An Ethical Analysis, 2008.
Retrieved from: https://repository.
library.georgetown.edu/bitstream/
handle/10822/548394/newborn_screening
.pdf?sequence=1

Pro Con. State-by-State Guide to Physician-Assisted Suicide, 2014. Retrieved
from: http://euthanasia.procon.org/view
.resource.php?resourceID=000132

Shepherd, L. "Terri Schiavo: Unsettling the
Settled," *Loyola University Chicago Law Journal* 37:297–341, 2006. Retrieved
from: http://www.luc.edu/media/lucedu/
law/students/publications/llj/pdfs/
shepherd.pdf

Stock, S. "In Vitro Fertilization," Medline,
2014. Retrieved from: http://www.nlm.
nih.gov/medlineplus/ency/article/007279
.htm

Thogmorton, J. Report of Autopsy, 2005. Retrieved from: https://umshare.miami.edu/
web/wda/ethics/documents/
schivao/061505-autopsy.pdf

Thomas, C., and Siela, D. "The Impaired
Nurse: Would You Know What To Do If
You Suspected Substance Abuse?" *American Nurse Today* 6(8), 2011. Retrieved
from: http://www.medscape.com/
viewarticle/748598

United States General Accounting Office.
Patient Self-Determination Act: Providers

Offer Information on Advanced Directives but Effectiveness Uncertain, 1995. Retrieved from: http://www.gpo.gov/fdsys/pkg/GAORE-PORTS-HEHS-95-135/pdf/GAOREPORTS-HEHS-95-135.pdf

Vermont State Legislature. Death with Dignity Act, 2013. Retrieved from: http://legislature.vermont.gov/

Washington State Legislature. Washington Death with Dignity Act, 2008. Retrieved from: http://euthanasia.procon.org/sourcefiles/EuthWashingtonStateLaw.pdf

CASES

Baxter v. Montana, WL 5155363 (Mont. 2009).

Robert Baxter v. State of Montana (2009 MT 449).

Cruzan, by Cruzan v. Harmon, 760 S.W.2d 408 (Mo.banc 1988).

Cruzan v. Director, Missouri Department of Health, 497 U.S. 261 (1990).

Long Island Jewish Medical Center (DOE), 168 Misc.2d 576 (1996).

Matter of Baby K, 16 F.3d 590 (4th Cir. 1994).

In re Quinlan, 70 N.J. 10 (1976).

Weber v. Stony Brook Hosp., 95 A.D.2d 587 (2d Dept. 1983).

GLOSSARY, APPENDICES, AND INDEX

GLOSSARY

A

AA *abbr* Alcoholics Anonymous

abuse of process A civil action in which it's alleged that the legal process has been used in an improper manner. For example, an abuse of process action might be brought by a physician attempting to countersue a patient, or by a psychiatric patient attempting to demonstrate wrongful confinement.

ad hoc committee A committee commissioned for a specific purpose.

adjudicated incompetent Declared incompetent by exercise of judicial authority. Note that a patient who has been adjudicated incompetent may still have the mental capacity to make an informed decision about his medical care. Compare *incompetence* and *mental incompetence.*

administrative review An investigation conducted by the state board of nursing when a nurse is accused of professional misconduct. The board first reviews the complaint and then may hold a formal hearing at which evidence is presented and witnesses examined and cross-examined. Court proceedings—and possibly legal penalties—may result from the board's findings.

admissible evidence Authentic, relevant, reliable information that's present during a trial and may be used to reach a decision.

ADN *abbr* associate degree in nursing

adult 1. One who's fully developed and mature and who has attained the intellectual capacity and the emotional and psychological stability characteristic of a mature person. 2. A person who has reached legal age (in most states, age 18 or 21 years).

advance directive A document (or documentation) allowing a person to give directions about future medical care or to designate another person(s) to make medical decisions if and when the individual patient loses decision-making capacity.

advance directive system A system implemented by health care institutions (including hospitals, extended-care facilities, and hospices) to ensure that every patient, at admission, is informed of his right to execute a living will or durable power of attorney for health care decisions.

advanced practice nurse (APN) An individual whose education and certification meet criteria established by each state's board of nursing, including current licensure as a registered nurse and a master's degree or post-basic program certificate in a clinical nursing specialty with national certification.

adverse reaction A harmful, unintended reaction to a drug administered at normal dosage.

affidavit A written statement sworn to before a notary public or an officer of the court.

affirmative defense A denial of guilt or wrongdoing based on new evidence rather than simple denial of a charge. For example, a nurse who pleads immunity under the Good Samaritan law is making an affirmative defense. The defendant bears the burden of proof in an affirmative defense.

against medical advice A patient's decision to leave a health care facility against his physician's advice.

age of majority 18 or 21 years, depending on the laws of each state or Canadian province.

agency A relationship between two parties in which the first party authorizes the second to act as an agent on behalf of the first.

agent A party authorized to act on behalf of another and to give the other an account of such actions.

AHA *abbr* American Hospital Association

Alcoholics Anonymous (AA) An international nonprofit organization founded in 1935 that consists of abstinent alcoholics whose purpose is to help other alcoholics stop drinking and maintain sobriety through group support, shared experiences, and faith in a power greater than themselves.

alcoholism The extreme dependence on excessive amounts of alcohol, associated with a cumulative pattern of deviant behaviors. Alcoholism is a chronic illness with a slow, insidious onset, which may occur at any age. The cause is unknown, but cultural and psychosocial factors are suspect. Also, families of alcoholics have a higher incidence of alcoholism. See also *drug addiction*.

AMA *abbr* against medical advice; American Medical Association

amendment An alteration to an existing law or complaint.

American Hospital Association (AHA) Founded in 1898, the AHA is a national association comprised of individuals and health care institutions, including hospitals, health care systems, and preacute and postacute health care delivery organizations. The AHA is dedicated to promoting the welfare of the public through its leadership and assistance to its members in the provision of better health services for all people.

American Medical Association (AMA) A professional association including practitioners in all recognized medical specialties as well as general primary care physicians. The AMA is governed by a Board of Trustees and House of Delegates. Trustees and delegates represent various state and local medical associations as well as such government agencies as the Public Health Service and medical departments of the Army, Navy, and Air Force.

American Nurses Association (ANA) The national professional association of registered nurses in the United States. It was founded in 1896 to improve standards of health and the availability of health care given in order to foster high standards for nursing, to promote the professional development of nurses, and to advance the economic and general welfare of nurses. The ANA is made up of 53 constituent associations from 50 states, the District of Columbia, Guam, and the U.S. Virgin Islands, representing more than 900 district associations. Members may join one or more of the five Divisions on Nursing Practice: Community Health, Gerontological, Maternal and Child, Medical–Surgical, and Psychiatric and Mental Health Nursing. These divisions are coordinated by the Congress for Nursing Practice. The Congress evaluates changes in the scope of practice, monitors scientific and educational developments, encourages research, and develops statements that describe ANA policies regarding legislation that affects nursing practice. Other commissions within the association include the Commission on Nursing Education, the Commission on Nursing Services, the Commission on Nursing Research, and the Economic and General Welfare Commission.

American Red Cross A nationwide organization that seeks to reduce human suffering through various health, safety, and disaster relief programs in affiliation with the International Committee of the Red Cross. The Committee and all Red Cross organizations evolved from the Geneva Convention of 1864, following the example and urging of Swiss humanitarian Jean-Henri Dunant, who aided wounded French and Austrian soldiers at the Battle of Solferino in 1859. The American Red Cross (one of more than 120 national Red Cross organizations) has more than 130 million members in about 3,100 chapters throughout the United States. Volunteers constitute the entire staffs of about 1,700 chapters. Other chapters maintain small paid staffs and some professionals, but depend largely on volunteers. See also *International Red Cross Society.*

ANA *abbr* American Nurses Association

answer The response of a defendant to the claims of a plaintiff. The answer contains a denial of the plaintiff's allegations and may also contain an affirmative defense or a counterclaim. It's the principal pleading on the part of the defense and is prepared in writing, usually by the defense attorney, and submitted to the court.

APN *abbr* advanced practice nurse

appellant The party who lost the case in the lower court and is appealing the appellate court to change the lower court's decision.

appellate court A court of law that has the power to review the decision of a lower court. An appellate court doesn't make a new determination of the facts of the case; instead, it reviews the way in which the law was applied to the case.

appellee The party in an appeal who won the case in a lower court. The appellee argues that the decision of the lower court shouldn't be modified by the appellate court.

arbitration The settlement of a dispute by an impartial person chosen by the disputing parties.

arbitrator An impartial person appointed to resolve a dispute between parties. The arbitrator listens to the evidence as presented by the parties in an informal hearing and attempts to arrive at a resolution acceptable to both parties.

assault An attempt or threat by a person to physically injure another person.

associate degree in nursing (ADN) An academic degree obtained after satisfactory completion of a 2-year course of study, usually at a community or junior college. The recipient is eligible to take the national licensing examination to become a registered nurse. An associate degree in nursing isn't available in Canada. Compare *Bachelor of Science in Nursing.*

attending physician The physician who's responsible for a specific patient. In a university setting, an attending physician usually also has teaching responsibilities and holds a faculty appointment. Also called the *attending* (informal), *physician of record.*

attorney of record The attorney whose name appears on the legal records for a specific case as the agent of a specific client.

audit A methodical examination; to examine with intent to verify. Nursing audits examine standards of nursing care.

authorization cards Cards employees sign to authorize a union election.

autonomy The principle of self-determination. The right to make decisions about one's own health care.

autopsy A postmortem examination of a body to determine the cause of death.

B

Bachelor of Science in Nursing (BSN) An academic degree awarded upon satisfactory completion of a 4-year course of study in an institution of higher learning. The recipient is eligible to take the national licensing examination to become a registered nurse. A BSN degree is a prerequisite for advancement in most systems and institutions that employ nurses. Compare *associate degree in nursing.*

bargaining agent A person or group selected by members of a bargaining unit to represent them in negotiations.

bargaining unit A group of employees who participate in collective bargaining as representatives of all employees.

BASIC abbr Beginners' All-purpose Symbolic Instruction Code, a programming language widely used on personal computers and small business systems.

battered woman syndrome (BWS) This syndrome is the "learned helplessness" that results from repeated but failed attempts to escape a batterer's violence. Eventually, the woman stops trying to escape the violence. Such violence tends to follow a predictable pattern. The first phase is characterized by the abuser's increased irritability, edginess, and tension. These feelings are expressed in the form of verbal criticism and abuse as well as physical shoves and slaps. The second phase is the time of acute, violent activity. As tension mounts, the woman becomes unable to placate the male abuser, and she may argue or defend herself. The man uses this as justification for his anger and assaults her, usually saying that he's "teaching her a lesson." The third stage is characterized by apology and remorse with promises of change on the part of the abuser. The calm continues until tension builds again. BWS occurs at all socioeconomic levels, and one-half to three-quarters of female assault victims are the victims of an attack by a lover or husband. It's estimated that up to 2 million women are beaten by their husbands each year.

battery The unauthorized touching of a person by another person. For example, a physician who has treated a patient beyond what the patient has consented to has committed battery.

bench trial A trial by a judge as opposed to a trial by a jury.

beneficence The promotion of good and prevention of harm.

benefits Nonsalary forms of compensation an employer provides for employees—for example, medical and dental insurance.

binding arbitration A process of settling disputes in which all parties agree to be bound by the determination of an arbitrator.

board of health An administrative body acting on a municipal, county, state, province, or national level. The functions, powers, and responsibilities of boards of health vary with the locale. Each board is generally concerned with the recognition of the health needs of the people and the coordination of projects and resources to meet and identify those needs. Among the tasks of most boards of health are prevention of disease, health education, and implementation of laws pertaining to health.

borrowed-servant doctrine A legal doctrine that courts may apply in cases in which an employer "lends" his employee's services to another employer who, under this doctrine, becomes solely liable for the employee's wrongful conduct. Also called *ostensible agent doctrine.* Compare *captain-of-the ship doctrine* and *dual agency doctrine.*

brain death Final cessation of activity in the central nervous system, especially as indicated by a flat electroencephalogram for a predetermined length of time. The cessation of all measurable function or activity in every area of the brain, including the brain stem. Compare *death.*

breach of contract Failure to perform all or part of a contracted duty without justification.

breach of duty Neglect or failure to fulfill in a proper manner the duties of an office, job, or position.

British Medical Association (BMA) A national professional organization of physicians in the United Kingdom.

BSN *abbr* bachelor of science in nursing

bullying Lateral or horizontal violence, also referred to as relational aggression, a form of psychological abuse.

BWS *abbr* battered woman syndrome

C

Canadian Association of University Schools of Nursing (CAUSN) A national Canadian organization of nursing schools affiliated with institutions of higher learning.

Canadian Nurses Association (CNA) This official national organization is a federation of professional nurses associations from 11 jurisdictions and territories. It represents more than 110,000 members and is the national voice of the profession in Canada.

capitation A per-member, monthly payment to a provider that covers contracted services and is paid in advance of delivery. In essence, a provider agrees to provide specified services to enrollees for this fixed payment for a specified term, regardless of how many times the member uses the service.

captain-of-the-ship doctrine A legal doctrine that considers a surgeon responsible for the actions of his assistants when those assistants are under the surgeon's supervision. Compare *borrowed-servant doctrine.*

care plans A charting format that shows the relationships of sets of interventions to sets of intermediate outcomes along a time line.

case management The process by which a designated health care professional, usually a nurse, manages all health-related matters of a patient. Case managers coordinate and ensure continuity of care. They develop a plan to use health care resources efficiently and achieve the optimum patient outcome in the most cost-effective manner. They also match the appropriate intensity of services to the patient's needs.

causa mortis Latin phrase meaning "in anticipation of approaching death."

The state of mind of a person approaching death.

CAUSN *abbr* Canadian Association of University Schools of Nursing

CCU *abbr* coronary care unit; critical care unit

CDC *abbr* Centers for Disease Control and Prevention

Centers for Disease Control and Prevention (CDC) An agency of the U.S. government that provides facilities and services for the investigation, identification, prevention, and control of disease.

certification A statement recognizing that a nurse is specially qualified, based on predetermined standards, to provide nursing care in a particular area of nursing practice.

CGFNS *abbr* Commission on Graduates of Foreign Nursing Schools

certified nurse-midwife See *midwife.*

chain of custody An evidentiary rule requiring that each individual having custody of a piece of evidence be identified and that the transfer of evidence from one custodian to another be documented so that all evidence is accounted for. Also called *chain of evidence.*

challenge An objection by a party (or his lawyer) to the inclusion of a particular prospective juror as a member of the jury that's to hear the party's cause or trial, with the result that the prospective juror is disqualified.

challenge for cause A challenge based on a particular reason (such as bias) specified by law or procedure as a reason that a party (or his lawyer) may use to disqualify a prospective juror.

child abuse The physical, sexual, or emotional mistreatment of a child. It may be overt or covert and commonly results in physical or psychological injury, mental impairment, or, sometimes, death. Child abuse results from complex factors involving both parents and child, compounded by various stressful environmental circumstances, such as poor socioeconomic conditions; inadequate physical and emotional support within the family; any major life change or crisis, especially those crises arising from marital strife; or a combination of these factors. Also called *battered child syndrome* for children younger than age 3. Compare *child neglect.*

child neglect Failure by parents or guardians to provide for the basic needs of a child by physical or emotional deprivation that interferes with normal growth and development or that places the child in jeopardy. Compare *child abuse.*

child welfare Any service sponsored by the community or special organizations that provide physical, social, or psychological care for children in need of that service.

chronic care A pattern of medical and nursing care that focuses on the long-term care of people with chronic diseases or conditions, either at home or in a medical facility. It includes care specific to the problem and measures to encourage self-care, promote health, and prevent loss of function.

circumstantial evidence Testimony based on inference or hearsay rather than actual personal knowledge or observation of the facts in question.

civil defense laws The body of statutory law that's invoked when the jurisdiction is under attack—for example, during a war.

civil penalty Fines or money damages imposed as punishment for a certain activity.

claims-made policy A professional liability insurance policy that covers the insured only for a claim of malpractice made while the policy is in effect.

claims review agency An agency that investigates claims for payment made to an insurance company. It determines whether the claim is legitimate, assesses how severe the loss is, and determines the amount the insurance company is required to pay.

clinical nurse specialist (CNS) A registered nurse who holds a master of science degree in nursing (MSN) and who has acquired advanced knowledge and clinical skills in a specific area of nursing and health care.

clinical pathways A clinical tool used by case managers to achieve better quality and cost outcomes by outlining and sequencing the usual and desired care for particular groups of patients. Clinical pathways incorporate care requirements from preadmission through postdischarge. Also called *critical paths.*

clinical practice guidelines A decision-making tool used to help practitioners determine how diseases or disorders can most effectively and appropriately be prevented, diagnosed, treated, and managed clinically. These guidelines include advice and information from recognized clinical experts.

closed shop See *union shop.*

CNA *abbr* Canadian Nurses Association

CNM *abbr* certified nurse-midwife; see *midwife.*

CNS *abbr* clinical nurse specialist

code 1. A published body of statutes, such as a civil code. 2. A collection of standards and rules of behavior, such as a dress code. 3. A symbolic means of representing information for communication or transfer, such as a genetic code. 4. *Informal.* A discreet signal used to summon a special team to resuscitate a patient without alarming patients or visitors. See also *no-code order.*

codes A system of assigned terms designed by a medical institution for quick and accurate communication during emergencies or for patient identification.

collective bargaining A legal process in which representatives of unionized employees negotiate with employers about such matters as wages, hours, and conditions.

collectively bargained contract A contract negotiated by a labor organization or union. Also called a *collective contract.*

Commission on Graduates of Foreign Nursing Schools (CGFNS) An organization established in 1977 to ensure safe nursing care for the American public and to protect graduates of foreign nursing schools from employment exploitation.

commitment 1. The placement or confinement of an individual in a specialized hospital or other institutional facility. 2. The legal procedure of admitting a mentally ill person to an institution for psychiatric treatment. The process varies from state to state, but usually involves judicial or court action based on medical evidence certifying that the person is mentally ill. 3. A pledge or contract to fulfill some obligation or agreement, used especially in some forms of psychotherapy or marriage counseling.

common law Law derived from previous court decisions as opposed to law based on legislative enactment (statutes). Also called *case law.* In the absence of statutory law regarding a subject, the judge-made rules of common law are the law on that subject.

comparative negligence Determination of liability in which damages may be apportioned among multiple defendants. The extent of liability depends on each defendant's relative contribution to the harm done as determined by the jury.

complaint 1. In a civil case, a pleading by a plaintiff made under oath to initiate a suit. It's a statement of the formal charge and the cause for action against the defendant. In a criminal case, a serious felony prosecution requires an indictment with evidence presented by a state's attorney.
2. *Informal.* Any ailment, problem, or symptom identified by the patient, member of the patient's family, or other knowledgeable person. The chief complaint is usually the reason the patient has sought health care.

confidentiality A professional responsibility to keep all privileged information private. In some instances, confidentiality is mandated by state or federal statutes and case law.

consent form A document that's prepared for a patient's signature, disclosing his proposed treatment in general terms.

consequential damages See *special damages.*

consumer A person who buys goods or services for his own needs and not for resale or for use in the production of other goods or services for resale.

continuum of care The full range of health care services, from health promotion and disease prevention through delivery of primary care, acute care, home health care, and long-term care.

contract defense An answer to an allegation that a breach of contract has occurred. Compare *impossibility defense.*

contract duties Duties defined in a contract such as an employment contract.

contract violations Actions that break mutually accepted contract provisions such as those of an employment contract.

controlled substance Any substance that's strictly regulated or outlawed because of its potential for abuse or addiction. Controlled substances include cannabis, depressants, hallucinogens, opioids, and stimulants. Compare *prescription drug.*

convalescent home See *extended-care facility.*

cooperation strategy A plan for bringing about change in which the person who initiates change influences others to adapt to the change, using open communication and interpersonal skills.

coronary care unit (CCU) A specially equipped hospital area designed for the treatment of patients with sudden, life-threatening cardiac conditions. Such units contain resuscitation and monitoring equipment, and are staffed by personnel specially trained and skilled in recognizing and immediately responding to cardiac emergencies with cardiopulmonary resuscitation techniques, administration of antiarrhythmics, and other appropriate therapeutic measures.

coroner A public official who investigates the causes and circumstances of a death occurring within a specific legal jurisdiction or territory, especially a death that may have resulted from unnatural causes. Also called *medical examiner.*

corporate liability The legal responsibility of a corporation and its officers. A corporation's liability is normally limited to its assets; the shareholders are thus protected against personal liability for the corporation.

counterclaim A claim made by a defendant establishing a cause for action in his favor against the plaintiff. The purpose of a counterclaim is to oppose or detract from the plaintiff's claim or complaint.

countersignature A signature obtained from another health care professional to verify that information is correct and is within the verifier's personal knowledge.

CPU *abbr* central processing unit

critical care unit (CCU) A hospital unit in which patients requiring close monitoring and intensive care are housed for as long as needed. A critical care unit contains highly technical and sophisticated monitoring devices and equipment, and the staff in the unit is educated to provide intensive care, as needed by the patients. See also *intensive care unit.*

critical paths See *clinical pathways.*

CRNA *abbr* certified registered nurse anesthetist; see *nurse anesthetist.*

cross-examination The questioning of a witness by the attorney for the opposing party.

custodial care Services and care of an unskilled nature provided on a long-term basis, usually for convalescent and chronically ill individuals. Custodial care may include providing board and personal assistance.

D

damages The amount of money a court orders a defendant to pay the plaintiff when the case is decided in favor of the plaintiff.

DEA *abbr* Drug Enforcement Administration

death 1. The final and irreversible cessation of life as indicated by the absence of heartbeat or respiration. 2. The total absence of meaningful activity in the brain and the central nervous, cardiovascular, and respiratory systems, as observed and declared by a physician. Also called *legal death.* Compare *brain death.*

declared emergency Situation in which a government official formally identifies a state of emergency.

decree of educational equivalency An official decision stating that a person's experience is of equal value to an academic degree.

default judgment A judgment rendered against a defendant because of the defendant's failure to appear in court or to answer the plaintiff's claim within the proper time.

defendant The party that's named in a plaintiff's complaint and against whom the plaintiff's allegations are made. The defendant must respond to the allegations. See also *answer* and *litigant.*

defense independent medical examination In malpractice litigation, a medical examination of the injured party by a physician selected by the defendant's attorney or insurance company. Compare *discovery device.*

delinquency 1. Negligence or failure to fulfill a duty or obligation. 2. An offense, fault, misdemeanor, or misdeed; a tendency to commit such acts.

delinquent 1. Characterized by neglect of duty or violation of law. 2. Behavior characterized by persistent antisocial, illegal, violent, or criminal activity; a juvenile delinquent.

deontology An ethical theory based on moral obligation or commitment to others.

dependent nursing function A function the nurse performs following another health care professional's written order on the basis of that professional's judgment and for which that professional is accountable.

deposition A sworn pretrial testimony given by a witness in response to oral or written questions and cross-examination. The deposition is transcribed and may be used for further pretrial investigation. It may also be presented at the trial if the witness can't be present or changes his testimony. Compare *discovery device* and *interrogatories.*

direct access The right of a health care provider and a patient to interact on a professional basis without interference.

direct contract model HMO A managed-care organization that contracts directly with individual physicians to provide services to its members.

direct examination The first examination of a witness called to the stand by the attorney for the party the witness is representing.

direct patient care Care of a patient provided in person by a member of the staff. Direct patient care may involve any aspect of the health care of a patient, including treatments, counseling, self-care, patient education, and administration of medication.

directed verdict A verdict given by a jury at the direction of the trial judge.

disclosure laws Legislation requiring that potentially confidential information be reported—for example, laws that mandate nurses report suspected child abuse or neglect.

discovery device A pretrial procedure that allows the plaintiff's and defendant's attorneys to examine relevant materials and question all parties to the case. Compare *deposition, defense independent medical examination,* and *interrogatories.*

discovery rule A rule stating that the time period for a statute of limitation begins when a patient discovers the injury. This may take place many years after the injury occurred and after the applicable statute of limitation has formally run out.

discretionary powers *The freedom of a public officer to choose courses of action within the limits of his authority.*

disease management An effort to provide cost-effective care for a chronic condition by emphasizing treatment protocols and changes in personal habits. It's a comprehensive approach to lowering costs and improving patient outcomes that's applied on a disease-by-disease basis.

dismiss To discharge or dispose of an action, suit, or motion trial.

dispense To take a drug from the pharmacy and give or sell it to another person.

distributive justice The principle that advocates equal allocation of benefits and burdens to all members of society.

DO *abbr* Doctor of Osteopathy; see *physician* **Doctor of Medicine (MD)** See *physician.*

Doctor of Osteopathy (DO) See *physician.*

documentation The preparation or assembly of written records.

drug abuse The use of a drug for a nontherapeutic effect, especially one for which it wasn't prescribed or intended. Some of the most commonly abused substances are amphetamines, barbiturates, tranquilizers, and cocaine. Drug abuse may lead to organ damage, addiction, and disturbed patterns of behavior. Some illicit drugs, such as lysergic acid diethylamide, phencyclidine hydrochloride, and heroin, have no recognized therapeutic effect. Use of these drugs can incur criminal penalties in addition to the potential for physical, social, and psychological harm. See also *drug addiction.*

drug addiction A condition characterized by an overwhelming desire to continue taking a drug to which one has become habituated through repeated consumption because it produces a particular effect, usually an alteration of mental activity, attitude, or outlook. Addiction is usually accompanied by a compulsion to

obtain the drug, a tendency to increase the dose, a psychological or
physical dependence, and detrimental consequences for the individual
and society. Common addictive
drugs are barbiturates, cocaine, crack,
and morphine and other opioids,
especially heroin, which has slightly
greater euphorigenic properties than
other opium derivatives. See also
alcoholism and *drug abuse.*

**Drug Enforcement Administration
(DEA)** An agency of the federal
government empowered to enforce
regulations regarding the import or
export of narcotic drugs and certain
other substances or the traffic of
these substances across state lines.

dual agency doctrine A legal doctrine
stating that both the agency and
the "borrowing" party may be held
liable for the actions of the agent.
Under this doctrine, a nurse from
a nurses' registry may be held to be
the agent of both the registry and
the hospital. Compare *borrowed-
servant doctrine.*

due process rights Personal rights based
on the principle that the government may not deprive an individual
of life, liberty, or property unless
certain rules and procedures required by law are followed.

durable power of attorney A legal document enabling an individual to
designate another person, called *an
attorney-in-fact,* to act on the individual's behalf, even if the principal
person becomes disabled or incapacitated. This power is revoked when
the principal person dies. Compare
power of attorney.

duty A legal obligation owed by one
party to another. Duty may be
established by statute or another
legal process, such as by contract
or oath supported by statute, or
it may be voluntarily undertaken.

Every person has a duty to avoid
causing harm or injury to others by
negligence.

duty-to-rescue laws Legislation that
requires certain people—those who
perform rescues as part of their
jobs—to rescue people in need.
These people include firefighters,
police officers, and emergency medical technicians. Only a few states
apply duty-to-rescue laws to nurses.

E

emancipated minor A minor who's
legally considered free from the custody, care, and control of his parents
before the age of majority. To be
considered emancipated, a minor
must meet one of three conditions:
be living separate from parents or
guardian and managing his or her
own financial affairs for any length
of time (with or without permission), be married, or be the birth
mother of a child. Emancipated
minors lose the right to parental
support but may gain certain other
rights, such as the right to consent
to their own medical care and the
right to enter into binding contracts.

Emergency Medical Service (EMS) A
network of services coordinated to
provide aid and medical assistance
from primary response to definitive
care, involving personnel trained in
the rescue, stabilization, transportation, and advanced treatment of
trauma or medical emergency patients. Linked by a communications
system that operates on both a local
and regional level, EMS is usually
initiated by a citizen calling an
emergency number. Stages include
the first medical response; involvement of ambulance personnel, me-
dium and heavy rescue equipment,
and paramedic units, if necessary;
and continued care in the hospital

with emergency department nurses and physicians, specialists, and critical care nurses and physicians.

EMS *abbr* Emergency Medical Service

EMTALA *abbr* the Emergency Medical Transfer and Active Labor Act, also known as the patient antidumping law.

endorsement 1. The act of giving approval, support, or sanction. 2. A policy whereby the state board of nursing will accept an out-of-state license to practice nursing.

EPO *abbr* exclusive provider organization

ethical diagnosis The determination that a moral dilemma exists, followed by classification of the dilemma by type.

ethics An area of philosophy that examines values, actions, and choices to determine right and wrong. The study of standards of conduct and moral judgments.

euthanasia Deliberately bringing about the death of a person who's suffering from an incurable disease or condition, either actively (e.g., by administering a lethal drug) or passively (e.g., by withholding treatment).

evaluation Determining the extent to which nursing care has achieved its goals.

exclusionary rule A constitutional rule of law that states that otherwise admissible evidence may not be used in a criminal trial if it was obtained as a result of an illegal search and seizure.

exclusive provider organization (EPO) EPOs limit health care benefits to participating providers. EPOs are regulated under insurance laws.

executing a contract Carrying out all the terms of a contract.

exemplary damages See *punitive damages.*

expert witness A person who has special knowledge of a subject about which a court requests testimony. Special knowledge may be acquired by experience, education, observation, or study and isn't possessed by the average person. An expert witness gives expert testimony or expert evidence. This evidence usually serves to educate the court and the jury about the subject under consideration. Compare *witness.*

express contract A verbal or written agreement between two or more people to do or not do something.

extended-care facility An institution devoted to providing medical, nursing, or custodial care for an individual over a prolonged period of time, such as during the course of a chronic disease or during the rehabilitation phase after an acute illness. Kinds of extended-care facilities are intermediate-care facilities and skilled nursing facilities. Also called *convalescent home* and *nursing home.*

F

false imprisonment The act of confining or restraining a person without his consent for no clinical or legal reason.

family nurse practitioner (FNP) A nurse practitioner possessing skills necessary for the detection and management of acute self-limiting conditions and the management of chronic stable conditions. An FNP provides primary ambulatory care for families in collaboration with primary care physicians.

FDA *abbr* Food and Drug Administration

Federal Tort Claims Act (FTCA) A federal law that regulates how and under what circumstances the U.S. government can be sued. Sections of the law include the statute of limitations for filing suits, the procedure for filing suits, and causes of action that may be alleged against the government.

fee-for-service 1. A charge made for a professional activity such as a physical examination. 2. A system for the payment of professional services in which the practitioner is paid for the particular service rendered rather than receiving a salary for providing professional services as needed during scheduled hours of work or time on call.

fidelity Faithfulness to agreements that one has accepted.

fiduciary A person having a duty, created by his undertaking, to act primarily for the benefit of another in matters connected with that undertaking.

fiduciary relationship A legal relationship of trust and confidence that exists whenever one person relies on another, as in a physician-patient relationship.

flexible staffing patterns Work schedules that vary—for example, 10- and 12-hour shifts, shorter work weeks, and special weekend schedules.

flextime, flexitime A system of staffing that allows flexible work schedules. A person who works 7 hours daily might choose to work from 7 to 3, 10 to 5, or other hours. Use of this system tends to improve morale and decrease turnover.

FNP *abbr* family nurse practitioner

Food and Drug Administration (FDA) The federal agency responsible for the enforcement of federal regulations regarding the manufacture and distribution of food, drugs, and cosmetics.

forensic medicine The application of medical science to legal problems and issues.

fraud Intentional deception resulting in damage to another, whether to his person, rights, property, or reputation. Fraud usually consists of a misrepresentation, concealment, or nondisclosure of a material fact, or at least misleading conduct, devices, or contrivance.

FTCA *abbr* Federal Claims Tort Act

G

general damages Compensation for losses that are directly referable to a legal wrong but abstract in nature, such as pain and suffering and a worsening change in lifestyle. Compare *punitive damages* and *special damages.*

gerontologic nursing Nursing care that provides for the physical, intellectual, and emotional needs of elderly people. As defined by the American Nurses Association, gerontologic nursing is the care and treatment of an older adult holistically, not just as a diseased or sick person. Nurses may choose gerontologic nursing as an area of clinical specialty.

good faith Total absence of intention to seek unfair advantage or to defraud another party; an intention to fulfill one's obligations.

Good Samaritan acts State or provincial laws that provide civil immunity from negligence lawsuits for individuals who stop and render care in an emergency.

grace period In general, any period specified in a contract during which payment is permitted, without penalty, beyond the due date of the debt.

grandfather clause A provision permitting persons engaged in an activity before passage of a law affecting that activity to receive a license without having to meet the new requirements.

grievance A complaint about working conditions or contract violations brought by an employee or union against an employer.

grievance procedure Steps agreed upon by employees and their employer to settle disputes in an orderly fashion. A labor contract may outline grievance procedures.

gross negligence The flagrant and inexcusable failure to perform a legal duty in reckless disregard for the consequences.

ground rules Rules governing a particular situation that describe legitimate behavior.

group model HMO A managed-care organization that contracts with a multispecialty group of physicians to provide all physician services to its members. The physicians are employed by the group practice—not the HMO—and may treat other patients.

guardian ad litem A person appointed by the court to safeguard a minor's or other incompetent person's legal interest during certain kinds of litigation.

H

health care consumer Any actual or potential recipient of health care, such as a patient in a hospital, a client in a community mental health center, and a member of a prepaid health maintenance organization.

health care industry The complex of preventive, remedial, and therapeutic services provided by hospitals and other institutions, nurses, physicians, dentists, government agencies, voluntary agencies, noninstitutional care facilities, pharmaceutical and medical equipment manufacturers, and health insurance companies.

health care professional Any person who has completed a course of study in a field of health care—for example, a nurse. The person is usually licensed by a government agency, such as a board of nursing,

and becomes registered or licensed in that health care field. In some instances, as in a certified nursing assistant, the person is certified by a state regulatory body.

Health Insurance Portability and Accountability Act (HIPAA) A federal law designed to make it easier for people to keep health insurance and protect the confidentiality and security of health care information.

health maintenance organization (HMO) An organization that provides basic and supplemental health maintenance and treatment services to voluntary enrollees who prepay a fixed periodic fee that's set without regard to the amount or kind of services received. Individuals and families who belong to an HMO are cared for by member physicians with limited referral to outside specialists.

health provider Any individual who provides health services to health care consumers.

HIPAA *abbr* Health Insurance Portability and Accountability Act

HIS *abbr* hospital information system

HMO *abbr* health maintenance organization

homestead laws Laws protecting any property designated as a homestead (any house, outbuildings, and surrounding land owned and used as a dwelling by the head of a family) from seizure and sale by creditors.

hospice A system of family-centered care designed to assist the chronically ill person to maintain a satisfactory lifestyle through the terminal phases of dying. Hospice care is multidisciplinary and includes home visits, professional medical help available on call, teaching and emotional support of the family, and physical care of the patient. Some hospice programs provide care in a center as well as in the home.

hospital information system (HIS) A computer-based information system with multiple access units to collect, organize, store, and make available data for problem solving and decision making.

hospital quality assurance program A program, developed by a hospital committee, that monitors the quality of the hospital's diagnostic, therapeutic, prognostic, and other health care activities.

hospital quality improvement program An approach to continuous study and improvement of the processes of providing health care services.

human investigations committee A committee established in a hospital, school, or university to review applications for research involving human subjects in order to protect the rights of the people to be studied. Also called *human subjects investigation committee*.

I

ICN *abbr* International Council of Nurses

ICU *abbr* intensive care unit

illegal abortion Induced termination of a pregnancy under circumstances or at a gestational time prohibited by law. Many illegal abortions are performed under medically unsafe conditions. Also called *criminal abortion*. Compare *legal abortion* and *therapeutic abortion*.

immunity from liability Exemption by law of a person or institution from a legally imposed penalty.

immunity from suit Exemption by law of a person or institution from being sued.

implementation 1. A deliberate action performed to achieve a goal, as in carrying out a plan in caring for a patient. 2. In the nursing process, a category of nursing behavior in which the actions necessary for accomplishing the health care plan are initiated and completed.

implied conditions Elements of a contract that aren't stated but are assumed to be part of the contract.

implied contract A contract manifested by conduct rather than words. An implied contract is based on an obligation created by law for reasons of justice and fairness. Also called *quasi contract*.

implied-in-law contract Obligations imposed upon a person by the law without his agreement and against his will or design because the circumstances between the parties render it just that the one should have a right and the other a corresponding liability similar to those that would arise from a contract between them.

impossibility defense A contract defense that says circumstances rendered the violation of a contract (such as not showing up for work) impossible to avoid. Compare *contract defense*.

incident An event that's inconsistent with ordinary routine, regardless of whether injury occurs.

incident report A formal, written report that informs a health care facility's administration (and its insurance company) about an incident and serves as a contemporary, factual statement of the incident in the event of a lawsuit.

incompetence The inability or lack of legal qualification or fitness to discharge the required duty. Compare *adjudicated incompetent* and *mental incompetence*.

indemnification Repayment or compensation for a loss. A person who has compensated another for injury, loss, or damage caused by a third party may file a suit seeking indemnification from the third party.

independent practice association (IPA) model HMO A managed-care organization that contracts with an association of physicians to provide physician services to its members. The physicians maintain their independent practices.

independent provider organization (IPO) A hybrid form of managed-care organization with characteristics of both IPAs and medical associations. They're commonly organized by community physicians to provide a mechanism for evaluating and negotiating participation in HMOs.

individual contract A contract negotiated with an employer by an individual employee.

informed consent Permission obtained from a patient to perform a specific test or procedure after the patient has been fully informed about the test or procedure.

injunction A court order restraining a person from committing a specific act or requiring the individual to do something.

in loco parentis Latin phrase meaning "in the place of the parent." The assumption by a person or institution of the parental obligations of caring for a child without adoption.

inpatient 1. A patient who has been admitted to a hospital or other health care facility for at least an overnight stay. 2. Pertaining to the treatment of such a patient or to a health care facility to which a patient may be admitted for 24-hour care.

insurance adjuster One who determines the amount of an insurance claim and then makes an agreement with the insured as to a settlement.

intensive care Constant, complex, detailed health care as provided in various acute, life-threatening conditions. Special training is necessary to provide intensive care. Also called *critical care.*

intensive care unit (ICU) A hospital unit in which patients requiring close monitoring and intensive care are housed for as long as needed. An ICU contains highly technical and sophisticated monitoring devices and equipment, and the staff in the unit is educated to give critical care, as patients need it. See also *critical care unit.*

intermediate care A level of medical care for certain chronically ill or disabled individuals at which room and board are provided but skilled nursing care isn't.

International Council of Nurses (ICN) The oldest international health organization, the ICN is a federation of nurses' associations from 93 nations and was one of the first health organizations to develop strict policies against discrimination based on nationality, race, creed, color, politics, sex, or social status. The objectives of the ICN include promoting national associations of nurses, improving standards of nursing and the competence of nurses, improving the status of nurses within their countries, and establishing an authoritative international voice for nurses.

International Red Cross Society An international philanthropic organization, based in Geneva, concerned primarily with the humane treatment and welfare of the victims of war and calamity and with the neutrality of hospitals and medical personnel in times of war. See also *American Red Cross.*

interrogatories A series of written questions submitted to a witness or other person having information of interest to the court. The answers are transcribed and are sworn to under oath. Compare *deposition* and *discovery device.*

intervention 1. Any act performed to prevent harm from occurring to a patient or to improve the mental, emotional, or physical function of a patient. A physiologic process may be monitored or enhanced, or a pathologic process may be arrested or controlled. 2. The fourth step of the nursing process. This step includes nursing actions taken to meet patient needs as determined by nursing assessment and diagnosis.

invalid contract Any contract concerning illegal or impossible actions; no legal obligation exists.

JK

JCAHO *abbr* Joint Commission on Accreditation of Healthcare Organizations

Joint Commission A private, nongovernmental agency that establishes guidelines for the operation of hospitals and other health care facilities, conducts accreditation programs and surveys, and encourages the attainment of high standards of institutional medical care. Members include representatives from the American Medical Association, American College of Physicians, and American College of Surgeons.

joint practice 1. The (usually private) practice of a physician and a nurse practitioner who work as a team, sharing responsibility for a group of patients. 2. In inpatient nursing, the practice of making joint decisions about patient care by committees of physicians and nurses working in a division.

joint statement A statement, opinion, or recommendation issued jointly by two or more organizations or committees.

judicial bypass statutes Statutes that allow a minor to go before a judge to avoid a strict requirement of parental notification or consent to obtain an abortion.

just cause A lawful, rightful, proper reason to act. A defendant establishes a cause for action in his favor.

L

law 1. In a field of study: a rule, standard, or principle that states a fact or a relationship between factors, such as Dalton's law regarding partial pressures of gas, and Koch's law regarding the specificity of a pathogen. 2. *a.* A rule, principle, or regulation established and promulgated by a government to protect or to restrict the people affected. *b.* The field of study concerned with such laws. *c.* The collected body of the laws of a people derived from custom or from legislation.

lay jury A jury made up of people who aren't from a particular profession. For example, a lay jury in a medical malpractice trial wouldn't include physicians, nurses, or other members of the medical profession.

lay-midwife See *midwife.*

legal abortion Induced termination of pregnancy by a physician before the fetus has developed sufficiently to live outside the uterus. The procedure is performed under medically safe conditions prescribed by law. Compare *illegal abortion* and *therapeutic abortion.*

legal guardian An officer or agent of the court who's appointed to protect the interests of minors or incompetent persons and provide for their welfare, education, and support.

liability Legal responsibility for failure to act or action that fails to meet standards of care that causes another person harm.

liable Legally bound or obligated to make good any loss or damage; responsible.

liaison nurse A nurse who acts as an agent between a patient, the hospital, and the patient's family and who speaks for the entire health care team.

libel A tort consisting of a false, malicious, or unprivileged written publication aiming to defame a living person or to damage the memory of a deceased person. Compare *slander.*

licensed practical nurse (LPN) A person trained in basic nursing techniques and direct patient care who practices under the supervision of a registered nurse or other health care provider. An LPN must complete a course of training that usually lasts 1–2 years, pass the NCLEX-PN examination, and meet the requirements set forth by the board of nursing for licensure in her state. In Canada, an LPN is called a *nursing assistant.* In the United States, an LPN is also called a *licensed vocational nurse.*

licensed vocational nurse (LVN) See *licensed practical nurse.*

licensure Permission granted by a competent authority (usually a government agency) to an organization or person to engage in a practice or activity that would otherwise be illegal. Kinds of licensure include the issuing of licenses for general hospitals or nursing homes, for health care professionals such as physicians, and for the production or distribution of biological products. Licensure is usually granted on the basis of education and examination rather than performance. It's usually permanent, but a periodic fee, demonstration of competence, or continuing education may be required. Licensure may be revoked by the granting agency for incompetence, criminal acts, or other reasons stipulated in the rules governing the specific area of licensure.

litigant A party to a lawsuit. See also *defendant* and *plaintiff.*

litigate To carry on a suit or to contest a suit.

living will A witnessed document indicating a patient's desire to be allowed to die a natural death, rather than be kept alive by heroic, life-sustaining measures. The will applies to decisions that will be made after a terminally ill patient is incompetent and has no reasonable possibility of recovery. Compare *testamentary will.*

living will laws Laws that help to guarantee that a patient's documented wishes regarding terminal illness procedures will be carried out. Living will laws may set forth testator and witness requirements for executing a living will and medical requirements for terminating treatment. Living will laws may also address other issues, such as authorization of a proxy for health care decisions, immunity from liability for following a living will's directives, and the withholding or withdrawal of life-sustaining treatment. Also called *natural death laws* and *right to die.*

locality rule Allowance made, when considering evidence in a trial, for the type of community in which the defendant practices his profession and the standards of that community.

LPN *abbr* licensed practical nurse

LVN *abbr* licensed vocational nurse; see *licensed practical nurse.*

M

malfeasance Performance of an unlawful, wrongful act. Compare misfeasance and nonfeasance.

malpractice A professional person's wrongful conduct, improper discharge of professional duties, or failure to meet standards of care that results in harm to another person.

managed-care organization (MCO) A system that integrates the financing and delivery of appropriate health care services to covered individuals by means of contracts with selected providers.

mandatory bargaining issues Issues, such as wages and working conditions, that an employer must address during collective bargaining.

master's degree program in nursing A postbaccalaureate program in a school of nursing based in a university setting that grants the degree Master of Science in Nursing (MSN) to successful candidates. Nurses with this degree usually work in leadership roles in clinical nursing, as consultants in various settings, and in faculty positions in certain schools of nursing. Some programs also prepare the nurse to function as a nurse practitioner in a specific specialty.

MCO *abbr* managed-care organization

MD *abbr* Doctor of Medicine; see *physician.*

Medicaid A program that subsidizes medical care for low-income women and children, some men, and people with certain disabilities. Although passed by Congress in 1965, Medicaid is a state-level program, with each state defining income levels and other standards of eligibility and the federal government subsidizing a portion of the expenses.

medical directive A comprehensive advance care document that covers preferred treatment goals and specific scenarios of patient incompetence. It also includes the option to designate a proxy decision maker or power of attorney for the event of incompetence, the option to record a personal statement, and a place to designate wishes for organ donation. Also called *physician's directive.*

medical record A written, legal document that includes every aspect of the patient's care. A record of a person's illnesses and treatment.

medical release form The form an institution asks a patient to sign when he refuses a medical treatment. The form protects both the institution and the health care professional from liability if the patient's condition worsens because of his refusal.

Medicare Federally funded national health insurance authorized by the Social Security Act for persons aged 65 years and older.

medicolegal Of or pertaining to both medicine and law. Medicolegal considerations are a significant part of the process of making many patient-care decisions and in setting policies about the treatment of mentally incompetent people and minors, the performance of sterilization or therapeutic abortion, and the care of terminally ill patients. Medicolegal considerations, decisions, definitions, and policies provide the framework for informed consent, professional liability, and many other aspects of health care practice.

mental competence The ability to understand information and act reasonably. A mentally competent person is capable of understanding explanations and is able to comprehend the results of his decisions.

mental incompetence The inability to understand the nature and effect of the action a person is engaged in. A mentally incompetent person is incapable of understanding explanations and is unable to comprehend the results of his decisions. Compare *adjudicated incompetent* and *incompetence.*

mental status examination A diagnostic procedure for determining the mental status of a person. The trained interviewer poses certain questions in a carefully standardized manner and evaluates the verbal responses and behavioral reactions.

midwife 1. In traditional use: a person who assists women in childbirth. 2. According to the International Confederation of Midwives, the World Health Organization, and the Federation of International Gynecologists and Obstetricians: "a person who, having been regularly admitted to a midwifery educational program fully recognized in the country in which it's located, has successfully completed the prescribed course of studies in midwifery and has acquired the requisite qualifications to be registered or legally licensed to practice midwifery." Among the responsibilities of the midwife are supervision of pregnancy, labor, delivery, and puerperium. The midwife conducts the delivery independently, cares for the neonate, procures medical assistance when necessary, executes emergency measures as required, and may practice in a hospital, clinic, maternity home, or in a woman's home. Also called *lay-midwife, nurse-midwife,* and *certified nurse-midwife (CNM).*

minor A person not of legal age; below the age of majority. Minors may not be able to consent to their own medical treatment unless they are legally emancipated. However, in many jurisdictions, parental consent is no longer necessary for certain types of medical and psychiatric treatment.

misdemeanor An offense that's considered less serious than a felony and carries with it a lesser penalty, usually a fine or imprisonment for less than 1 year.

misfeasance An improper performance of a lawful act, especially in a way that might cause damage or injury. Compare *malfeasance* and *nonfeasance.*

misrepresentation The statutory crime of giving false or misleading information, usually with the intent to deceive or be unfair.

moral dilemma An ethical problem caused by conflicts of rights, responsibilities, and values.

moral distress A condition that occurs when the internal environment of nurses—their values and perceived obligations—is incompatible with the needs and prevailing views of the external work environment.

moral relativism An ethical theory that holds there are no ethical absolutes and whatever an individual feels is right for him at that moment is indeed right.

moral turpitude Vileness, intentional violence, deceit, fraud, or dishonesty of a high degree. A crime of moral turpitude demonstrates depravity in the private and social duties a person owes to others, contrary to what's accepted and customary. The act is considered intentionally evil.

MSN *abbr* Master of Science in Nursing; see *master's degree program in nursing.*

N

National Council of Licensure Examination (NCLEX) An examination, administered separately by licensing authorities of each state, that measures competency to practice as a licensed RN or LPN. The test is commonly referred to as the "state boards." All 50 states (and some Canadian jurisdictions) require candidates for RN licensure to take the NCLEX-RN test. Candidates for LPN licensure must take the NCLEX-PN test. The NCLEX-RN consists of about 375 multiple-choice and alternative-format items involving multiple-response–multiple-choice, fill-in-the-blank, and point-and-click diagrams, which appear as case situations. Most test questions require the examinee to apply nursing knowledge to patient-care situations.

National Council of State Boards of Nursing (NCSBN) An independent, not-for-profit organization through which boards of nursing act and counsel together on matters of common interest and concern affecting public health, safety and welfare, including the development of nursing licensure examinations.

National League for Nursing (NLN) An organization concerned with the improvement of nursing education, nursing service, and the delivery of health care in the United States. Its members include nurses and other health care professionals, nursing educational institutions, agencies, departments of nursing in hospitals and other health care facilities, home and community health services, and community members interested in health. Among its many activities are accreditation of nursing programs at all levels, provision of preadmission and achievement tests for nursing students, and compilation of statistical data on nursing manpower and on trends in health care delivery.

negligence Failure to act as an ordinary prudent person would under similar circumstances. Conduct that falls below the standard established by law for the protection of others under the same circumstances.

negligent nondisclosure The failure to completely inform a patient about his treatment.

negotiation A meeting at which an employer and employees confer, discuss, and bargain to reach an agreement.

network model HMO A managed-care organization that contracts with more than one group practice to provide physician services to its members.

next of kin One or more persons in the nearest degree of relationship to another person.

NLN *abbr* National League for Nursing

no-code order An order, written in the patient record and signed by a physician, instructing staff not to attempt to resuscitate a patient if he suffers cardiac or respiratory failure.

nonfeasance Failure to perform a task, duty, or undertaking that one has agreed to perform or that one has a legal duty to perform. Compare *malfeasance* and *misfeasance.*

nonmaleficence An ethical principle based on the obligation to do no harm.

NP *abbr* nurse practitioner

nurse 1. A person educated and licensed in the practice of nursing. The nurse acts to promote, maintain, or restore the health of the patient. The American Nurses Association defines nursing as the "diagnosis and treatment of human responses to actual and potential health problems." The nurse may be a generalist or a specialist and, as a professional, is ethically and legally accountable for the nursing activities performed and for the actions of others to whom the nurse has delegated responsibility. 2. To provide nursing care. 3. To breast-feed an infant. See also *nursing* and *registered nurse.*

nurse anesthetist A registered nurse qualified by advanced training in an accredited program in the specialty of nurse anesthetist to manage the anesthetic care of the patient in certain surgical situations.

nurse clinician A nurse who's prepared to identify and diagnose patient problems by using the expanded knowledge and skills gained by advanced study in a specific area of nursing practice. The specialist may function independently within standing orders or protocols, and collaborates with associates to implement a care plan that's focused on the patient.

nurse-midwife See *midwife.*

Nurse Practice Act A law enacted by a state's legislature outlining the legal scope of nursing practice within that state.

nurse practitioner (NP) A nurse who, by advanced training and clinical experience in a branch of nursing (as in a master's degree program in nursing or a certification program), has acquired expert knowledge in a specialized branch of practice.

nurses' notes A means of documenting the care the nurse provides and the patient's response to that care; a legal document that can be submitted as admissible evidence in a court of law.

nurses' registry An employment agency or listing service for nurses who wish to work in a specific area of nursing, usually for a short period of time or on a *per diem* basis.

nursing 1. The professional practice of a nurse. 2. The process of acting as a nurse and providing care that encourages and promotes the health of the person being served. 3. According to the American Nurses Association, the "diagnosis and treatment of human responses to actual and potential health problems." 4. Breast-feeding an infant. See also *nurse* and *registered nurse.*

nursing administrator A nurse who's responsible for overseeing the efficient management of nursing services.

nursing assessment The first step of the nursing process, which involves the systematic collection of information about the patient from multiple sources, including the history, physical examination, and laboratory findings. This information is analyzed and used by the nurse to formulate inferences or impressions about the patient's needs or problems.

nursing audit A thorough investigation designed to identify, examine, or verify the performance of certain specified aspects of nursing care using established criteria. A concurrent nursing audit is performed during ongoing nursing care. A retrospective nursing audit is performed after discharge from the care facility, using the patient's record. In many instances, a nursing audit and a medical audit are performed collaboratively, resulting in a joint audit.

nursing care plan A plan devised by a nurse and based on a nursing assessment and a nursing diagnosis. It has four essential components: the identification of the nursing care problems and a statement of the nursing approach to solve those problems; the statement of the expected benefit to the patient; the statement of the specific actions taken by the nurse that reflect the nursing approach and the achievement of the goals specified; and the evaluation of the patient's response to nursing care and the readjustment of that care as required. See also *nursing assessment* and *nursing diagnosis.*

nursing diagnosis Descriptive interpretations of collected and categorized information indicating the problems or needs of a patient that nursing care can affect. According to the North American Nursing Diagnosis Association, "a clinical judgment about individual, community, or family responses to actual or potential health problems or to life processes. Nursing diagnoses provide the basis of selection of nursing interventions for which the nurse is accountable."

nursing home See *extended-care facility.*

nursing process An organizational framework for nursing practice, encompassing all the major steps a nurse takes when caring for a patient. These steps are assessment, diagnosis, planning, implementation, and evaluation.

nursing skills The cognitive, affective, and psychomotor abilities a nurse uses in delivering nursing care.

nursing specialty A nurse's particular professional field of practice, such as surgical, pediatric, obstetric, and psychiatric nursing. Compare *subspecialty.*

O

occurrence policy A professional liability insurance policy that protects against an error of omission occurring during a policy period, regardless of when the claim is made.

ombudsman A person who investigates complaints, reports findings, and helps to achieve equitable settlements.

open shop A place of employment where employees may choose whether to join a union.

oral contract Any contract that isn't in writing or isn't signed by the parties involved.

ordinary negligence The inadvertent omission of the care that a reasonably prudent nurse would ordinarily provide under similar circumstances.

original position The underlying principle of the social contract theory, which states that people in a society determine the principles of justice by which all members are bound to live.

ostensible agent doctrine See *borrowed-servant doctrine.*

outcomes management A process of systematically tracking a patient's clinical treatment and responses. The system encourages caregivers to follow a set of guidelines (practice guidelines or clinical pathways) that research has shown to be the "one best way" to treat a medical condition.

P

PA *abbr* Parents Anonymous; physician's assistant

parens patriae A doctrine that appoints the state as the legal guardian of a child or incompetent adult when a person hasn't been appointed as guardian.

paternalism The practice of a person in authority restricting the freedom of subordinates in the belief that doing so is in the subordinate's best interest.

Parents Anonymous (PA) An international organization, founded in 1970, dedicated to the prevention and treatment of child abuse.

patient 1. A health care recipient who's ill or hospitalized. 2. A client in a health care service.

patient advocate A person (typically a nurse) who seeks to protect a patient's rights from infringement by institutional policies.

patient antidumping laws Amendments to the Social Security Act intended to prevent hospitals from turning away patients who are uninsured or unable to pay. They require that hospitals participating in Medicare provide medical screening and stabilizing treatment for any patient who has an emergency condition or is in labor, and provide guidelines and require documentation for transfers to other facilities or for hospital discharge.

patient classification systems Ways of grouping patients so that the size of the staff needed to care for them can be estimated accurately.

patient overload The situation that occurs when the number of patients exceeds an institution's medical, nursing, and support staff resources to care for them properly. Also called *staffing shortage.*

patient record A collection of documents that provides a record of each time a person visited or sought treatment and received care or a referral for care from a health care facility. This confidential record is usually held by the facility, and the information in it is released only to the person or with the person's written permission, except in certain situations, such as when release is required by law. It contains the initial assessment, health history, laboratory reports, and notes by nurses, physicians, and consultants as well as order sheets, medication sheets, admission records, discharge summaries, and other pertinent data. A problem-oriented medical record also contains a master problem list. The patient record is usually a collection of papers held in a folder, but, increasingly, hospitals are computerizing the records after every discharge, making the past record available on visual display terminals. Also called *patient's medical chart* (informal).

Patient's Bill of Rights Documents that define a person's rights while receiving health care. Bills of rights for patients are designed to protect such basic rights as human dignity, privacy, confidentiality, informed consent, and refusal of treatment. The American Hospital Association, the National League for Nursing, the American Civil Liberties Union, and other organizations and health care institutions have prepared patients' bills of rights. Concepts expressed in these documents may be incorporated into law. Although bills of rights issued by health care institutions and professional organizations don't have the force of law, nurses should regard them as professionally binding.

PC *abbr* professional corporation

pediatric nurse practitioner (PNP) A nurse practitioner who, by advanced study and clinical practice, has gained expert knowledge in the nursing care of infants and children.

peremptory challenge A right given to attorneys at trial to dismiss a prospective juror for no particular reason; the number of times an attorney can invoke this right is usually limited.

persistent vegetative state A state of severe mental impairment in which only involuntary bodily functions are sustained.

physician 1. A health professional who has earned a degree of Doctor of Medicine (MD) after completion of an approved course of study at an approved medical school and satisfactory completion of the National Board Examinations. 2. A health professional who has earned a degree of Doctor of Osteopathy (DO) by satisfactorily completing a course of education in an approved college of osteopathy.

physician of record See *attending physician.*

physician assistant (PA) A person who's trained in certain aspects of the practice of medicine and provides assistance to a physician. A physician's assistant is trained by physicians and practices under the direction and supervision and within the legal license of a physician.

Training programs vary in length from a few months to 2 years. Health care experience or academic preparation may be a prerequisite for admission to some programs. Most physician's assistants are prepared for the practice of primary care, but some practice subspecialties, including surgical assisting, dialysis, or radiology. National certification is available to qualified graduates of approved training programs. The national organization is the American Association of Physician Assistants (AAPA).

physician's associate See *physician assistant.*

physician's directive See *medical directive.*

plaintiff A person who files a civil lawsuit initiating a legal action. In criminal actions, the prosecution is the plaintiff, acting on behalf of the people in the jurisdiction. See also *litigant.*

PNP abbr pediatric nurse practitioner

policy A definite course or method of action selected from among alternatives and in the light of given conditions to guide, and usually determine, present and future decisions. Compare *rule.*

policy defense Rationale for denying coverage given by professional liability insurance carriers when a client submits a claim. Reasons for denial may include failure to pay a premium on time or failure to renew the policy.

POLST abbr. Physicians Orders for Life Sustaining Treatment

power of attorney A legal document enabling an individual to designate another person, called an *attorney-in-fact,* to act on the individual's behalf as long as the individual doesn't become disabled or incapacitated. Power of attorney continues to operate only with the continued consent of the person who granted it. If the grantor of the power should become incompetent, the power of attorney is automatically revoked. It's also revoked when the grantor dies. Compare *durable power of attorney.*

PPO abbr preferred provider organization

practicing medicine without a license Practicing activities defined under state or provincial law in the Medical Practice Act without medical supervision, direction, or control.

practicing pharmacy without a license Practicing activities defined under state or provincial law in the Pharmacy Practice Act without pharmacist supervision, direction, or control. These laws give pharmacists the sole legal authority to prepare, compound, preserve, and dispense drugs.

practitioner A person qualified to practice in a special professional field such as a nurse practitioner.

preferred provider organization (PPO) Entity through which an employer health benefit plan and insurance carrier purchase health care service for members from a select group of providers.

prescription drug Any drug restricted from regular commercial purchase and sale. Compare *controlled substance.*

presumed consent A legal principle based on the belief that a rational and prudent person would consent in the same situation, if able to. Applies primarily to emergency care of unconscious patients, but may be expanded to cadaver organ donors.

privacy One's private life or personal affairs. The right to privacy refers to the right to be left alone and to be free from unwanted publicity.

privileged communication A conversation in which the speaker intends the information given to remain private between himself and the listener.

privilege doctrine A doctrine that protects the privacy of persons within a fiduciary relationship, such as a husband and wife, a physician and patient, or a nurse and patient. During legal proceedings, a court can't force either party to reveal communications between them unless the party who would benefit from the protection agrees.

probate 1. The act of proving that a purported will was signed and executed in accordance with the law and of determining its validity. 2. The combined result of all procedures necessary to establish the validity of a will.

probation period A period of time during which an individual is observed and evaluated to ascertain fitness for a particular job or duty.

pro-choice The philosophy that a woman has the right to choose to either continue or terminate her pregnancy.

professional boundaries Spaces between the nurse's power and the patient's vulnerability

professional corporation (PC) A corporation formed according to the law of a particular state for the purpose of delivering a professional service.

professional liability A legal concept describing the obligation of a professional person to pay a patient or client for damages caused by the professional's act of omission, commission, or negligence, after a court determines that the professional was negligent. Professional liability better describes the responsibility of all professionals to their clients than does the concept of malpractice, but the idea of professional liability is central to malpractice.

professional liability insurance A type of liability insurance that protects professional persons against malpractice claims.

professional organization An organization created to deal with issues of concern to its members, who share a professional status.

professional RN Defined by the American Nurses Association as a registered nurse who has graduated from a baccalaureate or higher degree program. Professional RNs develop policies, procedures, and protocols, and set standards for practice. Compare *technical RN.*

pro-life The philosophy that an unborn fetus has the right to develop to term and to be born.

proprietary hospital A hospital operated as a profit-making organization. Many are owned and operated by physicians primarily for their own patients, but they also accept patients from other physicians. Others are owned by investor groups or large corporations.

protocol A code providing and prescribing strict adherence to guidelines for and authorization of particular practice activities.

Provincial Territorial Nurses Association (PTNA) An association of nurses organized at the provincial or territorial level. The Canadian Nurses Association is a federation of the 11 PTNAs.

proviso A condition or stipulation. Its general function is to except something from the basic provision, to qualify or restrain its general scope, or to prevent misinterpretation.

proximate cause A legal concept of cause and effect, which says a sequence of natural and continuous events produces an injury that wouldn't have otherwise occurred.

proxy The recipient of a grant of authority to act or speak for another.

PTNA *abbr* Provincial Territorial Nurses Association

punitive damages Compensation in excess of actual damages that are a form of punishment to the wrongdoer and reparation to the injured. These damages are awarded only in rare instances of malicious and willful misconduct. Also called *exemplary damages.* Compare *general damages* and *special damages.*

Q

qualified privilege A conditional right or immunity granted to the defendant because of the circumstances of a legal case.

quality of life A legal and ethical standard that's determined by relative suffering or pain, not by the degree of disability.

R

RCP *abbr* Royal College of Physicians

RCPSC *abbr* Royal College of Physicians and Surgeons of Canada

RCS *abbr* Royal College of Surgeons

reasonably prudent nurse The standard a court uses to judge a nurse being sued for negligence. The court considers whether another nurse would have acted similarly to the defendant under similar circumstances.

rebuttable presumption A presumption that may be overcome or disputed by contrary evidence.

Red Cross See *American Red Cross* and *International Red Cross Society.*

redefinition A rewriting of the fundamental provision of a nurse practice act. This changes the basic premise of the entire act without amending or repealing it.

registered nurse (RN) 1. In the United States: A professional nurse who has completed a course of study at an approved school of nursing, passed the NCLEX-RN, and met the requirements for licensure set forth by the board of nursing in her state. A registered nurse may use the initials RN following her signature. RNs are licensed to practice by individual states. 2. In Canada: A professional nurse who has completed a course of study at an approved school of nursing and who has taken and passed an examination administered by the Canadian Nurses Association Testing Service. See also *nurse* and *nursing.*

registered nursing assistant In Canada, a person trained in basic nursing techniques and direct patient care who practices under the supervision of a registered nurse.

registry 1. An office or agency that maintains lists of nurses and records pertaining to nurses seeking employment. 2. In epidemiology: a listing service for incidence data pertaining to the occurrence of specific diseases or disorders, as in a tumor registry.

relativism A theory holding that morality is relative to the norms of one's culture.

remand To send back. An appellate court may send a case back to the lower court that considered the case, ordering that further action be taken there.

res ipsa loquitur Latin phrase meaning "the thing speaks for itself." A legal doctrine that applies when the defendant was solely and exclusively in control at the time the plaintiff's injury occurred, so that the injury wouldn't have occurred if the defendant had exercised due care. In addition, the injured party couldn't have contributed to his own injury. When a court applies this doctrine to a case, the defendant bears the burden of proving that he wasn't negligent.

respondeat superior Latin phrase meaning "let the master answer." A legal doctrine that makes an employer indirectly liable for the consequences of his employee's wrongful conduct while the employee is acting within the scope of his employment.

resuscitative life-support measures Actions taken to reverse an immediate, life-threatening situation (e.g., cardiopulmonary resuscitation).

review committee A group of individuals delegated to inspect and report on the quality of health care in a given institution.

right-of-conscience laws Based on freedom of thought or of religion, these laws allow a health care provider to refuse to care for a patient when an objection to the care or lack of care exists.

right-to-access laws Laws that grant a patient the right to see his medical records.

right-to-die law Law that upholds a patient's right to choose death by refusing extraordinary treatment. Also called *living will law* and *natural death law.*

right to notice 1. A due process right requiring that the accused receive timely notification of both the pending charges and the hearing date. 2. An employee's right to receive sufficient notification or warning before termination. This allows the employee time to protest or appeal the termination and to seek employment elsewhere.

risk management The identification, analysis, evaluation, and elimination or reduction—to the extent possible—of risks to an organization's patients, visitors, or employees. Risk management programs are involved with both loss prevention and loss control, and handle all incidents, claims, and other insurance- and litigation-related tasks.

risk manager A person who identifies, analyzes, evaluates, and eliminates or reduces an organization's potential accidental losses. This job entails systematically and continually answering three questions: "What can go wrong in this situation?" "What are the options?" and "Which option minimizes adverse effects for the organization?" Almost always, a risk manager deals with situations in which the only possible outcome is a loss or no change in the status quo. Examples of the responsibilities of a risk manager include purchasing and managing insurance policies, inviting engineering professionals to examine the structural integrity of a building, and examining policies and procedures to eliminate unnecessary risks.

RN *abbr* registered nurse

Royal College of Physicians (RCP) A professional organization of physicians in the United Kingdom.

Royal College of Physicians and Surgeons of Canada (RCPSC) A national Canadian organization that recognizes and confers membership on certain qualified physicians and surgeons.

Royal College of Surgeons (RCS) A professional organization of surgeons in the United Kingdom.

rule A guide for conduct that describes the actions that should or shouldn't be taken in specific situations. Compare *policy.*

S

sanctions A punishment for violation of acceptable norms or rules.

scope of practice In nursing, the professional nursing activities defined under state or province law in each state's (or Canadian province's) nurse practice act.

service of process The delivery of a writ, summons, or complaint to a defendant. The original document is shown; a copy is served. Service of process gives reasonable notice to allow the person to appear, testify, and be heard in court. See also *summons*.

settlement An agreement made between parties to a suit before a judgment is rendered by a court.

signature code A code of letters or numbers that are entered into a computer to identify the user.

skilled nursing facility (SNF) An institution or part of an institution that meets criteria for accreditation established by the sections of the Social Security Act that determine the basis for Medicaid and Medicare reimbursement for skilled nursing care, including rehabilitation and various medical and nursing procedures.

slander Spoken words that may damage another person's reputation. Compare *libel*.

slippery slope principle An ethical principle based on the belief that, when an ethical or legal barrier has been lowered, desensitization to the ethical or legal principle occurs.

slow-code order An illegal verbal or implicit order from a physician instructing staff to refrain from resuscitating a patient until cardiopulmonary resuscitation is unlikely to be successful.

SNF *abbr* skilled nursing facility

SNP *abbr* school nurse practitioner

socialized medicine A system for the delivery of health care in which the government bears the expense of care.

source-oriented records A record-keeping system in which each professional group within the health care team keeps separate information on the patient.

sovereign immunity doctrine A privilege granted to the elected government and its appointed agents—government employees—giving them immunity from lawsuits.

special damages Compensation for indirect loss or injury, such as present and future medical expenses, past and future loss of earnings, and decreased earning capacity. Also called *consequential damages*. Compare *general damages* and *punitive damages*.

specialty standard The standard of care that applies to a given nursing specialty.

spoliation The action of ruining or destroying something.

staff 1. The people who work toward a common goal and are employed or supervised by someone of higher rank such as the nurses in a hospital. 2. A designation by which a staff nurse is distinguished from a head nurse or other nurse. 3. In nursing education: the nonprofessional employees of the institution, such as librarians, technicians, secretaries, and clerks. 4. In nursing service administration: the units of the organization that provide service to the "line," or administratively defined hierarchy, such as the personnel office is "staff" to the director of nursing and the nursing service administration.

staffing pattern In an institution or nursing administration: the number and kinds of staff assigned to the particular units and departments of an institution. Staffing patterns vary with the unit, department, and shift.

staffing shortage See *patient overload*.

staff model HMO A managed-care organization in which the physicians who serve the HMO are its salaried employees.

standard 1. A criterion that serves as a basis for comparison for evaluating similar phenomena or substances, such as a standard for the practice of a profession. 2. A pharmaceutical preparation or a chemical substance of known quantity, ingredients, and strength that's used to determine the constituents or the strength of another preparation. 3. Of known value, strength, quality, or ingredients.

standard death certificate A form for a death certificate commonly used throughout the United States. It's the preferred form of the U.S. Census Bureau.

standards of care Criteria that serve as a basis of comparison when evaluating the quality of nursing practice. In a malpractice lawsuit, a measure by which the defendant's alleged wrongful conduct is compared—acts performed or omitted that an ordinary, reasonably prudent nurse, in the defendant's position, would have done or not done.

standing orders A written document containing rules, policies, procedures, regulations, and orders for the conduct of patient care in various stipulated clinical situations.

state of emergency A widespread need for immediate action to counter a threat to the community.

statute of limitation Law that sets forth the length of time within which a person may file a specific type of lawsuit.

statutory law A law passed by a federal or state legislature.

statutory rape Sexual intercourse with a person below the age of consent. (Age of consent varies from state to state; usually, age 18.)

subacute care Designed for patients who don't need acute-care hospitalization but instead more hours of nursing care per day than the typical nursing home resident.

subpoena A writ issued under authority of a court to compel the appearance of a witness at a judicial proceeding; disobedience may be punishable as contempt of court.

subspecialty A subordinate field of specialization. For example, dialysis nursing might be considered a subspecialty of renal care. Compare *nursing specialty.*

substantive laws Laws that define and regulate a person's rights.

substitute consent Permission obtained from a parent or legal guardian of a patient who's a minor or who has been declared incompetent by the court.

substitute judgment A legal term indicating the court's substitution of its own judgment for that of a person the court considers unable to make an informed decision such as an incompetent adult.

sudden emergency exception Defense used by hospitals in liability cases involving understaffing when staffing shortages couldn't have been anticipated, as opposed to chronic understaffing.

summary judgment A judgment requested by any party to a civil action to end the action when it's believed that there's no genuine issue or material fact in dispute.

summons A document issued by a clerk of the court upon the filing of a complaint. A sheriff, marshal, or other appointed person serves the summons, notifying a person that an action has been begun against him. See also *service of process.*

support group People in whom a person confides and draws on for support, either as individuals or in a group setting.

T

technical RN Defined by the American Nurses Association as a nurse who has graduated from an associate degree program. Technical RNs follow policies, procedures, and protocols developed by professional RNs. Compare *professional RN.*

teleology An ethical theory that determines right or good based on an action's consequences.

temporary practice permit Permission granted by a state board of nursing to an out-of-state nurse enabling her to legally practice nursing until she can obtain a license from that state.

terminate In contract law, to fulfill all contractual obligations or to absolve oneself of the obligation to fulfill them.

termination The procedure an employer follows to fire an employee.

testamentary Any document, such as a will, that doesn't take effect until after the death of the person who wrote it.

testamentary will A will whose provisions take effect after death. Compare *living will*.

testator One who makes and executes a testament or will.

therapeutic abortion Induced termination of pregnancy to preserve the health, safety, or life of the woman. Compare *illegal abortion* and *legal abortion*.

therapeutic privilege A legal doctrine that permits a physician to withhold information from the patient if he can prove that disclosing it would adversely affect the patient's health.

third-party reimbursement Reimbursement for services rendered to a person in which an entity other than the giver or receiver of the service is responsible for the payment. Insurance plans commonly pay third-party reimbursement for the cost of a subscriber's health care.

time charting A method of charting in which the care administered to a patient at a particular time is detailed at regular time intervals—for example, every half hour.

tort A civil wrong outside of a contractual relationship.

traditional staffing patterns Work schedules that follow 8-hour shifts, 7 days per week, including evening and night shifts.

trial de novo A proceeding in which both issues of law and issues of fact are reconsidered as if the original trial had never taken place. New testimony may be introduced, or the matter may be determined a second time on the basis of the evidence already produced.

U

unfair labor practices Actions taken by an employer that are prohibited by state and federal labor laws. This term commonly refers to tactics used by an employer to discourage employees from participating in union activities. For example, under the National Labor Relations Act, unfair labor practices include interfering with, restraining, or coercing employees who exercise their right to organize.

Uniform Anatomical Gift Act A law in all 50 states that allows anyone older than age 18 to sign a donor card, donating some or all of his organs after death.

union shop A place of employment in which employees must join a union.

U.S. Public Health Service (USPHS) An agency of the federal government responsible for the control of the arrival from abroad of any people, goods, or substances that may affect the health of U.S. citizens. The agency sets standards for the domestic handling and processing of food and the manufacture of serums, vaccines, cosmetics, and drugs. It supports and performs research, aids localities in times of disaster and epidemics, and provides medical care for certain groups of Americans.

USPHS *abbr* United States Public Health Service

Utilitarianism A theory supporting what is best for most people.

utilization management Evaluation of the necessity, appropriateness, and efficiency of the use of medical services, procedures, and facilities. This includes review of admissions, services ordered and provided, length of stay, and discharge practices on a concurrent and retrospective basis.

V

values Strongly held personal and professional beliefs about worth and importance. The social principles, goals, or standards held by an individual or society.

verbal order A spoken order given directly and in person by a physician to a nurse.

voluntary bargaining issues Issues such as noneconomic fringe benefits that an employer or union may or may not address during collective bargaining.

WXYZ

whistle-blowing The reporting of the unlawful, unethical, or unsafe practices of providers or organizations.

witness 1. One who gives evidence in a case before a court and who attests or swears to facts or gives testimony under oath. 2. To observe the execution of an act, such as the signing of a document, or to sign one's name to authenticate the observation.

workers' compensation Compensation to an employee for an injury or occupational disease suffered in connection with his employment, paid under a government-supervised insurance system contributed to by employers.

writ of habeas corpus Literally means "you have the body"; a process whereby an individual detained or imprisoned asks the court to rule on the validity of the detainment or imprisonment. If the person is granted the writ, he must be released immediately.

wrongful death statute A statute existing in all states that provides that the death of a person can give rise to a cause of legal action brought by the person's beneficiaries in a civil suit against the person whose willful or negligent acts caused the death. Prior to the existence of these statutes, a suit could be brought only if the injured person survived.

wrongful life action A civil suit usually brought against a physician or health care facility on the basis of negligence that resulted in the wrongful birth or life of an infant. The parents of the unwanted child seek to obtain payment from the defendant for the medical expenses of pregnancy and delivery, for pain and suffering, and for the education and upbringing of the child. Wrongful life actions have been brought and won in several situations, including unsuccessful tubal ligations and vasectomies. Failure to diagnose pregnancy in time for abortion, and incorrect medical advice leading to the birth of a defective child have also led to malpractice suits for a wrongful life.

Understanding the judicial process

The judicial process in the United States is based on court jurisdiction and consists of state and federal court systems. Court jurisdiction refers to a court's authority to hear a case and determine judicial action in a given place at a given time. Jurisdiction is determined by several factors,

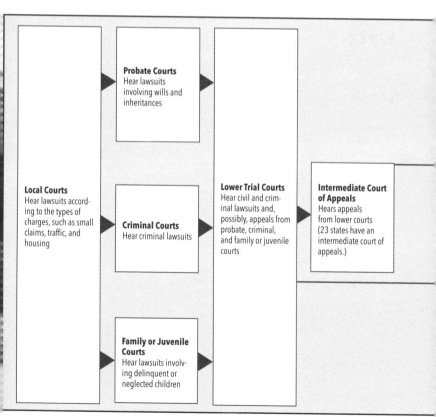

Local Courts
Hear lawsuits according to the types of charges, such as small claims, traffic, and housing

Probate Courts
Hear lawsuits involving wills and inheritances

Criminal Courts
Hear criminal lawsuits

Family or Juvenile Courts
Hear lawsuits involving delinquent or neglected children

Lower Trial Courts
Hear civil and criminal lawsuits and, possibly, appeals from probate, criminal, and family or juvenile courts

Intermediate Court of Appeals
Hears appeals from lower courts (23 states have an intermediate court of appeals.)

including the type of case (e.g., a tort action or a criminal case) and the location of the transgression or dispute.

Appeal is a legal process whereby a party dissatisfied with the decision of a lower court can seek a more favorable decision from a higher court. Either the plaintiff or the defendant can appeal an unfavorable decision from a lower court.

JUDICIAL PROCESS FLOW CHART

This flowchart depicts selected courts within the federal and state judicial systems. The arrows indicate pathways for appeal. Note that this flowchart doesn't include the complete federal court structure and that not all states follow the model depicted here.

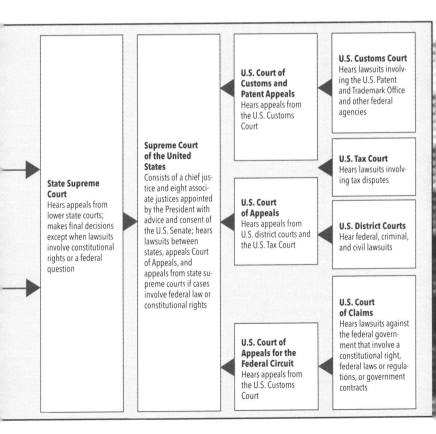

APPENDIX B

Types of MCOs

The era of the managed-care organization (MCO) is upon us. Created as a method to deliver health care by integrating resource utilization, financial spending, and desired patient outcomes through strict regulations on the provider used and the procedures performed, MCOs are controversial. However, their huge growth makes it likely that you work for an MCO-associated physician or hospital and that most of the patients you provide care for belong to an MCO.

MCOs often create guidelines for patient care; if health care providers want to be paid for their services, they must follow these guidelines, which are usually based on what's most cost-effective rather than what's best for the individual patient. This makes it necessary for all nurses to be aware of the types of MCOs, such as the health maintenance organization (HMO), preferred provider organization (PPO), exclusive provider organization (EPO), and point-of-service (POS) provider, and how their differences may affect nursing practice.

HMOs are the most well known of the MCOs. The most popular models of HMOs in use today are the *staff model*, the *group model*, the *network model*, and the *independent practice*

association (IPA). Additionally, some HMOs are formed on the basis of direct contract.

Kaiser Permanente is a classic example of a staff model HMO, in which physicians who serve the HMO enrollees are employed by the HMO. Staff model HMOs are having difficulty maintaining their profitability because they're unable to reduce the compensation to their physicians rapidly enough to keep up with the declining payments being made to physicians in group, network, and IPA-model HMOs.

Group, network, and IPA-model HMOs are in a much better competitive position in the marketplace. They require that the HMO contract with physicians, either individually or on a group or network basis, for the services needed to cover those enrolled in the HMO. The HMOs are left with the upper hand as physicians struggle to respond in a competitive marketplace.

Somewhere between the traditional fee-for-service program and the HMO is the PPO. PPOs are the most popular form of MCOs, with 50% of all workers insured by large- and medium-sized companies enrolled in this type of insurance plan. In a PPO, an employer or a health care insurance carrier contracts with a group of preferred or selected participating providers. These providers typically agree to accept the PPO's discounted reimbursement structure and payment levels, in return for which the PPO limits the size of its participating provider groups and provides incentives for its covered individuals to use the participating providers instead of other providers. Most recently, PPO plans for Medicare beneficiaries (Medicare combined with choice private fee-for-service plans) have been developed to help control Medicare costs.

EPOs are similar to PPOs and HMOs, but in EPOs, patients must select their provider from a list given to them by the EPO. In contrast are the POS organizations, which allow patients to select out-of-network providers at a reduced reimbursement rate.

Disease-management companies

Some HMOs contract with disease-management companies, which manage all aspects of treating a specific disease. Major pharmaceutical companies (including Merck, Eli Lilly, and SmithKline Beecham), major providers of health care (including The Johns Hopkins Hospital, Mayo Clinic, and Memorial Sloan-Kettering Cancer Center), third-party payers, and others have joined forces or have gone into disease management on their own.

In a typical disease-management arrangement, an HMO, employer, or insurance company contracts with a disease-management company for coverage of its enrollees when they're diagnosed with a specific disease, such as cancer. Components of a disease-management program include clinical pathways or treatment guidelines designed to provide the best possible care in the most streamlined environment. Disease-management companies usually guarantee that payments won't exceed a maximum amount. At best, the arrangement may provide high-quality care at the lowest possible cost.

Health care networks

Conceptually, health care networks are similar to disease-management companies. A typical health care network includes a major hub hospital; several smaller, community-based hospitals; a long-term–care facility; and perhaps a rehabilitation center, home health care agency, and subacute-care center.

In smoothly functioning health care networks, patients benefit from the reduction or elimination of fragmented delivery of care. Such networks can provide a continuum of care from one stage of illness to the next. Duplication of services is limited, and both preventive and outpatient care can be encouraged.

However, health care networks may become so powerful that they eliminate competition from alternative health care providers. This can cause substantial controversy. Ethical issues regarding patient referrals may be raised when there is cross-ownership of different components of the health care network.

Interpreting legal citations

You may obtain information on a specific court case or law (statute or regulation) from your county courthouse law library or local law school library. If you're looking for an overview or summary of a court case or law, look up the citation in a standard legal reference, such as a legal encyclopedia *(Corpus Juris Secundum)* and a legal text *(Restatements of Law)*.

If you have a full citation, you can locate the complete text of a court case. A full citation includes the name of the court case and a series of identifying numbers and letters. If you're missing some or all of the identifying information, you can look up the case name in the index of a legal reference.

In the court case citation index of this handbook, most of the court cases on the state level will have two complete series of identifying numbers. The first series is the *official citation*, indicating where the case can be found in that state's set of court case decisions. The second series is the *unofficial citation*, indicating where the case can be found in a commercially published set of court case decisions grouped by region. Keep in mind that

an "unofficial" legal reference doesn't have any less authority than an "official" legal reference.

Each citation includes an abbreviation for the legal reference that contains the law or case. For example, "U.S.L.W." stands for *United States Law Week*. To find out what the abbreviations used in the Nurse's Legal Handbook, Fifth Edition, stand for, see the list of legal reference abbreviations at right. For more information on legal citations, see *The Bluebook: A Uniform System of Citation*, 17th Edition (The Harvard Law Review Association, 2000).

The number that precedes the abbreviation indicates either a volume number or title classification within the legal reference. A title classification is a body of laws or cases on a particular subject such as malpractice. A title can be one book or many books, depending on the amount of cases that bear on the titles.

Two sets of numbers follow the abbreviation. The first set indicates the page where you'll find the case. The second set, in parentheses, indicates the year of the decision.

Law or case	Legal reference	Abbreviation
Federal court decisions	United States Law Week (unofficial reporter containing recently issued Supreme Court decisions)	U.S.L.W.
	United States Reports (official reporter containing Supreme Court decisions)	U.S.
	Supreme Court Reporter (unofficial reporter containing Supreme Court decisions)	S. Ct.
	Lawyers Edition, United States Supreme Court (unofficial reporter containing Supreme Court decisions)	L. Ed.
	Federal Reporter (contains court of appeals decisions)	F., F. 2d
	Federal Supplement (contains Federal District Court of Appeals decisions)	F. Supp.
State court decisions	Published state court decisions in official state sets for about two-thirds of U.S. states (The *Uniform System of Citation* lists all state reporters and instructs how to cite them.) Commercially published National Reporter System, which includes all state and group state court decisions by region:	Standard state abbreviations
	North Eastern Reporter	N.E., N.E. 2d
	Atlantic Reporter	A., A. 2d
	South Eastern Reporter	S.E., S.E. 2d
	Southern Reporter	So., So. 2d
	North Western Reporter	N.W., N.W. 2d
	South Western Reporter	S.W., S.W. 2d
	Pacific reporter	P., P. 2d
Miscellaneous abbreviations	New York Supreme Court, appellate division	A.D.
	New York Miscellaneous Reports	Misc. 2d
	West's New York Supplement	N.Y.S. 2d
	Dominion Law Reports (Canada)	D.L.R.
	Western Weekly Reports (Canada)	W.W.R.
	Ontario Reports	O.R.
	Ontario Law Reports	O.L.R.
	Labour Arbitration cases (Canada)	L.A.C.
	Canadian Cases on the Law of Torts	CCLT
	Reports of Family Law (Canada)	RFL
	National Labor Relations Board	N.L.R.B.
Federal statutes	*United States Law Week* (contains chronologic list of recently enacted statutes)	U.S.L.W.
	United States Statutes at Large (contains chronological lists of all statutes enacted during a single legislative session)	STAT. or STAT. AT L.
	United States Code (contains all statutes arranged by title)	U.S.C.
State statutes	Published state statutes in official state sets	Standard state abbreviations
Federal regulations	*Code of Federal Regulations* (contains federal regulations arranged by title)	C.F.R.
	The Federal Register (contains updates to the C.F.R.)	F.R.
State regulations	Published state regulations in official state sets	Standard state abbreviations

APPENDIX D

Court case citations

A

American Hospital Association v. NLRB, *111 S. Ct. 1539, 59 U.S.L.W. 4331 (1991)*

Application of the President and Directors of Georgetown College, Inc., *331 F.2d 1000 (D.C. Cir. 1964); cert. denied, 377 U.S. 978 (1964)*

Ashley v. Nyack Hospital, *412 N.Y.S.2d 388, 67 A.D.2d 671 (1979)*

B

Babits v. Vassar Brothers Hospital, *732 N.Y.S. 2nd 46 (N.Y. App. 2001)*

Bailie v. Miami Valley Hospital, *8 Ohio Misc. 193, 221 N.E.2d 217 (1966)*

Barber v. Reinking, *68 Wash. 2d 139, 411 P.2d 861 (1966)*

Barber v. Time, Inc., *348 Mo. 1199, 159 S.W.2d 291 (1942)*

Battocchi v. Washington Hosp. Center, *581 A.2d 759 (D.C. App. 1990)*

Bellotti v. Baird II, *443 U.S. 622, 99 S. Ct. 3035 (1979)*

Big Town Nursing Home v. Newman, *461 S.W.2d 195 (Tex. Civ. App. 1970)*

Brookover v. Mary Hitchcock Memorial Hospital, *893 F. 2d 411 (1st Cir. 1990)*

Brown v. State, *391 N.Y.S.2d 204, 56 A.D.2d 672 (1977)*

Burdreau v. McDowell, *256 U.S. 465, 41 S. Ct. 574 (1921)*

Butler v. South Fulton Medical Center, Inc., *215 Ga. App. 809, 452 S.E.2d 768 (1994)*

Byrne v. Boadle, *159 Eng. Rep. 299 (1863)*

C

Cannell v. Medical and Surgical Clinic S.C., *21 Ill. App. 3d 383, 315 N.E.2d 278 (1974)*

Canterbury v. Spence, *464 F.2d 772 (D.C. Cir. 1972)*

Carey v. Population Services International, *431 U.S. 678, 97 S. Ct. 2010 (1977)*

Carr v. St. Paul Fire and Marine Insurance Co., *384 F. Supp. 821 (W.D. Ark. 1974)*

Cline v. Lund, *31 Cal. App.3d 755, 107 Cal. Rptr. 629 (1973)*

Claypool v. Levin, *Wis. 562 N.W.2d 584, 209 Wis. 2d 284 (1997) No. 94-2457*

Collins v. Davis, *254 N.Y.S.2d 666, 44 Misc. 2d 622 (1964)*

Collins v. Westlake Community Hospital, *57 Ill. 2d 388, 312 N.E.2d 614 (1974)*

Colorado State Board of Nurse Examiners v. Hohu, *129 Colo. 195, 268 P.2d 401 (1954)*

Commissioner of Correction v. Myers, *379 Mass. 255, 399 N.E.2d 452 (1979)*

Commonwealth v. Gordon, *431 Pa. 512, 246 A.2d 325 (1968)*

Commonwealth v. Porn, *196 Mass. 326, 82 N.E. 31 (1907)*

Commonwealth v. Storella, *6 Mass. App. 310, 375 N.E.2d 348 (1978)*

Cooper v. National Motor Bearing Co., *136 Cal. App. 2d 229, 288 P.2d 581 (1955)*

Crowe v. Provost, *52 Tenn. App. 397, 374 S.W.2d 645 (1963)*

Cruzan v. Director, Mo. Dept. of Health, *110 S. Ct. 2841, 111 L. Ed. 2d 224 (1990)*

D

D. v. D., *108 N.J. Super. 149, 260 A.2d 255 (1969)*

Darling v. Charleston Community Memorial Hospital, *33 Ill. 2d 326, 211 N.E.2d 253 (1965)*

Dembie, *21 RFL 46 (1963)*

Derrick v. Portland Eye, Ear, Nose and Throat Hospital, *105 Ore. 90, 209 P.2d 344 (1922)*

Dessauer v. Memorial General Hospital, *96 N.M. 92, 628 P.2d 337 (N.M. Ct. App. 1981)*

Doe v. Roe, *400 N.Y.S.2d 668, 93 Misc. 2d 201 (Sup. Ct. 1977)*

In re Doe Children, *402 N.Y.S.2d 958, 93 Misc. 2d 479 (1978)*

Dowey v. Rothwell, *[1974] 5 W.W.R. 311 (Alberta)*

E

Eastern Maine Medical Center v. NLRB, *658 F.2d 1 (1st Cir. 1981)*

Edith Anderson Nursing Homes, Inc. v. Bettie Walker, *232 Md. 442, 194 A.2d 85 (1963)*

Eisenstadt v. Baird, *405 U.S. 438, 92 S. Ct. 1029 (1972)*

Emory University v. Shadburn, *47 Ga. App. 643, 171 S.E. 192 (Ct. App. 1933)*

Estelle v. Gamble, *429 U.S. 97, 97 S. Ct. 285 (1976)*

F

Farrell v. Snell, *2 S.C.R. (Ct. App., New Brunswick, 1990)*

Feeney v. Young, *181 N.Y.S. 481, 191 A.D. 501 (1920)*

G

Garcia v. Bronx Lebanon Hospital, *731 N.Y.S. 2nd 702 (N.Y. App., 2001)*

Garcia v. Presbyterian Hospital Center, *92 N.M. 652, 593 P.2d 487 (1979)*

Geransy, *13 R.F.L.2d 202 (1977)*

Griswold v. Connecticut, *381 U.S. 479, 85 S. Ct. 1678 (1965)*

Gugino v. Harvard Community Health Plan, *380 Mass. 464, 403 N.E.2d 1166 (1980)*

HI

Hammonds v. Aetna Casualty and Surety Co., *237 F. Supp. 96 (D.C. Ohio 1965)*

Harrell v. Louis Smith Memorial Hospital, *3975 E.2d 746 (Ga. 1990)*

Henry By Henry v. St. John's Hospital, *512 N.E.2d 1044 (Ill. App. 4 Dist. 1987)*

Hernicz v. Fla. Dept. of Professional Regulation, *390 So. 2d 194 (Dist. Ct. App. 1980)*

Hiatt v. Groce, *215 Kan. 14, 523 P. 2d 320 (1974)*

H.L. v. Matheson, *450 U.S. 398, 101 S. Ct. 1164 (1981)*

Hodges v. Effingham County Hospital, *355 S.E.2d 104 (Ga. 1987)*

Hodgson v. Minnesota, *110 S. Ct. 2926, 111 L. Ed. 2d 344 (1990)*

Horton v. Niagara Falls Memorial Medical Center, *380 N.Y.S 2d 116, 51 A.D.2d 152 (1976)*

Hudock v. Children's Hospital of Philadelphia, *Civil Action No. 98-929, 1999 U.S. Dist. LEXIS 19269 (3d Cir. 1999)*

Hunt v. Palms Springs General Hospital, *352 So. 2d 582 (Fla. Dist. Ct. App. 1977)*

Hunter v. Hunter, *65 O.L.R. 586 (1930)*

J

Jefferson v. Griffin Spalding County Hospital Authority, *247 Ga. 86, 274 S.E.2d 457 (1981)*

Jones v. Hawkes Hospital, *175 Ohio 503, 196 N.E.2d 592 (1964)*

Justice v. Natvig, *178, 381 S.E.2d 8 (Va. 1989)*

K

Kansas State Board of Nursing v. Burkman, *216 Kan. 187, 531 P. 2d 122 (1975)*

Karp v. Cooley, et al., *493 F.2d 408, 419 (1974)*

Keyes v. Humana Hospital, Alaska, Inc., *750 P.2d 343 (Alaska 1988)*

Kyslinger v. United States, *406 F. Supp. 800 (W.D. Pa. 1975)*

L

Laidlaw v. Lions Gate Hospital, *[1969] 70 W.W.R. 727 (B.C. 1969)*

Lama v. Boras, *16 F.2d 473 PR (1994)*

Lane v. Candura, *6 Mass. App. 377, 376 N.E.2d 1232 (1978)*

Larrimore v. Homeopathic Hospital Association, *176 A.2d 362, aff'd, 54 Del. 449, 181 A.2d 573 (1962)*

Leib v. Board of Examiners for Nursing, *177 Conn. 78, 411 A.2d 42 (1979)*

Leigh v. Board of Registration in Nursing, *395 Mass. 670, 481 N.E.2d 1347 (1985)*

Lopez v. Swyer, *115 N.J. Super. 237, 279 A.2d 116 (1971)*

Loton v. Massachusetts Paramedical, Inc., *Mass. Sup. Ct. 1987, 4 National Jury Verdict Review and Analysis 5 (1989)*

Lott v. State, *225 N.Y.S.2d 434, 32 Misc. 2d 296 (1962)*

Lovato v. Colorado, *198 Colo. 419, 601 P.2d 1072 (1979)*

M

Manning v. Twin Falls Clinic and Hospital, *830 P. 2nd 1185 (Idaho, 1992)*

Mapp v. Ohio, *367 U.S. 643, 81 S. Ct. 1684 (1961)*

Maryland v. Buie, *494 U.S. 325, 110 S. Ct. 1093 (1990)*

Mathias v. St. Catherine's Hospital, *212 Wis. 2d 540, 569 N.W.2d 330 (1997)*

May v. Broun, *261 Ore. 28, 492 P.2d 776 (1972)*

McCarl v. State Board of Nurse Examiners, *39 Pa. Cmwlth. 628, 396 A.2d 866 (1979)*

McCutchon v. Mutual of Omaha Insurance Co. , *354 So. 2d 759 (La. Ct. App. 1978)*

McInnes v. Dillard Department Stores, Inc., *736 So. 2d 1190; 1999 Fla. App. LEXIS 6322*

McIntosh v. Milano, *168 N.J. Super. 466, 403 A.2d 500 (1979)*

In re Melideo, *390 N.Y.S. 2d 523, 88 Misc. 2d 974 (Sup. Ct. 1976)*

Methodist Hospital v. Ball, *50 Tenn. App. 460, 362 S.W.2d 475 (1961)*

Misericordia Hospital Medical Center v. NLRB, *623 F.2d 808 (2d Cir. 1980)*

Mohr v. Jenkins, *393 So. 2d 245 (La. Ct. App. 1980)*

Mohr v. Williams, *95 Minn. 261, 104 N.W. 12 (1905)*

Moore v. Guthrie Hospital, *403 F.2d 366 (4th Cir. 1968)*

Moore v. Willis-Knighton Medical Center, *720 So. 2nd 425 (La. App. 1998)*

In re Mount Sinai Hospital and Ontario Nurses Association, *17 L.A.C.2d 242 (1978)*

Mutual Insurance of Arizona v. American Casualty Co. of Reading, PA, *189 Ariz. 22, 938 P.2d 71 (1997)*

N

Nathanson v. Kline, *186 Kan. 393, 350 P.2d 1093 (1960)*

Nelson v. Trinity Medical Center, *419 N.W.2d 886 (S. Ct. N.D. 1988)*

New York v. Class, *475 U.S. 106, 106 S. Ct. 960 (1985)*

NLRB v. Baptist Hospital, *442 U.S. 773, 99 S. Ct. 2598 (1979)*

NLRB v. Health Care & Retirement Corporation, *114 S. Ct. 1778 (1994)*

NLRB v. Health Care & Retirement Corp., *511 U.S. 571 (1994)*

NLRB v. Kentucky River Community Care, Inc., *532 U.S. 706 (2001)*

Norman v. Good Shepherd Medical Center, *2001 Tex. App. LEXIS 5571, August 17, 2001. Filed.*

Norton v. Argonaut Insurance Co., *144 So. 2d 249 (La. Ct. App. 1962)*

N.Y.C. Health and Hospitals Corporation v. Sulsona, *367 N.Y.S.2d 686, 81 Misc. 2d 1002 (1975)*

N.Y. State Association for Retarded Children, Inc. v. Carey, *438 F. Supp. 440 (E.D. N.Y. 1977)*

O

O'Connor v. Donaldson, *422 U.S. 563, 95 S. Ct. 2486 (1975)*

Ohio v. Akron Center for Reproductive Health, *110 S. Ct. 2972, 111 L. Ed. 2d 405 (1990)*

Oliff v. Florida State Board of Nursing, *374 So. 2d 1054 (Fla. Dist. Ct. App. 1979)*

O'Neill v. Montefiore Hospital, *202 N.Y.S.2d 436, 11 A.D. 2d 132 (1960)*

In re Osborne, *294 A.2d 372 (D.C. 1972)*

P

Pedersen v. Zielski, *Adv 3785, 822 P.2d 903 (Ak. 1991)*

People v. Doe, *410 N.Y.S.2d 233, 96 Misc. 2d 975 (1978)*

People v. Kraft, *3 Cal. App. 3d 890, 84 Cal. Rptr. 280 (1970)*

Planned Parenthood of Central Missouri v. Danforth, *428 U.S. 52, 96 S. Ct. 2831 (1976)*

Planned Parenthood of Northwest Ind. v. Vines, *543 N.E.2d 654 (Ind. App. 1989)*

Planned Parenthood of S.E. Pennsylvania v. Casey, *127 L.E.2d 352, 114 S. Ct. 909 (1992)*

Pommier v. ABC Insurance Co., et al., *715 So. 2d 1270 (La. App. 3d Cir. 1998)*

Poor Sisters of St. Francis Seraph of the Perpetual Adoration, et al. v. Catron, *435 N.E.2d 305 (Ind. Ct. App. 1982)*

Pounders v. Trinity Court Nursing Home, *265 Ark. 1, 576 S.W.2d 934 (1979)*

Powell v. Columbia-Presbyterian Medical Center, *267 N.Y.S.2d 450, 49 Misc. 2d 215 (Sup. Ct. 1965)*

Prairie v. University of Chicago Hospitals, *298 Ill. App. 3d 316, 327 (1998)*

Q

In re **Quinlan**, *137 N.J. Super. 227, 348 A. 2d 801 (Ch. Div. 1975); modified, 70 N.J. 10, 355 A.2d 647 (1976)*

R

Ramos v. Lamm, *639 F.2d 559 (10th Cir. 1980)*

Richardson v. Brunelle, *119 N.H. 104, 398 A.2d 838 (1979)*

Roach v. Springfield Clinic, *Ill., App. 4 Dist., 166 Ill. Dec. 48, 585 N.E.2d 1070, 223 Ill. App.3d 597, appeal allowed 173 Ill. Dec. 13, 596 N.E.2d 637, 145 Ill. 2d 644, aff'd in part, rev'd in part 191 Ill. Dec. 1, 623 N.E.2d 246, 157 Ill. 2d 29 (1992)*

Rochin v. California, *342 U.S. 165, 72 S. Ct. 205 (1952)*

Roe v. Wade, *410 U.S. 113, 93 S. Ct. 705 (1973)*

Rogers v. Kasdan, *612 S.W.2d 133 (Ky. 1981)*

Rohde v. Lawrence General Hospital, *34 Mass. App. Ct. 584, 614 N.E.2d 686 (1993)*

Rust v. Sullivan, *59 U.S.L.W. 4451 (1991)*

S

Salgo v. Leland Stanford Jr. Univ. Board of Trustees, *154 Cal. App. 2d 560, 317 P.2d 170 (1957)*

In re **Sampson**, *328 N.Y.S.2d 686, 278 N.E.2d 918 (1972)*

Sanchez v. Bay General Hospital, *116 Ca. App. 3d 776, 172 Cal. Rptr. 342, Cal. App. 4 Dist., (1981)*

In re **SAS**, *1 LMQ 139 (1977)*

Schloendorff v. Society of New York Hospitals, *211 N.Y. 125, 105 N.E. 92 (1914)*

Schmerber v. California, *384 U.S. 757, 86 S. Ct. 1826 (1966)*

Schneckloth v. Bustamonte, *412 U.S. 218, 93 S. Ct. 2041 (1973)*

Sengstack v. Sengstack, *4 N.Y.2d 502, 176 N.Y.S.2d 337; 151 N.E.2d 887 (1958)*

Shannon v. McNulty and HealthAmerica Pennsylvania, *718 A.2d 828; 1998 Pa. Super LEXIS 2383, filed October 5, 1998*

Simonsen v. Swenson, *104 Neb. 224, 177 N.W. 831 (1920)*

Snelson v. Culton, *141 Me. 242, 42 A.2d 505 (1949)*

Stack v. Wapner, *368 A.2d 292, 244 (Pa. Super. Ct. 278, 1976)*

Stahlin v. Hilton Hotels Corp., *484 F.2d 580 (7th Cir. 1973)*

State v. Brown, *8 Ore. App. 72, 491 P.2d 1193 (1971)*

State v. Perea, *95 N.M. 777, 626 P.2d 851 (1981)*

State v. Riggins, *348 So. 2d 1209 (Fla. Dist. Ct. App. 1977)*

Stefanik v. Nursing Education Committee, *70 R.I. 136, 37 A.2d 661 (1944)*

Stevenson v. Alta Bates, *20 Cal. App. 2d 303, 66 P.2d 1265 (1937)*

Stone v. Commonwealth, *418 S.W.2d 646 (Ky. 1967); cert. denied, 390 U.S. 1010*

Story v. McCurtain Memorial Management, Inc., *634 P.2d 778 (Okla. Ct. App. 1981)*

Story v. St. Mary Parish Service District, *La. No. 77, 471C (January 17, 1987)*

St. Paul Fire and Marine Insurance Co. v. Prothro, *266 Ark. 1020, 590 S.W.2d 35 (Ark. Ct. App. 1979)*

St. Germain v. Pfeifer, *637 N.E.2d 848 (Mass. 1994)*

Sweet v. Providence Hospital, *881 P.2d 304, Alaska (1995)*

T

Tarasoff v. Regents of the University of California, *131 Cal. Rptr. 14, 551 P.2d 334 (1976)*

Thompson v. The Nason Hospital, *527 Pa. 330, 591 A.2d 703 (1991)*

Thor v. Boska, *38 Cal. App. 3d 558, 113 Cal. Rptr. 296 (1974)*

Tighe v. State Board of Nurse Examiners, *40 Pa. Cmwlth. 367, 397 A.2d 1261 (1979)*

Tuma v. Board of Nursing, *100 Idaho 74, 593 P.2d 711 (1979)*

U

Ullo v. State Board of Examiners, *41 Pa. Cmwlth. 204, 398 A.2d 764 (1979)*

United States v. Montoya de Hernandez, *473 U.S. 531, 105 S. Ct. 3304 (1985)*

United States v. Winbush, *428 F.2d 357 (6th Cir. 1970)*

Utter v. United Health Center, *160 W. Va. 703, 236 S.E.2d 213 (1977)*

V

Viletto v. Weilbaecher, *377 So. 2d 132 (La. Ct. App. 1979)*

Vinnedge v. Gibbs, *550 F.2d 926 (CA 4 VA 1977)*

WX

Warden v. Hayden, *387 U.S. 294, 87 S. Ct. 1642 (1967)*

Washington State Nurses Ass'n v. Board of Medical Examiners, *93 Wash. 2d 117, 605 P.2d 1269 (1980)*

Webster v. Reproductive Health Services, *492 U.S. 490, 109 S. Ct. 3040 (1989)*

Whalen v. Roe, *429 U.S. 589, 97 S. Ct. 869 (1977)*

Whitney v. Day, *100 Mich. App. 707, 300 N.W.2d 380 (Ct. App. 1980)*

Widman v. Paoli Memorial Hospital, *No. 85-1034 Pa 1989*

Winters v. Miller, *446 F.2d 65 (2nd Cir. 1971)*

Woodward v. Myres, Dean, and Correctional Medical Services of Illinois, *2001 WL 506863 (N.D. Ill. 2001)*

Wyatt v. Stickney, *325 F. Supp. 781 (M.D. Ala. 1971); 344 F. Supp. 387 (M.D. Ala. 1972)*

YZ

Ybarra v. Spangard, *154 2nd 687 (California, 1994)*

Younts v. St. Francis Hospital and School of Nursing, *205 Kan. 292, 469 P.2d 330 (1970)*

Young v. Board of Hospital Directors, Lee County, *#82-429 (Fl. 1984)*

INDEX

---

t refers to a table.